Learning Online

D0172878

Whether you are taking classes in school, college or university, or in a corporate training setting, it is likely that you will be expected to do at least part of your studies via the computer. This book provides realistic guidelines to ensure your success in the virtual learning environment. From detailing tools such as WebCT and Blackboard, to overcoming personal barriers to success in distance learning, this handy text deals with issues that readers of any age, stage or situation are likely to encounter by:

- demystifying terms and concepts common to online learning;
- addressing issues of online ethics such as netiquette, plagiarism and software piracy;
- offering practical advice on interacting effectively online, submitting assignments, and doing research;
- furnishing numerous links to Web pages and other resources for further study and research.

The author offers anecdotes to help you avoid the pitfalls and capitalize on opportunities that will help you become a successful online student.

Both current and prospective online learners will greatly benefit from this practical book filled with clear, detailed assistance for learning online.

Maggie McVay Lynch is currently Manager of Distributed Education at Portland State University.

Learning Online

A guide to success in the virtual classroom

Maggie McVay Lynch

LIBRARY 15237
Argosy University
San Francisco Bay Area
1005 Atlantic Ave.
Alameda, CA 94501

NEW YORK AND LONDON

First published 2004
by RoutledgeFalmer
29 West 35th Street, New York, NY 10001

Simultaneously published in the UK
by RoutledgeFalmer
11 New Fetter Lane, London EC4P 4EE

RoutledgeFalmer is an imprint of the Taylor & Francis Group

© 2004 Maggie McVay Lynch

Typeset in Bembo by
HWA Text and Data Management Ltd, Tunbridge Wells
Printed and bound in Great Britain by
Biddles Ltd, Guildford and King's Lynn

All rights reserved. No part of this book may be reprinted or reproduced or utilized in any form or by any electronic, mechanical, or other means, now known or hereafter invented, including photocopying and recording, or in any information storage or retrieval system, without permission in writing from the publishers.

Library of Congress Cataloging in Publication Data
A catalog record for this book has been requested

British Library Cataloguing in Publication Data
A catalogue record for this book is available from the British Library

ISBN 0–415–70005–1 (hbk)
ISBN 0–415–70000–0 (pbk)

For Michele and Patricia who continue to demonstrate that a commitment to life-long learning and embracing technology is necessary at every age

Contents

Figures

Tables

Acknowledgments

No book of this scope is written without help. First, I am thankful for the community of distance educators and online students who have freely shared their issues, concerns, advice, and experiences with me over the past five years of surveys and interviews. It is from these postings that I determined what would be important to include in this book. Specific individuals who have been particularly valuable in answering questions, providing Web page resources, and assisting in locating research articles have been Patricia Cornman, Stephen Downes, Lya Visser, Michele Gester, Misty Hamideh, Steve McCarty, Arun Tripathi, and Michael Warner. Finally, this book would not be nearly as complete without the undying dedication of my husband and first-reader, Jim, who agreed to read and do a first edit of everything I wrote, even though it often involved late nights, weekends, and sometimes trying to find a nice way to tell me a particular section didn't make any sense.

Chapter 1

The future is now

> The proper artistic response to digital technology is to embrace it as a new window on everything that's eternally human and to use it with passion, wisdom, fearlessness, and joy.
>
> (Ralph Lombreglia, 'The right mix', *The Atlantic Unbound*, 4 June 1998)

Shaping our world – living and learning with technology

Technology is a tool that is affecting the way we work, play and communicate. From simple tools like can openers and magnifying glasses to complex machines like computers and jet airliners, technology can help in our work and give us more ways to keep in touch with friends and family. Technology is changing our lives; it's up to us to decide how to use it, how to make it work for – rather than against – us.

Tools that use technology, useful gadgets, and disposable items surround us, entertain us, provide useful services, and make our lives easier. We can do things every day that would have been considered impossible (or perhaps magical) not so long ago. The modern woman is able to awake precisely at 5:45 am to an electronic buzzer, a favorite radio station, a CD, or even recorded sounds of birds, the ocean, or a rainforest. Her home, cool during sleep hours, is warm and coffee is already brewing in the electronically programmed coffeepot. A quick flick of the remote control tunes the television to the local morning news where she can get a weather report while deciding what to wear for the day. After getting dressed, she may login to her personal computer, connect to the Internet, and check her email, review a calendar of appointments and projects planned for the day, and check her stock portfolio. All of these Internet resources have been configured *just* for her needs. She then leaves the house, gets in the car, stops at an automatic teller machine (ATM) on the way to deposit a birthday check. Just before getting to the office, she visits the local florist to send flowers to her sister who just had a baby. She pays for the flowers with a credit or debit card, not neeeding to carry cash with her. Finally, she calls her administrative assistant from a cell phone to get some copies made for her first meeting of the day. This all happens before 8:00 am.

Society is expecting more and more of these things, and these same expectations cross into the realm of education and learning. Furthermore, employers now expect that new hires will have the ability to use technology to learn faster, produce more products, and network with people around the globe to solve problems.

The next 50 years will see a learning revolution unlike anything witnessed since the beginning of the printing press. Adults want and need to be able to learn things on-demand – whether it is at 3:00 am or 10:00 pm. Students are more mobile now and thus desire to learn in their homes, in their cars, in their offices, on the manufacturing floor, and while traveling. In particular, people want to obtain the required knowledge just before or right at the time they have the need for it.

Education and training's response to technological change

Traditionally, mainstream education and training has embraced technology at a slower pace than business. The belief that face-to-face instruction or tutoring is the most effective way to teach is still the accepted tenet of quality education at most institutions. Certainly, most learners would love to have the luxury of personalized instruction in a one-on-one setting – in effect a private instructor. However, that is possible only for a very few special or particularly wealthy learners. The typical college course ranges from a a seminar with as few as 12–15 students to a large lecture with 500 or more students. Furthermore, a traditional college education in many parts of the world is very teacher-centered. In other words, the teacher provides the expertise and the knowledge to the student who then repeats it – in a recitation of some type – to commit it to memory. In some instances the students are asked to synthesize information and reformulate the material for their own needs – but this is rare in most courses. In this traditional education system, the application of knowledge occurs in lab sections that are separate from the lecture class. In many instances the application of knowledge is not tracked within the educational environment but instead left to each student to struggle on his or her own after completing the course.

In a very few universities the opposite approach is taken. For example, at Cambridge in the UK, the student does attend limited class sessions (lectures); but the larger part of the student's time is spent independently in study and reflection around a self-selected group of topics. In this environment, the student must choose what to study from multiple resources given by the instructor as well as additional resources found by the student. Students then meet regularly (4 to 5 times per week) in a "supervision" group with up to six other class members and an instructor to discuss their progress and to hand in work accomplished in their individualized study pursuits. The supervision session may include additional questions asked by the instructor to help expand the student's knowledge. This is what is often referred to as a "student-centered" approach to learning.

A good online learning environment is much more like the Cambridge experience than the typical learning environment of other institutions around the world. It relies on a student-centered methodology that requires students to be responsible for their own learning and to be motivated to study in a continuous and consistent manner without the structure or requirement of attending physical class sessions.

As budgets decrease and student populations increase, the need for serving larger classes and more diverse people becomes an absolute necessity in the struggle to provide equal access to education around the globe. Online learning has become one of the responses to this need. Consequently, more and more training options are being developed using online learning as a part of, or the whole of, the education experience.

Though many people believe online learning is a new phenomenon brought about the spread of the Internet, the fact is that computer-based learning goes back about four decades, when large mainframe computers began to become a mainstay of government and business. In the 1960s extensive programs were written for a variety of training or research purposes, with an emphasis on development of simulations and thinking tools.

The overall philosophy of computer-assisted education through the 1960s and 1970s focused on electronic curriculum materials – self-study programs that students could use to learn specific content. Computers were used to provide a series of interactions consisting of content followed by a problem or question. The student would respond and some type of feedback would be presented. This instructional design was based on a sound theoretical basis of behavioral and early cognitive learning theory. Furthermore, there was ample empirical evidence to show that students studying in this manner did achieve the objectives or learning outcomes. However, as computer technology became more sophisticated and personal computers (PCs) became more the norm both for business and for individual home use, it became clear that the previous computer-assisted approach was too limited and did not provide sufficient learning beyond memory and recall. In order for educators to truly embrace the use of computers, there was a need to provide more complex problem-solving and critical thinking opportunities.

With the advent of the Internet in the early 1990s, computers became accepted as superb devices for communication and information sharing. What really impressed students and teachers was the capability to interact electronically, search through databases, and work together to solve problems. So, interactivity remained of utmost importance. However, it was no longer the student-to-computer interaction that was prized. Instead, it was the person-to-person interaction with the computer serving only as an intermediary.

In higher education and corporate training, quality online education is now shaped by exploration and discovery, collaboration, connectivity, community, multi-sensory experiences, and authenticity related to student-centered needs. Let's look at a few examples of how online education is being used today and how these initiatives are characterized in online courses.

Initial physician training via online courses

A worldwide group of medical schools is collaborating to build an "International Virtual Medical School," allowing students to begin work toward a medical degree thousands of miles from a classroom. The virtual medical school project, known by the acronym IVIMEDS, is based at the University of Dundee in Scotland, but is actually an international collaborative comprised of over 50 institutions in 16 countries. Many of the participating institutions are in the United Kingdom; other contributing universities are located in Portugal, Italy, Singapore, Israel, and Saudi Arabia.

The goal of the program is to replace the conventional lecture-and-textbook approach of medical school, which some believe is "dehumanizing." The new curriculum emphasizes the value of problem-solving over memorization, and, because it will rely heavily on computers, it can be used both on campus and off-site.

Supporters of this approach also see broader potential in long-distance medical education. Doctors from poor communities would be more likely to practice medicine at home, where they are needed, if they haven't been forced to relocate for four years. Even in more developed areas, some medical educators worry that there won't be enough doctors in 20 years to serve an aging and growing population.

The program is based on the concept of a "virtual practice," where the computer presents students with patients to treat. For example, a video patient may appear in the course complaining that his leg hurts. He believes it started when he was jabbed in the leg with a rusty nail while mending his fence. First he just needs a tetanus shot and antibiotics, but he comes back the next week complaining about the deteriorating state of his farm and wondering if his family would be better off without him. The students then must examine him for depression. When students present their diagnoses, the computer will provide some automated feedback and direct the students to background reading. Faculty will also closely monitor students' performance. Students and teachers will interact over email or on discussion boards, and at some point in the program students may be required to volunteer in local clinics or hospitals.

The plan is for students to be able to finish their first two years of medical school by completing a series of computer-based assignments as well as some hands-on work at local institutions. Then, like all medical students, they would finish their degrees by spending two years doing hands-on clinical work in a teaching hospital.

Science Learning Network for K-12 schools

In online education for children the major value of the Internet is to provide a link to many resources. This is done through special projects such as the Science Learning Network or through individual, instructor-developed WebQuests – inquiry-oriented activities in which most or all of the information used by learners is drawn from the Web – that lead the students through a series of Web site explorations along with questions or study points.

The Science Learning Network (http://www.sln.org) is an online community of educators, students, schools, science museums and other institutions that demonstrate a new model for inquiry science education. The project provides an opportunity for young students to explore science on their own, through inquiry-based teaching approaches, or as part of their classroom experience. The site allows for collaboration among geographically dispersed teachers and classrooms, and a large variety of Internet content resources.

For example, the museum section allows students to visit museums in Finland, the United Kingdom, Japan, Singapore, and the United States. The "Exploratorium" keeps students updated on the top ten "cool sites" that cover topics as diverse as hunting crabs, exploring race and prejudice, and understanding engineering challenges (see Figure 1.1).

Virtual foreign exchange program to provide global student experience

In an attempt to improve students' understanding of global issues, schools are seeking new ways to incorporate international education into their curriculum. In the United States, the University System of

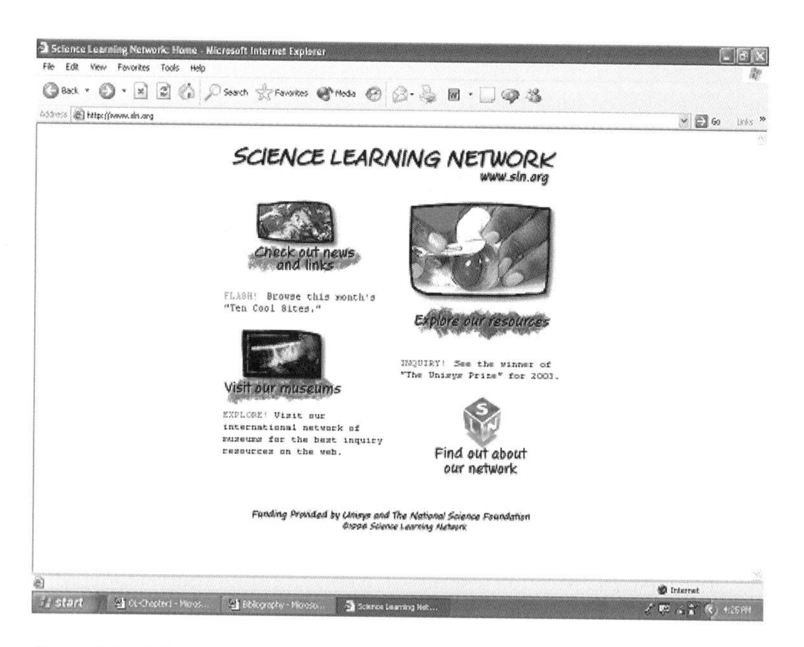

Figure 1.1 **Science Learning Network** (courtesy of The Science Learning Network, www.sln.org).

Georgia (USG) and the University of Munich in Germany have developed and implemented a unique collaborative approach that provides students with a global education experience, while giving them the opportunity to participate in a "virtual" foreign exchange program. During the fall 2001 semester, the institutions jointly offered their first two interdisciplinary, intercultural online courses. Over the next 18 months, a total of nine online courses – all focused on some aspect of the European Union – were offered to students from both universities. All nine courses were developed and team-taught in English by faculty members from a USG institution and the University of Munich.

The courses are part of a European Union Studies Certificate program, which provides undergraduate students from USG campuses and the University of Munich with the opportunity to earn a combined certification from both institutions (see Figure 1.2). The certificate is a collaborative program of USG and its European Union Center (www.inta.gatech.edu/eucenter), as well as the European Council. By taking part in the program, students learn about the European Union, gain knowledge of European history and culture, exchange ideas about business practices, and communicate electronically.

Figure 1.2 European Union Center University System of Georgia

Britain's e-University

UK e-Universities Worldwide (UKeU), which opened its doors in April 2003, is a joint initiative between the UK Government, 12 universities and private industry. UkeU was given £62m of funding from the government and has created a set of online courses for students around the globe. Undergraduate, post-graduate and life-long learning courses will be offered in subjects such as English language, science and technology and business. There is also an ongoing project with three Chinese universities to offer teacher training resources online.

Initially, the courses will be offered by Cambridge University, the University of York and Sheffield Hallam University. Students can complete some of the courses wholly online while others require them to take a traditional exam in a location near to their homes. Study seminars are held as online chats with instructors monitoring individual input to such discussions.

Online corporate training for all types of employees

The business world is also a prime candidate for online learning opportunities. In a global knowledge economy, businesses are under pressure to get new products and services to the marketplace ever more quickly, and to respond to increasingly demanding customers. To remain competitive businesses need to improve every aspect of their performance and ensure that they are benefiting from the economies of scale available through online training.

Many commentators have acknowledged that the speed at which an organization learns is its only sustainable source of competitive advantage. This has made the knowledge of how individuals and organizations learn a key business issue. Thus, corporations are taking a more critical view of how they develop their people.

In some areas traditional sources of education – colleges, universities and training organizations – continue to provide what is required. But just as the needs of corporations are rapidly changing, so are the ways that learning opportunities are delivered; mobile-telephony, electronic simulation, interactive and modular delivery of instructional tutorials, the Web, and digital television are some of the more obvious examples. Learning centers and corporate universities are just two instances of how online learning impacts the business world. In addition, online learners can enroll in Internet-based learning programs with commercial providers thousands of miles away (sometimes even in a different country). Or, a corporation may choose to have training designed specifically to meet its needs, allowing the topics to be tailored to an individual's requirements while still maintaining the corporate philosophy and strategic goals that are desired for each course. Businesses now rely on online learning to develop skills and knowledge faster and when needed by employees, that is "just-in-time" learning.

The types of corporate training and online courses favored by businesses range from complete MBA programs, in partnership with major universities, to skill-training programs for specific job positions in an organization. Let's look at these two extremes of online training that meet corporate needs.

MBA training worldwide

In June 2003, Universitas 21 Global (http://www.universitas21.com), Asia Pacific's premier e-University headquartered in Singapore, opened its doors to MBA aspirants. Students from around the world can register with Universitas 21 Global, which uses the Internet to deliver a world-class education experience for its global students.

A joint venture between Universitas 21 and Thomson Learning Corporation, Universitas 21 Global is a consortium of 17 world-renowned universities. In 2002, five of Universitas 21's member universities were ranked among the top 20 MBA schools by Asia Inc, including the National University of Singapore, University of New South Wales, University of Queensland, University of Hong Kong and University of Melbourne. Other member universities are recognized as being among the top business schools ranked by *The Financial Times*, the *Economist* Intelligence Unit and *The Wall Street Journal*.

Universitas 21 Global students are required to demonstrate their analytical thinking and understanding of coursework through problem-based assignments that are set in a virtual environment. Students can engage in online discussions that connect them to their counterparts around the world and access the Universitas 21 Global library for learning resources. Active interaction between students and lecturers occurs through real-time Internet chat, threaded discussions and similar Web-based communications tools. Other learning applications are provided through Universitas 21 Global's proprietary Learning Management System. This system includes online announcement boards and special notepad functions where students can create their own lecture notes.

Universitas 21 Global is not the only online MBA program, but it is

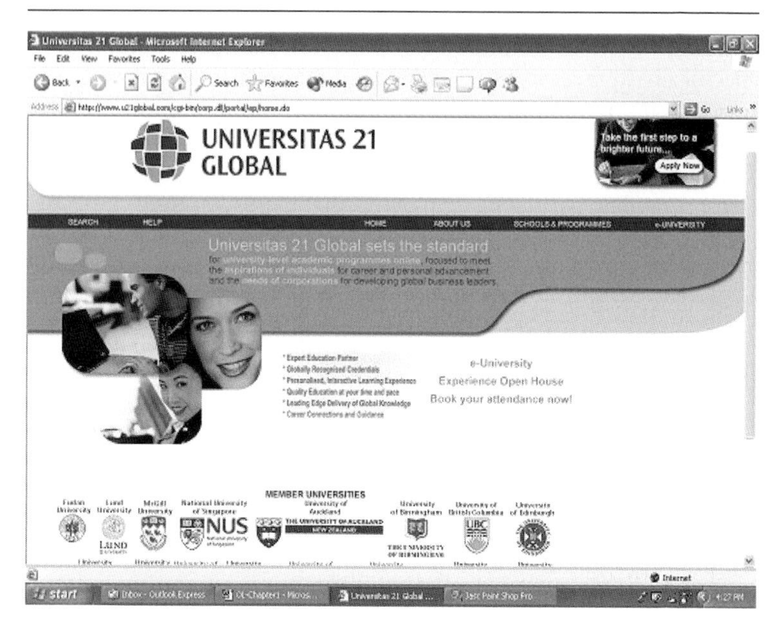

Figure 1.3 **Universitas 21 Global:** In addition to academic programs, Universitas 21 Global offers the full range of student services online, including academic counseling, career guidance and technical support.

probably one of the largest consortiums. MBA programs are frequently the first online degrees offered by a university; consequently, there are hundreds of programs worldwide, including 103 accredited online MBA programs in the US alone.

Specific job training for an American newspaper conglomerate

At an American newspaper conglomerate, Lee Enterprises, new district managers now receive an orientation to their job responsibilities and to the company through an online course. Lee Enterprises is a 113-year-old company that owns 44 daily newspapers in 18 different states. In addition, they own over 175 weekly newspapers and special publications, and employ approximately 6,700 people across the United States.

District managers (DMs) are responsible for ensuring that newspapers are delivered on time and in the right place for every customer. Each DM is responsible for contract newspaper carriers – both youth and adults – and accountable for the training and performance of these

Test your knowledge by completing this fill-in-the-blank quiz about carriers as independent contractors. When you have completed the quiz correctly, close the window and you will return to this page.

Retention of Carriers Through Good Communication

When there is a good carrier in your district, you want to keep the person on route as long as possible and have the person continue to grow in skill.

Figure 1.4 Lee Enterprises district managers course

carriers. District managers typically do not have college degrees and work long, hard hours (with a morning paper, their shift begins at 2:00 to 4:00 am). Because of the hours and frustrations inherent in this job, the company experiences a great deal of employee turnover and is therefore faced with training new employees on a regular basis. To meet this need Lee Enterprises opted to have a course designed and delivered totally online to provide DM training. The online course presents needed information, practice quizzes to reinforce the information, video examples of appropriate techniques to use for a variety of management responsibilities, and online discussions with other DMs across the country to resolve common problems and to create a sense of community among fellow district managers. The online course served more than 400 people in the first six months of its release.

Specific job training for British food manufacturers' employees

Food manufacturing companies in the United Kingdom can now opt to train their staff in "lean manufacturing techniques" online. Lean manufacturing is a performance-based process used to increase competitive advantage in manufacturing organizations. The basics of lean manufacturing employ continuous improvement processes to focus on the elimination of waste or non-value-added steps within an organization.

The Manufacturing Institute is an organization formed in 1994 of leading UK manufacturing companies and universities. The institute develops productivity improvement programs to help build greater capacity for skilled manufacturing competitiveness. To date, over 9,000 manufacturers have participated in its programs.

An Internet-based training program launched by the Manufacturing Institute allows staff from a variety of companies to access training remotely from their workplace. As well as having to complete a number of exercises, trainees can also use the program to add their own site or departmental data to help them measure and track performance across key performance indicators. In addition, the training program also uses an online discussion forum where trainees can login and share knowledge, post messages to a threaded discussion board and discuss ideas with other manufacturers or with experts in using lean techniques.

The Lean On-line™ program has been designed as a business improvement tool as well as a training course. While employees are learning about "lean manufacturing," their company can be using the self-assessment and audit tools, provided in the training, to determine how to best implement lean manufacturing and tracking in its business.

Companies around the world are now using online education options to provide immediate training for a large variety of positions, ranging from the new receptionist to technicians and managers. Topics may be very specific (how to use a word processor) or more generalized (how to provide good customer service). In the past, online learning was seen primarily as a venue for training computer workers; but now it is being used effectively for all types of training. The use of the Internet to deliver in-company courses is now well established. Flexibility and economies of scale are powerful factors for the educational establishments and commercial providers who are significant players in the burgeoning business education market.

New schools, structures, and enterprises spanning the globe

The most notable impact of online learning has been in the adoption of this technology at colleges, universities, and industry training centers around the world. Projections for 2025 suggest that 160 million people will be seeking education. Compare that to the current 45 million students enrolled in higher education today. Online delivery of education has been seen as an important way to meet this growing need for higher education. Furthermore, many countries with large rural populations, or large illiterate and poorly-educated populations, coupled with an enormous shortage of trained teachers, see online education delivery as an important means to providing consistent educational opportunities to large numbers of people.

As an example, in the India Vision 2020 educational plan, it is predicted that country-wide learning systems will encourage more private industry participation that will be complementary to the existing government education programs and policies. These private-public partnerships will be involved in setting priorities, gaining institutional commitment, determining organizational structures with re-engineered processes, and creating better management and leadership within education. Furthermore, the Vision 2020 plan documents that these partnerships will be driven by learner needs and educational choices that maintain student autonomy and job mobility. They will allow adult learners to move easily from one location to another and to still be able to continue their education without losing forward progress toward a degree or program completion.

The India Vision 2020 plan covers all levels of education. It proposes strategic alliances between universities, colleges, schools, industry, subject experts, cable operators, communication service providers, and many others. The partnerships are multi-level to reduce government dependency on funding. Multi-communication technologies that can provide multi-lingual and multi-cultural options for education are to be used.

Some might ask, "Why are countries, such as India, Sri Lanka, China, and many in South America embracing technology so readily when it seems much of the population hardly has electricity, not to mention computers?" The answer is that these countries understand that knowledge and technology independence – enhanced by universal education – is a key strategy for their economic survival, their future growth and competitiveness in a global economy. Furthermore, these nations and many other proponents of technology see this global education as a way of removing the disparity between rich and poor, between developed and less-developed countries, and through shared learning and communication between disparate people eventually, perhaps, even make a difference between peace and war.

Although online learning opportunities are offered by thousands of colleges and universities, a growing number of consortia and brokering arrangements have developed among traditional institutions, hundreds of corporate universities, and the military branches to serve a larger and more diverse population of learners. Some of the first institutions established solely and specifically to provide technology-mediated distance learning were established outside of the United States in countries such as China, France, India, Indonesia, Iran, Korea, Spain, and South Africa. One of the first institutions of this kind was the Open University in the UK, which was established in 1969. Since then, 30 other open universities have been established throughout the world. The number of students served is impressive. For instance, in 1995, the China TV University System enrolled 530,000 students, the Anadolu University in Turkey enrolled 577,804 students, and the Universitas Terbuka in Indonesia taught 353,000 students. These institutions are all major higher education providers in their countries.

Mingle (1995), a researcher who studies computers and education, earlier identified four interrelated phenomena accompanying the rapid growth of information technology's impact upon global postsecondary education. These phenomena certainly seem to be the harbingers of growth today. They are described in detail below.

Lifelong learning

The world has changed in ways that make lifelong learning more of a necessity than an appealing phrase. In their book, *The Monster Under the Bed*, Davis and Botkin note that in an agrarian economy, education for young people between 7 and 14 was sufficient to last 40 years of a working life. The industrial economy expanded the age range of students to between 5 and 22. In the information economy, the rapid pace of technological change requires education to be updated throughout an individual's working life. People have to increase their learning power to sustain their earning power. Lifelong learning is the norm that is augmenting school-age education.

Learner-centered instruction

Mingle (1995) also points out that, traditionally, higher education is organized around the needs of the providers, where a "place" to conduct research and teach is supplied. The standards for conducting research and teaching, including faculty workload, space for labs, etc. are centered on the provider and professional needs. A "learner-centered" delivery system possesses three fundamental characteristics: it is, to a greater degree, self-directed; it is more focused and purposeful; and it employs the appropriate level of faculty mediation. The real roles of the instructor in an information-rich world will not be to provide information, but to guide students wading through the deep waters of the information flood. Instructors in this environment thrive as mentors. They use the best skills they have to encourage students through the educationally crucial task of processing information, problem solving, analysis, and synthesis of ideas – the activities in which a student's time can be best spent.

Providing access

For several years it has been recognized that learning does not have to take place only on a college or university campus. In 1994 the US government announced its intention to establish by the year 2000 the National Information Infrastructure (NII), which is essentially a broadband digital network. One fundamental requirement is that the applications of the NII extend into homes and workplaces as well as colleges and universities. A plethora of courses and entire academic programs are already being provided to students in venues away from the campus, particularly in a student's home or workplace. Many other countries have undertaken similar efforts to provide network infrastructures. Rich information technology, the worldwide push toward global standards, ever-increasing customer demands, and growing international competition are key forces behind the emerging multimedia revolution and the evolution of national information infrastructures in every country. Many of these countries are now also participating in the development and acceptance of standards through the global information infrastructure. These advances hold the promise of a broad range of information-age benefits to virtually every citizen of the world.

Knowledge media

The term "knowledge media" was proposed by Marc Eisenstadt to describe the convergence of telecommunications, computing, and the learning or cognitive sciences. He defined knowledge media as the "capturing, storing, imparting, sharing, accessing and creating of knowledge" (Eisenstadt 1995). The combination of technologies coupled with our understanding of the learning process will fundamentally change the relationship between people and knowledge. This medium is not just a technical format, such as a CD-ROM or email, but encompasses the entire presentational style, how the user interfaces with the media, the accessibility of the medium, and the degree of interactivity. Knowledge media provide the opportunity to change the emphasis from the classroom and teaching to the individual and learning. In short, with good learning materials, effective networks, and proper support, students can learn better at home than in class.

Many students are drawn to online courses because they both want and need to determine the time and place of their learning. Many recent researchers have predicted that online learning will make its greatest contribution through hybrid courses that combine the classroom and the computer. Electronic interaction already extends learning beyond classroom walls; it is likely that by 2010 the vast majority of courses in higher education will have some online components associated with them.

Making connections across virtual space and time

At this point you might be thinking "This is all fine, but how do I know if online learning is right for me?" Certainly, if you are working full or part time, or have multiple community or family obligations, you are a good candidate for online learning. If you are an adult returning to higher education after being away, you may really enjoy the independence of online learning. If you are in a job where you are required to update your skills on a regular basis, it is likely that you will be encountering online learning in training – whether through a computer-based software tutorial or in an actual facilitated online class. Finally, if you are a student in a traditional college or university, the chances are that you will be required to use the Internet and do some of your learning online, and it is likely this will become even more the case in the near future.

So, almost everyone will be encountering online learning at some time. However, there is a way to evaluate your *readiness* for this environment. Take a moment to complete the survey (Table 1.1) and you can begin to reflect on how prepared you might already be for this setting or where your strengths and weaknesses lie and thus, on what sections of this book would be most beneficial for you to focus.

Student self-evaluation checklist

This survey (see Table 1.1) is designed to assist you in rating your current readiness to pursue online education courses. Answer honestly by rating your agreement with each statement. Tick the box that best matches your feelings. The feedback from this survey may assist you in the areas where you need to focus prior to enrolling in an online degree program.

Any questions where you answered "rarely" reflect areas where you should particularly focus on those topics in this book. As you read through this book, continue to evaluate yourself as a potential online learner and carefully reflect on your reasoning and your personal learning preferences. For example, many students who enjoy the social aspects of learning or who learn more effectively by interacting with other students face-to-face might answer "rarely" to question 12. This means you will want to pay special attention to the section on building a learning community, and you will want to carefully evaluate online programs to ensure they provide many opportunities for you to be in a more supportive and interactive environment.

Once you are convinced you want to pursue online learning more actively, you need to locate courses, programs, or entire degrees online that fit your needs. There are many ways to search for these options. One way is to go to your local college or university and ask what online learning opportunities are available. Another is to search Web sites of institutions that you already know have a good reputation for delivering the types of courses or majors in your interest. It is possible that some or all of those courses are online. If you do not already have local resources or a personal knowledge of what is available in your country, there are a number of good resources on the Web to help you with this process.

There are many Web-based resources to help you research institutions, online course providers, and their reputation. It would be impossible to list all of them. However, the three sites below will provide excellent information about accredited programs or links to reputable resources for programs around the world.

The International Center for Distance Learning (http://icdl.open.ac.uk/)

The International Centre for Distance Learning (ICDL) of the Open University, UK, maintains distance education databases containing information on over 31,000 distance learning programs and courses

Table 1.1 Student self-evaluation checklist

		Rarely	*Sometimes*	*Most of the time*	*All of the time*
1	I am able to easily access the Internet as needed for my studies.	☐	☐	☐	☐
2	I am comfortable communicating with others over the Internet.	☐	☐	☐	☐
3	I am willing to communicate actively with my classmates and instructors electronically.	☐	☐	☐	☐
4	I am willing to set aside an amount of time each week to effectively engage in study.	☐	☐	☐	☐
5	I feel that online learning is of at least equal quality to traditional classroom learning.	☐	☐	☐	☐
6	I feel that using my background and experience in my studies will be beneficial to new learning.	☐	☐	☐	☐
7	I am comfortable with online written communication.	☐	☐	☐	☐
8	When it comes to learning and studying, I am a self-directed person.	☐	☐	☐	☐
9	Reviewing what I have learned in a course helps me with new learning.	☐	☐	☐	☐
10	In my studies I am self-disciplined and find it easy to set aside reading and homework time.	☐	☐	☐	☐
11	I am able to manage my study time effectively and easily complete assignments on time.	☐	☐	☐	☐
12	As a student, I enjoy working by myself with minimal support or interaction.	☐	☐	☐	☐
13	In my studies I set goals and have a high degree of initiative.	☐	☐	☐	☐
14	I believe I am the only one responsible for my learning.	☐	☐	☐	☐

and over 1,000 institutions teaching at a distance worldwide. It is the most inclusive distance learning site on the Web.

Distance Education Clearing House at University of Wisconsin (http://www.uwex.edu/disted/home.html)

The Distance Education Clearinghouse is another comprehensive and widely recognized Web site bringing together distance education information from both US and international sources. New information and resources are being added to the Distance Education Clearinghouse on a continual basis.

Degree.Net (http://www.degree.net/guides.html)

This site attempts to demystify accreditation, identify "diploma mills" and other disreputable institutions, and report on some of the latest developments in the industry.

Get Educated.Com (http://www.geteducated.com/onlineguides.htm)

This site offers free downloads of their directories of online universities arranged as PDF documents by speciality. These manuals detail accredited online programs and degrees throughout the US and Canada.

Chapter 2

Deciding to pursue online learning

If I should not be learning now, when should I be?
(Lacydes, *c*.241 BC, from Diogenes Laertius, *Lives of Eminent Philosophers*, Lacydes, sec. 5)

An introduction to online learning

Since the introduction of the personal computer in 1981, the possibilities for learning online have grown rapidly. Though some online learning did occur before that time, it was primarily the province of large software company training programs or military programs where men and women were deployed at great distances and needed tutorials to learn a specific skill. These efforts were limited to computer-mediated instruction (CMI) or computer-assisted instruction (CAI), where courses were designed as self-study tutorials in a particular subject or topic. They typically included some questions which required a response and then the computer generated immediate feedback. Though heralded as excellent at the time, they did not afford the student an opportunity to interact with other students or with an online instructor. Furthermore, the tutorials were very limited in scope and the amount or type of interaction with the computer that could occur.

Large-scale interest in computer instruction waned quickly. The time and effort required to develop the curriculum, as well as the necessary technical sophistication, was out of reach for most businesses and educational institutions. Estimates of course creation timelines averaged between 150 and 300 hours of development time for each hour of delivery time. Consequently, the price to purchase courses commercially was also expensive. A typical 10 -or 12-hour course would cost $5,000 or more.

The use of computers for online learning didn't really begin on any large scale until 1996, four years after the introduction of the World Wide Web. In 2000, reflecting the increase in computer users both at home and at work, many government census bureaus began reporting statistics regarding the number of computers available to a population, their location, individual and business access to the Internet, and if the computer was used for educational purposes.

Today, traditional colleges and universities around the world offer individual courses and entire degree programs online – both undergraduate and graduate. When you complete your degree online from an accredited traditional institution, you receive the same diploma as you would for taking all the courses at the campus. In other words, an MBA at Harvard (whether completed online or on campus) is the same thing. Your transcripts do not state where the courses were taken.

In addition to traditional colleges entering the online market, we are now seeing entire "virtual" universities – institutions that do not have a physical campus. These schools offer all their courses completely online, with instructors, and administrative staff working from their homes or small business offices. It is still unclear how these entirely virtual universities will be accepted. It is important to check carefully the accreditation of these programs and their offerings before spending your money to get a degree. This will be discussed in greater detail later in this chapter.

Courses taught via the Internet have now become quite common, as computers are widely distributed throughout libraries, schools, businesses, and homes. In 1992 fewer than 10 US states were using Web-based learning; today, all 50 states have significant efforts in online learning, both at the grammar school and at the college level. Even in countries with poorer economies (e.g. many African countries, India and Sri Lanka, and much of Latin America) the Internet has become a key ingredient in economic growth and education. Many of these countries have been given assistance to build the computing infrastructure needed to support Internet commerce and education. As a Ghanaian instructor commented:

> I see young children taking their lunch money to go into Internet cafes because it provides them with a freedom to learn and their curiosity can range widely. The Internet as an educational tool can become an equalizing force for all countries and levels of people.
>
> Dr John Afele
> (Lynch, 2003)

How is online learning delivered today?

Online learning encompasses a large variety of offerings, from individualized topical searches to single-issue tutorials (for example, "How to Build A Web Page") to individual college courses and full degree programs at the bachelors, masters, and doctorate levels. Today an online course can incorporate a wide range of technologies and use a great number of software programs in its creation. However, the experience for the student falls into five basic categories described below. Having a basic understanding of each of these areas will help you become a successful student in the virtual classroom. These categories of technology will be revisited throughout this book several times and in greater detail in the ensuing chapters.

Hyperlinked web pages

Web pages are based on print materials that are available over the Internet. What makes these pages interesting for learners is the ability to move from one page of content to a related page of content easily. This movement is called "hyperlinking." When you hear the term "surfing the Web" it usually means someone is moving from one page of interesting information to another by selecting "links" to new material. These links are provided by the page author and allow the user to easily find additional information without having to look it up each time.

Another reason Web pages provide the foundation for online learning is that they are the underpinning for content. Many students prefer to have content on the Web, instead of in a paper study guide or class notes, because it is easy to search.

Audio interaction

One of the links that can be provided on a Web page is audio content. This might include the ability to hear an instructor's lecture, listen to music, or listen to another language being spoken in order to learn the accent.

In addition to Web-based audio content, many online classes also include the use of other audio technologies. For example, you may be asked to participate in a telephone audioconference or a computer audiobridge as part of the class. This is an opportunity to have a two-way conversation with your instructor or your classmates.

Video interaction

Instructional video tools include still images such as slides, pre-produced moving images (film or videotape), and real-time moving images delivered to your desktop computer combined with audio tools. Some typical examples of video used in an online course would include film of the instructor lecturing, video demonstrating a procedure (e.g., how to give a shot to a patient), and a tutorial that demonstrates how a piece of software works – typically showing the cursor moving to certain functions and then showing what happens when a button is clicked.

Some online programs also allow for video-conferencing which allows you to see the instructor and your classmates (and for them to see you) and talk to them while sitting at your home computer. The video-conferencing capabilities are not yet widely used because of the differing speeds of computers. However, there is no doubt that as computers and the data lines become faster, video conferencing will become much more ubiquitous.

Dynamic data

One of the functions of a traditional classroom environment is to provide constant feedback to the instructor as to how the students are learning. This is accomplished in different ways. First, instructors constantly scan their students to look for body language that indicates they are engaged in the learning or that they are confused – for example, frowning or that "glazed" look in the eyes. Second, instructors ask questions and test student understanding by having them respond or discuss. This type of interaction can happen online as well.

Computers send and receive all information electronically. The term "data" is used to describe this exchange. "Dynamic" means that the data can change forms or be passed from one program to another. This may take place via email, discussion boards, online quizzes or tests, or chat rooms. The exchange may take place at the same time (synchronously) as in a chat room, or be posted to be downloaded later (asynchronously) such as in a discussion board.

Print materials

Printed material is still a foundational element for all instruction, including the online classroom. Textbooks and study guides are still distributed to students through bookstores and mail. The Web-based content in a class usually consists of the logistical materials and supplemental materials. For example, you would typically find static pages containing information such as the syllabus, calendar, course descriptions and grading rubrics. Many instructors also provide hyperlinked materials such as instructor notes, presentation slides, and links to additional articles to read or library resources. However, most online classes still require a textbook, and the chapter readings are integral to the learning process. For example, you may be asked to read Chapter 2 and then discuss key points in the online discussion board.

The primary skill needed to be a successful online learner is to be an independent learner. This means someone who enjoys researching information and finding the links on his or her own. For example, if you are interested in learning how to create a beautiful English garden for your backyard, but don't have the time or money to take a formal class, you might approach it by going to the library and checking out books on the topic, asking friends who have gardens you admire, or going to a local nursery and soliciting advice. All of this is independent learning. Many of these same skills can be used electronically as well. A typical sequence to an individualized learning approach using the Internet might include the following steps:

- use a search engine to gain access to the topic areas
- read Web pages and follow their links
- subscribe to newsgroups or discussion lists which relate to the topic
- participate in chat rooms with that topical theme
- exchange emails with individuals who appear to be knowledgeable in the topic.

In the context of courses offered through a formal mechanism, such as a college or a corporate training online course, the learning approach is not necessarily different than that above. The primary difference is that your learning would be guided to specific areas and knowledge bases that you probably would not find on your own. Whereas individualized learning or research using Internet resources exclusively is often a "hit and miss" affair, quality online education programs provide you with only "hits."

Selecting learning/training opportunities – fully online vs. hybrid courses

There are a variety of ways you might encounter online learning. Certainly, one way is in a distance course, where all of the learning is online and you never need to go to the campus. The history of academic programs delivered fully online is a recent one. The Sloan Foundation – a funding organization for online learning in the US – has been supporting the development of fully online programs for over a decade. Recently, however, they have documented an increased interest in blended or hybrid courses – those that combine online components with face-to-face instruction. A survey of 50 institutions in the US found that online learning directors expect hybrid course enrollments to triple over the next three years, while the growth in fully online offerings will increase about 25 percent.

Hybrid courses have an online learning component associated with a campus-based course. In some cases, the online learning component allows the attendance requirement on campus to be significantly reduced (e.g., instead of attending class three days per week, you only attend one day and the remaining time is spent in online learning). In other cases, a hybrid course means that you may still be required to attend all classroom sessions, but some of the learning will be online. In the latter case, most often readings and some discussions are done online while the lecture or practice and labs are done on campus.

What you select will be based on your personal needs for face-to-face communication as well as your scheduling needs and the offerings at your institution.

Ensuring training or degree value

Unfortunately, the ease of putting information online and the access it provides to a worldwide population has also produced a noticeable increase in the numbers of "diploma mills" or online training that does not provide a quality learning experience.

Consider the following:

- There are more than 300 *un*accredited universities now operating in the US alone. While a few are genuine start-ups or online ventures, the great majority range from merely dreadful to outright diploma mills that will sell people any degree they want at prices from $3,000 to $5,000.
- It is not uncommon for a large fake school to "award" as many as 500 PhDs every month.
- The aggregate income of these crooks is reported to be in excess of $200 million a year. Data show that a single phony school can earn between $10 million and $20 million annually.

- With the closure of the FBI's diploma mill task force, the indifference of most state law enforcement agencies, the minimal interest of the news media, and the growing ease of using the Internet to start and run a fake university, things are rapidly growing worse.
- A fair chunk of that $200 million is being spent by people who really want and need a legitimate degree but don't know enough to tell the difference. It's tuition that should be going to legitimate schools.
- The literature and the sales pitch of some of these phony schools is really slick. The catalog is frequently more attractive than some real schools. For example, a typical catalog is replete with photos of campus scenes, happy alumni (all from stock photo companies) and even two Nobel laureates listed with honorary doctorates – though these awardees may be unaware of the use of their picture in the school catalog.

What is accreditation?

Quite simply, it is a validation – a statement by a group of persons who are, theoretically, impartial experts in higher education, that a given school, or department within a school, has been thoroughly investigated and found worthy of approval. Accreditation rules and procedures vary from one nation to the next. In some countries all colleges and universities either are operated by the government or gain the full right to grant degrees directly from the government, so there is no need for a separate, independent agency to say that a given school is acceptable. Other countries have formed accrediting bodies or agencies that provide some oversight or approval of schools.

The United States

In the United States, accreditation is an entirely voluntary process, done by private, nongovernmental agencies. As a result of this lack of central control or authority, there have evolved good accrediting agencies and bad ones, recognized ones and unrecognized ones, legitimate ones and phony ones. So when a school says, "we are accredited," that statement alone means nothing. You must always ask, "Accredited by whom?" It is all too frequent that one hears from a distressed person who says, about the degrees they have just learned are worthless, "But the school was accredited; I even checked with the accrediting agency." The agency, needless to say, turned out to be as phony as the school. The wrong kind of accreditation can be worse than none at all.

In the US the proper accreditation process takes about two years to become a "candidate" and a total of 4 to 8 years to become fully accredited. Once a school is accredited, it is visited by inspection teams at infrequent intervals (every five to ten years is common) to see if it is still worthy of its accreditation. The status is always subject to review at any time, should new programs be developed or should there be any significant new developments, positive or negative.

Note Everything in the foregoing section applies to accreditation as done by recognized agencies. Many of the other agencies, even those that are not illegal, will typically accredit a new school within days, even minutes, of its coming into existence.

In the US the best way to ensure the school is accredited is to check for *regional* accreditation. Regional accreditation bodies are set up as commissions and serve the purposes of quality assurance and improvement, as well as being gatekeepers for the US Department of Education. These bodies attest to the required level of quality of their member institutions for receiving federal funds to support teaching, research, and student financial aid. These commissions are recognized by the US Department of Education and by the Council on Higher Education Accreditation as the regional authority on the quality of institutions of higher education

The six regional accrediting bodies in the US are listed in Table 2.1 and the states within their responsibility. Each of the regional associations may also accredit American/international schools around the globe.

The United Kingdom

The university structure in the United Kingdom is different from that of the United States. All universities in England are controlled by government regulations and protocol. This ensures a consistent standard and quality of programs that is continuously monitored by the government's Quality Assurance Agency for Higher Education, the QAA. Universities operate under royal charter, which is the government's approval that gives legal powers to call themselves a university and award degrees.

The award of degrees or related qualifications in the UK is illegal without the proper authorization. Authorization is granted under royal charter or act of Parliament. Institutions seeking permission to award degrees must demonstrate they have a commitment to quality and

Table 2.1 Regional accreditating bodies

Regional Accrediting Association	*States under Purview*
Southern Association of Colleges and Schools (www.sacscoc.org/)	Alabama, Florida, Georgia, Kentucky, Louisiana, Mississippi, North Carolina, South Carolina, Tennessee, Texas, Virginia
Middle States Association of Colleges and Schools (www.msache.org/)	Delaware, Florida, Maryland, New Jersey, New York, Pennsylvania, Puerto Rico, US Virgin Islands
New England Association of Schools and Colleges (www.neasc.org/)	Connecticut, Maine, Massachusetts, New Hampshire, Rhode Island, Vermont
North Central Association of Schools and Colleges (www.ncahigherlearningcommission.org/)	Arkansas, Arizona, Colorado, Iowa, Illinois, Indiana, Kansas, Michigan, Minnesota, Missouri, North Dakota, Nebraska, Ohio, Oklahoma, New Mexico, South Dakota, Wisconsin, West Virginia, Wyoming
Northwest Association of Schools and Colleges (www.nwccu.org/)	Alaska, Idaho, Montana, Nevada, Oregon, Utah, Washington
Western Association of Schools and Colleges (www.wascweb.org/senior/)	California and Hawaii, the territories of Guam, American Samoa, Federated States of Micronesia, Republic of Palau, Commonwealth of the Northern Marianas Islands, the Pacific basin, and east Asia, and areas of the Pacific and east Asia where American/international schools or colleges may apply.

adequate systems for safeguarding academic standards. The government is advised on all issues by the QAA for Higher Education. The royal charter is the highest level of accreditation attainable and is recognized and respected throughout the world.

Each country has its own accrediting standards. If you are pursuing education outside of your country, it is best to do good research first and determine if the school from which you wish to take classes is legitimate, and thus your degree or certificate will be recognized by others around the world.

What constitutes quality in an online course or program?

There is quite a range of online education offerings, from no-name colleges to offerings from Harvard, Cambridge, and Queensland. Additionally, most countries operate Open University programs that are also government certified. People want these online degree programs because of convenience and flexibility. However, many programs, even at legitimate schools are not very mature, and therefore the actual quality of the course or program may vary from school to school and from instructor to instructor. Then again, with increasing emphasis, demand, and investment, the legitimate schools are becoming better at using online learning technology effectively, especially those programs that combine the online experience with collaboration and provide on-campus activities and networking opportunities. To get the full benefit, you need to look for a high degree of interaction (whether face-to-face or online), high-quality assignments, and online mentoring from experienced faculty rather than teaching assistants.

There is no universal agreement within the international higher education community regarding the definition of quality. Debate continues about the relative merits of online interactivity, communication with instructors and classmates, and how much self-directed learning is important to student success and institutional effectiveness. Nevertheless, it is tempting, and in many ways convenient, to use the instructional processes and activities of "traditional" higher education as the benchmark upon which online learning is judged. The teaching–learning process of higher education has long been a combination of face-to-face meetings ranging from tutorials to large lectures, asynchronous communications (such as written assignments), and guided independent work (like reading and laboratory assignments). Through the application of information technology, however, a wide variety of options are now available and, although these fundamental pedagogies are still part of the teaching–learning process, they are reconfigured and enhanced.

The following practices are offered as appropriate quality assurance strategies to be considered when learning takes place online. Each of these strategies focuses particularly on the needs of the learner, enjoys support from a number of practitioners of online learning, and is found in a growing body of literature. When evaluating an institution's online offerings, you might consider talking to a faculty member, a student who has taken courses at the institution, and/or an administrator. Ask them to describe how the courses address these key areas. The quality assurance strategies below represent many of the best practices used by experienced providers of online learning combined with teaching–learning methods that have withstood the test of time in colleges and universities around the world.

Teaching methods

There are four key areas to consider (listed below) when evaluating the quality of online teaching methods for a particular course or entire curriculum.

Interactivity

Course interactivity is the key to a quality online learning experience. A substantial body of evidence suggests that the more interactive the instruction, the more effective the learning outcome is likely to be. The key ingredients appear to be the availability of the instructor – whether through direct person-to-person contact or through electronic means – and the intellectual engagement of the student, regardless of the method of engagement. Interactivity can take place with the content, through quizzes, short questions, simulations, and examples. Interactivity

Modularity

Considerable evidence exists that individualized instruction emphasizing small, modularized units of content, mastery of one unit before moving to the next, immediate and frequent feedback to students on their progress, and active student involvement in the learning process are consistently effective in enhancing subject matter learning over more traditional learning formats such as lecture and recitation. Even in the case of advanced subjects, it is important that concepts be presented in a manner that allows the student to build on past experience and to apply each step of the process along the way. This enhances retention and application.

Collaboration

Learning is enhanced through cooperation and reciprocity among students. The learning process involves collaboration and a social context, with students working together. This is particularly true online because of the absence of some or all of the face-to-face opportunities for teamwork. Sharing ideas in a group setting improves thinking and deepens understanding. Study groups, collaborative learning, group problem solving, and discussion of assignments can be dramatically strengthened through the use of discussion boards, chat rooms, electronic whiteboards, and effective email collaboration.

Learning styles

Students learn in many different ways and bring varied talents and experiences to the learning activity. Technology has the enormous potential to enable students to learn in a variety of ways. Online learning can provide dramatic visuals and well-organized print, demonstrate process and procedures with simulations and interactive objects, encourage self-reflection and self-evaluation, and promote collaboration and group problem solving. It is important that any online course does not get bogged down in one method of delivery. The use of physical textbooks, along with visuals (both online and in other forms), as well as direct application in the student's real world environment are all helpful to a robust learning experience.

Faculty involvement

A good online course is much more than the content of a subject area or the online examples of a process. Key to any good course experience is the involvement of faculty. Some institutions mistakenly believe that online learning can cut down on the use of faculty or completely cut out faculty from the teaching process. On the contrary, many studies have indicated students learn to more depth and effectiveness with significant faculty involvement. Although no longer lecturing in person, the instructor is still crucial to guiding students toward proper questions, research, problem-solving, and further exploration in the field. Faculty expertise and mentoring are vital to a great online learning experience.

Faculty contact in and out of class is very important to student motivation and involvement. The concern of faculty often helps students get through rough times, making it easier to continue their studies. Through electronic conferencing, email, discussion boards and chat rooms opportunities for conversation between students and their instructors actually increase. Researchers have found that students and faculty converse and exchange work much more speedily than before and more thoughtfully and "safely" than when confronting each other in a classroom or during busy faculty office hours.

Knowledge media are replacing the instructor as the student's primary source of information. These media usually produced by the faculty or in conjunction with the course instructor, become integral to the online delivery of the course. Much of this media is provided through links to a myriad of resources both in the faculty's repertoire and in the collections of other institutions, libraries, or faculty sites. Since any individual instructor is no longer the only source of information, particular importance is placed on the ability of the instructor to guide students through the morass of the Internet and the reliability of information. In addition, faculty should be capable of identifying or creating courseware that boosts student motivation, and encourages interactivity, collaboration, and modular learning activities.

Support services

An integrated team – such as computer service technicians, counselors, site administrators, distribution clerks, and library resource personnel – is needed to support effective online learning. When evaluating the quality of a program or an institution, it is important to check on each of these resources and how effectively they can respond to your needs as a student who may not be able to come to campus on a regular basis.

Libraries

Libraries are being transformed by technology. An institution that is geared toward the online learner will already be engaged in replacing traditional library resources with digital collections, online journal and media databases, and information literacy tutorials. All of this should be easily accessible through a user-friendly online retrieval system available to students 24 hours a day, seven days a week. If the institution you are considering does not have online access or digital collections, it is important for you to determine how it will get you needed research articles, books, or other media in a timely manner. If the institution requires you to use the resources of your local library, you need to evaluate if that is reasonable. Many local libraries have neither the resources nor the staffing necessary to accommodate typical higher education studies.

Student services

All student services, including registration, tuition payment, financial aid, and bookstore functions should be electronically available to the online learner. Check to see that the institution you are considering is diligent in ensuring that online students receive clear, complete, and timely information at least as quickly and easily as any on-campus student. Of particular importance is technical assistance for students so that the technology becomes a "transparent" conduit of knowledge.

Assessment of learning

Though many students might wish they never had to take another test or prove that they had met the learning objectives for a course, it is important to know that the institution you are selecting has consistent and effective assessment criteria. Certainly, you want to know that you are learning what is necessary to progress in a field or master a topic. Furthermore, you want to be assured that your degree is worth the time and energy you are putting into it. Effective assessment of learning is critical to ensuring that graduating students can be successfully compared to students of similar majors around the world.

Almost two decades ago Howard Bowen observed that in higher education true outcomes in the form of learning and personal development of students are on the whole unexamined and only vaguely discerned. It is becoming increasingly important (and some would say imperative) for institutions participating in online learning to identify a clearly understood set of outcomes, and especially student knowledge, skills, and competency levels. Once these student learning outcomes are identified, reliable and valid methods for measuring their achievement should be developed. As the concept of "seat-time" becomes less and less relevant, especially as a proxy for student learning, externally validated outcomes – preferably determined through multiple measures – provide both the institution and the student with evidence that learning has taken place.

Checklist for evaluating online programs

It is helpful to begin looking at institutions in your location first, and then branch out to other institutions based on your subject needs. Before committing any money or resources, be sure you thoroughly acquaint yourself with the institution. Consult their academic advising services and ask several questions. Below is a checklist of questions to ask any institution or organization that is providing online education. The checklist is divided into five categories.

1 Basic information any online education provider should make clear
2 Important technical considerations
3 Day-to-day operations and experience of the course or program
4 Costs of the course/program
5 The course delivery system

Checklist for evaluating online programs

Basic information any online education provider should make clear

1 *How credible is the course or institution?*
Do they have a good reputation? Can you check references?
2 *What are the qualifications of the course designers, instructors, delivery personnel?*
Do they have proper licensure or accreditations for your needs?
3 *Exactly what are you expected to learn?*
Is this what you want to learn? Do the outcomes match your needs?
4 *What are the "intended learning outcomes" for each and every course and the entry level knowledge or skills necessary for your success?*
Do you have the necessary preparation to be successful in this course or program?
5 *What will you get when you finish the course or program? e.g. college credit, completion certificate or professional designation.*
Can you do anything with it? Will it be recognized by another institution? Will it help you get a job, raise, promotion, or into a degree program?
6 *Who or what accrediting body recognizes the institution and its programs or degrees?*
Are the courses and programs reputable? Have they been recognized by a government entity or a well-known professional organization?
7 *Is the timeline/timeframe flexible for completion or mandatory?*
If there is a mandatory timeframe (e.g. within a typical term of 15 weeks) how much flexibility is available within those weeks? If you are traveling and don't have computer access for two weeks, will you fail the course? If the completion timeframe is extremely flexible (e.g. one year) is that too much flexibility for you? Are you able to keep yourself on task without an impending deadline?

8 *Who are the teachers/instructors and what are their credentials? How will they interact with you online?*
Is their any human interaction in the course or is it all computerized? Is the instructor credible? You might try sending the instructor an email and see if you get a response in a timely manner.
9 *How will you be assessed? What is the criteria for evaluation and success?*
Is this done through objective testing (e.g. a multiple-choice test), writing papers, or doing a project? Is it individual assessment or group assessment?

Important technical information

1 *What are the minimum computer and operating system requirements? Are there any options?*
Is it Mac or PC compatible? Does it require a high-bandwidth connection or is a 56K dial-up modem sufficient?
2 *What are the software requirements?*
Do you need to purchase or download special software? Is there additional cost for this software?
3 *What technical skills do you need? Is there an orientation to get you started?*
If you don't have the technical skills, do they provide a way for you to get them? Does that cost extra?
4 *Is there a help desk or other technical support option?*
How do you get technical support? Is there a toll-free number or is it all by email? Is it available late at night or on the weekends when you might need it most?

Day-to-day operation and experience of the course or program

1 *How skilled do you need to be at reading, taking exams, managing your own time? What are the learning skills you need for success in this course/program?*
Is there an orientation course or some instructional tutorial available to help you prepare for learning online?
2 *What is the type of material you'll cover in the course/program? Why is it important to the field or to your profession?*
Is the content current and relevant or is the syllabus filled only with old citations? Is the required textbook's publication date within the last three to five years?

3. *Is the content relevant, well-organized and presented in an interesting manner?*
   Is it easy for you to read? Are there options for learning in addition to reading? Are there helpful explanations or other interactions that help clarify concepts? Do you see examples that you can apply to your life or work?
4. *How do you get started and connect with the supplier? Are the complete instructions and registration procedures and services available online?*
   Is it easy to register? Can you track your registration? How do you order books or other needed supplies? How to you access advising or financial aid services?
5. *How do you get help during the course (technical assistance or content expertise)?*
   If you have questions, who do you contact and how? What is the response time? Is there instructor assistance if you have problems during the course/program? Is that free or an additional cost?
6. *Are there optional paths to learning? Can you personalize the course for maximum benefit or is it one size fits all?*
   If you are having a problem, are there links to remediation? If the course is too easy for you, is there a way to learn more in-depth?
7. *Are various approaches to learning styles included – reading, doing, listening, viewing, demonstrating competency?*
   Is the way you like to learn a major or minor part of the course? (e.g., if you need pictures to understand concepts, are there sufficient pictures for you?) Are you willing to adapt your learning style to this course/program if it is different?
8. *How is communication conducted during the course?*
   Is it in "real time" (synchronous) requiring you to be online at specific times of the day or night? If so, how often is this required? Or, are communication requirements more flexible (asynchronous) allowing you to login when you have an opportunity?
9. *Are there a required number of "check-ins" online (e.g. you must login every day or five days out of seven) and are they reasonable?*
   Do you have to meet a specific schedule? If so, why and is it reasonable?
10. *Do you have frequent and sustainable opportunities to communicate with teachers, content experts, process experts, and other students as needed?*
    Is the majority of the learning self-directed and independent, or are you in a learning community where your instructors and classmates are working together to learn a topic? How important is it to you to be in communication with others in your class? With your instructor?

11 *Is there a regular and systematic way for you to evaluate your experience and provide feedback to the provider? Can you evaluate instructors, curriculum, processes and resources?*
Is the instructor or institution actively seeking your feedback? Do they provide evaluations to the user/student? Do you feel like a valued customer? Are students treated as important individuals?

Costs of the program

1 *What will be the total cost – registration, tuition, books and materials, equipment, other fees?*
Can you afford it? Are there special technical fees or access fees that are not usually included with tuition?
2 *Are the cost options (e.g. taking a course for university credit may be more than taking a course for noncredit) clearly stated?*
Do you need college credit in order to transfer to a degree program? If you take it noncredit, are there different expectations for passing the course/program?
3 *Is there financial aid available? How is it accessed?*
Are there limitations on the financial aid in terms of the number of courses, the timeframes for completion, or the level of the course? Are there scholarships or grants, as opposed to loans?
4 *How do you get out of the course if you are not satisfied? What are the policies for withdrawal and refunds?*
Check specific rules for refund timelines and amounts. If you withdraw with the intention of returning at a later date, are there special fee arrangements?

Course delivery system

1 *Is there a demo of a course or how the course delivery system works that you can practice with and evaluate first?*
Some online course delivery systems require special browser configurations, passwords, or security protocols. How do these work with your computer configuration?
2 *Is the navigation logical and well-organized? Can you find the materials you need when you need them?*
Is it easy to use? Can you practice with all the course options (e.g., discussions, quizzes, reading, simulations, etc.)

3 *Do you need to download software to interact with the course or must you be on the Internet to interact with the course?*
If software is downloaded is it compatible with your computer system? If you must be on the Internet, what is the time requirement and does that affect your overall cost (e.g. per minute charges for Internet access).

Financing your online education

The cost of education varies widely around the world. In some countries the government has determined that higher education is key to their economic stability and competitiveness in the global market. In these countries higher education tuition is free for selected students who have already shown their ability to compete at university or, in other countries, free for all citizens who pass entrance exams. For example, in Sri Lanka, public university tuition is free through the bachelor's degree for all citizens who are able to pass exams. Of course, students must still find a way to pay for books, materials, and room and board. Other countries, such as the US require that all students pay for education whether at public colleges and universities or private institutions. Even in countries where the cost is minimal, such as Germany, there are still students who need financial assistance. Some students, based on need or academic merit are provided financial aid to help defray the costs of tuition or living expenses while attending school.

The rules of financial aid differ from nation to nation and sometimes from school to school. It is best to check with high school and college advisors about the specifics in your local area. When online learning was in its infancy some national financial aid offerings were not available to online learners because there was not a means of ensuring quality control or institutional audits. However, now that online learning has become a major offering in most traditional institutions, this stricture seems to be gone in most cases.

For example, in October 2001, the US Congress voted 354 to 70 in favor of a bill to allow colleges and universities to offer more of their courses online (exceeding the previous 50 percent rule) and still participate in federal financial aid programs. Furthermore, the bill no longer required distance students to satisfy the residency requirement of physically being on campus a certain number of days. Now, students meet an institutional residency requirement in an online class by being required to login to the course a minimum of one day a week.

In both the European Union and the US most financial aid programs are offered on one or more of four criteria.

Ability to benefit

Most countries do not allow financial aid monies to be granted to students without a high school (secondary) diploma or equivalency unless the student has demonstrated that he or she can benefit from the education offered. This is accomplished by receiving a passing score on an independently administered test approved by the government.

Academic credit

This is the unit of measurement an institution gives to a student when he/she fulfills course or subject requirement(s) as determined by the institution. Most financial aid programs require that the student be engaged in a minimum number of academic credits to prove he/she is making progress toward a diploma, degree, or certification.

Financial need

It seems universal that all nations want to be sure that financial hardship is not a barrier to a good student to attend university. If a student proves scholarship through testing, high marks in secondary education or previous college education, but lacks the finances for tuition there are a multitude of packages available to help ensure that the student receives an education. Note, however, that need alone does not necessarily qualify the student. One must also demonstrate promise or scholarship.

Scholarship

This criterion reflects the desire of all nations and higher education institutions to support those people who have shown a true talent or extensive background in a particular field. Financial aid packages based on scholarship may be awarded purely on high scores on tests or in previous courses, or may be combined with identification of financial need.

General advice about applying for financial aid

If there are government monies available in your country, there is generally a universal application process – for example the FAFSA form in the US or the EU3 in the European Union. This is frequently the key application necessary to receive full consideration for federal aid as well as other private or local aid. Filing the appropriate paperwork and applying for aid at colleges in which you are interested is the best way to get a full picture of your likely annual costs and options available to meet them. The aid packages may include grants, scholarships, loans, or work-study options. Be sure to accurately determine the due dates for this paperwork and get it in as early as possible prior to the due date.

Don't be afraid to apply for any and all scholarships! Many students do not fully realize their scholarship potential. Everyone is good at something, and often there is money that goes unclaimed because there were no applicants. Many scholarships are set up by private groups, industry interests, or individuals based on criteria that may not be keyed to good grades. For example, in the US there are scholarships specifically for individuals returning to college in midlife (age 40 or older). There are also many scholarships set up by unions for children of parents or grandparents who were members of those unions. Begin searching and applying for scholarships the year before you plan to apply. Check with school advisors at any institution where you wish to apply. Also check with your employers and your parents' employers and with charitable and service organizations. Below are links to good information about obtaining financial aid in the European Union and the US.

- Students in England and Wales: http://www.dfes.gov.uk/student support/students/index.shtml.
- Students in the European Union and UK: http://www.dfes.gov.uk/studentsupport/.
- Students in the EU wishing to study abroad with Erasmus/Socrates Mobility Grants: http://europa.eu.int/comm/education/programmes/socrates/erasmus/answers_en.html; http://www.oasis.gov.ie/education/european_education_programmes/erasmus.html.
- Students in the United States: http://www.fafsa.ed.gov/.

Chapter 3

Communicating electronically

> The great end of learning is nothing else but to seek for the lost mind.
>
> (Mencius, *c*.372–289 BC, *Works*, bk. II, 1:11.4)

Though some online students may access courses via CD tutorials or only through email communications, the primary interface for online students is through Web pages and a variety of communication tools used on the Internet. Learning in an online environment differs significantly from a traditional face-to-face setting. The electronic medium lends itself very well to discussion, brainstorming, sharing understandings, clarifying misconceptions, and developing knowledge in a collaborative way. The online environment is also a wonderful medium in which to promote critical thinking.

There are other advantages to online learning. For example, you can connect to a host computer from the comfort of your own home and at a time that is most convenient to you. The medium provides greater access to learning opportunities at a distance and as a way to reduce the number of hours you have to sit in a classroom at a school away from your office, your home, or your family. Using chat rooms, discussion boards, and email creates a permanent transcript that provides you with a record of all interactions. The group collaborations available electronically promote the development of multiple perspectives and shared understandings among learners.

Electronic communication offers you *and* the instructor flexibility, an important consideration for those participants with multiple roles and obligations. Learners who are geographically distant from an educational institution can connect socially with others participating in the same experience. For example, in 2001, after the destruction of the World Trade Center, many Arab students at Portland State University were called home in the middle of the term by parents who feared that they would no longer be safe in the US. These students were able to complete their studies in several classes that had online components by keeping in touch with their classmates and their instructors through online discussions and chats, and sending their homework assignments by email attachments. They continued to take many classes online for the remainder of the year so that when they returned to their studies in the US the following year, they were not far behind their peers. In this way, electronic communication reduced, and in many cases, dissolved, feelings of social isolation frequently associated with other forms of online delivery (for example, with traditional print-based correspondence courses).

The online environment offers a great many advantages. It can promote a sense of equality by granting each participant an equal voice. This may not be the case in traditional classrooms, where students may feel intimidated or shy about voicing opinions due to competition for "air time." Also, the subtle and sometimes not-so-subtle influences of non-verbal cues are missing online. Responses have a greater likelihood of being judged on the basis of their substance and merit rather than by the appearance of the person commenting. This non-visual atmosphere can be highly motivating, as well as liberating. Sharing information through active, ongoing dialogue and constructing knowledge through mutually-shared understandings all contribute to the development of a sense of community online.

However, communicating electronically may take some adjustment, especially if you are accustomed to a more teacher-centered, traditional approach to learning. In this section, typical new student difficulties are highlighted.

"Did you get my email? Did you? Did you? Did you?"

The seeming immediacy of the online environment can be deceiving and lead to bad habits. For example, you may feel that you need to get immediate answers to questions or to emails. In the beginning some students fear that if they don't get an immediate response from the instructor it means their email has been lost in cyberspace. These students make the mistake of sending three or four messages a day asking instructors the same question: "Did you get my paper?" or "I need to know about this assignment right now." This is not necessary and it may quickly give you the reputation of being a pest. Just as you wouldn't go to your instructor's office four times in one day to ask the same question, you need to also trust the Internet.

Allow a reasonable amount of time for people to respond to your email, and give yourself the same leeway. Remember, the flexibility of online learning permits everyone to fit learning into their personal schedule. It is wise to wait 24 to 48 hours before sending another email message requesting the same information. Remember to consider time zone differences and also give time for reflection. Some people may be logging onto the system at midnight or at 4:00 in the morning, and your instructor is not online 24 hours a day. He or she probably has a few hours each day scheduled to login and get emails, so you need to be patient. This also gives you permission to answer messages at a time which fits your schedule and outside activities.

"I'm afraid everyone will see my typos, or grammar errors and think I'm stupid."

It is not uncommon for the new online student to feel vulnerable or inadequate when communicating online. Instructors and students alike may not be skilled at keyboarding and may feel somewhat frustrated with having to type out their thoughts. These thoughts may also become transformed as they are written, and once recorded and forwarded to others online, may reflect ideas that have since changed. Commitment to ideas documented in writing can sometimes contribute to a sense of risk for the participant.

Some students have also expressed a sense of vulnerability in regard to the adequacy of their online contributions. They worry about whether their contributions to the dialogue will be well-received and respected by the instructor and their peers. At first, you may be tentative and reluctant to express yourself freely, knowing that all contributions will be seen, and to some degree, evaluated by everyone. The following excerpt from a recent online student captures these thoughts:

> When I first began my online course I was really scared to say anything – to type anything. I knew that immediately everyone would know how stupid I was. They could see if I misspelled a word or if I didn't know what I was talking about. I found that very stressful ... Even though I'm an adult I still worry about what people think of me. How will I do? Am I too old to learn this stuff? What if I fail? Even though I've been taking courses for a year now, at the beginning of each course I get that same feeling.

It is true that one of the most difficult aspects of online learning is sharing your thoughts and work with others in the class. Whereas in a classroom the instructor may let you get away without speaking, it is nearly impossible to do that in an online learning environment. Many programs require you to participate in chats, post to bulletin boards, and even post your completed papers on Web pages or share them with classmates via email.

Try to think of your contribution as a member of a team. Remember, all of your classmates will have some trepidation about sharing their work as well. It is through sharing and working together that each member of the class improves and becomes a better student. There are many benefits to finding out how other people approach the assignment or how their thinking process works in response to a particular question or problem.

Learners benefit from an approach which involves them in the learning process ... in other words, active learning. It is important to recognize that each person brings his or her own expertise to a class, and each contribution enriches everyone's experience. Perhaps, one time a particular concept you read in the text takes longer than usual for you to grasp. Then you might need to ask a classmate for an explanation. Yet another time you may be the one who immediately understands a visual model presented online and you will be able to clarify it for someone else. In another class, you may be assigned a project that is similar to one you have already completed on your job; then you will look like an expert. Good instructors will see you as an individual who will help them explore the information that they bring to the class and gain from your personal and professional experiences to make that information applicable to the real-world environment in which you live.

Technology and the learning process

Online education has the ability to take advantage of the changing forms of communication. With the World Wide Web offering differing communication perspectives, the learning context is increasingly technologically rich. You will have access to a wide range of both media and sources of education. Online learning makes it possible for you to communicate in dual modes: that of receiver and communicator. Online students work in cyberspace, looking at content, surfing for information, utilizing Web pages, conferencing in chat rooms and receiving/sending content on listserves. As video technology progresses and becomes more accepted on the computer desktop, you will also have opportunities to see, hear, speak, and even raise your hand for acknowledgment.

At the University of Twente, in the Netherlands, Dr Betty Collis teaches classes that consist of some face-to-face meetings as well as extensive use of the Web for resource material, collaborative activities, and discussions. Collis (1996) identified four basic patterns of communication in the learning environment: telling, asking, responding, and discussing. Each of these patterns of communication is affected by technology.

- *Telling*: In the asynchronous mode, telling has traditionally been communicated through the printed text, but increasingly it is taking on a new form in Web pages. Many conventional linear texts, articles, reports and original works are now available on the Internet, as well as multimedia graphics with descriptive text and links to other resources. Telling is the only online experience that does not require human interaction with the student.
- *Asking*: When you need an answer, you naturally request interaction. This can take place through text messages via email, through real-time text chat systems, or through any of the audio or video conferencing systems (including telephones). Asking requires a response and thus human interaction.
- *Responding*: Responding online is supported in delayed time through asynchronous systems such as email or discussion boards, and much more immediately through synchronous systems such as chat and instant-messaging and telephones.
- *Discussing*: Collaborative work among small groups of students, with or without the instructor present, can take place over an extended time through discussion boards or listservs, or for much shorter periods via instant-messaging, chatrooms, whiteboards, or video/audio-conferencing. Discussing also requires human interaction.

Synchronous vs. asynchronous communication

Communication in an online environment may be synchronous or asynchronous. With synchronous communication, all participants are connected at the same time (e.g. in a chat room or using instant-messaging). This environment promotes a feeling of coming together and simulates being part of a more traditional concept of a class. It also means that everyone has to be at a computer at the same time. Many online programs have at least one or two mandatory synchronous activities during a course. This requires you to coordinate with the instructor and classmates and plan your schedule to be available at a prescribed time.

The most common type of communication in online learning is asynchronous. Asynchronous communication means that participants contribute to the class at times that are convenient to them – though usually within a specified timeframe, such as one week. This is also referred to as delayed-time messaging (as opposed to real-time messaging). For example, email is a typical asynchronous activity. You can log into your email, download the messages, log off, read and reflect upon the messages, construct responses, and finally log in and upload your replies. A similar process takes place with listservs or newsgroups.

When accessing discussion boards, you usually cannot download the information. Some students, therefore, elect to read the information and respond right then. However, if you are the type of person who prefers to think about it, you can copy the information to your computer (using the copy and paste commands) then log off. Next you can compose a response on your word processor, log back on to the bulletin board and copy and paste your response into a posted message. Most students are very comfortable with asynchronous communication because it provides a great deal of flexibility and gives them time to reflect and think through their answers before posting.

Synchronous delivery has a significant role to play in the developing world of virtual and online education. Though most current online education programs are delivered asynchronously (e.g. discussion board, email, Web pages), synchronous delivery is that aspect which creates a true sense of virtual community. While asynchronous delivery provides instruction that is free of time, place, and scheduling constraints, the synchronous approach adds immediacy, live interaction and personal contact. Both systems peacefully co-exist in a group of online learning strategies that focus on online access to learning through common cyberspace technologies. In the near future, these common technologies will become as prevalent as the family television and CD player.

Asynchronous delivery

There are four crucial advantages to the asynchronous media approach:

1 *Flexibility*: access to the teaching material, on the Web or in computer conference discussions, can take place at any time and from any location with an Internet-capable computer.

2 *Time to reflect*: rather than having to react immediately, asynchronous systems allow you time to mull over ideas, check references, go back to previous messages and take any amount of time to prepare a comment.
3 *Situated learning*: because the technology allows access from home and work, you can easily integrate the course concepts and materials into your working environment.
4 *Cost-effective technology*: text-based asynchronous systems require little bandwidth and low-end computers to operate, thus access, particularly global access, is more equitable.

Synchronous delivery

There are also four compelling advantages to synchronous systems:

1 *Motivation*: synchronous systems focus the energy of the group, providing motivation to online learners to keep up with their peers and continue with their studies.
2 *Instantaneous interaction*: real-time interaction with its opportunity to convey tone and nuance helps develop group cohesion and the sense of being part of a learning community.
3 *Quick feedback*: synchronous systems provide quick feedback on ideas and support consensus and decision-making in group activities; both enliven online education.
4 *Pacing*: synchronous events encourage students to keep up-to-date with the course and provide a discipline to learning that helps people prioritize their studies and manage their time more effectively.

There are many online teaching programs that are entirely asynchronous (for example, those using print plus email, or those using the Web for both course delivery and interaction), and others that are primarily synchronous (for example, those using videoconferencing for delivery and interaction). However, the trend is to combine synchronous and asynchronous media in an attempt to capitalize on the obvious benefits of both modes.

Pretesting

It is common practice for many online education courses to offer pretests prior to the beginning of the course or of a lesson. Pretests are used for three purposes: to provide instructional information regarding the mix of student skills; to provide feedback to the student regarding his or her current knowledge level; or to provide an opportunity for the student to skip a course or section.

Some instructors give an ungraded, online pretest at the beginning of a course to evaluate the skill and knowledge level of students in the class. Analysis of the pretest results is then used to modify the emphasis of the curriculum and adapt assignments to reflect the needs of each group of students.

Colleges and universities are very attuned to ensuring that specific course outcomes are met by all passing students. However, gathering information from a pretest does allow the instructor to develop case studies or simulation examples that are most meaningful to a specific group of students. For example, if the majority of students are working in government jobs, the instructor will select different case scenarios than if the majority of students were working in small entrepreneurial businesses.

Pretests that are designed to provide the student with feedback may be used as a screening tool for prerequisite skills required for success in the study area. For example, a computer systems design class requires the student to have Computer Science 101 and a certain level of programming skills. Though you may have taken these classes in the past, your memory of key concepts may be rusty. A pretest would provide you with feedback on the expectations of your knowledge level prior to the beginning of the course. You could then make the decision whether to continue with the course and do some preliminary self-study and review, or decide to drop the course until after you have taken a refresher course to bring you up to speed.

Online pretests are now being used even more often for allowing a student to test out of a class or a lesson. This is particularly true of technical courses, like programming. Some of these pretests are also linked to specific online tutorials that match the areas in which the student needs additional help. The beauty of online learning and its integration with pretests is that it often allows students to accelerate their completion time if they already have mastered the knowledge requirements of a particular section.

Receiving lecture materials and assignments

Contact with your teacher and with other students is conducted primarily through the use of email, bulletin boards and chat rooms.

Using email and Web pages will probably be the most convenient and fastest way for you to transmit and receive materials from your instructor and your peers. Most lecture materials are transmitted via Web pages in online education. Instructors prepare their materials and post them to the Web well in advance of your class assignments. Once the initial Web page has been posted, it varies from instructor to instructor as to how updates or continued materials are distributed.

Some will regularly update their Web pages throughout the term of a course. Others will provide updates by emailing them to their students, and still others will send them via the postal service. No matter how updates are transmitted, it is important for you to take responsibility for receiving them.

If you already use a word processor, you will be accustomed to reading text on screen and should know how to scroll up and down pages. Reading Web pages for lecture materials or assignments is no different. They are usually presented as text and pictures. In addition to your scroll bars, you can also use the page up and page down keys to move through the material one screen at a time. The reading style you employ may also determine which method of scrolling you use (see Table 3.1).

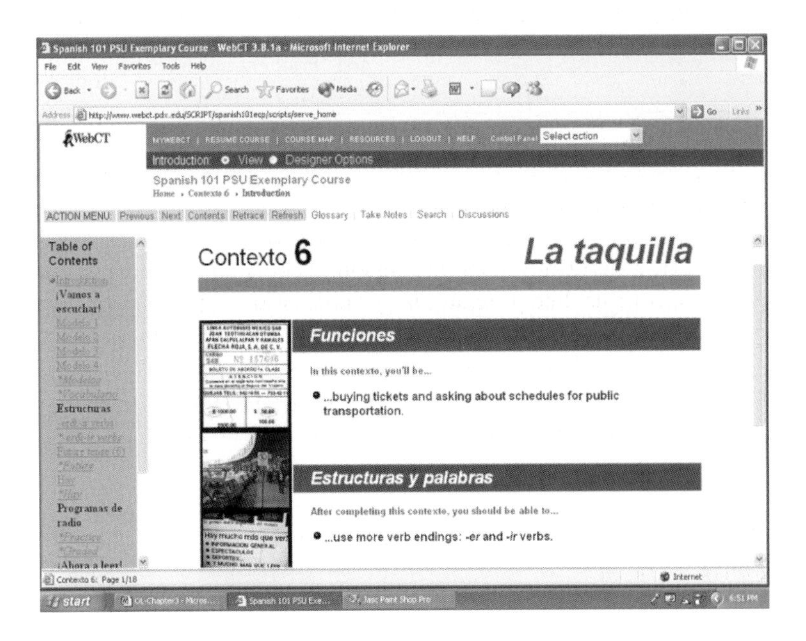

Figure 3.1 **Online Spanish course**. A Web page in an online Spanish course.

Table 3.1 Methods for online learning

Style	*Description*	*Use this method*
Scanning	Glancing at text very quickly to find a specific item.	"Find" in page; most browsers have the ability to search for a text string in a Web page. This function is commonly found under the "Edit" menu.
Skimming	Quickly looking through each section to get a general idea.	Use the "Page down" and "Page up" keys. If the page provides sectional or targeted navigation tools, use those as well.
Surface reading	Reading everything but not stopping to think about the information.	Use the "Page down" and "Page up" keys.
Study reading	Making sure you understand the text fully, often re-reading the information and deciphering new or unfamiliar words.	Most students will choose to print out the page in this case. Then you have it to mark up, write questions, make notes. There is also note-taking software now available that allows you to open a pop-up window to take notes while you read. Tip: If the page is using "frames," first make sure that the cursor is placed in the frame you wish to print. Then choose "File" and "Print Frame" from your browser's menu.

Some Web pages may also contain animations and sound. Depending on how those pages are developed, you may be required to download certain browser plug-ins (e.g. Real Audio, Shockwave, or Acrobat Reader). It is also possible that lecture materials will be available as a file to download to your computer. (For example, a Microsoft Word™ document, a spreadsheet template, or a Microsoft PowerPoint™ presentation.) Instructions for downloading information and/or installing free browser plug-ins to your computer are available in your browser documentation.

Note-taking for online courses

Taking notes during lectures in the classroom is something most students do during their studies. However, studying online requires a different set of skills. If you are reading course materials or information you have found on the Internet and wish to take notes, use your word processor or special note-taking software to record your ideas. If you want to *copy* a section of text that you are reading, use your mouse to highlight the text and do a copy and paste from the Web page into your word processor.

Finally, lecture materials may contain a number of Web sites and their links. To help manage these multiple pages, it is useful to keep track of them through a process called "bookmarking." When you wish to do this, select "Bookmarks" and "Add" from the drop down menu (in Netscape). The title of that Web page is recorded as a bookmark and choosing its bookmark name from that same menu can then access the page in the future. (In Internet Explorer bookmarks are called "Favorites".) If you collect a lot of bookmarks, start grouping them into folders containing Websites with similar information.

Tip It is handy to bookmark the login point of your course to make it easier to find each day.

Transmitting homework assignments

Most homework assignments will be sent to your instructor as attachments to email. However, some instructors are beginning to request that you put your homework assignments into a Web page (particularly research papers and design work). Making your completed assignments available to the Web enhances student learning and collaboration. You will have the opportunity to see how other students approached a particular problem or what additional research they did to answer a question. This may prove useful in your next assignment. Chapter 4 addresses how to easily design web pages.

Some universities have settled on a standard transmittal sheet that must accompany all assignments. This electronic sheet acts as a cover page for you and the instructor. Typically, it includes your name, course name and number, assignment name and number, and any other specific identifying materials to that project or assignment. The instructor then uses this same cover page to return you a grade and/or comments about your assignment.

Some schools also ask you to include a written verification that this is your own work and has not been taken from other sources, except where cited according to research protocols. With the ease of copying and pasting information from the Web, there has been an increased concern regarding plagiarism. The key to transmitting any homework assignments is to follow the rules set up by your college or course instructor.

Tip If your school does not have any policies about assignment transmittal, keep in mind that the name of your file should include your last name and a descriptor (e.g. lynch-paper1.doc). This will help your instructor differentiate your paper from all of the other files named "paper1.doc."

Receiving instructor feedback on assignments

Depending on the administrative structure of your college or university, instructor feedback may be received during a synchronous session (on the phone, in a chatroom), via email or via the postal service. Some courses will provide multiple alternatives. Many courses today also have a special online grade book. The instructor is able to see all the student records and put in the appropriate grades, but each student may only access his or her own grade with a password.

If you have been engaged in a graded synchronous session, such as a chat room discussion, the instructor may take the opportunity to critique the discussion or comment on specific points both during the discussion and at the end of the session. Depending on the instructor's style, he or she may also include specific detailed comments to each participant in the discussion. Even when this is done, however, instructors rarely give grade information publicly.

It is becoming more common for online instructors to give specific assignment and grade feedback via email. The instructor will usually send you an email with comments regarding what went well and where you could improve, then assign a grade. If you did not pass the assignment, some instructors may also give you instructions on how to rework the assignment and resubmit it, or what to do for future assignments to make sure you have an opportunity to meet the outcomes and pass the class.

The use of "electronic comments" within written papers is becoming more popular as software tools for editing are more widely accepted. For example, Microsoft Word™ allows the recipient to insert corrections and comments directly into the document, then return it to the sender with that feedback. You then have the option to incorporate or ignore those comments in your paper.

Asynchronous written communication

Education programs that are delivered in an online environment rely on written communication as the primary interface among students and between students and the instructor. Every electronic communication, except some audio or video conferencing, requires some aspect of writing to be effective on the Web. You are communicating with writing in email, on discussion boards, in listservs, and in chat rooms. Even when using the shared white boards, you will probably need to use some written communication along with the diagrams you draw.

The better your skills in written communication, the more successful you will feel in an online environment. Each of the forms of electronic communication contains certain common requirements. The foremost rule for any communication on the Web is to keep it brief. Write with as much clarity and brevity as possible. Let's look at some good and bad examples of Web-based communication.

Listservs

In a class environment you may have many occasions when you want to send the same message to everyone or to a list of people. A listserv is a mail list of specific individuals who regularly participate in discussions. You become a member of that mail list by "subscribing" to the list – just like subscribing to a free newsletter or magazine. To subscribe, you send an email to the listserv moderator asking to become a member of the list. Once you subscribe to the list, you automatically receive email messages from anyone who responds to the server until you "unsubscribe".

Email

When using regular one-to-one email, it is best to keep in mind that most people don't want to read more than one screen of information. Email has become so ubiquitous that people are inundated with mail and try to get through it as quickly as possible. If you have more than one screen of information to share, it is better to write it in a word processor and attach the file to your email message. In that way, you can present your written communication in an organized and formatted document that is easy to read, instead of many lines of unformatted email.

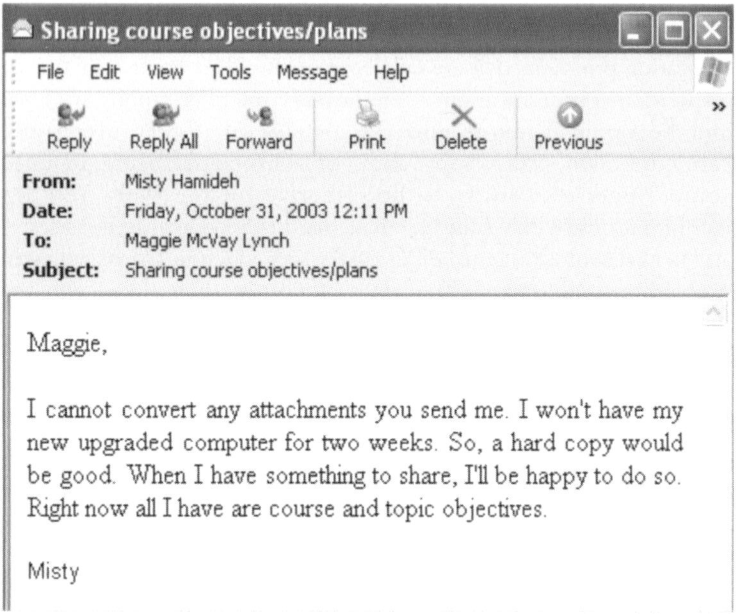

Sharing course objectives/plans

From: Misty Hamideh
Date: Friday, October 31, 2003 12:11 PM
To: Maggie McVay Lynch
Subject: Sharing course objectives/plans

Maggie,

I cannot convert any attachments you send me. I won't have my new upgraded computer for two weeks. So, a hard copy would be good. When I have something to share, I'll be happy to do so. Right now all I have are course and topic objectives.

Misty

Figure 3.2 Sharing course objectives/plans

The email in Figure 3.2 is short and to the point. The writer needed to pass along a reply without going into a lot of detail. Note that she doesn't continue with an explanation of why she won't have her computer for two weeks, or how difficult it has been for her to be using a computer that is not at the same level as someone else. She simply states the facts, requests a solution, a hard copy of the document, and offers to participate in the sharing process when she has prepared her lessons.

The email example in Figure 3.3 would have worked better as a wordprocessed attachment to a brief email. Though the information is all there, it would have been better presented as a formatted document with bold headers, indented sections, key words highlighted, etc.

Even if the reader were to print out this long email (which is actually about 5 or 6 pages) it would still be difficult to read and to follow all the important sections of information. Each email program has its own formatting protocols, so you do not know how it will appear on the readers' screens. At best, it would still be difficult to use as a reference document because nothing stands out to catch your attention.

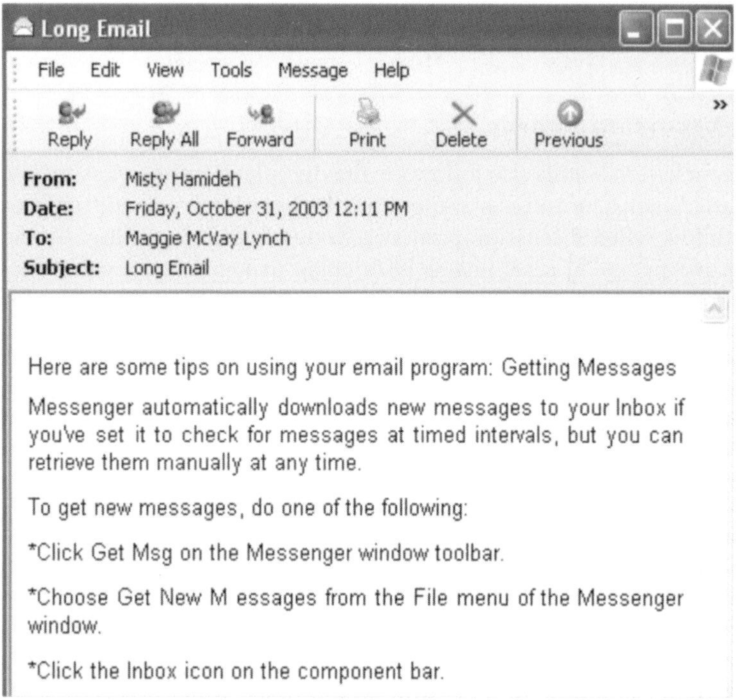

Long Email

File Edit View Tools Message Help

Reply Reply All Forward Print Delete Previous

From: Misty Hamideh
Date: Friday, October 31, 2003 12:11 PM
To: Maggie McVay Lynch
Subject: Long Email

Here are some tips on using your email program: Getting Messages

Messenger automatically downloads new messages to your Inbox if you've set it to check for messages at timed intervals, but you can retrieve them manually at any time.

To get new messages, do one of the following:

*Click Get Msg on the Messenger window toolbar.

*Choose Get New M essages from the File menu of the Messenger window.

*Click the Inbox icon on the component bar.

Figure 3.3 Long email

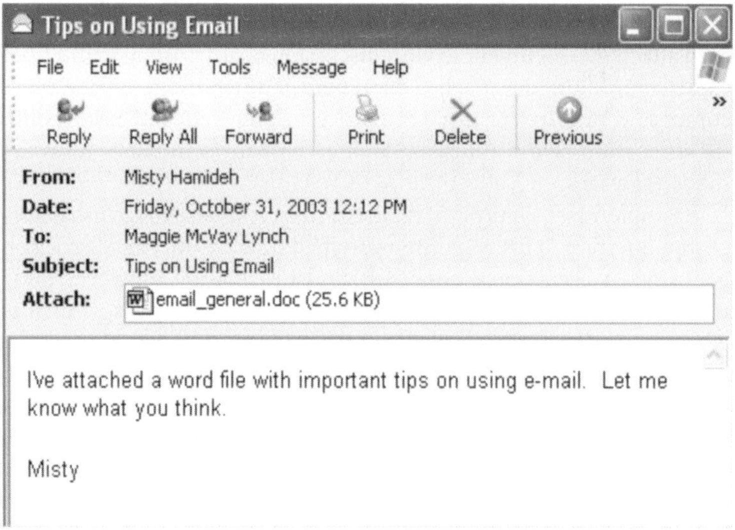

Tips on Using Email

File Edit View Tools Message Help

Reply Reply All Forward Print Delete Previous

From: Misty Hamideh
Date: Friday, October 31, 2003 12:12 PM
To: Maggie McVay Lynch
Subject: Tips on Using Email
Attach: email_general.doc (25.6 KB)

I've attached a word file with important tips on using e-mail. Let me know what you think.

Misty

Figure 3.4 Tips on using email

Note the panel in Figure 3.4 where the email message is once again brief and now has an attachment for the tips on using email.

Discussion boards

Discussion boards also follow the brevity rule. Because many people are posting to a discussion group, the board becomes difficult to follow when discussion points are long or several postings by the same person appear. Just as with email, it helps to provide some format to your thoughts if they are more than one screen. As most discussion boards provide the capability to link to Web pages, it would be best to format longer comments on a Web page and provide a link. (How to make *easy* Web pages is in Chapter 4.) Alternatively, you could attach a document.

Discussion boards are a favorite tool for asynchronous class discussions. Frequently, instructors will post questions or points to ponder. They are also used as a place to ask general questions and see the instructor's or your classmates' responses. When a discussion board is used for a class discussion, you are frequently graded both on your willingness to participate and on what you actually post. As this is an asynchronous communication tool, you have time to formulate your response and post it in whatever format works best for you.

There are three ways to approach posting long discussion items. One way is to format your response(s) on a Web page and provide a link. The second is to compose your response in your word processor, then attach the document to your discussion board posting with a brief explanation about the attached document. The third is to organize and compose your response in a word processor, then cut and paste it onto the discussion board. An example of each of these methods is on the following pages.

Example 1 (see Figure 3.5) depicts a short response to an instructor-posted question. This response was typed directly into the discussion board. Most discussion postings are similar to this one. However, there may be a situation where you need to create a longer posting – such as when you are presenting a topic on the discussion board, or you have several items of discussion. In the case of longer postings, as in Example 2 (see Figure 3.6), it is best to compose your message in your word processor, then cut and paste it to the discussion board or attach your word document to your post. In this way you have the opportunity to organize it, format it, and spell check. Examples 3 and 4 depict referencing a URL (Web address) and attaching a document

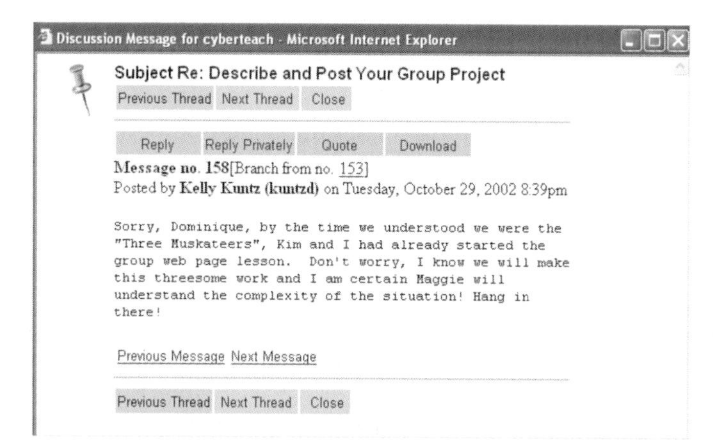

Figure 3.5 **Brief discussion board message.** Example 1: a brief message within the discussion board when you only have a few lines to post.

Discussion Message for cyberteach - Microsoft Internet Explorer

Subject Re: Kim De Costa

Previous Thread | Next Thread | Close

Reply | Reply Privately | Quote | Download

Message no. 49[Branch from no. 12]
Posted by Maggie Lynch (cyberteach) on Friday, October 11, 2002 12:11pm

This sounds like a great class and I like your idea of it being only partially online given your population. However, don't sell them short either. YOu may find certain things that are central to helping your population that can be provided in the online environment.

1. Shy students or students with low self-esteem often "talk" more online because they don't have to deal with all the social expectations of the classroom. So give them lots of opportunities to share online.

2. Some students really love the opportunity to be creative. Consider giving them a way to build an electronic portfolio that can be shared online not only in class but with potential teachers, parents, partners, etc. that reflect what they've learned. This can be done through webpage postings, posting attachments to discussion board, or even some type of class newsletter that is shared more globally. This gives some instant recognition and feedback for their efforts. (Even adults really appreciate positive strokes)

3. Like other courses mentioned here, this one is ripe for some video. Consider doing brief tapes of potential situations (e.g., angry response that can be reframed, self-defeating attitudes) and make them available on the web with discussion questions to follow. These should

Figure 3.6 **Long discussion board message.** Example 2: a long description submitted by the instructor. In order to maintain formatting and ensure you have spell-checked your document, it is easier to compose this type of posting in your word processor and "cut and paste" it to the discussion board.

(see Figures 3.7 and 3.8). Using a Web page or an attached document is best for longer postings or sharing of your assignments.

Most discussion board programs today do provide some basic formatting options and spell-checking capabilities. However, it depends on the system your school is using. Finally, if formatting and pictures are important to your message, posting to a Web page or attaching a word-processed document is an excellent way to get your point across.

Tip Not all discussion boards allow for the posting of URLs with a link. But certainly you can include the URL as part of the text in your posting. Then others may type it into their browsers to see your full message.

Web pages

Written communication using Web pages is an art in itself. Web pages can be as simple as a word-processed document (e.g. a student paper) that is posted in HTML format, or as complex as an interactive and graphic site with written words to enhance the meaning.

The primary rule in developing Web pages, just as in writing a report, is to identify the purpose of the page. If the purpose is to provide a research or opinion paper for viewing, then it is best to complete the paper in a word processor, save the file as a Web page (or as HTML), and then post it "as is." If the purpose is to provide a Web page for teaching or interaction, it is best to develop the page within some type of HTML editor which allows for the easy insertion of graphics, animation, hot links, email responses, and other identified interaction devices. With the myriad of editors available today and the tools available in most word processors, any student is able to post pages to the Web with minimal training.

Synchronous collaboration

Effective collaboration with other students requires you to plan in advance and come to sessions well organized. Most online collaboration is accomplished either through email or through chat rooms. Recent advances in online whiteboard technology (the ability to interactively create drawings online) make it another medium used for collaboration – particularly in the corporate environment. Using email for collaboration is no different from sending assignments to instructors or attaching documents for your classmates to review. This section will elaborate on techniques for collaboration via synchronous communication methods: chat and electronic whiteboards.

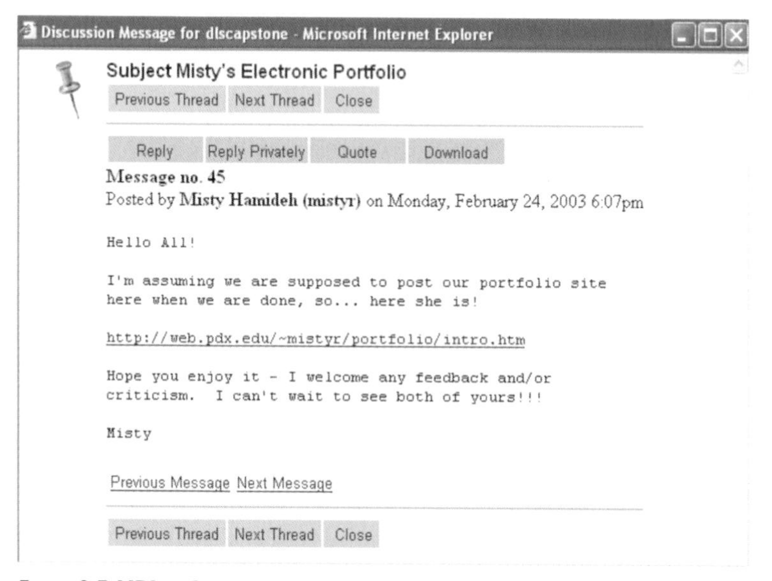

Figure 3.7 **URL reference posting.** Example 3: reference to a URL for a Web page. When presenting a great deal of information, or a unique format, posting to a Web page and providing a link from the discussion board is the best method.

Discussion Message for dlscapstone - Microsoft Internet Explorer

Subject Vita Draft #2, Web Document

Previous Thread Next Thread Close

Reply Reply Privately Quote Download

Message no. 59

Posted by Patricia Cornman (cornmanp) on Wednesday, March 12, 2003 11:14am

Here is the latest iteration of the Vita. Any/all comments or suggestions are appreciated. After I have received any comments I will post it to my Electronic Portfolio. We are all getting closer all the time, girls!!! patricia

See Attached

Previous Message Next Message

Previous Thread Next Thread Close

Figure 3.8 **Document attachment.** Example 4: attachment of a document. When presenting a great deal of information, or sharing an assignment or project with your classmates, using an attachment to the discussion board is another alternative.

Collaboration via chat

Chat provides an excellent opportunity for people to communicate in short sentences or words in real-time. In addition to class discussions, this technology is frequently used for small group planning. The rules for chat are twofold: 1) keep your sentences short, as they are one of many being seen by everyone; 2) if you have a large amount of information, or you know you are a slow typist, come prepared with it pre-typed somewhere else so it can be "cut and pasted" into the chat window at the appropriate time. Preface any large posting with a single line that warns a long post is coming. For example: "Long answer to Philosophy Question 1." This allows the other members of the chat room to prepare to read several lines/screens of text.

Some chat rooms also have protocols for moderated participation. This means that there is a defined way in which to "raise your hand" and wait to be called on for your input. One way this occurs is to depress your space bar and then hit return. This places only your name in the chat window. The instructor then gives you permission to speak by typing your name with a question mark. Another method is to set a protocol of specific symbols that indicate your input. In the example below, an exclamation point (!) means the student has a comment or answer. A question mark (?) means the student has a question about the topic. Generally, the instructor gives permission to speak in the same order in which your comment or question is placed in the chat (see Figure 3.9).

Many colleges provide multiple spaces on their servers for chat collaboration. If you are partnered with someone not in your local area, negotiate specific times when you will meet in the chat area. If you are unsure of how to access the chat at your school, be sure to contact your instructor or designated technical support person for that information.

The chat environment offers the advantage of real-time conversations through typing information, questions and answers. The first key to collaboration during chat is to establish an agenda and goals. Plan to use your time in the chat room as if you were conducting a business meeting. It is wise to select a moderator for the chat (similar to a meeting chairperson) who will be responsible for setting the agenda, encouraging discussion and closing the topic to ensure time schedules are kept. Be aware that moderating can be difficult and all participants must cooperate to achieve success. Even if your collaboration effort only involves two or three people, it is still advantageous to have an agenda distributed in advance. A good facilitator can make the difference

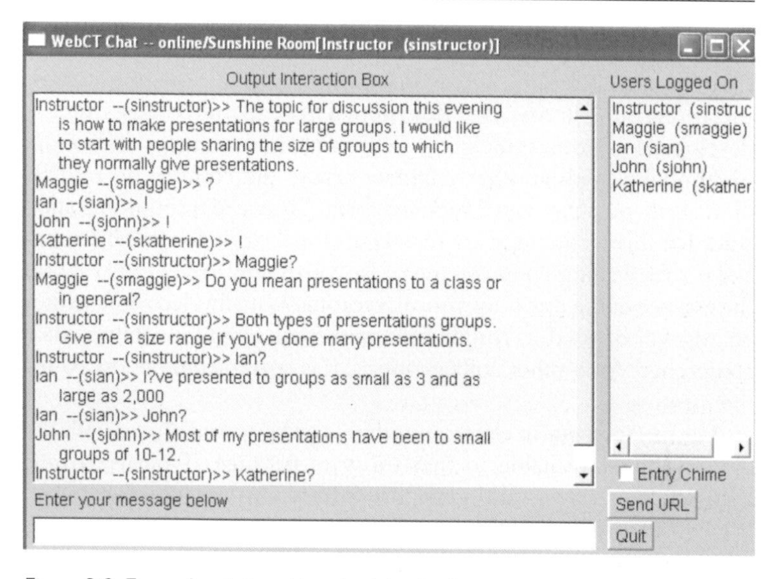

Figure 3.9 Example of virtual hand-raising in chat

between a productive chat session and time wasted by scattered energy and thoughts.

If you are presenting information during the chat session, develop your presentation in advance by typing it in your word processor, preparing a Web page, or having appropriate URLs ready for viewing. If you have typed information in your word processor, you can upload it to the chat environment (if your software allows) or cut and paste it into your chat window as the conversation develops. If your information presentation is more formal, including pre-designed graphics or photographs, it is best to prepare that portion of your presentation and post it to a temporary Web page. During the chat, advise the group of the URL and give them time to view your Web page; then return to the chat room for discussion and feedback.

Tip Chat requires all parties to be typing their responses. Because the differences in typing ability may vary significantly from person to person, the more information that can be presented in advance, the more effective the chat session will become. If participants have an opportunity to read information prior to attending the chat, the entire session can then be spent in productive questions, answers, and resolution or action toward project completion.

Collaborating via electronic whiteboard

Electronic whiteboards are used to communicate real-time graphic interpretations across the Internet. This capability was initially developed for business meetings. For example, an engineer could share his thoughts with another engineer across the country by actually drawing them as they typed back and forth. The written communication rules for this technology are few. Use whiteboards for graphic input and not for writing/typing memos. Use words only to label and capture the essence of the drawings you are creating. Usually electronic white-boards will be used in conjunction with a chat window or an audio-conference. As in other collaborations, it is best to come prepared for the meeting.

The key to using an electronic whiteboard is to be familiar with the drawing tools available to that software package. Typically, ovals, triangles, lines, arrows, and some type of freeform drawing are available. If you are unsure of which whiteboard software will be used at your school, you might practice using the drawing tools in the Windows Paint program or any similar basic drawing program available to most computer users.

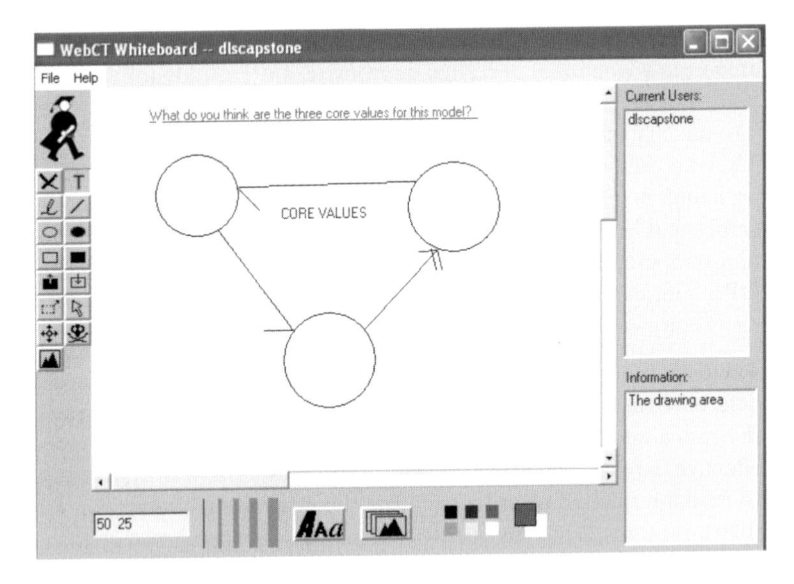

Figure 3.10 **Whiteboard**

Tip When using the electronic whiteboard DO NOT worry about producing a diagram that will be in final form. Think of the whiteboard as a napkin you might quickly draw on during a lunch conversation, or over coffee at breakfast.

Because the whiteboard is sending graphics from one location to another, the transmission time is significantly slower than using chat or email for collaboration. Keep in mind that it is best to draw one or two shapes, then wait for feedback before drawing again. If you are designated to begin with a completed diagram, it should be prepared in advance then cut and pasted to the whiteboard. Do not spend the time recreating the diagram in the real-time collaborative environment.

If you are collaborating with a group, have each participant use a different color when making additions or deletions to the whiteboard. In that way, everyone will know who is making the suggestion without having to take the time to write their name on the diagram or type in their name in the chat window. As with all of these collaborative technologies, it helps to practice with a friend well in advance of your need to participate effectively in a conference.

Chapter 4

The media you need to understand

Learning occurs in the mind, independent of time and place.
(Plato, 428–348 BC, *The Greek Anthology* (1906), 111,197)

As indicated in the previous chapter, online learning takes place in two modes: asynchronous and synchronous. Each of these modes has a variety of technologies that help you learn the content and communicate with your instructor and classmates. This chapter will provide more specific detail of each of these technologies.

Managed learning environments

Many schools now use managed learning environments (MLE) – as they are called in Europe – or course management systems (CMS) – as they are called in the US – to make the integration of both asynchronous and synchronous tools easier for the student and the instructor. An MLE is usually a software system that houses course Web pages, email communications, discussion boards, chat rooms, and whiteboards all in one place and supported by one software company. The nice thing about these environments is that everything is consistent from one course to another or even from one university to another using the same program. Though the course design may vary significantly from one course to another, the easy availability of tools and easy access to class materials remains similar.

The top commercial examples available today are WebCT and Blackboard. As an example, WebCT is currently used by thousands of colleges and universities in over 85 countries around the world. Throughout this chapter, all the examples of tools are with WebCT. Though the actual implementation may differ slightly from one MLE to another, the functionality and use of the tools is the same. In other words, the way the discussion board works in WebCT is very similar to the way a discussion board works in Blackboard or in any other tool. So, no matter what software your institution may elect to use, the skills you will employ and the way in which these tools work vary little (see Figures 4.1 and 4.2).

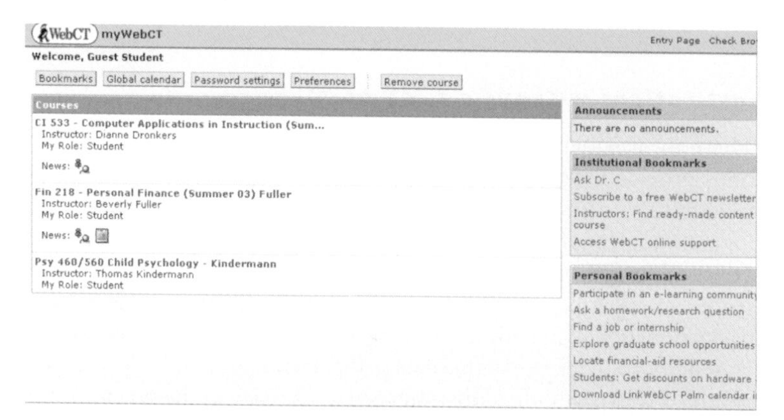

Figure 4.1 **WebCT opening page.** Here is a typical opening student page for WebCT. This student has three online courses. Notice that the system provides immediate access to announcements, links to help, and personal bookmarks. This is typical of a managed learning environment.

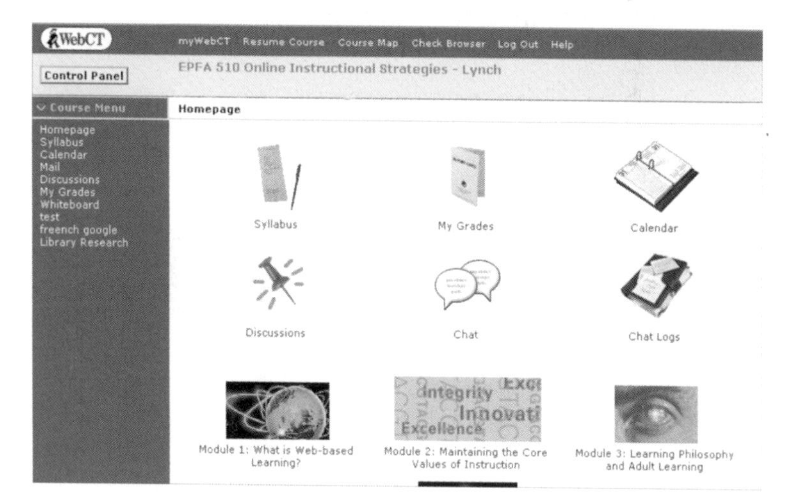

Figure 4.2 **Class page in WebCT.** Here is a class page in WebCT. Note that in addition to each of the learning modules, there is also a link to the class syllabus, a calendar, a discussion board, and private e-mail. You navigate to each piece by clicking on the item.

If you are interested in how these courses may vary and wish to try your hand at navigating, one place to go is the WebCT Exemplary Course Project pages (http://www.Webct.com/exemplary/home). These are courses that have been selected as good examples of online learning. You can access the sample lessons for free and get a sense of how easy it is to move around in the course.

Institutions without a CMS or MLE

There are also many institutions that do not use a MLE. These institutions provide their online courses through a series of Web pages that have links to communication tools and use your own email software for communication. The example in Figure 4.3 is from a training course designed for a newspaper enterprise in the US. Though this is all presented via Web pages, note how the student still has access to easy navigation as well as communication tools such as a discussion board.

Whether you take an online course that uses a MLE or builds a group of linked Web pages, the skills you need to use each of the synchronous and asynchronous tools will remain the same. Once you understand the basics of navigating and using these tools you will be able to move easily from one MLE to another or from one Web-navigated course to another.

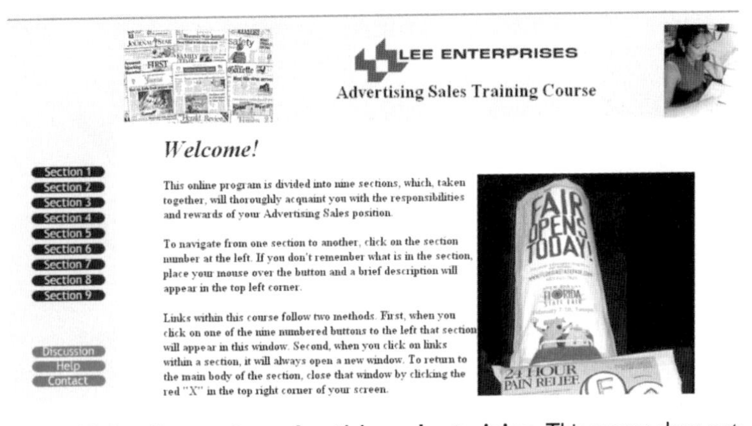

Figure 4.3 **Lee Enterprises advertising sales training.** This course does not use an MLE, instead it uses Web pages with a navigation bar and a link to a discussion board.

Using email

For most online education courses you will need to have a minimum set of email skills. The list below identifies these skills.

- Enter personal details for email address and mail server
- Collect email from the mail server
- Receive an attachment and store it on your computer
- Open and print a word processor attachment
- Reply to an email message
- Create and send a new email message
- Address a new email message
- Attach a word-processed document to an email message

If these skills are beyond your capability at the moment, you may wish to do a short course through your college or to try one of the many tutorials available online.

- http://www.learnthenet.com/english/section/email.html.
- http://www.domaincarecenter.com/microsoft_outlook_ email_ help_guides.htm.
- http://visualtutorials.com/email.htm.
- http://wp.netscape.com/browsers/using/newusers/messenger/.

While there are no "rules" relating to sending email, there are guidelines (or netiquette) that you should follow. In general, rules of common courtesy for interaction with people should be in force for any situation, and on the Internet it is doubly important where body language and tone of voice must be inferred. The following 20 email tips are good ones to remember whenever you use email.

1. Unless you have your own Internet access through an Internet provider, be sure to check with your employer about ownership of electronic mail. Laws about the ownership of electronic mail vary from place to place.
2. Unless you are using an encryption device (hardware or software), you should assume that mail on the Internet is not secure. Never put in a mail message anything you would not put on a postcard.
3. Respect the copyright on material that you reproduce. Almost every country has copyright laws. If you are forwarding or re-posting a message you've received, do not change the wording. If the message was a personal message to you and you are re-posting to a group,

you should ask permission first. You may shorten the message and quote only relevant parts, but be sure you give proper attribution.

4 A good rule of thumb is to be conservative in what you send and liberal in what you receive. You should not send heated messages (called "flames") even if you are provoked. On the other hand, you shouldn't be surprised if you get flamed. It is prudent just to ignore it.

5 Beware your personal reactions when reading email. Remember, you cannot see the person's body language or hear a tone of voice. Before reacting to a possible insult, consider that the sender did not intend it that way. For example, in one email the sender said "I disagree with your logic and can't see how you came up with that response." The receiver immediately took that statement as a personal affront to her level of intelligence, and thought the sender was questioning her educational training in the topic. In fact, the sender was merely disagreeing with a statement.

6 In general, it's a good idea to at least check all your new mail subject headers *before* responding to a message. Sometimes a person who asks you for help (or clarification) will send another message a few minutes later which effectively says "Never Mind."

7 Make things easy for the recipient. In order to ensure that people know who you are, be sure to include a line or two at the end of your message with contact information. You can create this file ahead of time and automatically add it to the end of your messages (known as a "signature" file).

8 Be careful when addressing mail. Some group addresses look like it is just one person. Know to whom you are sending. Watch "cc"s when replying. Don't continue to include other people if the messages have become a two-way conversation with one person.

9 Remember that people with whom you communicate are located across the globe. If you send a message requesting an immediate response, the person receiving it might be at home asleep when it arrives. Give recepients a chance to wake up, come to work, and login before assuming the mail didn't arrive or that they don't care.

10 Verify all addresses before initiating long or personal discourse. It's also a good practice to include the word "Long" in the subject header so the recipient knows the message will take additional time to read and respond. Anything over 25 lines is considered "long."

11 Remember that the recipient is a human being whose culture, language, and humor have different points of reference from your

own. Remember that date formats, measurements, and idioms may not travel well. Be especially careful with sarcasm.

12 Use mixed case. ALL UPPER LETTERS LOOKS AS IF YOU'RE SHOUTING.

13 Use asterisks for emphasis. "That *is* what I meant." Use underscores for underlining "_Fahrenheit 451_ is my favorite book."

14 Use smileys (a colon followed by a parentheses) to indicate tone of voice, but use them sparingly. :) is an example of a smiley (look sideways). Don't assume that the inclusion of a smiley will make the recipient happy with what you say or wipe out an otherwise insulting comment. Another way to indicate emotion is carots around a word. For example, after a joke you might type <giggle>. Or after a story that touches you type <teary eyed>.

15 Wait overnight to send emotional responses to messages. If you have really strong feelings about a subject, indicate it via FLAME ON/OFF enclosures. For example:
FLAME ON:
"This type of argument is not worth the bandwidth it takes to send it. It's illogical and poorly reasoned. The rest of the world agrees with me." FLAME OFF

16 Be brief without being overly terse. When replying to a message, include enough original material to be understood but no more. It is extremely bad form to simply reply to a message by including all of the previous message. Edit all the irrelevant material.

17 Mail should have a subject heading which reflects the content of the message.

18 Just as email may not be private, mail (and news) are subject to forgery and spoofing in various degrees of detectability. Apply common-sense "reality checks" before assuming a message is valid.

19 If you think the importance of a message justifies it, reply briefly and immediately to let the sender know you got it, even if you will send a longer reply later.

20 "Reasonable" expectations for conduct via email depend on your relationship with a person and the context of the communication. For example, the norms accepted with your close friends may not apply in your email communication with people in online classes. Be careful with slang or local acronyms, and using swear words is almost always forbidden.

Using listservs or a discussion list

Another form of email service is a listserv or discussion list. These lists are different from a discussion board because they are operated through a mail server instead of a Web server. Any type of listserv or discussion list works by having a computer keep a list of all the email addresses of people in your class or organization. When you send a message to the list, the computer automatically resends your message to everyone on that email list. When anyone responds to the email, the entire list of people also receive that response. In other words, every posting and response are public to everyone on the list. Today, most institutions providing online courses prefer to use discussion boards or Webboards for class discussions rather than the email discussion list.

Tip To join or subscribe to a listserv or discussion list, you actually have to send an email message to the service coordinating the dispensing of the messages. The typical way to subscribe is to leave the subject line blank, and to type in the body of the message the word SUBSCRIBE and the name of the listserv. For example, to subscribe to an online education listserv for biology students, you might type the following in the body of the message:

SUBSCRIBE BIOLOGY-LIST

When your subscription has been confirmed, you will then begin automatically receiving all messages from the list in your email inbox.

When participating in a list be careful what personal information you choose to display. For example, your email address and any other identifying information you send with email (e.g. a signature line) is automatically displayed to everyone on the distribution list. This also impacts you as a representative of a business or institution. Many organizations have made policies regarding accepted participation in a list. For example, if you are giving a response that is your own opinion, and not that of your organization, you may need to make that statement explicitly.

The list moderator is the controlling authority for all submissions. When you submit anything to a list the moderator has the option of reading it, editing it, or choosing not to let it get posted (depending on the rules under which the list was established). It is unusual, however, for most moderators not to post your messages unless you have used bad language or are caught "flaming" a previous posting.

There are thousands of public lists on the Web. If you would like to practice participating in one, or simply have an interest in a particular topic the easiest way to find one is to search Web pages for the topic name followed by the words "listserv" or "discussion list". Given below are two sites that provide list information in searchable directories covering many topics:

- CataList http://www.lsoft.com/lists/listref.html
- H-net http://www.h-net.org/lists/

Using discussion board systems

Discussion boards are also referred to as "webboards" or "bulletin boards." This communication board provides a way for you to contact all the members of your class by posting only one message. In an online learning environment, it is common for instructors to have a discussion board set up for each class with several topic areas where you can post information or respond to questions. Discussion boards are accessed via the Web and are similar to Web pages in appearance. The primary difference is that when you post a message it is immediately posted to the discussion board for all to view (see Figure 4.4).

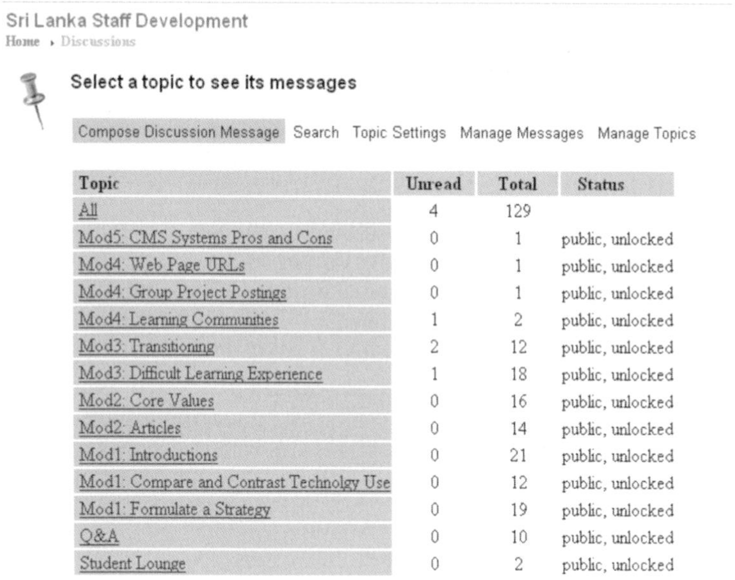

Sri Lanka Staff Development
Home › Discussions

Select a topic to see its messages

Compose Discussion Message Search Topic Settings Manage Messages Manage Topics

Topic	Unread	Total	Status
All	4	129	
Mod5: CMS Systems Pros and Cons	0	1	public, unlocked
Mod4: Web Page URLs	0	1	public, unlocked
Mod4: Group Project Postings	0	1	public, unlocked
Mod4: Learning Communities	1	2	public, unlocked
Mod3: Transitioning	2	12	public, unlocked
Mod3: Difficult Learning Experience	1	18	public, unlocked
Mod2: Core Values	0	16	public, unlocked
Mod2: Articles	0	14	public, unlocked
Mod1: Introductions	0	21	public, unlocked
Mod1: Compare and Contrast Technolgy Use	0	12	public, unlocked
Mod1: Formulate a Strategy	0	19	public, unlocked
Q&A	0	10	public, unlocked
Student Lounge	0	2	public, unlocked

Figure 4.4 Discussion board topics

In this discussion board there are 13 individual topics. The instructor has them divided by modules. Module 1 responses were required during the first week of classes. Module 2 responses required to the second week, and so on. There are also two freeform discussion topics – topics that don't pertain to specific areas – that are typical of many boards. One is a Q&A topic. This is a place where students can post general questions about the course that may not relate to any of the required postings. For example, a student might ask "When will the grading be completed from the mid-term exam?" In this way, the instructor only needs to read one question like that and respond once for the entire class to view, instead of responding to the same question 10 times in emails. The second freeform topic is called "student lounge." The student lounge is a place that some instructors set aside as a social meeting place for students to get together and talk about anything unrelated to the course. Typical conversations might be about upcoming vacations, where to find information about university services, or even arranging times to meet in person at a conference or a local restaurant.

Most online courses now require a login-id and password to access the course and subsequently the discussion boards. This security will ensure that your instructor and classmates, as well as special designated guests, will be the only ones participating in discussions. Public discussion boards outside of your class, on the other hand, allow anyone to access them and welcome postings from all over the world.

Discussion boards vary in style from program to program and campus to campus. However, they all function similarly. The main page of each board lists various topics from left to right (as seen in Figure 4.4). To enter a topic, you click on the topic name and a list of messages pertaining to that topic will appear.

To read a message, you need only click on the text that interests you. In Figure 4.5, most of the topics have the same subject line because each is a response to the instructor's initial posting. If the student does not change the default entry it will automatically post "Re:" and the previous subject line. Once you have clicked on the linked text you will have an opportunity to read the pertinent posting and to respond. Notice the indentation with the arrow. This is called "threading." A thread is a response to a particular posting. When you follow a thread, you are clicking on the major topic and then following the subtopics to the end.

All discussion boards have some type of form for responses. In the examples in Figures 4.6 to 4.8, the format maintains a response button on the top of each page. Other formats will provide a link – through a button or in words – to the response form at the bottom of the page.

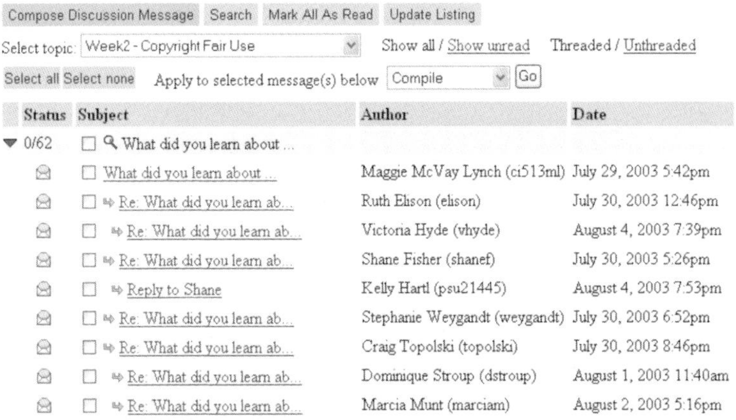

Compose Discussion Message | Search | Mark All As Read | Update Listing

Select topic: Week2 - Copyright Fair Use   Show all / Show unread   Threaded / Unthreaded

Select all Select none   Apply to selected message(s) below Compile Go

Status	Subject	Author	Date
0/62	What did you learn about ...		
	What did you learn about ...	Maggie McVay Lynch (ci513ml)	July 29, 2003 5:42pm
	Re: What did you learn ab...	Ruth Elison (elison)	July 30, 2003 12:46pm
	Re: What did you learn ab...	Victoria Hyde (vhyde)	August 4, 2003 7:39pm
	Re: What did you learn ab...	Shane Fisher (shanef)	July 30, 2003 5:26pm
	Reply to Shane	Kelly Hartl (psu21445)	August 4, 2003 7:53pm
	Re: What did you learn ab...	Stephanie Weygandt (weygandt)	July 30, 2003 6:52pm
	Re: What did you learn ab...	Craig Topolski (topolski)	July 30, 2003 8:46pm
	Re: What did you learn ab...	Dominique Stroup (dstroup)	August 1, 2003 11:40am
	Re: What did you learn ab...	Marcia Munt (marciam)	August 2, 2003 5:16pm

Figure 4.5 **Discussion board postings.** In this example, students are responding to a teacher posted question about copyright and fair use.

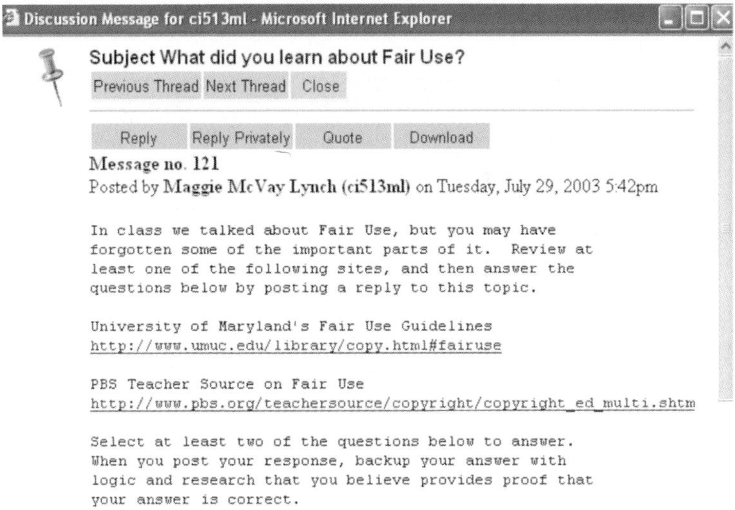

Discussion Message for ci513ml - Microsoft Internet Explorer

Subject What did you learn about Fair Use?

Previous Thread | Next Thread | Close

Reply | Reply Privately | Quote | Download

Message no. 121

Posted by **Maggie McVay Lynch (ci513ml)** on Tuesday, July 29, 2003 5:42pm

```
In class we talked about Fair Use, but you may have
forgotten some of the important parts of it.  Review at
least one of the following sites, and then answer the
questions below by posting a reply to this topic.

University of Maryland's Fair Use Guidelines
http://www.umuc.edu/library/copy.html#fairuse

PBS Teacher Source on Fair Use
http://www.pbs.org/teachersource/copyright/copyright_ed_multi.shtm

Select at least two of the questions below to answer.
When you post your response, backup your answer with
logic and research that you believe provides proof that
your answer is correct.
```

Figure 4.6 **Instructor initial posting.** From the messages listed above, here is part of the instructor's initial posting to the class that is displayed when you click on the first post in the thread.

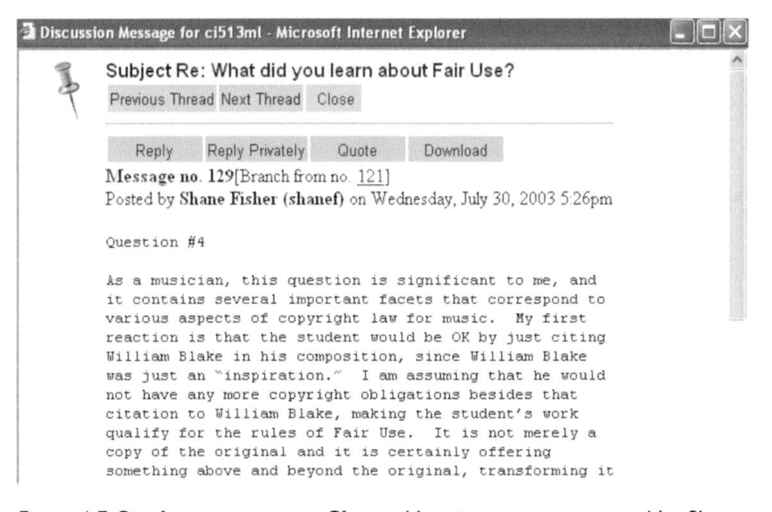
Discussion Message for ci513ml - Microsoft Internet Explorer

Subject Re: What did you learn about Fair Use?

Previous Thread Next Thread Close

Reply Reply Privately Quote Download

Message no. 129[Branch from no. 121]
Posted by Shane Fisher (shanef) on Wednesday, July 30, 2003 5:26pm

Question #4

As a musician, this question is significant to me, and it contains several important facets that correspond to various aspects of copyright law for music. My first reaction is that the student would be OK by just citing William Blake in his composition, since William Blake was just an "inspiration." I am assuming that he would not have any more copyright obligations besides that citation to William Blake, making the student's work qualify for the rules of Fair Use. It is not merely a copy of the original and it is certainly offering something above and beyond the original, transforming it

Figure 4.7 **Student response – Shane.** Here is a response posted by Shane, one of the students in the class. Note that each time you click on a message to read it, you are presented with the opportunity to immediately send a reply by clicking on the reply button at the top.

Discussion Message for ci513ml - Microsoft Internet Explorer

Subject Reply to Shane

Previous Thread Next Thread Close

Reply Reply Privately Quote Download

Message no. 256[Branch from no. 129]
Posted by Kelly Hartl (psu21445) on Monday, August 4, 2003 7:53pm

Shane, I like the way you approached #4. It is a bit tricky since we don't know if he used the text of the poem or created an instrumental work or a work with different lyrics than the poem. I also wonder though, about the "essence" of a work. If he used the text of the poem at all, I would think he would need to credit his source. Hmmm... Kelly H.

Previous Message Next Message

Previous Thread Next Thread Close

Figure 4.8 **Reply to Shane by Kelly.** Following the discussion thread one step more, above is a student's reply to the first student's posting. Note you also have the ability to move up and down the thread with the "previous thread (previous message)" and "next thread (next message)" buttons.

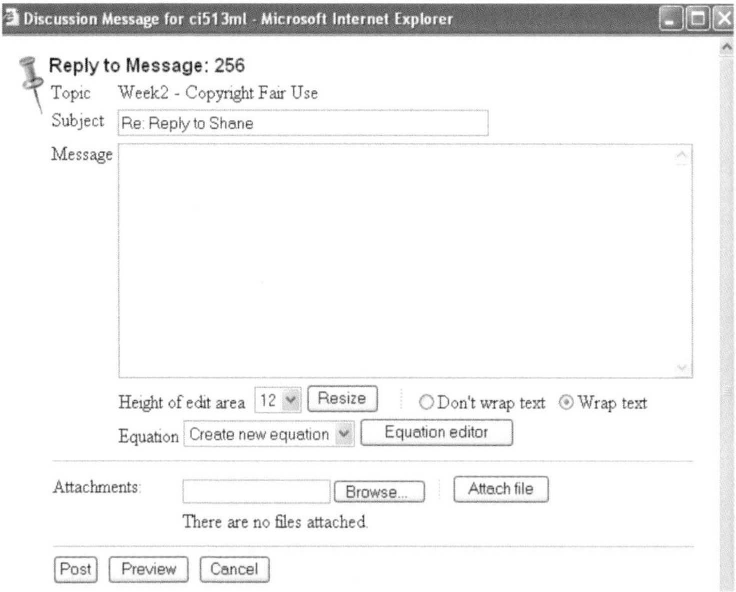

Discussion Message for ci513ml - Microsoft Internet Explorer

Reply to Message: 256
Topic Week2 - Copyright Fair Use
Subject Re: Reply to Shane
Message

Height of edit area 12 Resize Don't wrap text Wrap text
Equation Create new equation Equation editor

Attachments: Browse... Attach file
There are no files attached.

Post Preview Cancel

Figure 4.9 **Reply form.** In this example when you click on reply, the form above is presented. It is comprised of two required boxes (subject and message) which must be filled in by those wishing to post new material. An additional box allows for including an attached file. An attached file may be a document, a picture, a spreadsheet, or other type of electronic document that you know can be read by your classmates.

In any case, the form will guide you to post your comments, questions, and suggestions.

In most reply forms, you move from one box to the next by using the "tab" key after entering your text. In this example (Figure 4.9) you would:

- type an appropriate subject line in the "Subject" box, then hit "tab".
- in the "Message" box enter the body of your message.

Tips Some discussion boards also require you to enter your name and email address. If this is the case use your common name (e.g. Maggie Lynch), and for email be sure to include your entire email address (e.g. mmlynch@pdx.edu). If you want to enter a Web address, be sure to enter the entire URL (e.g. http://www.pdx.edu). That will often make it clickable, allowing the reader to click on the address and immediately go to the location you indicated.

If your message contains more than one paragraph, leave a blank line between paragraphs. Most discussion boards now have text wrapping (automatic return to the left margin). This means you *do not* want to use the "enter" key when your text approaches the right scroll bar of the message box because this will make the message display awkwardly in the recipients browser. Once your message is complete, click on the "Post" or "Submit" button (usually at the bottom of the form). Your message will then immediately appear on the Discussion board.

Tip If you do not see your message on the discussion board, click the "reload" button of your Web browser. You should then see your entry without a problem.

If you are familiar with HTML, you can use tags in the body of your message. For example, if you want to emphasize a word or idea, you can bold it by inserting the <b> and </b> around the words. Also, some discussion boards have formatting options for your message included with the software as in the example in Figure 4.10.

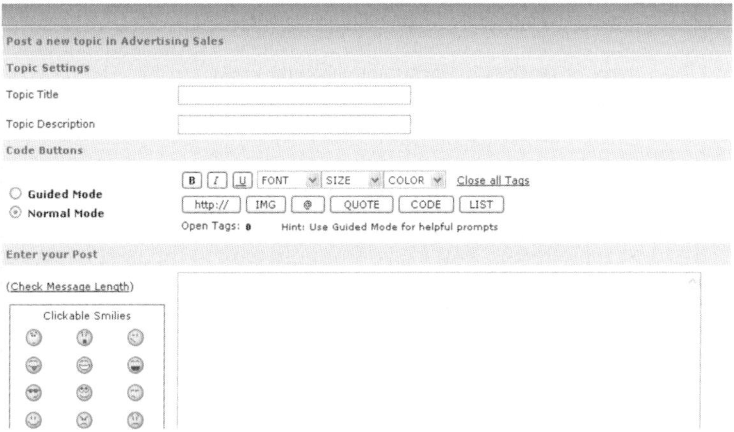

Figure 4.10 **Discussion board formats – HTML.** Note this example of a discussion board from InVision™ allows for several formatting options – the B for bold or the I for italics. It also provides ways to easily enter a Web page address (http://) or a picture (IMG), and allows you to click on a "smilie" if you want to indicate an emotion or mood with your post.

Posting web pages

Today anyone can create a Web page thanks to the quality of HTML editors and the ability of word processors to save documents as Web pages. These editors and word processors allow you to design your pages by just typing in the text and "dropping" the images where you want them. The software then writes all the HTML code behind the scenes. Check with your institution as to which type of editor they prefer you to use.

Tip for Microsoft Word™ users It is easy to save your files as HTML. Depending on the version of Word you are using. You can either select from the menu line "File – "Save as Web page" or select "File – "Save as" and in the "type" window select Web page or HTML page.

Remember, links are the primary interface mechanism within Web pages. When using links it is important to provide the entire URL address (including the http:// or other locator).

Once you have completed your page, you need to publish it to your on-campus Web site or through your own Internet service provider (ISP). There are several software packages that can help you do this. Check with your institution as to what to use and where to publish.

If your school uses a course management system, such as WebCT, it may also provide a way to publish your pages within the course. This course tool is usually called something like "student presentation tool" or "shared space." Ask your instructor whether he or she is using this tool in your course.

Asynchronous audio and video

As computer speeds increase and dial-up modems give way to cable and satellite access, you will begin to see more and more use of audio and video in online courses. Currently, these technologies are used in a very limited fashion because the download times can be frustrating.

One way in which courses that contain audio within a Web page designate that use is with an icon that looks like a loud-speaker or bullhorn. The student clicks on the audio image to listen to whatever is being presented. The two types of presentations most often heard are music that relates to the topic or a reading that may enhance the topic (e.g. a poem or a brief speech).

Another use for audio is pre-recorded announcements or greetings. Some courses contain a database of remarks and greetings that change on a regular basis based on particular criteria relating to the course and/

or the student's performance. By clicking on the audio icon you would get a different announcement or greeting each time. For example, one week you may hear your instructor say, "The homework for this week has been changed to include Chapters 3 and 4 in your textbook." The next week, the same icon click would say, "Congratulations, you received an A on your last assignment."

Streamed videos or QuickTime™ movies are finding their way into more and more online courses. Again, because of long download times, this technology is not used in places where students don't have access to fast modems. The most common uses of video are in 15 to 30 second clips that usually display a place, thing, or type of interaction the students may not otherwise have an opportunity to experience. For example, an online history course might have a short clip of the Parthenon or of a person examining a particular relic found at an archaeological dig site. Another example might be seen in a counseling course, where the student can view the "patient" discussing a difficult situation. The video then stops and the student reacts by writing what he or she would do or say in that instance.

As with asynchronous audio, video is designed to enhance the online experience by providing another stimulus to the learning process. As bandwidths and speed increase, it is likely you will see more frequent use of both these asynchronous technologies in online courses.

CD-ROMs are another way you may get audio or video information for your online course. In fact, frequently your class textbook will come with a CD-ROM. These CDs may contain case studies, real-world simulations or role plays, special software (e.g. a statistical program) that will help you work problems, or movies and video situations that relate to your course. The key to integrating a CD into your learning process is to make use of it as much as possible. Most CDs are loaded on your computer with a self-executing program. Typically, you place the disc in your CD Drive, then click on the CD Icon under "My computer." The program then automatically begins to install whatever is needed on your hard drive. If an automatic install program is not included with your CD, instructions are often found printed on the back of the case or in a handout. These instructions would provide a step-by-step process for installing the CD or for viewing the files required for your class.

Tip Although the CD may install a program on your hard drive that doesn't mean you can always run the program without the CD. CDs containing numerous graphics or videos will often run in conjunction with the program installed on your computer. The program on your computer then directs the CD to access the graphic or video at the appropriate time.

Using chat

Chat is a set of protocols that allows two or more people to have an interactive dialogue via computer. In the online education environment, chat is one of the primary synchronous interfaces used to interact with your entire class during an activity. (See example of a chat session in Figure 4.11.) As with other written messages, the primary rule for using chat is to be considerate of others. Realize that not all participant machines are running at the same speed, nor do all participants have the same typing capability. If you are a fast typist, be sure to allow opportunities for others to chat. Patience will go a long way toward providing the interactive classroom environment desired in a chat session.

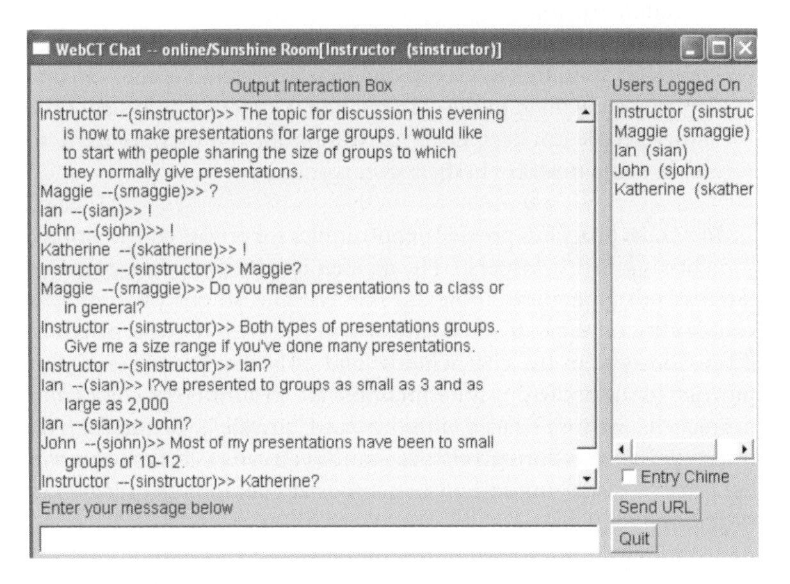

Figure 4.11 **Chat window.** In this example, you type your message in the window at the bottom. When you have typed everything you want to say, you press the "Enter" key. Your message immediately appears in the window at the top for all to view. Each chat program has different options regarding sending URLs (Web pages) or entering private chats. Check with your institution on the specifics of your program.

A few reminders about using chat:

- Use mixed case and proper punctuation, as though you were typing a letter or sending mail.
- Remember that other people have to read what you write, so be brief. A good rule of thumb is to write out no more than 12 lines (since you're using a split screen).
- If you prepare in advance, you can have ideas already typed in your word processor, then cut and paste that typing into the input window of the chat.
- Always say goodbye, or some other farewell, and wait to see a farewell from the others (particularly your instructor if he or she is participating) before exiting the session. This is especially important when you are communicating with someone physically far removed. Remember that your communication relies on the speed of your connection, the computers connecting along the route, and the recipient's modem. This means it may be a couple of minutes before your response is viewed.
- Chat shows your typing ability. If you type slowly and make mistakes, it is often not worth the time to correct them as you will quickly fall behind in the conversation. Don't worry! Usually, the other people can decipher what you meant and they are likely to make some mistakes in their own typing.

Most chat programs provide opportunities for private conversations, sometimes called "whispers." The manner in which you engage in this differs from program to program. For example, in one program you simply click on the individual with whom you wish to speak privately. Then you type in the chat window and only that person sees your message (usually these private messages are in a different color from normal chat or are prefaced with the word "private"). Be careful how much you use this during a class session as you can easily fall behind in the primary discussion and miss an important point or be called on to respond.

Using electronic whiteboards

Corporations are abandoning the paper, markers, easels and traditional whiteboards as methods of boardroom note-taking and diagramming, and schools are tossing out their chalkboards. They're turning instead to electronic whiteboards – input devices that allow for interactive collaboration, application-sharing and remote conferencing, in addition to importing hand-written notes directly into the computer.

"Whiteboarding," in electronic terms, also refers to a wide range of software packages (see Figure 4.12). Those applications may allow two or more computers to share typing and mouse-controlled sketching. Both users can type and draw together, as if they were sharing one computer, and that work is immediately seen on each computer screen. More complex software packages also include application-sharing, voice communications and even videoconferencing over the Internet. A variety of software products are available for interactive whiteboard use, and most managed learning environments include a whiteboard as one of the communication tools.

Audioconferencing

Audioconferencing is the most common and least expensive form of teleconferencing. All participants in an audioconference (also known as an audiobridge) are connected via a telephone call. This call may be made using normal telephone lines, or it may be made using the computer.

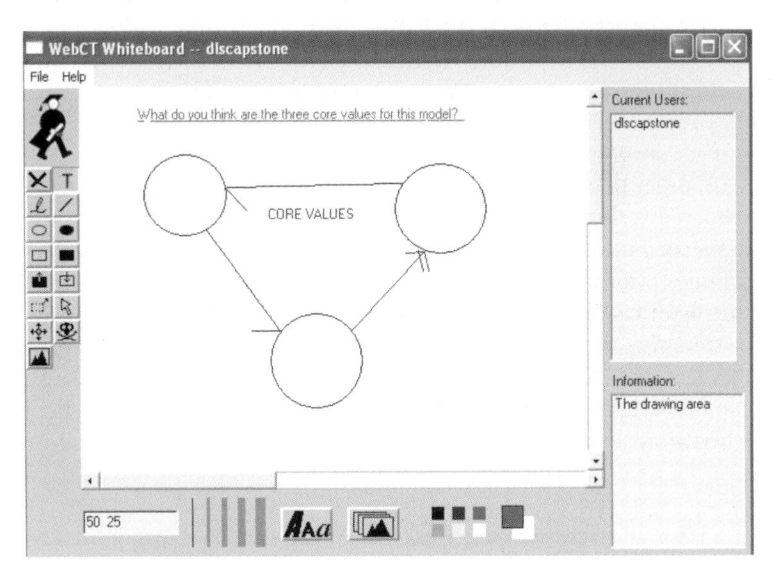

Figure 4.12 **Whiteboard.** Similar to a chat room, the whiteboard will usually list all of the users on the right, and provide a space for drawing in the center. The drawing tools are usually on the left or the bottom of the screen.

If your course uses normal telephone lines, this call is routed through an operator. Typically, individual students use their regular home or office telephones and dial into a toll-free number. The operator then creates a "bridge" to connect all the lines and allow everyone to speak and to hear each other. The key is to respect the order of speaking and to be careful not to interrupt when someone else is talking.

If the audioconference is taking place over the computer, you will need to have a microphone installed with your computer. You would be directed to login to a particular Web site where the conferencing facilities are available. Then you would talk through your microphone to participate in the discussion. If at all possible, it is best to participate in this type of conference with a headset. In that way, you don't have to worry about your speakers being turned on or disturbing others near you.

Audioconferencing is used for lectures, discussions of a particular topic, student oral presentations, and question-and-answer periods. If you are in an online education environment that never meets face-to-face, an audioconference gives you the opportunity to hear the voices of your instructor and participants and to gain information through their tone and inflection which you may not accurately interpret in emails, discussion boards, or chat. Some students find that once they have identified the voice and nuances of another person's speech pattern, in the future they associate that same pattern with the written messages they receive over the Internet. This pattern provides a context for all future communication.

In order to get the most out of an audioconference, it is wise to be prepared well in advance of the call. You should also call into the designated number (or login to the designated site) a minimum of five minutes prior to the beginning of the session. Many schools have the instructor take roll call prior to the beginning of a session. Also many conferences are set up so that if you are late you will not be admitted to the session. A transcript can sometimes be provided of the entire conference, depending on the conference options selected by the school when arrangements were made.

Tips

- Have all textbooks, instructor notes, copies of Web pages marked and available before the conference begins.
- Read the agenda prior to beginning the conference.
- Prepare, in advance, your specific questions or responses regarding assignments or the topic of discussion.

- If you are giving a presentation during the conference, have your notes in front of you while you speak. This will help you to not stumble with words.
- Be sure to eliminate any distractions from the room. They not only disrupt you, but also everyone else who is listening.
- Make arrangements for children, parents, friends, not to interrupt you.
- Remove potential barking dogs from the room.
- Don't eat or chew gum while on the conference. Everyone will hear it clearly.
- Don't play music in the background.
- It is hard for most people to differentiate more than four different voices, so you should always state your name each time you speak (e.g. "Maggie here. I think the best approach to this...).

MUDs and MOOs

What is a MUD or MOO?

MUD was first used in the "virtual reality" game dungeons and dragons. Most MUDs still retain this game-like atmosphere with players moving to higher levels or earning points, often by eliminating (shooting) the other players' characters. MUD stands for multi-user dimension, or Dungeon, reflecting its origin. MOO is an acronym for MUD, but keys on the "object oriented" aspect. MOO is frequently referred to as multi-user object oriented dimension. MOOs, usually developed as more social spaces, lend themselves readily to use in the classroom or as spaces for conferences and meetings. Many people uses the terms MUD and MOO synonymously.

Proponents of the use of MOOs in the classroom come from a wide variety of disciplines. Part of the attraction of these virtual spaces is that they allow for classes from different geographic regions to connect in real time. In most MOOs, teachers, and often students, can create the virtual world to suit their needs and desires. And, especially in writing-intensive courses, a large part of the attraction of MOOs is that they are text-based.

An educational MOO has an academic theme and uses a variety of MOO communication tools such as internal email, newspapers, documents, blackboards and classrooms to accommodate a variety of teaching styles. Teachers use these tools in harmony with the goals for the class while exploiting the nature of MOO as a student-centered learning environment. For example, one instructor teaches a Middle-Eastern History class using a MOO. The instructor designed the space as a story with a mystery flavor and divided the story into discrete items. Each item had a clue for solving the mystery of a particular piece of pottery, or art, or a location where something might have happened. There was no importance to the sequence of browsing around. The MOO provided an interesting and interactive way for students to learn more than dates and times in history.

Below are links to some of the types of MOOs used in education

- **Diversity University, Inc.**: a non-profit organization providing MOO environments for innovative approaches to learning. Click on "Visit DU MAIN" to access the MOO, or see their web gateway: http://www.du.org/.
- **MundoHispano**: a well-populated, virtual representation of dozens of cities in the Spanish-speaking world, written entirely in Spanish for learners, teachers, and native speakers. http://www.umsl.com/~moosprog/mundo.html/
- **MOOfrancais**: modeled after Paris, a well-organized MOO for learners, teachers, and native speakers of French, entirely in French. http://www.umsl.com/~moosprog/moofrancais.html
- **schMOOze University**: built to resemble a small college, learners can practice English and socialize with other learners as well as native speakers of English. http://members.at.infoseek.co.jp/schmooze
- **PennMOO**: the virtual classroom site in the English Department of the University of Pennsylvania. http://dept.english.upenn.edu/~afilreis/88/moo-home.html

A MOO is very similar to a chat room. People participate at the same time (synchronously), it is text-based, and you get a sense of immediacy in the discussions. The difference between a chat and a MOO is that a MOO also has pre-programmed environments, messages, and objects with which students may interact. Participation in a MOO involves the same two basic activities as reading and taking notes in a book – as you MOO you will read, and you will write in response to what you have read. Participants read descriptions of locations, objects, characters, and other participants, and they read what the other characters and participants have to say. Their writing consists of simple commands, and also of dialogue, as they interact with one another and with the objects and characters in the MOO.

What can different kinds of users do on a MOO?

Those who first connect to a MOO are called guests. Guests have the ability to "talk," send messages across the MOO by "paging," use MOOmail for sending messages, and move around the MOO. They cannot make any permanent changes in their guest "character," nor can they create objects. Those who want a permanent character with password access need to request this, usually by sending email or MOOmail to the registrar (often the instructor) of the MOO. Permanent characters can name themselves, describe themselves, and set their gender. Users come to know one another, forming friendships and a sense of community. These relationships can be one of the most rewarding aspects of the MOO experience.

Builders are users that have programming permissions for creating rooms, exits, and objects which they can describe in any way that is consistent with the MOO's theme. They can also write customized, durable "messages" that automatically appear when certain commands are used. For example, when a user pages "MariLuz" at MundoHispano, that user will see a line of text in Spanish stating that a kangaroo puts the message in its pocket and carries it to MariLuz.

Those who learn the MOO programming language can become programmers who create more elaborate features such as that created by a student named Gregor, at the schMOOze University. He created a monkey that hands out dry towels to swimmers. This program causes lines of text describing the monkey's actions to appear at regular intervals on the screens of all the users in the same virtual room. The ability to create objects, "messages" and programs gives the user a sense of ownership, an outlet for creative writing, and motivation to return. The wizards (usually the teachers) are at the top of the hierarchy. They create new characters, monitor connections, teach new users, and deal with problems, often with the help of teacher-administrators. They also do deep-level programming and uniquely have access to information such as the users' email addresses.

What difficulties can I expect when using a MOO?

Some MOO users have quite an emotional response, positive or negative, to the experiences they have. Students have been known to fall in love with or be very offended by other users. While the sense of place and permanence that is achieved on MOO can contribute to the meaningfulness of the learning experience, some users simply have difficulty adjusting to having a virtual self (their "character") somewhere in cyberspace. Many instructors who use MOOs regularly also schedule in-class discussions that focus on student reaction to MOO use.

Tip Why use a MOO?

In a MOO, you can:

- move between distinct places (called rooms)
- manipulate objects (e.g. get, drop, activate)
- chat with people or 'bots' (robots)
- create new virtual places (rooms)
- describe your character, the places you create and the objects you build
- mail electronic messages
- conduct classes.

In a MOO, you have instant communication

- with each other
- with distant students
- with distant experts.

A MOO extends natural collaboration

- text-based discussion leads to collaborative work
- individual and collaborative identities
- immediate audience response.

Mooing is fun and it is educational

- the activity relies on problem solving and creative writing.

Many MOOs have evolved into sophisticated and flexible environments, full of objects and rooms and people who can be anything or anyone and can interact in a variety of ways. Today, these programs are used for social communities, scientific forums, educational environments, process control systems, business conferencing systems, and many other collaborative endeavors. Many MOO servers have been adapted to work with graphical Web interfaces and even 3D Virtual Reality perspectives. Artificially intelligent "bots" (automatic programs for specific functions or responses) interact with users and with the environments. Users can build and shape their environments and share information, ideas, resources, and communities online with people around the world.

Accessing a MOO

Although MOOs have a higher learning curve than chat programs, the time is well-spent as it will engage your interests. If you find you really love this virtual environment, you may build your own MOO. The underlying code to build your own virtual environment (with a little expertise) is available for free downloading on the Internet, thanks to Pavel Curtis of Xerox Corporation. Many MOOs already have programming in place (via generic objects) to allow for such virtual reality features as blackboards and slide projectors, moderated panel discussions, and more. Most of them also allow you to customize the environment to suit your needs.

The best way to understand this form of communication and educational "gaming" is to try some of them. Try some of the links mentioned previously and determine if this is something you might enjoy. As you enter these spaces as a guest, remember that just as there are "netiquette" rules in email, discussion boards, and chat, virtual environments also depend upon the people in it treating each other with consideration and respect. As a virtual environment, the nature of a MOO is determined by the interactions among the members and visitors who participate in it. Some physical life situations have little bearing on a virtual community. You won't, for instance, have to fuss about who should open a door to let the other pass. Some situations requiring consideration and respect in physical life are of equal or greater importance in a virtual environment. If you wouldn't barge into someone else's office at your job, then perhaps you should think twice about joining someone in a private space without asking first.

Because educational MOOs are designed for learning purposes, the interactions among people should reflect personal and professional respect. Identify yourself and your interests. In fantasy MOOs, players may take on fantastic names, identify their gender as neutral, and otherwise indulge themselves in the magical possibilities of a virtual environment. However, in educational MOOs you need to identify yourself with your true name. Most institutions have adopted this policy, as using your true identity you are less likely to act inappropriately. Below, are a few guidelines for your initial contact in a virtual environment interaction.

- Describe yourself the first time you log on. Here is an example using the typical MOO commands: @describe me as <brief description> "I'm Maggie McVay Lynch from Oregon. I am an instructor teaching courses about online learning."

- It also helps to describe yourself as a physical character. It is up to you what details you want to include. Example: <a character's description> "Brown hair, brown eyes, dressed in casual clothes with a cup of tea and a sesame bagel."
- Identify your gender. Example: @gender "female"
- Describe your interests. When you have been given a character name and a password, you should create an information file. Some typical things to include would be your name, school affiliation, your field of study, your email address and any major interests you would like to share. Example: @info me "My name is Maggie McVay Lynch from Oregon where I am an instructor. My hobbies are hiking, golf, tennis, and reading science fiction. I can be reached at mmlynch@pdx.edu."

We have spent all our lives developing our social skills by picking up cues about others from their reactions to us. In a virtual space, you are held to much the same standards of consideration, but with fewer of the familiar cues. You can't depend on closed doors, raised eyebrows, or voice inflection. Only typewritten words are presented. Again, here are some guidelines to help ease the way:

- Before trying to page or join anyone, find out first where they are, what they are doing, and who they're with (the command may be @who or @crowd). The person you would like to see may be in a class or having a private conversation. If they are in a public space you can join without paging first.
- Page first. Once you've determined that a person is logged in and not apparently busy, page her or him as a greeting with an invitation to join you.
- Respect private space. One of the greatest frustrations is having someone barge right into a private space without paging to ask if he or she may join the person or group there. You can usually tell when people are in a private space, once you have logged on and checked @who a few times and noticed where they tend to be. Also, don't leave objects in or take objects from the private space.
- Be mature, professional, and friendly. One of the banes of non-educational cyberspace is the freedom some people feel to harass, insult, or otherwise offend people over the net in ways they wouldn't consider in person. Fortunately, it doesn't happen much in educational environments. Certainly, you can joke around, enjoy people's company, be playful as well as serious – but always be

sensitive both to the other people with whom you are interacting and to the sense of purpose in the educational MOO.

- Getting around the MOO can be confusing at first. *Before* asking every character you meet for help, read the "help" texts provided in the environment. Nearly every command has a help text associated with it. Most MOOs make it clear how to access help. Typical commands are: "HELP" or "911" for emergency procedures, or "?". Also most MOOs have people with authority (i.e. the instructor). These people may be called "moderators" or "wizards." They usually respond to email quickly, but if you find them online you can certainly ask for help.

Basic commands that apply to most MOOs

First, it is important to know that each MOO is different from all other MOOs – a different look and frequently different commands. It's very important that you read every screen presented to you from the moment you log in. These screens will usually provide important information as to how you may proceed. Once you have entered the room or shared space, the following 10 simple commands should get you started in most MOO environments.

1. **co guest** should get you on, but some have different entry commands. Read the opening screen.
2. **@who** usually shows you who else is in the environment, where they are, how long they have been on and how long they have been idle or not entering commands.
3. **help** shows an index of help files.
4. **help [object or verb]** shows the help file on a specific object or verb.
5. **look** by itself will show you the description of the "room" you are in.
6. **look [object]** without the brackets will show you the description of the specific object you name.
7. **say** allows you to talk to someone in the same room with you.
8. **page [comment]** without the brackets allows you to talk to someone who is not in the same room with you.
9. **@join [someone]** without the brackets allows you to teleport yourself to the same room someone else is in. *Do not do this without paging them and asking permission beforehand.*
10. **@quit** quit or log off the MOO site.

Exits are ways for you to move from one room to the next. It is important to look for exit names in each room (e.g. lounge or library). To leave (exit) the room you are in and go to another room, type that room name.

For additional MOO resources including downloads for software, documentation, programming resources, and lists of MOOs you can visit http://metaverse.net/moo.html.

Visual chats or avatar chats

Visual chats, sometimes called multimedia chat or GMUKS (graphical multi-user konversations), and "habitats," are something of a cross between a MOO and a traditional chat room. As social environments, they are unique in that they are graphical. Rather than limiting users to text-only communications as in most chat rooms, multimedia programs add a visual dimension that creates the illusion of movement, space, and physicality. It allows people to express their identity *visually*, rather than just through written words. The result is a whole new realm for self-expression and social interaction with subtleties and complexities not seen in text-only chat rooms. Though not yet used in an educational arena, there are several ongoing efforts to create these type of environments for students.

One example of a multimedia environment is a program called the "Palace" (see Figure 4.13). There are many "palace" rooms on the Internet, each with its own personality. The Palace software is free. It can be downloaded to your computer from http://practice.chatserve.com/ or to a school's server and then customized for whatever graphics the school wishes to present. There are two visual components to this environment. The first is the backdrop or "room" in which people interact with each other. Users can move freely within and between the rooms. Like characters in comic strips, you communicate with others via typed text that appears in balloons that pop out from your head or body (see Figure 4.14).

Head? Body? How do you want to appear? This is the second visual feature of this multimedia environment: "avatars" or "props." Although these words often are used interchangeably, there is a slight distinction in the minds of some users. Avatars refer to pictures, drawings, or icons that users choose to represent themselves. Props are objects that users may add to their avatars (say, a hat or umbrella), place in the room, or give to another person (say, a glass of water or a bouquet of flowers).

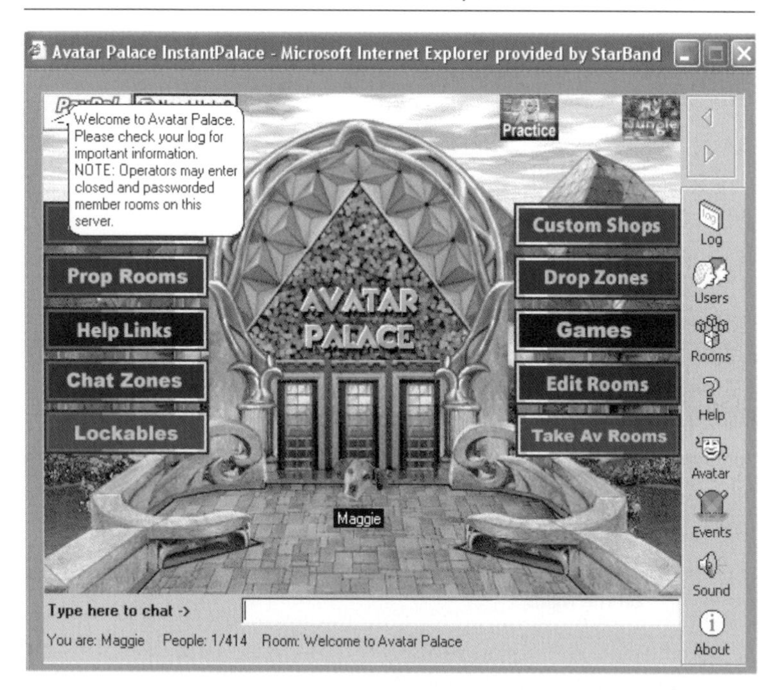

Figure 4.13 **Avatar chat-Palace.** The Avatar Palace entry page at http://www.avatarpalace.net/. From here you can navigate to a number of different rooms. There are many different "palace" locations on the Internet – each with its own themes, social structures, and likely topics of conversation. The Avatar Palace is a safe place for an initial exploration of visual chat because the monitors are strict about language use, acceptable behavior, and the types of avatars that can be displayed. Palace members range in age from 8 to 50 with an average age of between 12 and 15.

Avatars – or "Avs," as visual chat users affectionately call them, fall into two general categories. The first is the standard set of "smileys" that come with most programs. They display basic human emotions and behavioral signals – happy, sad, angry, winking, sleeping/bored, blushing, head-nodding, head-shaking. The user also can change the color of the face or add to it one or more props, such as hats, wigs, scarves, devil horns, a halo, a glass of beer, a bicycle, etc. Because the faces and props can be mixed and matched, users have at their disposal an almost infinite array of combinations to express themselves.

However, advanced visual chat fans rarely use the smileys. Instead they choose the second major category of avatar creations – those

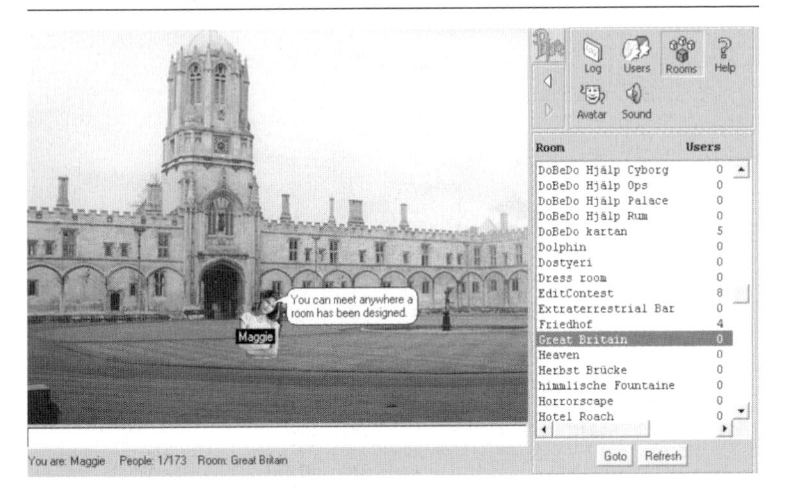

Figure 4.14 **Avatar communication bubbles.** Communicate by typing in the chat window. This is displayed as a balloon for all in the room to see. You can move from room to room by clicking on your choice on the right.

designed by the members themselves (see Figure 4.15). Visually, you can be anything you want. Only your graphics skills and imagination limit you. In cyberspace, most people don't want to be totally anonymous, but they *do* like control over how their identity is expressed. Some people choose pictures or icons borrowed from internet archives, scanned from hardcopy, or taken from other digital sources. Students may choose to present a true picture of themselves, a celebrity face, animals, cartoon characters, or even an outdoor scene. Users might edit or combine these pictures according to their particular tastes.

Educational video games

Over the past two decades electronic games have become ingrained in our culture. Children's fixation with these games initially alarmed parents and educators, but educational researchers soon questioned whether the motivation to play could be tapped and harnessed for educational purposes. A number of educational electronic games have been developed and their success has been mixed. The great majority of these games are designed for single players; if there is more than one player, the players are usually required to take turns playing. Although learning within a cooperative group setting has been found to be extremely effective, designing educational games to support multiple players working together has received little attention.

Figure 4.15 **3D Planet Avatar create.** 3D Planet's 3D Assistant Internet Utilities allow you to take any picture, cut and paste features you like or don't like, and change each of those individual features with others from their database.

Already there are many educational video games that can be purchased or used in school. Games like SimCity or Civilizations provide interesting interactions on specific topics. One can easily imagine a game called Wall Street where each student in the class is given shares of stock to trade or buy and learn about the machinations of the market. A UN simulation game might assign each student in the class a specific political role and country. All students then work together to solve a global problem. Several colleges and universities have received grant money to look more closely at how best to take advantage of this video gaming potential.

Desktop videoconferencing

Many desktop videoconferencing products have been introduced that have the ability to project an image of the person who was called in a small window on the computer screen. The software programs allow users to see one another and to work on documents at the same time. Common components include a software program and tiny cameras that sit on top of the computer screen. Each product enables you to see another person with the same equipment.

Video establishes a strong connection among participants. Since a teacher can see and hear remote learners in real time, he or she can use conversation and body language to enhance communication. Frequent interaction increases understanding and encourages more personalized instruction. Interactive teaching strategies, such as questioning and discussion, can also help engage and motivate learners by making them active participants. Videoconferencing also allows for connection with external resources. Remote experts can help validate understanding, provide feedback, and introduce practical examples. This real-world connection can greatly improve motivation, especially if students participate and the expert is able to demonstrate practical applications of the theory. Video can support use of diverse media. Photos and color graphics look great on video and can help convey a difficult concept or simplify instructions. Room-based systems usually include an attachable document camera that allows transmission of a high-quality still image. This feature can be used to show objects as well as photos and graphics, and many instructors also project "slates" – simple text displays with a few sentences (usually instructions). Slates are an easy way to shift learner focus from the video screen to a learning activity.

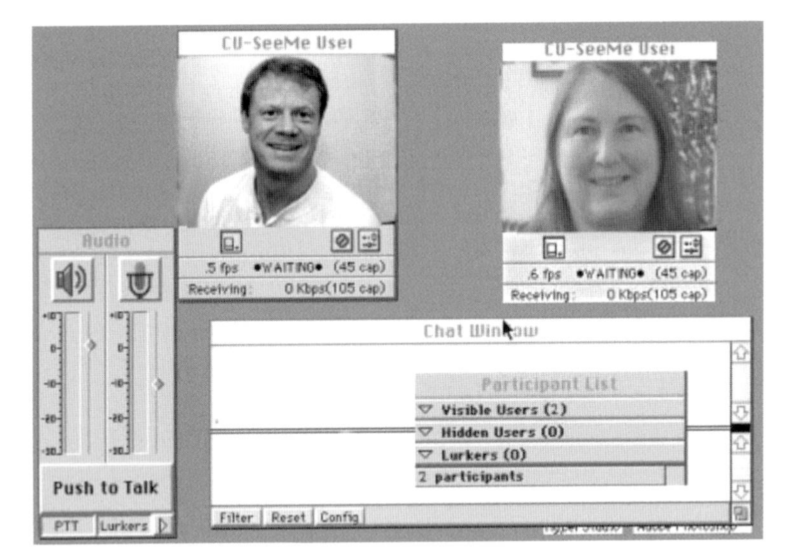

Figure 4.16 CUworld

One of the most popular video chats is CUworld. It allows you to see multiple people, hear them, and run a text-based chat room at the same time. To use it requires each person to have a Web camera, a microphone, sound card and video card.

CUworld began as the free CUSeeMe software. It is no longer free; you register for a three-month trial membership, purchase your materials, link to other schools, and get going. The sessions are hosted by CUworld and they now provide monitors and helpers, which makes the membership cost worthwhile if you use this tool frequently. Note: it is Windows only; Macintosh users will not be able to connect. After the three-month trial you must select a membership level ranging from $5 to $30 per month depending on your needs.

Desktop videoconferencing is still rarely used in online education today because of the degradation of video quality over regular phone lines. Though CUworld has provided some inroads to the technology, it still has its problems. Good quality videoconferencing uses a great deal of bandwidth, making interaction slow. The picture can become so jumpy or irregular that it is frequently difficult to see what the other person is doing. However, with the increasing use of satellite links for the Internet and media centers set up on college campuses, it is likely that this technology will become a key interface in the near future.

Chapter 5

Overcoming isolation and building community

The psychology of being online

> Learning is not attained by chance, it must be sought for with ardor and attended to with diligence.
>
> (Abigail Adams, 1744–1818, Letter to John Quincy Adams, May 8, 1780)

As a world structured by machines rather than the physical environment, the online experience may have some rather unique psychological features – such as reduced or altered sensory experience, the opportunity for identity flexibility and anonymity, the equalization of social status, the transcending of spatial boundaries, the stretching and condensation of time, the ability to access numerous relationships, the capacity to make permanent records of one's experiences, and the "uninhibition" effect, to name a few. Fortunately, some of these psychological effects are limited in the online course environment. Outside of the classroom, however, the cyberspace experience can become even more foreign. It can be a world with its own language. As a virtual reality, it can offer you true-to-life experiences as well as highly imaginative scenarios, such as in the video game experience – where people interact in imaginative visual scenes while shifting their image and identity through the use of chosen characters.

Some people thrive in the cyberspace environment of minimal face-to-face interaction, while others feel isolated from their classmates and their instructor. If you are someone who feels comfortable online and is already very involved in the social aspects of online chats, discussions, and gaming, this chapter will help ground you in the expectations of your behavior in the online classroom environment. The online classroom is not as free as the rest of the Internet (for example, you must use your true name and identity in class – not a made up one). On the other hand, if you have not been online very much or feel uncomfortable with the freeform social environment that seems to exist online, this chapter may help to set your mind at ease. It begins with some practical tips about setting up a physical and psychological space for you to be successful in the online learning environment. Then it explores some of the psychology behind individual and group dynamics online and how you can interact safely and successfully.

Setting your learning expectations

Whether your class experience is fully online or only partially, it is important that your expectations are realistic when you enter the course. When students register and then attend a course of their choice, they arrive with a set of preconceptions about what they can expect from the institution, from the instructor, and from their classmates. Typically, online students anticipate they will communicate with their instructor via email, discussion groups, and Web pages. Onsite students expect the instructor to appear at the appointed room at the appointed time, and there deliver a lecture on the topic of the day, or at least manage the class while they engage in learning activities.

Some students report difficulty in the online environment because they get insufficient information to direct their learning, and without attending lectures find some difficulty in staying on-task with their studies and thus assimilating the many things to be learned. When taking an online course, students must accept a larger responsibility for difficulties they encounter and for their own learning. Students who need the discipline of regular face-to-face meetings to keep them engaged and on-task may never be successful at online learning. Let's look at some practical tips for setting up your environment and tracking your progress with your studies.

Create your own learning space

It is important that you have a place to study that is quiet and away from distractions (e.g. the television, your children, other students). You may have to consider moving your computer to another room if it is located in the same room as your family television or stereo. If you are sharing a computer, in a library or campus environment, you will need to work out a timetable for sharing with other users.

Your study area needs to be comfortable, with adequate lighting and ventilation. It is important to pay close attention to ergonomics to ensure you don't overstress your back, neck, or eyes. Your computer desk should be large enough to handle the computer, monitor, printer and mouse pad and still give you room for a notebook. A copyholder is a good idea for reading text at eye level while typing. A height and back adjustable chair is essential for correct posture and to keep your eye level in line with the top part of the monitor. Being able to look straight ahead reduces tension on your spine.

Tip Do not slouch in your chair. Be sure to get up and have a stretch break at least once per hour! Make a conscious effort to blink regularly!

When you work in a properly arranged environment, it is much easier to develop good learning, time management, and self-discipline skills. By controlling your environment, you take the first step toward controlling your online learning experience. The way you arrange your furniture, the positioning of your computer and your chair, the accessibility of your books and paper materials, and even the visual aids on your wall and bulletin board are all keys to creating an optimal learning environment at home.

If possible, claim a separate space for yourself somewhere in your home. If you don't have an extra bedroom or home office, simply find a quiet corner you can section off. Choose an area that doesn't get too much traffic and where you can instruct other family members to leave you alone when needed.

After you've set aside your learning space, get to work making it reflect a comfortable and creative environment for you. Some people need a space that allows everything to be neatly filed, categorized, and cubby-holed. Others only need flat surfaces for piles. Think of situations in which you are able to concentrate easily and do a great amount of work without much stress. Is it sitting at a desk facing the wall? Looking out a window? Sprawling on a sofa or on cushions on the floor? Maybe you need a combination of spaces – a sofa for reading and making notes and a desk for writing and communicating on the computer. Below is a list of some important learning environment considerations:

- type and arrangement of furnishings
- lighting
- temperature and air circulation
- organizational tools (bulletin boards, file cabinets, supply storage)
- plants and/or pictures
- background noise vs. total quiet.

The tools of online learning

In addition to the obvious need for a computer, there may be a number of other tools required in your online learning program. For example, many programs also use CDs, videotapes, and faxes. You need to determine what policies your college or university may have about using these ancillary devices. Do you have a VCR to play tapes? Does your computer include a CD drive? Do you have access to a fax machine? Carefully evaluate all the technologies required for your courses.

Your home computer, of course, will be your primary tool. Students new to this environment may be wondering exactly how "fancy" a computer they need. Would your 10-year-old computer work? Do you have to have a PC or a Mac? Again, these are questions you would need to ask the college offering the online courses. Most have a minimal configuration that they will support with their course management system. Because the Internet's capabilities are changing so rapidly and programmers continue to take advantage of new protocols, it is wise to have a computer that is no more than three years old (two is even better). Below is a listing of the minimum requirements for most online study programs:

- modem or cable access to the Internet at 56K or higher
- reliable connection to the Internet
- adequate hard drive space for your classes (recommend 500MB+).
- a CD Drive
- a sound card
- an Internet browser program that is Java enabled.
- a word processing program (Microsoft Word™, WordPerfect™, LotusNotes™).

Some schools will have very specific hardware or software requirements that they will support. In this case, they usually provide a list to you or include the computer purchase as part of your tuition for the program. Others provide a wide variety of support options, including Macintosh computer compatibility. In addition to the above minimum configuration, a variety of browser plug-ins is commonly required. These browser plug-ins are free and easily downloaded from the Internet as indicated below:

- Real Audio to hear sound recordings on Web pages http://www.real.com/

- Acrobat Reader to download PDF files http://www.adobe.com/products/acrobat/readstep2.html
- QuickTime™ to view online video clips http://www.apple.com/quicktime/download/
- Flash or Shockwave to view certain animations and 3-D technologies http://www.macromedia.com/downloads/.

Study routines and time schedules

A timetable will assist you with your learning by organizing your study routine. Map out a weekly schedule that shows academic, work and family commitments, as well as your leisure activities. For a longer-term picture, you might use a term planner (quarters, semesters, or trimesters as they match your school environment). Pin it on the wall or a corkboard near your desk. This is also a good place to post the learning goals you have set for your course.

You are not tied to a study routine based on attending campus at certain times. However, always check when online tests are due, reading assignments should be completed, and papers sent to your instructor. Be sure to give yourself plenty of time to complete any tasks. Map out the due dates on your calendar. Be sure to also mark all dates for required synchronous activities (chat, whiteboard, video or audioconferencing). As your instructor or other students may be in a different time zone from you, double-check the correct time that your attendance is required. Studying online means that you have the opportunity to plan your study routine around other commitments, but even with this flexibility you must schedule specific hours for study if you are to be successful.

When planning the best time to login to your course, you might also need to consider what is the best time to be on the Internet. Depending on the amount of Internet traffic in your local area, certain times of the day will be faster download times than others. For example, many areas have traffic problems between the hours of 7:00pm and 9:00pm when most people are home from work and finished with dinner. You may need to try at different times and adjust your study routine accordingly. If you share a computer with other users, you will have to negotiate your online time with them.

Tip Some users may be connected through an Internet provider that charges for use by the hour or the minute (especially rural students who might not have local call connection). In that case, look for ways to minimize this time.

- Download email messages and disconnect from the Internet before you read them. Answer them offline then connect again to upload them.
- Download some of your course files or Web pages to your hard drive to read later.
- If you are paying by the minute or hour for your online time, be sure to let your instructors know. Perhaps they can help you with other ways to accommodate your budget.

Often students interpret online learning as freedom from a schedule. Though the online student does not attend classes at a building on a regular timetable, the successful student does, in fact, set up and maintain a strict plan of reading, participation, and assignments. In fact, due to the lack of classroom lectures, the work of learning can be perceived as actually "harder" in an online environment. If you do not set up and stick to a schedule of learning activities, you will quickly find yourself too far behind to successfully complete your class.

Most students have a tendency to procrastinate studying. It is common to find a group of college students "cramming" for a test the day before, instead of studying a little each week throughout the class. Similarly, it is common for students to put off writing a paper until one or two days before it is due; then stay up for 24 or 48 hours straight to complete it. In the online learning environment, these same commonalities occur. However, procrastination may put you in danger of not completing the project on time.

In the classroom, you have the benefit of *hearing* the instructor's lectures. If you didn't read the textbook, chances are you can "cram" for the test by skimming your notes and skimming the book. In online learning, you *must* read the textbook and the ancillary materials because that is what comprises the lecture. For most people it is not possible in an online environment to "cram" all of the learning into a few days before a project is due.

Remember, you are responsible for your own learning. Most online programs require that you explore the vast information and communication opportunities of the Internet and that you become an active participant in the construction of more opportunities. Only through the creative acts required in the course activities and the electronic collaboration with classmates will you begin to see the value and the challenge of this learning medium.

Tip One difficulty, with the plethora of online resources available for research, is knowing where to draw the line at *enough* research. Set yourself a schedule for how much time you can afford to follow your

research path. When that time is up, *stop* and move on to the actual writing of your paper.

As an online student, you must be an independent and self-directed learner. The following checklist may assist you in preparing for and successfully completing each class.

- Purchase all class materials well in advance of the class.
- Be thoroughly familiar with the syllabus and course structure.
- Check the Internet often for weekly updates and new assignments.
- Log into asynchronous online course conferences and resources (e.g. discussion boards, your email account, course Web pages) at least five out of seven days a week.
- Familiarize yourself with the instructor's electronic office hours.
- Read each assignment sheet thoroughly.
- Note all due dates, including those for the rough drafts, preparatory work, or discussion postings.
- Complete all assigned reading. If you have difficulty reading online, print out the assigned readings and keep them well-organized to help with your studies.
- Email the instructor with any questions well in advance of due dates.
- Follow all instructions and rules for the course precisely.
- Learn and follow the assigned guidelines for email etiquette.
- Type all assignments on a word processor.
- Turn in "readable" exercises and drafts via email attachments of your word-processed document.
- Plan to hand in assignments a minimum of four to five hours *before* they are due to ensure Internet processing time. This type of advance planning will take into account potential computer down time, and time-zone differences.
- Attend all scheduled synchronous sessions.
- Actively access online resources, initiate and guide discussions, encourage cooperation, collaboration, and growth for all participants.
- Serve as an instructor for peers needing help as you are able.

Self-direction

Self-direction is an integral part of independent learning. Many of the items in the checklist above mirror the organization of a self-directed person. One of the most important characteristics of a self-directed person is the ability to set and meet goals.

Meeting goals requires developing objectives, timelines, strategies, problem-solving, accepting challenge and change. As a student, successful learning is your primary goal. Keeping a journal of your goals, strategies, performance criteria, and how you met the goals can be very useful. At the end of a course, or a degree program, you can use those notes to include in a portfolio, on a resume, in interview discussions and many other places which capture your entire learning experience. Below are a few concepts to consider and write down in your educational journal.

Learning goals and objectives

Write down your learning goals for each class. Make sure they are clearly defined and appropriate to your entry level skills, knowledge, and interests. You may begin with the stated course goals, but you should restate them in relationship to your own experience. Please remember that your goals and objectives may change over time. If they do, your journal should record the changes as well as the thought process you went through to determine the changes.

Example If a course goal for management communications is to make a presentation using PowerPoint, you might modify it for your personal goal to be "make a PowerPoint presentation to my department regarding Internet training."

Learning strategies

Write a short description of the methods and resources you plan to use in order to achieve your stated goals and objectives. Be specific relative to each goal and objective. Again, some of the strategies may be derived from your online education course. You need to relate these strategies to your personal life or work environment and make the course meaningful to you.

Example Using the same PowerPoint presentation example above, you might write, "I will practice finding appropriate graphics for my presentation. I will define the types of transitions I want to use."

Performance criteria

Describe how you plan to demonstrate that you achieved your goals and objectives. Certainly getting a good grade in the class will demonstrate some achievement. However, what will make you feel good about what you have learned? Using the skills on your job? Teaching your new skills to someone else?

Example: "I will use my PowerPoint skills in each management presentation I do."

Diversity of perspective

A self-directed learner is able to view a problem from several directions. Frequently you will be faced with difficult assignments or concepts. Keep track of the number of types of ways you approach problems and solutions, including analysis of various technologies. These notes will help you in the future when you face similar problems or circumstances. Also, taking notes is one way to solidify the process in your mind.

Example: "It was difficult to determine how the page should look. Viewing other classmates' presentations and comparing them to my previous overhead slides was helpful."

Individual effort and contribution

At the end of each project, or at the end of a course, write a short description of what you actually did to achieve your goals and objectives. Be sure to include input and involvement on group projects. In our daily lives, we are inundated with data, projects, and problems to solve. Sometimes, after a few weeks or months pass, we no longer remember what our effort or contribution was to that project. These notes will help you again in sharing information, putting together experience essays, writing your resume, and speaking in interviews about your education.

Example: "The presentation was the combined effort of Jack, Sharon, and Barb. Each of us brought ideas and old overheads to the table to begin the process. Then we..."

Individual reflection

The process of reflective learning is discussed in detail later in this chapter. However, for your journal, the ability to be both self-congratulatory and self-critical will illustrate that you have thought about what you learned and identified what you need to learn relative to your personal goals as well as class activities and projects.

Example "My presentation was well-received by the management team. They particularly liked the graphics I selected. However, I was not as well prepared as I would have liked for the discussion and questions that followed. In the future I will…"

The learning experience provided in higher education has been changing to encompass ways to immediately apply your learning to "real-world" environments. Unlike traditional education paradigms of the past, which train students only in theory and historic practices, many colleges and universities now incorporate opportunities for direct application of skills to specific jobs or to your current work context. This education paradigm allows you the opportunity to synthesize your studies with both your personal and professional life.

It is becoming a common practice, particularly in adult online education, to have your homework assignments relate directly to your professional work experience. For example, instead of doing a presentation for your classmates, you will be required to do a presentation at your office and have your boss verify that it took place. In a leadership class, you may be asked to analyze your specific work environment, considering management styles, stakeholders, and processes.

The synthesis of your personal and professional life with your educational pursuits requires some advance planning on your part. First, you need to identify what bridges you need to build at your office to accommodate any assignments. It might be advisable to let your boss and other co-workers know about your continuing education efforts and get advanced permission to occasionally do special projects for the office.

Traditional "one right answer for all students" types of assessments have been done through worksheets, reports, and tests completed during a face-to-face class session. This type of knowledge testing has proven difficult to monitor in an online environment. Therefore, as much as possible, online education programs have been working to obtain student results through products that are meaningful and meet practical application standards. Instead of a final exam, you may be asked to produce a final project that you were able to apply to your work life. (If you are not working the instructor would provide a work scenario for you.) A part of your final paper would describe how you used it at work and how effective it was. In this way, no two papers are alike and it is more difficult for students to "cheat" to find the right answer.

The Chinese character representing the word "learning" combines a symbol that means "to accumulate knowledge," with a symbol meaning "to practice constantly." Together these suggest that learning could be the "mastery of the way of self-improvement." Using a reflective learning technique is an important key to success as an online student.

Research suggests that individuals and teams learn in a cyclical fashion consisting of four phases: reflecting, connecting, deciding, and doing. (Veterans of the quality movement will also recognize the "plan-do-study-act" cycle, popularized by Deming.) Students need to tap into this cycle to create not only time to think and notice feelings, but time for questioning assumptions and brainstorming solutions. The key to reflective learning is to become a powerful observer of your own thinking, feeling, and acting.

Reflective learning is a "process skill" that invites you to direct your attention in a different way. One way to observe your learning process is to ask yourself questions around for key areas:

1 **Data:** Reflect on actions. What happened? What did you do? What caught your attention? What did others do?
2 **Associations and emotions:** What did you feel? What worked? What energized you? What were the low points? What frustrated you?
3 **Interpretations:** What new knowledge emerged? What has become most significant to you? What are the implications of that new knowledge? How does this apply to your success?
4 **Decisions:** How will you be different? What will you do differently as a result?

You might actually write down your associations and feelings by using two columns labeled "What I liked" and "What I didn't like." After celebrating what is going well under the "liked" column, use the "didn't like" column to decide what you will do to enhance your learning process in future classes. An example of these types of associations, along with the third column, is given in Table 5.1.

By using a similar chart, you may discern a pattern of behavior you have used to learn but of which you were unaware. Your pattern of learning also reflects your ability, or inability, to take action and improve the process. In Table 5.1 the "what I will do" column reflects both behavior and thinking, giving keys to changing the learning pattern to be more effective.

To understand and improve how you learn, you must become explicitly aware of what processes you use to assimilate, examine, and incorporate new knowledge into your daily life. Reflective practice is a

Table 5.1 Associations and feelings

What I liked	*What I didn't like*	*What I will do*
Working in chat to discuss concepts with my classmates.	If too many people were in chat, I couldn't type quickly enough to get a word in edgewise.	Work on a typing tutorial to improve my speed. Find a quick word to let people know I need to slow down – like "Wait!"
Taking time to reflect on a question then posting it to the discussion board.	Sometimes it's hard to follow the thread of conversation on the discussion board.	Suggest to the instructor to provide some type of category organization to the discussion board to make it easier to follow.
Seeing a picture which describes the process I am studying.	Only reading about processes.	Make pictures of processes for myself as I read, or ask the instructor to depict the process in a picture for me.
When I could see how the subject directly applied to my work environment.	When it seemed that the subject didn't apply to anything in my life.	Look for applications to my life and when I can't find them, ask a classmate or the instructor for real-life examples.
The ability to research things on the Internet.	How long it takes to get things through my campus library.	Talk to the campus library and see how I can speed things up. Look into my local library and any inter-library loan programs they may have.

technique to help you think about *how* you think. It is the practice of observing yourself learning. In one loop you are doing the learning and in the second loop you are observing yourself learning.

One way to practice reflective thinking is to keep a journal while you are learning. Choose a time schedule for contemplating your learning process on a regular basis – daily, weekly, bi-weekly. For example, each time you are at the computer write down quick notes about how you are learning a new concept. Include what you feel about this new knowledge. At the end of each week, reflect on your learning activities and describe what techniques or patterns of behavior you might be using to learn. Were you guessing? Asking for help? Using trial and error? If you didn't ask for help, why not? Were you embarrassed? Lost? Frustrated? Angry? Excited? Did you feel good?

Did you gain energy or were you worn out? Did you keep bashing your head against a brick wall? Were you flexible or rigid? Did you learn better with others or by yourself?

If you don't have clearly formed ideas, put down impressions and feelings. After your first online course, you will be able to look back over your notes and certain patterns will begin to emerge. These are your *actual* learning patterns. At the end of that first course, you should be able to accurately identify your behavior when faced with learning challenges. Please note there are no *correct* patterns, just your own patterns. Understanding your own patterns gives you the power to change them or improve them if you desire.

Keeping a journal is difficult. As you get wrapped up in your studies, you will forget to observe yourself. If you miss a session, give yourself permission to skip it and write what is fresh. Remember, you are seeking an overall pattern. Just gently remind yourself to observe and continue learning. Stay balanced by focusing equally on both loops. Sometimes you will resist this reflective process, and that resistance is also important to note in your journal. It is vital to acknowledge how you feel about the learning. If you write in your journal, "This is stupid" or "I'll fake this later" you have expressed important fundamental qualities of your learning pattern. Acknowledge it. It is neither bad or good, it is simply how you learn right now.

Reflective learning is a process that should be used anytime you are acquiring new knowledge. As you reflect, you change. As you change, new reflections become evident. The end product is your ability to learn effectively. With each class you will come to some conclusions about what, if anything, you might want to alter in your learning approach. As you continue through your courses, monitor your actual behavior by thinking reflectively about your particular style. Keep questioning yourself about your underlying assumptions in regards to how and what you should be doing to learn something new. When you know how you learn best, you will be able to let your instructors and work supervisors know; perhaps they will agree to allow you to identify ways to integrate your tasks with your personal style.

Constructing knowledge

Think about learning as a collaborative experience where understandings are developed. Constructing knowledge is not the one-way transmission of information from the instructor to the learner. It is not the "empty vessel" theory of learning, where the learner's brain is perceived to be an empty container, ready to be filled. Constructing knowledge involves the opportunity to critically analyze information, converse with others about its meaning, reflect upon how the information fits within your personal belief and value structures, and arrive at a meaningful understanding of that information. In this process, information becomes transformed into knowledge.

Constructing knowledge involves active learning through participation and dialogue. It shifts away from a prescriptive to an engaging approach to learning. This method is particularly important, and lends itself well, to the online learning environment because learning online supports dialogue and the collaborative development of understandings.

In this environment, you can work together with other learners to solve problems, argue about interpretations, and negotiate meaning. While conferencing, you are electronically engaged in discussion and interaction with peers and experts in a process of social negotiation. Knowledge construction occurs when you explore issues, take positions, discuss positions in an argumentative format, and reflect and evaluate your position. As a result of contact with new or different perspectives, these activities may contribute to higher level learning.

Think about how rich the discussion in your course can be in the online environment if everyone is involved in shaping the experience. Everyone has something to offer. Therefore, it is of utmost importance that you participate fully in the discussions and interactions with your online class. Think of this environment as the equivalent of sitting with your classmates on the lawn or in the student center and bandying about the concepts covered in class. Try to make your online discussions just as free, just as informal. Don't worry about your writing being perfect in discussions. Leave that for your formal papers. Take the opportunity to get out ideas, argue points, and ultimately construct your own knowledge of the subject.

Applying learning outcomes to your daily life

Graduates of both traditional classes and online education programs will face an increasingly complex society in their personal, social, and professional life. To be successful in the future, you need to develop a high level of competency in multi-faceted reasoning strategies, effective communication skills, interpersonal skills, and lifelong learning strategies. These key strategies have rarely been a systematic component of the curriculum design in college education in the past and their development has been mainly left to chance. However, the trend in both traditional and online education is to explicitly teach and assess these more complex learning outcomes instead of testing memorization capabilities.

Online education programs lend themselves to these goals. It is apparent that giving students the usual multiple choice or true/false tests is ineffective over the Web and requires an intricate setup of test proctoring wherever the student is located. Therefore, online education programs tend to be more performance-based in their assessment of student knowledge. This means that instead of "regurgitating" the material you have studied, you will be required to perform the skills identified as learning outcomes. For example, in a written communications class you would be required to write a "real-world" business proposal in the context of your own work life, rather than simply discuss what should go into a proposal or identify the parts of a business proposal on a test.

This student-centered method allows you, the student, to tap into the advice, experience and support of the instructor and your classmates. In the process, you are also learning how to advance your ability to learn from others. It's not about getting a grade – it's about attempting a task and getting immediate, knowledgeable feedback, then having the opportunity to *use* that feedback to experiment and improve until you have a usable product – your improved ability to learn.

A performance task is an opportunity for you to demonstrate your ability to integrate and fluently use knowledge and skills and good judgment in a meaningful activity. In the online learning environment, many programs relate these performance tasks directly to your own professional environment or provide you with actual case studies of professional environments to use as your background. The following characteristics can be recognized in a performance task:

- It requires you to use knowledge and skills in the context of real life situations or issues.
- It reveals how you go about dealing with a given situation, not only the end result.
- It integrates the demonstration of multiple learning outcomes.
- It requires the use of complex reasoning strategies.
- It focuses on multiple dimensions of your learning.
- It requires you to select a form of representation to display what has been learned.

This performance-based orientation affords you the opportunity to immediately apply your learning to your professional life. Frequently students are encouraged to include real work projects as a part of applying their studies. This allows them to accomplish both class and work goals at the same time.

Psychological, individual, and group dynamics

Digitizing people, relationships, and groups has stretched the boundaries of how humans interact. In different online environments you may experience variations of the psychological features discussed here. Just as in the face-to-face world, each group with which you interact has its own distinct psychological quality – an environment which determines how people experience themselves and others. How people behave online will always be a complex interaction between the dynamics of cyberspace and the individual characteristics of the person.

Individual cyberspace psychology

Who are you in cyberspace? Do you act the same in person as you do online? One of the interesting things about the Internet is the opportunity it offers to present yourself in a variety of different ways. In the non-classroom environment, you can alter your persona just slightly or indulge in wild experiments with your identity by changing your age, history, personality, physical appearance, even your gender. The username you choose, the details you do or don't indicate about yourself, the information presented on your personal Web page, the persona you assume in an online community – all are important aspects of how you manage your identity in cyberspace. Identity is a very complex aspect of human nature.

In the online course these chameleon-like qualities are restricted. In most classes you are required to be truthful about your name, your personal history, your goals, and your reason for being in the class. You are also required to do your own work, identify yourself when communicating online, and follow the rules of online etiquette. However, beyond these basic identity characteristics you are still free to choose how you wish others to perceive you in this environment.

For example, if you are a normally shy person in class – perhaps because you feel uncomfortable speaking in front of others – you may discover that you are more assertive online. Many students find that without having to worry about their physical appearance they are freed to express themselves more completely. Another common personality change online regards the perception of race or age. Depending on your circumstances, you may feel that people have preconceived ideas about you before you speak because you are of a different race or age than the majority in the group. Again, these characteristics are not evident online (unless you tell them) and thus some students feel freed of those prejudices.

In each class, you decide how much you wish to reveal about yourself. For some people this is confusing, particularly as you try to determine how to react to others. Yet others also use the online environment to fully express who they are and take advantage of being the student they always wanted to be. Suler (2002) identified several specific characteristics of cyberspace psychology that are discussed in the next few pages.

Reduced sensations

Can you see a person in cyberspace – his or her facial expressions and body language? Can you hear voice inflections? Whether an environment in cyberspace involves visual and/or auditory communication will greatly affect how people behave and the relationships that develop among people. Though the promise of audio and video conferencing will give us some of these cues in the future, most online communication today is still text-based and, thus, seeing and hearing is very limited. For the most part people communicate through typed language. Even when audio-video conferencing becomes efficient and easy to use, people will never be able to physically interact with each other – no handshakes, pats on the back, or hugs of encouragement. The limited sensory experiences of cyberspace has some significant disadvantages, as well as some unique advantages (see Table 5.2).

Identity flexiblity

The lack of face-to-face cues has a curious impact on how people present their identity in cyberspace. Communicating only with typed text, you have the option of being yourself, expressing only parts of your identity, assuming imaginative identities, or remaining completely anonymous – in some cases, being almost invisible, as with the "lurker" (someone who is able to observe all communications but does not participate). Anonymity has an uninhibiting effect that works two ways. Sometimes

Table 5.2 Advantages and disadvantages of cyberspace communication techniques

Advantages	*Disadvantages*
1 When the interaction is asynchronous, it doesn't occur in "real time" so you can respond to your classmates whenever you wish (within the due date time-frame) and at whatever pace you wish. This gives you time to think about what you want to say and to compose your reply exactly the way you want.	1 If you are a person who works out your thought processes by talking things out with someone, you may find this time lag difficult to handle. People who learn by asking a lot of questions and build knowledge by checking it against other opinions may be frustrated.
2 Chat and instant messaging systems, which also involve typed text, are much more synchronous than email and message boards. However, they too often involve a slightly but meaningfully longer delay than face-to-face interactions.	2 Though instant-messaging meets the needs of a "talk-it-through" personality, it also requires you to be a decent typist and someone who feels comfortable writing down thoughts.
3 The written dialogues of online learning may involve different mental mechanisms than in-person talk. It may reflect a style that enables some people to be more expressive, subtle, organized, or creative in how they communicate. Some people feel that they better express themselves in the written word.	3 Some people feel they don't express themselves well in writing. In fact, their expression relies very heavily on emotion transmitted through their body language or voice tone. These same people would suggest that they cannot ever express their whole meaning in written words alone.
4 Online communication tools enable you to save the typed text. You can preserve everything that has been said and then, at your leisure, review it. This kind of reevaluation of communication is impossible in a face-to-face environment, where you almost always have to rely on the vagaries of memory.	4 When reading a typed message, there is a strong tendency to project – consciously or not – your own expectations, wishes, anxieties, and fears into what the person wrote. This may lead to further conflict and, because it is written, sometimes builds a feeling of resentment that lasts longer.

people use it to act out some unpleasant need or emotion, often by verbally abusing other people. Or it allows them to be honest and open about some personal issue that they could not discuss in a face-to-face encounter.

As discussed previously, in the online classroom you normally don't pretend to be someone other than your true identity. However, there may be instances – such as in a visual chat where your avatar choices are limited, or in a role-play simulation where you assume an imaginary persona – where your identity is purposely obscured. If your school has a multimedia chat community, you have no choice but to wear an imaginative looking avatar to represent yourself. Many other environments fall somewhere in between reality and fantasy.

The tricky issue with the real versus fantasy self is this: what is one's *true* identity? Most people assume it must be the self that is presented to others and consciously experienced in their day-to-day living. But is that the true self? Many people walk around in their face-to-face lives wearing "masks" that are quite different from how they think and feel internally. It is likely that the "face" you present to your family is different from the one you present at work, and that is also different from your school persona. Once online, people sometimes begin discovering things about their personality that they never realized before. Their daydreams and fantasies often reveal hidden aspects of what they need or wish to be. Online this may bring about surprising results – even from people you thought you knew. If people drop the usual face-to-face persona and bring to life online those hidden identities, might not that be in some ways *more* true or "real"?

MEDIA AND IDENTITY

We express our identity in the clothes we wear, in our body language, through the careers and hobbies we pursue. We can think of these things as the media through which we communicate who we are. Similarly, in cyberspace, people choose a specific communication channel to express themselves. There are a variety of possibilities and combinations of possibilities, each choice giving rise to specific attributes of identity. People who rely on text communication prefer the semantics of language and perhaps also the linear, composed, rational, analytic dimensions of self that surface via written discourse. They may be the "verbalizers" who have been described in the cognitive psychology literature, as opposed to "visualizers" who may enjoy the more symbolic, imagistic, and holistic reasoning that is expressed via the creation of avatars and Web graphics. Some people prefer synchronous communication, like chat, which reflects the spontaneous, freeform, witty, and temporally "present" self. Others are drawn to the more thoughtful, reflective, and measured style of asynchronous communication, as in discussion boards and email. There are personalities that want to show but not receive too much by using Web cams or creating Web pages; or those who want to receive but not show too much by lurking or Web browsing; and still others who want to dive into highly interactive social environments where both showing and receiving thrive.

The media chosen can intimately interlock with the extent to which a person presents a real or imaginary self.

Equalized status

In most cases, everyone on the Internet has an equal voice. Everyone – regardless of status, wealth, race, gender, etc. – starts on a level playing field. Some people call this the "net democracy." Although your status in the outside world ultimately will have some impact on your life in cyberspace, there is some truth to this net democracy ideal. What determines your influence on others is your skill in communicating (including writing skills), your persistence, the quality of your ideas, and sometimes your technical know-how.

Temporal flexibility

In previous sections of this book, there has been a discussion of "time stretching." During chat you have from several seconds to a minute or more to reply to the other person – a significantly longer delay than in face-to-face meetings. In email, you have hours, days, or even weeks to respond. Cyberspace creates a unique dimension where ongoing, interactive time stretches out. This provides a convenient zone for reflection.

In other ways, cyberspace time is condensed. If you are a member of an online community for several months, you may be considered an "old-timer." Internet environments change rapidly because it is a lot easier to write and rewrite software infrastructure than it is to build with bricks, wood, and iron. Because it is easy to move around in cyberspace, the membership of online groups also changes rapidly. Your subjective sense of time is intimately linked to the rate of change in the world in which you live. With the context of sights, sounds, and people changing around you so quickly in cyberspace, the experience of time seems to accelerate.

Social multiplicity

With relative ease you can contact individuals from all walks of life and communicate with hundreds, perhaps thousands, of people. When "multitasking" you can juggle many relationships in a short period of time – or even *at* the same time, as in chat or instant messaging, without the other people necessarily being aware of your juggling act. By posting a message on a discussion board read by countless numbers of users, you can draw to yourself others who match even your most esoteric interests. Using a Web search engine, you can scan through millions of pages in order to zoom your attention onto particular people and groups. The Internet will get more powerful as tools for searching, filtering, and contacting specific people and groups become more effective. The ability to sift through so many online possibilities for developing relationships amplifies an interesting interpersonal phenomenon well-known to psychologists. A user will act on unconscious motivations – as well as conscious preferences and choices – in selecting friends, specific classmates to be in a study group, or identifying perceived "enemies." This process, called transference, guides you toward specific types of people who address your underlying emotions and needs. Pressed by hidden expectations, wishes and fears, this unconscious filtering mechanism will help you to choose the best online classmates who will meet your needs, become good study partners, and challenge you intellectually.

Recordability

Most online activities, including email correspondence and chat sessions, can be recorded and saved to a computer file. Unlike real world interactions, the user in cyberspace can keep a permanent record of what was said, to whom, and when. These records may come in very handy to the user. You can reexperience and reevaluate any portion of the relationship you wish. You can use quoted text as feedback to your study partner. It's fascinating to see how different your emotional reactions to the same exact record can be when you reread it at different times. Depending on your state of mind, you may invest the recorded words with all sorts of meanings and intentions.

Media disruption

It is natural to expect the Internet to cooperate with you whenever you desire. After all, most of the time you turn on your computer and it responds immediately. Much of the time, you send an email and you get a response back much more quickly than if you sent a letter by post. Nevertheless, no matter how complex and sophisticated electronic tools become, there will always be moments when software and hardware don't work properly, when noise intrudes into the communication, and connections break. There will be moments when the telecommunication system gives you nothing, not even an error message. The frustration and anger you may experience in reaction to these failures is a reflection on the natural dependency any online user now has on them.

When the system fails, that lack of response also opens the door for many students to project all sorts of worries and anxieties onto the machine that gives no reply. It is at this time that some students are prone to suddenly drop their classes. Sometimes it is out of a sense that they can never depend on the connection again. Other times it is out of worry that others in the class will think poorly of their skills or ability to participate effectively. It is important to remember that the best way to handle this situation is to turn off your computer and walk away for a while (maybe even a couple of hours). Then return and try again. Most disruptions are relatively short in duration – lasting only a couple of hours. In some countries, however, the disruptions can last up to a day or a week. If this is a problem for you, the best thing to do is to let your instructor know of your access situation. Agree to a plan, in advance, as to how you will contact him or her regarding long outages or how you will make up any time that is lost in your studies.

Group dynamics

The same types of group dynamics that occur in face-to-face environments also occur in the online environment – issues concerning leadership, communication patterns, group boundaries, cohesion, alliances and sub-groupings.

However, given the special psychological features of cyberspace, online groups can also be quite different from in-person groups. Text-only communications, equalization of status, and the opportunity for altering or hiding one's identity are all unique dilemmas tossed into the online group process. The stretching of temporal boundaries also makes asynchronous groups unique not only as compared to in-person groups, but in relation to online chat sessions as well.

Anyone who has participated often in a work group in business, education, or a volunteer organization has experienced the hassles of scheduling meetings, as well as the sometimes frustrating complexities of how small groups function. Extending the group into cyberspace can eliminate the discontinuity due to scheduling problems. In groups where people need to speak to each other more often or maintain contact during vacation, holiday, or summer breaks, an email list or discussion board can be the perfect solution. The asynchronous communication of these tools allows members to participate in the ongoing virtual meeting at their own convenience and at their own pace. Some of the unique features of asynchronous, typed-text communication also may alter the interpersonal dynamics of the group, which offers the opportunity to better understand and improve how the group functions.

Some practical tips for group work online

It is likely you will be asked to work in small groups with any online class you take. This group may be as small as you and one other person, or as large as seven or eight members. No matter the group size, these tips can be useful in helping you to work together effectively and meet deadlines in a timely manner.

ASYNCHRONOUS GROUPS

1. It's a good idea to have a facilitator or leader for the group. If the group is using email to communicate, it is the leader's responsibility to gather all the members' email addresses, to create a distribution list, and to make sure all members have a copy.
2. Whenever any member replies to an email or a discussion board posting, he or she should quote enough of the previous communication to set the context for the reply. This will help build group cohesion and keep everyone understanding the nature of each communication.
3. The first order of business should be to set some ground rules about how work will be distributed, what are the interim due dates, and how the overall paper or project will be evaluated and changed by the group prior to submittal.
4. If there are members who are not participating fully in the discussions or planning, it is best to first talk to them privately (private email or call them on the phone if they live in your local calling area). Politely ask if everything is OK and remind them of their agreement to participate. See how to handle conflict detailed later in this chapter.
5. If a member seems to be "bossy" or not treating you or another member fairly, follow the same structure. First talk to him or her privately.

6 Stick to your timeline and insist that others do so as well. If your group is having continuous unresolved problems and it is affecting your ability to meet your homework deadlines, bring it to the attention of your instructor.

SYNCHRONOUS GROUPS

Synchronous groups follow all of the same tips above. However, because of the synchronous nature there are some of additional requirements for the group leader. Leading online groups is a skill that will, hopefully, be demonstrated by your instructor. If not, the group and group leader may want to ask for assistance.

1 When you meet with your group for the first time, you should send a short message saying "Hello" and asking for a roll call. In that roll call, ask everyone to reply and indicate that they have received the message and can participate in the synchronous discussion. Don't start any formal discussions until you verify that everyone can send and is receiving the text.
2 Once it is clear everyone is on board, send an introductory message containing some suggestions about how to use the tool. Don't assume that everyone understands the technical and social aspects of participating in a chat or instant-messaging forum. Some experienced online users may see the suggestions as old hat, but it's a good idea to make sure everyone is starting on the same page. Also clarify what will happen if someone is suddenly disconnected. Will the group wait for him or her to return? When that person reconnects, will you review what happened? Or will you simply continue with your work and ask him or her to read the transcript later?
3 During the session, if someone is not participating, directly ask him or her if everything is OK. You might type something like, "Maggie, I notice you haven't contributed something for a while. Can you still see these messages? Is everything OK with your computer?" This helps to put Maggie on notice that you are paying attention to each contribution and it helps you to know if there is a technical problem she might be having.
4 At the close of the session, the leader should review what was agreed among the members and what the next steps will be. Set a time for meeting again, and thank everyone for participating.

As a rule of thumb, whether participating synchronously or asynchronously, it is a good idea to always be encouraging of your classmates. Remember, many of them worry about their technology, the quality of their postings or statements, and contributing successfully to the group project. Usually, if you confirm their efforts they will in turn be supportive of you.

Group boundary differences and issues

PACING

Because email involves asynchronous communication, people can speak to the group whenever they want and as frequently as they want. Avid email users may have more input into the discussion than casual or inexperienced users, possibly altering in a dramatic way the usual in-person pattern of participation. Set realistic expectations for email (e.g. once a day).

WRITING, NOT TALKING

Typed text usually forces people to be more concise and to-the-point, resulting in a filtering out of extraneous conversation that typically pads a face-to-face meeting. The discussion may feel more efficient to some people, or blunt to others. Some members may be frustrated by the tedium of having to type everything they want to say, feeling a face-to-face dialogue is easier and more thorough. Because online communication involves writing and not speaking, those with superior writing skills will have a communicative advantage. They may not be the same people who have the verbal advantage in an in-person meeting. Those who are ignored, interrupted, or talked-over during a face-to-face meeting may have a stronger voice in cyberspace. Those who dominate an in-person meeting may lose some of their influence online. It is important for each member to help ensure that others have equal opportunity for expression and that those who struggle with written communication are not ridiculed, but helped and supported in their efforts.

UNINHIBITION

The inability to hear or use voice tone and inflection results in a "masking" effect that may make people more willing to express thoughts and feelings that they otherwise would keep to themselves during an in-person meeting. As a result, new ideas may pop up. Surprising opinions are expressed. Conflicts that were previously warded off now rise to the surface. In an ideal situation, this uninhibiting effect can jostle a group into new and productive lines of discussion. In unfortunate circumstances, the uncovering of hidden problems may destabilize the group, reducing its ability to communicate and work effectively. If possible, an in-person meeting is one way to remedy that situation. If that is not possible, you may need to bring the instructor into the group to help work through the issues.

PERMANENT RECORD

Any member can easily save all of the group messages to an archive. This permanent record is handy for reviewing who said what and when, how decisions were made, and for attaining a bird' s eye view of the course of a discussion. Without visual and verbal cues, it's sometimes easy to misread the meaning or emotion within someone's message – particularly if you happen to be having a bad day. Going back to read a message at a later date can help you see it in a fresh light, with a new mind set and a bit more objectivity.

On the other hand, using those same messages to aggressively prove a point is disruptive. Remember, no one writes perfectly online. Give your classmates the benefit of the doubt. Instead of accusingly sending back a copy of their typed response with an angry written comment, consider quoting their response and then saying something like, "I'm confused. When I read your response quoted here I thought you meant … now it seems you have changed your mind. Did I misunderstand the first time?" This gives people an opportunity to clarify their true meaning and doesn't immediately put them on the defensive or escalate bad feelings.

Resistance to being online

Because group work is difficult, and online group work is very different from being in-person, some people may show resistance to participating – even if it is required by the instructor. Even if someone in your group is uncooperative, you need to find ways to work through the resistance and still get the required projects completed. Understanding why some people have problems with online learning is an important first step to this process.

A person's resistance may manifest itself in several ways: infrequent messages sent to the group, brief or unsubstantial discussions, frequent pleas for in-person meetings, habitual private (backchannel) email or private in-person discussions (rather than bringing issues to the group), critical comments about using online communication, and other assorted direct and indirect expressions of hostility. In rare circumstances some people may staunchly refuse to participate, which can create considerable uneasiness and distrust in the group. There are a variety of possible reasons for resistance:

- *Being unfamiliar or uncomfortable with using computers, email, or discussion boards* Some people may need time and experience to adapt; a little bit of training could be helpful. A requirement to be posting email or discussions constantly may be frightening for new users. Limiting the number of postings may be helpful in easing their fear.
- *A fear of displaying one's writing abilities* It's very helpful to establish a norm where all writing styles are accepted – including being casual and making errors in spelling and grammar. Strict standards about "correct" writing will not be productive.
- *A fear of "going public"* People may worry that someone might save their messages for later use as "ammunition" against them. This anxiety may coincide with the worry that people outside the group may have access to the list or may be given email by a group member. Such concerns may be a low-level symptom of preexisting distrust within the group. From the beginning, emphasizing the importance of confidentiality can help alleviate some of these worries.
- *Angry withdrawal, indifference* These barriers are most likely a symptom of preexisting interpersonal dynamics within the group. The uninhibiting effect of online communication may help people discuss and resolve these issues, but don't count on it.

Integrating online with offline

Because many students will be participating in online classes as only part of their class experience, it is possible they will do some assignments as a group online and then be expected to come back to the classroom and do something with that same group in-person. Because online discussions are a very different style of communicating from being in-person, the two channels may become disconnected from each other. What is said in one domain may not be said in the other. Sometimes the discussions occurring in email or on a discussion board may even evolve into a kind of "subconscious" voicing of issues that are actively avoided in-person.

It is possible to work through these issues through electronic communication, allowing the beneficial effects to seep into the face-to-face meetings without openly discussing them in those meetings. However, the best approach is to head off the potential problem before it becomes too deeply embedded. Make an attempt to discuss important issues in both domains and, if possible, try to understand the psychological barriers that might prevent people from doing that. Understanding those barriers will lead to valuable insights into the interpersonal dynamics of the group.

Under ideal conditions, in-person and online discussions will complement and enrich each other. The group will come to recognize the pros and cons of each realm. It will learn to maximize the advantages and minimize the disadvantages of each, effectively integrating the two. When the group moves fluidly from one realm to the other, when both realms give expression to all important group functions – brainstorming, decision-making, problem-solving, socializing, conflict resolution – then the group has fully succeeded in extending itself into cyberspace.

Online conflicts and constructive criticism

Sometimes conflict can get blown out of proportion online. What may begin as a small difference of opinion, or misunderstanding, becomes a major issue very quickly. Conflict can be difficult at the best of times, but something about online communication seems to ignite "flaming" and make conflicts more difficult to resolve.

There are a number of reasons why conflict may be heightened online. One is the absence of visual and auditory cues. When you are in a face-to-face environment, you see facial expressions, body language, and hear tone of voice. Someone can say the exact same thing in a number of different ways, and that usually effects how you respond. For example, someone could shout, and shake his or her finger at you, or speak gently and with kindness. Another person could stand up and tower over you, or sit down beside you. How you feel, interpret, and respond to someone's message often depends on how he or she speaks to you, even when it's a difficult message to hear.

Online, all you have are the words on a computer screen, and *how you hear those words in your head*. While people who know each other have a better chance of accurately understanding each others' meaning and intentions, even they can have arguments online that they would not have in-person. While many people are convinced that how they read an email is the only way it *can* be read, the truth is, how you read a text, or view a work of art, often says more about yourself than it does about the message or the messenger.

All of your communications, online and in real-time, are filled with projections. You perceive the world through your expectations, needs, desires, fantasies, and feelings, and you project those onto other people. For example, if you expect people to be critical of you, you will perceive other people's communication as being critical – it *sounds* critical even though it may not be. You do the same thing online; in fact you are more likely to project when you are online precisely because you don't have the visual or auditory cues to guide you in the interpretations. How you "hear" an email or discussion posting is how you hear it in your own head, which may or may not reflect the tone or attitude of the sender.

You usually can't know from an email or post alone whether someone is shouting, using a criticizing tone, or speaking kindly. Unless the tone is *clearly and carefully* communicated by the messenger, or you are very skilled at understanding text and human communication, you most likely hear the voice you hear, or create in your head and react to that. This is one of the reasons why controversy and potential conflicts are best dealt with by using great care and *explicit expressions of tone, meaning, and intent.*

Projections come from your life experiences – how you have been treated, how important figures in your life have behaved, how you felt growing up, how you responded and coped, etc. Everyone projects or transfers feelings and views of important figures into their daily lives and onto other people.

To take a look at your own projections or transference with people online, think back to the last time you felt angry at someone online. What was it about the email that made you so angry? What did you believe that he or she was doing to you or someone else? How did you react internally and externally? Was your reaction to this person (whether spoken or not) influenced by someone or something from your past? While it certainly happens that people are treated with disrespect and anger online, if there are any parallels between this experience and any of your past experiences, it's likely that how you felt and responded was colored by your past. When your past is involved, particularly when you are unaware of it, you invariably project and transfer old feelings onto the present situation.

Tips for resolving online conflict

The following are tips for handling conflict online with respect, sensitivity, and care:

1 *Don't respond right away* You may want to write a response immediately, to get it off your chest, but don't hit send! Wait 24 hours. Sleep on it and then reread and rewrite your response the next day.

2 *Read the post again later* Sometimes, your first reaction to a post is influenced by how you're feeling at the time. Reading it later – and sometimes a few times – can bring a new perspective. You might even experiment by reading it with different tones (matter-of-fact, gentle, non-critical) to see if it could have been written with a different frame of mind than the one you initially heard.

3 *Discuss the situation with people you trust and who know you* Ask them what they think about the post and the response you plan to send. Having input from others who are more objective can help you step back from the situation and look at it differently.

4 *Choose whether or not you want to respond* You do have a choice, and you don't have to respond. You may be too upset to respond in the way you would like, or it may not be worthy of a response. If the post is accusatory or inflammatory and the style tends to be aggressive or bullying, the best strategy is to ignore it.

5 *Assume that people mean well, unless they have a history or pattern of aggression* Everyone has bad days, reacts insensitively, and writes an email without thinking it through completely. It doesn't mean that they don't have good intentions. On the other hand, some people pick fights no matter how kind and patient you are with them. They distort what you say, quote you out of context, and make all sorts of accusations to vilify and antagonize you. Don't take the "bait" by engaging in a struggle with them – they'll never stop.

6 *Clarify what was meant* Online, it is easier to misinterpret what is heard and read, particularly when you already feel hurt or upset. It's a good idea to check if you understood the email or post correctly. For example, you could ask, "When you said … did you mean … or, what did you mean by …?" Or, "when you said … I heard … is that what you meant?" It is possible that what you think was said is not even close to what was meant. Give each person the benefit of the doubt and the chance to be clear about what he or she meant.

7 *Think about what you want to accomplish by your communication* Are you trying to connect with this person? Are you trying to understand him or her and be understood? What is the message you hope to convey? What is the tone you want to communicate? Consider how you can convey that.

8 *Verbalize what you want to accomplish* Here are some examples, "I want to understand what you're saying." "I feel hurt by what you said. I want to talk about it in a way that we both feel heard and understood." "I want to find a way to work this out. I know we don't agree about everything and that's okay. I'd like to talk with you about how I felt reading your post." "I hope we can talk this through because I really like you. I don't want to be argumentative or blaming."

Tip Use "I" statements when sharing your feelings or thoughts. For example, "I feel ..." versus "You made me feel ..." Choose your words carefully and thoughtfully, particularly when you're upset.

9 *Place yourself in the other person's shoes* To avoid unnecessary conflict or a lot of hurt feelings, it helps to take into account to whom you're writing. One person might be able to hear you say it exactly how you think it, and another person would be threatened by that style of communication. Think about the other person when writing your email or post. Do your best to communicate in a way that is respectful, sensitive, and clear. People often feel that they should be allowed to express their anger when someone hurts them and not have to control these feelings. Of course you can respond any way you want, especially online, but if you want to communicate with this person and have it accurately heard and understood, it helps to think about how he or she will hear it.

10 *Use emoticons to express your tone* In online communication, visual and auditory cues are replaced by emoticons, for example, smiles, winks, and laughter. It helps to use emoticons to convey your tone. Having a conflict or misunderstanding doesn't mean you don't like the person any more, but people often forget that reality, or don't think to say it. It may be most needed during a tense interaction.

11 *Start and end your post with positive, affirming, and validating statements* Say what you agree with, what you understand about how they feel, and any other positive statements at the beginning of your email or discussion posting. This helps set a positive tone. End on a positive note as well.

Handling conflict constructively is hard at the best of times, and it can be even more difficult online. It can take a great deal of effort, care, and thoughtfulness to address differences, tensions, and conflicts online. Paradoxically, some of the same things that contribute to heightened conflict online can contribute to peaceful resolutions as well. The Internet is an ideal place to practice communication and conflict resolution skills. It is your choice whether to take advantage of the uninhibiting status of electronic communication and say what ever *negative* thing you want, or to feel free to try new, and more positive communication styles and to take all the time you need to do that. As with any new technology, the Internet can be used to enhance your personal growth and relationships, or to alienate you from others. It is your choice.

Chapter 6

Adapting your learning style to the online environment

> A little learning is a dangerous thing;
> Drink deep, or taste not the Pierian spring:
> There shallow draughts intoxicate the brain,
> And drinking largely sobers us again.
> (Alexander Pope, 1688–1744, *Essay on Criticism*, part ii, line 15)

Assessing your learning style

To gain a better understanding of yourself as a student, you need to evaluate the way you prefer to learn or process information. Strengths and weaknesses can have a strong impact on your academic success in certain tasks. It is important to identify your preferred learning style so that you can develop a set of strategies to capitalize on strengths and compensate for weaknesses.

Many researchers divide learning style into three broad categories: auditory, visual, and kinesthetic. Auditory learners need to *hear* what is going on. They quickly pick up concepts from lectures. When auditory learners solve a problem, they tend to talk it out. Visual learners need to *see* or make pictures of concepts. In a lecture, they might take notes, draw a diagram of the concepts or make a table of the important points. Kinesthetic learners need to *do* things physically to understand concepts. They may build a model to physically simulate the problem. People may, however, use different styles together or in different situations. No one style is better than any other but it is important to be aware of your preferred style so you can help yourself when information is not presented in that style and you are having difficulties understanding the content.

Many students who perform well in the traditional classroom/lecture environment have highly developed auditory learning. The online environment tends to favor students with a visual learning style. Web-based courses contain more visual instructional tools, requiring more reading and graphic interpretation. Therefore, auditory and kinesthetic learners need to find ways to accommodate this new medium.

The following puzzle is designed to help you analyze your problem-solving style and see how others may differ from you in their approaches. As you work through the problem, try to be aware of how you think while you are solving it, specifically:

1. Which strategies work and which ones don't?
2. What do you do when an approach doesn't work?
3. How do you feel about the problem?

If possible, have someone observe you as you solve the problem. You may be unaware that you are speaking aloud, making motions with your hands, or closing your eyes to "see" the action.

Problem

A man and a woman are standing side by side with their weight on their right feet. They begin by walking so that each steps out on his or her left foot. The woman takes three steps for each two steps of the man. How many steps does the man take before their right feet simultaneously reach the ground?

Write down your work as you solve the problem, then analyze your process using the above questions and any other observations you wish to make.

Once you have your answer and your list of how you went about solving the problem, compare them to the different approaches used below.

Two visual approaches

1. Visualize two walkers including the imagery, sounds, smells, and footprints. As you watch them walking, determine the answer.
2. Draw a diagram of the footsteps and determine the answer.

Two kinesthetic approaches

1. Simulate the walkers by using your fingers on the desk
2. Simulate the walkers by asking a friend to reconstruct the problem with you.

An auditory approach

Talk through the problem with someone else, each of you sharing difficulties and potential solutions, until you have determined the correct solution.

Using multiple approaches

Some problem solvers limit themselves to one approach; others jump around between approaches without spending enough time with each to develop an adequate solution. Problem solving is frequently an unconscious process, which makes it difficult to determine your preferences and patterns. With practice this thinking can be made conscious through identifying strategies used and strategies avoided.

To analyze your personal learning style, it helps to take an inventory which identifies these patterns for you. Many inventories exist both in books and on the Internet. A learning style inventory, based on sensory input, looks at your preferences for an auditory, visual, or kinesthetic style. Before proceeding in this book, go to http://web.pdx.edu/~mmlynch/learningstyle to take a survey of your style. It will take you about one half-hour to complete. When you press "Submit", your responses will be analyzed and the survey will provide some feedback on your preferred learning style.

As you analyze your results, you may wish to make some notes regarding specific strategies you will undertake to ensure success in your online learning program.

Analyzing the learning styles inventory results

There is no right or wrong scores in the inventory. Totals for each category range from 0 to 100, with most categories averaging counts between 30 and 70. If your score in any one category is more than 50 it shows you are adept at using that style. Some people will find that they have a strong preference for one style, with tallies over 75 in a particular category. Others will find they have a balance of scores across two or more categories (e.g. 58 in Visual and 62 in Auditory). This indicates you are equally comfortable in each of those areas.

Remember *You adapt your learning style to the situation in order to be successful. Gaining awareness and knowledge of your style preferences is the first step. The second is identifying strategies that work for you without completely giving up your preferences.*

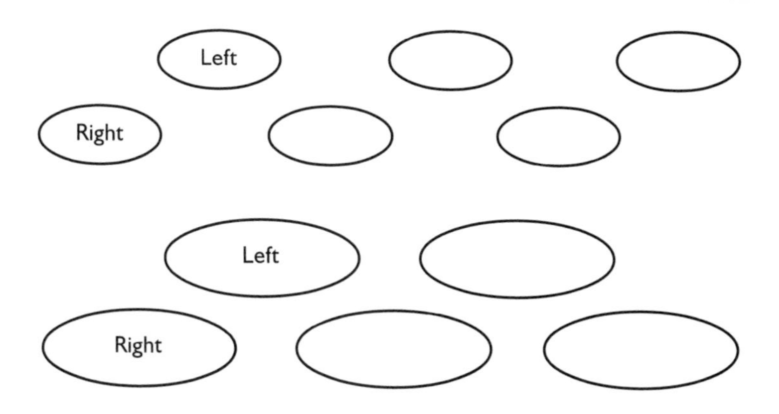

Figure 6.1 Using a visual approach

Research shows that approximately 60 percent of the population has a preference for visual learning. This would lead one to wonder then how all these visual learners were successful in school. The answer is successful adaptation. Through practice and some learned strategies, visual learners were forced to adapt and increase their auditory skills to survive the lecture environment. On the other hand, preferences often lead to career choices. For example, those who chose a profession that involves use of their hands (e.g. mechanic, plumber, electrician, carpenter) are often showing a preference to be a kinesthetic learner.

If you are a visual learner, you will probably enjoy classes in an online environment. To enhance your success online, use charts, maps, notes, and flashcards as you study. Putting your thoughts on paper will also enhance your visual memory. Writing out questions, answers, and discussions, will give you frequent, quick visual reviews. Practice visualizing or picturing words/concepts in your head.

Auditory learners may wish to use tapes. As you read something, say it aloud and tape your reading. Because online learning is very visual, you will need to work hard to bring that medium into your auditory style by talking with others. Any time your online course offers an opportunity for sound, be sure to take advantage of that option. If your preference is very high (a score of 50 or more) you might consider purchasing a voice recognition software package, which will read the words from your screen. Unfortunately, current technology makes the voice sound very mechanical, but can still be a wonderful adaptation for those who are primarily auditory learners.

A kinesthetic learner will have the most difficulty in the online environment. You will need to work to bring visual stimuli into a kinesthetic reality. Trace words as you are saying them or point to them as you read. Writing facts and concepts down several times will help you retain the information. The motion of writing helps translate concepts in your mind. Keep a supply of scratch paper near you and always take notes as you read, listen, or watch presentations. Make study sheets. Most importantly, develop ways to apply your learning to a tactile world. In the problem-solving example above, the kinesthetic learners used their fingers to solve the problem or actually went out and walked with someone. These are the same adjustments you will need to make to ensure success in your online education program.

Multiple intelligences

Conceived by Howard Gardner, Multiple Intelligences are nine different ways to demonstrate intellectual ability. The Multiple Intelligence Learning Styles table (Table 6.1) describes each of these intelligence types in terms of three categories: how you think or solve problems, what you love to do, and what you need to be successful. As you review the table and find where your preferences fit, carefully evaluate the "need" column associated with your intelligence type(s). This may provide some initial clues as to how to improve your studies in the classroom. For example, the linguistically intelligent person needs books, tapes, writing tools, etc. Alternatively, the musically intelligent person needs music playing, singing, concerts. This would suggest that this person would be more successful if they study with music in the background, or study and memorize facts by putting them into a musical jingle.

Look over Table 6.1 and evaluate where you fit best. Once you have identified your preferred style or intelligence type, you can plan your studies better and adapt information presentations to your own style. Online education has the advantage of providing information in a variety of approaches. However, any one part of a course, or an entire course, may be presented in a method that doesn't work best for you. It is up to you, then, to adapt it and make yourself successful in that course.

There are many other ways to measure learning styles – more than can be covered in one chapter. If you have an interest in gaining more knowledge in this area, a useful Web site that describes many models and has links to some online inventories can be found at Indiana State University: http://web.indstate.edu/ctl/styles/ls1.html

Table 6.1 Multiple intelligences learning types descriptors

Learners who are strongly	*Think ...*	*Love ...*	*Need ...*
Linguistic	In words	Reading, writing, telling stories, playing word games, etc.	Books, tapes, writing tools, paper, diaries, dialogue, discussion, debate, stories, etc.
Logical, mathematical	By reasoning	Experimenting, questioning, figuring out logic puzzles, calculating, etc.	Things to explore and think about, science materials, manipulatives, trips to the planetarium and science museum, etc.
Spatial	Images and pictures	Designing, drawing, visualizing, doodling, etc.	Art, videos, movies, slides, imagination games, mazes, puzzles, illustrated books, trips to museums, etc.
Bodily, kinesthetic	Through body sensations	Dancing, running, jumping, building, touching, gesturing, etc.	Role play drama, movement, things to build, sports and physical games, tactile experiences, hands-on learning, etc.
Musical	Via rhythms and melodies	Singing, whistling, humming, tapping feet and hands, listening, etc.	Sing-alongs, trips to concerts, music playing, musical instruments
Interpersonal	By bouncing ideas off other people	Leading, organizing, relating, manipulating, mediating, socializing, etc.	Friends, group games, social gatherings, community events, clubs, mentoring, apprenticeships
Intrapersonal	Deeply inside themselves	Setting goals, meditating, dreaming, being quiet, planning	Secret places, time alone, self-paced projects, choices, etc.
Naturalistic	Notices patterns, picks up on similarities and differences in their surroundings	Collecting, classifying, caring for the environment, animals	To use sensory skills, to create, keep or have collections, scrapbooks, logs, or journals about natural objects
Emotional/intuitive	With feelings, respond intuitively	Motivating others, getting groups to work together, making and implementing decisions	Aesthetically pleasing environments, opportunities to experience awe and wonder

The variety of models used to characterize learning styles can sometimes seem confusing. There are many layers of human learning preferences. Think of exploring these layers as peeling an onion, each layer having a particular purpose but all important to the overall flavor of your personality.

Instructional and environmental models are those that describe the most observable traits. Dunn *et al.* (1982) describe five dimensions that mark various environmental preferences:

1 Environmental preferences regarding sound, light, temperature, and class design
2 Emotional preferences addressing motivation, persistence, responsibility and structure
3 Sociological preferences for private, pair, peer, team, adult or varied learning relationships
4 Psychological preferences related to perception, intake, time, and mobility
5 Psychological preferences based on analytic mode and action.

While the latter category overlaps with subsequent layers in the onion, each of these preferences can be mapped through tests, observations, and productivity studies that illustrate how different approaches to the same subject or task can result in very similar gains.

Social interaction models describe the outer layer of the onion and consider ways in which people in specific social contexts will adopt certain strategies. William Perry's (1970) well-known model showed how college students developed through different intellectual maturation levels as they went through college. Mary Belenky (1986) illustrated how women preferred different strategies from those recognized and rewarded in typical universities. More recently Marcia Baxter Magolda (1992) has described how strategies used by students varies by gender and by maturity and is responsive to the teaching context in which students find themselves.

Information processing models describe the middle layer in the onion and are an effort to understand the processes by which information is obtained, sorted, stored, and used. Probably the most recognized idea about information processing is the right brain/left brain discussion. A more complex approach is Kolb's (1984) approach to experiential learning which has become a much-used model. He maps out four quadrants and shows how they can serve as stages of holistic learning (individual styles are seen as particular strengths in the process). Howard

Gardner's theory of multiple intelligences, presented earlier in this chapter, is another popular model for information processing.

Personality models describe the innermost layer of the onion, the level at which your deepest personality traits shape your orientation toward the world. The popular Myers- Briggs type indicators categorize people as extroverts/introverts, sensing/intuiting, thinking/feeling, and judging/perceiving. This model anchors your preferences in your very make-up.

Adapting your style to the online environment

There are a number of strategies you can use during your learning experience. Some are the same ones you would choose in a traditional classroom. Others may be unique to the online environment. You will not be listening to lectures and taking notes, so you must adapt your style by taking notes as you read, write, and interact online. You must be more self-directed and independent. You must plan how to learn.

This section provides some suggested study strategies, many of which you have probably already used. As you read through them, evaluate which ones work for you given your preferred learning style and which ones need to be expanded or adapted to the online environment you are pursuing.

There are a number of other strategies to consider in independent work: thinking, questioning, reading, and writing. Each of these will have an impact on your success as an online student.

Study strategies

Advanced organization

Preview what you are going to learn. For example, if you want to improve your understanding of general concepts before an interactive chat or meeting with your class for the first time, look through the introduction in advance or read the first few chapters in your textbook.

Direct your attention

Pay attention to studying something, and not doing other things like surfing the Internet. In an online study environment it is easy to get caught up in the links on a topic and to wind up far afield.

Selective attention

Study things you can remember easily, for example because they are useful in your job or have immediate impact on an assignment. If you need to do a presentation for your course, you can study presentations; if you need to write a report at work, you can learn how to write a report. Don't worry about learning the whole course in one sitting.

Self-monitoring

Correct yourself if you make a mistake or ask for help immediately when you find you are not understanding what is going on in a class. Remember, the instructor cannot look at you and see that "glazed" look of incomprehension. You have to communicate via email or chat or posting your question to the class discussion board.

Delayed production

When you first start to learn a new concept or topic, you may need to take it slowly. In the beginning you may feel overwhelmed with written information both online and in your text. Don't try to use all the jargon words immediately or combine all the concepts at once. You may want to just listen at first, or discuss and clarify concepts with a classmate or instructor before completing your first assignment.

Self-evaluation (self-assessment or testing)

Prior to taking a test or participating in a discussion where you are evaluated, test yourself first. Get together with a classmate via chat and go through some of the topics in advance to be sure you have the concepts, and the phrasing you need, clear in your mind. Then you will perform significantly better during the assessment.

Self-reinforcement

Give yourself a present when you have successfully learned something. For example, take a break for 10 minutes and play a computer game. It is important to give yourself breaks and reinforce all the hard work you are doing.

Working alone or with other people

There are reasons for working with other people as well as working alone. In an online environment, you may choose to work with other people through email and chat.

REASONS FOR WORKING WITH OTHER PEOPLE

- You get additional ideas from your peers.
- They may suggest improvements.
- They may be able to identify your mistakes.
- They can encourage you to do better.
- Explaining things to a classmate can broaden your understanding.
- Sharing the work helps you do it more quickly.
- You can share your thoughts and feelings.
- Teamwork skills and experience are important for your career.

REASONS FOR WORKING ALONE

- To set your work apart from that of your classmates.
- Sharing a task might teach you only part of the task, not how to do it all.
- You don't want to be influenced by, or share your ideas with, other people.

Thinking strategies

One of the most useful thinking strategies is to categorize concepts as you read or learn. Without an instructor lecturing and providing groupings for you, it is up to you to do this. You will get part of this classification process from the organization of your textbook or your online learning units. But you may need to sort the concepts in a way that helps you to understand them. Putting things into groups and in order helps you to build a framework for learning. This process also reflects the way your brain organizes information. For example, in an administration class you can group concepts together according to categories like human resources, communication, management styles, and reports. You can also use this same process to solve a problem or design a writing assignment.

If you are a visual learner, you can process conceptual information with a picture. Some people like to draw flow charts or hierarchical groupings, or simply doodle on a page and put the concepts within those pictures. These visual images, often called mind maps or concept maps, are merely drawings of how you are thinking and organizing your thoughts.

An example of a mind map for finding a job is given in Figure 6.2. In this example, the map begins in the middle with the main concept, then adds a second level of primary categories and finally the sublevels to those general categories.

Note that the map does not have to be in a traditional hierarchy like an organization chart. It is simply a way to see how things are related. This may then help you understand not only the concept you are mapping, but also the relationships within that concept. In working with others, it is also a good brainstorming tool, and can help you see others' thinking processes.

Question strategies

The most common reason for a question is simply clarification. Online, ask someone to repeat, paraphrase, elaborate or give examples by typing

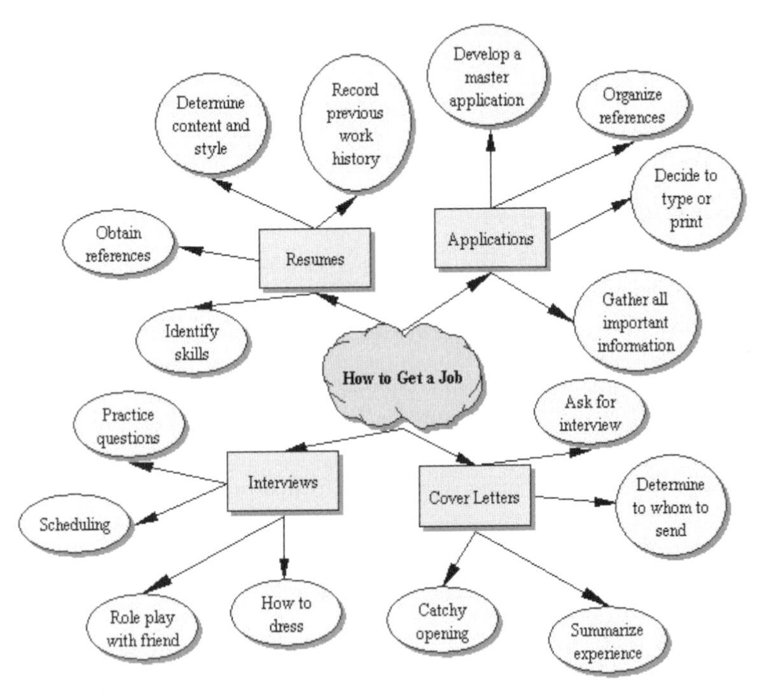

Figure 6.2 **Mind map – find a job.** Example of a mind map or concept map.

a quick note to the effect of "I'm not sure what you mean. Can you tell me again?" Or you may ask for further explanation: "Could you explain that for me?" or "Could you give me an example?" If this is taking place during a chat session, these examples alone will work. In an email, you may wish to preface your question with what was specifically said or presented previously. You may do this by quoting the previous message or by copying a section from a page that needs more clarification.

If you have several questions, it is best to present the entire list at one time. For example, you may wish to get specific clarification on how the instructor is going to grade an assignment. Rather than ask a general question like, "How is the assignment going to be graded?" You might make a list of specific questions and number them in order of importance.

1 Are different sections weighted differently in terms of points?
2 Is there a specific format for margins, font sizes, and length for term papers?
3 Do you need to see my work on the calculations?
4 Do you want my paper submitted as an email attachment or posted as an attachment to the discussion board?
5 Does grammar count?

Reading strategies

Online programs require more reading than any other form of learning. Because you are not listening to lectures, it is up to you not only to read the textbook, but also to read articles and web pages that relate to the topic you are studying. The following strategies may help you to understand and retain information more readily.

1 *Highlight.* Highlight text or passages that capture the essence of the concept or topic. Write brief notes in the margins. For example, in a chapter on business ethics you might make margin notes of each important concept or how that concept relates to your business environment.
2 *Outline.* Another strategy is to outline the book chapter or article. Studies have shown that writing concepts while you are reading or listening help you to remember. Outlining also provides a way to organize the concepts in your mind.
3 *Infer.* You can also use the strategy of making predictions as you read, based on your knowledge of the world, of how people think,

write and talk, and of what the author is like. For example, if you are reading a book about communication styles, you already have a great deal of personal knowledge about communication in your daily work life. You can take the information presented and already predict the outcome. This helps you to learn more quickly. The concept "tag" may be all you need to get from the information (e.g. anger is associated with conflict management in communication. The concept tag is "conflict management"). It is also a good idea to read any sections about the authors and their work, as well as the table of contents to help you make predictions about their beliefs.

Writing strategies

Note-taking or outlining is always a good writing strategy. The same reading strategies of highlighting and outlining also apply here, as reading and understanding your research is the first step toward writing a good paper. Another strategy is to write down the main ideas, important points, or a summary of a topic on index cards. In this way, it is easy to return to these cards as you organize your paper. It is also easy to use these cards to remember the large variety of research articles you have used for the paper.

As you review these methods and pay attention to how you learn, you may develop other strategies that work well for you. Be sure to write them down and then consciously make an effort to use them as you proceed through your online education program.

Adapting to different teaching strategies online

Traditional teaching, as we now know it, i.e. a instructor lecturing to a large assembly of students, is of medieval origin. In an age when books were scarce, it made sense for the learned instructor to broadcast knowledge in a lecture. However, it was probably true then – and it is certainly true today – that talking alone is not an efficient learning method. The physical set-up promotes student passivity; students are treated as empty vessels to be filled up with knowledge from the expert instructor. Second, lecturing leads to a view of learning as memorizing and conquering a multitude of facts. This is particularly true in the sciences where "truth" evolves and the number of facts increases rapidly in order to keep up with the latest research, producing shallow understanding at best.

The modern student's response to this lecture, memorize, restate method is to engage in a process of learning only enough to get by. In their minds the goal becomes not wisdom but passing the course. Their overarching concern becomes "What does the instructor want me to know for the test?" In this teaching paradigm, universities are locked in a vicious cycle. Teachers continue to teach using the methods by which they were taught; their students arrive with an expectation of this same method of education, and so it continues.

Student-centered teaching

The ineffectiveness of the traditional lecture and test approach has become ever more apparent in our rapidly changing world. Even in the traditional classroom, but particularly online, student-centered approaches to instruction are finding widespread adoption today. This paradigm seems to be inherently more suited to producing deep understanding because it is based on the principle that learning must be personally constructed. In other words, understanding does not exist inside the brain but is an outward expression of some kind of performance, usually writing, verbalizing or problem-solving. This view of understanding sharpens and changes the traditional education methodology because it must be aimed at the very specific goal of flexible performance rather than regurgitation of facts.

Although the student-centered learning paradigm is elegant and convincing to most educators, switching to a student-centered approach is fraught with difficulties for both instructors and students. Some students find self-directed education easy, but these are the exceptions as most need structures to help them learn in this mode. Partly it is the switch from passivity to activity, which requires more energy. Partly, the difficulty is in the discomfort of changing something many have accepted unquestioningly throughout their educational experiences, and partly it is a question of not knowing where to begin. Some examples follow of processing tasks that you may find commonly used in an online, student-centered learning environment.

Problem-solving by triads

Triads are groups of three students in which each has an assigned role. Two are problem-solvers, whose task is to try to solve the problem by discussing it out loud, and the third is a scribe whose job is to record the unsuccessful and successful paths followed by the problem-solvers. After 4–5 minutes the scribes report to the class publicly – on the discussion board or in a chat – and the general methods tried are compared and discussed.

Concept maps

This is a tried-and-true approach, and very effective at pinpointing underlying strengths and weaknesses in understanding. The instructor asks students to create their maps on a whiteboard in a small group. These maps are then posted, as attachments or Web pages, and then discussed in a larger class group.

Commentaries

Students are asked to provide a substantial commentary on an opinion piece they read in the newspaper. These commentaries are posted to the discussion board and then other students are asked to critique the commentary, and to add their agreement and disagreement to the commentary.

Problem expansion

Problem expansion invites the student to break up the problem into all its component words and phrases, examine them, and question their significance. Once the bulk of the knowledge is identified, the way to solve the problem becomes more obvious.

Student resistance to student-centered learning

People generally shy away from things that do not conform to their perception of the way education should be. Students are particularly resistant because the university seems to be set up to promote traditional lectures. Some students even complain, "I have paid a lot of money to study at this university and to be taught by an expert." One could argue that, in fact, students are getting even more return on their investment because in the student-centered, online environment the teacher is working to meet their specific learning needs. This allows for more one-on-one time with the instructor, which may help you to learn more thoroughly and to be even more successful in your studies.

Peer learning and teaching

One of the techniques sometimes used in online education is to have the class participants actually teach a lesson to each other. This technique is used not only to enhance your retention of the information; but also as an opportunity for you to demonstrate critical thinking, leadership, and collaboration skills. Research has demonstrated that peer interaction improves the academic performance and attitudes of the students who receive instruction and those who provide it.

Peer teaching may take a variety of forms in online education, such as:

- teacher assistants leading discussion groups, seminars, or tutorial groups
- senior students assisting individual students (called the proctor model)
- student learning groups that are instructor-less or self-directed.

You, as a student, bring a lot of invaluable life experiences into the classroom; these should be acknowledged and used. You can learn much from dialogue with respected peers and they can learn from you.

Teachers as facilitators or mentors

If you haven't been involved in education for a while, or you are moving from a very traditional method of instruction, you may be in for a surprise with the online education style of classes. Actually, both traditional and online education have been changing the role of the teacher from one of distributing information to one of facilitation and mentorship. In the online education environment, this is even more pronounced. Online students must be more independent, because the technology provides an overwhelming amount of information, making it essential that teachers guide and advise. In addition, your instructors will not know when you are having trouble unless you inform them. They depend on you to supply this information, as they can no longer "see" your confusion by non-verbal cues.

As an adult, your life experience is a rich resource for learning. Though instructors also have their own expertise, online learning tends to focus more on your knowledge and its relationship to the course. Although an instructor might share what works and what does not work, it is more likely they will take on the role of providing resources, and will expect you to learn by integrating your life experiences with new information to construct meaning. You will need to experiment.

Sometimes you will make mistakes, but mistakes are an opportunity for learning. The online teacher is there to facilitate your learning process, not to tell you how to learn.

Adult learning is linked to what the learners need to know or do in order to fulfill their roles and responsibilities. As each adult is at a different stage in the career cycle, it is possible that every assignment given by an online teacher is different for each student. Many higher education curriculums now include the option for developing your own homework assignment with instructor approval. For example, instead of giving specific instructions for the topic of a written assignment, the instructor will ask you to write a 2,000-word paper which reflects what you have learned in the class as it applies to your professional life. This requires you not only to understand the content of the class, but also to actually use it.

Adult learners are problem-centered rather than subject-centered. The nature of all learning provides for some type of content-centered section. However, in the online environment, this section is usually brief and limited only to summaries and to links to additional reading resources. Instructors still rely heavily on the textbook and then provide online or interactive resources to round out your learning experience. While students are encouraged to ask questions about the content of their instruction, the emphasis is on the *process* of their learning.

Instructors who are guides and mentors will emphasize problem-solving skills. Rather than giving you information, they now assist you in finding your own answers. They may help you generate lists of possible options and then encourage *you* to experiment to find what works best. Some of the best mentors/teachers answer many questions with a question. Though this may seem frustrating, it ensures that you are finding the answers on your own instead of memorizing a set of responses given by the instructor.

Multiple teachers/multiple locations

It is becoming common practice for colleges and universities to take advantage of the global access to instructors. Schools frequently hire an instructor for only one or two classes to be offered online. The global accessibility of the World Wide Web allows for education to be facilitated by multiple teachers at multiple locations. For example, in a recent course offered at Nova Southeastern University in Florida, one of the instructors was in the Netherlands, another instructor (co-teacher) was in Indiana, and the 30 students in the class were scattered through many different countries – Canada, Jamaica, Israel, the United States, and Switzerland.

The advantage to you in this arrangement is the opportunity to receive instruction from some of the top people in your field of study without attending the university where they reside. Additionally, a course may be offered in conference or symposium style. This allows exposure to many instructors during the term. You may have one instructor for the first three weeks, then another for the next three weeks, and so on. This has become particularly popular with courses regarding "trends." Each instructor will cover the material that pertains to his or her expertise.

Due to the physical distance between some instructors and the school, some universities have implemented a system of class coordinators who assist with the day-to-day administrative work for a course. This person's role is to act as a liaison between the students, the instructors, and the university at the physical campus. The actual functions of these coordinators vary from campus to campus. Some of the duties may include student advising, collecting final grades and posting them to the registrar's office, informing instructors of student profiles for each class, processing course registrations and tuition payments, acting as a liaison with the bookstore and library, and answering or forwarding questions to the appropriate on-campus resource. In general, these coordinators are the individuals assigned to assist you and to ensure you are not lost in the university bureaucracy because you are not physically at the campus.

Other colleges add to the coordinator concept by keeping enrolled students in specific groups, known as clusters or cohorts. This concept is somewhat similar to being a part of "class" that will move through the curriculum together and graduate together. This is particularly popular in graduate programs, but is becoming more prevalent in undergraduate programs as well. The advantage to the cohort or cluster concept, usually a group of 15 to 30 students, is that you have more opportunity to get to know a few people very well over the course of your studies. Your cohort members will become your study partners and you will share the same frustrations and joys as you undertake your program together. The cohort concept helps to make the online community very much like a residential community and often helps in retaining students throughout their degree program.

Chapter 7

Doing research online

> When you steal from one author, it's plagiarism; if you steal from many, it's research.
>
> (Wilson Mizner, 1876–1933, quoted in A. Johnston, *The Legendary Mizners*, Chapter 4)

Certainly the skills required to do research do not change for the online student. You need to locate relevant books, journals, magazine articles, newspapers, academic publications and conference proceedings. Though you are not physically on a college campus, you still have access to your public libraries, local community college and university libraries, as well as bookstores in your area. The primary difference is not being able to walk into your campus library to look for books or articles. Or can you?

Perhaps the greatest impact on civilization since the creation of the printing press will come from the ability to digitize information regardless of format. Digitization allows for the transformation of information from one form to another (e.g. print to sound) and for a range of retrieval options. Technological advances have resulted in many changes in the traditional library, and are both a cause and cure for the information explosion. Digital technology generates information at faster rates, and 90 percent of all information produced since 1979 has been transformed to digital format. Digital retrieval systems offer the only hope of managing this much information.

The focus is now shifting from acquisition to access. Rather than every library in a system buying a periodical or book, only one will need to buy it – in electronic form – and make it available, through inter-library loan, to others on the system. Libraries will be able to build virtual collections and reference works specifically tailored to their users. As the ability to amass comprehensive printed collections declines, the importance of virtual collections using the relative strengths of several libraries will grow.

New electronic access software programs make it easier for you to do your own reference searches, then download the abstracts or full text articles from databases or digitized library collections. Electronic access means that libraries can remain "open" 24 hours a day. More journals and magazines are becoming available for electronic access because of the move to electronic desktop publishing and the inexpensive alternative of scanning document pages to a PDF format (portable document format) – a standard form for storing printed publishable documents on the Web. If the materials you need are not digitized, many libraries will provide fax or mail service for specific pages if necessary.

Many public and college libraries now have access to large electronic journal databases, such as First Search, Academic Search Elite, and ProQuest. To access these databases you must be enrolled in the college programs and receive special logins and passwords. These databases provide a wealth of online full-text articles, thus not requiring the library personnel to send you anything separately. Check with your university facility to see what the availability is for online research.

Basic Web searching using search engines

Because the Web is not indexed in any standard manner, finding information can seem difficult. Search engines are popular tools for locating Web pages, but they often return thousands of results. Using special software, search engines constantly explore the Web and log the words from the Web pages they find into their databases. Because some search engines have logged the words from over a billion documents, results can be overwhelming. Without a clear search strategy, using a search engine is like wandering aimlessly in the stacks of a library trying to find a particular book.

Successful searching involves two key steps:

1 You must have a clear understanding of how to prepare your search. You must identify the main concepts in your topic and determine any synonyms, alternate spellings, or variant word forms for the concepts.

2 You need to know how to use the various search tools available on the Internet. Search engines, such as Google (http://www. google. com), are very different than subject directories, for example Yahoo! (http://www.yahoo.com). Even search engines themselves can vary greatly in size, accuracy, features, and flexibility.

Internet search engines have become very important to general users and students, and are now multi-million dollar businesses. Choosing the best search engine for your needs, and then determining how to enter the words or phrases which work best, will make your research go much more quickly. Some estimates put the number of Internet search engines available at nearly 150. This chapter will touch on a few of the most popular ones.

Search engines use software robots to survey the Web and build their databases. Web documents are retrieved and indexed. When you enter a query at a search engine Website, your input is checked against the search engine's keyword indices. The best matches are then returned to you as hits. The key is to keep your query as specific as possible. If you enter something very general, like "baby," you will get hundreds of thousands of hits – everything from "naming babies" to "baby animals" to "making babies." You need to learn to narrow your search.

Remember You must provide the most information possible to obtain an accurate search result. Unlike a librarian, search engines don't have the ability to ask a few questions to focus the search. They also can't rely on judgment and past experience to rank Web pages in the way humans can.

Search engines determine relevancy by following a set of rules, with the main rules involving the location and frequency of keywords on a Web page. With the "baby" example, search engines first look for the word "baby" in the title or toward the top of the Web page. Those that work on the frequency rule will analyze how often keywords appear in relation to other words in a Web page. Those with a higher frequency are often deemed more relevant than other Web pages.

So, why do some search engines seem to give back more results than others? To begin with some search engines index more Web pages than others. Some search engines also index Web pages *more often* than others. The result is that no search engine has the same collection of Web pages to search through. Search engines may also give Web pages a "boost" according to certain criteria. For example, WebCrawler (http://www.webcralwer.com) uses popularity as part of its ranking method.

It can tell which of the pages in its index have a lot of links pointing at them. These pages are given a slight boost during ranking, since a page with many links to it is probably well regarded on the Internet. Some hybrid search engines, those with associated directories, may give a relevancy boost to sites they've reviewed. Yahoo! uses this method. The logic is that if the site was good enough to earn a review, chances are it's more relevant than an unreviewed site.

Subject directories

A subject directory is a catalog of sites collected and organized by humans. Subject directories start with a few main categories and then branch out into subcategories, topics, and subtopics. Subject directories are useful when you do not know exactly what you need. For example, if you knew there was a well-known football (soccer) team in Manchester, England but could not remember the name, you might use subject directories to research it. You would begin by selecting "Sports" at the top level, then "soccer" at the second level, "by region" at the next level, then "countries," then "United Kingdom" then "cities and towns", then "Manchester," then finally "Manchester United." This may seem like an arduous task, but it is similar to how you would approach many research projects – looking for connections among topics or ideas.

Because humans at Yahoo! organize the Websites in subject directories, you can often find a good starting point if your topic is included. If you have more information at the beginning, you can use keyword indexing to find records much more quickly. Keyword search options usually eliminate the need to work through numerous levels of topics and subtopics. In this case, it would have been faster to enter "Manchester football" in the keyword search instead of working through the levels.

Because directories cover only a small fraction of the pages available on the Web, they are most effective for finding general information on popular or scholarly subjects. If you are looking for something specific, use a search engine.

Keyword indexing

If Yahoo! can't give you a hit, it automatically sends your query to its partner Google for a search through a keyword index. Google is one of the newer search engines, but it has rapidly become a favorite. In fact, the word "google" is now frequently being used as a verb, a synonym for searching, as in "I'm going to google the Web to find the info I need." Google combines keyword searching with ranking importance. Its technology considers pages that are linked to it from other sites as more important than pages that only have a few links from other sites. In other words, if many Webmasters consider a Web site valuable enough to create a link to it, Google deems that a good reason to justify a high ranking for that site.

Unless the author of a Web document specifies the keywords for the document (this is possible by using special HTML code when building the webpage), it's up to the search engine to determine them. Essentially, this means that search engines pull out words that are believed to be significant. Words that are mentioned toward the top of a document and words that are repeated several times throughout the document (location and frequency of keywords again) are more likely to be deemed important.

Some sites (like AltaVista (http://www.altavista.com) and Open Text (http://www.opentext.com)) simply index every word on every page. Others index only part of the document. For example, Lycos (http://www.lycos.com) indexes the title, headings, subheadings and the hyperlinks to other sites, along with the first 20 lines of text and the 100 words that occur most often. InfoSeek (http://infoseek.go.com) uses a full-text indexing system, picking up every word in the text except commonly-occurring stop words such as "a," "an," "the," "is," "and," "or," and "www." Inktomi (http://inktomi.com) also ignores stop words.

The problem with keyword indexing is that search engines have a tough time distinguishing between words that are spelled the same way, but mean something different (e.g. hard cider, a hard exam, and the hard drive on your computer). This often results in hits that are completely irrelevant to your query. Some search engines also have trouble with so-called stemming. For example, if you enter the word "big," should they return a hit on the word, "bigger?" What about singular and plural words? What about verb tenses that differ from the word you entered by only an "s," or an "ed"? Search engines also cannot return hits on keywords that mean the same, but are not actually entered in your query. A query on "romance" would not return a document that used the word "heart" or "love" or "intimacy, " if it did not include the word "romance."

Tips for working with keyword indexing

- Enter synonyms, alternate spellings and alternate forms (e.g. dance, dancing, dances) for your search terms.
- Enter all the unique terms that are likely to be included in the document or site you are seeking.
- Avoid using very common terms (e.g. history, painting) which may lead to an avalanche of irrelevant search results.
- Using the "Help" feature, determine how your search engine uses capitals and plurals, and enter capitalized or plural forms of your search words if appropriate.
- Use a phrase or proper name if possible to narrow your search and therefore retrieve more relevant results.
- Use multiple operators (e.g. AND, NOT) if a search engine allows you to do so.
- If you receive too many results, refine and improve your search. (After perusing the results, you may become aware of how to use NOT e.g. – Boston AND hockey AND NOT Bruins.)
- Pay attention to proper spacing and punctuation in your search syntax (i.e. no space when using the plus sign means+term).

Concept-based indexing

Unlike keyword indexed-based systems, concept-based indexing systems try to determine what you mean, not just what you say. Essentially, they do this by checking documents for the dominant themes or concepts, which are then indexed. A concept-based search returns hits on documents that are about the subject/theme you're exploring, even if the words in the document don't precisely match the words you enter into the query. Excite (http://excite.com) is currently the most popular, general purpose search engine site on the Web that relies on concept-based searching.

How does it work? There are various methods of building concept-based indices, some of which are highly complex, relying on sophisticated linguistic and artificial intelligence theory. Excite sticks to a numerical approach. Excite's software determines meaning by calculating the frequency with which certain important words appear. When several words or phrases that are tagged to signal a particular concept appear close to each other in a text, the search engine concludes, through statistical analysis, that the piece is "about" a certain subject.

Using our previous example, the word "heart," when used in the romance context, would be likely to appear with such words as love, flowers, candy, passion, and valentine. In that case, the search engine would return hits on the subject of romance. On the other hand if the word "heart" appeared with words like, artery, cholesterol, or blood, a very different context is established, and the search engine would only return hits relevant to a medical inquiry.

Tip Concept-based indexing is a good idea in theory, but it's far from perfect in practice. The results are best when you enter a lot of words, all of which roughly refer to the concept about which you are seeking information.

Refining your search

Most engines offer two different types of searches – basic and refined. In a basic search, you just enter a keyword without sifting through any pull-down menus of additional options. Depending on the engine, though, basic searches can be quite complex. Refining options differ from one search engine to another, but some of the possibilities include the ability to look for more than one word, to give more weight to one search term than to another, and to exclude words that might be likely to muddy the results. You might also be able to search proper names, phrases, and words that are found within a certain proximity to other search terms.

Some search engines also allow you to specify the form in which you'd like your results to appear, and whether you wish to restrict your search to certain fields on the Internet or to specific parts of Web documents (e.g. the title or URL). Many, but not all search engines allow you to use Boolean operators to refine your search. These are the logical terms *and*, *or*, and *not* and the proximal locators, *near* and *followed by*. All the search engines have different methods of refining queries. The best way to learn them is to read the help files on the search engine sites and practice.

A synopsis of some of the common Boolean search operators is below.

AND	All the terms you specify must appear in the document, e.g. computer *AND* hard *AND* drive. If you were looking for computer hard drives you might use this if you wanted to exclude common hits that would be irrelevant to your query.
OR	At least one of the terms you specify must appear in the document, e.g. education *OR* learning. You

	might use this if you didn't want to rule out too much. This is particularly useful when you are using synonyms in a topic that is not frequently researched.
NOT	The terms you specify must not appear in the document. You might use this if you anticipated results that would be totally off-base, e.g. nirvana *AND* Buddhism *NOT* rock *NOT* music.
+ and –	Some search engines use the characters plus (+) and minus (–) instead of Boolean operators to include and exclude terms. The + works the same as *AND*. The – works the same as *NOT*.
NEAR	The terms you enter should be within a certain number of words of each other. For example, science fiction *NEAR* novel.
FOLLOWED BY	One term must directly follow the other. At present, only the Open Text engine allows the use of the term *FOLLOWED BY*, although several other search engines allow you to query on phrases.
Phrase query	These require that you enclose the phrase in quotation marks, "space, the final frontier" – the engine will then search only for the phrase exactly as written. It would omit anything about space as a new frontier.

Now that you know some of the secrets of using search engines for your research, how do you choose which directory to use? First, you want to evaluate what you are looking to do. Choose a search engine, directory or library in accordance with the kind of search you are doing and the kind of results you are seeking. Are you looking for a Web site? Are you looking for information that might be contained in a news server? Are you looking for academic articles that may only be retrievable through old archived sites?

Determine your goal. Do you want a specific hard-to-find document on an esoteric subject, or general information on a broader topic? Do you need to search the entire Web, or is what you are seeking likely to be found on a number of sites, or only the most popular sites? In making your choice, determine whether the information you are looking for is likely to be in a page's title or first paragraph, or buried deeper within the document or site.

Another class of search engine is the metasearch or multiple search engine. These engines allow you to perform a keyword query in many search engines at the same time. MetaCrawler (http://www.metacrawler.com) is probably the best known for this. However, other popular ones are Dogpile (http://www.dogpile.com), Cyber411 (http://euklid.mi.uni-koeln.de/~jbe/ref/www.cyber411.com/), and Savvy Search (http://www.search.com/). These engines will explore Yahoo!, InfoSeek, AltaVista and many others at the same time. Most meta-search engines will give you only the top ten hits from each engine. Others will allow you to set the number of hits you want to get from each. This can be a quick way to survey the entire Web for content on a topic.

Finally, the newest development in the search engine arena is specialized search engines that are subject specific. For example, DejaNews (http://groups.google.com/) indexes only the content of newsgroups. InfoSpace (http://infospace.com/) contains an index of addresses and phone numbers for anyone in the US listed in a phone book. Some of the specialized engines are also being included in the metasearch engines mentioned above.

Selecting a search engine

At this point, you may be thinking, "How do I make a choice among all these search engines?" Below are brief descriptions of some of the most popular search engines, as reported by Search Engine Watch (http://searchenginewatch.com/).

AltaVista

(http://www.altavista.com/) A large search engine with a number of advanced search features. Also useful for locating multimedia files, such as images, audio, and video files. AltaVista includes a directory which categorizes Websites according to broad categories. Most intriguing is the Babel Fish translation feature that currently handles Chinese, Japanese, Korean, French, German, Italian, Portuguese, and Spanish translations to and from English, plus one-way translation from Russian to English. You're guaranteed to find lots of results with AltaVista, but will probably need to sift out ephemeral pages from the authoritative ones. A good choice when you need to find that needle in a haystack.

AlltheWeb

(http://www.alltheweb.com/) Another very fast, award-winning, and popular search engine. AlltheWeb is a good choice for finding all kinds of information and file types. It currently offers excellent support for locating multimedia files such as images, music, and videos on the Web.

Ask Jeeves

(http://www.askjeeves.com) Jeeves lets you search either by keyword or in plain English and presents answers in an uncluttered format. The site also offers channels focusing on shopping, travel and mobile phone content. Jeeves gets more intelligent all the time as staff process repeated queries and create specific answers. The human-created answers appear at the top of the list of possible responses. If Jeeves doesn't have a human-created answer, it connects to an automated search index or other search partners to find the answer.

Google

(http://www.google.com/) One of the largest and quickest search engines, and a good choice for research. Works on the principle that important, authoritative pages will tend to be those that are heavily linked by other pages. Useful for finding well-known and well-cited Web pages, organized by most- to least-cited pages on your topic or search terms. Other search services, such as HotBot, have arranged with Google to use its software or portions of its index. You'll get similar (but not necessarily identical) search results using such search engines, but only searching Google directly will produce comprehensive results from their service.

HotBot

(http://hotbot.lycos.com/) This search engine now offers users a choice between four widely-known Web crawlers – FAST (now called AlltheWeb, http://www.alltheweb.com/), Google, Inktomi, and Teoma (http://www.teoma.com) – to search the Web for your terms. Advanced search features differ according to which crawler is chosen.

Overture

(http://www.content.overture.com/) Previously known as GoTo.com, this search engine is primarily focused on "pay for placement" results, meaning that companies or individuals pay money for their Web pages to appear high in search result lists. Overture describes this service as "commercial search," and uses the phrase "pay for performance" to describe this advertising emphasis. Because of its pay for placement organization, this search engine is good for research on topics such as commercialism of the Internet, advertising, business, popular culture, and similar topics. As of July 2003, Yahoo! had acquired Overture, which could signal changes in store for Yahoo! as well.

Yahoo!

(http://www.yahoo.com/) Easily one of the most recognizable and popular Web directories, and as of 2002 also a Web search engine. The directory portion of Yahoo! relies on people to submit and to categorize sites. The Web search engine portion is powered by Google (and previously by Inktomi). Since late 2002, Yahoo!'s default search is the Web search feature; directory results must explicitly be chosen by the user.

Tips for successful searching

Remember, you are smarter than a computer. Use your intelligence. Search engines are fast, but dumb.

A search engine's ability to understand what you want is very limited. It will obediently look for occurrences of your keywords all over the Web, but it doesn't understand what your keywords mean or why they're important to you. To a search engine, a keyword is just a string of characters. It doesn't know the difference between cancer the astrology sign and cancer the disease ... and it doesn't care.

Know where to look first

Are you looking for information about a person? A company? A software product? A health-related problem? Do you need to research a term paper? Document a news story?

There are various databases containing specific information that might be more useful to you than a general search engine (e.g. news servers). However, you can find these databases by using a search engine.

Fine-tune your keywords

If you're searching on the name of a person, place or thing, remember that most nouns are subsets of other nouns. Enter the smallest possible subset that describes what you want. Be specific. Try to meet the search engine halfway by refining your search *before* you begin.

For example, if you want to buy a car, don't enter the keyword "car" if you can enter a brand name such as "Toyota." Better still, enter the phrase "Toyota Dealerships" *AND* the name of the city where you live.

Be refined

Read the help files and take advantage of the available search refining options. Use phrases, if possible. Use the Boolean AND (or the character +) to include other keywords that you would expect to find in relevant documents.

Also learn to EXCLUDE with the Boolean NOT. Excluding is particularly important as the Web grows and more documents are posted. Run your initial query over again several times, each time adding further refinements to narrow down your list of relevant hits.

For example, if you want to find medical details about how to diagnose Alzheimer's disease, try entering "Alzheimer's" AND "symptoms" AND "diagnosis." If you want to find Alzheimer's care and community resources, query on "Alzheimer's" AND "support groups" AND "resources" AND NOT "symptoms."

Query by example

Take advantage of the option that many search engine sites are now offering for "query by example," or "find similar sites," to the ones that come up on your initial hit list. Search engines provide this option based on a set of criteria that can help you expand your hits.

Creating an effective search statement

When structuring your query, keep the tips in Table 7.1 in mind.

Internet references for top search engines

http://www.northernwebs.com/set/setsimjr.html
http://www.monash. com/spidap2.html
http://searchenginewatch.com/

Table 7.1 Tips for structuring search queries

Tip	*Example*	*Description*
Be specific	Noritake dinner plates	Whenever possible use nouns, proper names, and objects as keywords
Important words first	+hybrid +electric +gas +vehicles	Put the most important terms first in your keyword list. To ensure they are searched, put a + sign in front of each one
Use more keywords	Interaction vitamins drugs	Use at least three keywords in your query
Phrase query	"search engine tutorial"	Combine keywords, whenever possible, into phrases and offset them with quotation marks
No common words	"bottled spring water"	Avoid common words, e.g. water, unless they are part of a phrase query
Write it down first	+"portland state university" + "financial aid" +applications +grants	Write down your search statement and revise it before you type it into a search engine query box

Evaluating Internet resources

When researching a topic for your course, it is easy to locate a wealth of information using search engines on the Web, but how reliable is this information? The old saying, "Don't believe everything you read" holds especially true for the Internet. Any person or group with any agenda can post articles, books, or images to the Internet. There is no assurance that what has been posted is rooted in academic inquiry or real-world experience. It is wise to have a consistent procedure for evaluating anything you read online.

Tips:

- **Purpose:** Based on the content, tone and style, does the purpose match your research needs?
- **Audience:** Who is the intended audience for the document? School teachers, parents, children, science fiction fans?
- **Source:** Are the authors identifiable? Do they introduce themselves and give some background information? Academic authors or professionals will often provide a résumé or credentials page, or site affiliations with a recognized educational institution or other organization.
- **Site Sponsor:** The sponsor of the site is identified by the URL extension: .edu for educational sites; .gov for government sites; .org for organizational sites; .com or .net for commercial sites.
- **Content:** Do the authors present logical arguments? Look for point-of view and evidence of bias. Sources of information (references) should be clearly stated and you should be able to trace them to books, articles, or reputable organizations or individuals.
- **Depth:** Is the site comprehensive? Determine if the content covers a specific time period or aspect of the topic, as compared to a historical review or specific research on a population relating to the topic.
- **Current:** Has the site been updated recently? Are the links still working and are they relevant and appropriate. If the site is extensive, does it provide a search capability or targeted links within the page.

There is an informative tutorial online, "The Internet Detective," which was created in Europe specifically for students and faculty doing academic research. You can find it at: http://www. sosig.ac.uk/desire/internet-detective.html. The tutorial is free to use, but you need to register your own personal ID so that the system can remember your quiz scores and your place in the tutorial. The tutorial takes around two hours to complete, but your ID means you can do it at more than one sitting. You also have the option to download it to your computer. However, if you download it you won't get the full interactive functionality of the tutorial.

Finding and contacting experts on the Web

Although the Internet is a great research resource, it cannot answer all your research questions. Sometimes the volume of information is just too large, or the complexity of the search makes it difficult to use the search engines provided. But many times the Internet cannot give the answer you are looking for because your question is subjective. For example, you're looking for advice on whether a five-year-old child can learn to use a mouse effectively. It is possible you'll find that answer somewhere online, but it's more likely you'll find only general information about computers and children, leaving you to apply it to the question in which you're interested.

In a case like the one above, it would be best to ask a human. Just as you might include the talents of a research librarian in your local college or public library, you can access an expert via the Web. Fortunately, the Internet is not short of humans, and some of them are experts who encourage questions!

If you find a Website that covers your area of interest, and you have a question, you will need to email the expert and ask. But before sending an email, be sure to check the expert's Website to make sure the question isn't already answered in a FAQ (frequently asked questions) section. Sometimes the FAQ will say, "I'm very busy! Please don't send me questions!" If you still don't find your question answered, then prepare a brief email message describing your question and thanking the expert, in advance, for assisting you. Be sure to include some of the following information:

- Make sure your email address is enclosed with your message. Even though it is in the email header, you should not count on the expert automatically noticing that. You want to make it as easy as possible for the expert to get the answer to you.
- If you are gathering information for an assignment, let the expert know. He or she might be able to point you to additional sources of information.
- Be sure to double-check any information sent by the expert; don't assume it's true because you heard it on the "Net." At the very least the information should give you a lead to further research.

- Remember, experts do not have an obligation to answer your question. If you don't hear back, don't take it personally; they might be very busy. Sometimes if you ask a question that's already answered in their FAQ, they won't answer.

Online news articles

The research you do on the Internet frequently involves comparing the theory you learn in class with experience in the "real-world." Class assignments may ask you to provide a news story that demonstrates a concept or illustrates how a theory does not apply. Fortunately, the Web provides a number of resources for news and news archives.

National and major stories news resources

If the news in which you're interested is national or global, you can start with the AP Newswire (http://www.ap.org). From the front of this page click on the "Product and Services" button then choose the gateway to the wire at http://wire.ap.org/specials/bluepage.html. You'll be given a choice of different gateways to the wire service, broken down by state. Once you've picked a wire gateway, you'll get a chance to browse by subject or search a week's worth of stories. If you are trying to find how a story of national interest evolved over several days, the AP wire will get you a lot of information. Two other organizations to consider are BBC News at http://news.bbc.co.uk/ and CNN at http://www.cnn.com/. If you need to do research outside of Europe and the US, the News Voyager service provides coverage of major newspapers in every country around the world at http://www.newspaperlinks.com/home.cfm.

For a story of local interest, such as a mayor's future political ambitions, be sure to pick a wire service in the area in which you're interested. Often newspapers which carry the AP wire break out the stories by region and topic, which makes things easier to find.

Another resource for wire and large-scale stories is Yahoo! News (http://dailynews.yahoo.com/). Yahoo! News carries reports from AP, Reuters, National Public Radio, and more. They carry ten days' worth of stories, so there's not a lot of depth to the archive, but when you're looking for something that happened recently, it's quick and easy to use.

Archived news and wider searches

If the news you are researching isn't recent, you need to check "after wire" indexes and other resources. Several are available, each with its own unique indexing system. The different resources are summarized below.

BBC World News Archive (http://www.bbc.co.uk/worldservice/)

The BBC News Service makes many news stories from Europe and the world available for free. You may also search their past articles archive, dating back to the site's launch in November 1997. Available in 43 languages; many stories and articles are available in audio or video versions. Provided by the British Broadcasting Corporation.

The Irish Times (http://www.ireland.com/newspaper/archive/)

The archives contain all articles published on ireland.com, including The Irish Times online, Breaking News, Sports, Jobs, Property, Motors, Business and Special news and event sites.

Newstracker (http://news.excite.com/index/id/home.html)

Indices over 300 publications and offers them for free lookup. Newstracker also tracks particular news topics of current interest. For more esoteric concerns, you can create your own free "clipping service" which will track keywords you specify.

NewsHub (http://newshub.com)

Adds content every 15 minutes. Its sources do not seem to be as extensive as Newstracker, but it lists updated stories on its front page and has a feature called "MiniHub" that lists the latest stories in a particular area of interest.

Total NEWS (http://www.totalnews.com)

Arranged by categories, it becomes a nice search engine once you get some experience using it. This site doesn't have an extensive clipping service, but it does seem to contain a deeper archive than you might find other places.

NewsTrawler (http://www.newstrawler.com/)

A search engine of news sources divided by region and by topic. You can mark checkboxes to indicate which resources you want. This is a good source if you're looking for information from one particular geographic area.

TotalNews (http://www.newsindex.com)

Does not maintain an archive – they only index current news. With over 300 sources it provides a broad check for current reports or ongoing stories.

Conducting research with online library databases

A quick way to get the ball rolling on your research is to ask yourself the following five questions:

1 What do you already know about your topic?
2. What do you want to know about your topic?
3 What keywords can you think of that are related to your topic? (You will use these when you search the online catalog and journal databases)
4 Does your topic fit into a specific discipline? If so, what? (See tip below)
5 What research tools does the library offer on this subject?

Tip Academic scholarship tends to be divided into one of the three disciplinary areas – social sciences, sciences, and humanities. The library's resources are also organized this way. Identify some databases or subject guides that might be helpful for your topic.

Social Sciences: psychology, sociology, anthropology, education, business, etc.

Sciences: biology, chemisty, geology, engineering, computer science, etc.

Humanities: art, music, literature, dance, theater, etc.

Locate background information

Two key sources of background information on your topic are:

- *Your course materials*: Be certain to review the bibliographies in your textbook or other course readings.
- *Reference books and other reference sources*: Get to know your library's reference collection and where it is located. In most places, the Reference desk is always staffed by knowledgeable librarians. Please ask if you need help locating reference materials on your topic.

Develop a research strategy

Developing a research strategy means identifying some initial parameters to your research. You may stray far and wide from your initial search plan, but it will help you get started by narrowing down your topic to a reasonable size. Here are some things to consider in your analysis:

- Determine the scope of your topic: is it too broad for a short paper? Too narrow for a long paper?
- Should you narrow the scope to a specific aspect, set of aspects, or time period?
- Should you broaden the scope by selecting a wider range of topical aspects?
- What is the time frame?
- What is the geographic area? Is it local, national, international?

Once you've answered these questions you will want to:

- Collect background information
- See if there is an online subject guide
- Check the online catalog for books
- Check the databases for articles
- Based on what you've found, revise your search strategy

Finding journal articles online

There are thousands of possible databases that your school or public library may use. Databases are often purchased with negotiated contracts for the number of users. This is a means for libraries to carry significantly larger collections of journals and papers than they could previously afford, because they are only charged by the usage.

It is critical that you take time to get to know your library resources and how they are accessed. These databases are usually updated monthly with new articles and information. Two types of databases can be used to assist in your research.

General databases

These are interdisciplinary and will work for finding just a few articles on a topic or beginning research on a more in-depth project. General indexes are interdisciplinary and cover a broad range of topics. Academic libraries select indexes that catalog periodicals appropriate for academic-level research. These indexes may include some magazines (e.g. *Time*, *The Economist*, etc.) and newspapers but also comprise many key journals from a wide range of subject areas (e.g. *College Literature*, *Journal of Psychology*, etc.). A typical general database is Academic Search Elite.

Subject-specific databases

These are better for finding articles from journals in a specific discipline. You will turn to these when you have exhausted your findings in a general index such as Academic Search Elite, or when you're doing an in-depth project in a specific discipline.

Some databases provide full-text articles, while others provide only the citation for an item. If an article is not full-text, you will need to check your library to see if they subscribe to the journal. Many library catalogs can also be searched online. If the library does carry the journal, selected articles can usually be emailed, printed and scanned, saved to a disk, or sent via post to your home.

A description of some of the more popular databases is summarized in the Appendix.

Searching databases follows many of the same rules as using search engines.

Tips

Break your topic down into keywords

"I want to know how oil leaks from the Exxon Valdez have affected fish populations"

Keywords for searching: oil AND Exxon Valdez AND fish

Combine your keywords with AND or OR. This works for almost all databases
Combine different concepts with AND: oil **AND** fish **AND** Exxon Valdez
Combine similar concepts with OR: oil **OR** pollution OR leaks

Put phrases into quotes
"Mississippi River Delta"
"chicken-fried steak"
"war on terrorism"

Use the "Help" menu
Every database has extensive online help screens. Look for a "help" button in the upper navigation bar of the database.

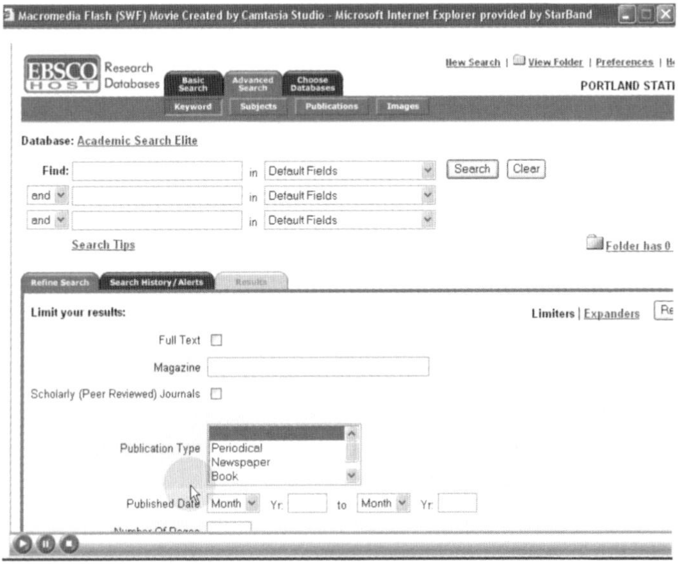

Macromedia Flash (SWF) Movie Created by Camtasia Studio - Microsoft Internet Explorer provided by StarBand
EBSCO HOST Research Databases
Basic Search | Advanced Search | Choose Databases
New Search | View Folder | Preferences
PORTLAND STATI
Keyword | Subjects | Publications | Images
Database: Academic Search Elite
Find: in Default Fields Search Clear
and in Default Fields
and in Default Fields
Search Tips
Folder has 0
Refine Search | Search History / Alerts | Results
Limit your results:
Limiters | Expanders
Full Text
Magazine
Scholarly (Peer Reviewed) Journals
Publication Type: Periodical, Newspaper, Book
Published Date Month Yr: to Month Yr:

Figure 7.1 **Initial search criteria.** In the top fields you enter your search criteria by keywords, author, or title. The drop-down boxes allow you to select the Boolean operators you desire (AND, OR, NOT). In the bottom fields you may limit your results to full text, specific publications, and dates of publication.

Evaluate your results
It's tempting to grab the first three full-text articles that come up in a search, but be careful. You want to choose articles that are high-quality and substantial enough for your paper or project.

The screens in Figures 7.1–7.3 demonstrate how these databases are used. Though these screens show Academic Search Elite, most of the databases work using the same steps and search formats.

Citing online resources

When you read an article and then use the author's words or ideas in your paper you *must* give the author credit in the form of a *citation*. This is true for online sources such as Academic Search Elite, just as it is for printed sources. When you download articles, you may want to make a note of the information needed, so that you can use it to create citations in your work.

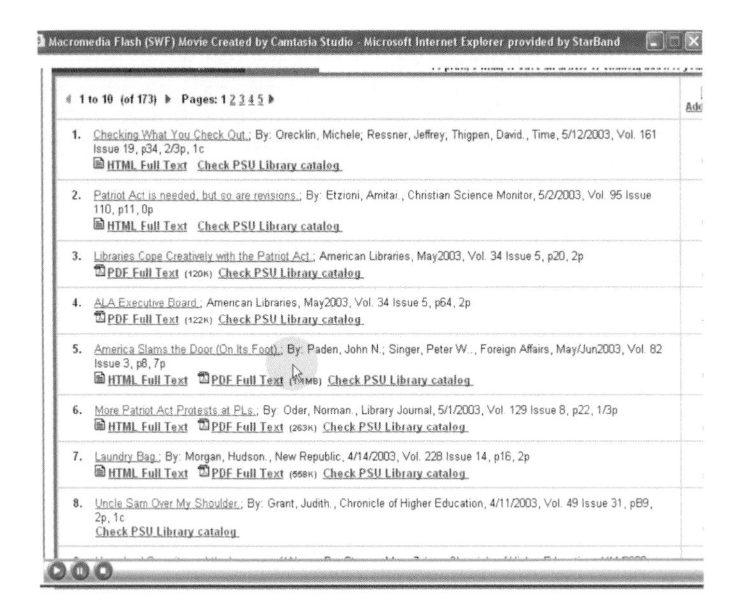

Figure 7.2 **Article List.** The articles meeting your search criteria are then displayed. The various availability types (HTML, PDF, Abstract only, etc.) are indicated. You click on the article(s) you wish to view. You may select multiple articles by using a checkbox on the far right (not in this picture.

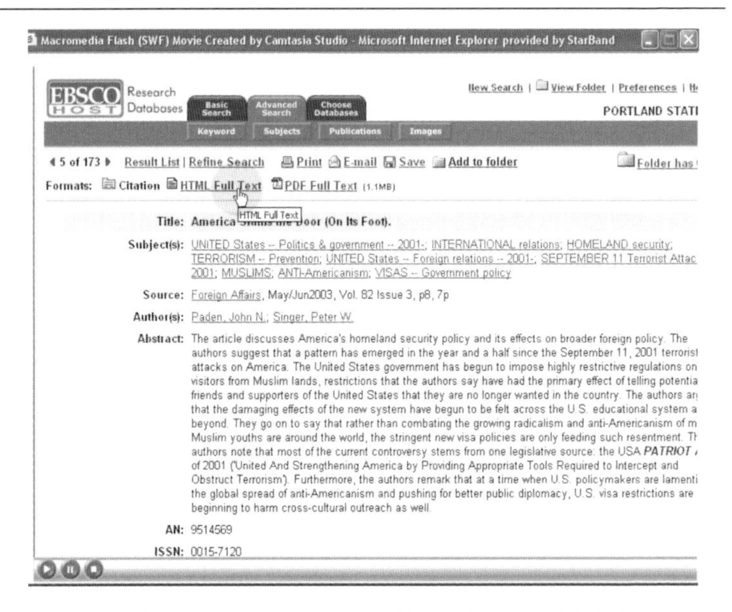

Figure 7.3 **Article citation and abstract.** Each selected article is displayed in turn. The full citation and abstract is provided. If you are interested in the article, you next select the format in which you wish to receive the article (HTML Full Text is selected above). If, after reading the abstract you determine this article is not of interest, you may move forward to the next citation or press your "back" button to return to the list of articles.

There are two parts to citations of articles you research from an online service such as Academic Search Elite:

- The first part of the citation reflects the nature of the publication in which the article was published. For example, newspaper, magazine, or scholarly journal. The formatting for each type of source publication is different.
- The second part of the citation references Academic Search Elite and, if known, the specific online database available in which you found the article. The formatting for this part of the citation remains the same, regardless of the publication type.

If you're citing an article or a publication that was originally issued in print form but that you retrieved from an online database to which your library subscribes, you should provide enough information so that the reader can locate the article either in its original print form or retrieve it from the online database (if they have access).

Provide the following information in your citation:

- Author name(s) (if not available, use the article title as the first part of the citation)
- Article title
- Publication name
- Publication date
- Page number/range
- Database name
- Service name
- Name of the library where service was accessed
- Name of the town/city where service was accessed
- Date of access
- URL of the service (but not the whole URL for the article, since those are very long and won't be re-used by someone trying to retrieve the information).

Below are two examples of how a citation differs depending on the style. These may not be exactly what your college or university requires. As new technology is introduced, citation styles frequently change and manuals are updated. It is always wise to check with your instructors as to the current requirements at your institution.

APA Example:

Schaefer, Bradley E. (1998, December). Meteors that changed the world. *Sky and Telescope*, [8 pages]. Retrieved October 29, 1998 from Academic Search Elite (Research Library Periodicals) on the World Wide Web: http://academicelite.lib.pdx.edu.

MLA Example:

Schaefer, Bradley E. "Meteors That Changed the World." *Sky and Telescope* Dec. 1998. *Research Library Periodicals*. Academic Search Elite. Portland State University Lib., Warren. 29 Oct. 1999 http://academicelite.lib.pdx.edu.

Different citation styles – which should you use?

It is best to ask your teachers which citation style they want you to use. If they have no preference, you may wish to follow these general guidelines:

- APA: psychology, education, and other social sciences.
- MLA: literature, arts, and humanities.

- AMA: medicine, health, and biological sciences.
- Chicago: used with all subjects in the "real world" by books, magazines, newspapers, and other non-scholarly publications.

Good resources for learning more about proper citations:

- The Evidence Network: http://www.evidencenetwork.org/bibliocitations.asp
- University of Nottingham site: http://www.nottingham.ac.uk/www/citation.html
- Columbia Guide to Online Style: http://www.columbia.edu/cu/cup/cgos/idx_basic.html
- APA Style.org: http://www.apastyle.org/elecref.html
- Online! A reference guide to using Internet sources: http://www.bedfordstmartins.com/online/citex.html

Chapter 8

Ethical issues

> If you take away ideology, you are left with a case by case ethics which in practise ends up as me first, me only, and in rampant greed.
> (Richard Nelson, 1950–, *Independent*, London, July 12, 1989

The root word for ethical is the Greek "*ethos*," meaning character. The root word for moral is Latin "mos," meaning "custom." Both words are broadly defined in contemporary English as having to do with right and wrong conduct. Character and custom, however, provide two very different standards for defining what is right and what is wrong. Character would seem to be a personal attribute, while custom is defined by a group over time. People have character. Societies have custom. To violate either can be said to be wrong, within its appropriate frame of reference.

This chapter will look at both ethics and morals in online education and in online communities. The first section of this chapter discusses the personal ethics of treating others with respect, sincerity, and fairness. The second section looks into illegal behavior in the use of online resources, and the ethics of participating in those actions or looking the other way when others participate in them. In the end it is up to you and your own sense of character as to how you conduct yourself.

Culture, language, and the ethics of discourse

Discourse ethics are motivated by the values of respect, truth, sincerity, fairness, equity participation, and accountability. For the norms to be valid within a group, community or culture, they must be regulated through the protection of practice that enhances mutual understanding of the norms from other cultures.

The Internet is a melting pot in which people of different races, religions, nationality, and abilities meet to share experiences and skills with each other, and to learn from each other. It is one of the challenges of an online community to establish how these differences and similarities can be used to help achieve the needs of the group. Furthermore, language differences can be a major obstacle to clear expression. Often online students whose native language is not English have concerns and questions about how they will be perceived online.

Most intercultural miscommunication is caused by well-meaning statements, where each person behaves according to his or her own cultural norms, rather than by deliberate unpleasantness. To help prevent such difficulties, all participants need to recognize that cultural, gender, and religious identity constitute an important part of each person in the class.

Another problem is that some people do not know how to engage in supportive discourse. A competitive culture teaches adversarial communication. An unhelpful result is a tendency for people to ignore other belief systems because they don't match their own rather than work together to help one another learn. When adversarial communications stray into a fight for domination, the result is usually either "flaming," which generates anger and more need for control, or withdrawal by some members who refuse to participate in this type of environment.

In online communities as in any other, the ethical issues of respect for individuals are paramount for the effective operation and survival of the group as an entity. One way to ensure this ethical participation is to agree to a code of conduct or ethics in discourse from the beginning. This code should include issues such as:

- the unacceptability of lying
- the amount of self-disclosure required
- judging the borderline between controversial and offensive
- how to handle conflict

Language

Language is an important element of cultural identity. It enables us to communicate ideas, beliefs, values and feelings. The Internet offers the potential for international collaboration and the provision of courses, which attract participants with a wealth of different languages and cultures from around the world. Many providers of internationally available online learning opportunities use English as the common language.

However, even with the choice of a common language, there are still variations and differences that continue to cause problems. For example, any traveler will quickly point out that English has many differences in its use among countries like the US, the UK, Australia, New Zealand and Canada. As an example, throughout this book the term instructor was used to indicate a person who heads the class and is responsible for ensuring student mastery of a topic. In some parts of the world, this person is called the "tutor," in others it is the "teacher," and in yet others the "professor." One can't even use them as synonyms because each term has its own nuances of different meanings in each of the English-speaking countries named above.

Native and non-native speakers

The difficulties of language and communication are magnified when the class members consist of both native and non-native English speakers. A key problem is finding the right level of communication with which all of your classmates are comfortable. The use of jargon or colloquialisms may be a source of misunderstanding and confusion for some non-native speakers. Therefore, it is very important for you to use plain language and to be as clear and brief as possible. Furthermore, you need to show patience in supporting the language attempts of others in your course.

One way of reducing problems is to get to know your classmates early on. Ask them about their native language and how comfortable they feel communicating online. Whenever non-native speakers post, it is up to you to offer encouragement and support of their efforts. Below is an example of a non-native speaker's first posting in a class and the supportive response from another student. It is this type of support that will continue to help the discourse remain positive.

Non-native speaker's first post

Buenos Dias Fellow Class Members!

Please forgive my writing skills to this board. My native language is Spanish and thus it is difficult for me. It took me houres to get here! I am worry my expressions are not clear and maybe foolish. But my bigger wish to share my ideas makes me not regret a post. If something is not clear, people must ask me for clearafication. It helps me sort out my own mind but theirs as well. I even dare to hope I will improve my english along the road.

Native-speakers ethical reply

Buenos Dias Jaime (I hope I spelled your name right).

I find your first post to be clear and to the point. I admire that you can write English so well. I must admit that my Spanish capabilities are limited to "buenos dias," "buenos noches," and "gracias." So you are already far ahead of me in your language abilities. Please do contribute frequently and don't worry about your skills. I for one promise to ask for clarification if you are unclear.

Netiquette

Cross-cultural learning groups present a wonderful opportunity for participants to benefit from diverse views and experiences, often far beyond what they might find in their local community. Online groups, like all learning communities, need ground rules to guide how they interact with each other. These rules, known as "netiquette," are sometimes established by the university and other times established within each course. The ground rules should address how participants wish to identify themselves, the community's mode of operation and style of communication (formal/informal), and frequency of participation. These rules can help reduce students' worries about offending each other by overstepping unknown boundaries. Many of these rules have been discussed in previous chapters, but it is also helpful to take into consideration the depth of cultural beliefs and ethics around some specific rules.

Most online forums adopt an informal style of address in which participants including the instructor are addressed by their first names. However, this may not be true in all contexts. There could be a cultural or social need for some to remain formal. For example some national groups feel reassured with a preamble to open discussions, and others have specific requirements for discussion that all greetings must include titles. i.e., "Good morning, Dr. Lynch," as opposed to "Good morning, Maggie." Some may prefer a period of relationship building while others are accustomed to getting right to work. Whatever the online conversation style participants prefer, some may have deeply held feelings concerning the written text.

In many non-Anglo cultures the written text is seen as something more than an individual presentation or personal opinion. Differences of opinion about such postings may be seen as an attack on the writer or the person's group. This can be explained by the fact that in some cultures the written text is seen as a fixed form of expression in which everything is important and thus worth reading. In this situation additional emphasis is also placed on the status of the author of the text. The higher the status of the author, the more authoritative the text, and the less acceptable that it be challenged. This makes the task of producing written text based on personal opinion particularly challenging for some learners. These students will tend to rely more on collective opinion or that based on someone of higher recognized status than their own, or even choose not to participate in discussions because they believe their opinion cannot possibly have value.

If you have classmates in this situation, you can be helpful by pointing out the cultural norms within the required communications in the group. Both by example, and your explanations, you can show your classmate(s) how to:

- contradict someone politely
- join conversation
- draw attention to common points of view
- come to a conclusion
- depersonalize opinions and arguments

Tips for communicating with non-native speakers of English

- Use uncomplicated language and clear explanations.
- Write clearly and avoid slang and idioms.
- Summarize what each person has written to assure each that you have understood.
- Clarify and confirm that your explanation has helped the participant understand.
- Check for understanding, avoiding "Yes/No" questions.
- Pause longer when waiting for responses; allow time for the other person to reply. Pause time varies in each culture and if we neglect to allow enough pause time it is almost the same as interrupting the other person.
- Allow non-native speakers to finish their sentences by themselves (many cultures are extremely comfortable with silence).
- Remember that language fluency does not equal cultural fluency and neither is it a reflection of intelligence.

- Encourage co-mediation as a positive approach to take advantage of different mediators' styles.

Based on Myers and Filner (1997).

Silences and humor as online interaction issues

Silences

In online intercultural communication, silences can occur either in the texts themselves, where certain topics are avoided, or in the irregular contribution of messages to the discussion board. Depending on the culture, these silences can mean disapproval, approval, neutrality, an admission of guilt, or a sign of incompetence. In Germanic countries, for example, the emphasis is on personal and explicit verbal messages for which the writer assumes responsibility for its clarity. Words serve as a form of social control, while silence tends to be used as a form of tacit consent or a sign of failure. In many Asian countries, on the other hand, meaning is based on an indirect style emphasizing the implicit connotation of words in a given social context (e.g. the high/low status of the writer). The onus is on the reader to decode meaning and not for the writer to send an explicit message that can be understood by all. This ability to read between the lines includes the understanding of the various registers of silence. In this way silence is used as a means of social control.

In some Asian contexts silences can be a sign of respect for the expertise of the other, or of displeasure. While in other cultures, like that of France, silence can be a form of neutral communication to keep a respectful distance from strangers. Even with this generalized information, you must not assume this is true of everyone within a culture. There will always be a range of diversity in a group. For example, in online learning some students gradually become aware of a reduction of traditional cultural barriers. Given this, no one person can fully understand a phenomenon like silence. It would be wiser to check with your classmate and ask. This can be done in the online group environment, or behind the scenes in individual emails.

It is important to allow for silences. Silence could mean the learner is:

- too busy
- not present for the moment, e.g. holiday, illness, pressure of work
- following along just fine

- having difficulties,
- waiting to be called upon
- uncomfortable responding to something, for example, with which the person disagrees
- in a position where the person feels there is nothing appropriate to say
- waiting for a difficult situation to 'cool down' before responding, (e.g. conflict, embarrassment)
- taking the time to carefully word what to say
- unable to access the course.

Asking your classmate to reply or to give the reason for their silence should be done regularly, but with tact and explaining why the subject is raised. Some people are often not aware of the impact of their silence on other participants in the group.

Humor

Humor is another difficult area in online intercultural communication. Humor is both culturally specific and personal. Some expressions of humor can be appropriate in one culture and completely inappropriate in a different culture. Also, within any culture some individuals are less comfortable with humor than others. Humor is also language specific, especially humor that relies on plays on words (puns) or slang.

Even with these difficulties, we should not give up humor as it is a way in which we can communicate our humanness online, helping to bridge the distance and lack of physical communication cues. When used appropriately, humor can help provide a "safe" place to learn new online tools and to make mistakes without fear of ridicule.

Consider these points before interjecting humor into your online communications.

- Does the humor rely on language/slang that may not be understood across the group?
- If the humor involves ridicule, however mild, is it self-deprecating and free of implications for others in the group?
- Is the humor used at an appropriate time? Do not make a joke in the middle of a serious dialogue. Save it for a more social time.
- Start slowly and pay attention to the reception. If someone comes back with "hehee" or "lol" (laughing out loud) you will know the comment was read in the spirit intended. If not, then you might

need to check to see if anyone has understood your attempt at humor or has been offended by it. Ask, do not assume.

- Use humor with intent. If working on developing a sense of warmth in a group, a warning ahead of time about one's own style of humor is in line.
- If you used humor and it was misinterpreted or ended up hurting someone's feelings, recognize it, admit your mistake, and apologize.

Tip Use emoticons or parenthetical statements to make sure the readers are clear you are making a joke or using humor.

Cheating on assessments

One of the more pervasive issues that an educator faces is the age-old concerns about students cheating on assessment. In fact, recent studies indicate that academic dishonesty is on the rise. A 1998 survey from *Who's Who Among American High School Students* reported that 80 percent of the students surveyed admitted to cheating on an exam. Furthermore, 50 percent of them did not believe cheating was necessarily wrong. Such statistics clearly reveal the pervasiveness of unethical behavior in schools.

Below is an abbreviated list of the ways in which students cheat in the traditional classroom:

- Looking at another pupil's test paper during a test.
- Dropping ones' paper so that other pupils can get answers off it.
- Developing codes such as tapping the floor three times to indicate that a multiple-choice item should be answered "C."
- Using crib notes or small pieces of paper. Crib notes can be hidden in many ingenious places.
- Writing test information on the desktop and erasing it after the test; a variation is to write information in allowed reference or textbook pages prior to the test and use the information during the exam.
- Changing answers when teachers allow pupils to grade each other's papers.
- Using resources forbidden by the teacher in take-home tests or work.

In considering the issue of ethics and online education, these same concerns take on a new twist. Students are no longer in close proximity. In fact they may be separated by thousands of miles. Distance, however, does not diminish the possibility of students cheating, with or without an accomplice, on online assessments. Instead of developing codes or dropping papers, students pass private emails, which instructors have no means of intercepting. In some cases, students can also download a test, look up the answers before actually taking it, and share those answers with classmates. Instead of using crib notes or writing answers within the margins of the textbook or on the desktop, students simply use the forbidden resources during the examination.

Certainly, a number of cheating prevention strategies are used online, but ultimately it is up to you and your sense of moral conduct to decide whether cheating is acceptable or not. It is up to you not only to monitor your own behavior but also to report known dishonest behavior by your classmates. Unfortunately, cheaters not only undermine their own education but may also undermine your education as well.

How cheating is curtailed online

Instructors have devised a number of methods to help curtail cheating while at the same time increasing learning.

1. Assignments are made that require some degree of cooperation and coordination among students. Tasks such as small group discussions, group papers, and group projects make it difficult for a student to find consistent help throughout a project of some duration and complexity.
2. A high level of instructor–student interaction is required in the course, through frequent email contact and occasional synchronous chats that are substantive in nature. Regular student–instructor contact will have two advantages: first, a student will have difficulty finding someone else to respond to frequent instructor emails. Second, through ongoing dialogue, the instructor will get a better "feel" for a student's ability.
3. All assessments become open-book instead of trying to limit allowed resources, and are also more substantive nature.
4. Writing assignments are submitted electronically so that the instructor can archive them for future reference, and run them through a plagiarism search service that identifies all the places on the Internet where words were copied exactly.
5. Many of the packaged courseware products, such as Blackboard and WebCT, have the ability to set availability dates and times for all assessments. Time limits and the number of permissible accesses

can also be set by the instructor, forcing students to work through online tests quickly, demonstrating their knowledge without having time to look up answers.

6 Many managed learning systems also have the capability of creating large question pools for randomized testing. Randomized question pools ensure that no two students will take exactly the same examination.

Finally, course systems, such as WebCT, can track the time, duration, and number of times that a student opens any sections of an online course. This is particularly true with assessments. Multiple accesses for short durations are definitely suspect.

Plagiarism

Plagiarism is using the ideas and writings of others and representing them as your own. Even if you do not copy another source word-for-word, but rather rephrase the source without attributing it to the original author by including a footnote, citation, or reference, you are guilty of plagiarism. Plagiarism is a serious violation of academic standards and, in most universities, is punishable with a failing grade and possible expulsion from the institution.

Using online sources ethically

One of the most important ethical issues which online learning raises is that of giving due credit or acknowledgement to the work of others. Online students sometimes have the misconception that copying things from online sources is acceptable. *That is not true*! Online communications, just like all other sources are automatically copyrighted at the moment they are created. The fact that you can access them easily or don't have to pay to use them does not mean it is acceptable for you to copy them without attributing citations to the author. This includes all online communications (e.g. emails, listservs, chat room transcripts, discussion board postings, etc.), as well as online content such as Web pages, images, music, videos, and flash animations. Whenever you are copying any content, even if it is to rephrase or summarize someone else's online writings or comments, you must properly cite the writer in your papers. If you do not cite the sources upon which your research is based, you will be guilty of plagiarism.

Remember Everything on the Internet is copyrighted at the moment of its creation. Even if it doesn't carry a copyright symbol or statement, it is still the property of the creator and needs to be properly cited.

Dynamic nature of online documents

The Internet is a rich repository of knowledge as well as a large source of teaching and learning materials. However, its dynamic state accounts for some of the confusion about the nature of online content, particularly when compared to the permanent status of paper-based resources. The Web presents the advantage of ease in updating and altering documents. Unfortunately, this flexibility also makes it simple to illegally copy documents.

These features could create an ethical dilemma for a student who in good faith may have cited materials from a URL listed in his or her research paper without realizing that the material may have been pirated. Similarly, the impermanence of Web-based resources, for example Web sites and documents being taken offline without notice of how to further gain access to such materials, makes it difficult for students to use them. If a student has quoted one such source in his or her work and it is no longer there when the instructor checks the site for accuracy and relevance, it may seem that the student has cheated or quoted a source incorrectly. Such a scenario, may call to question the moral integrity of the student.

Tip Use correct electronic citation techniques, as described in Chapter 7, to indicate the location online. Including the actual date you accessed the online material will also help verify your intent in making a proper citation.

As covered in Chapter 7, proper citations for online sources such as Web pages, FTP sites, listservs, discussion boards, and email correspondence include much of the same information as a print source. However, you must also add information about format, availability, and the date you viewed the site.

Minimum citation requirements

- author (if available)
- title
- publishing information (if available): city, publisher, year of publication

- format (online, CD-ROM, etc.)
- availability (address for site such as URL or telnet address)
- date of access (online sources only).

Example of an online article in APA format:

McVay, M. (1998, December). Facilitating knowledge construction and communication on the Internet. *The Technology Source*. Accessed Online August 15, 2003 at http://ts.mivu.org/default.asp?show=article&id=60

Remember Be sure to check with your instructors as to the exact requirements for citing online sources and the citation style you should use.

As you find resources on the Internet you will need to keep track of them so that you can record them in your assignments. Software programs such as EndNotes™ can help you with this if you have a lot to record. EndNotes provides a mechanism for accurately generating both internal references and bibliographies for a number of the most popular writing styles (e.g. APA, MLA, Chicago). The citation style you choose may depend on the style your instructor prefers or the discipline in which you are doing research. Though style is important to learn, what is more important is that you are consistent throughout your paper. There are many style manuals available that provide detailed explanations of how to format your citation. These style manuals have been published by professional organizations, such as the American Psychological Association (APA), or by an individual who is well regarded in academia. In addition to providing guidelines for how to cite sources, these manuals give background information on other elements of style such as page layout, punctuation, basic grammar, etc.

Additionally, there are a number of Websites that describe how to cite electronic resources. The Bedford St. Martins site mentioned in Chapter 7 is an excellent online resource for providing quick citation examples and sources. http://www.bedfordstmartins.com/online/citex.html.

File sharing with music and videos

Music and video file sharing has become a major problem at universities around the globe. Students downloading MP3 files, or running their own networks on university servers, have been using up bandwidth and in some instances not only slowing down but disabling the schools computer services. Furthermore, entertainment companies have been aggressively contacting university legal offices and serving subpoenas on computer records of student Internet access in order to catch those who are illegally downloading these files.

Many students mistakenly consider free downloads of music files from the Internet, whether unauthorized by the artist or not, an inalienable right. In a recent survey, American college students were asked if it was acceptable to arrest someone who stuck a dozen CDs under his jacket and tried to walk out of a record store, 96 percent of students indicated the arrest was deserved. However, when asked if downloading unlicensed MP3s or music files from KaZaA was also thievery, 72 percent said it was not and that no arrest would be warranted.

KaZaA and other peer networks make sharing files – particularly music and videos – seem painless. This type of sharing is in direct violation of copyright laws. It's easy to say something like, "The big rich music company won't miss my measly $15 to buy an album." Or "It's OK to download just a couple of songs because I don't want to buy the whole album." However, millions of people have been following this same logic and music and video companies have lost tens of millions of dollars in sales. Now entertainment companies are aggressively pursuing people who use these file-sharing networks, having them arrested, and filing expensive law suits to recoup their losses.

A recent article at CNN's news site describes the plight of a bright 17-year-old Princeton University student who downloaded music and videos and has now been arrested, convicted of theft, and is working to repay a fine of $15,000. http://www.cnn.com/2003/TECH/internet/06/27/music.sharing.column/ In Europe software companies joined with the film and music industry to launch an integrated anti-piracy hotline called FAST (The Federation Against Software Theft). The hotline was the first of its kind. It provides a single point of contact for members of the public, law enforcement agencies, the Internet and creative industries to get advice and information about film, music and software copyright issues, and to report piracy.

Remember It is illegal to make a copy of a music or film recording without the permission of the copyright owner, even for personal use. Court decisions worldwide consider economic and moral impacts of a breach. Industry is now aggressively pursuing thousands of violators around the world and serving notices. If caught, both you and the university may have to repay thousands of dollars. The way to your protect yourself is simply not to engage in this type of activity.

Software use and abuse

An overwhelming majority of students feel that software piracy and similar forms of unethical behavior are acceptable. The most commonly pirated software is the Windows™ operating system, followed by typical programs such as word processors, spreadsheets, image manipulation tools, and then special software required for a class. Not only do many students feel that it is okay for them to pirate software (particularly for use in their education) but they feel that piracy is normal behavior.

When you purchase a piece of software, you do not own that software. You have purchased the *right* to use the software. This right is usually limited to one machine (i.e., your personal computer). You cannot share it with a friend, copy it to another computer, or send it in the mail for someone else in your family to use.

What's the harm in making a few extra copies?

When extra software copies are used on university-owned computers, the harm could be great. Software publishers take piracy very seriously and have held many universities and the students involved liable for large monetary damages. Also, even for continued minor infringements, the university could lose its eligibility for educational discount pricing on software.

In the larger picture, copying cheats the publisher, the software authors, and everyone who uses the software. It makes software more costly and denies the publisher the sales it needs (and earned) to improve its product and finance new ones.

Should I report other people who share software?

Students usually know who is pirating software and who is not, but they don't want to be seen as a traitor. Most universities have posted standards of ethical conduct regarding computer usage on the Internet and in their school catalogs. As a student you agree to follow this ethical conduct. By staying silent, you'd violate those standards and could face disciplinary action yourself.

The ethical conduct policy will protect you from anyone else who might be upset by your honesty. Most schools endeavor to shield the identity of individuals providing information concerning possible violations, including fraud, as much as allowed within legal limits.

Misuse of computer resources – identification and authentication fraud

As students become more technologically savvy, some take advantage of their knowledge and use college and university systems for unethical purposes. One way you can help to stop this problem is to safeguard your personal computer identifications and passwords. Many students have unwittingly given their username and password to a "trusted" friend, only to find out their account was then the center of illegal activities. *Do not* let anyone know your username and password, even a friend.

Examples of computer misuse:

- Using a computer account that you are not authorized to operate.
- Giving someone else access to your computer account.
- Obtaining a password for a computer account without the consent of the account owner.
- Using the campus network to gain unauthorized access to other computer systems.
- Knowingly performing an act that will interfere with the normal operation of computers, terminals, peripherals, or networks.
- Knowingly running or installing on any computer system or network, or giving to another user, a program intended to damage or place excessive load on a computer system or network. This includes but is not limited to programs known as computer viruses, Trojan horses, and worms.
- Attempting to circumvent data protection schemes or uncover security loopholes.
- Violating terms of applicable software licensing agreements or copyright laws.
- Deliberately wasting computing resources.
- Using electronic mail to harass others.
- Masking the identity of an account or machine.
- Posting materials on electronic bulletin boards that violate existing laws or the university's codes of conduct.
- Attempting to monitor or tamper with another user's electronic communications, or reading, copying, changing, or deleting another user's files or software without the explicit agreement of the owner.

At the beginning of this chapter, ethics was defined as character. When you act in an ethical manner your good character is on display. If you engage in any of the unethical behaviors discussed in this chapter you may not get caught or get arrested, but your character will be on display to your instructors and your peers. Your behavior broadcasts your ethics; what they are is up to you.

Chapter 9

The future of learning technology

> We should all be concerned about the future because we will have to spend the rest of our lives there.
>
> (Charles Franklin Kettering, 1876–1958, *Seed for Thought*, 1949)

Approximately two decades ago, the common rule for keeping up to speed with changing technology in any career was to recommend investing one day a month on personal growth in your field. Today it is estimated that the half-life of technical knowledge in the computer field is about 18 months. General knowledge is 3 to 4 years. In order for companies to remain competitive, they require employees to be constantly learning and changing. Though you may not be a computer "wiz," your career is definitely linked to computers; and your company's success is linked to technology. You need to be in a continuous learning and change mode to be successful today.

So how do you establish an environment that helps you to continue your learning – to accurately assess what knowledge you will need before it is required? How do you know what courses to select, or in which certificate or degree programs to enroll? The first step is to set some career goals and then list what you need to know to get there. For example, you may be an auto mechanic who wants to become the shop foreman. In addition to keeping up to date on changes in technology with automobiles, you would benefit from taking courses in business principles, interpersonal management skills, and perhaps purchasing or budgeting. If you have a ten-year-old degree in business, it may be time for you to pursue an MBA in order to move up in your organization. Or maybe you just need to update your computer skills and can do so through a four-course certificate program offered at your local school or online. If you are unsure as to the next steps, make an appointment with a career counselor and get professional advice on expectations in the business world today.

Here are some tips for evaluating curriculum as you select the next steps in your continuous learning plan.

Tips

- Look for specific new technology and operational training opportunities that relate directly to your job. Training courses vary in length from one or two hours to several months and are generally technology specific.
- Evaluate the educational and experience credentials of your instructors. In the corporate marketplace, educational credentials may be sparse but experience is often greater. In academia, educational credentials are always present, but you need to evaluate whether the experience of the instructor fits your needs.
- Assess how your performance in the course will be evaluated. It's important to have a knowledgeable instructor who ensures you are mastering the concepts and skills. What are the course goals/objectives? Do they match what you want to learn?
- In the case of degrees, check the college or university accreditation. It offers some assurance as to the quality of education you will be receiving.

Learning technology in the near future

The future of technology in online education is toward diversification, increasing functionality and overlapping modes of learning. The benefit of participating in an online learning program is having the opportunity to access and use cutting-edge communication technology in your studies. Providers are offering more integrated options, such as text and video on the same channel, synchronous or asynchronous modalities, and one-on-one access to faculty (email and videoconferencing). For the undergraduate market, the fundamental need is to serve as wide as possible a community of users. This student group will grow even more rapidly as job options move from one nation to another and more developing countries have their network infrastructures in place. Online undergraduate education, as well as specific vocational skills training, will become the norm in the not too distant future.

As new technologies such as computer conferencing, virtual reality, artificial intelligence, and other media become more available, researchers in online education will be examining their use and effectiveness within instructional settings. This research will focus on learner characteristics, effective instructional strategies, and cost/benefit issues. Which media attributes are effective for certain learning tasks when learning online? Which learners are more likely to succeed in online education programs? How much structure and interaction is enough or too much for successful programs? What is the nature and meaning of interaction for the learners and teacher? What makes learners feel socially present in online environments? These are some of the questions that will be of central focus for future studies in the field of online education and will then impact the delivery of online education throughout the world.

Multiple-campus schools and independent instructors will become the norm

The competition for students, as well as the desire to serve a larger diversity of student learning needs, has already created an interesting trend toward partnerships among universities and community colleges, or outright merger and acquisition of smaller institutions in order to quickly gain expertise and faculty in particular subjects. Affiliations between institutions both nationally and internationally have proven to be especially valuable, providing a match of special subject matter expertise with multi-media instructional support and marketing experience spread across institutions. Additionally, technology alliances with corporations are already becoming the norm for many colleges looking to just-in-time learning opportunities for their employees.

The use of adjunct (part-time or independently contracted) instructors will become the norm rather than the exception, allowing schools to hire online professors from anywhere in the world without worrying about office space, location, or maintaining a permanent affiliation with the university. It is possible that some future instructors will choose to market their international reputation, well-known teaching skills, and special expertise without having to partner with only one university – netting themselves several teaching contracts at a variety of universities. This use of faculty has the potential to benefit both the university and the student. The university would have the advantage of a large potential pool of instructors for popular courses requiring more sections to be opened, as well as the capability to offer specialized courses beyond the capacity of its current staff. The student may have the opportunity to interact with professors who are well-known in the field, but don't necessarily reside at the home university. The diversity of experience and perspective will only enhance the teaching/learning mix.

The growing challenge of online education in the future is globalization. It is already conceivable that students will cross national borders as they select educational opportunities to pursue. Canadians, for example, are enrolling in US online programs in large numbers. Adding to the international flavor are residents of the Caribbean and Mexico. US citizens, on the other hand, may choose to enroll in online education courses offered in Canada, Europe, Asia or Australia. Education accreditation, transfer, and qualification will become a global concern, instead of just a regional or national one.

The Open University of the UK has already tackled many of the issues of global partnership. With its current student base of over 200,000 it already makes its courses available throughout Europe. In addition, it manages other institutional partnerships in over 30 non-EU countries. Today, about 26,000 students participate in Open University courses outside the UK.

Bandwidth possibilities

In the future, bandwidth will be almost unlimited. Bandwidth is the amount of information that can be quickly delivered from all servers to a computer. Today that standard falls around 48,000 to 52,000 bits per second. This equates to roughly a page of text, a medium-sized image, or a few video frames. Unfortunately, most dial-up connections are even slower than this. Bandwidth limitations preclude the use of innovative software programs that allow for more interaction, as well as multimedia and videoconferencing.

We are already seeing a change in the availability of bandwidth. In many Canadian and American cities cable television services are offering high speed access. Telephone companies are responding with better data compression technologies and special "clean" lines that don't compete with voice traffic. At the end of the 1990s, several governments partnered with private corporations have launched a network of low-earth-orbit satellites allowing for high-speed connections to be made available to improve communications and information exchanges in the fields of public health, medicine and the environment. Today, wireless technologies are appearing in airports and even in town squares. With many governments around the world investing heavily in high-speed data infrastructures, it points even more surely that greater bandwidth will become ubiquitous and inexpensive in the not too distant future.

Internet2

Internet2 is a consortium of universities, corporations, and affiliated organizations working together with various government funding packages around the world to develop and deploy advanced network applications and technologies. Begun in 1996, Internet2 developers were tasked with accelerating the creation of the next-generation Internet. Within only four years, Internet2 had already changed the way many do business in terms of research and distance education. The bandwidth available through participation in Internet2 provides universities, corporations, museums, libraries, hospitals, and others almost unlimited resources to move vast quantities of data internationally. Current applications focus primarily on research among universities and select institutions outside of the university setting. However, distance education is likely to be an even more widespread application in the long run. And for schools interested in attracting top notch faculty, Internet2 is rapidly becoming a benchmark for successful recruitment in many disciplines.

The Internet2 backbone only carries traffic related to university education and research. No commercial or personal traffic is allowed thereby ensuring sufficient capacity for high-bandwidth applications. The minimum connection to an Internet2 point of presence (PoP), is a 155 megabit per second OC-3 connection. Today and in the near future bandwidth is described in terms of optical carrier circuits (OC). Already OC48 connections (2.488 Gbps, 1,000 times faster) are common with large companies and national Internet service providers.

Internet2 is working to enable applications, such as telemedicine, digital libraries and virtual laboratories that are not possible with the technology underlying today's Internet. The following four categories exemplify some of the areas that are undergoing the most rapid development and will enhance teaching and learning.

Managed learning environments

Very little high quality instructional software is available to serve as the content basis for distributed instruction. Most educational software has been designed for stand-alone use, especially that which incorporates sound, image or video. Much of this is dependent on a single operating system. Internet2 provides an opportunity to work on a high-bandwidth architecture that will push the boundaries of interactive learning in multimedia and online distribution.

Digital libraries

The services and capabilities envisioned for Internet2 offer important opportunities to move the digital libraries program into new areas. Very high bandwidth and bandwidth reservation will allow continuous digital video and audio to move from research use (such as in the Carnegie-Mellon University Digital Library Project) to much broader application. Still images, audio and video can, at least from a delivery point of view, move into the mainstream currently occupied almost exclusively by textual resources. This will also facilitate more extensive research in the difficult problems of organizing, indexing, and providing intellectual access to these classes of materials.

Tele-immersion

Tele-immersion has the potential to significantly change educational, scientific and manufacturing paradigms. A tele-immersion system would allow individuals at different locations to share a single virtual environment. For example, participants would interact with a virtual group at a conference table approximating what would be possible in a physical room. The individuals could share and manipulate data, simulations and models of molecular, physical or economic constructs, and jointly participate in the simulation, design review or evaluation process.

Virtual laboratories

A virtual laboratory is a heterogeneous, distributed problem solving environment that enables a group of researchers located around the world to work together on a common set of projects. As with any other laboratory, the tools and techniques are specific to the domain of the research, but the basic infrastructure requirements are shared across disciplines. Although related to some of the applications of tele-immersion, the virtual laboratory does not assume the need for a shared immersive environment.

Electronic books

Many people have now seen, or at least heard about, the new consumer electronics appliances popularly called "e-books" or "electronic books" or (more accurately) "electronic book readers," though few have actually been sold. The traditional print book publishing houses, online booksellers such as Amazon.com and distributors such as Barnes & Noble are announcing a series of commercial ventures and alliances to produce material for electronic distribution.

New technologies – both in hardware appliances and in software for general purpose computers – will facilitate the use of e-books. With strong innovative companies, such as Adobe and Microsoft, championing the evolution of e-books, these new technologies should make digital books more convenient and more readable.

Functionality is the key driver of e-book acceptance. There are many benefits to using digital books. You can search 500 pages in a few seconds and you can carry a thousand books in a lightweight laptop. E-books are typically less expensive than printed books, and you can buy an e-book any time of the day or night and download it immediately to your reader.

Currently, the downloading process needs to be simplified and the reading platforms have to be stable and more lightweight. However, as more publishers come onboard and more consumers become used to reading online instead of holding a printed book, it is likely e-books will become more popular.

The cyborg millennium and interaction in the farther future

Revolutions in information technology and genetics continue to change and shape our lives. As these two fields become more entwined, the impact on diverse cultures becomes more evident. Change is occurring more quickly than most can comprehend – change in relationships, work, privacy, and personal responsibility. From workplace surveillance to mail retrieval, from pre-natal genetic screening to cloning, from human consciousness to artificial intelligence, there lurks both dangers and opportunities, as well as ethical ambiguities inherent in new technologies.

When most people think of cyborgs (part machine and part human), it is usually about the Borg in *Star Trek* or the Terminator in *Robocop*. But the metaphor of the cyborg already exists in our lives today. It is no longer simply the realm of science fiction. George Landow, at Brown University, estimates that at least one in every ten Americans are "fully endowed" cyborgs – people living with machines such as pacemakers, artificial joints, drug implant systems, implanted corneal lenses – the list increases daily. We live in an age of artificial hearts, cochlear implants and soon-to-be retinal implants (which utilize electronic-to-neural connections). We have artificial hips, legs, feet and even skin. Severely disabled people are using neurotrophic electrodes to move mouse cursors with their brain. And chips are being placed into humans while neurons grow and connect to them. We are beginning to physically bridge the physical gap between ourselves and our technologies.

In addition to the obvious physical adaptation to technology, many people also use machines for specific social, psychological, occupational, or behavioral purposes. For example, biofeedback machines are frequently used to manage stress or illness. Surgeons use lasers, airplane mechanics use augmented reality, pilots use flight simulators, and don't forget the millions of people around the world who go into a machine – their computer and access the Internet – to experience reality in cyberspace. The cyborg metaphor addresses the essence of high-technology life, defining complexity without excessive oversimplification, establishing a pattern that explains the human relationship to machines. It assumes that humans will strive to master their environment, both inside and outside their bodies, through the use of technology.

And this is just the embryonic stage of a much larger trend: our future will be inexorably tied to the cyber realm. Some scientists maintain that the human species will evolve into cyborgs. As engineer and futurist Bart Kosko proclaimed, "Biology is not destiny. It was never more than tendency. It was just nature's first quick and dirty way to compute with meat. Chips are destiny" (Kosko 1999).

Our integration with computers is moving at a quicker pace each day. Steve Mann, pioneer of wearable computing, has long immersed himself in various technologies. In examining his own experiences with the wearable computer, he recognizes both the dangers and possibilities of being constantly connected to cyberspace and makes important observations on such things as technology's existential impact, the difference between privacy and solitude and the threat of corporate and government surveillance. If one "wears" a computer at all times, how does that change learning and performance in the future? Would you be constantly learning?

Children in developed countries are growing up with technology surrounding them. The typical teenager in America can be found using Instant Messenger on the computer, while listening to a CD with a headset, simultaneously doing homework with a word processor while monitoring an online interactive game. All of this occurring with his or her cell phone at the ready. It is already hard for many to imagine what life was like before the microchip. Educators are already looking to take advantage of these technologies by delivering educational opportunities to cell phones, PDAs (personal digital assistants like Palm Pilots™) and, yes, to wearable computers.

Delivering education in the cyborg millennium

If computers become lightweight, wearable, and integrated into all parts of daily life it is likely that the expectations for education delivery will be that it is also completely integrated by being easy to access and available at any time. Students will also demand that they be allowed to customize learning by selecting how much or how little of any topic they need. Instead of registering for an entire class, a student would register for a topic or list of topics, or for an objective or goal to meet. The model of a group of people starting at the same time, studying the same materials at the same pace, and ending at the same time will be rare. Education in the future will be topic-based, and learning will not be paced by the teacher but by the student's own capacity to master the material. For example, rather than electing to take an entire course on statistics a student may elect only to take the topic on analysis of variance, because that is the only statistical analysis required to meet his or her immediate career goal. Any given student may at any time be taking any given topic, and progressing at a pace through that material appropriate to his or her learning ability.

Topics will be selected based on student interest, aptitude, educational level, and societal need. The menu of available topics will be determined by the individual's demonstrated prior learning. Selecting a topic will be as easy as selecting a channel on television is today. The daily menus will be varied to build on each day's achievement.

Artificial intelligence software will continually monitor the student's actions. In the process, it will identify optimal learning conditions in order to generate similar study conditions in the future and avoid strategies that prove ineffective. It will note areas of weak achievement or knowledge, then customize the program to include remedial material and/or to adjust the nature and speed of the delivery of instruction. The software's analysis of learning patterns and assessment data will also take into account the students' style preferences, problem-solving techniques, and stimulus requirements. It will adjust for these variations and thus, with newly developed learner-specific teaching materials, improve the individual performance of each user.

Imagine that most learning will be based on realistic simulations in three-dimensional environments. Stephen Downes, a Canadian researcher on the future of online learning environments, suggests that students will engage in knowledge quests – games and simulations presented at a variety of levels, based on their new understanding of concepts and skills. As students select a quest, they are joined by fellow-travelers attempting the same mission. Each role in the simulation serves different levels of the various players by presenting theories, models, and problems appropriate to them. Students will also be awarded points for leadership and demonstrating mastery knowledge by mentoring lower-level players. Some quests may be short – just a few minutes – while others may require a sustained commitment over several days.

The opportunities for education will definitely change. Before the microchip not a single science fiction writer had foreseen its invention. It is likely that technology and the delivery of education will go in a direction none of us can imagine. The question is will you fight this change or embrace it? Will you be ready to take advantage of it?

Remember You are responsible for your own learning. Grab for the gold ring of education wherever you find it!

Appendix

Academic Search Elite

Provides full text for over 1,500 journals covering the social sciences, humanities, general science, multicultural studies, education, and current affairs.

Access UN

Internet access to UN Documents and Publications since 1991. Bibliographic database and links to full-text of selected UN documents. Full text of Resolutions and Preliminary Verbatim reports.

America History and Life

Citations to articles on the history and culture of the United States and Canada from prehistory to the present. Citations drawn from over 2,000 journals in history, related humanities, and the social sciences. Includes citations to book reviews (appearing in 100 major history journals) and dissertations.

Anthropological Literature

Describes articles and essays on anthropology and archaeology, including art history, demography, economics, psychology, and religious studies. Updated quarterly, it indexes articles two or more pages long in works published in English and other European languages from the late 19th century to the present

Annual Reviews

In-depth literature and research reviews on topics of importance in the disciplines.

Biomedical science

Biochemistry, biomedical engineering, biophysics and biomolecular structure, cell and developmental biology, ecology and systematics, entomology, genetics, genomics and human genetics, immunology, medicine, microbiology, neuroscience, nutrition, pharmacology and toxicology, physiology, phytopathology, plant physiology and plant molecular biology, psychology, public health.

Physical science

Astronomy and astrophysics, biomedical engineering, biophysics and biomolecular structure, earth and planetary sciences, energy and the environment, fluid mechanics, materials science, nuclear and particle science, physical chemistry.

Social science

Anthropology, energy and the environment, political science, psychology, public health, sociology

Art Full Text

Provides indexing and abstracting of art periodicals published throughout the world. Full-text coverage for selected periodicals is also included. In addition to articles, it catalogs reproductions of works of art that appear in indexed periodicals

Avery Index to Architectural Periodicals

Indexes more than 1,000 periodicals published worldwide on archeology, city planning, interior design, and historic preservation, as well as architecture. Coverage reaches from the 1930s (with selective coverage dating back to the 1860s) to the present. With more than 229,000 records, it is updated daily.

CINAHL

The CINAHL (Nursing and Allied Health) database provides comprehensive coverage of the English language journal literature related to nursing and the allied health disciplines.

Dissertations Abstracts International

Includes citations for materials ranging from the first US dissertation, acknowledged in 1861, to those accepted as recently as last semester; those published from 1980 forward also include 350-word abstracts, written by the author. Citations for masters theses from 1988 forward include 150-word abstracts ... The database represents the work of authors from over 1,000 North American graduate schools and European universities.

EBSCO Host Web

Provides citations and full text articles, and in some databases reference materials from books and pamphlets. Databases include: Academic Search Elite, MasterFILE Premier, Health Source Plus, Business Source Elite and Newspaper Source.

Education Abstracts Full Text

Covers 423 core periodicals, monographs, and yearbooks in the field of education. Topics include a wide range of contemporary education issues, including government funding, instructional media, multicultural education, religious education, student counseling, competency-based, and information technology.

EI CompIndex Web

Supplies coverage of the world's engineering literature. It corresponds to the printed publication *Engineering Index*, plus additional conference records from the *Engineering Meeting* file.

Essay & General Literature Index

Citations to essays and articles contained in collections of theses and miscellaneous works published in the United States, Great Britain, and Canada. It focuses on the humanities and social sciences, with subject coverage ranging from economics, political science, and history to criticism of literary works, drama, and film.

Geobase

Provides citations to journals, books, monographs, conference proceedings, and reports. Subject coverage includes: cartography, climatology, energy, environment, geochemistry, geophysics, geomorphology, hydrology, meteorology, paleontology, petrology, photogrammetry, sedimentology, volcanology.

Global Access (Disclosure Inc.)

Database provides access to financial and management data for US and international companies. Data include 10-year financial histories, company profiles, and stock market performance.

Grangers World of Poetry

Provides citations to poems published in poetry anthologies. Also includes approximately 13,000 poems in full text as well as added reference material – biographies, bibliographies, commentaries and a glossary.

Grove Music

Includes full text of dictionary articles supplemented with sound clips, images and links to relevant Web materials.

Health Source Plus

Citations and some full text for medical journals, consumer health magazines, health newsletters, reference books, referral information, topical overviews, pamphlets and newspaper articles.

Historical Abstracts

Citations and abstracts for articles from 2,000 journals published worldwide in history, the social sciences, and related humanities. Includes citations to new books reviewed in key English-language history and review journals and to relevant dissertations.

Humanities Index

Citations to ±500 English-language periodicals in the areas of archaeology, classical studies, art, performing arts, philosophy, history, music, linguistics, literature, and religion. Provides article citations to the major journals in these disciplines.

Inter-Play

Indexes plays in collections, anthologies, and periodicals. It presently contains more than 17,500 citations to plays in many languages.

Lexis-Nexus

Provides a variety of full text sources including: regional, national, and international newspapers; magazines; wire services; business publications (trade journals, corporate annual reports, tax sources); legal resources (law reviews, court cases, briefs, federal and state codes); government documents; medical information (medical journals); and reference sources (directories, biographical information).

MathSciNet

Covers research literature from all areas of mathematics, both theoretical and applied, and also covers related areas such as computer science, engineering, physics and statistics. This database corresponds to the printed indexes, *Mathematical Reviews* and *Current Mathematical Publications*. Abstracts and indexing.

MedLine

Covers the international literature on biomedicine, including the allied health fields and the biological and physical sciences, humanities, and information science as they relate to medicine and health care.

Music Index

Citations and indexing drawn from 640 international music periodicals.

Oxford Reference Online

Multidisciplinary database of approximately 100 dictionaries, handbooks and other reference books published by Oxford University Press.

PAIS

Database contains abstracts of journal articles, books, statistical yearbooks, directories, conference proceedings, research reports and government documents covering topics in public and social policy, business, economics, finance, law, international relations, public administration, government, political science, and other social sciences – with emphasis on issues that are or might become the subjects of legislation.

Political Science Abstracts

Citations, indexing and abstracts for journal articles in political science and its complementary fields, including international relations, law, and public administration/policy. The database, published since 1967, covers over 1000 journals drawn from the international serials literature.

PsychINFO

Covers the professional and academic literature in psychology and related disciplines including medicine, psychiatry, nursing, sociology, education, pharmacology, physiology, and linguistics.

Zoological Record

Coverage of the world's zoological and animal science literature, covering all research from biochemistry to veterinary medicine. The database provides an easily searched collection of references from over 4,500 international serial publications, plus books, meetings, reviews and other non serial literature from over 100 countries.

Glossary

Adapted from *Glossary of Internet Terms*, Copyright © 1994–2003 by Matisse Enzer. Used by permission under the Creative Commons and Open Content Licenses. The URL of the complete document is: http://www.matisse.net/files/glossary.html which is where you can look for the latest, most complete version. SMALL CAPITALS indicate a corresponding entry elsewhere in the glossary.

applet A small JAVA program that can be embedded in an HTML page. Applets differ from fully-fledged Java applications in that they are not allowed to access certain resources on the local computer, such as files and serial devices (modems, printers, etc.), and are prohibited from communicating with most other computers across a network. The common rule is that an applet can only make an Internet connection to the computer from which the applet was sent.

backbone A high-speed line or series of connections that forms a major pathway within a network. The term is relative as a backbone in a small NETWORK will likely be much smaller than many non-backbone lines in a large network.

bandwidth How much stuff you can send through a connection. Usually measured in bits-per-second. A full page of English text is about 16,000 bits. A fast modem can move about 57,000 bits in one second. Full-motion full-screen video would require roughly 10,000,000 bits-per-second (BPS), depending on compression.

blog – (web log) A blog is basically a journal that is available on the WEB. The activity of updating a blog is "blogging" and someone who keeps a blog is a "blogger." Blogs are typically updated daily using software that allows people with little or no technical background to update and maintain the blog.

Postings on a blog are almost always arranged in chronological order with the most recent additions featured most prominantly.

bps – (bits-per-second) A measurement of how fast data is moved from one place to another. A 56K MODEM can move about 57,000 bits-per-second.

browser A CLIENT program (software) that is used to look at various kinds of Internet resources.

CGI – (common gateway interface) A set of rules that describe how a Web SERVER communicates with another piece of software on the same machine, and how the other piece of software (the CGI program) talks to the Web server. Any piece of software can be a CGI program if it handles input and output according to the CGI standard.

client A software program that is used to contact and obtain data from a SERVER software program on another computer, often across a great distance. Each client program is designed to work with one or more specific kinds of server programs, and each server requires a specific kind of client. A Web BROWSER is a specific kind of client.

cookie The most common meaning of "Cookie" on the Internet refers to a piece of information sent by a Web SERVER to a Web BROWSER that the browser software is expected to save and to send back to the server whenever the browser makes additional requests from the server.

Depending on the type of cookie used, and the browser's settings, the browser may accept or not accept the cookie, and may save the cookie for either a short time or a long time.

Cookies might contain information such as login or registration information, online "shopping cart" information, user preferences, etc.

When a server receives a request from a browser that includes a cookie, the server is able to use the information stored in the cookie. For example, the server might customize what is sent back to the user, or keep a log of particular users' requests.

Cookies are usually set to expire after a predetermined amount of time and are usually saved in memory until the browser software is closed down, at which time they may be saved to disk if their "expire time" has not been reached.

Cookies do not read your hard drive and send your life story to the CIA, but they can be used to gather more information about a user than would be possible without them.

cyberspace Term originated by author William Gibson in his novel *Neuromancer* the word cyberspace is currently used to describe the whole range of information resources available through computer networks.

DNS – (domain name system) The domain name system is the system that translates Internet DOMAIN NAMES into IP numbers. A "DNS server" is a SERVER that performs this kind of translation.

domain name The unique name that identifies an Internet site (i.e. www.pdx.edu). Domain names always have two or more parts, separated by dots. The part on the left is the most specific – naming a location, whereas the part on the right is the most general – referring to the type of entity using the name (e.g. "edu" for education or "com" for commercial).

download Transferring data (usually a file) from a another computer to the computer you are using. The opposite of UPLOAD.

DSL – (digital subscriber line) A method for moving data over regular phone lines. A DSL circuit is much faster than a regular phone connection, and the wires coming into the subscriber's premises are the same (copper) wires used for regular phone service. A common configuration of DSL allows downloads at speeds of up to 1.544 megabits (not megabytes) per second, and uploads at speeds of 128 kilobits-per-second. Another common configuration is symmetrical: 384 kilobits-per-second in both directions.

email – (electronic mail) Messages, usually text, sent from one person to another via computer. Email can also be sent automatically to a large number of addresses.

FAQ – (frequently asked questions) Documents that list and answer the most common questions on a particular subject. There are hundreds of FAQs on subjects as diverse as pet grooming and cryptography. FAQs are usually written by people who have tired of answering the same question over and over.

fire wall A combination of hardware and software that separates a NETWORK into two or more parts for security purposes.

flame Originally, "flame" meant to carry forth in a passionate manner in the spirit of honorable debate. Flames most often involved the use of flowery language and flaming well was an art form. More recently flame has come to refer to any kind of derogatory comment no matter how witless or crude.

flame war When an online discussion degenerates into a series of personal attacks against the debators, rather than discussion of their positions. A heated exchange.

FTP – (file transfer protocol) A very common method of moving files between two Internet sites. FTP is a way to LOGIN to another Internet site for the purposes of retrieving and/or sending files. There are many Internet sites that have established publicly accessible repositories of material that can be obtained using FTP, by logging in using the account name "anonymous", thus these sites are called "anonymous ftp servers."

GIF – (graphic interchange format) A common format for image files, especially suitable for images containing large areas of the same color. GIF format files of simple images are often smaller than the same file would be if stored in JPEG format, but GIF format does not store photographic images as well as JPEG.

gigabyte 1000 or 1024 MEGABYTES, depending on who is measuring.

home page – (or homepage) Several meanings. Originally, the WEB page that your BROWSER is set to use when it starts up. The more common meaning refers to the main Web page for a business, organization, person or simply the main page out of a collection of web pages, e.g. "Check out so-and-so's new home page."

host Any computer on a NETWORK that is a repository for services available to other computers on the network. It is quite common to have one host machine provide several services, such as SMTP (email) and HTTP (web).

HTML – (hypertext markup language) The coding language used to create HYPERTEXT documents for use on the World Wide Web (www). HTML looks a lot like old-fashioned typesetting code, where you surround a block of text with codes that indicate how it should appear.

The "hyper" in hypertext comes from the fact that in HTML you can specify that a block of text, or an image, is linked to another file on the Internet. HTML files are meant to be viewed using a "Web browser".

HTTP – (hypertext transfer protocol) The protocol for moving HYPERTEXT files across the Internet. Requires a HTTP CLIENT program on one end, and an HTTP SERVER program on the other end. HTTP is the most important protocol used in the World Wide Web (www).

hypertext Generally, any text that contains links to other documents – words or phrases in the document that can be chosen by a reader and which cause another document to be retrieved and displayed.

IRC – (internet relay chat) Basically a huge multi-user live chat facility. There are a number of major IRC SERVERS around the world which are linked to each other. Anyone can create a channel and anything that anyone types in a given channel is seen by all others in the channel. Private channels can (and are) created for multi-person conference calls.

ISDN – (integrated services digital network) Basically a way to move more data over existing regular phone lines. ISDN is available to much of the USA and in most markets it is priced very comparably to standard analog phone circuits. It can provide speeds of roughly 128,000 BITS-PER-SECOND over regular phone lines. In practice, most people will be limited to 56,000or 64,000 bits-per-second.

ISP – (internet service provider) An institution that provides access to the Internet in some form, usually for money. Your university may also be considered an ISP if it allows students to access the Internet from off campus by using the university SERVER.

Java Java is a NETWORK-friendly programming language invented by Sun Microsystems. Java is often used to build large, complex systems that involve several different computers interacting across networks, for example transaction processing systems. Java is also becoming popular for creating programs that run in small electronic devices, such as mobile telephones.

A very common use of Java is to create programs that can be safely downloaded to your computer through the Internet and immediately run without fear of viruses or other harm to your computer or files. Using small Java programs (called "APPLETS"), Web pages can include functions such as animations, calculators, and other fancy tricks.

JPEG – (joint photographic experts group) JPEG is most commonly mentioned as a format for image files. JPEG format is preferred to the GIF format for photographic images as opposed to line art or simple logo art.

kilobyte A thousand bytes. Actually, usually 1024 (2^{10}) bytes.

LAN – (local area network) A computer NETWORK limited to the immediate area, usually the same building or floor of a building.

Listserv ® The most common kind of maillist, "Listserv" is a registered trademark of L-Soft International, Inc. Listservs originated on BITNET but they are now common on the Internet.

login Noun or a verb.

- Noun: The account name used to gain access to a computer system. Not a secret (contrast with PASSWORD).
- Verb: the act of connecting to a computer system by giving your credentials (usually your "username" and "password").

megabyte A million bytes. Actually, technically, 1024 KILOBYTES.

meta tag A specific kind of HTML tag that contains information not normally displayed to the user. Meta tags contain information about the page itself, hence the name ("meta" means "about this subject").

Typical uses of meta tags are to include information for SEARCH ENGINES to help them better categorize a page. You can see the meta tags in a page if you view the pages' source code.

modem – (*mo*dulator, *dem*odulator) A device that connects a computer to a phone line. A telephone for a computer. A modem allows a computer to talk to other computers through the phone system. Basically, modems do for computers what a telephone does for humans.

MOO – (MUD, Object Oriented) One of several kinds of multi-user role-playing environments.

MUD (multi-user dungeon or dimension) A (usually text-based) multi-user simulation environment. Some are purely for fun and flirting, others are used for serious software development, or education purposes and all that lies in between. A significant feature of most MUDs is that users can create things that stay after they leave and which other users can interact within their absence, thus allowing a world to be built gradually and collectively.

netiquette The etiquette on the Internet.

netizen Derived from the term citizen, referring to a citizen of the Internet, or someone who uses networked resources. The term connotes civic responsibility and participation.

network Any time you connect two or more computers together so that they can share resources, you have a computer network. Connect two or more networks together and you have an internet.

newsgroup The name for discussion groups on USENET.

password A code used to gain access (LOGIN) to a locked system. Good passwords contain letters and non-letters and are not simple combinations such as *virtue*7.

plug-in A (usually small) piece of software that adds features to a larger piece of software. Common examples are plug-ins for the Netscape® BROWSER and Web SERVER. Adobe Photoshop® also uses plug-ins.

PNG – (portable network graphics) PNG is a graphics format specifically designed for use on the World Wide Web (WWW). PNG enable compression of images without any loss of quality, including high-resolution images. Another important feature of PNG is that anyone may create software that works with PNG images without paying any fees – the PNG standard is free of any licensing costs.

POP – (point of presence, also post office protocol) A point of presence usually means a city or location where a NETWORK can be connected to, often with dial-up phone lines. So if an Internet company says they will soon have a POP in Belgrade, it means that they will soon have a local phone number in Belgrade and/or a place where leased lines can connect to their network.

A second meaning, post office protocol refers to a way that email CLIENT software such as Eudora gets mail from a mail SERVER. When you obtain an account from an INTERNET SERVICE PROVIDER (ISP) you almost always get a POP account with it, and it is this POP account that you tell your email software to use to get your mail. Another protocol called IMAP is replacing POP for email.

port This term has three meanings.

- First and most generally, a place where information goes into or out of a computer, or both, e.g. the serial port on a personal computer is where a MODEM would be connected.
- On the Internet port often refers to a number that is part of a URL, appearing after a colon (:) right after the DOMAIN NAME. Every service on an Internet server listens on a particular port number on that SERVER. Most services have standard port numbers, e.g. Web servers normally listen on port 80. Services can also listen on non-standard ports, in which case the port number must be specified in a URL when accessing the server, so you might see a URL of the form: webct.pdx.edu:8900. This shows a WebCT server running on a non-standard port (the standard Internet port is 80).
- Finally, port also refers to translating a piece of software to bring it from one type of computer system to another, e.g. to translate a Windows program so that it will run on a Macintosh.

portal Usually used as a marketing term to describe a Website that is or is intended to be the first place people see when using the Web. Typically a "portal site" has a catalog of Websites, a SEARCH ENGINE, or both. A portal site may also offer email and other service to entice people to use that site as their main "point of entry" (hence "portal") to the Web.

posting A single message entered into a NETWORK communications system.

proxy server A proxy server sits between a CLIENT and the "real" SERVER that a client is trying to use. This often happens with online library services. The client makes all of its requests to the proxy server, which then makes requests to the "real" server and passes the result back to the client. In a library system this is important to protect access to expensive resources like online journal databases.

search engine A system for searching the information available on the Web. Some search engines work by automatically searching the contents of other systems and creating a database of the results. Other search engines contains only material manually approved for inclusion in a database, and some combine the two approaches.

server A computer, or a software package, that provides a specific kind of service to *client* software running on other computers. The term can refer to a particular piece of software, such as a WWW server, or to the machine on which the software is running, e.g. "Our mail server is down today, that's why email isn't working." A single server machine can (and often does) have several different server software packages running on it, thus providing many different servers to clients on the NETWORK. Sometimes server software is designed so that additional capabilities can be added to the main program by adding small programs known as servlets.

spam – (or spamming) An inappropriate attempt to use a mailing list or other networked communications facility as if it was a broadcast medium (which it is not) by sending the same message to a large number of people who did not ask for it. The term probably comes from a famous Monty Python skit which featured the word spam repeated over and over. The term may also have come from someone's low opinion of the food product with the same name. (Spam® is a registered trademark of Hormel Corporation, for its processed meat product.)

T-1 A leased-line connection capable of carrying data at 1,544,000 bits-per-second (BPS). At maximum theoretical capacity, a T-1 line could move a MEGABYTE in less than 10 seconds. That is still not fast enough for full-screen, full-motion video, for which you need at least 10,000,000 bps. T-1 lines are commonly used to connect large LANs to the Internet.

T-3 A leased-line connection capable of carrying data at 44,736,000 BPS. This is more than enough to do full-screen, full-motion video.

TCP/IP – (transmission control protocol/internet protocol) This is the suite of protocols that defines the Internet. Originally designed for the UNIX operating system, TCP/IP software is now included with every major kind of computer operating system. To be truly on the Internet, your computer must have TCP/IP software.

Trojan horse A computer program that is either hidden inside another program or that masquerades as something it is not in order to trick potential users into running it. For example, a program that appears to be a game or image file but in reality performs some other function. A Trojan horse computer program may spread itself by sending copies of itself from the host computer to other computers, but unlike a VIRUS it will (usually) not infect other programs.

upload Transferring data (usually a file) from the computer you are using to another computer. The opposite of DOWNLOAD.

URL – (uniform resource locator) The term URL is most often used to describe an Internet address (i.e. http://www.pdx.edu), file, or other resource on the Web. The URL contains the protocol of the resource (e.g. http:// or ftp://), the domain name for the resource (e.g. www.pdx.edu), and the hierarchical name for the file (e.g. index.html).

virus A chunk of computer programming code that makes copies of itself without any concious human intervention. Some viruses do more than simply replicate themselves, they might display messages, install other software or files, delete software of files, etc.

A virus requires the presence of some other program to replicate itself. Typically, viruses spread by attaching themselves to programs and in some cases files, for example the file formats for Microsoft word processor and spreadsheet programs allow the inclusion of programs called "macros" which can in some cases be a breeding ground for viruses.

Web Short for "World Wide Web." See WWW.

Web page A document designed for viewing in a WEB BROWSER. Typically written in HTML.

worm A worm is a VIRUS that does not infect other programs. It makes copies of itself, and infects additional computers (typically by making use of NETWORK connections) but does not attach itself to additional programs; however a worm might alter, install, or destroy files and programs.

WWW – (World Wide Web) World Wide Web (or simply Web for short) is a term frequently used (incorrectly) when referring to "The Internet", WWW has two major meanings:

- First, loosely used: the whole constellation of resources that can be accessed using Gopher, FTP, HTTP, telnet, USENET, WAIS and some other tools.
- Second, the universe of HYPERTEXT SERVERS (HTTP servers), more commonly called "web servers", which are the servers that serve web pages to web browsers.

Bibliography

Andrusyzyn, M.A. and Davie, L. (1995) Reflection as a design tool in computer-mediated education. *Proceedings of the Distance Education Conference: Bridging Research and Practice*, San Antonio, TX: Texas A&M University.

Baxter Magolda, M. (1992) *Knowing and Reasoning in College: Gender-related Patterns in Students' Intellectual Development*, San Francisco: Jossey-Bass.

Beaudoin, M. (1990) The instructor's changing role in distance education. *The American Journal of Distance Education,* 4(2), 21–9.

Belenky, M.F. (1986) *Women's Ways of Knowing: The Development of Self, Voice, and Mind*, New York: Basic Books.

Brey, R. (1991) *U.S. Postsecondary Distance Learning Programs in the 1990s: A Decade of Growth*. Washington, DC: The Instructional Telecommunications Consortium/American Association of Community and Junior Colleges.

Collis, B. (1996) *Tele-learning in a Digital World: The Future of Distance Learning*, London: International Thomson Publications.

Croasdale, M. (2002) Virtual medical school may become a reality. *Amednews.com*, 45(45) December 2. Available online http://www.ama-assn.org/amedews/2002/12/02/prsa1202.htm.

Daniel, J. (1999) *Mega-Universities and Knowledge Media: Technology Strategies for Higher Education*, London: Kogan Page.

Davis, S. and Botkin, J. (1995) *The Monster Under the Bed*, New York: Simon and Schuster.

Downes, S. (1998) *The Future of Online Learning*, Brandon, Manitoba, Canada. Available online http://www.atl.ualberta.ca/downes/future.

Dunn, R., Dunn, K., and Price, G. (1982) *Manual: Productivity Environmental Preference Survey*, Lawrence, KS: Price Systems.

Eisenstadt, M. (1995) *The Times Higher Education Supplement*, Multimedia Section, April, vi–vii.

Hartley, D. (2000) *On-Demand Learning: Training in the New Millennium*, Amherst, MA: HRD Press.

ITAA (October 2002) e-health: virtual medical school created by colleges in 16 countries. Available online http://www.itaa.org/isec/pubs/e200210-04.pdf.

Jonassen, D.H., Davidson, M., Collins, M., Campbell, J. and Haag, B.B. (1995) Constructivism and computer-mediated communication in distance education. *The American Journal of Distance Education*, 9(2), 7–26, 33.

Kasko, B. (1999) *Heaven in a Chip: Fuzzy Visions of Society and Science in the Digital Age*, New York: Random House.

Kearsley, G. (2000) *Online Education: Learning and Teaching in Cyberspace*, Toronto: Wadsworth/Nelson Thompson Learning.

Kolb, D.A. (1984) *Experiential Learning*, Englewood Cliffs, NJ: Prentice-Hall.

Kuwait Institute for Medical Specialization Bulletin (2002) The International Virtual Medical School (IVIMEDS), 1, 9–44. Available online http://kims.org.kw/bulletin/Issues/issue2/IVIMEDS.pdf.

Latham, S., Slade, A.L. and Budnick, C. (1991) *Library Services for Off-Campus and Distance Education: An Annotated Bibliography*, Ottawa: Canadian Library Association.

Lynch, M. (July 2003) Member profile – focus on Africa, Dr. John Afele. *WAOE Electronic Bulletin*, 3(2). Available online http://waoe.org/communication/webframe3-july.htm.

McVay, M. (2000) *How to be a Successful Distance Learning Student: Learning on the Internet*, Needham Heights, MA: Pearson.

Mingle, J. (1995) Vision and reality for technology-based delivery systems in postsecondary education. Paper presented at the Governor's Conference on Higher Education, St Louis.

Moore, M.G. and Thompson, M.M., with Quigley, A.B., Clark, G.C. and Goff, G.G. (1990) *The Effects of Distance Learning: A Summary of the Literature*, Research Monograph No. 2. University Park, PA: The Pennsylvania State University, American Center for the Study of Distance Education.

Myers, S. and Filner, B. (1997) *Conflict Resolution Across Cultures: From Talking it Out to Mediation*, Amherst, MA: Amherst Educational.

Perry, W.G., Jr. (1970) *Forms of Intellectual and Ethical Development in the College Years: A Scheme*, New York: Holt, Rinehart and Winston.

Reiser, R.A. (1987) Instructional technology: a history. In R. Gagne (ed.) *Instructional Technology: Foundations*, Hillsdale: Lawrence Erlbaum.

Sachs, S.G. (1991b) Teaching thinking skills to distant learners. *Tech Trends*, 36(1) Jan/Feb, 28–32.

Slavin, R.E. (1987) *Cooperative Learning: Student Teams*, Washington, DC: National Education Association.

Slavin, R.E. (1990) *Cooperative Learning: Theory, Research and Practice*, Englewood Cliffs, NJ: Prentice Hall.

Subramanian, K. (2000) Education for all in the new millennium – vision for India 2020. Available online: http://www.tenet.res.in/commsphere/s9.4.pdf.

Suler, J. (2002) The basic psychological features of cyberspace. In *The Psychology of Cyberspace*. Available online: http://www.rider.edu/suler/psycyber/basicfeat.html.

Turner, S.J. (2002) Dean shapes curriculum for virtual medical school. *Brown University George Street Journal*, November 15. Available online http://www.brown.edu/Administration/George_Street_Journal/vol27/27GSJ12a.html.

Werry, C. and Mowbray, M. (eds) (2001) *Online Communities: Commerce, Community Action, and the Virtual University*. Upper Saddle River, NJ: Prentice Hall/Hewlett Packard Professional Books.

Index

Best of

TIN HOUSE

STORIES

Foreword by Dorothy Allison

CONTRA COSTA COUNTY LIBRARY

3 1901 04037 1405

Copyright © 2006 by Tin House Books

Additional copyright information can be found on pages 446–47.

All rights reserved. No part of this book may be used or reproduced in any manner whatsoever without written permission from the publisher except in the case of brief quotations embodied in critical articles or reviews. For information, contact Tin House Books, 2601 NW Thurman St., Portland, OR 97210.

Published by Tin House Books, Portland, Oregon, and New York, New York
Distributed to the trade by Publishers Group West, 1700 Fourth St., Berkeley, CA 94710, www.pgw.com

ISBN 0-9773127-1-2

First U.S. Edition 2006

Cover and interior design by Laura Shaw Design, Inc.

www.tinhouse.com

Printed in Canada

CONTRA COSTA COUNTY LIBRARY

CONTENTS

FOREWORD

MY SON TELLS ME he never wants to be a writer "because writers work all the time." He wants to be a chiropractor, he thinks. That way he can help people and have regular office hours.

I understand. Regular office hours and measurable sources of validation—money earned or thank you notes—all are fine things but are far from how most storytellers determine their worth. Money earned is uncertain, and fairly irrelevant to the quality of a story. Great writers often go begging and facile storytellers sometimes fall into small fortunes. A writer's fate seems as fickle as lust or weather, and not the point anyway.

If one believes in a world of story, a terrain in which short stories, novels, and memoirs intersect to create a reality as powerful and as full as human history itself, then being part of that creation offers a sense of validation and purpose that subsumes awards bestowed or money paid. You want your story to meet all other stories, to become part of the great human narrative, to shape how people think about themselves and their history. I truly believe that human change takes place through story, that we can only become what we can imagine, and that imagination is constantly in the process of being augmented, enlarged, or diminished. Small narratives, reductively cruel stories, and mean-spirited tales diminish us. Large-souled narratives—attempts to fully understand individuals and communities, to portray us fully and with compassion—enlarge us, making us more than we have been seen to be before. It is how we imagine ourselves that can be changed, and no political slogan, no matter how catchy or rhythmic, is as powerful as a narrative that takes us inside someone we have never imagined before or pulls us inside someone we have always dismissed or held in contempt and makes us see that person in new and deeper ways.

A short story opens the door to a brightly lit room. It calls us out of darkness, makes sense of what cannot be explained, and validates the most commonplace choices of our daily lives. Of course every now and then a story does another thing entirely. It stops us cold and leaves us sitting stunned. But there are lifetime truths to which sitting stunned is the only response—certainly preferable to burying ourselves in distraction or loud noisy babble.

Loud noisy babble is in fact what we seem to have far too much of these days.

I grew up with the notion that democracy was maintained and strengthened by the writer. I believed that a free and critical press was always out there examining and exposing what lay behind the big events of the day. I believed that lies would be revealed and nefarious plots exposed. I believed that truth would trigger an awakened citizenry to act to restore free and open process. But these days it seems our national dialogue is choked by a massive onslaught of misrepresentation, a steady tide of argument and counterargument buried in irrelevant or misleading opinion. What comes through most of our media these days are reductionist caricatures that serve only simple-minded social or political agendas. What seems trustworthy one day is debunked or buried the next, and it grows more and more difficult to sort out advertisement and propaganda from genuine research or carefully verified intelligence. There is so much information, and so little of it that we can genuinely trust or know how to interpret. It comes in waves that almost drown any sense of how we can recognize what is true, meaningful, or revelatory. How then can we know how to act as citizens of this complicated new state?

I counter the news by talking to people all the time—young women trying to decide whether to sign up for another stint in the National Guard, middle-aged men worrying about what is going to happen to their teenagers in another five or six years, aging baby-boomers trying to figure out what is going on by comparing today's struggles to their own youth during the anti-Vietnam War campaigns or the civil rights movements of the sixties and seventies. *It's all different, isn't it?* they say. And it is.

I need to refute the black hole of meaninglessness that is carried along on the conviction that we are living in the end-time, the prelude to the apocalypse that becomes the excuse for doing nothing, or the explanation for the short-sighted, self-centered, "me and mine first" mentality that dominates so much of what we hear and see from our news media these days. In the midst of a daunting sense of being deliberately led into fearful anxiety, I try to shore up my sense of a resilient, compassionate citizenry still striving to live with integrity and social conscience. To manage this, I need to believe that individual lives matter, that individuals have the capacity to affect national events, and that what each and every one of us chooses to do or not do in his or her daily life has meaning for the greater number of us. In this most embattled of times, I'm trying to maintain a semblance of optimism, or, at the least, hopeful pragmatism. And always I am surrounded by people doing the same thing, all of us fighting off a sense of dread and uncertainty.

How can we do this?

Some days we don't. Some days despair seems reasonable indeed. But fighting it is vital. Not giving up seems the least I can do, and some days I only manage by stepping out of the fray, by picking up a magazine or journal or paperback anthology. I shore myself up with story, reading as widely as I can narratives that strengthen my sense of justice, purpose, and meaning. It is in story that I find what I so desperately need—the refutation of despair, the clarion call of hope—not sanitized, one-note, bleached-out depictions of robotic indistinguishable caricatures, but multilayered, deeply compassionate portraits of the complicated, difficult people I see all around me and love with my whole heart. In times like these it is to art that we look for understanding—to find the passionate rebel voice that speaks honestly, the perspective not steered by the desire for wealth and fame but by the need to put on the page a genuinely true portrait of the hidden and unseen lives all around us. It is how I shape my sense of the world, our times, and what is really going on against an onslaught of misrepresentation, disdain, and outright falsehood. I need this multilayered complex view of human nature if I am to continue to try to be my own kind of full citizen, good mother, and responsible member of society.

Rereading the stories that have been pulled from *Tin House* magazine to compile this anthology, I remembered what it is I love about fiction: the way that story—the deliberate act of making up lives—can become an act of truth. How extraordinary that these writers should, through telling lies, be countering the great lies that are stalking and misshaping our democracy. Here you will find stories that refute the simple line-driven narrative of a callous, contemptible, self-absorbed culture. Here are stories that complicate what has been reduced, minimized, or denied—the way individuals choose to make their lives extraordinary, to resist despair or fall to it after struggling against it, to value their own lives and those around them, or to deny what they know or fear or hope to accomplish.

I need the full range of the stories you will find in this collection, tales by Deborah Eisenberg, Pinckney Benedict, Marshall N. Klimasewiski, Elizabeth Tallent, Robert Olen Butler, Frances Hwang, Jim Shepherd, Martha McPhee, Denis Johnson, and Stacey Richter. I need the Chinese grandfather, the grown-up damaged boy-child, the stubborn young woman with a death sentence flirting with the woman across the table from her, and the black-hearted, despairing soldier asking himself questions he cannot answer. I stack full-color creations against black-and-white headlines—the pogue in Anthony Swofford's grief-stricken Iraqi landscape, the mechanical boy leaking tears in Ryan Harty's "Why the Sky Turns Red When the Sun Goes Down," or the farmer in Pinckney Benedict's "Mudman" fashioning his golem with a wasp-wing heart. What is most unexpected is the way that the unreal can redefine the real, as with Aimee Bender's little man who reveals the grotesque in his full-size captor or the breathless stubbornness of the security officer in Julia Slavin's "Squatters" who takes me back to my childhood dreams of moving into the Sears, Roebuck store and sleeping between fresh clean sheets every night. Nothing here is what you thought it would be. Every new story turns the prism and shines new color on how the world around us is both what it was and yet startlingly, astonishingly new.

Here you will find complicated, deep portraits of the human that sing of worth and hope and endurance. Here are surprises, introductions to people who cannot be rendered by a few sound bites on the evening news or through downloading someone's Podcast or reading an online blog. Ellen Litman, Jung H. Yun, and Natasha Radojcic will show you women you won't find in the headlines. David Benioff, Steve Almond, and Howard Luxenberg will take you beyond the cardboard stereotypes of young men on reality television. Few of the characters are in control of their lives, few have the energy to worry about why.

Still, they startle me, and win me over—sometimes in spite of my resistance. I have no impulse to sympathize with the gout-ravaged aging lover in Amy Bloom's "I Love to See You Coming, I Hate to See You Go," but by the time he lies miserably in that icy bed while his now ex-girlfriend gives him a cold eye, I am shivering myself. And, truly, I want to stand apart from the matter-of-fact rage expressed by the daughters in "Shades of Mango" by Natasha Radojcic and "End of Messages" by Lucia Nevai. Their sharp-toothed misery burns over decades and the protagonist of the latter wants me to believe that she and her father are unjustly punished for being wealthy. "Rich people," she tries to tell me, "are an emotionally deprived, persecuted minority." *Right*, I think. But by her final shouts, I see how she is right.

Open the door and step into these lives. See here what will remake all your notions of who the people around you are and what they might become. Find here what you need most—your soul enlarged, your consciousness remade. Here is your membership to the largest community we share—each of us alone reaching out to understand most deeply all the others of us. In the world of story, stubborn human beings are still trying to understand themselves and each other. It is enough to make you take a deep breath and go back to fighting a little harder.

DOROTHY ALLISON

I said she seemed fine.

I'd meant to give her shin a fleeting inspection, but Val closed her eyes and let her head fall back and this gave me a chance to consider her neck. Or, more precisely, the soft hollow at the base of her neck where, in the final moment of release, the tendons seized up and the skin flushed with blood.

My fingers drifted up her shin and Val let her other leg sag open a bit.

"You should get going," she said.

"Right. Going."

"Because you said you had to go. And I want to respect that."

Val plucked at her dress. She did this sometimes, when she was nervous, the result being, in this case, that the hem rode up to the tops of her thighs. I could have accused her of subconscious sadism but she didn't believe in the subconscious. She would have said that she was hot, that she'd had too much wine, that I thought about these things too much.

"So anyway," she said. "Thanks."

She gave me a peck on the cheek. Then she leaned down to grab her camera and I could see her breasts struggling to free themselves, the prim pale bands that cut down from her shoulders and gracefully broadened above the nipple and the round outward swell, which made me want to suckle her, there in the fizzy yellow light of the front seat, in the motionless August night.

I reached for her thigh, the smooth expanse of the inner half, and she let out a shivery moan and we were going down once more, once more at least, in a tangle of black underwear and salty skin and dumb teenage lunging—the colliding teeth, the muscle spasms—and we didn't stop, couldn't stop, until I was all the way up inside and her ass was pounding the horn in a vibrant staccato. She looked how she always looked naked: she looked sautéed.

The problem, obviously, is that we were broken up. Not freshly, but a month or so in, during that phase when you're still trying to be pals—hey pal!—while also searching desperately for an excuse to leap into the sack. This wasn't the first time we'd backslid. It was more like the

The Breakup Vows

STEVE ALMOND

WE WERE IN MY little shitbox of a sedan, coasting past the reservoir. Val was wearing a sundress the color of bubble gum. Most women, nine out of ten, would have looked dippy in this thing. But there was almost nothing Val couldn't wear. She had the kind of beauty that made the rest of the world seem completely irrelevant. The tops of her knees were brown with August sun.

She and her pals had borrowed my car to attend a wedding reception in Milton, and I'd given them a ride home. Now I was pulling up across the street from her place and she was thanking me.

"No problem," I said.

"Really," she said. "I owe you one, Mark."

"You don't owe me anything."

It was one in the morning and the street lamps had all but given up. Val smelled like a wedding: wine, cigarettes, a pleasing confusion of perfumes.

"I should probably go," I said.

Val nodded and set her foot on the gearshift. She was wearing these plastic sandals with straps that wound around her ankles and up her calves.

"Nice," I said.

"These things?" She smiled. "At least I shaved my legs. Here. Feel."

"Nice."

It was nice. Everything about her was nice. There wasn't a single aspect of her body or spirit I wouldn't have described, at that very moment, as nice.

Val observed that she might have drunk a bit too much at the reception. She meant by this that she had wept at some point, shy tiny sobs that had the perverse effect of making her more beautiful.

third or, okay, the fourth. Fifth, I guess, if you count the day we broke up, which, after all the tears and vows of sorrow, required that we do it standing up in the foyer of her apartment house.

Val and I had broken up mutually, and for all the right reasons. I know how lame this sounds, but it's true. We weren't afraid of commitment. We certainly didn't lack chemistry. But our personalities didn't square. She was one of those people lousy with sufficiency, the strong silent type. I was more like the insecure loud type.

I made fusses in public, stiffed rude waiters, nearly wept at the late-season ineptitude of the Red Sox. Val loved that I wasn't afraid to show my feelings. And I marveled at her poise, the way she could soothe the people around her *without even speaking*. Even the way she shopped astounded me, the quiet dignity of her selections, boneless chicken thighs (from which she assiduously trimmed the fat), whole wheat tortillas, avocados only if ripe.

Eventually, though, my rants stopped seeming so funny. And her silences began to grind me down. On long drives, I'd turn off the radio and wait for her to say something, anything, a perfectly idiotic ploy for which I was invariably rewarded with the question: "Are you mad at me?" But nobody was mad at anybody. That was the whole problem. We were just too stubbornly ourselves.

It would have been easier, I guess, if we'd had some big blowout. Or one of us had been unfaithful. But no, we were incompatible, a couple of crazy young incompatible horndogs panting through the endless sultry afternoons.

A week or so after the wedding, we met up at a free concert on the Common, the Boston Symphony doing Beethoven's Ninth—not exactly Barry White, but you take what you can get. The conductor was one of these old Japanese hipster dudes with a hairstyle like he'd just stuck his thumb in a socket.

Val was wearing cutoffs and a halter top. Was it inappropriate for me to slip my hand down the front of this garment during the rousing third movement (*adagio molto e cantabile*)? Or to blow warm air onto the nape of her neck as the woodwinds huffed out their mournful glissandos? Given that we were surrounded by ten thousand classical music nuts, many of them no more than a few feet away and all of them rocking on their blankets, ever so slightly, with eyes half-closed . . . I would say yes.

It was the chorale that really got us bothered, though, all that gothic hollering, those mouths stretched with doom, which made us feel as if we were being watched by God Himself while our hands drifted toward the hidden places.

The mezzosoprano stepped forward. "All creatures drink of joy at nature's breast," she sang. "Just and unjust alike taste of her gift."

I couldn't argue with that.

"Do you want to get out of here?" Val whispered.

"Now?"

"*Now.*" Her eyes were starting to glaze over.

And of course I wanted to say yes, *hell yes*, let's go. *Taxi!*

But suddenly it seemed quite a strange thing to be diddling my ex in the middle of a huge public lawn, with all that religious music pouring down around us. Val and I had never even gone to church together. A church was where you got married, after all. And what would a priest have to say to us, exactly?

Then it occurred to me that a priest was exactly what we needed—someone with the moral clout to make our breakup stick. Someone prepared to administer vows:

We are gathered here today to witness the dissolution of this lovely couple. Do you, Mark, swear to remain apart from Val in solitude and drunken revel, in healthy erections and heartsickness, even as your desire for her exceeds all human expectation?

I do.

And do you, Val, make these same grim and holy vows?

I do.

Then, by the power vested in me by the Holy State of Romantic Woe, I declare you ex and ex.

The singers were belting out their final, aching refrain and Val was running her fingers through the soft hair at my temples.

"We can still beat the crowd," she said.

I didn't know what the hell to say.

"Come on, Mark."

"It's not that I don't want to," I said. "It's just . . ."

But Val wasn't the sort to beg. She despised ambivalence. Her hand fell away from my cheek. I could see her jaw in profile, tensing.

biceps and I could smell her, the sweet salty center of her, through the damp cotton of her panties.

"That hurts a little," I said. "Actually."

Val reached behind her and squeezed me.

"Ready for love," she said. "How sad. What did you think was going to happen, Mark? That I'd just melt at the sight of you?"

She let go of me and raised herself up on her knees, so that her full weight pressed on my arms. I tried to kick my feet free. But they were tangled in the cuffs of my trousers. Val slid her pelvis forward, sort of nudged at my chin, then lowered her intimate parts over my mouth.

If all this sounds alluring to you, in a rough-sex sort of way, I can only ask that you consider the reality of the situation: Yes, I could taste her through the cotton. Yes, my limbic brain was registering that most joyful sense message: *pussy, pussy, pussy*. But my right arm had started to go numb and I was snorting like a heavyweight in the late rounds.

I wondered, briefly, what would happen if I asphyxiated, there in her front room. Would the sexy TV coroner discover the true cause of death? Would she find the pubic hairs nestled under my tongue? The cotton fibers embedded in my nasal passages? Would she stand up in court and point dramatically to Val's lovely snatch and say: *What you are looking at, ladies and gentleman of the jury, is the perfect murder weapon.*

But now, all fooling aside: *I couldn't breathe.* It was like when I was a little kid and my big brother smothered me with a pillow. And just like back then, at that exact moment when I was sure I was going to pass out and die, I began to buck violently. Val stumbled forward and my right arm came free and I slashed my elbow through the air, felt a glancing blow land.

I was sputtering, trying not to cry, and Val was leaning against the wall, holding one side of her mouth and smirking with the other.

"You think that's funny?" I said.

I wasn't so much bigger than Val. But I had the advantage of rage—a pure, humiliated rage—and I pushed her to the floor and yanked her wrists over her head and I could see the veins rising in my arms. Her panties came off in two torn halves.

She'd shaved recently and the flesh around her sex was a pebbled red. Val brought her knees up and raised her head. She wanted to watch me was her point, as she had back in the tender days of love, when each motion had felt like a gentle gift. But I was in no mood for gifts. I braced my feet against the wall behind me and slammed forward. Her eyes widened and she sucked in a sharp breath. She looked almost comic for a moment, like a silent film star shot in the gut.

"You still think that's funny?" I said. "You think it's funny to be a pricktease?"

I pressed in, quick and to the hilt, until I felt the soft thump of our pelvic bones.

Val smiled at me and there was blood on her teeth, red blood, happy blood, and her mouth reached for mine. This was what we'd been waiting for after all, the chance to vent our rage, to mark our bodies with what our hearts had been suffering. And these bodies, all the miraculous systems of organs, clamored with their sudden capacities for pleasure, the sprung rhythm and the vital descent, the flushed and sucking walls.

None of this took long, a few minutes maybe, while we banged at the walls and gasped and clenched our fists. And later, when all the venom had been sucked out of us, we lay exhausted on her bed, like pelts, with our palms open and our bruises laid out for kisses and together wept a terrible confusion of tears.

I kept expecting Val would find someone new. She was this smart, gorgeous woman breezing through her twenties with fabulous skin, and she worked in a field (advertising) that seemed dedicated to a rigorous schedule of cocktail parties. Every few weeks, she called me to tell me all about it.

"My God," she'd say. "This guy had his hard-on pressed against me the whole night. I mean, is it normal for a guy to have a hard-on for three hours? It felt like a brick."

Or: "He offered to fly me to Maui on his private jet. How nineties is *that*?"

Or: "He really was an incredible dancer. I guess I might have kissed him. You know how I get when I drink tequila. Thank God Andrea was there!"

This meant I was allowed, encouraged even, to conjure up an image of what Val was like when she drank tequila, meaning uninhibited, meaning spilling from her top, her wide mouth thrown toward the action.

This particular brand of cruelty was allowed, you see, because we were back to being pals. So she fed me these guys, draped all over her, pressing their brick dicks against her long flanks. Her basic message being: though I am desirable, and many men would like to fuck me, I am not yet fucking them, you dumb shit.

Always, afterward, there would be an ominous silence, while I tried to figure out what to say. I had no stories of my own to tell. There were no women (that I could recall) sliding their sopping pussies down my thigh or inviting me onto their privately owned aircraft.

Then two or three weeks would pass without any dispatches and I was sure that Val had moved on and I would suffer those inevitable twinges of regret, because I wasn't ready yet to give my body to a new lover, to enter that half-lit kingdom of risk.

But then Val would call with her latest atrocity and my heart would leap at the news that she was still conceivably mine (mine! mine!), then plunge into a sudden, disorienting disappointment.

Val was moving to another apartment, in a nicer part of town. She needed help with the bed, she said. She and Andrea could handle everything else. Really, she should have called a moving company. She had enough dough socked away. But it was part of her solid, midwestern sense of things to be frugal and self-depriving.

So I swung by and flexed my arm muscles for an hour while Andrea hovered over us with a big doubtful grimace and asked how my work was going and tried not to scoff when I explained that my latest grant had fallen through. She was what I would call a *breakup vigilante*, part of the larger *breakup posse* dedicated to keeping Val from another sensational misstep.

The same Val, mind you, who was wearing a calfskin miniskirt and a simple cotton blouse and a choker of colored beads and who had parted her hair down the middle. Who looked, in short, like a horny little porno squab.

Andrea was determined to get me out of there. But what was she against the power of breakup sex? A cobweb of doubt. A nun with a broken ruler.

Val sent her to pick up some batteries while she and I assembled the bed frame, which meant we had twenty minutes at the outside. It was all a little frantic. She flipped her skirt up and shucked her panties, lickety-split, and bent herself over the mattress. There was her ass, shapely, splendidly pale . . . not so many months ago I had seriously considered moving in to this ass, just subletting my place and taking the plunge.

But there was the matter of her legs, those endless brown legs, which required that I spend several mortifying seconds on tiptoe, hoping somehow to achieve the desired point of entry. (Was I supposed to leap, *then thrust?*)

"The bed frame," Val said. "The bed frame, you idiot."

"Right."

I stepped up and reached for the bundled flesh of her hips, pulled her toward me and watched the entire hot slick swallowing. Val pressed her face into the mattress and sighed elaborately. Her breasts swayed beneath her. I could smell the cocoa butter that Val used to moisturize—she was a world-class moisturizer—which rose from the soft indentations above her hip bones and softened the musk of our exertions.

I gazed down at myself, at the motion of our bodies in congress. Val's head slowly bobbed. The line of her part glowed in the dusk, like an ancient scar. And the small of her back trembling with sweat, her hand reaching down to touch herself, and her happily gobbling ass . . . it was all a bit much.

I closed my eyes and tried to think of something else, anything.

But what came to mind was a memory of Val, lying with her hair fanned across my pillow. It was a Sunday morning early on, one of those lazy mornings that unravels with such languor you never quite accept that it will come to an end. We'd been gorging ourselves on strawberries and cream and the bedroom smelled of fruit and sex.

Val looked at me for a long moment. Then she said: "Where do you want to be in five years?"

I'd thought she meant geography and murmured something idiotic about California, sunny California. But I could see now that she'd wanted to know about us, whether we were headed anywhere real.

It was a fair question, and we both knew the answer—and we both knew, given the answer, that we had no business letting our affair drag on.

The bed frame was cutting into the ball of my foot. I could tell I was going to have a nasty bruise, though I was so close now that the pain was just an afterthought.

"We should slow down," I said. "Just a little, baby."

Val shook her head. I could see the tendons on the back of her hand flexing as she caressed herself. "Go," she whispered.

"Give me a second."

Val rocked back and clenched something inside and just at that moment my foot slipped off the bed frame and I popped out of her.

"Get back here," she said. "Mark. *Mark.*"

But it was too late: that last maneuver—the way her insides had seemed to grip me—sent me over the edge. I could see my hopeless cock releasing itself onto the moving boxes, the scabbed wood floor, the backs of her thighs.

Val flinched. "Goddamn you," she said. "I was close. I was so close."

"I'm sorry," I said.

It wasn't like her to hold such things against me. But I could see now that Val was crying. And suddenly, it made me sick with shame to see her bent over the bed, swaying on her elbows, with her skirt bunched up around her ribs and the imprint of a mattress button on her cheek—so sick that I felt like throwing up, though what I did instead was stagger backward and pull on my trousers.

"I'm sorry," I said. "We'd better, you know . . . She's gonna be back pretty soon."

"You son of a bitch," Val whispered. "You goddamn son of a bitch."

You all know how this story ends, anyway. One of you moves out of town. Or gets into a decent therapy. Or meets someone new. And a year later, you get word that Val, your Val, is getting married. Yeah, to some doctor who works with deformed children. A plastic surgeon with a heart of gold.

It was Andrea who delivered the news. I'd run into her at the café where Val and I used to come for coffee and scones after weekend sleepovers.

"That's great," I said. "I'll have to give her a call."

"Not such a good idea," Andrea said.

"Why not? I'm allowed to congratulate her."

"Mark." She exhaled through her nose. "Just use your brain."

But I called anyway. She had a new number and this fellow's voice was on the answering machine, a soothing voice, the kind of voice you'd want speaking to you if your kid was having her jaw rebuilt. I hung up and tried Val at work.

She agreed to meet me downtown, but only for lunch. I'd never heard of the place. It was loud and crowded with businessmen. Val had let her hair grow out and gained a few pounds. She looked softer, more content.

I did most of the talking, because I wanted to convey how happy I was for her and because I didn't want to hear too much about her new happiness. Toward the end of the meal, I asked her if she still ever thought about me.

"Stop being dramatic," she said. "You sound like a cliché."

"I'm just asking a question."

"No, Mark. You're trying to stir things up."

But Val wasn't angry. She only wanted to keep me from making things worse for myself.

I said, "Don't you ever wonder about the feelings that passed between us?"

"We were lonely," she said. "Loneliness."

"But the physical part," I said. "There was such a charge."

"Only because we kept pushing each other away. It was the loss that got us all crazy." Val sighed. "That's what loss does, Mark. It makes people crazy."

"Yeah, I know. I'm not saying we were right for each other. I mean, obviously. I'm just saying we had some good times."

Val gazed at me across the table and her mouth was smiling, and though her eyes had taken on the opposite emotion, her hand seemed poised just then to reach out and touch mine, so that it took me a moment to recognize what was actually happening: Val was feeling pity for me.

The businessmen were yammering away, telling their polite lies and gulping down their watery booze. Val sat back and looked away from me and gestured, a little too eagerly, for the waiter.

"Let me pay for this," I said quickly. "I'll pay for this."

That night I went home and sat in a tub of scalding water and waited for the knots behind my shoulder blades to loosen up. And after I'd soaked for long enough to realize it was no use, I dried myself off and lay on my bed and thought about how Val looked in that pink dress, the way her knees glowed under the street lamp, and I wondered about this marriage, just how solid it might prove, whether there was still some chance, any chance, that she might be mine again to lose.

End of the Line

AIMEE BENDER

THE MAN WENT to the pet store to buy himself a little man to keep him company. The pet store was full of dogs with splotches and shy cats coy, and the friendly people got dogs and the independent people got cats and this man looked around until in the back he found a cage, inside of which was a miniature sofa and tiny TV and one small, attractive brown-haired man, wearing a tweed suit. He looked at the price tag. The little man was expensive, but the big man had a reliable job, and thought this a worthy purchase.

He brought the cage up to the front, paid with his credit card, and got some free airline points.

In the car, the little man's cage bounced lightly on the passenger seat, held by the seatbelt.

The big man set up the little man in his bedroom, on the nightstand, and lifted the latch of the cage open. That's the first time the little man looked away from the small TV. He blinked, which was hard to see, and then asked for some dinner in a high, shrill voice. The big man brought the little man a drop of whiskey inside the indented crosshatch of a screw, and a thread of chicken with the skin still on. He had no utensils, so he told the little man to feel free to eat with his hands, which made the little man irritable. The little man explained that before he'd been caught he'd been a very successful and refined accountant who'd been to Paris and Milan multiple times, and that he liked to eat with utensils, thank you very much. The big man laughed and laughed, he thought this little man he'd bought was so funny. The little man told him in a clear, crisp voice that dollhouse stores were open on weekends and he needed a bed, please, with an actual pillow, please, and a lamp and some books with actual pages if at all possible. Please. The big man chuckled some more and nodded.

The little man sat on his sofa. He stayed up late that first night, laughing his high, shrill laugh at the late-night shows, which annoyed the big man to no end. He tried to sleep and could not, a wink. At four a.m., exhausted, the big man dripped some antihistamine in the little man's water drip tube, so the little man finally got drowsy. The big man accidentally put too much in, because getting the right proportions was no easy feat of mathematical skill, which was not the big man's strong suit anyway, and the little man stayed groggy for three days, slugging around his cage, leaving tiny drool marks on the couch. The big man went to work and thought of the little man with longing all day, and at five o'clock he dashed home, so excited he was to see his little man, but he kept finding the fellow in a state of murk, drooling all over the cage. When the antihistamine finally wore off, the little man awoke with crystal-clear sinuses and by then had a fully furnished room around him, complete with chandelier and several very short books, including *Cinderella* in Spanish, and his very own pet ant in a cage.

The two men got along for about two weeks. The little man was very good with numbers and helped the big man with his bank statements. But between bills, the little man also liked to talk about his life back home and how he'd been captured on his way to work, in a bakery of all places, by the little-men bounty hunters, and how much he, the little man, missed his wife and children. The big man had no wife and no children, and he didn't like hearing that part. "You're mine now," he told the little man. "I paid good money for you."

"But I have responsibilities," said the little man to his owner, eyes dewy in the light.

"You said you'd take me back," said the little man.

"I said no such thing," said the big man, but he couldn't remember if he really had or not. He had never been very good with names or recall.

After about the third week, after learning the personalities of the little man's children and grandparents and aunts and uncles, after hearing about the tenth meal in Paris and how le waiter said the little man had such good pronunciation, after a description of singing tenor arias with a mandolin on the train to Tuscany, the big man took to torturing the little man. When the little man's back was turned, the big man snuck a needle-thin droplet of household cleanser into his water and watched the little man hallucinate all night long, tossing and turning, retching small pink piles into the corners of the cage. His little body was so small it was hard to imagine it hurt that much. How much pain could really be felt in a space that tiny? The big man slept heavily, assured that his pet was just exaggerating for show.

The big man started taking sick days at work.

He enjoyed throwing the little man in the air and catching him. The little man protested in many ways. First he said he didn't like that in a firm, fatherly voice, then he screamed and cried. The man didn't respond, so the little man used reason, which worked briefly, saying: "Look, I'm a man too, I'm just a little man. This is very painful for me," and also, "Even if you don't like me it still hurts." The big man listened for a second, but he had come to love flicking his little man, who wasn't talking as much anymore about the art of the baguette, and the little man, starting to bruise and scar on his body, finally shut his mouth completely. His head ached and he no longer trusted the water.

He considered his escape. But how? The doorknob was the Empire State Building. The backyard was an African veldt.

The big man watched TV with the little man. During the show with the sexy women, he slipped the little man down his pants and just left him there. The little man poked at the big man's penis, which grew next to him like Jack's beanstalk in person, smelling so musty and earthy it made the little man embarrassed of his own small penis tucked away in his accountant pants. He knocked his fist into the beanstalk, and it grew taller and, disturbed, the big man reached down his pants and flung the little man across the room. The little man hit a table leg. Woke up in his cage, head throbbing. He hadn't even minded much being in the underwear of the big man, because for the first time since he'd been caught, he'd felt the smallest glimmer of power.

"Don't you try that again," warned the big man, head taking up the north wall of the cage entirely.

"Please," said the little man, whose eyes were no longer dewy, but flat. "Sir. Have some pity."

The big man wrapped the little man in masking tape, all over his body, so his feet couldn't kick and there were only little holes for his mouth and his eyes. Then he put him in the refrigerator for an hour. When he came back, the little man had fainted and the big man put him in the toaster oven, at very, very low, for another ten minutes. Preheated. The little man revived after a day or two.

"Please," he said to the big man, word broken.

The big man didn't like the word "please." He didn't like politesse and he didn't like people. Work had been dull, and no one had noticed his new coat. He bought himself a ticket to Paris with all the miles he'd accumulated on his credit card, but soon realized he could not speak a word of the language and was too afraid of accidentally eating veal brains to go. He did not want to ask the little man to translate for him, as he did not want to hear the little man's voice with an accent. The thought of it made him so angry. The ticket expired, unreturned. On the plane, a young woman stretched out on her seat and slept since no one showed up in the seat next to hers. At work, he asked out an attractive woman he had liked for years, and she ran away from him to tell her coworkers immediately. She never even said no; it was so obvious to her, she didn't even have to say it.

"Take off your clothes," he told the little man that afternoon.

The little man winced, and the big man held up a bottle of shower cleanser as a threat. The little man stripped slowly, folded his clothing, and stood before the big man, his skin pale, his chest a matted grass of hair, his penis hiding, his lips trembling so slightly only the most careful eye would notice.

"Do something," said the big man.

The little man sat on the sofa. "What?" he said.

"Get hard," said the big man. "Show me what you look like."

The little man's head was still sore from hitting the table; his brain had felt fuzzy and indistinct ever since he'd spent the hour in the refrigerator and then time in the toaster oven. He put his hand on his penis and there was a heavy sad flicker of pleasure, and behind the absolute dullness of his mind, his body rose up to the order.

The big man laughed and laughed, at the erection of his little man, which was fine and true but so little! How funny to see this man as a man. He pointed and laughed. The little man stayed on the sofa and thought of his wife, who would go into the world and collect the bottle caps strewn on the ground by the big people and make them into trays; she'd spend hours upon hours filing down the sharp edges and then use metallic paint on the interior, and they were the envy of all the little people around, so beautiful they were and so hearty. No one else had the patience to wear down those sharp corners. Sometimes she sold one and made a good wad of cash. The little man thought of those trays, trays upon trays, red, blue, and yellow, until he came in a small spurt, the orgasm pleasureless, but thick with longing.

The big man stopped laughing.

"What were you thinking about?" he said.

The little man said nothing.

"What's your wife like?" he said.

Nothing.

"Take me to see her," the big man said.

The little man sat, naked, on the floor of his cage. He had changed by now. Cut off. He would have to come back, a long journey back. He'd left.

"See who?" he asked.

The big man snickered.

"Your wife," he said.

The little man shook his head. He looked wearily at the big man. "I'm the end of this line for you," he said.

It was the longest sentence he'd said in weeks. The big man pushed the cage over, and the little man hit the side of the sofa.

"Yes!" howled the big man. "I want to see your children too. How I love children!"

He opened the cage and took the little floral-print couch into his hand. The little man's face was still and cold.

"No," he said, eyes closed.

"I will torture you!" cried out the big man.

The little man folded his hands under his head in a pillow. Pain was no longer a mystery to him, and a man familiar with pain has entered a new kind of freedom. "No," he whispered into his knuckles.

With his breath clouding warmly over his hands, the little man waited, half-dizzy, to be killed. He felt his death was terribly insignificant, a blip, but he still did not look forward to being killed, and he sent waves of love to his wife and his children, to the people who made him significant, to the ones who felt the blip.

The big man played with the legs of the little armchair. He took off the pillow and found a few coins inside the crevices, coins so small he couldn't even pick them up.

He put his face close to the cage of his little man.

"Okay," he said.

Four days later, he set the little man free. He treated him well for the four days, gave him good food, and even a bath and some aspirin and a new pillow. He wanted to leave him with some positive memories and an overall good impression. After the four days, he took the cage under his arm, opened the front door, and set it out on the sidewalk. Unlocked the cage door. The little man had been sleeping nonstop for days, with only a few lucid moments staring into the giant eye of the big man, but the sunlight soaked into him instantly, and he awoke. He exited the cage door. He waited for a bird to fly down and eat him. Not the worst death, he thought. Usually the little people used an oil rub that was repellant-smelling to birds and other animals, but all of that, over time, had been washed clean off him. He could see the hulking form of the big man to his right, squatting on his heels. The big man felt sad but not too sad. The little man had become boring. Now that he was less of a person, he was easier to get along with and less fun to play with. The little man tottered down the sidewalk, arms lifting oddly from his sides, as if he had wet hands or was covered in paint. He did not seem to recognize his own body.

At the curb, he sat down. A small, blue bus drove up, so small the big man wouldn't have noticed it if he hadn't been looking at foot level already. The little man got on. He had no money, but the bus revved for a moment and then moved forward with the little man on it. He took a seat in the back and looked out the window at the street. All the little people around him could smell what had happened. They lived in fear of it every day. The newspapers were full of updates and new incidents. One older man with a trim, white beard moved across the bus to sit next to the little man, and gently put an arm on his shoulder. Together, they watched the gray curbs passing by.

On the lawn, the big man thought the bus was hilarious and walked next to it for a block. Even the tires rolled perfectly. He thought how if he wanted to, he could step on that bus and smush it. He did not know that the bus was equipped with spikes so sharp they would drive straight through a rubber sole, into the flesh of the foot. For a few blocks, he held his foot over it, watching bus stops come up, signs as small as toothpicks, but then he felt tired, and went to the corner, and let the bus turn, and sat down on the big, blue plastic bus bench on his corner made for the big people.

When the big man's bus came, he took it. It was Saturday. He took it to the very end of the line. Here, the streets were littered with trash, and purple mountains anchored the distance. Everything felt like it was closing in, and even the store signs seemed too bright and overwhelming. He instantly didn't like it, this somewhere he had never been before, with a different smell, that of a sweeter flower and a more rustic bread. The next bus didn't come for an hour, so he began the steady walk home, eyes glued to the sidewalk.

He just wanted to see where they lived. He just wanted to see their little houses and their pets and their schools. He wanted to see if they each had cars or if buses were the main form of transport. He hoped to spot a tiny airplane.

"I don't want to harm you!" he said out loud. "I just want to be a part of your society."

His eyes moved across grasses and squares of sidewalk. He'd always had excellent vision.

"In exchange for seeing your village," he said out loud, "I will protect you from us. I will guard your front gates like a watchdog!" He yelled it into the thorny shadows of hedges, down the gutter, into the wet heads of sprinklers.

All he found was a tiny, yellow hat with a ribbon, perched perfectly on the yellow petal of a rose. He held it for a good ten minutes, admiring the fine detail of the handiwork. There was embroidery all along the border. The rim of the hat was the size of the pad of his thumb. Everything about him felt disgusting and huge. Where are the tall people, the fatter people? he thought. Where are the aliens the size of God?

Finally, he sat down on the sidewalk.

"I've found a hat!" he yelled. "Please! Come out! I promise I will return it to its rightful owner."

Nestled inside a rock formation, a group of eight little people held hands. They were on their way to a birthday party. Tremendous warmth spread from one body to the other. They could stand there forever if they had to. They were used to it. Birthdays came and went. Yellow hats could be resewn. It was not up to them to take care of all the world, whispered the mother to the daughter, whose yellow dress was unmatched, whose hand was thrummed with sweat, who watched as the giant outside put her hat on his enormous head and could not understand the size of the pity that kept unbuckling in her heart.

Mudman

PINCKNEY BENEDICT

Some people say a man is made out of mud.
A poor man's made out of muscle and blood.
Muscle and blood and skin and bone
A mind that's weak and a back that's strong.

—Merle Travis, "Sixteen Tons"

ON ANOTHER DAY, Tom Snedegar would have smashed the dirt dauber without a thought, but on this day—an overcast Sunday when thin greenish mist fluttered like cobwebs in the gullies and sinkholes of Snedegar's place—on this day, Snedegar just watched it come.

"You'd bite me if you was to get the chance, wouldn't you?" he asked the wasp. It buzzed its wings. It was only maybe a foot from the steel-capped toes of his boots on the cold concrete floor of the milking parlor. Snedegar decided that he liked the wasp, liked it for its truculence, liked it for its solitary ways. "Bite hell out of me," he said.

He rummaged briefly in the cabinet on the wall until he came up with the measuring cup that he sometimes dipped into the cooling tank, to sample the sweet raw milk. He had used the same cup since he was a boy. The glass of the measuring cup was thick and slightly yellow. He upended the cup and bent to put it down over the wasp, but the wasp was gone.

Snedegar looked over the milking parlor. He had just finished hosing it down after the morning milking, and it looked clean and pleasing to him, with its ranked feed bunks and its overhead network of pipes and its solid concrete block walls. He checked the floor again, the measuring cup dangling by its handle from his fingers. No wasp.

"Slipped me," he said, and the wasp buzzed in response. It had found its way onto the leg of his coveralls, its abdomen bobbing dangerously. Snedegar brushed at it with the back of his hand and it fell to the floor. Snedegar plopped the measuring cup over it. The wasp's wings blurred, their whirring muted.

He got on his hands and knees to look at the trapped wasp. He squinted his weak left eye so that he could focus more sharply with the right and put his face close to the measuring cup. The wasp reared up on its hind legs and returned his gaze between the faded seven-eighths and the full-cup markings. It was a great, glossy dauber, and it had extraordinarily long wings.

Snedegar took a minute to admire the gorgeous black-pearl curve of its thorax, which was the size of his pinkie finger's first joint. He examined the neat articulation of the wasp's small body, its oily limbs and agile antennae, the deftness of its armor. Its depthless eyes. He tapped the glass, and the wasp droned. It seemed content to wait.

Snedegar wanted a mudman. He needed it to help him out around the farm. He worked the operation alone: two milkings a day, feeding, chopping the corn, maintaining the buildings and the equipment. The list of things to be done was endless, but money was always short, and it was almost impossible to hire anybody to do the sort of work that Snedegar did.

"I'll never get to Heaven," Snedegar said to himself as he dug. He was getting the mud to make the mudman. Sundays were the Sabbath, but Snedegar worked anyway. The cows didn't know what day of the week it was. They had to be milked, they had to be fed. When he had a mudman to help him, he could begin keeping the day holy. He could accompany his wife to the church she attended in the county seat, and on the rounds of pleasant errands and visits she always undertook afterward. She was doing those errands right then, and he couldn't tell when she might be back.

Snedegar's thoughts wandered briefly to the trapped wasp. A wasp didn't get tired. A wasp needed nothing. A wasp never wasted time mooning about what to do. He had watched this particular one for weeks as it built its nest under the eaves of the dairy barn, rolling up little pills of mud at the edges of puddles and then hauling them aloft.

Stinging fat spiders and taking them away, too, to feed its babies, the spiders' long spindly legs dangling as the dauber bore them upward.

Time to get back to digging. Snedegar put the shovel blade into the dirt of the field again. A couple of his Holstein heifers watched him with mild eyes as he burrowed.

Snedegar's wife was town-bred and not made for farm life. She was young and pretty. Sensible shoes, tidy bosom. She worked part-time at a travel agency in the county seat. She worked for a man named Carlson, the youthful guy who owned the travel agency. Snedegar chopped at a stray root that blocked his digging, sank the sharp blade of the shovel deep into the loam, and added another wet spade-load to the growing pile. The dirt was rich with fat nightcrawlers.

Without the mudman, Snedegar would never get to Heaven, because he worked on the Sabbath. He did pretty well on the other Commandments, if he said so himself: No strange gods, no cursing, honored his father and mother, both dead for years. Had no reasons to lie, no one to lie to. No murder, and he wanted no woman other than his wife—he wanted her so fiercely that he thought sometimes he would go blind or die with the wanting. Coveted nothing, needed nothing other than this place, these acres that were his and his alone. Couldn't imagine needing anything else. Except the mudman.

Carlson the travel agent would get to Heaven because he took Sundays off from the office. Carlson was well scrubbed and he dressed handsomely. Snedegar had no one to work with him, but Carlson had Snedegar's wife. Snedegar laughed to himself, thinking of his orderly wife working alongside him as he grubbed in the dirt of the field.

He was sweating heavily. He had enough dirt piled up to make his mudman; he had plenty, but he kept on going. The hard ground yielded up valueless detritus: a sharp flint spear point, a scattering of hog's teeth, shards of glazed crockery, a length of greasy chain, a glistening rib. Snedegar's shoulders and arms and back bent eagerly to the task of excavation, as they always had to difficult physical labor, and the dirt flew.

At last, the edge of the shovel's blade scraped against bedrock, sending up a flurry of short-lived sparks. Snedegar paused. He was standing in the hole that he had made, and he felt mildly shocked to find how deep it was, only his head rising above the lip. The dark shape of a hawk rode the thermals overhead, cruising, looking to dine on the mice that throve in the dairy barn, or to hook one of the portly groundhogs that populated the farm, that tunneled endlessly through the dirt of the fields.

Snedegar hated the groundhogs because they made their dens in his fields, made craters that were a danger to his livestock and that threatened to damage and destroy his machinery. He killed them whenever he was able, and hung their limp, furry bodies on his fence posts for the crows to pick at. He silently wished the hawk good hunting.

Up to his neck in dirt, Snedegar realized that he had pretty much a groundhog's view of things. Stones loomed like mountains. The horizon was inches away from his nose. He felt like prey.

A cruciform shadow swept over him, and he glanced upward. The hawk cupped its broad wings, stroking its way upward into the flat, colorless sky, and Snedegar closed his left eye so that he could focus his right on it. He saw then, as it flared and circled toward open ground, that it wasn't a hawk at all. It was a horned owl, its curved beak slightly open, its feathers rumpled and dirty looking. One of its legs was crippled, the claw drawn up and withered. It gave Snedegar the creeps, to see a night bird out in the middle of the day. The owl disappeared over the ridgepole of the dairy barn.

Snedegar bent to his shovel again, but the impulse to dig had left him. He felt tired. He felt so tired suddenly that he thought he might just fall asleep, leaning on his shovel handle. It occurred to him to lie down in the foot of the hole. He could just forget about the mudman, forget about the Sabbath and the wasp in the milking parlor and his wife. He could simply lie down and stare upward. Maybe the hawk—no, the owl, the daylight owl—would return to sail over him, to relieve the monotony of the lowering sky, the deck of clouds that promised more rain to come.

Mudmen had once done a lot of the labor in amongst the hills where Snedegar had his dairy. When hardwood was king, a hundred years and more ago. They had worked the clear-cuts, snaking the giant sawlogs out of the woods, dense white oak trees fourteen feet in diameter, logs that could acquire a coltish life of their own when a man chained them and skidded them down the hillsides, into the bottoms where the whining sawmills and the boomtowns squatted. Logs that could turn on a man and stave in his ribcage, smash him to pieces without warning, grind him into the earth like an insect.

You could see them, the mudmen, in the blurry sepia photographs that had come down from Snedegar's grandfather and his great-grandfather. The pictures lined the upstairs hallway of Snedegar's house: groups of bandy-legged, barrel-chested timber cutters. Snedegar's grandfather, who had worked the last stands of virgin oaks, had called them "timber apes." The timber apes grinning like boys, teeth gleaming in their pale faces, axes and two-man saws on their shoulders, ranged in a semicircle around the sundered trunk of whatever enormous oak or black locust they'd just brought thundering down.

And in the background, always at the edge of the light, looking as though it might be no more than an awkward-falling shadow, or maybe some hulking, shy, ugly fellow who didn't care to have his picture made: a mudman. Eyes like slits in the broad, flat face, mouth a silent gash above the lantern jaw. Sometimes two of them, or three, standing shoulder to shoulder, close together as though for companionship.

Great Caesar's Ghost—that was the name of Snedegar's bull—knew that something was up. As Snedegar, up in the nearly empty hayloft, hammered together the crude mold that had the shape of a man, the bull slammed its ponderous head against the tightly fitted boards of its stall, keeping time with the strokes of the hammer. Even after Snedegar was done hammering, the blows of the bull's head continued on, slow and perfectly rhythmic.

The frame of the dairy barn jolted with every impact, and the chittering swifts in the haymow left their comfortable perches in the rafters and swept out through the wide north window of the loft and back in again from the west. Snedegar watched the birds as they flashed from daylight into the dusk of the loft. They were marvelous, he thought, better than Chinese acrobats, the way they never so much as touched one another, though maneuvering so close and in such a confined space.

He left off his hammering for a bit, descended the steep staircase to the ground floor of the barn, and went to the stall where Great

Caesar's Ghost stood confined. The bull was a monster, well over a ton in its prime, heavier now, bloated, head like a beer keg, chest as broad as a snowplow. It shifted its great shoulders when it caught sight of Snedegar, blew out a vast gust of breath before slamming its skull into the barn wall again.

"Howdy, old man," Snedegar said. The bull had been done with breeding back in the time of Snedegar's father, but Snedegar could somehow never bring himself to do the needful thing, and so Caesar's Ghost continued on here in the half light of the stall. From where he stood, Snedegar could see the small vacuum tank of liquid nitrogen where he kept the straws of bull semen he used for breeding his cows. It stood in a corner of the unused stall next to the bull's. "Cryo-Bio," read the brightly colored label on the side of the canister. The canister itself was made of burnished aluminum, and the logo on its side bore the cartoon picture of an appealing cow—she looked more like a deer, really—surrounded by snowflakes.

Snedegar knew that if a man stuck his hand into the LN2 and then shook it, his fingers would fall off and shatter like glass. He'd had numerous dreams about just that, dreams in which he slowly, deliberately inserted his hand into the tank. It was like he wanted to do it. In the dream, there was no pain as his hand froze, only a rising numbness and a sense of wonder. When he withdrew it, the fingers and fingernails were a delicate shade of blue and they glittered like jewels.

In fact, a time or two, he'd had to fight to keep himself away from the canister, to fight the impulse to plunge his hand into it, his arm up to the elbow, just to see if it would become numb and beautiful, like the hand in the dream.

Caesar's Ghost bashed its head into the boards again, and Snedegar grabbed the ring in the bull's nose and twisted it fiercely toward him. "Stop it," he said. Something passed from the bull to him. He felt it pass to him through his hand on the nose ring, felt it travel like hot acid up through his arm and into the center of his chest, into the dense muscle of his heart, and from there to his limbs, his cock, his brain, and he saw what he would do when his wife came home that afternoon, that evening: he would pull her close, his hands hard on her shoulders, and she would laugh at his urgency. "Careful," she would say, giggling, "don't muss me," and he would laugh along with her. He would laugh as he jerked her blouse open, laugh as he ignored her protests, frightened of him now, laugh as he rucked her demure skirt above her waist, as he tumbled her to the floor.

There had been mudwomen too, at the logging camps and up in the hardwood forests. It was inevitable, so few women in the region, which was a wilderness then, and so many randy, uncouth men. That was what had ended it, finally, the mudwomen. They awakened something that had not previously exhibited itself in the stolid, silent mudmen, who were made exclusively for work, a sort of sympathy. Sympathy that quickly bloomed into what could only be called love.

The unanswerable love of the mudmen, the unrelenting sexual desire of the timber apes: mayhem ensued, deadly violence that spread swiftly and terribly and ineluctably from one teeming sawmill town to the next, swept through the hollers and down the creeks and raced along the ridges. Axes and splitting mauls and whirling band-saw blades and rotgut liquor and pistols and fire. When it was over, a dozen of the timber apes lay in shallow graves in the stony bottoms, their arms and legs and spines fractured by the awesome, impassive strength of the mudmen, their ears and noses and mouths stopped up with silt, their lungs filled with the suffocating stuff; and the mudmen had been utterly purged from the face of the earth.

Snedegar finished cobbling together the form for the mudman out of two-by-fours. He hauled the earth up into the loft bucket by bucket, dumped it into the mold, added water until it achieved what seemed to him an appropriate viscosity, tamped it down, shaped it with his hands. He was covered in it.

He had made the mold large. There wasn't much to it, really—two arms, two legs, heavy body, blocky squared-off head. He was no artist. He had lugged, all told, probably four hundred, maybe five hundred pounds of earth to fill the mold, but he figured that the mudman would weigh a good bit less when it had dried out some.

He knelt down beside the head of the mold, extended his index finger, poised it over the great flat face. A poke for the left, a poke for the right, and a pair of dark, beady eyes stared up at him. He stood back from the mold so that he could observe his handiwork. The mudman's gaze seemed to follow him. Snedegar grinned. Leaning down, he slashed his forefinger across the face, a hand's span beneath the eyes. A lopsided, unsmiling mouth.

Snedegar balanced precariously atop his ladder, jabbing at the delicate panpipes of the dirt dauber nest with a paint spatula. He worked the thin edge of the spatula under the nest where it adhered to the unpainted wall of the dairy barn, just beneath the eaves of the sharply sloping roof. He wanted the nest, with its sleepily murmuring cargo of baby wasps, to serve as the mudman's heart. The nest began to pull loose, and Snedegar moved too quickly with the spatula.

Bits of the brittle nest broke free and spiraled to the ground thirty feet below, and Snedegar imagined that the muttering within increased in volume and intensity. The dried bodies of garden spiders, the wasps' larder, sifted out like shell corn. He had watched the dauber build the nest and fill it with dauber eggs and paralyzed spiders. The eggs hatched, and—Snedegar's mind did not like to go to what happened next, what happened to the spiders there in the muddy dark. He was no great fan of spiders, but some things did not bear much thinking about.

"Hush now," Snedegar told the babies, and he crooned a brief lullaby to them. It was a song that he recalled his mother singing, but the memory was a distant one and it contained no words, so he could only hum the tune as well as he remembered it and hope for the best. He sang in time to the monotonous banging that rose once again from Caesar's Ghost, and Snedegar believed that the wasp babies inside could hear him, that they knew he meant them no harm, that he was going to put them to a good use. He believed that they were humming along with him.

From up near the barn roof, he could see out over the breadth of his operation, with its little clusters of silos and outbuildings, the pole barn and the granary and the machine shop. Along the eastern fence line, a couple of crows did noisy battle over the week-old carcass of a groundhog, spiked to a leaning post. Their screeches floated to him like the voices of bickering children.

The wet soil of the field looked soft as a featherbed. It seemed inviting, as though it wanted him simply to loose his hold on the ladder, to spread his arms, and drop down sprawling onto it. The hole that he had made looked bottomless to him, filled with moving shadows. He glanced around for the cruising owl, thinking that it might be drawn by the squabbling of the crows, but it was nowhere in sight.

There were other wasps' nests under the roofline, dozens of them, decades' worth, but they had been broken open over the years and emptied by the ravenous beaks of barn swifts. This one, the last whole one, would have to suffice. He slowed his breathing and steadied the hand with the spatula, working with the concentration of a surgeon. The ladder wobbled beneath him, and he stopped scraping at the wall for a moment to brace himself and to get a new grip on the ladder. He had a gallon-size freezer bag with him, into which he planned to drop the nest when he had freed it. He thought that the nest and the baby wasps and the freezer bag all together would make a most satisfactory heart. Growing. Feeding. Tireless.

A swift landed on the edge of the tin roof, fluttering its wings momentarily for balance, its claws clattering like light rain against the slick metal. It turned a bright eye on him. He thought that it looked hungry. "Get your own," he said to the bird, which flicked its head so that it could look at him with its other eye. "These ones are mine." He went back to work.

The dauber nest gave slightly, and the spatula slipped another half inch beneath it, a full inch, two. Snedegar put his hand on the crumbling surface of the nest, and he could feel the young daubers waking within, ceasing to batten on the still-living spiders, hauling themselves reluctantly over one another's compact bodies there in the trembling dark. In the warm enclosure of its stall, Caesar's Ghost ceased to beat its head against the wooden walls, and the silence was a blessing.

The nest released its hold on the wall with shocking suddenness, and Snedegar went after it as it slipped away from him. The extension ladder rocked and threatened to telescope itself, taking Snedegar down with it. His fingertips recalled the rough terracotta exterior of the nest, recalled it so keenly that he felt he could almost will it back into his grasp, but the clatter of the frail mud pipes against the hard ground below told him that the nest was gone.

The birds came. They swooped through the air like little fighter planes, the swifts, and they plucked up the struggling young wasps and ate them. They ate the shrunken, quivering spiders, too. In their greed, they grabbed up bits of the mud nest and flung them down again. Snedegar beat at the birds, and they twittered furiously as they circled his head, avoiding his swatting palms without difficulty. They pecked at the plastic bag, they gobbled wasps, they jabbed at Snedegar's hands, beat their wings against his brow, clung to his back, their tiny claws pricking his flesh through the fabric of the coveralls.

Snedegar crawled on the packed earth, racing against the birds, sweeping the baby wasps and the shattered pipes of the nest and the spiders into the baggie. Sometimes he slipped and his hands or his knees crushed this or that wasp, and the wasps stung him as he saved them. He wanted to cry out but he didn't, swifts caught in his clothes, swifts trapped in the tangle of his hair.

Snedegar tapped at the upturned bottom of the measuring cup. "I'll never get to Heaven," he told the trapped wasp. He wondered what his face looked like to it as he gazed in through the distorting lens of the glass. Vast and cratered as the moon. He knew that a wasp's eyes saw differently from a man's.

He wondered if maybe the wasp thought that he was God. What it would be like if he were under the measuring cup. A dirt dauber god leaning over him, poison-filled stinger the size of a man, wings like the sails of a windmill. The notion filled him with horror. *Wasp god.* If God actually was a wasp, then he, Snedegar, was going to be in terrible trouble.

Every now and again, a bird would throw itself against the milking parlor window with a bone-crunching thump. They wanted more of the wasp larvae. The sound of their bodies smashing into the glass made Snedegar wince. Stunned or dead, they lay on their backs near the barn's foundation, their wings outspread, their dainty claws upthrust.

The wasp turned its back to Snedegar. "Don't you want to bite me?" Snedegar asked it. He held up the baggie, half-filled with baby daubers. "You wanted to bite me this morning. Remember?" He put his lips against the cool glass. "Don't you even remember?"

He thrust the plastic bag into the chest of the mudman. He pushed the remains of the dauber nest down deep into the dirt and the muck. Then he waited. He knelt by the mudman's form. From time to time he imagined that he could hear the buried wasp babies stirring in their renewed darkness. The cows were gathering at the wide door of the milking parlor; he knew it by the shuffling of their hooves, their soft lowing at the discomfort of their full udders. He realized with a start that he was, for the first time that he could remember, late for the afternoon milking.

Maybe, he thought, the mudman wasn't moving because it had nothing to do. Snedegar knew that without the constant nagging of the work, without the terror that something had been left undone, he himself would lie down and never arise again. Maybe the mudman was the same way. It needed a job to do. Snedegar needed to give it a job. He searched the pockets of his coveralls, came across a chewed-up stub of pencil, and tore a scrap from a feed sack to write on.

He licked the pencil tip, poised it above the triangular fragment of paper. His needs all crowded into his brain at once. The cows, the preparation of the fields for planting, the repairs of winter damage to the outbuildings, feeding, cleaning, the thousand things small and large that he did during any given day. How to pick one? He could hear the Holsteins shouldering against one another down at the dairy, and his breath grew short at the thought of his tardiness.

At the fence line, the crows continued to caw in harsh voices. It sounded like there were more than two of them now, three, four, a half dozen, screaming and fighting over the mummified remains of the groundhog. KILL GROUNDHOGS, he scrawled on the coarse paper in big block letters. The clamor of the crows increased. How hungry must they be, to fight over such food? Then, inspired, he struck out the word GROUNDHOGS with heavy, black strokes of the pencil lead and wrote in another: VERMIN.

At first, he placed the rough triangle of paper on the mudman's inert chest. Then he picked it up, put it down over one of the eyeholes. His wife would be home at any moment. The cows were waiting to be milked. The crows were at war in the lower field. The mudman was waiting for instructions. He took up the paper a third time and thrust it savagely, deeply into the mudman's grim mouth. Outside, the rain that had threatened all day began to fall, the water pooling on the surface of the soaked ground.

The upper-floor hallway of his house was ill lit, illuminated only by a clumsy wall sconce and a narrow slit of a window. The hallway had been dim and full of shadows for all of Snedegar's life. What light there was glinted unhelpfully off the glass that covered pictures of his family. In this picture his grandfather, standing atop the ridgepole of the half-finished dairy barn; in that one his great-grandfather at the center of a newly cleared pasture field; the tilt of their hats jaunty, their faces shaded by the deeply creased brims. They looked much alike, those two men. They looked much like Snedegar.

Snedegar took each one of the photographs from its place on the wall, examined it closely. The pictures left behind them lighter, unsoiled squares of wallpaper. Pictures older than the ones of the farm with its open fields, pictures from the time of the forests, the dark understory and the timber apes, their postures vain as they posed and preened before the toppled corpses of the great trees. Holding up their hands to show where the voracious band saws had taken various of their fingers. "There were giants in the earth in those days," Snedegar said to himself.

The shadows in the photographs twisted and slipped, capricious—or were those the shadows in the hall, moving? Shifting with the rain that sheeted across the single window. It seemed impossible to know what anything was for sure.

Downstairs, his wife moved from room to room, the soles of her shoes rapping smartly against the bare floorboards. He had not grabbed her when she had come home, had not wanted to smear her with the mud that covered him. He had twisted the ring in the bull's nose and he had felt the power that still lay within the animal, he knew that he had. He wanted to ravish her. But the notion had come to seem ridiculous with her standing there facing him, her clothes unwrinkled, her makeup fresh. How could he touch her?

"Will you come up?" he called to her. His voice sounded exhausted and weak in his own ears.

"After a while," she replied, her voice light and singsong. "I've got to ret up this mud you tracked in. You go on to bed. Go on to sleep."

He closed his left eye and brought his face close to the photographs, one after another. He wished for a jeweler's loupe. The tones of the photos were muted, and the timber apes swam in his vision, indecipherable blotches of light and dark. They faded even as he peered at them. The trees were vast, the hillsides steep. The men were small. The mudmen . . . Where were the mudmen?

He hauled himself into his bedroom. The wasp was there, sitting motionless beneath the measuring cup on his bedside table beside the clock, which he wound and set to wake him for the morning milking. The mudmen were a lie. There would be no mudman for Snedegar. The knowledge grieved him because of the time he had wasted this day. Grieved him, too, because he could no longer imagine how he was going to be able to keep the Sabbath holy, and so he would never get into Heaven. The wasp waved its antennae at him, and he leaned over to it. "Nighty-night," he told it, and the moisture in his breath fogged the glass.

Snedegar dreamed of the vacuum canister. In the dream, he carefully unscrewed the top of the tank and set it, just as carefully, to one side. The LN2 was precious stuff and not to be wasted. Wisps of vapor rose from the darkness within, along with a kind of hissing. A buzzing. Putting his ear to the tank, he thought that he could make out the voice of the mudman. The voice spoke to him with the droning of insects' wings. He could make out individual words, longer phrases, but not their meaning. This was an old language, the language of wasps, not meant for human ears, and it filled him with terror.

He stood over the mudman's form, the canister in his hands. The metal of the tank was cold, and he could feel himself beginning to freeze. Freezing was a relief. He welcomed the numbness, but he knew that it could prevent him from doing what he must. From doing his work. He braced himself to resist the creeping cold and raised the canister, tipped it so that the liquid nitrogen ran out in a heavy stream, seething as it struck the warm earth of the mudman's body, smoking and boiling as Snedegar laved it over the mudman's limbs, the dirt blanching and crystallizing, fracturing under the cascading stuff.

The wasps, grown now to maturity, two inches long and more, began crawling from the mudman's flesh; they pushed their way blindly outward from the buried heart to the surface. They knew that the end was coming, deep within the mudman's chest they felt it coming on like winter. Snedegar deluged them, and there was an astonishing pleasure in it, to see a gleaming wasp, pulling itself free, turn in an instant to blue smoldering glass, the perfect simulacrum of a wasp, before it burst and shattered and crumbled into dust. The mudman was screaming, shrieking imprecations in the voice of the wasp god, but its crude mouth never moved.

The dream shifted, and Snedegar no longer stood over the prostrate mudman. Now it was his own bed that was crawling with wasps. They blundered over the sheets that bore his grandmother's monogram, and over his pillows and the body of his wife. It was too late to stop the cataract of nitrogen that flowed from the canister, and Snedegar was not at all sure that he'd have called it back if he could. It was a hard job that he was doing, but it was his job, and he would see it done properly. His wife's lithe body writhed and twitched as he bathed her, as he baptized her, and the droplets of nitrogen that went astray and struck Snedegar burned him like fire.

Her breath smoked and she gargled with pain; she tore at the stiff frozen folds of her nightdress and the material collapsed like thinly beaten gold foil beneath her fingers, her delicate fingers that broke loose one joint at a time until she was left with nothing more than stumps. He splashed the nitrogen over her legs, and she howled, and he had never wanted her so much in his life, he was hard as a railroad spike, hard as a diamond. Her voice was gone now, and she arched her back like a gymnast until only the crown of her head and the tips of her toes touched the mattress.

Snedegar stepped back from the bed, in awe of what she had become. What he had made her. Her body was a perfect glimmering bow, of a blue so pure it pained his eyes to look at it.

He shook the canister, and it continued full. Which meant that his work was not done yet. It was heavy, and the muscles of his arms were tired, but he raised the yawning mouth of the tank, touched its unearthly cold to his blistered lips, and began eagerly to drink.

Snedegar woke in the night, thinking that it must be time for the morning milking, but the clock told him that it was not. That was hours off yet. His wife slept heavily beside him. He held his breath, listening for the sound that had brought him out of his dreams. The rain muffled everything. He could hear the settling of the farmhouse on its stone foundation and the ticking of his bedside clock and the slow creeping of the wasp beneath the measuring cup. Round and round the perimeter it went. Then, distantly, the metronomic rapping that he knew to be Great Caesar's Ghost. Snedegar kept track of the strokes until he reached thirteen, and then he left off counting.

When his alarm clock rang, Snedegar flung out an arm to shut it off. His fingers connected with the measuring cup, and it flew from the tabletop and thumped to the hooked rug that covered the floor. The wasp sat still for a moment, as though unsure of what to do with its newfound freedom, and Snedegar almost got a hand over it before it spread its impressive wings and darted away. The room was dark and he quickly lost sight of it, but he could still hear it bumbling around up near the ceiling.

Snedegar patted his wife on her warm hip. "You watch out now," he told her as he rose. "There's a wasp loose in the room."

Every fence post along the short lane between the dairy barn and the house bore the body of a groundhog, pinioned like a butterfly in a kid's collection. Crucified, their buck-toothed mouths comically agape, rodent eyes startled and bugging. The sight of them lining the road—ten, fifteen, more and more of them as Snedegar played the beam of his flashlight along the fence—staggered him. It was dark out, time for milking, and the rain was still falling, pattering off his cap and the shoulders of the slicker that he wore, catching like bright beads in the shaggy coats of the groundhogs.

He prodded the pudgy, out-thrust belly of the first groundhog with a forefinger, and the animal twitched and snapped its jaws at him, rolled its eyes, grunted. Still alive. Pinned through the body to the locust post with a square-headed iron nail, a handmade nail that must have been drawn by brute force from the timbers of the dairy barn itself; its spine was snapped, its blood staining the post and the ground beneath it, but it was still alive. He shone his light down the row of groundhogs and he could see that others among them—not all, but many—were alive as well, their paws paddling helplessly at the air. Snedegar marveled at the fantastic cruelty of it.

The wasp god.

The mudman.

He came near to laughing. This was the mudman's work. There was such a thing. He himself, Snedegar, had made it. He thought of the despair he had felt the night before with contempt. He wanted to shake that Snedegar, that exhausted Snedegar, and shout into his face, *You see? They were not lies. The stories were not lies.*

He trotted down the lane, sloshing his way through the puddles that had collected in the low places. He tried not to look at the struggling groundhogs, but his eyes were drawn back to them, again and again. He noticed that there were other creatures pinned to the posts as well: a pair of sleek red foxes, squirrels, blacksnakes, copperheads, a wrist-thick diamondback, its rattles still sizzling. On one post alone, two dozen of the little barn swifts, tacked up by their fragile wings. Possums, crows, a feral dog, its eyes shining green in the lamplight. The owl with the withered claw.

Snedegar felt queasy, numbering in his mind the fence posts that bordered the lane. Dozens. How many fence posts on the entire place? Hundreds. Thousands, all set by the hands of the Snedegar men. Spreading out into the darkness on all sides of him, where the beam of his light was too weak to illuminate. The sun would be up soon; the eastern sky was already beginning to pinken with the coming dawn. And then he would see. He knew now the meaning of the alarm from Great Caesar's Ghost in the night, and what would greet him when he reached the barn.

Something passed him in the lane moving toward the house, something massive and cold, something that moved in near silence and so swiftly that he couldn't bring the flashlight beam to bear on it before it was gone. On tottering legs, wishing that he had some other choice but knowing that he did not, he followed.

He found the mudman seated on a slight rise on the north side of the house, rain sluicing over its clumsy body. The mudman was smaller than Snedegar had thought it might be. Not much larger than he himself, in fact. Far heavier, though, packed mud denser than flesh, to judge by how deeply sunk it was into the hard ground of the bank. It appeared to be very much at its ease, leaning back on its elbows, its lumpy legs stretched out before it. Snedegar noticed that the liquid nitrogen canister rested on the sod of the bank an arm's length from the mudman, which made a generous gesture, as though to invite him to sit down beside it.

The rise looked in on the windows of Snedegar's bedroom. The mudman's eyes, which were, of course, nothing more than holes in the blank slate of its face, stayed fixed on the rectangles of light as though there were a particularly fascinating show going on behind them. Snedegar followed the mudman's gaze and was astonished to see his wife, in nothing but her nightie, leaping around the room like a dancer.

As he watched, she jumped up onto the bed, ran nimbly across it, dropped to the floor on the other side, then hopped up onto a chair. Had the mudman not been there with him, he'd have laughed out loud. She gripped a rolled-up magazine in her hand, and she waved it in the air, slapped it against the walls, twirled and squatted. There was an angry red lump on one of her smooth thighs and another high on her cheek. The asymmetry lent her face a new aspect, a charm that went well beyond mere prettiness, and Snedegar felt again how powerfully he desired her.

"Leave her alone," Snedegar told the mudman. The mudman chortled, a sound like water spattering in hot fat. A wasp crawled from its mouth, and the mudman sucked it soundlessly back in again. Snedegar thought of his dream, thought of going after the nitrogen canister, emptying it over the mudman, watching the mudman's frozen body shatter there on the bank. Even as he considered the notion, the mudman drew the canister close, uncapped it, and took a long draught.

Vapor billowed around its head. It offered the canister to Snedegar.

Snedegar considered. How easy, to take the canister and drink. How much easier than enduring what was to come. But Snedegar had never been much of a one for the easy road, and he knew that he could not simply leave his wife to the mercies of the mudman. She sprang over the bench of her vanity, magazine held high above her head, and knocked over a lamp. The room was plunged into darkness.

The mudman spoke for the first time, a low rumbling sentence that Snedegar couldn't make out. Another wasp tried to make its escape from the unmoving mouth and was drawn back. "Come again?" Snedegar said.

The mudman spoke more distinctly this time. "What's she doing?" it asked, and took another swig of liquid nitrogen. The dawn was coming on fast, and Snedegar switched off his flashlight.

"Chasing a wasp," Snedegar told the mudman.

It nodded. A moment later, it began to talk, then paused and seemed to clear its throat. When it spoke again, its words were clearer. It was learning. "She's fucking him," it said.

It was Snedegar's turn to nod. "I know," he said, and he guessed he had. He guessed he had known it for quite some time.

The light was stronger now, the sun rising and the overcast burning off some, though the storm still spat fretfully on Snedegar and the mudman. Snedegar's wife appeared at the darkened window of the bedroom, peering fearfully out at the two of them. She looked to Snedegar, and then to the mudman, and back to Snedegar again. Her left eye was weepy and nearly closed from the wasp sting, and Snedegar felt his own weak eye throb in sympathy. He figured that she could see them, but she couldn't tell who they were, couldn't tell one from another in the slanting morning light and the rain: the mudman slouching casually on the ground, Snedegar nearby in his wet-weather gear.

The mudman made as if to rise. "I expect I'll go in there," it said. "Not right now. But I will go in there, after a while."

Snedegar balled his fists and squared his shoulders. The mudman regarded him, then motioned toward the fence with its freight of carrion. *Join them if you want*, the gesture said. It reclined on its elbows again, and Snedegar saw that his wife was gone from the window. He was not going to get into Heaven, and his wife was not going to get into Heaven. That much was sure. And one other thing as well: when the time came, the mudman was going to rise and set about his work.

Zoanthropy

DAVID BENIOFF

WHENEVER A LION was spotted prowling the avenues, the authorities contacted my father. He had a strange genius for tracking predators; he made a lifelong study of their habits; he never missed an open shot.

There is a statue of him in Carl Schurz Park, a hulking bronze. He stands, rifle slung casually over his shoulder, one booted foot atop a dead lion's haunches. A simple inscription is carved on the marble pedestal: MACGREGOR/DEFENDER OF THE CITY. The statue's proportions are too heroic—no Bonner ever had forearms like that—but the sculptor caught the precise angle of my father's jawline, the flat bridge of his nose, the peacemaking eyes of a man who never missed an open shot.

In the old days, the media cooperated with the authorities—nobody wanted to spark a panic by publishing news of big cats in the streets. That attitude is long gone, of course. Every photographer in the country remembers the *New York Post*'s famous shot of the dead lion sprawled across the double yellow lines on Twenty-third Street, eyes rolled white, blood leaking from his open jaws, surrounded by grinning policemen, below the banner headline: BAGGED! My father was the triggerman; the grinning policemen were there to keep the crowds away.

So it's sacrilege to admit, but I always rooted for the cat's escape. A treasonous confession, like a matador's son pulling for the bull, and I don't know what soured me on my father's business. A reverence for exiled kings, I suppose, for the fallen mighty. I wanted the lions to have a chance. I wanted them to live.

All good stories start on Monday, my father liked to say, a line he inherited from *his* father, a Glasgow-born minister who served as a chaplain for the British troops in North Africa and later moved to Rhodesia, where my father was born. For my grandfather, the only story worth reading was the holy one, King James Version. My father rejected the God of the book in favor of empirical truth. He never understood my obsession with fictions, the barbarians, starships, detectives, and cowboys that filled the shelves of my childhood room. He purged his mind of fantasy only to watch his lone child slip back into the muck.

This story starts on Tuesday. I was twenty years old. On bad afternoons I sometimes found myself where I had not meant to go: lying on the dead grass in Bryant Park with a bottle of celery soda balanced on my chest; inside a Chinese herb store breathing exotic dust; riding the subway to the end of the line, Far Rockaway, and back. The bad days came like Churchill's black dogs; they paced the corridor outside my bedroom, raking the carpet with their claws. The bad days chewed the corners. When my corners got too chewed for walking, I took a taxi to the Frick museum, stood in front of Bellini's *Saint Francis*, waited for the right angles to return.

On this bad Tuesday I stared at Saint Francis and Saint Francis stared into the sky, hands open by his side, head tilted back, lips parted, receiving the full favor of the Lord. Bellini shows the man at the moment of his stigmatization, the spots of blood sprouting from his palms. I don't think I'm being vulgar or inaccurate when I say that the saint's expression is orgasmic—the rapture of divine penetration. The animals are waiting for him, the wild ass, the rabbit, the skinny-legged heron—they want to have a word with him, they see that Francis is in ecstasy and they're concerned. From the animal perspective, I think, nothing that makes you bleed is a good thing. The rabbit, especially, watches the proceedings with extreme skepticism.

After an hour things inside my brain sorted themselves out, the thoughts began to flow with relative order, my bladder swelled painfully. I went to the restroom, stopping on the way to take a photograph for a honeymooning German couple who thanked me effusively and gave me a business card from their bookstore in Düsseldorf. In the toilet stall I locked the door, did my business, closed the seat, and sat down for a smoke.

The stall door was scrawled with names and dates, a worldly graffiti: Rajiv from London, Thiago from Saõ Paulo, Sikorsky from Brooklyn. I leaned forward, the cigarette gripped between my teeth, the smoke in my lungs, pulled a ballpoint pen from my hip pocket, wrote my name in boxy capitals: MacKENZIE ALASTAIR BONNER, and then, in lieu of a hometown, LIVES!

Someone rapped on the door. "Occupied," I said.

"You'll have to put out the cigarette, sir. No smoking in the museum."

I took a final long drag, stood, lifted the toilet seat, and flushed the butt. When I opened the stall door the guard was still standing there, a tired-looking kid about my age, bat-wing eared, narrow shouldered, his maroon blazer two sizes too large. He stared at me sadly, hands in his pockets.

"You smoke Lucky Strikes," he said. "I could smell them from the hallway. They used to be my brand." He spoke with a forlorn air, as if the real meaning of his words were *You slept with Cindy. She used to be my girlfriend.* "Hey," he added, smiling, "the Saint Francis man."

I squinted at him and he nodded happily.

"You're the guy that always comes and stands by that Saint Francis painting. What's the matter, you don't like the other stuff?"

"I like *The Polish Rider*."

I was spending too much time in this place. The Frick made for a cheap afternoon with my student discount—I had dropped out of NYU after a term and kept my ID—but I hated the idea that people were watching me. Perhaps I had grown too dependent on Saint Francis. I walked over to the sink to wash my hands.

"Me too, I like that one. Well, listen, sorry about busting you. It's pretty high school. Detention! But I've only been working here a couple weeks and, you know."

He held the door open for me and I thanked him and exited the bathroom, drying my hands on the seat of my corduroys. The guard followed me, walking with a bowlegged strut as though he had six-guns strapped to his waist. "The thing about Lucky Strikes, they have this sweetness, this . . . I don't know how to describe it."

"You're not from New York, are you?"

"Huh?"

"Where are you from?"

He grinned, jangling the heavy key ring dangling from his belt. "Bethlehem, Pennsylvania. What, I have hay in my hair?" His Bethlehem had two syllables: *Beth-lem.*

We were in the garden courtyard now, a beautiful pillared room with an iron trelliswork skylight and a fountain in the center where stone frogs spitting water flanked a giant marble lily pad. I sat down on a bench and watched the frogs. The guard stood behind me, fiddling with his black tie. He seemed lonely. Or gay. Or both.

"So you're an artist?" I asked him. "You're in school here?"

"Nah. I don't think I could look at paint after being in this place all day. Nope, not for me."

"Actor?"

"Nope, nothing like that. It's—"

We both saw the lion at the same time, padding below the colonnade on the far side of the courtyard, yellow eyes glimmering in the shadows, claws click-clacking on the floor. He rubbed his side back and forth against a pillar before limping to the fountain. The lion looked unwell. His mane was tangled and matted down; an open red sore marred one shoulder; his ribs seemed ready to poke through his mangy fur. He stared at us for several seconds before dipping his muzzle to the water and drinking, huge pink tongue lapping up the frog spit. His tail swayed like a charmed cobra. After satisfying his thirst he looked at us again, and—I swear—winked. He left the same way he came.

"Lion," said the guard. What else could he say?

Neither of us moved for a minute. We heard screams from the other rooms. People ran through the courtyard in every direction, hollering in foreign languages. A small girl in a dress printed with giant sunflowers stood alone beneath the colonnade, hands covering her ears, eyes clenched shut.

They closed the museum for the remainder of the afternoon and all of us witnesses had to answer questions for hours—the police, the Park Service rangers, the television and newspaper reporters. I was interviewed on camera and then stood to the side, listening to the other accounts. A group of schoolchildren and chaperones from Buffalo had seen the lion walk out the museum's front door, search the sky like a farmer hoping for rain clouds, and walk slowly east. A bicycle courier spotted the lion on Park Avenue and promptly pedaled into a sewer grate, flipping over the handlebars and smashing his head against the curb. He spoke to the reporters while a paramedic wrapped gauze bandages around his forehead. After Park Avenue, the lion seemed to disappear. A special police unit had scoured the surrounding blocks and found nothing. New Yorkers were being advised to stay indoors until further notice, advice that nobody took.

After all the interviews were over, the guard found me sitting on the bench by the frog fountain. "That was something," he said. "I need a beer. You want to get a beer somewhere?"

"I do," I said. "I really do."

We went to the Madison Pub, a dark old speakeasy where the gold-lettered names of long-dead regulars scrolled down the walls. We didn't say much during the first beer, didn't even exchange names until the food came.

"Louis Butchko," I said, repeating the name to help me remember it. My father had taught me that trick.

"Mm." He was chewing on a well-done cheeseburger. "Most people call me Butchko."

"He winked at us. Did you notice that? The lion, he winked."

"Hm?"

"I'm telling you, I saw him wink. He looked right at us and winked."

"Maybe. I didn't see it. One thing's for sure," he said, licking his lips, "they didn't mention lions when I applied for the job. Mostly they're afraid of people touching the paintings."

"He winked."

"I thought maybe a lunatic splashing yellow paint on the Titians, something like that, but lions? I ought to get, what do they call it, danger pay? Hazard pay?"

The bartender, an old Cypriot with dyed-black hair who had worked in the pub since my father first took me there as a child, rubbed down the zinc bar top with a rag and a spray bottle. He whistled a tune that I could not place, a famous melody. It was maddening, the simple, evasive music.

"How long have you been here?" I asked Butchko.

"New York? Nine months. Down on Delancey."

"I like that neighborhood. You mind if I ask what you're paying?"

He took the pickle off his bun and offered it to me. It was a good pickle. "One fifty."

"One fifty? What does that mean?"

"One hundred and fifty dollars. A month."

I stared at him, waiting for an explanation.

"Come over and see the place sometime. I got a great deal. I met the superintendent and we worked it out. You know, New York is very expensive."

"Yes," I said.

"I didn't really have the money to move here, but it's one of the requirements. As a title holder."

"What title?" I examined his scrawny neck, his small white hands. "You're not a boxer?"

"Nope." He smiled, bits of blackened beef on his lips, in his teeth. "Nothing like that."

"You're going to make me guess? You're Anastasia, daughter of the Czar?"

"It's something I kind of have to keep a low profile about. No publicity."

I sighed and waited.

"All right," he said, "all right. But you can't go around telling people. It's part of the deal, I have to keep it undercover. I'm the Lover," he said, beaming a little in spite of himself.

"Okay," I said. "Whose lover?"

"No, *the* Lover. Capital *L*."

"Right," I said, finishing my beer. The bartender, quartering limes, kept whistling his one song. "You're a porn star."

"No," he said, offended. "Nothing like that." He looked around the shadowy barroom, making sure nobody was within hearing distance. "The Lover of the East Coast. I'm the Greatest Lover on the East Coast. Not counting Florida, they're independent."

I smiled at him happily. The great thing about New York, no matter how insane you are, the next man over is bound to be twice as bad.

"What is there," I asked him, "a tournament?"

"It's not something you compete for," said Butchko. "It's more like the poet laureate. The last guy, Gregory Santos, he lives up in the Bronx, near Mosholu Parkway. Really nice guy. He took me out for drinks when I got the title, told me how to handle certain situations. He said it would change my whole life. The pressure is—I mean, women have *expectations* now. It's like being the New York Yankees."

I was pondering that for a while. The New York Yankees? No other customers remained in the pub, just the two of us and the bartender whistling. I imagined the Cypriot coming to work on the subway, head buried in the newspaper, while a small black-eyed girl sitting next to him whistled notes she heard at breakfast from her father's razor-nicked lips, notes her father heard the night before as he stood in the crowded elevator and watched the lighted floor numbers count down.

I concentrated on Butchko's sallow face, the purple blooms below his eyes. Studying a face will keep things quiet for a while. I tried to imagine that this was the man millions of East Coast women fantasized about while doodling in the margins of crossword puzzles. I tried to imagine him mounting bliss-faced seducees from the northern tip of Maine to Georgia, whispering in their ears, making them go all epileptic, their skin stretched so tight over rioting nerves that one touch in the right place would send them ricocheting around the room like an unknotted balloon.

I could picture the rapturous women because I had read about them in novels, had seen them in movies, but I had never held one in my arms. I had not touched a naked breast since the day my mother weaned me. The only contact I had with women was incidental: the brush of a supermarket clerk's fingers as she handed me my change, or an old lady tapping my shoulder, asking me to move aside so she could step off the bus. Like my beloved Saint Francis, I was a virgin.

"So what happened," I asked Butchko, "your high school girlfriend said you were the greatest?" I was trying to figure the origins of his fantasy.

He seemed mystified by the question. "Well, yeah."

There was something appealing about him. His delusions had originality, at least. All the other New York immigrants think they're the greatest actor, artist, writer, whatever—it was nice to meet the greatest lover.

The whistling Cypriot would never quit. Verse chorus verse chorus verse. If there was a bridge, the man didn't know it. I dug my knuckles into the corners of my eye sockets and breathed deeply.

"Mackenzie? You okay?"

"This *song*," I whispered. "What is this song he's whistling?"

"'Paper Moon,'" said Butchko. He sang to the Cypriot's accompaniment: *"Say, it's only a paper moon, sailing over a cardboard sea, but it wouldn't be make-believe, if you believed in me."* Butchko's voice was gorgeous, a pitch-perfect tenor, and for a moment I believed everything, all of it, the cities, towns, and countrysides full of quivering women sloshing about their bathtubs, moaning his name, *Butchko, Butchko,* wetting a thousand tiled floors in their delirium.

"Lion," he said, plowing the ketchup on his plate with the tines of his fork. "My first lion."

As soon as I got home I began preparing the house for my father, transferring six steaks from the freezer to the refrigerator, vacuuming the carpet in the master bedroom, winding each of the antique clocks, stacking the logs and kindling in the library's fireplace, arranging the ivory chess pieces in their proper formations. I knew that he would have heard about the lion, that he would be on a plane crossing the Atlantic. We lived in a turn-of-the-century brownstone, the façade adorned with wine-grape clusters and leering satyrs. My room was on the top floor, beneath a skylight of pebbled glass. After the house was made ready for its master, I locked myself in my bedroom and turned off the lights.

Not counting the skylight there was only one window in my room, small and round as a porthole, facing south. Next to this window, mounted on a tripod, stood a brass telescope that my father had given me for my twelfth birthday. The telescope had once belonged to the Confederate general Jubal Early; his monogram was stamped into the brass below the eyepiece. Our house stood on the highest hill in Yorkville and the vista must have been pretty before the surrounding apartment towers rose up to steal the sunlight. The resultant view was of the building directly south of us, a redbrick Goliath of forty stories. The upper floors made for poor spying—I could only see into the apartments nearly level with my own room. Humbled telescope: once employed to track Union troop movements in the Shenandoah Valley, now trained on the cramped quarters of New Yorkers: a red-haired woman watching television with a thermometer in her mouth; four young girls sitting cross-legged on the living room rug, folding origami cranes; an old man, bare chested, arms folded on the windowsill, looking over me to Harlem; two women, one old, one young, slow dancing in the kitchen; a small boy with a bowl haircut, wearing Superman pajamas, lying in bed reading a book.

I was watching the night this boy's mother first brought him home from the hospital, bundled in blue blankets. I was watching when he learned to crawl, took his first steps, met his new puppy on Christmas morning. It sounds sinister, I know, the spying. It sounds creepy. Believe what you will, I cannot stop you, but the truth is I loved that boy as a baby brother. I've always been a coward but I would have been ferocious in his defense. Night after night I would look in on him, to make sure he slept safely, the Babar night-light glowing in his doorway, a cup of water by his bedside. When his mother held her hand against his damp forehead, I would feel the fever surge in sympathy through my own body.

I focused on the cover of the boy's book. *The Count of Monte Cristo*. He was awfully bright, this kid, he devoured novels in the nighttime while his parents slept. A real prodigy, making me proud. I watched over him until he switched off the light, and then I swept over the other rooms of the apartment to make sure everything was safe. Sometimes I half hoped to see smoke pouring from the toaster oven so that I could call the fire department and watch the snorkel truck raise its boom to the little boy's window, watch the fireman pluck him from danger. Sinister, creepy, I won't defend myself. I was lonely. If there is a witness to my soul, He knows the truth, and I am calm in that judgment.

When I was satisfied that the boy was safe I capped the telescope's lens and eyepiece, undressed, climbed into bed. It was a marvelous bed, with four tall cedarwood posts and hand-woven mosquito netting from the Ivory Coast. There weren't many mosquitoes in the brownstone, but I loved how the netting endlessly swayed in the air conditioner's breeze, pale lungs inhaling and exhaling.

Rain pounded the pebbled glass of my skylight, the hoof steps of a cavalry brigade heard from a great distance. It was almost dawn. The house was less empty than it had been. I pulled on a pair of green plaid pajamas and walked downstairs, knocked on the door of the master bedroom.

"Come in," called my father.

I opened the door. He sat cross-legged on the floor, the parts of his rifle disassembled, gleaming and oiled, on a spotted towel thrown over his steamer trunk. He wore his undershirt and a grass-stained pair of khakis; wire-framed glasses; a black steel wristwatch with a nonreflective face, the gift of a Ugandan general.

If you are sitting in your home, late at night, alone, strange noises echoing down the hallways, disturbing your mind, and if you look out across the street, look through the window of a stranger's apartment, the apartment lit only by the television's static, and the stranger's room glows a cool and eerie blue—that was the exact color of my father's eyes.

He wiped his hands clean on a corner of the towel, stood up, walked over, and clasped my shoulders, kissed me on the forehead. "You look thin."

"I was sick for a while. I'm okay."

"You're eating?" He watched me carefully. I was never able to lie to my father. I mean, I was able to lie to him but I never got away with it.

"I forget sometimes." That was the truth. On bad days the idea of food, of eating, seemed somehow ridiculous, or indulgent.

He walked over to his desk, a gorgeous rolltop of luminous mahogany that had supposedly belonged to Stonewall Jackson. Hanging on the wall above the desk were four masks—carved wood embellished with feathers and shredded raffia—that my father had bought in Mali. Each represented a figure from the old Bambaran saying: *What is a crow but a dove dipped in pitch? And what is a man but a dog cursed with words?*

My father pulled a sheaf of fax papers from his desktop and looked through them. "I saw your name in here. You were one of the witnesses?"

"He winked at me."

My father continued reading through the papers, holding them at arm's length because his prescription was too weak and he never bothered to get reexamined. Being farsighted had little effect on his aim, though. I remember reading a profile of my father in a glossy hunting magazine; accompanying the article was a photograph of a silver dollar that had been neatly donuted by a high-caliber bullet. The caption below the picture read: SHOT BY MACGREGOR BONNER AT 400 YARDS IN THE TRANSVAAL (PRONE POSITION). My father had bet a drunk Johannesburg socialite one thousand dollars that he could make the shot; when the woman paid up she told him, "I hope I never make you angry, Bonner."

My father read through the fax papers and I said again, "He winked at me. The lion. He was staring right at me and then he winked and then he walked away."

My father removed his glasses and hung them, by one stem, from the neck of his undershirt. He pinched the bridge of his nose for a moment and then laughed.

"All mammals blink, Mackenzie. It keeps the eyeballs from drying out."

"Wink, not blink. He winked at me."

"Okay, he winked at you. Why don't you go back to sleep for a while. I'll make us a big brunch later on."

I went to my room and burrowed deep beneath the sheets, listened to my own breathing and the morning rain. In the strange space between sleeping and waking I imagined myself lionized. I paced the avenues, mane dreadlocked by city dirt. I met my stone brothers on the public library's steps; I sat with them and watched the beat cop pass, orange poncho clad, walkie-talkie chattering on his hip. I went underground, below the sidewalks, prowled the subway tunnels. The big-bellied rats fled when they smelled my hide. I curled up beside a soliloquizing madman, a filthy bundle of piss-damp rags, once a babe in a cradle, a shiny possibility. I licked the tears from his face and he buried his head in my mane. Soon he slept, and it was the first good sleep he'd had in years. Nothing could hurt him now; he was safe between the lion's paws.

Nobody saw the lion for the next five days. Wildlife experts on television speculated on his disappearance and proposed various possibilities for his whereabouts, but nobody knew anything. My father met with the chief of police and the mayor to coordinate the hunt. He inspected the sites where the lion had been seen and carefully studied all the eyewitness reports. In the terse interviews he gave to carefully chosen members of the press, he urged the public to remain cautious. He believed that the lion was still on the island of Manhattan.

Six days after I first saw the lion, on a humid afternoon—the kind when every surface is wet to the touch, as if the city itself were sweating—Butchko called and invited me to come over. I had forgotten that I gave him my number, and at first I was reluctant to go all the way downtown in the miserable August heat. But I had nothing better to do and I was curious to get a look at his $150 apartment.

I met him on the stoop of his building. Before I could speak he raised a finger to his lips and motioned me to sit beside him. The hysterical dialogue of a Puerto Rican soap opera spilled from the open window of the first-floor apartment. I let the language wash over me, the rolling *r*'s, the sentences that all seemed to rhyme. Every few minutes I'd recognize a word and nod. *Loco! Cerveza! Gato!*

"*Te quiero,*" said Butchko, practicing the accent during a commercial break. "*Te quiero, te quiero, te quiero.*"

"You speak Spanish?"

"I'm learning. Gregory Santos said bilinguality is one of the seven steps to the full-out shudders."

Bilinguality? "What's the full-out—"

The soap opera came on again and Butchko hushed me. We listened to a hoarse-voiced man calm a distraught woman. A swell of violins and cellos seemed to signal their reconciliation and I imagined the kiss, the woman's eyes closed, tears of happiness rolling down her face as the darkly handsome man wrapped her in his arms. Butchko nodded solemnly, stroking his chin. When the show ended he led me into the brownstone and up a poorly lit staircase, pointing out various obstacles to avoid: a dog-shit footprint, a toy car, broken glass. At the top of the last flight of stairs he pushed open a graffiti-tagged door and led me onto the tar-papered roof. A water tower squatted on steel legs alongside a shingled pigeon coop.

"You hang out up here?" I asked.

"This is home," he said, closing the door behind me and securing it with a combination lock. "Look," he said, pointing. "That's a pigeon coop."

"I know it's a pigeon coop."

"Ask me why it has two doors."

The coop was windowless and low-slung, narrow and long, hammered together of weathered gray boards. Splits in the wood had been stuffed with pink fiberglass insulation. A yellow door hung crooked in its frame on one end; I circled around the coop and found an equally crooked red door on the opposite end.

"Why does it have two doors?"

"Because if it had four doors it would be a pigeon sedan."

He was so happy with the joke his face turned bright red. He opened up his mouth and shined his big white Pennsylvania teeth at me. "Oh, Mackenzie. You walked right into that one."

I opened the red door and stepped inside. There were no pigeon cubbies, just a green sleeping bag, patched in places with electrical tape, rolled out on the bare wood flooring; a space heater, unplugged for the summer; a clock radio playing jazz; a blue milk crate stacked with paperbacks; an electric water boiler; and a pyramid of instant ramen noodles in Styrofoam cups. The wires ran into a surge protector connected to a thick yellow extension cord that snaked down a neatly bored hole in the floor.

"The super sets me up with electric," said Butchko, standing in the doorway behind me. We had to stoop to fit below the steeply canted ceiling. "Pretty good deal, I think."

"Don't you get cold up here?" Even with the space heater at full blast, the coop could not be good shelter in the depths of winter.

Butchko shrugged. "I don't sleep here most nights, you know?"

I picked a paperback off the top of the pile. *The Selected Poetry of Robert Browning*. I read a few lines, then returned the book to its brothers. "There's a toilet somewhere?"

"Down in the basement. And a shower, too. If I need to pee I just go off the roof, see how far I can get. Here, look at this." He ushered me out of the converted coop to the edge of the roof. We leaned against the parapet and looked at the brick wall of the building opposite us. "See the fire escape? I hit it the other day. What do you think, twenty feet across?"

With my eyes I followed the ladders and landings of the fire escape down to the alley below, deserted save for a blue Dumpster overflowing with trash.

"It's just rats down there anyway," said Butchko. "They don't mind a little pee. Or maybe they do, but screw 'em, they're rats. And then, here, this is the best part. Come over here."

In the cool shadow of the water tower he grabbed a canteen off the tar paper and began climbing the steel rungs welded onto one of the tower's legs. I walked back into the sunlight to watch his ascent. At the upper lip of the tower he turned and waved to me, thirty feet below, before pulling himself over the edge and disappearing from view. A minute later he started climbing down. He jumped with five feet to go and hit his landing perfectly.

"Here," he said, offering me the canteen. I drank cold water.

"There's a tap up there for the inspectors. They come twice a year and check things out, make sure there's no bacteria or whatnot floating around."

I handed him back the canteen and watched him drink, watched his heavy Adam's apple bob in his throat.

"Are you ever going to tell me what the full-out shudders are?"

Butchko grinned. "Come on, Mackenzie, you've been there."

"Where?"

He capped the canteen and laid it down in the shade of the tower. "The shudders are reality," he said, and by the way he said it I knew he was quoting. "The shudders are the no-lie reality. Listen, women are very different from men."

"Oh! Ah!"

"Well, okay, it sounds obvious, but it's important. For a man, sex is simple. He gets in and he gets off. But it's not automatic for a woman."

It wasn't automatic for me, either, but I kept my mouth shut.

"The thing is, women are more sensitive than men. They don't want to hurt our feelings."

"Ha," I countered.

"In general," he said. "So they act, sometimes. They pretend. Now, for me, given my circumstances, it's very important that I know exactly what works and what doesn't. And I can't rely on what she's saying, or the groaning, the moaning, the breathing, none of that. Arching the back, curling the foot, biting the lip—none of that is a sure thing. Only the shudders. There's no faking the full-out shudders. You see those thighs start to quiver, I mean *quiver*, you know you found the pearl. Oysters and pearls, Mackenzie. Everybody knows where the oyster is—finding the pearl is what makes a good lover."

I stared at the water tower looming above us. The kid was a genuine lunatic, but I liked him.

"I'll tell you the first thing I learned, living in the city," said Butchko. "Puerto Rican women are excellent lovers."

"All of them?"

"Yes," he said. "All of them."

I smoked Lucky Strikes on the rooftop and talked with Butchko about women and lions until he told me he had to get ready for his date. Twenty minutes later I was riding the First Avenue bus uptown. "Air conditioner's broken," the driver told me before I stepped on. "There's another bus right behind me." He said the same thing to everyone, and everyone besides me grunted and waited for the next bus, but I paid the fare and sat in the back row. My decision displeased the driver. I think he wanted to drive his hot empty bus at high speeds, slamming on the brakes at red lights with no passengers to complain. I wouldn't have said a word. He could have cruised up the avenue at ninety miles per hour, swerving around the potholes; it didn't matter to me. I was easy.

When we passed under the Queensboro Bridge I saw the lion. I shouted, a wordless shout, and the driver looked at me in his mirror and hit the brakes, as simple as that, as if he were used to riders shouting when they wanted to get off. I shoved through the heavy double doors at the rear of the bus and ran back to the bridge, under the shadowy barrel vault.

It could be that I read too much in a wink, and I wouldn't have been the first, but it seemed to me that the lion knew who I was. I believed that. I believed that the lion had a message for me, that the lion had come Lord knows how many miles in search of me, had evaded countless hunters in order to deliver his intelligence. Now he was here and my father had been hired to kill him. The lion would never make it back to Africa.

He waited for me on the sidewalk below the bridge. Flies crawled in the tangles of his mane. He watched me with yellow eyes. His hide sagged over his bones; the sore on his shoulder was inflamed, graveled with white pustules. His belly was distended, bloated from hunger. I thought of how far he was from home, how many thousands of miles he had traveled, so far from the zebras and wildebeests, the giraffes and antelopes of his native land, his nourishment. Here there were only people to eat. I could not imagine this lion stooping to devour the neighborhood mutts or the blinkered carriage horses.

I wondered how long it would take him to gobble me down, and how much it would hurt, the long white teeth, the massive jaws, how long, and would he strip me to the wet bone or leave some meat for the pigeons to peck at, would he spit out my knuckles and watch them roll like gambler's dice, would he chew through my spine and suck out the marrow, would he look up from my carcass, his muzzle painted red, watch the taxis race by like stray gazelles frantic for their herd?

"Speak to me," I pleaded, hungry for revelation. "Speak to me."

If you have ever stood near a lion, you understand humility. Nothing that lives is more beautiful. A four-hundred-pound lion can run down a thoroughbred, can tear through steel railroad car doors with his claws, can hump his mate eighty times in one day.

The lion rose to all fours and walked closer, until his whiskers were nearly brushing against my shirt. I closed my eyes and waited. The carnivorous stink of him, the low purr of his breathing, the mighty engine of him—I was ready. I got down on my knees on the sidewalk, below the Queensboro Bridge, and the lion's breath was hot as steam in my ear.

When I opened my eyes the lion was gone and I was shivering in the August heat. I hailed a taxi and directed the turbaned driver to the Frick Museum, but when I got there the front doors of the old robber baron's mansion were bolted shut. It was Monday, I remembered. The museum was closed. That's why Butchko was home. It was the worst possible time to be Monday, and I imagined that all days would now be Monday, that we would suffer through months of Mondays, that the office workers would rise day after day and never come closer to the weekend, they would check the newspaper each morning and groan, and the churchgoers would find themselves, perpetually, a day too late for the Sabbath.

I needed Bellini's Francis. I needed to stand with the virgin saint and experience the ecstasy, to feel the rapture driven through my palms, my feet. I needed to understand the language of animals, the words of the beasts, because when the lion whispered in my ear it sounded like nothing but the breath of a big cat. I needed translation.

I walked all the way home. The house was empty, every clock ticking solemnly until—in the space of a terrifying second—they yodeled the hour in unison. Whenever my father was in Africa I would quit winding the clocks; in every room their dead hands would mark the minute the pendulum stopped swinging. He always synchronized them the day he came home.

In my bedroom I uncapped the telescope's lens and eyepiece and studied the apartments across the street. My little brother was away—at a baseball game, I imagined. He rooted for the Mets and had their pennant on his wall. In the next apartment over, the old man leaned against his windowsill, gazing toward Harlem. The redhead one floor below him seemed healthier; she lay belly down on her carpeted floor, propped on her elbows, chewing a pencil, still working on Sunday's crossword. Behind her, on the television, Marlon Brando smooched Eva Marie Saint. The redhead never turned the TV off: not when she was away at work, not when she was sleeping. I understood—voices comforted her, even strangers' voices.

These people were my friends, my comrades, I cared about them, but I wanted that building to slide aside for the afternoon. I wanted a clear prospect of the entire city. I was looking for a lion and a blue-eyed hunter.

The redhead finished her crossword and began checking her answers against the solution in Monday's paper. The television behind her flashed an urgent graphic: BREAKING NEWS. A reporter wearing a safari hat and sunglasses began speaking into his microphone, gesturing to the crowd surrounding him. I tried to read his lips. Bored of the game, I was about to swing the telescope away when I saw the lion, *my* lion, staring into the camera. He sat by a fountain, a great round fountain with a winged angel standing above the waters.

I ran. Down the stairs, out the door, west on Eighty-fourth Street, dodging the street traffic, dashing across the avenues, York First Second Third Lexington Park Madison Fifth, into Central Park, panting, sweat pouring into my eyes. All the way to Bethesda Terrace, at least a mile, farther than I had run in years. When I got there the crowd bulged way back to the band shell, hundreds of yards from the fountain. A man with a pushcart sold Italian ices and sodas. A news helicopter circled above us.

I shoved and sidled my way to the front lines, ignoring the dirty looks, the muttered heys, watchits, and yos. Blue police sawhorses barricaded the way, a cop stationed every ten feet. Two curving stone staircases flanked by balustrades swept down to the terrace. The lion sat patiently by the angel fountain. Behind him was the stagnant pond where paddleboating tourists typically photographed the bushes and collided with each other and cursed in every language known to man. They had all been evacuated. I saw my father, halfway down the steps, on one knee, holding his rifle. Two Park Service rangers stood next to him, high-powered dart guns aimed at the lion. Police sharpshooters ringed the terrace.

At the back of the crowd people yelled and whistled and laughed, but up close, in view of the lion, there was cathedral silence. My father gave the order and the rangers pulled their triggers. Darts fly far slower than bullets; I could trace their black flight from gun barrels to lion shoulder.

The lion roared. His jaws swung open and he roared. All the birds sitting in the trees burst from their branches and squawked skyward, a panicked flight of pigeons and sparrows. Everyone leaning against the barricades fell back, the entire crowd retreating a step as instincts commanded: *run, run, run!* A lion's roar can be heard for five miles in the emptiness of the savanna. Even in Manhattan his protest echoed above the constant squall of car alarms and ambulance sirens, above the whistles of traffic cops and the low rumble of subway trains. I imagine that sunbathers in the Sheep Meadow heard the roar, and tourists in Strawberry Fields; that bicyclists squeezed their hand brakes and stood on their pedals, squinted through their sunglasses in the direction of the noise; that old men, piloting their remote-controlled miniature schooners across the algae-filmed water of the Boat Pond, looked north, leaving their ships to drift; that dog walkers watched their charges go rigid, prick up their ears, then bark madly, until all the dogs in the borough were howling; that every domestic cat sitting on a windowsill stared heartlessly toward the park and licked its paws clean.

The lion stood unsteadily, blinking up at the sun. He began to walk, headed for the staircase, but stumbled after a few paces. Everyone in the crowd inhaled at the same moment. My father gave another command and two more darts pierced the lion's hide, releasing their tranquilizers. The rangers cradled their guns in their arms and waited; four darts were enough to put a rhino to sleep.

The lion charged. He reached the steps so quickly that none of the sharpshooters had time to react; he bounded up the broad stone stairs, white fangs bared, while the rangers fumbled with their guns and the cops standing near me said *Jesus Christ* and backed into the sawhorses and mothers in the crowd covered their children's eyes.

In midleap the lion seemed to crash into an invisible wall; he twisted in the air and landed heavily on his side, front paws two steps above his hind paws. The rifle shot sounded as loud and final as a vault door slamming shut. My father ejected the spent shell and it glittered in the air before bouncing off the balustrade and into the vegetation below. I ducked under the sawhorse, evading the dazed policemen, and ran down the stairs. My father saw me coming and shouted my name, but I was past him before he could stop me. I knelt down beside the lion and held his furred skull in my palms, my forearms buried in his dirty mane. He seemed smaller now, shrunken. The blood puddling beneath him began to drip down the steps.

"Tell me," I begged him, looking into his yellow eyes. My father was coming for me. I lowered my head so that my right ear rested against the lion's damp muzzle. "Tell me."

A series of violent spasms ran down the length of his outstretched body. Each breath exited his lungs with an unnerving whistle. His jaws slowly parted. I closed my eyes and waited. He licked my face with his mighty tongue until my father collared me and dragged me aside. I did not watch the mercy shot.

Hours later, when I stood in the shower and let the hot water beat down on me, I picked three blue splinters from my palms. It took me a while to figure out that they came from gripping the police sawhorse by Bethesda Terrace. After the shower I toweled myself dry, pulled on my pajamas, climbed the stairs to my bedroom, locked the door behind me, and switched off the lights. A pale moon shone weakly through the pebbled glass. I tried to remember how many miles away she was, how many cold miles of sky I would need to climb. It seemed impossible to me that men had ever walked there, had ever cavorted in her loose gravity.

When I was young I had known the number, known her distance to the mile. I had known her diameter, her weight in metric tons, the names of her major craters, the precise duration of her rotation around the earth. I forgot everything.

I uncapped General Early's telescope and scanned the apartments opposite. Whatever the old man was looking for in Harlem, he had quit for the night—the lamps were all out and the shades drawn. My little brother was awake. He sat beneath his sheets with a flashlight—a one-boy tent—furtively reading when he was supposed to be sleeping. I watched him for an hour, until I felt the calm blood return, flowing through the arteries and capillaries, delivering peace and oxygen to every living cell.

I checked the other rooms in my customary search for fire, and this night I found it. Not in the boy's apartment but one flight down, candles burning atop the stereo speakers and bookshelves, the coffee table and turned-off television, the windowsill and mantle. The redhead, naked, straddled a man on her sofa, her hands resting on his narrow shoulders. In the candlelight her flanks were mapped with copper trails of sweat. She rose and fell like a buoy in the sea, bobbing with the waves. Before I turned away, to give them their privacy, the woman flung her head back and stiffened for an instant, her hands falling from Butchko, her fingers spread wide. Her mouth opened but I'm sure no words came out, no words at all, nothing but ecstasy.

I Love to See You Coming, I Hate to See You Go

AMY BLOOM

WILLIAM HAS GOUT.

It is the worst and most embarrassing pain of his life. His true nature, his desires and hidden history are now revealed. By his foot.

Before he can get to the phone, the machine picks up.

"It's me. I heard the gout's back. Call me."

Claire's messages are always like this, concerned and crabby, as if having to make the call will cause her—probably has caused her, the plane is pulling away even as she speaks—to miss her flight.

"I'm here," William says.

"Okay, do you want to just get Thai in Worcester?"

Worcester is halfway between Claire's house and his. William doesn't have the energy even for Thai in Worcester.

"Worcester? Baghdad, without the dignity. Why don't you just drive up here and bring lunch?" He would like to patch things up with Claire, but just holding the phone drives long, thick needles of uric acid deep into his joints. He should have flowers in the house. He should shave. It won't be romantic.

Claire gets her car washed and drives up. She has to make sure that her visit takes place when Charles won't want to come, and there are things she cannot cancel and things she doesn't want to cancel, and in the end she sticks a note on her door, changing her office hours, and she loads up the car. Usually she brings William corned beef on rye, or paté and pumpernickel, and a big can of Guinness, and once, when they were right in the thick of things, she brought a box of Krispy Kremes and a bottle of Sancerre, but none of that is right for someone with gout. She packs two cooked, skinless chicken breasts, blanched broccoli, a basket of Maine blueberries (she read up after the first attack, and every Web site said blueberries), a box of chocolate soy shake, and a little tub of tofu. It's not romantic.

Claire knocks twice and comes in. If Isabel were there, they'd hug and kiss before she was ushered into the Presence. And if Isabel were upstairs, but not too close by, William would kiss Claire hard on the lips and then he'd ask her to do things that he wouldn't ask of Isabel. If Isabel were there, she'd make Claire stay over when it got late, and lend her her own ivory linen pajamas, and Claire would lie awake, under the faded pink comforter in his daughter's old room, listening for William and imagining him listening for her. Neither one of them would slip down the hall at two a.m., they wouldn't expect it of each other, but at breakfast, while Isabel showered, Claire would look at William with a sort of friendly disdain, and he would look at her as if she were selling drugs to schoolchildren.

William calls her name from the living room. He would get up, but it hurts too much. He usually shaves twice a day. He usually wears custom-made shirts and mossy, old-fashioned cologne, and he would prefer not to have Claire see him in backless bedroom slippers and green baggy pants, dragging his foot from room to room like roadkill, but when he says so, she laughs.

"I've seen you worse," she says, and there is no arguing with that. It seems to William that Claire last saw him looking good, well-dressed and in control of himself, a year and a half ago, before they were lovers. Now she's seen him riddled with tubes, hung left and right with plastic pouches, sweating like a pig though a thin hospital gown that covered about a third of him.

Claire puts her groceries away in Isabel's kitchen. Isabel has been telling William to change his ways for twenty years, and now he has to. Claire puts the chicken breasts in the refrigerator and thinks that that must be nice for Isabel.

William sits back in his armchair, moving his right foot out of harm's way. If Claire gently presses his foot or lets the cuff of her pants just brush against his ankle, it will hurt worse than either of his heart attacks. He sees Claire angling toward him and moves his leg back a little more.

"Don't bump me," he says.

"I wasn't *going* to bump you."

Claire sits on the arm of the chair and glances at his foot. It's her job not to take any notice of it. She can notice the slippers and green gardening pants, and she can say something clever about it all, if she can think of something clever, which she can't. Isabel says clever, kind things to William when he's under the weather. Claire's seen her do it. Isabel arranges him beautifully, she flatters him into good behavior, she buys chairs that fit him and finds huge, handsome abstracts to balance the chairs; she drapes herself around him like wisteria and she carries his hypertension pills, his indomethacin, his cholesterol pills, and his prednisone in an engraved silver case, as if it's a pleasure. The last time William and Claire had sex, William rested above Claire, just for a minute, catching his breath. He slipped off his elbows, and his full weight fell onto her. "Jesus Christ," she'd said, "you could kill someone." William did laugh but it's not something she likes to remember.

"God, it's like a giant turnip," Claire says, putting her hand over her mouth.

It is exactly like a giant turnip and William is happy to hear her say so. His heart rises on a small, breaking wave of love just because Claire, who says the precisely wrong and tactless thing as naturally as breathing, is with him, and will be right here for almost twenty-four hours.

"Really, cooked turnip."

"Well, the skin begins peeling in a couple of days, the doctor says, so it'll be even more disgusting. Hot, peeling, naked turnip." He leans forward and kisses the shoulder closest to him.

"Did Isabel leave food for you?"

"Hardly any. Well, the three things I can eat. When she comes back the two of you can have a big party, tossing back shots of vodka, eating caviar out of the jar."

"Isabel wouldn't do that to you."

"You would."

"Probably," Claire says, and bends to kiss him. Everything she thought about while driving up, how much trouble he is and how selfish and where all that shameless piggery has gotten him (gout and her) is nothing when he kisses her, although even when their lips touch, even as the soft, salty tip of his tongue connects to hers, they are not the best kisses she's ever had.

When they stop kissing, William says, "Take off that ugly brown coat and stay awhile, won't you?"

A month before the gout attack, Claire made William come with her to visit her uncle David. William clutched the staircase with both hands and made her carry his hat, his jacket, and the bottle of wine.

"You didn't say it was a walk-up."

"It's two flights, William, that's all. Just rest for a minute."

It was a bad idea. William said it, panting up the stairs, and he said it again when Uncle David went into his kitchen to get William a glass of water. And Uncle David said it when William went to use the bathroom. William washed his face with cold water and took his hypertension pills. He looked at the Viagra pills he'd been carrying around, in a tiny square of plastic wrap twisted like the wax-paper salt shakers his mother had made for picnics. He'd been hoping for several weeks that he and Claire would go for a very elegant autumnal picnic in the Berkshires and that afterward they would stop into one of the seedy motels on Route 163. When they do finally have the picnic and they do find the Glen Aire Motel, the Viagra mixes badly with William's hypertension pills, and right after getting the kind of erection the online pharmacy had promised, he passes out. Claire will have to drive them home in her aggressive, absentminded way, blasting the horn and sprinkling the remaining six blue pills out the window as William rests, his face against the glass.

"What do I want to meet him for?" Uncle David said. "He seems like a nice man, but I like Charles."

"He's my best friend. That's all. I wanted my best friend to meet my favorite relative."

"Only relative." David shrugged.

It was so clearly a bad idea, and so clearly understood by all parties to be a bad idea, that Claire thought she should just take William back downstairs and send her uncle a box of chocolates and a note of apology.

William came out of the bathroom, mopping his face, and shook Claire's uncle's hand again.

"Nice place. I'm sorry Claire made me come."

"Me too. She's hard to argue with."

The two men smiled, and William picked up his coat.

"Those stairs'll kill you," David said. "Why don't you have a beer, and then go."

They had their beers as if Claire wasn't there. They talked about baseball, as the season was under way, and they talked about electric cars, which was even more boring than baseball. Claire sat on the windowsill and swung her feet.

William used the bathroom again before they left. David and Claire looked at each other.

David said, "You can't hide someone that big. Where would you put him, sweetheart? He'd stick out of the closet, and you can't put a man like that under the bed."

Claire believed that Charles would never walk in on her and William. It was probably not a great idea to sleep with William; she knew it wasn't a great idea almost immediately after it happened. She knew she had managed to upend something that had sat neatly and four-square beneath them, and even if William shouldered the blame, even if Charles was good enough to blame William, Claire's never thought you could fault a man for taking sex when it was offered, any more than you'd blame the dog for flinging himself on a scrap that missed the plate. She knew she'd done more than just tilt the friendship between the four of them, but she was not ruining their lives with brilliantined paramours, sidecars, and cuckolds, the way her uncle made it sound. She was not ruining their lives at all, and you might think that the man known in her family as the Lord Byron of Nyack would understand that.

"What can I say?"

"He makes you feel so young?" David sang. "He makes you feel like spring has sprung, songs must be sung? Like that?"

"No. You don't have to be ugly about it. I think . . . I make him feel alive."

David shook his head. "I'm sure you do. That's what these things are for."

Claire looked out the living room window and counted three women pushing strollers, four boys smoking cigarettes, seven bags of garbage.

"Don't bring him again."

"I get it," Claire said. "I'm sorry."

"You're not listening to me. Stop."

"All *right*."

William walked in to see Uncle David whispering in Claire's ear and Claire pulling on her coat. William would rather have danced naked in a Greyhound bus station, he would rather have danced naked wearing a big pink party hat and matching pink boots, than stay another minute in Claire's uncle's apartment.

The men shook hands again and Claire kissed her uncle on the cheek, and he patted her face. They didn't like to fight.

In the car William said, "What was that for?"

"I thought you'd like each other."

"You embarrassed him," William said, and he thought it was just like her to make that perfectly decent old man meet her lover and force him—not that she ever thought she forced anything upon anyone—to betray Charles by saying nothing or betray Claire, which of course he would never do. It was just exactly like Claire to act as if it had been a pleasant visit under normal circumstances.

William dropped Claire off at the university parking lot and drove back to Boston. She watched him pull away, the gray roof silver from the halogen street lamps, the inside brightened for just a second by the green face of his phone and the deep yellow flare of his lighter.

At four o'clock, William takes the round of pills Isabel left in a shot glass by the kitchen sink. At five, he falls asleep, and Claire reads their newspaper and then William's old *Economists*. At six, while William snores in his recliner, she calls Charles to say that William is under the weather, Isabel is still on duty with her mother, and she, Claire, will stay overnight with William. As she talks, Claire gets her coat out of the kitchen and her sweater out of the dining room and kicks her shoes into the rattan basket in the front hall.

"Don't kill him," Charles says. Claire is not famous for her bedside manner.

"He's a pain in the ass," Claire says, and it's not just her faint reflexive wish to throw Charles, and everyone, off the track. Isabel and Charles and all of their combined children could walk through the house right now, looking for trouble, and there'd be no sign, no scent, no stray, mysterious thread, of anything except an old, buckling friendship.

William snorts and wakes up, his hair wild and waving like silver palm fronds. He looks like he might have had a bad dream, and Claire smiles to comfort him. He looks at her as if he's never seen her, or never seen her like this, which isn't so; he's seen her a hundred times just like this, seated across from him deep in thought, flinging her legs over the arm of the chair to get comfortable.

"Oh, you're here," he says.

Claire drops the magazine on the floor and stands up.

"Do you want some dinner?"

"How can you?" William asks. "What kind of dinner?"

"Aren't you the most pathetic thing." Claire walks over to smooth his dream-blown hair. They stay like this so long, her hands on his head, his head against her chest, that neither one of them can think of what the next natural thing to do is.

"We could go to bed," William says.

Claire goes into the kitchen, gathers up everything that wasn't eaten at lunch and every promising plastic container, including a little olive tapenade and a lot of pineapple cottage cheese, and lays it all on the coffee table in front of William with a couple of forks and two napkins.

"You do go all out," he says.

"I don't know how Isabel caters to you the way she does. If Charles were as much of a baby as you, I'd get a nurse and check into a hotel."

"I'm sure you would."

He doesn't say again that they could go to bed; she heard him the first time. That lousy picnic might have been the last time. This might not be the farewell dinner (and you could hardly call it dinner, it's not even a snack, it's what a desperately hungry person with no taste buds might grab while running through a burning house), but it has that feeling. She's brought him sensible food, and no wine; she hasn't made fun of his slippers or the gardening pants; she's worn her ugly brown coat and not the pretty blue one they bought together in Boston. An intelligent, disinterested observer would have to say it doesn't look good for the fat man.

"Let's go to bed," Claire says. Husbands and wives can skip sex, without fuss, without it even being a cause for fuss, but Claire can't imagine how you say to the person whom you have come to see for the express purpose of having sex, Let's just read the paper.

"You look like a Balthus," William says. "Nude with Blue Socks."

"Really? I must be thirty years too old. Anyway, Balthus. Ugh." She pulls the socks off and throws them on William's nightstand. They're his socks. He must have a dozen pair of navy cashmere socks and he's never asked to have these back. And Charles has never said, Whose are these? They cover Claire almost to the knee, the empty heel swelling gently above her ankle. She wears them all the time.

William lies under the sheets and the comforter, leaving his foot uncovered and resting, like the royal turnip on a round velvet pillow taken from Isabel's side of the bed.

"Is it better?" Claire asks.

"It is better. I hate for you to have to see it."

Claire shrugs, and William doesn't know if that means that seeing his foot grotesquely swollen and purple cannot diminish her ardor or that her ardor, such as it is, could hardly be diminished.

"I don't mind," she says. She doesn't mind. She didn't mind when her kids were little and projectile vomiting followed weeping chicken pox, which followed thrush and diarrhea; she didn't mind the sharp, dark, powdery smell of her mother's dying or the endless rounds of bedpan and sponge bath. She would have been a great nurse if the patients never spoke.

"You looked very cute in those socks, I have to tell you." William puts a hand on Claire's stomach.

"I don't know," Claire says. "I think . . . we might have to stop . . . I think . . ."

William laughs before he sees her face. This is exactly what he has hoped not to hear, and he had thought that if she were naked beside him, bare even of his socks and her reading glasses, they would get through the night without having this conversation.

Claire turns on her side to look at him. "You don't think I might have a guilty conscience?"

William sits up and puts on his glasses. He doesn't think Claire has a guilty conscience; he doesn't think she has any kind of conscience at all. She loves Charles, she loves her sons, she is very fond of William. She found herself having sex with William when they were bombing

Afghanistan and it seemed the world would end, and now they are bombing Iraq and the evening news is horrifying, rather than completely terrifying, and whatever was between them is old hat; it's an anthrax scare, it's Homeland Security; it's something that mattered a great deal for a little while and then not much.

"You might have a guilty conscience. Sometimes people confuse that with a fear of getting caught."

Claire does not say that she would cut William's throat and toss his body in the dump before she would let Charles find them and that there is clearly something wrong with William that he would even mention the possibility.

"I don't want to get a guilty conscience. Let's just say that."

William pushes the socks off the nightstand. There is nothing to be gained by arguing. What they have is nothing to their marriages. Claire to Isabel, him to Charles: two cups of water to the ocean. There's no reason to say: Remember the time you wore my shirt around the motel room like a trench coat and belted it with my tie to go get ice? Remember when you sat on top of me in East Rock Park and you pulled off your T-shirt and the summer light fell through the leaves onto your white shoulders and you bent down close to me, your hair brushing my face, and said, "We're in trouble now." And I have never known another woman who can bear, let alone sing, all of *The Pirates of Penzance*, and who else will ever love me in this deep, narrow, greedy way?

"We'll do whatever you want," he says.

Now Claire laughs. "I don't think so. I think what I want, in this regard, is not possible."

"Probably not."

Oh, put up a fuss, Claire thinks. Throw something. Rise up. Tell me that whatever this costs, however pointless this is, the pleasure of it is so great, your need for me is so tremendous that however this will end—and we are too old not to know that it'll end either this way, with common sense and muted loss and a sad cup of coffee, or with something worse in a parking lot somewhere a few months from now and it's not likely to cover either one of us with glory—it is somehow worth it.

William closes his eyes. I would like it if seeing you would always make me happy, Claire thinks. I would like to have lost nothing along the way.

"What do you think?" she says.

William doesn't open his eyes and Claire thinks, Now I have lost him, as if she has not been trying to lose him, without hurting him, for the last hour. She crosses her arms on her chest, in the classic position of going to bed angry (which William may not even recognize—for all she knows, he and Isabel talk it out every time, no matter how late), and she thinks, Maybe I just want to hurt him a little, just to watch him take the hit and move on, because he is the kind of man who can and does. Except in matters of illness, when he sounds like every Jewish man Claire knows, William's Presbyterian stoicism makes for a beautiful, distinctly masculine suffering that Charles can't be bothered with. She uncrosses her arms and puts a hand on William's wide, smooth chest. He looks at her hand and breathes deeply, careful not to shift the comforter toward his foot.

"I don't know," he says. "Farewell, happy fields?"

"You're not helping."

"I'm not trying to help."

"Oh," Claire says.

"It's late," William says.

"I know." Claire rolls toward him.

"Watch out for the turnip."

"I *am.*"

Her head is on his chest, her chin above his heart. His hand is deep in her hair. They sleep like this, a tiny tribe, a sliver of marriage, and in their dreams, Claire is married to Charles and they are at Coney Island before it burned down, riding double on number seven in the steeplechase, and they are winning and they keep riding and the stars are as thick as snow. And in their dreams, William is married to Isabel and she brings their daughter home from the hospital, and when William sets her down in the crib, which is much larger and prettier than the one they really had on Elm Street, he sees she has small sky-blue wings and little clawed feet.

William kisses the baby's pearly forehead and says, to his wife in the dream and to Claire beside him, It's not the end of the world, darling.

Severance

ROBERT OLEN BUTLER

After careful study and due deliberation it is my opinion the head remains conscious for one minute and a half after decapitation.

—Dr. Dassy d'Estaing, 1883

In a heightened state of emotion, we speak at the rate of 160 words per minute.

—Dr. Emily Reasoner, *A Sourcebook of Speech*, 1975

VALENTINE

Roman priest and saint, beheaded by Emperor Claudius II, circa 270

in she pads and crouches over me, quietly, the she-wolf, I am in her cave, not beneath the fig tree where Romulus and Remus cry in hunger, she has abandoned them to give me her tit and the cave is my jail cell and I wake ready to die for my Lord, His name on my lips, the dream a dream from my childhood before Christ and I crouch tiny in our doorway and naked men run by striking the backs of women who willingly bare their flesh to receive the lash of goatskin, receiving fertility on the day of Lupercalia, and Julia appears now at my cell door, daughter of Asterius my jailer, her eyes sightless from birth, I rise and cross to her and take the cup of water and the crust of bread and I drop them at once, knowing this time my hands are filled with the Spirit and I need only touch her eyelids and she will see, and her hair falls soft about her shoulders and I hesitate, my loins filling and in my head the sound of naked men rushing past and we bare our backs, we priests, ready for the lash of God, and her face is lambent, turned slightly aside, and I slough off my clothes: I am naked, visibly filled with the ache of men, and I lay my thumbs lightly on her eyes so she can see her Valentine

GOOSENECK (GANSNACKEN)

Court jester to Duke Eberhard the Bearded, beheaded by his master, 1494

quickly, my lord arrives soon, I tether the goat and place the crest of my lord's defeated enemy round its neck and put my oft-merrily-used floppy crown on my ass-eared hat its bells jingling as if in laughter already at my jest and I have secured the rope in the ceiling beam and I stretch and draw myself up, hanging for a moment, breathless from my own wit, my father places his hand on my shoulder and pushes me toward the Duke descended from his horse and laughing at the belt of choked geese around my waist, me wishing to keep their feet dry I say, and he laughs loud and I am excited by this sound, my jokes are my lovers thrilling me, and he takes me to Wurtemburg and a life of mirth and he will soon be here I begin to swing on the rope, pulling hard at it and I am swinging faster and the goat looks up at me and I wave at him whom I will, as the great Duke, shortly leap upon in antic triumph and the door opens and it is the Duke and I am a jester not a sailor the goat breaks his knot and bolts just as I leap from the rope and fly at my stricken lord and fall heavy upon him, crotch to face, and alas I am already full excited at my joke, like a lover

ANNE BOLEYN

Queen of England, beheaded after the displeasure of her husband, King Henry VIII, 1536

tiny and gray is the boy and I am undone, him being no living boy and no heir to my husband, though I hold his body close and I am breathless with love for him, and the next is merely a lump of blood between my legs and he was my last chance to live, this clot this stain this wet-cleansed spot in my place of sex, but still there is my sweet girl my

Elizabeth her pale face and her hair the color of the first touch of sun in the sky, the pale fire of her hair, she turns her gray eyes to me and I know I am soon to leave her and she is dressed in russet velvet and a purple satin cap with a caul of gold and the candlelight thrashes about the walls and I say to her *Lady Princess I will always be your mother* and she says in her wee voice *Madam you are my Queen* and she bows as she has been taught and I ache to take her up but she is right, of course, we are who we are to each other and I am who I am to the man who must cast me off now, and I say *Rise my sweet child* and she straightens and lifts her face and I bend to her, I draw near to her, I cup my daughter's head in my hands

MARIE ANTOINETTE

Queen of France, guillotined by order of the
French Revolutionary Tribunal, 1793

softly on the arm he touches his wife and they hesitate in the dim corridor I a few steps behind holding tight to nurse's petticoat and I know how never never again will I be present in a moment like this because there is always the great goose-flock of my brothers and sisters and always there are courtiers and ladies-in-waiting and I am but a little girl a little little girl with a lute I can play and satin shoes with such elegant thin soles I feel the cold stone on my toes and he touches his wife's arm, he who is Emperor of Austria, King of Jerusalem, Hungary, Bohemia, Dalmatia, Croatia, and even more, that's as far as I can remember I am small as small can be I could crawl into the belly of my lute and stay there looking between the strings he touches his wife's arm and he is my father and she is my mother the Empress of Austria and Queen of Jerusalem and Hungary and so forth and her skirts are bright and enormous I could live inside them and bring my three dogs and my pony too and all my clothes and the skirts are a problem for my father who has touched my mother's arm because he leans far over far across them and nearly falls but she turns her face to him knowing he is her beloved and he kisses her

NGUYEN VAN TRINH

Viet Minh guerilla leader, guillotined by French Colonial authorities, 1952

very still, I hold my rifle drawn across my chest and I am careful even in the breath I draw I am pressed against a mangrove tree my knees tucked close I move my eyes but I can see none of my comrades and of course I cannot hear them for we all wait on the noisy French wait till they are between the two columns of us and I should at least be able to see my friend Ky I know his place forward in a closing of vines but he is not there and I wait for the French and I think of my father in his collar and cravat and the way his head would draw down like a tortoise when he spoke of the Frenchman who ran his lycée *pull your collar off, my father, seize by the throat that man who shames you* and my father is a vase of ashes and my mother prays in the bourgeois myth that his spirit lives yet in another realm, and I hear them nearby, breaking dry leaves beneath their feet, and it is time and I make a sharp bird cry and I leap now but there is no rifle in my hands I have come from the trees onto the path and these are not Frenchmen but Vietnamese in mandarin dress and one turns his face and it is my father and he offers his hand

LYDIA KOENIG

Chicago woman, decapitated by her son, 1999

baby Mama calls me baby on my lap a lump of cloth baby doll and then a freckled face, Howdy Doody baby, I hum his name his puppet strings folded under, not a doll but I like his hard legs and arms beneath his clothes like real bones, Lake Michigan at twilight the color of tarnished brass a hand inside my lap and he asks me that night atop the Prudential Building the lake too dark to see and then my baby my own baby boy his bones deep and untouchable inside him, I dress him in pink thinking it makes no difference I hold him baby and then in plaid and he has freckles on his nose and he stinks of urine from his bed I carry the great lump of soiled cloth and the Tide waiting, the cleaning power of Tide and Oxydol and Clorox, and the man is gone and my baby cries all night through, though he is no baby he is returned and he says *help me find a vein help me tap this vein* and I cannot, I take his load of piss sheets to the Maytag in the basement and it is cool here and smells of the lake on a bad day and I wash them and dry them sitting in the dimness of the basement and I hold these sheets in my lap my baby my baby's voice is behind me

Revenge of the Dinosaurs

DEBORAH EISENBERG

HI, BARBARA, I said. You're Barbara?

Eileen, said the nurse who answered the door. Nights.

I'm the granddaughter, I said.

I figured, Eileen said. Barbara told me you'd be showing up. So where's that handsome brother of yours?

Bill? I said. I beat Bill? That's a first.

Traffic must be bad, she said.

Traffic, traffic . . . I was goggling past Eileen at Nana's apartment—the black-and-white tile, the heavy gold-framed mirror, the enormous vases or whatever they are, the painting of a mysterious, leafy glade I'd loved so much from the time I was a child, the old silver-dust light of Nana's past. I was always shocked into sleepiness when I saw the place, as if a little mallet had bonked me on the head, sending me far away.

Or in Connecticut, Eileen said. I looked at her. Isn't that where they drive in from? she said. He's a wonderful man, your brother. So kind and thoughtful. And his wife, too. They always know just how to cheer your grandmother up. And that's one cute little girl they've got.

How's Nana doing? I asked.

Awhile since you've seen her, Eileen commented.

I live on the other side of the country! I said.

I know that, dear, Eileen said, I've seen your picture. With the trees. Before the second stroke she liked me to sit with her and go over the pictures.

I stared. Nana? Bill had told me to prepare myself, but still—family souvenirs with the nurse? It's supposed to mean something to be one person rather than another.

Eileen accompanied me into the living room. Nana was dozing in one of the velvet chairs. I sneezed. Soldiers were marching silently toward us across the black-and-white desert of an old television screen. An attractively standardized smiling blond woman in a suit replaced them. Does Nana watch this? I asked. She seems to like having it on, Eileen said. I keep the sound off, though. She can't really hear it, and I'd rather not. Wake up, dear, your granddaughter's here to see you. Don't be surprised if she doesn't recognize you right off, Eileen told me. Dear, it's your granddaughter.

It's Lulu, Nana, I said, loudly. Nana surveyed me, then Eileen. Neither Bill nor I had inherited those famous blue eyes that can put holes right through you, though our father had, exactly, and so had our brother, Peter. Where does all that beauty go when someone finishes with it? If something exists how can it stop existing, I recently mused aloud to Jeff. Things take their course, Jeff said (kind of irritably, frankly). Well, what does *that* mean, really—*things take their course*? Jeff always used to be (his word) charmed that I wasn't a (his word) sucker for received (his phrase) structures of logic. Anyhow, if something exists, it exists, is what I think, but when Nana turned back to the TV she did actually look like just any sweet old lady, all shrunk into her little blanket. I bent and kissed her cheek.

She winced. It's Lulu, dear, Eileen shouted. One of Nana's hands lifted from the pale cashmere blanket across her lap in a little wave, as if there were a gnat. I'll be in the kitchen, Eileen said. Call me if you need me. I sat down near Nana on the sofa. I was not the gnat. Nana, I said, you look fabulous.

Did she hear anything at all? Well, she'd never gone in for verbal expressions of affection, either. Someone sighed loudly. I looked around. The person who had sighed was me.

The last time I'd seen Nana, her hearing was perfect and she was going out all the time, looking, if not still stunning, still seriously good, with the excellent clothes and hair and so on. She was older, obviously, than she had been, but that was all: older. It's too drastic to take in—a stroke! One teensy moment, total eclipse. In my opinion, all moments ought to contain uniform amounts of change: X many moments equal strictly X much increase in age equal strictly X much change. Of course, it would be better if it were X much decrease in age.

Oh, where on earth was Bill? Though actually, I was early. Because last week when I'd called my old friend Juliette and said I was coming to the city to see Nana, she said sure I could stay at her place and naturally I assumed I'd be hanging out there a bit when I got in from the airport and we'd catch up and so on. But when I arrived, some guy, Juliette's newish boyfriend, evidently—Wendell, I think his name might be—whom she'd sort of mentioned on the phone, turned out to be there too. *Sure, let's just kill them, why not just kill them all,* he was shouting. Juliette was peeling an orange. I'm not saying kill *extra* people, she said, I'm just frightened; there are a lot of crazy, angry maniacs around who want to kill us, and I'm frightened. *You're frightened,* he yelled. *No one else in the world is frightened?* Juliette raised her eyebrows at me and shrugged. The orange smelled fantastic. I was completely dehydrated from the flight because they hardly even bring you water anymore though when I was little it was all so fun and special, with the pretty stewardesses and trays of little wrapped things, and I was just dying to tear open Juliette's fridge and see if there was another orange in there, but Wendell, if that's what his name is, was standing right in front of it shouting, *What are you saying? Are you saying we should kill everyone in the world to make sure there are no angry people left who want to HURT anyone?* So I waited a few minutes for him to finish up with what he wanted to get across and he didn't (and no one had ever gotten anything across to Juliette) and I just dropped that idea about the orange and said see you later and tossed my stuff under the kitchen table and plunged into the subway. When Juliette and I were at art school together, all her boyfriends had been a lot of fun, but that was three or four years ago.

Happy laundry danced across the screen on a line. Little kids ate ice cream. A handsome man pumped gasoline into a car, jauntily twirled the cap back on the gas tank, and turned to wink at me. A different standardly attractive woman in a suit appeared. It was hard to tell on this ancient black-and-white set what color we were supposed to believe her hair was. Red, maybe. She was standing on the street, and a small group of people, probably a family, was gathered around her. They were black, or anyhow not specifically white, and they were noticeably fatigued and agitated. Their breath made lovely vapor in the cold. One of them spoke distractedly into a microphone. The others jogged up and down, rubbing their arms. Someone was lying on the pavement. The possibly redheaded newscaster looked serene; she and the family appeared to have arrived at the very same corner from utterly different planets by complete coincidence. She had a pretty good job, actually. A lot better than selling vintage clothing, anyhow. And maybe she was getting some kind of injections. Then it was the blond newscaster again, bracketing a few seconds in which a large structure burst slowly open like a flower, spraying debris and, kind of, limbs, maybe. The blond newscaster was probably getting injections, herself. I might have caught some lines trying to creep up around near my eyes, lately. But even when I was a little child I felt that people who worry about that sort of thing are petty. Of course, when I was a little child I wasn't about to be getting sneak attacks from lines anytime soon. Hi, Nana, I said, sure you're okay with this stuff? But she just kept gazing at the images supplanting one another in front of her.

One way or another it had gotten to be a few months since Bill had called to tell me about Nana's initial stroke. I'd intended to come right out to see her, but it wasn't all that easy to arrange for a free week, and Jeff and I were having sort of vaguely severe money problems, and I just didn't manage to put a trip together until Bill called again and said that this time it was really serious. I reached over and rested my hand on Nana's. Nana had pretty much looked out for us—me and Bill and Peter—when our mother got sick (well, died, really) and our father started spending all his money on cars and driving them into things. If it hadn't been for Nana, who knows what would have happened to us.

Nana gave my hand a brief, speculative look that detached it from hers, and then she turned back to the TV. From what closet had that old apparatus been unearthed? Nana had always gotten her news from the *Times*, as far as I knew, and other periodicals. I wondered what she was seeing. Was it just that the shifting black-and-white patterns engaged her attention, or did she recognize them as information and find solace in an old habit of receiving it? Or did she still have some comprehension of what was happening in front of her?

Enormous crowds were streaming through streets. Refugees! I thought for an instant, my hands tingling—Evacuations! But a lot of the people were carrying large placards or banners, I saw, and I realized this must be one of the protests—there was the Capitol building, and then something changed and the Eiffel Tower was in the distance, and then there was something that looked like Parliament, and then for a second, a place I couldn't identify at all, and then another where there were mostly Asians. The apartment was stifling! Despite the horrible freezing weather I got up to open the window a crack. When I sat down again, Nana spoke. Her voice used to have a penetrating, rather solid sound, something like an oboe's, but now there were a lot of new threadlike cracks in it—it was hoarse, and strange. I suppose you have no idea how I happen to be here, she said. This is where you live, Nana, I said, in case she'd been speaking to me; this is your home. Nana examined my face—*dispassionately*, I think would be the exact right word. No wonder my father had been terrified of her when he was growing up! *Thank* you, she said, apropos of what, who could say. She folded her hands primly and ceased to see me.

My brain rolled up into a tube, and my childhood rushed through it, swift pictures of coming here to this apartment with my mother and father and Peter and Bill—swift-moving, decisive Nana, smelling simply beautiful when she leaned down to me, and her big, pretty teeth, and all the shiny, silver hair she could twist up and pin in place in a second with some fantastic ornament. The ornate silver tea service, the delicate slice of lemon floating and dreaming away in the fragile cup, the velvet chairs, the painting of the mysterious, beautiful, leafy world on the wall that you could practically just *enter* . . . the light, as soon as you opened the door, of a different time, the lovely, strange, tarnished light that had existed before I was born . . . translucent scraps of coming to see Nana went whirling through the tube and were gone. Nana, I said.

Doll-like figures sprayed into the air, broke open and poured out blackness. There was a bulldozer, and stuff crumbling. Eileen came in. Would I like a cup of tea, she asked me. Thanks, I told her, no. She paused for a moment before she went away again, squinting at the screen. Well, who knows, she said. But I'm glad I don't have sons.

Nana had come into the world at the end of one war and lived through part of another before she left Europe, so she must have seen plenty of swarming crowds in her time and crumbling stuff and men in uniforms and little black pinpricks puncturing the clear sky and swelling right up. Jeff and I don't have a TV. Jeff doesn't like anything about TV. The way the set looks, or the sound it makes, or what it does to your brain. He says he's not so dumb that he thinks he can outsmart the brainwashing. He likes to keep his brain clean all by himself, and it does have a sparkly, pristine quality, despite the fact that it's a bit squashed by events at the moment, which occasionally causes him to make remarks that could be considered vaguely inappropriate. For example, the other day we were going up in the elevator of the office building where Jeff and his team do their research, and there was a guy standing next to us, wearing a sort of light blue, churchy suit, and Jeff turned to him and said to him in a low voice, It's sunset. The guy glanced at Jeff and then at his watch. He had really nice eyes—candid, I think you'd say. He glanced at Jeff again and said, Would you mind pushing seven? Jeff said, Yup, the sun is setting, you guys at the helm. He pushed seven and turned back to the guy. See it sink toward the horizon, he said, feel the planet turn? Hear the big bones crunch at the earth's hot core? The wooly mammoths, the dinosaurs, hear that? The fossil fuels sloshing? Crunch, crunch, slosh, slosh, Dinosaur Sunset Lullaby? I nodded to the guy when he got out at seven, but he wasn't looking. Normally, Jeff is very cogent, and he's amazingly quick to spot the specious remark or spurious explanation, especially, these days, if I'm the one who's made it. I don't especially mind having a TV around myself, but my concentration isn't all that terrific in certain ways and I really can't get myself to sit down and follow what's going on in that little square window, so maybe I'm not as vulnerable to assault as Jeff is. But if someone turns on a TV in a bar, for example, I don't just have to run out screaming.

In fact, I never actually see a TV unless we happen to go out, which we really can't spare the money to do these days, even if we were to feel like it (which Jeff certainly doesn't). But TV or not, I had no trouble, as I sat there next to Nana, recognizing those faces appearing in front of us with their veiled and decorous expressions appropriate to serious matters. I suppose everyone knows those faces as well as if they were tattooed on the inside of one's eyelids. There they are, those guys, whether your eyes are open or shut.

Gigantic helicopters were nosing at some mountains. I felt worn out. Flying is no joke at all these days! The interrogations at the airport, and worrying about the nail scissors, and those dull boomings, even though you know it's only luggage getting vaporized, and then when you finally do get mashed into place on the clanking, rickety old thing, with your blood clotting up, and the awful artificial, recirculated whatever it is, air or whatever, who doesn't think of great chunks of charred metal falling from the sky? Oh, well. I'd gotten to Nana's in any case.

A recollection of my father and Nana sitting in this room back when they were on viable terms, drinking something from fragile, icy little shot glasses, pressed itself urgently upon me. Though of course, when Bill finally did stride in, allowing his overcoat to slip off into Eileen's hands, Peggy behind him, I was glad enough not to be sprawled out hiccuping. You beat me, Bill said, and kind of whacked me a bit on the back, that's a first. Unfair, I said, when am I ever late these days? How would I know? Bill said. You live on the other side of the country.

Peggy was carrying an enormous vase full of lilies, a funereal flower if ever there was one. Hi, Peggy, I said, some flowers you've got there. Melinda here, too? Hi, Aunt Lulu, Melinda called from the hall, where she was studying the magical glade. I had a sudden memory of the guy who'd given Nana that painting—Mr. Berman. What a handsome old man! He was one of Nana's suitors after she booted out Dad's dad. Dad used to refer to Mr. Berman as the Great Big Jew. Mr. Berman was very nice, as I remember, and rich and handsome, but Nana was sick of getting married, so he moved on, and Nana never looked back, I think. It wasn't in her nature.

Peggy was staring at the TV. Goodness me, she said, and jabbed at the remote until a few sluttish teenagers appeared, flouncing around a room with studio décor. That's better, Peggy said. She chuckled wanly. I calculated: the big gloomy bouquet must have cost about what I make in a week. Hey, Melinda, I said, as she wandered into the room, they brought you along, great. My sitter's mad at me, she said, they didn't have any choice—she looked at me—alternative? Sure, I said, that's fine: They didn't have any alternative. The hell we didn't, Bill said, we could have left her on a mountain with her ankles pierced. Melinda swiveled her head toward him, then swiveled it back. Your father's just being funny, I said. You thought that was funny, Aunt Lulu? Melinda said. Cute outfit, hon, Peggy told me, fanciful. The fun shirt is what? Pucci, I said, early seventies? An as-is—there's a cigarette burn, see?

Hey, Granana, Melinda said, watchin' a show, huh. She peered at Nana scientifically, and waggled her fingers in a little wave. Then she walked backward into the sofa and plopped down, showing her teeth for a moment as though she'd performed a trick. So what's going on? she asked no one in particular.

There were about five teenagers. One was a boy. They were all making faces and pausing for the silent audience to laugh, apparently. Peggy, who had a gift, rubbed Nana's hands and sort of chattered. Nana looked around, and spoke, in the strange voice that sounded like it had been shut away, gathering dust. Everyone, she said. Hi, Nana! we all said. Hello, Lulu, dear, she said, are you here? She blinked once, like a cat, and yawned. It was an odd sight, our elegant Nana's body and its needs taking precedence that way. She looked back at the TV, and said, What.

What the hell is this? Bill said, squinting at the flouncing, mugging teenagers. He flicked the remote, and there were those familiar guys again, standing around a podium beneath a huge flag. Bill grunted, and set the remote back on the table with a sharp little click. He forgot about the TV and started ranging around the room, absently picking up objects and turning them over, as though he was expecting to see price tags. Poor Bill. He was frowning a frown, which he'd no doubt perfected in front of his clients, that clearly referred to weighty matters. Terrible, he was muttering, terrible, terrible, terrible, terrible. His feelings for Nana were complicated, I knew (though he didn't seem to), heavily tinged with rage and resentment, like his feelings for everyone else. Our brother Peter was the quote unquote outstanding one, so Bill, as the other boy, had naturally suffered a lot growing up and was kind of arrested, being so compensatorily dutiful. He looked as if he was incredibly tired, too. Poor Nana, he said. Poor, poor, poor Nana.

Trip okay, hon? Peggy asked me. Where are you staying? One-two punch, huh, I said. You're so funny, Peggy said vaguely. You always make me laugh. She looked tired herself. Outside, someone was making some sort of commotion. Screaming or something. Bill went to the window and closed it. Listen, he said to me, I want to thank you for coming. He had already acquired a drink, I noticed—how had he managed that? I'm glad to be here, I said, it's natural, isn't it? You don't have to thank me. Good, he said. He frowned his frown again. I'm glad you decided to come. Because decisions have to be made, and I wanted us to be united. Against? I said.

Against? he said. Decisions have to be made and I wanted you to be part of the process.

I've had a lot of practice in not getting pissed off at Bill, who can't help his patronizing, autocratic nature. I reminded myself severely that (a) he's just a poor trembling soul, trying to keep himself together in whatever way he can and I should appreciate that it was Bill, obviously, who was dealing with Nana's whole thing here, and (b) that I wouldn't want to start regressing all over the place. Thanks, I said. Thanks for including me.

Bill nodded, I nodded.

Thanks for including me, I said again. But I don't have anything to contribute, remember?

I never *said* that, he said. I *never* said that you don't have anything to contribute. Be straightforward for a moment. Do you think you could be straightforward for a moment? That's merely the construction you chose to put on a perfectly harmless suggestion I made once—once!—that you might try just a little harder, in certain circumstances. We'll go into another room for a minute, shall we, you and I?

Melinda and I will stay right here with your nana, said Peggy, who has a sort of genius for pointless remarks. Bill and I strolled down the long hall to the dining room. I don't suppose you happen to know where the, um, liquor cabinet is, I said. What is it you require, Bill said, absinthe? There's not enough stuff right over there on the credenza? Huh? I said. He said, That's what it's called, a credenza; is that all right with you? I said, Maybe you could be a little straightforward yourself. He said, Sorry. I'm under a lot of, um . . .

Poor Bill. Obviously Dad wasn't going to be pitching in here. Or Peter, who's in Melbourne these days. Peter left the whole scene practically as soon as he could *walk*. When Peter was little everyone thought he'd be the one to find a cure for cancer, but he became sort of an importer instead, of things that are rare wherever he happens to be living, so he can be away all the time. From anywhere. Away, away. Away away away away away. Bill at least gets some satisfaction in thinking Peter's work is trivial—which really makes Jeff snicker, since Bill works for insurance companies, basically figuring out why they don't have to pay the policyholders. Now, *there's* something trivial, Jeff said. But then he said no, actually, that it wasn't trivial at all, was it—it was huge. And that Peggy was even worse than Bill, because Bill was born exploitative and venal and he can't help it, but Peggy actually *cultivates* those qualities.

I remember once, in this very apartment, overhearing Nana telling my father that he was weak and that he resorted to the weapon of the weak—violent rage—and that he used his charm to disguise the fact that he was always just about to do whatever would make everyone most miserable. I provided you with grandchildren, Dad told her. Does that make you miserable? I thought that was what every mother wanted from her child. How can you complain about your grandchildren?

How? Nana said. Peter is brilliant, but damaged. Lucille is certainly well-meaning, and she isn't a ninny, despite appearances, but she's afraid of reality just like you. Only *she* expresses it in immaturity, laziness, confusion, and mental passivity.

Well, that was a long, long time ago, of course, but I still remember feeling kind of sick and how quiet it was. It was so quiet I could hear the foliage in the painting rustle and the silvery dust particles clashing together. What about Bill, my father said. Surely you don't intend to spare Bill? Even from behind the door where I was hiding, I could hear Nana sigh. Poor Bill, she said. That poor, poor Bill.

Hey, that's my brother you're talking about, I told Jeff when he criticized Bill, but the fact is, I guess I did that thing that people say people do. Which is that one quality I evidently sought out in my lover is a quality that runs in my family—the quality of having a lot of opinions about other people. Low opinions, specifically.

And Nana would have to recognize now, if she were only compos, that Bill had taken charge of her well-being all by himself, and that he was doing a pretty good job of it. Eileen, for example, Eileen seemed terrific, nothing wrong with Eileen. Listen! I said to Bill. Listen, I want to tell you this with complete sincerity: I know you've had to deal with a lot here, and I'm really, truly sorry I haven't been much help. How could you have been any help? Bill said. You live on the other side of the country.

And besides, I said.

Bill did something with his jaw that made it click. There were dust covers over the chairs. He pulled one aside and sat down. Then he got up and pulled another aside for me. When did she stop going out? I said. When did she stop going out, he said, hooking the words up like the cars of a little toy train, when did she stop going out. When she stopped being able to walk, Lucille? After her first stroke? Kind of hard to get around if you can't walk.

Well, I guess I assumed she'd use a wheelchair or something, I said. Or that someone would take her. A driver, or someone.

Anyhow, she didn't want to see anyone, he said. I told you that, I know I told you that. And more to the point I suppose, she didn't want anyone see her.

Bill was looking stricken. The fact is, Nana was an amazing person, even if she had been pretty rough with our father, who obviously deserved it anyway. She had seen a lot in her life, she'd experienced a lot, but from all those experiences there weren't going to be many, you might say, artifacts, except for, oh, the tea service and maybe a bit of jewelry and a few pamphlets or little books, I guess, that she'd written for the institute (foundation?) she worked with. At. With. At. *The tradition of liberal humanism*, I remember Dad saying once, with hatred, as though something or other. Anyhow, there wasn't going to be much for the world to remember our shiny Nana by, except for example her small, hard, rectangular book on currency. It's incredible, I can't ever quite wrap my head around it—that each life is amazingly abundant, no matter what, and every moment of experience is so intense. But so little evidence of that exists outside the living body! Billions of intense, abundant human lives on this earth, Nana's among them, vanishing. Leaving nothing more than inscrutable little piles of commemorative trash.

I could see that Bill was suffering from those thoughts, too. I put a hand on his arm and said, She didn't want people to see her, but she let *you* see her, I said.

Bill flushed. I don't count, he said.

As far back as I can remember, Bill was subject to sudden flashes of empathy that made him almost ill for a moment, after which he was sure to behave as if someone had kicked the kick-me sign on his rear end. Anyhow, you and I have to make some decisions, he said. Like what? I said.

He gave me plenty of time to observe his expression. Do you know how much this sort of private care costs? he said. Sure, she was well-to-do by your standards. And by mine. But you might pause to consider what will have happened to her portfolio in this last year or so. Mine will go back up in due course, yours will go back up— Portfolio? I said. But hers won't, Bill said. She doesn't have the time. In another year, if she lives, she'll be propped up over a subway grating in the freezing cold with a paper cup to collect change. So the point is, that every single thing here has to be decided. And it has to be decided either by *us*, or by *me*. None of it's going to happen automatically. Honestly, Lulu—You still don't seem to get it. How do you think Nana came by her nurses? Do you think they just showed up on the doorstep one morning?

Bill rubbed the bridge of his nose as if *I* were the one having the tantrum. The point is, he said, there seems to be no chance of significant recovery. So what will happen with her things, for example? Who will go through her papers? Can we find a better place for her to be? These are decisions.

These were *not* decisions, I didn't bother to point out to Bill, who was looking really *so* pathetic with his silly jacket and premature pot-belly, they were questions. This is Nana's apartment, I said. This is where she lives. We can't just, what, send her off on an ice floe.

I appreciate your horror of the sordid mechanics, Bill said. But stay on task, please, focus. I mean, driver! Good lord, Lulu, *what* driver? You know, Geoff is a fine man, I like Geoff, and it's a big relief to see you settled down, finally, with someone other than a blatant madman. But Geoff is as impractical as you are. More impractical, if possible. He takes an extreme view of things, and I know he encourages you in that as well.

I'm capable of forming my own extreme views, I said. And if you're referring to the tree painting project, it was hardly *extreme*. We all just picked one tree that was going to be deforested, and commemorated that particular tree in paint. I don't call that *extreme*.

I agree, Bill said. It's perfectly harmless. And that's great, because you have to be prudent. Courage is one thing, and simplistic rashness is another. There are lists, you know. Lists, lists, lists.

Simplistic *rashness*? I said. You know what Jeff has been doing, you know what he's been studying! I was shouting at Bill but I was thinking about poor Jeff, lying in bed this last month or so, scrawling on sheets of paper. When I'd urge him to eat, he'd start intoning statistics—how many babies born with this, how many babies born with that. I know, I said the other day, I know; don't tell *me*, tell *them*. We've *told* them, he said, that's why they cut off the funding! He did manage to write a song or two about it, at least, and he sang one on his friend Bobby Baines's six a.m. radio slot. You'd be surprised what Jeff can wrap a good tune around. I wish he'd get back to his music. It used to be so much fun, hanging out with his band. My mouth was still open, I noticed, and yelling at my brother. The funding's been cut off, my mouth was yelling. For the whole study! And now they're saying, Depleted uranium, wow, it's great for you, sprinkle it on your breakfast cereal! Is it any wonder Jeff isn't a barrel of laughs these days? Is it any wonder he's on a short fuse? Extreme! You're the one who's extreme! I can absolutely *hear* how you're trying to pretend his name is spelled! Jeff is *Jewish*, okay? Do you think you can handle it? His name is Jeff with a *J*, not waspy, waspy Geoff with a G, but every time you send us so much as a note, it's Dear Lulu and Geoff with a G!

Bill was just standing there with his arms folded. At least I send the occasional note, he said. And please don't pretend you don't know what a portfolio is. Please, please don't.

We looked at each other for a long, empty moment. The Corot will have to be sold, he said.

Sold, I said.

Well, I don't know why it should have made a difference to me. Sold, not sold—it wasn't as if I could have hung the thing up on our stained, peeling wall or whatever. But still! That word—sold! It's like inadvertently knocking over a glass!

Sold, Bill said. The jewelry's already been sold. Eek, I said. Who knew. Oops, sorry, you did, I get it, I get it, I get it, honest I do. Bill cleared his throat. Anyhow, he said.

He gestured at the cloth-draped room. Obviously, there's a lot of stuff left, but none of it's worth anything to speak of. Peggy's researched pretty thoroughly. Still, if there's anything you want, now's the time to claim it.

"Now's the time. " "Now's the time." Who wants to hear that about anything? Thanks, I said.

Was there anything of Nana's I'd ever particularly coveted? I closed my eyes. Wow, to think that Nana had been showing Eileen that clipping of me and my tree and my painting! Okay, so, maybe the project hadn't been that effective, but at least there'd been a clipping! Had Nana been proud? Did she think I looked nice? Wait a minute, I said, Nana's still alive! You get no argument from me there, Bill said. But how much of this stuff do you think she's going to be using from now on? Do you think she'll be using the tea service, for example?

The tea service? I said. Do you want the tea service? he said. The tea service! I said. That great big hulking silver thing? What on earth would I do with the tea service? How on earth do you think Jeff and I are living, out there in the woods? Calm down, Lucille, Bill said, for heaven's sake. Please don't go Dad's route.

Why on earth are we talking about the tea service? I yelled. Excuse me a minute.

I went into the kitchen, where Eileen was sitting, grabbed a glass from the cupboard, and clattered some ice cubes into it from a tray in the freezer. Excuse me, I said. Help yourself, dear, Eileen said.

There was a printed notice stuck to the door of the fridge with a magnet that looked like a cherry. Do Not Resuscitate, the notice said. Oh, shit, I said. Eileen nodded. She's a lovely lady, your grandmother, she said, but I just kept looking at Eileen, as though I were going to see something other than a nurse in a white uniform sitting there.

When I went back out to the dining room it appeared that Bill had gone back to the others, so I made a pit stop at the cruh-*den*-za to fill my glass and returned to the living room myself. Anyhow, we weren't talking about the tea service, Bill said, *you* were talking about the tea service. The tea service? Peggy said.

Want it? I said.

That's so sweet of you, hon, Peggy said.

Bill flashed an expression just like one of Dad's—pure gleeful, knowing malevolence. He'd obviously stopped by the good old credenza himself again, and was gulping away at his tumbler. Eileen came in and helped Nana drink a glass of water with something in it to make it thick enough for her to swallow, and gave her a pill. A little water dribbled from the corner of Nana's mouth. Nana didn't appear to notice it. Eileen wiped it away, and then wiped at something leaking from Nana's eye. Melinda had her hands over her ears. Those *airplanes*!

she said, I can't stand the sound of those *airplanes*! Why are there so many airplanes here?

Oh, don't fuss, Melinda, Peggy said, there are airports in New York City, and so naturally there are airplanes. And in any case, that's a helicopter, Bill said. Is it going to drop a bomb on us? Melinda said. Don't be silly, sweetie, Peggy said, they're not dropping bombs on us, we're dropping bombs on them.

Helicopters don't drop bombs, Melinda, Bill said, they're probably looking for someone. Who? Melinda said. The police, Bill said, hear those sirens? No, but who are the policemen looking *for*? Melinda said with her hands over her ears again. How would your mother and I know who the policemen are looking for, Bill said. Some criminal, I suppose.

Melinda flopped over, face down onto the sofa, and let out a muffled wail. Just calm down, please, Melinda, Peggy said. You're upsetting your great-grandmother. Melinda cast a glance at Nana, who was gazing levelly at the images I'd seen earlier of the gracefully exploding building. I wondered where the building was—what country, for instance.

Things were always occurring suddenly and decisively inside the TV. Another building, for example, was just getting sheared off as we watched, from an even taller one standing next to it. Why is everyone always so mad at me? Melinda said.

I'm not mad at you, I said. Are you mad at Melinda? I asked Bill and Peggy. Of course not, Peggy said. You are, too, Melinda said.

We are not angry with you, Peggy said. And I've told you repeatedly that when you pay for the paint job, you can put tape wherever you like.

I was doing it for you! Melinda said. I was just doing it for you! She turned to me. It said to do it, she said. It said to get tape and put plastic over the windows because of the poison, and my sitter was up in my room with her boyfriend so I got the tape from the drawer and some garbage bags, and then Stacy was mad at me too, even though I didn't tell that she and Brett were upstairs having—

I don't want you talking like that, Peggy said. About Stacy or anyone else, young lady. Girls in real life don't behave like television floozies. I'm limiting your viewing time.

What did I *say*, what did I *say*, Melinda said and lapsed into loud, tearing wails that sounded like she was ripping up a piece of rotting fabric. Stop it, Melinda! Peggy said. Stop that right this instant—You're getting hysterical!

She's so theatrical, Peggy said to me, rolling her eyes. She put her arms around Melinda, who continued crying loudly. There's no reason to get so *excited*, Melinda, she said, you're just overtired.

Soldiers were marching across the screen, again. Peggy was gazing at them absently, her chin resting on Melinda's soft hair. Was Melinda going to be a numbskull like her parents? I wondered, but then I reminded myself how much stress Peggy and Bill were under, worrying about Nana all the time, and whatever. Peggy was looking so tired and sad, just gazing droopily at the screen. She sighed. I sighed. She sighed. Do you remember when people could have veal chops whenever they wanted? she said. Bill had a yen for veal chops yesterday, so I went to the market and I practically had to take out a *mortgage*.

Are we poor? Melinda said, and hiccuped. Ask your mother, Bill said, looking like Dad again. Peggy glared at him.

I was trying to remember what Nana had written in her little book on currency . . . *fixed, floating, imports, exports, economies* . . . And then I tried to remember what exactly had happened in the last wars we'd fought, or anyhow, in the last vaguely recent ones—just who exactly was involved, and so on. So many facts! So much information always coming out about these things, after they've occurred. It's pretty hard to keep straight just what's been destroyed where, and how many were killed. Well, I guess it's not that hard for the people who live in those places. And Jeff always has a pretty solid grasp on that stuff, and Nana sure used to. I wondered what she thought she was looking at now, if she thought she was actually seeing back, seeing pictures from her own life— memories, the inside of her own head . . . She seemed to be focusing on the screen so intently, as if she were concentrating on some taxing labor. Really working out what that screen was showing. Well, that was Nana! Always work work work work work work. There was the sheared-off building, and the tall one still standing right next to it. I wondered what that tall building was, and I wondered what she thought it was. It looked like an office building, with black windows. Maybe Nana thought Death's office was there, behind those black windows. Maybe she pictured Death as a handsome old man in uniform, sitting at his desk and going over his charts and graphs. Behind him she'd be seeing a huge map with pins in it and his generals, with those familiar, familiar faces, their expressions bright, now, in private, as they reviewed their sleek and potent devices. But Death himself would look tired—so much to do!—and sad. He wouldn't notice the glass tear leaking from his glass eye.

Guess we'll all be going together one of these days, Bill said. Swell, I said. You know, guys, I'm really tired. I'm going to go back downtown to Juliette's. We can talk over everything tomorrow, okay?

Do you have enough money for a taxi, Lulu? Bill said.

Do I have enough money for a taxi? Of course I have enough money for a taxi, I said. I was wishing I hadn't spent most of my last check before Jeff's funding was cut on those white Courrèges go-go boots. But discounts are about the only perk of my job, and I do have to say that the boots look pretty fabulous. Anyhow, I said, I'm going to take the subway.

The subway! Peggy said. Don't be *insane*, Lulu.

Don't die, Aunt Lulu! Melinda said.

For pity's sake, Melinda, Peggy said. No one's going to *die*.

Was I ever hoping that Wendell had finished trying to tenderize Juliette, so I could just flop down on her futon! *No rest for the wicked*, Dad used to say, chortling, as he'd head out for a night on the town. (Or for the saintly, is what Jeff has to say about *that*, or for the morally indecipherable.)

Oh, look—Peggy said, pointing to the screen, where a grinning person in a white lab coat was standing near some glass beakers and holding what looked like a little spool—I think they must be talking about that new thread!

What new thread, what new thread? Melinda said.

That new thread, Peggy said. I read an article about this new thread that's electronic. Electronic? I think that's right. Anyhow, they've figured out how to make some kind of thread that's able to sense your skin temperature and chemical changes and things. And they're going to be able to make clothes that can monitor your body for trouble, so that if you have conditions, like diabetes, I think, or some kind of dangerous conditions, your clothes will be able to register what's going on and protect you.

That's *great*, huh, Granana, Melinda said. She threw her little arms around Nana, who closed her eyes as if she were finally taking a break.

Why the Sky Turns Red When the Sun Goes Down

RYAN HARTY

I GET THE CALL as my wife is setting the table for dinner. It's our neighbor Ben Hildeman, who tells me in a breathless voice that my son has had a problem.

"This is bad, Mike," Ben says, and in the background I hear his boys Tanner and Phillip talking in excited tones. "He fell and hurt his leg, is I guess what happened, but then he just sort of lost control. By the time I got there he was in the Kohlers' yard, banging his head against their air-conditioning unit."

"God, you're kidding," I say.

"I'm afraid it's pretty bad, Mike. Some of the kids are upset now. I wish you'd come down."

"I'll be right there," I say, and hang up the phone.

Dana comes into the doorway with a bunch of utensils in her hand. "It's not about Cole?" she says, but she can see in my face that it is. "You should go, Mike. Hurry."

Running down Keehouatupa, past the subterranean houses, I'm hoping that whatever happened to Cole will have nothing to do with the trouble we had in Portland. I know Dana is thinking the same thing back at the house. We came to Arizona at the height of the D3 crisis, with high hopes that the desert air would be good for Cole. Amazingly, in the seven months we've been here he's had not a single problem—no shutdown or twitching hands, no problems with speech or movement. We've only just begun to believe that things might be all right again.

Ben's house comes into view, a newly built subterranean with smoke-tinted skylights, a couple of date palms shimmering in the day's waning heat. Ben stands atop the grassy dome, a stocky man in jeans. Behind him are the red peaks of the Superstition Mountains. A half dozen boys in shorts and tank tops stand at his side. Cole, I see, is not among them.

Ben jogs down and puts a hand on my shoulder. "I didn't want to touch him, Mike," he says. "He's around the back now. I think he might be unconscious."

"That's good, actually. It means he's in shutdown."

We climb the hill. From the top I see Cole lying belly down on the back slope, his legs splayed out behind him. He is in shutdown—there's that stillness about him—and I'm relieved to see it, though it's clear he's in horrible shape. His neck has twisted around so far that his chin seems to rest in the shallow valley between his shoulder blades. His right arm has come off completely and lies, bent at the elbow, a few yards away, multicolored wires curling out of the torn end. I get a light-headed feeling and have to crouch for a moment and catch my breath.

"You all right?" Ben asks.

"I'll be okay."

"He just—" Ben gives me a squint-eyed look. "It's hard to describe it, Mike. It was crazy."

"So all this happened when he fell? The arm and everything?"

"That's what I was saying." He jerks a thumb at a metal box at the edge of the Kohlers' yard. "When I came out he was just banging against that thing like he wanted to knock it down or something. He made an electrical noise in his throat, sort of, a whirring sound."

I glance at the boys, who are all studying me carefully—six boys in a line on the hill.

"Everybody all right?"

They nod.

"I asked them to go home, but they wouldn't go," Ben says. "They're worried about their friend."

"Sure," I say. "Well, listen, guys, Cole's gonna be all right, you hear me?"

They nod again and glance at one another. These are good kids, all of them—Ben's son Tanner and our next-door neighbor Sean Ho, and a Devin something whose parents I've met a few times. One of them, a red-haired boy I haven't seen before, looks as though he might be D3 himself; his skin seems to reflect the sun a little more directly than the other boys'. He holds his shoulders unusually straight. Most people can't see the difference, but D3 parents can more often than not. This kid looks as stunned as the rest of them.

I walk down the grassy slope and kneel beside Cole. His eyes are wide open and staring at nothing, and that's something I hate to see. I lay a hand on each of his cheeks, turn his head to the side and feel a pop—things seem looser inside him than they should be. I brush his bangs from his forehead, roll him to his back and slip a hand under his T-shirt, feeling for the power button. I give it a push.

Cole's head jerks just slightly. His eyes change, almost imperceptibly, as if the dimmest light has gone on behind them. It's enough, though: he looks like my son again.

"Hey, buddy," I say.

He blinks at me. "Hey, Dad. What are you doing here?"

"I came to take you home."

He glances around, and I see the disappointment in his eyes, the look of understanding. "I had an accident," he says.

"I'm afraid so, kid. Do you remember what happened?"

"We were playing kick the can," he says, and draws his lips in, concentrating. "I was running, I think. I had a bad headache. I don't remember anything else."

I'm relieved he's come out of it alert and lucid, much better than at times in the past. During the bad period in Portland there were always problems upon switchback—inability to focus, slowed-down speech and movement.

"So listen, there are a few things I need to tell you," I say. "Things you may not want to hear." I help him to a sitting position, a hand at the small of his back. "For one thing, your arm's come off."

He touches his shoulder where the arm should be. A look of panic overtakes him.

"It's all right," I say. "It's just down the hill. We'll get it fixed up as soon as we can. I just want you to know what's going on, okay? The other thing is that I think there might be a little problem with your neck, but that'll be fine, too, I promise."

He swallows hard and looks at me. "What about my arm?" he says. "Aren't you going to put it on again?"

"I can't, pal. I wish I could. We'll have to bring it along to the hospital tomorrow."

He glances up at his friends on the hill. I know he's embarrassed about what's happened.

"Maybe you ought to say something to them," I tell him. "Let them know you're all right."

"I don't know what to say," he says.

"Just whatever you want. It'll make it easier when you see them the next time."

He seems to think for a moment, his tongue poking out between his lips. Then he glances up the hill and says, "Hey, guys, I'm all right and everything. I gotta go home, but I can probably come back tomorrow."

"Hey, that's terrific," Ben says, and glances around at the boys. "Isn't that great, guys?"

"Yeah," Tanner Hildeman says quietly. "That's great, Cole."

"We just hope you're okay and everything," Sean Ho says, then glances at Cole's arm where it lies on the grass. He turns to the other kids, and as if given a signal they all start down the hill. A couple of them raise their hands to Cole and Cole waves back.

"That wasn't so bad, was it?"

"I guess not," he says.

"You ready to go home to Mom now?"

"All right," he says, but there's a hint of hesitation in his eyes.

"What's the matter, kid?"

He shakes his head, then says, "Does Mom know what happened?"

"She knows you got hurt," I say. "She'll be glad to see you."

He glances up at the date palms in front of the house.

"What's the matter, pal?"

"Nothing," he says, but I can see there is. For the first time it occurs to me that he might know more about Dana and me than I've imagined.

Dana is outside when we get home, standing at the edge of the lawn with an uneasy look on her face. I try to give her a reassuring nod, but there's little use in that with Cole's arm tucked under my own like a rolled-up newspaper.

"Oh boy," she says, glancing from Cole to me and back. "You all right, kid?"

"I guess," he says, and looks at me.

"He's disappointed," I say.

"Of course," she says. "Who wouldn't be?" She brushes her hands down her sides, glances at the house. Dana is an attorney at an intellectual property firm in Phoenix and makes a good living appearing composed when everything is going to hell around her. But I can see she's flustered now and it makes me feel suddenly tender toward her. Together we go into the house, where the air is cool and smells of pork chops and mashed potatoes.

While Cole goes upstairs to get cleaned up, I walk into the kitchen. Dana is washing her hands and staring out the window. It's six o'clock and the sky has taken on the pinks and silvers of an abalone shell.

"Don't you think we ought to shut him down?" she says, and turns to me. "I can't stand to see him with his arm like that."

"I think it's better to keep him running if we can," I say. "We don't want him to get any more disoriented than he has to."

"I guess not," she says.

"He seems pretty good in most ways. This is probably nothing too serious."

"He's torn his own arm off, Mike," she says. "Of course it's serious."

"All right. I just mean it might be a mechanical problem. It's not necessarily anything chronic."

Her face is doubtful, weary. "Well, let's hope so," she says.

At the top of the stairs I hear the faucet running in the bathroom. Cole bumps a knee against the cabinet under the sink and says, "Ouch," then the faucet shuts off with a knock. I walk into the master bathroom, where the face I see in the mirror is so pale it shocks me. I have to sit on the toilet for a while with my head between my knees. It's that echoey feeling I had in the Hildemans' yard, a feeling I had a lot as a kid—at swim meets and at summer camps, and later during final exams in college. A doctor put me on Zoladex for a while when I was in my twenties, but I didn't like the way it made me feel—sedate and strangely detached from my life. I sit blotting my forehead with toilet paper, breathing deeply until my heartbeat slows.

I had these symptoms back in Portland, too, when Cole was at his worst and Dana and I disagreed about how to handle it. Dana wanted to get a new center chip for Cole then, one of the D4 units that seemed to work well for people at the time. To me that would have been like getting a new child altogether, since his personality wouldn't be the same. In D-children, experience affects development the way it affects a human child: D-children become who they are because of the lives they've lived. While it's possible to transfer memory, you cannot transfer a personality that's been formed over the years. We'd been told that the engineers could *approximate* Cole's personality type, which to me was worthless, though a lot of people disagreed with me. My wife happened to be one of them.

Dana's brother Davis had a D3 child of his own, a boy named Brice who suffered for years from the same kinds of problems as Cole—intermittent breakdown, loss of motor control. A year before we moved to Arizona, on the Tuesday before Thanksgiving, Brice disappeared after a martial arts class, and it was almost a week before they found him in a wooded field two miles north of Davis's house, where he'd apparently collapsed taking a shortcut home. A week later, Davis had a new center chip installed. The results were so positive he couldn't help calling us about it during our worst stretch with Cole. He knew how I felt about center chips; we'd discussed it many times. Davis had always been protective of Dana, and I'd never got the feeling he approved of me. I began to see his calls as a way of stirring up trouble between Dana and me.

And it worked, too. Brice was a high school junior then, a scholar-athlete and a truly fine kid, a boy Dana and I had always liked. But it was less his personality and accomplishments that impressed Dana, I think, than the sheer absence of D3-related problems. I remember Davis being worried about drugs at one point (he'd found a marijuana cigarette in Brice's underwear drawer), and even that became a selling point, because it was a *normal* problem. You couldn't miss the pride in Davis's voice when he told us about it—about the awkward talk he'd had with Brice, the two of them hashing it out for nearly an hour before finally hugging and crying. The point seemed to be that Brice was living a life of uninterrupted normalcy, and the insinuated question was, Why settle for a child who breaks down all the time when you can have a new one who won't?

I was dead set against it. It mattered absolutely to me that Cole be *my* child, the boy I'd come to know over the years. Dana and I fought about it more than we'd ever fought about anything, and in the end I think it changed the way we saw each other. She came to seem harder to me, less nurturing; I must have come to seem weak and sentimental. We'd met during our final year at the University of Oregon, and for the longest time had been amazed by how much we had in common—a penchant for old books and antiques, a respect for nature, a desire to have kids while we were still young enough to do everything with them. But as problems with Cole became worse, Dana receded, took on longer hours at work, grew distant when she was home. We argued about small, unrelated things, like the antiques we'd collected over the years. She said she felt hemmed in by them, even suggested we sell the old gas-powered Bonneville we'd loved to drive in college. For a few months that fall, I became convinced she was having an affair with a man named Stuart Solomon, a high-tech consultant at her firm. I never had solid evidence. Stuart's name turned up a few times on the caller ID, though he and Dana worked on different accounts. Twice, when Dana was supposed to be working late, I drove to her office and found that her car was not in the parking lot. I tried to confront her about it a few times, but always lost my nerve. There's no describing the relief I felt when the reports came in about D3 kids going problem-free in the Southwest. Suddenly there seemed reason to hope our lives could return to normal if we moved.

I stand and walk to the window. Outside, the rows of subterranean houses lie spread out like the fairways of a golf course. Mine is one of the few two-story houses left in the neighborhood now, and it costs so much to cool I'm sure I won't be able to keep it long—though I hate to think of giving it up, since it's a link to my past, to the two-story colonial my family still owns in Eugene. From where I stand, I can see the other two-story on the street, a big stucco home with a pool in the back. A light goes on in an upstairs window, and a man passes through a room. I've never spoken to this man before, but now I find myself thinking about him, wondering if he's anything like me, wondering if he feels himself being ushered into the future, away from the things that brought him comfort in the past.

Downstairs, Cole is carrying a basket of rolls to the table with his one good hand, singing "My Bonnie Lies Over the Ocean." It's a song he learned at summer camp, but he seems to have gotten some of the words wrong. Instead of singing "Bonnie," he sings "body." "My body lies over the ocean / My body lies over the sea." He sets the rolls on the table and goes back for more.

"Sit, honey," Dana says from the kitchen. "I'll get the rest."

"I don't mind," he says.

He takes a pitcher of water from the counter and starts into the dining room. Dana touches the back of his neck. I give her a look meant to say, "Doesn't he seem fine?" and she gives me a more doubtful look, which says, I suppose, "We'll see." But she comes over and puts her arms around me—an offering of peace.

"All right, break it up," Cole says, hurrying back in. "Can't you see I'm starving here?"

We bring the rest of the food to the table. As we begin to pass dishes and talk I feel a little better. It seems as if we've gotten past the day's bad luck and tension.

"Good dinner, Mom," Cole says, forking up a bite of pork chop.

"Flattery will get you everywhere," she says, and gives him a small smile.

"Listen," I say, passing the rolls, "how'd you guys like to take the Bonneville out tomorrow? After we get everything taken care of at the hospital, we could head out to Papago Lake and have a picnic. Maybe drive around Tortilla Flats."

"All right," Dana says. "Sounds like a good idea."

"Cool with me," says Cole, and glances up from his plate.

Something is wrong with his eyes, I see. One of them points directly at me while the other seems to shoot off at a crazy angle toward the kitchen. I glance at Dana, who's noticed it too.

"What?" Cole says, looking from me to Dana. "What's wrong?"

"Nothing," Dana says, carefully. "It's just—can you see all right?"

"Yeah," he says, "why?"

I set the bowl of broccoli down and say, "Listen, kid, try this." I put a hand in front of his face, then slowly move it until my fingers enter the line of his wayward eye. "Can you see my fingers now?"

"No," he says, and a flash of panic comes over him. "What's happening, Dad?"

"Well, I don't think it's anything to worry about. It looks like you've lost vision in one of your eyes, is all. But we're going to the hospital tomorrow anyway, right? They can fix this in a snap."

For a minute I think Cole might start to cry. "Gaw!" he says and throws his balled-up napkin on the table. "I can't believe this!"

"Hey, come on," Dana says, her tone gentle but firm. She goes to Cole and kisses the crown of his head, and says, "Don't let it get you down." Then she gives me a look and walks into the kitchen. Cole and I keep on with our dinners. When Dana's been gone for a minute, I get up and go after her. She's at the sink, staring out the window at the fading sunset.

"We've got to shut him down, Mike. This is just scary. It's scaring *him*."

"I know," I say, because it's scaring me, too. I can't think of anything else to do about it.

"Hey, Dad," Cole calls from the dining room.

"What's up, pal?" I wait for an answer, but it doesn't come. "Be out in a second, all right?"

"Hey, Dad, what makes the sky red when the sun goes down?"

Dana breathes out a small laugh. Her face softens. For a moment she looks like the young woman I met in Oregon. I give her a kiss on the cheek and go into the dining room.

"That's just dust," I say. "Dust and pollution, actually."

But Cole isn't looking at me. He's pushing food across the table with his fingers, staring at the mess he's made. An electric drone comes from his throat.

"Cole?"

"I gotta go to the bathroom," he says, staring at the table. "I don't feel so hot." The drone in his throat gets louder.

"What's the matter, kid?"

He glances up, his expression suddenly sly. "I'll bet you a dollar," he says.

"What are you talking about, pal?"

Dana comes into the doorway. "What's going on, Mike?"

"Jesus H. Christ," Cole says, and suddenly laughs. "Holy-frickin'-shit!"

"Cole! Look up here," I say. "Look at me."

He raises his head, but his eyes veer in different directions. His jaw makes a clicking noise. Then he suddenly raises his head high and brings it down with a violent crack against the table.

"Cole!" I say.

He lifts his head again, his face covered with pork chop grease and broccoli. I try to get around the table to hold him down, but before I can get there his head hits the table with another crack, rattling the silverware. Dana shrieks. This time, when Cole's head comes up, it swings way back over one shoulder, loose and wild.

"My God, his neck!" Dana says.

"I see it! Help me hold him down."

I get a hand on his shoulder and try to reach under his shirt for the power button, but it's hard to get to with his head lolling around like a jack-in-the-box.

"Whoa!" he says. "Help me, Dad."

The smell of burning wires comes off him. He breathes out an electric wheeze, his head lolling, and then his face seems to fill with wonder and he goes perfectly still in my arms. He turns to me, eyes clear and perfectly aligned.

"This is the best Christmas ever," he says.

I shut him down. His head thumps against the table. The electric drone cuts out. I wipe his face with a napkin and go into the kitchen, where I get a bottle of beer from the fridge. When I come back Dana is at the table, arms folded across her chest. She glances out the window.

"That's it, Mike," she says. "I mean it. This has got to stop."

The next morning I pull the Bonneville out of the driveway and carry Cole downstairs. Even with the seat belt over his shoulder, it's hard to prop him up in a way that looks natural. His head tips forward, making his mouth fall open. Dana and I have not talked about taking the Bonneville out since last night, and a picnic no longer seems like the best idea, but I'm in the mood to feel the thrum of the big gasoline engine, the vibration of the catalytic converter under my legs.

After a few minutes, Dana comes down and we take Highway 1073 past the mall and the hydroponics yards. The D-pediatric is twelve miles way, a sprawling complex on the outskirts of Olberg. As we drive,

Dana stares out the window, her eyes steady and serious, her mouth drawn into a line.

Last night, after I shut Cole down and we cleaned up the mess in the dining room, Dana went into the den and called her brother Davis, and through the door I heard her talking softly. I couldn't make out what she said, though I'm certain it was something she couldn't say to me, since we went through the evening without another word about Cole. Sometime late in the night I woke to the sound of her crying and put a hand on her shoulder, and she moved into my arms for a while. It was like holding an injured animal; I couldn't help feeling she just needed a little time to heal, and then she'd be out of my arms for good.

Afterward I lay awake, looking at the tiny red light of a smoke detector, listening as the wind pulled an ocotillo branch across the window. Dana was asleep, and Cole, I knew, was much farther away than that, gone in a sense, so that he was not even dreaming and would not wake up and call my name. I waited until the sky whitened in the window, then got up and walked down the hall and into his room. Cole lay dressed on top of the covers, his eyes closed, an inappropriate smile on his face. I had an urge to put his pajamas on him and tuck him into bed, but I knew it wouldn't make me feel better. Eventually I went down and started coffee and made bacon and eggs as the sky whitened through the windows.

We pass Mesa now, and the ground opens up to uncultivated fields and cacti. Just past Alvarado, I catch a glimpse of a coyote between the clumps of sage, golden brown and moving quickly, nose to the ground. It makes me think of driving out to Salmon Creek with Dana when we first got the Bonneville, years ago, laying a blanket across the backseat and making love right in the car with the windows open, the sound of the wind coming through the firs.

In the rearview mirror I see Cole propped against the door, his eyes closed, his mouth open. Dana is staring out the window. For some reason I imagine she's thinking of Davis, and it makes me angry.

"So suppose things get bad again," I say, and glance at her. "What do you think would happen then?"

"What do you mean, Mike?"

"Suppose this is the beginning of more bad times with Cole. We'd have to make some decisions then, right?" I know my voice is sharp, but it seems beyond my power to control it.

"Of course," she says.

"But you already know what you'd want to do," I say. "Isn't that right, too?"

"Come on, Mike, don't do this," she says. "I'm not in the mood for an argument right now."

"But suppose I need to know. Suppose it's important for me to know where we stand on this."

She sighs and glances out at the fields of brush. "Why do you have to push things all the time? What if I *can't* say what I'd do in every single situation? Can you?"

"I think I can. Yes."

"Can you, really, Mike? You can say what you'd do no matter what happens to him or to us?"

"What do you mean 'to us'?"

"Oh, God, I don't know," she says, and shakes her head wearily. "I just get tired of waking from the dream, don't you? Don't you get tired of being reminded he's not real?"

"He's as real to me as you are," I say, but when I glance at Cole in the rearview mirror he looks like what he is—a mechanical boy, a sophisticated doll for adults.

The desert floor runs out to a line of purple mountains. A ranch house slips past, then an electric plant, huge and complicated. For a moment I feel as if I don't know what's important to me, what matters the most. Dana has closed her eyes and is leaning back against the headrest.

"There was a coyote back there in a field," I say in a small voice. "I should have pointed him out to you."

We wait for hours in the air-conditioned lobby, sitting on a vinyl couch, trying to read magazines while other parents come and go with their children. Through a tinted window, I see a slice of blue sky. A peregrine falcon dips into view now and then. Finally Dr. Otsuji comes down the hall in a crisp white coat and yellow tie. He gives us his doctor's smile and sits on the chrome magazine table across from us.

"He's fine," he says. "We've fixed the arm and the neck, and right now he's just going through some tests to make sure everything's in good shape. He seems terrific."

Dana nods the way she does in court when conceding a point made by the opposition. "Do you have any idea what happened?" she asks.

The doctor turns up his eyes in concentration. "I'd call it an anomaly," he says, "though it could be more than that. It's like if you have an arrhythmia—unless we can check your heart when it's happening, we have a hard time knowing what causes it."

"But, in your opinion, is it likely we'll have more problems?" she asks. "Now that this has happened?"

Dr. Otsuji looks from one of us to the other, as if he'd just noticed the tension between us. "He's not showing any symptoms that would point to that, no," he says, "but to be honest, I don't see it as a good sign. For someone with Cole's history, you want as few problems as possible. Problems can lead to problems, is one way of looking at it."

Dana nods.

"Can we see him?" I ask.

"In a few minutes. He's a little upset, as you might expect. He's had a rough day. What I'd like to do is to put him out for a few minutes and run some numbers, then let him wake up naturally. I'll have the receptionist tell you when you can see him." He smiles in his professional way, then stands and shakes our hands and walks down the hall.

"Well, there it is," I say.

"I should call Davis," Dana says, and takes her bag up from the floor. "He'll want to know what happened."

She opens her cell phone, but before dialing she looks at me with an expression I've never seen before—her face hard, her eyes narrowed with what seems like pity. It's as if she's far away and needs to squint just to see me. "Listen, if you still want to go for a drive, that's fine. We can do that."

"Forget it. I don't really feel like it anymore."

"Well. Whatever. We'll go if you want to."

"I said I don't want to." The tone of my voice makes us both fall silent. She stands and walks down the hall.

Outside, clouds move across the sky, changing the light. A young family rushes into the lobby, the man carrying a blond, catatonic-looking girl in his arms. The child stares straight ahead with vacant eyes.

I pick up a magazine, but there's no use trying to read or even think about anything before I'm able to see Cole. Finally, the receptionist calls my name and I get Cole's room number and go down the hall.

Cole's in a bed in a pale yellow hospital gown, asleep with his arms at his sides. His cheeks are flushed, his hair a little tousled. I stand above him and watch his chest rise and fall. He opens his eyes and glances around, then nods in a resigned way. "The hospital," he says.

"I'm afraid so, pal. They've fixed your arm, though. Check it out."

He raises the arm and rolls his shoulder. I can see he's trying to appear calm for my sake.

"Does it feel all right?"

"Pretty good," he says.

"We'll test it out with a game of catch. How's that sound?"

"All right."

"Maybe we'll drop your mom off at home and head out to Papago Park. I've got the Bonneville. We can just grab some mitts and go."

"Where *is* Mom?" he says, and gives me a worried look.

"Down the hall. Talking to your Uncle Davis."

"Is she mad at me?"

"Of course not. Why would you say that?"

"I don't know," he says. "I know she doesn't like it when I break down all the time."

"You don't break down all the time," I say. "And anyway, none of this is your fault."

He seems distracted, as if he's trying to listen to Dana's voice down the hall. I can just hear her, a low, familiar sound coming over the tiles.

"Let's get you dressed and get your hair combed," I say. "We don't want people to think you were raised by wolves now, do we?"

He lifts the covers away and lowers his legs to the floor. I help him with the ties at the back of his gown. His clothes are on a chair by the window, and as he puts them on I see the seam where his arm has been reattached, a thin band where the skin is a little lighter, nothing you'd notice unless you were a parent or a doctor. I comb his hair, crouching in front of him, watching his eyes, which are alive with private thoughts and worries.

"Now you look like a gentleman," I say. "You ready to go?"

"I guess so," he says, and together we walk into the hall.

On the ride home, we play a game called Blackout. The object is to find the letters of each other's names in the license plates of passing cars, then call them out before the other person does. If you call them all, the person is out of the game. There's very little traffic until we hit the highway, and then we're suddenly in a sea of sedans and sport utility vehicles. Cole picks up a *D* for Dana and an *M* for Mike. I get an *A* for Dana, who seems not to be paying attention to the game.

"You better hurry up, Mom," Cole says, leaning over the front seat. "You've got two letters already."

She gazes straight out the windshield, a distant look on her face. Ever since our exchange in the hospital, she's been stiff and far away. I've seen the effect on Cole—the way he keeps his eyes on her, the way he won't stop trying to draw her attention.

"There's an *I*, Dad," he says, and glances at Dana.

We get off the highway and drive down Auwatukee, past the golf course and the hydroponic yards. At a red light, I call an O and an *N*, and then Cole and I both see a Honda in front of us, the license plate ALA-36940. We meet each other's gaze in the mirror, but neither of us calls the *A*.

At home I park on the street and kill the engine. Dana steps out of the car. She pretends not to hear Cole when he asks if she's coming to the park with us. He watches her walk up to the house with a stricken look on his face.

"She's having a rough time," I say. "It's not your fault, pal. I'll go get the mitts."

He nods, his face tight and willfully composed.

When I go inside, Dana is at the dining table, staring out the window. The sky has burst into color and filled the room with yellow light.

"So what's the plan?" I say. "Treat him badly? Make him feel like he doesn't have a mother?"

She turns, and I see that she's been crying. Her cheeks shine where the light strikes them from the side. "Are you really going to do this?" she asks. "Would you really take him and leave me?"

"I guess I don't know what my legal options are," I say.

"No one said anything about legal options," she says, "though I guess I shouldn't be surprised if you're thinking in that direction." She gives her head a small shake and glances up at me in a surprisingly open way, her eyes soft and even. "If I try hard enough, I can almost imagine how I look to you right now."

"Can you really?"

"Yes, I can," she says. "And it's not pretty."

"I don't think either of us looks very good to the other right now," I say, and try a smile.

"I guess not," she says.

"Of course, we don't know what will happen. He might be fine. He might just get better and surprise both of us."

"Do you think it would even matter?" she asks, smiling sadly.

"Why wouldn't it?"

"I just think you reach a point where you can't go on. Don't you? I feel as if we've gotten close to that point."

"Have we really?"

"I was very in love with you," she says, and puts a hand on top of my own. "You know that, right? I still love you very much."

"I love you, too," I say, and let out a laugh, because it all seems so crazy. "It's not as if we've lost everything, is it? It's not as if everything's gone."

"I don't know," she says. "That's what I worry about sometimes."

Cole and I drive out Clementine Road, past orange groves and fields of yuccas. Cole takes his mitt up from the floorboard and socks the ball into the pocket. He's been quiet and somber since I returned to the car, but now he seems to be cheering up under the influence of the drive. We pass an old stable building, the wood planks faded to silver-gray. He asks if I remember a drive we took a couple of winters ago, when it hailed so hard I had to pull to the side of the road and wait for it to stop.

"We were on our way to see the rodeo," I say, remembering.

"I thought the hail would dent the car," he says, and gives a small laugh. "There was a little dog out in the street, remember? You went out and brought him back to the car."

"I remember he smelled like rotten garbage."

Cole laughs. "He did not." He's excited, and seems to be coming to the point of his story, which I'm guessing will be that we should allow him to have a dog. It's an argument he's been making the last few months. Before he can get to that, though, the fingers of his right hand begin to twitch and he slips the hand into his mitt. As we drive past the arboretum, I see the tendons of his forearm jumping. I don't say anything. It's not like him to hide anything from me.

I'm thinking of Dana, of course, thinking she seems like a different person now, though I suppose we'll both have to change if we intend to go our separate ways. Our conversation has made it necessary to imagine raising Cole by myself. I imagine taking him to the grocery store, having him break down in the produce aisle, carrying his inert body back to some empty apartment. It's hard to be optimistic when you know you'll be alone, when you know it will be only you in the D-Pediatric waiting room, waiting to hear whether your son will seem like a child again.

At the park we walk across a field of fresh-mowed grass, the sun cutting over a long line of oleanders. A Mexican family barbecues flank steak under a picnic stand, and the smell of charred beef is in the air. Cole's hand seems to have improved enough for him to play catch, so we take our usual positions on a strip of grass near the snack bar.

"So, Dad," he says, winding up like a big-league pitcher, "you think I'll be able to play Little League next year?" He looks an imaginary runner back to first.

"You'll be eligible. You can try it if you want to."

His sidearm pitch skids on the ground. "Sorry about that," he says.

"Your arm all right?"

"Little sore," he says, and takes his mitt off and massages the shoulder. Even from twenty feet I can see the hand twitching, though he's playing it cool. "I'm trying to decide if it would be too much to do baseball *and* soccer," he says, and puts the mitt back on.

"What are Tanner and Sean going to do?"

"Tanner's gonna do both. Sean hasn't decided yet."

"Maybe you should just play baseball and see how it goes." I throw him a grounder and he fields it and makes a pretend throw to first.

"Soccer's my main sport, though," he says with intensity. "I want to play soccer for sure." He throws a pitch that hits the grass a few feet in front of him, then hustles up like a catcher going after a bunt. But his throwing arm is shaking so badly he can hardly hold the ball, let alone make the throw. He falls abruptly to a sitting position on the grass, pressing his bad hand into the mitt.

"Let's take a break," he says.

I walk over and sit down beside him.

He's gazing off at the covered picnic tables, watching a young Mexican girl in a white lace dress swing at a piñata with a broomstick. He hunches over his mitt, rocking back and forth. What seems remarkable is not that he's having problems, but that he's been able to throw a ball at all, ever—that we've stood here and played catch and it's seemed normal.

"Maybe we ought to go home," I say. "It's been a long day for everyone."

"I'll be all right in a second," he says.

I lean into him, touch his face. When he's looking at me, I say, "It's really all right if you're having problems. You don't have to hide anything from your dad."

"I'm not hiding," he says, but his eyes suddenly fill with tears and he has to glance off at the picnic tables, where the girl has opened up the piñata now and kids are clamoring underneath. He watches, his jaw set tight. His voice, when he speaks again, is as thin and frightened as I've heard it before. "What's going to happen, Dad?" he asks. "What'll become of me?"

"You'll be fine," I say, because sometimes it's a father's job to lie. "Don't worry, kid. You'll be great."

Sovietski!

HOWARD HUNT

WE ARE IN THE SNOW near the Czech/Slovak border, looking up at the mountains and hissing steam with excitement. The air is murderously cold, facilitating a dialogue-balloon landscape of excitable steam as we stand around Dusan's Skoda XL and watch the three Honzas attack the front tires. Boy, is it cold! The Slovak roads have not yet been plowed, so it's definitely time to affix snow chains to tires, and the reason we're so excited is that we've acquired the very latest in snow chain technology but have absolutely no clue how this technology works. Before we left Prague, we stopped off at TESCO (where Honza P and Vitek work in public relations) to purchase consumables and upgrade our equipment, and the German-made snow chains were just too funny to resist, packaged as they were in industrial rubber, the color and texture of a basketball squashed flat. Big, goateed Libor (whose boutique agency handles TESCO, Ikea, Globus, and Carrefour—the new French hypermarket to go up in town) deemed the snow chains "*Sovietski!*," so the Honzas and Dusan and Jiri the Philosopher were quick to Frisbee a package into their well-stocked shopping carts. A good call from Libor, who neither owns a car nor the inclination to buy one, as there is mad snow in the Slovak highlands this winter, and the road to the chalet is very slippery indeed.

We defer to Libor in all things sportif (he is, after all, the most radical snowboarder), but his vehicular disinterest leaves the chaining of Dusan's tires in the loose and capable hands of the three Honzas, who are glamorous and have streaked hair and thick gold bracelets and the muscular confidence of American NHL stars, and they go at it in shifts, trying to master the new German system of wrapping chain around wheel. It goes without saying that the Honzas will ace this, in much the same way they mastered C++ and Xcel and the many other computer languages they code in, however after much puffing and panting, it transpires that the German snow chains, which we admire enormously and are very much taken by the style of, differ in basic functionality from the drab and rather ordinary Czech snow chains, which we can throw on our cars pretty much with our eyes closed. In the end, Jiri the Philosopher is summoned, and after some deliberation, it is he who cracks the puzzle by suggesting we refer to the instructions on the packaging.

"Can anyone read German?" he asks.

Martina C, the ice queen (recently promoted to senior management at Globus, the German hypermarket that stands directly opposite TESCO and Ikea on the other side of the Plzenska highway, and which features, truth be told, a far more comprehensive and competitively priced liquor section than either TESCO or Carrefour, which we do not patronize out of loyalty to Honza P and Vitek, but also because of that thing with the Germans occupying our country and coming back as tourists and speaking loudly in German and tipping poorly), is, of course, the woman for the job, and she translates fluently, making a big deal of the verb declinations but otherwise casting light on the non-insurmountable problem of Czech v. German industrial design. The Honzas are quick to act. Crouching in the snow like huskies, their blue eyes keenly appraising the mechanical integrity of this new locking system, they set to work, and the chains go on Dusan's tires as quick as Greased Lightning.

Dusan's Skoda is the corporately luxurious Octavia XL, mint green and covered with signage for L&M Menthols, the American blend cigarette that is taking Europe by storm. It is by far the best car in the convoy, and the prestige girlfriends—Magda, Monika, and Martina C, the ice queen—have elected to ride in it, choosing comfort over proximity to their nondriving boyfriends. Dusan is a journalist at TV Nova, the most popular and hard-hitting news station in Prague, and the car (and many others like it) are but a few of the enviable perks he enjoys with his job. Each year as we prepare to head off to the mountains, it has become something of a tradition to gather in the parking lot at TESCO and wait for Dusan to drive up in the latest Octavia, and this year's model is something to die for! L&M cigarettes have recently changed their campaign, so the computer-generated and dead sexy photographic imaging that covers the hood and roof and back and side windows features a new girl smoking provocatively, crooking her finger and blowing heart-shaped smoke rings, setting in train much jocular and, in the case of the prestige girlfriends, bitchy discussion as to whether she (the new girl) holds a candle to the old girl in terms of sultry provocation and smoke-ring-blowing technique, and the debate is still raging as we chain all five cars, and then the convoy is ready for the slow drive uphill.

The prestige girlfriends in place, Dusan guns the engine, and we climb into the mountains. Our chalet is in Habovka, a tiny resort town in the High Tatras where our parents used to ski in the time of Communism. It is cheap and dirty, with few amenities and none of the class of the French or Swiss Alps, but we are here to snowboard, and the collective opinion is that the inferior slopes and downmarket ski traffic (lots of Poles and Slovaks in silly tam-o-shanters) will afford us a more discreet place to learn the discipline of snowboarding, as, with the exception of Libor, who is truly radical and "bad," none of the group have ever snowboarded before. On the bright side, we have made a killing in currency exchange, trading robust Czech crowns for heavily depreciated Slovak crowns, precipitating an across-the-border frenzy through a drive-in liquor mart and subsequent bulk acquisition of Bohemia Sekt, the excellent "sparkling champagne" served in restaurants in Prague. While the jury may be out on the new L&M girl, one thing upon which we have all reached consensus is that we love the campaign slogan—"Join Me on the L&M CRAZY HOTEL Tour"—which has a behind-closed-doors edgy feel, like there's a party going on if only we could find it, and, despite the fact that discreet inquiries by Libor and Dusan have yielded the disappointing news that there is no "tour" budgeted into the L&M campaign (i.e., that the CRAZY HOTEL tour is just a registered trademark, not an actual party we can locate and crash), we have rebounded quickly by appropriating both name and concept as the central theme of our skiing vacation. With Dusan leading the convoy, his bass-enhanced stereo blasting vintage Eminem with an avalanche-starting low-end frequency, we look for all the world like a CRAZY HOTEL tour on tour, and for the next two hours, heads turn in our direction as we traverse the steep slope up the sprawling Alpine range.

The roll call is as follows: Honzas P, C, and J. Dusan. Jiri the Philosopher. Vitek (the joker). Marek C (the good Marek), Marek P (the bad Marek), big goateed Libor and homeboys Mikael and Martin. The girls are Magda, Monika, Martina C, the ice queen. Veronika J. Veronika K. Sarka, Klara, Lenka, Petra, and Libor's new girlfriend, *Spy* magazine "sexy girl" Daniela Zalesakova, who is five feet tall and downright surly. Considerable friction between her and the ice queen, pretty much from the moment they met outside TESCO, resulting in much car shuffling and black looks and the packing and unpacking of snowboards, and once again, it looks like sex is off the menu for poor old Marek C. (Truth be told, Marek C is not much longer for this world. Since making the jump from TESCO to Carrefour, his status has diminished in the eyes of the group, and while our sympathies are with him, the sad fact is that he has priced himself out of our entertainment median. He also doesn't drive, which doesn't help.) With the exception of Jiri (who is in fact a philosopher and heads the Departments of Philosophy and Creative Writing at the Greek-owned University of New York in Prague), our driving convoy is entirely comprised of new model Skodas, the three Honzas having been "hooked up" by Veronika J, who works for a dealership in Andel. Jiri, by contrast, drives a Volkswagen Passat, and has been delegated the responsibility of transporting the majority of snowboards (he has roof racks: the three Honzas do not), as well as Libor and Daniela Zalesakova and Marek P (the bad Marek). A core and likable member of our group, Marek P requires constant surveillance, as his sloe-eyed charm and pop-star good looks are a constant source of heartbreak for the ladies. Right now, just outside the ski lodge, flicking L&M ash into the pristine snow, he cuts a dangerous figure in his Marc O'Polo windbreaker and American-brand designer jeans, and the flow of female traffic is steady around him as we meet the landlord and move into the chalet.

The chalet is, of course, absurdly furnished. Each of the six rooms has a homemade cut-glass chandelier mounted off-kilter in the ceiling, the wiring visible, the wallpaper harsh, with bad shag carpet and regulation Communist-era boxy wall units replete with Samovar tea sets and ugly china. The sofa in the living room is orange, and the coffee table in front of it has, for some reason, been meticulously covered with little stickers from the American teen drama *Beverly Hills 90210*.

As we kick off our boots and carry our backpacks through the lodge, a most humorous discovery, revealed to us by Vitek, is that the feature wall of each room showcases a magnificently hideous home-knitted picture—not needlepoint, *wool*—which has turned furry and decrepit with age, and harks back to a time when entertainment was very much a DIY affair. The Honzas and Vitek are simply loving the pictures, and there is the usual good-natured squabbling between them as to who will claim which room based upon their preference in home-knitted art. But common sense prevails and strategic billeting takes place. Libor and Daniela Zalesakova have the west wing to themselves; Marek P is placed under the watchful eye of Jiri the Philosopher, while Veronikas J and K occupy the big room, along with Sarka, Klara, Lenka, Petra, and prestige girlfriend Monika Navratilova. One big pajama party in there, observes Vitek (a tad ruefully, we think), as he accepts the inevitable and bunks in with homeboys Mikael and Martin.

The Honzas in the meantime have discovered a convenient snowdrift outside the kitchen window, and are expertly refrigerating 120 bottles of Bohemia Sekt. There's nothing quite like watching the Honzas at work. On and off the rink, there is a synergy between them; a reflexive meld of thought and action that has been characteristic of their behavior since they were little boys growing up in the industrial town of Zlin. Ferocious on the ice, yet surprisingly warmhearted, the Honzas have charmed parents and girlfriends alike with their quiet mystery and earthy competence, and we are expecting great things from them on the snowboard slopes tomorrow.

Tonight, however, we will drink. It is the tradition. We are three days away from St. Sylvester, the festive night of New Year's Eve, when colorful folklore has it that your behavior during this evening will dictate your fortune in the oncoming year, and while we are not the slightest bit superstitious (or traditional), the unspoken consensus is that Sylvester is a time for sober contemplation. Hence we do our drinking early. The big table in the kitchen is ideal for this purpose, and chairs are brought in from the living room and bottles of slivovitz are produced from backpacks, and the phat beats of Eminem are transferred from car to chalet, transforming the kitchen into the Official Party Zone. It should be said that we are enormous fans of Eminem and everything he stands for. The two homeboys, Mikael and Martin (whose English, admittedly, is not so good), are particularly enamored of his style, and it's fun to watch them rap along with him, shouting any old thing, but with such attitude! By day, Mikael and Martin work for a company that specializes in promotional signage on the side of ballpoint pens, but at night they are hip-hop desperadoes, spray painting their "tags" on the sides of buildings many hundreds of years old. It is through them that we have access to an impressive collection of American rap CDs, and as the girls filter into the room with their homemade Christmas biscuits, we relish the prospect of taking in such genre classics as Cypress Hill, Shaggy, Baha Men, and Ice-T.

Veronika J and the ice queen, both of whom view the manufacture of Christmas biscuits a bit too competitively for our liking, have, as usual, outdone themselves on the Christmas biscuit front, however unexpected psychic turmoil is unleashed on the group when tiny Daniela Zalesakova appears in full makeup, brandishing her own Christmas biscuits, which are *moc delíkátní*, or very delicious. The blood drains from Marek's face as the factional pull of Libor prompts Vitek and Dusan to issue the most hesitant of compliments, and then it's a free-for-all among the nonprestige girlfriends, who have never liked Martina C and are making a big show of gorging themselves on Daniela's biscuits, rolling their eyes and going "Mmm," and "Oh yeah."

The tension is palpable. It's an inauspicious start to the CRAZY HOTEL tour, particularly as the twin-engine sulking prowess of not just Martina but Veronika J is well documented and feared, and it's obvious right off the bat that the raven-haired and highly volatile Veronika J is not going to stand for any *Spy* magazine "sexy girl" cutting in on her turf. In the typology of Czech women, Veronika is what we call a "gum-chewing girl," in that, along with the continuous chewing of gum, she's brisk and all business and one of the guys. She knows her Skodas and is not afraid to shout, and Sarka, Klara, Lenka, and Petra are treading thin ice viz the biscuits. With Libor and Dusan in tacit agreement (and Marek C destabilized by his suicide jump to Carrefour), the stage is set for a major uprising, and it is here that the Honzas shrewdly broker detente. A faction unto themselves, the Honzas will brook no unpleasantness when it comes to festive drinking, and they defuse the tension by shaking up and uncorking many snowdrift-chilled bottles of Bohemia Sekt and spraying "sparkling champagne" at all and sundry.

The girls squeal and protect their hair while the guys launch a spirited assault on the Honzas, and of course the alcohol is now out on the table so we're One Big Party once again. Glasses are lined up and more champagne is uncorked, and Magda, the most prestigious of the prestige girlfriends (also at TESCO, but in the fabled Foreign Acquisitions and Leasing department), heats up a big pan of *svarák*, or hot wine. Shot glasses of slivovitz are downed. Christmas biscuits are eaten unilaterally. Eminem is temporarily off the airwaves, and we are enjoying (and trying to decipher) the Jamaican rap style of the "advisor" character to whom the more easily understandable African American "confessor" character confesses his sexual transgressions in Shaggy's "Wasn't Me," when Sarka, Klara, Lenka, and Petra, who have snuck outside to smoke L&M Menthols, come rushing in with the news that a party of Slovaks is bogged in our driveway and their car needs a push ASAP.

The Slovaks are a bedraggled crew in an ancient Ford Sierra—two guys and two girls with the hungry and confused look of impoverished E-bloc shoppers ("air shoppers," as we call them in Prague)—and what they're doing in our driveway is something of a mystery until it turns out they're renting a room in the basement. The chalet is split-level, we're surprised to discover, and the Slovaks are tucked away beneath the crook of the stairwell, where they've been partying nonstop since the Sixth Day of Christmas. This new development opens a veritable Pandora's box of agendas, the first being that of Vitek (the joker), who wants to know if said basement apartment is festooned with hideously knitted wall decorations, and if so, can we see them?—the answer is yes—which in turn thin-edges the signature wedge of Marek P, who has his comb out and is vigorously up-combing his hair, as the Slovak girls are drop-dead gorgeous. Libor, Dusan, and the Honzas venture out into the snow and assist the guys with the pushing of their car, and then it's either a gratitude round of hot wine in the basement (we think not) or else please welcome Roman, Ondrej, Lucie, and Anna to the sensory dynamism of the kitchen upstairs!

The prestige girlfriends have been watching from the balcony, and are clearly not liking this influx of culture, but the die has been cast and the chips have fallen where they may. After a quick tour of the basement in which the hideous wall hangings have been deemed *Sovietski!* we repair to the kitchen with the Slovaks in tow, and are embarrassed by their sharp intake of breath and wide-eyed survey of our well-stocked Party Zone. Aside from Magda's big pan of *svarák*, the CRAZY HOTEL tour boasts more Becherovka, absinthe, vodka, slivovitz, and "sparkling champagne" than we know what to do with, and the ambient mood is definitely festive as hands are shaken and introductions are made.

The Slovak guys are wolflike and lean, with angular features and sleek, glossy hair, and while they both have the Slavic NHL look of the Honzas, theirs is of the Socialist Olympiad variety, the kind that involves being hit with a stick. The girls are lovely (prettier than the Czech girls, we are troubled to conclude), and as Marek P attends to his hair, Shaggy is jerked from the airwaves and Eminem is back on deck, and homeboys Mikael and Martin (who are painfully shy to the point of blushing as they speak) are suddenly rapping along in a flamboyant gangsta style. Significant looks are exchanged by the Honzas. Unpleasantness will not be brooked. But it is Vitek (the joker) who comes to the rescue, standing up and declaring that the time has come to debut this year's "anthem," which he has selected with great care and is possibly even more hilarious than last year's anthem, the much-loved and highly amusing "Mr. Bombay." (Each year, having scoured the bargain bin at TESCO, the increasingly quirky Vitek sources and burns an outlandish theme song on his CD-Rewritable. Last year it was "Mr. Bombay," the closing number from a Bollywood romance, the wrought emotion of which was truly absurd and had us in stitches the first five or six listens.) Before the homeboys can react, the joker has taken charge of the Boom Box, prompting groans of protest from the prestige girlfriends (it is Vitek's practice, especially after he's had a few drinks, to put the song on high rotation, and the majority of us are of the opinion that we would rather strangle a goat than sit through "Mr. Bombay" again). As the Slovaks look on in disbelief, Vitek cues up this year's anthem, which is, as far as we can tell, some kind of bizarre German polka with really bad falsetto singing (actually it's kind of catchy, but these are early days), and we are given a brief rundown of its origin (the soundtrack to a recently released and lighthearted German WWII-era drama), which makes us smile extra-grimly at those tuba oom-pah-pahs.

Martina C is on her feet, champagne glass in hand, testing the water with an old return to power. Her eyes are sparkling with devilish irony as she loudly proposes a toast to "The Germans!" but who can tell what she's thinking? She scares us, frankly, and for all we know she could be proposing a toast to Globus senior management. But we're quick to rise and charge our glasses and toast the Germans, our voices as one. The Slovak girls have huge furry eyebrows, undisciplined teeth, and ugly clothes, but their beauty is remarkable, and a few of the guys can't help but shake their heads at the cultural injustice of the Czech/Slovak split. Here are these girls who could be modeling Marc O'Polo, who could (with a bit of prudent dental work) be presenting the news or hosting any number of popular shows on TV Nova, but who are instead destined to wear brown Adidas track suits and drink hot wine in below-snow-level basements, purely as the result of a line drawn in the sand. (Are there hypermarkets in Bratislava? Martina C is moved to ask. The answer is yes, but merely supermarket-size.) More slivovitz is opened and champagne poured, and the talk naturally turns to snowboarding. The Slovaks have never seen a snowboard up close, so the Honzas and Libor and Marek C (the good Marek) retrieve their decks from the stairwell and haul them upstairs. Our American-brand snowboards have hardcore names like "Radical Power" and "Bitchin' Machine," and the head Slovak guy, Roman, is obviously somewhat at a loss with all this hardware on display. The question he asks, hunched forward in his chair, is: What's up with our use of the word *Sovietski!*? Correct him if he's wrong, but wasn't *Sovietski!* a Russian putsch-imposed word, a word dripping with Stalinist reeducation camp and Socialist-despot connotations, meaning "even more excellent than the already-existing Czechoslovakian word for excellent," *Vyborny!* (which literally translates as "of the highest esteem"), and if this is the case, then why are we using it? Why are we using a Stalinist word? Roman is rib-cage thin in the manner of Jack London's wolves, and he's pulling the filters off our L&M Menthols. The Slovak girl/Czech guy attraction scenario does not exist between the Czech girls and Roman, but there is something compelling about his patriotic outburst, so the decision is made to bring the poor guy up to speed.

Libor would be the logical spokesman, as he deals in cool and is an advertising man, but he's a bit big and stupid when he's had a few drinks, and the *Sovietski!* question is a contextual grenade. Jiri the Philosopher is thus our man in the box, and the German tuba music is turned off completely. Knuckles are cracked. The tension is electric. Face-to-face across the table from Roman, Jiri quietly debunks the Slovak head guy's terminological opposition to the use of *Sovietski!* on the grounds that, for the duration of the Stalin-through-Brezhnev years of E-bloc occupation, everyone without exception in the formerly unified country of Czechoslovakia knew that the Russians sucked bigtime and were a bunch of hapless clowns. Thus the original *Sovietski!*, forced at gunpoint by this most ignorant and non-*vyborny* of regimes, presented something of a paradox to the Czech/Slovak mind. Driving a tractor was better than excellent? Okay, Boris. Whatever you say. By not taking the Russians seriously (while doing their bidding at gunpoint), the occupied Czechs/Slovaks were able to deflect the potentially lethal trajectory of Socialism (subjugation of the will) with a kind of fatalistic humor—"Yessir, we are loving driving this tractor,"—and thus accommodate the paradox with a minimum of fuss. In the case of hideous wall hangings and garishly packaged German snow chains, the deployment of *Sovietski!* is a just throwback to those times. The world is filled with hideous wall hangings. What are you going to do? Complain to management?

Marek P (the bad Marek) has finished his hair, and he unexpectedly comes to Roman's defense. "We could have fought," he observes dryly, his upswept quiff and cigarette behind ear connotating a dangerous blend of ideals and defiance, and if we didn't know him better (he works at Citibank in credit analysis and has, to date, refused MasterCards to Honzas P, C, J, and Veronika K), we might be thoroughly entranced by this Luke Perry–style rebellion. But no. This is a shameless play for the lovely Slovak girls' attention, and the Honzas (who take a dim view of Marek's romantic posturing, and who are understandably nonplussed by this business with the MasterCards) have primed a veritable arsenal of Bohemia Sekt, and the sloe-eyed Marek is rather brutally hosed down.

The homeboys and Vitek make a play for the Boom Box, but the prestige girlfriends have rallied behind Monika Navratilova and the compilation tapes she always puts on when she's drunk. We secretly like these tapes (and we're very fond of Monika), but there's that thing where the songs are censor-approved rock from the late seventies/early eighties, featuring lyrics about tractors and stout women baling hay. Jiri and Roman trade points of difference as the kitchen is briefly plunged backward in time, and we find ourselves singing along with fifteen-year-old Pavel Hornak, one of the great voices of the "normalization" era. Not a whole lot of fatalistic humor to be heard (although Pavel does sound like he's singing at gunpoint), but Roman is clearly on the ropes re: the *Sovietski!* question and defensively throws back a double shot glass of vodka. "What are *you* looking at?" he growls at Marek C.

A squeal from Sarka, Klara, Lenka, and Petra heralds an unexpected but welcome infusion of cuteness, and we turn to find a kitten nuzzling in through the window. It has climbed up the snowdrift, negotiated the forest of Bohemia Sekt, and can be heard purring hopefully above the wail of Pavel H. The girls leap on the kitten and bring it into the kitchen, where it starts working the room in the manner of tiny kittens worldwide. Shins are rubbed up against. The purring is incessant. It's obvious the poor creature hasn't eaten in days, so Lenka and Petra crumble up a handful of Martina's Christmas biscuits while the two Veronikas pour milk into a bowl. It is snowing outside and the couples are on their feet, swaying drunkenly to a slow ballad (about love) by Hana Hegerova, and after a couple of false starts, even the ice queen gets up and slow-dances with her boyfriend. The sadness of which is inescapable, as the engagement is off and Marek C is on the verge of moving back in with his parents. He's playing a long career game, buying a piece of Carrefour with a salary cut and equity, but the time it will take for his investment to yield is a couple of years the ice queen intends to spend elsewhere. Don't get her wrong. She's as forward-thinking as the next girl. It's just that the economy right now is one huge game of musical chairs where when the music stops you just know it will stay stopped, and, as is always the case with multinational corporations, it's the little guys like Marek who end up relinquishing their chairs so some overseas guy with a huge ass can sit down. The fundamental problem with the new Czech economy is that the second the Russians rolled out of Prague in '91, the country's former Communist leaders put on their capitalist hats and sold state-owned industry under the table to the West. Kickbacks were pocketed. Many of these guys now live in Switzerland. All well and good, except that for clear-eyed realists like Martina C, for whom government-level graft was not an option, the only profitable game now worth playing involves getting in bed with foreign investment. In bed as in procreational with. As in "my kids will speak a language other than Czech." This is the reality. She's sorry. And if it means she's going to have to stand around and watch the likes of Lenka and Petra feeding her biscuits to a kitten, well, feed away!

Marek C (oblivious to this internal monologue, but under no illusions as to where he stands in the relationship) is a really good slow-dancer, and he re-creates old magic in his corner of the kitchen, bump-and-grinding the ice queen with a hint of cruelty in his eyes. The homeboys are loving this (it's dead sexy), and would be loving it a whole lot more if the Slovak girls would only look in their direction. The Slovak girls are not as cool as the Czech girls, so it's endearing to watch them play with a kitten instead of exploring the plethora of romantic possibilities around them, and Mikael and Martin, who have used the words *yo* and *word* concurrently and unpacked their spray cans and rotated their Kangol hats and mimed the "scratching" of vinyl on invisible turntables, feel that they have no choice but to "keep it real" and impress the girls with some spray-painting wizardry. With no further ado, they brandish their cans and run out into the night. Vitek (who has not been dancing) seizes control of the Boom Box, ejecting the slow ballad and switching function to CD, and bad German polka assails the Party Zone once more. Uproar from the prestige girlfriends, who demand that Vitek be silenced, but Vitek has already climbed out the window with the Boom Box in his arms and appears to be stuck headfirst in the snowdrift, clanking around in all those bottles of champagne.

Spy magazine "sexy girl" Daniela Zalesakova is on the floor with the Slovak girls, fussing over the kitten as it laps milk from the bowl. The kitten is *in* the bowl, in fact, purring heartily and prompting no end of girlish chatter from the Slovak girls and Daniela, who is dressed more or less exactly the way you imagine a "sexy girl" would dress. Lucie and Anna wear tragic brown track suits and big fleecy boots that scream "Farm!" but they seem much more comfortable in their kitten handling than the Prague girls, for whom the handling of kitten seems oddly cinematic. A quick appraisal of the kitchen table reveals a dense wall of empty slivovitz bottles, slivovitz being a kind of vodka made from plums instead of potatoes. The big bottle of absinthe is also empty, which possibly accounts for why Vitek is fighting a losing battle with the snowdrift, and why Libor has removed his shirt and is striking poses by the window. On the vodka front, Jiri the Philosopher is fielding a reverse-Socratic line of questioning from Roman and Ondrej, who have dispensed with the shot glasses and are chugging straight from the bottle, the thrust of their questioning apparently directed at the Philosopher's much-coveted Harry Potter hat. Once again the Slovaks aren't getting it, and patience is stretched thin explaining the validity of a grown man wearing a lurid purple baseball cap with the name of a prepubescent British wizard in big gold letters above the bill. No Stalinist guns to heads here, comrade. The cheesiness of Potter is to be embraced and celebrated for the simple reason that we know it is cheesy. This knowledge empowers us. The U.K. marketing hordes may think they have foisted this wizard upon us unawares, but we're on to them, and by wearing the hat and sporting the merchandise, what we are in fact saying is "Globalist consumerism is kind of stupid, no?" "Yessir, we are loving this Potter," is Roman's icy retort, and to our dismay, he rallies the lovely Slovak girls and shepherds them out the door. The energy level of the kitchen is immediately cut in half, and many reproachful glances are cast in Jiri's direction. The bad Marek P is particularly distraught, as he has showered and changed into a silk dressing gown with flaming Chinese embroidery, the sight of which sets off a wave of recognition-shuddering from most of the women in the room. Veronika K is crimson with fury—refusal of MasterCard being the proverbial straw—and she stalks from the room with a bottle of vodka, followed by Sarka, Klara, Lenka, Petra, and the raven-haired and volatile Veronika J.

Vitek is still half buried in the snowdrift, but his legs have gone limp and the Honzas laugh themselves silly as they retrieve their kooky friend from the world's largest icebox. The joker's face has turned blue, but the first thing he does is recue the German music. "What happened to the chicks?" he wants to know.

The chicks have decided to call it a night. Ice queen Martina C and "sexy girl" Daniela Z have whisked their boyfriends away to respective bedrooms, conveying the idea that slow-dancing v. shirtless posturing is but an inkling of what they're in for, bedroom-action-wise. And Magda and Monika have wandered off to play Scrabble. In their absence, the Party Zone takes on a no-BS men's-locker-room ambience that facilitates the start of CRAZY HOTEL-style drinking. Bottles of champagne are opened and glasses are charged, and then vodka is poured into the open champagne bottles, creating a kind of Ur-champagne, which we're knocking back with great vigor and speed, when the door crashes open and the homeboys rush in with the news that the town is completely covered with snow, and spray painting snow is "wack" and "jiggy." It's below zero out there. A blizzard, by all accounts. And since the Slovak girls are no longer in the room, removing any motivational justification for a Napoleonic romp through waist-deep snow, the decision made by homeboys Mikael and Martin is to change forthwith into their flannel pajamas and hit the booze like there's no tomorrow.

At the far end of the table, the three guys with receding hairlines (that would be Vitek, Dusan, and Jiri the Philosopher) are playing an amusing game that consists of them peeling soggy labels off Bohemia Sekt bottles and slapping the labels in the middle of their foreheads. There's a point-scoring system involved, which Vitek is trying to enforce, but he's also getting up and recueing the polka, and when we tell him to knock it off with the polka, he unplugs the Boom Box and threatens to climb onto the roof. The homeboys are in their pajamas and clamoring for beats, but a compromise is struck where we agree to sing along with the latest Karel Gott CD—Karel Gott being the Czech Sinatra, although he actually bears more of a resemblance to the late Roy Orbison in the high-pitched, creepy vocal department. He's been around since the sixties and has recently been outfitted with Cher-style big disco production, which makes his contemporary work a total "hoot" to sing along with. We're spectacularly drunk by this point, and a boisterous toast is proposed to bad Communist rock and Christmas biscuits and the prettiest girls who walk the earth. "To the Czech hockey team!" the Honzas cry. "To Ivana Trump and Milos 'Amadeus' Forman!" A patriotic warmth fills the kitchen to the brim, and Marek P, who has been roving the chalet in search of "possibilities," returns with the tiny kitten he has found sleeping on the couch. "To the kitten!" we roar, and for reasons we later find hard to recollect (but which seem logical and funny at the time), the decision is made to spray paint the kitten in the red, white, and blue of our national flag. "Mascot kitty" is what we're probably thinking, and the homeboys rush off to retrieve their spray cans while a mat of paper towels is assembled in the bathroom. The kitten is charcoal gray with white socks, prompting the ever-practical Jiri to suggest an undercoat of white paint followed by the red and blue layers once the undercoat has dried. This seems like a good plan until we discover that Mikael has left his blue can in Prague ("No one uses blue," he points out). Red and white is too Swiss for our liking, so we end up settling on a basic white with black stripes. The dextrous Mikael takes care of the painting while we hold and turn the kitten on the mat of paper towels, and "zebra kitty" is created in no time. We set it free and watch it tear ass through the chalet, dotting the carpet with paint like tiny footprints in snow.

Absinthe has taken its toll on the joker. We find him passed out on the kitchen table, a Bohemia Sekt label still stuck to his forehead. The experienced drinkers in our crew tend to avoid absinthe as it's high octane and defies the various booze groups, but Vitek just loves it as it comes replete with the requisite cross-cultural baggage. It's a tourist drink, basically. You can't buy it in the West, as it's extremely harmful to the brain, which of course is a red rag to a bull where backpackers are concerned. A trip to Prague is not truly complete unless you've endured the industrial-grade hangover absinthe tends to produce, and thus the act of drinking absinthe in the Czech Republic has, for a certain type of individual, the same kind of illogical-but-predictable similarity to the act of, say, buying I ♥ NY merchandise in NYC (which Vitek swears he will do if he ever travels to the States). The Honzas transfer the sleeping joker to the couch, while the homeboys locate his CD and wordlessly snap it in half, and then we settle in for one last drink before bed. Marek P makes a final circuit of the lodge and seems surprised to discover that the bedroom doors are closed to him. With his hair greased up, he looks like Elvis, but he's removed his contact lenses and tends to bump and move slowly on account of poor eyesight, which makes his late-night prowls more disabled than seductive. Dusan and Jiri are howling along with Karel Gott, who is many hundreds of years old and looks as creepy as he sings, and then the room tilts off its axis and the Party Zone is suddenly plunged into the roller-coaster downtrack of a vodka/champagne spin. Visibility in triplicate. The rotor whir of impending pain. Homeboys M and M, in their flannel pajamas, laughing at something, we don't quite know what, but the opinional consensus is that we're credibly hammered and have covered ourselves with glory on CRAZY HOTEL day one.

We therefore call it a night and crowd into the bathroom, avoiding the mirrors and lifting our voices in song, and the big closing number is "*My Mame Ocelove Ptaky*," a Soviet tune our parents sang in the fifties, which goes: "We have birds made of steel / We are flying above the clouds," which just cracks us up (as it did our parents), as *bird* in our language is a popular euphemism for *penis*. We have penises made of steel and we are flying above the clouds. How thoroughly appropriate! How hilarious indeed!

The following morning, we follow the trail of tiny paw prints and find the zebra-striped kitten frozen solid in the driveway. Its eyes are shut and its teeth are snarled up in pain, and the fumes have either killed it outright or else the undercoat has smothered the pores of its skin and it has suffocated slowly in the snow outside the lodge. The girls are teary (and in a few cases, reproachful) as we dislodge and wrap the kitten in a plastic shopping bag, and then we throw it in the trash and load snowboards into cars, and drive down the hill to the big ski barn for breakfast.

The Old Gentleman

FRANCES HWANG

AS A YOUNG GIRL, Agnes was often embarrassed by her father. Her family lived on the compound of a girls' high school in Taipei where her father worked as principal. On Monday mornings, after the flag had been raised and the national anthem sung, he liked to give speeches to the students assembled in the main courtyard. To get their attention, he stood with silent, aggrieved humility, his arms dangling at his sides, his limp suit already wrinkled from the humidity, the front pockets stuffed with his reading glasses, a spiral notebook, a pack of cigarettes, and a well-used handkerchief. When he opened his mouth, he did not immediately speak, desiring that slight pause, that moment of breath in which everyone's attention was fixed on him alone. He quoted regularly from Mengzi, but his favorite writer was Cao Xueqin. "'Girls are made of water and boys are made of mud,'" he declared. Or, "'The pure essence of humanity is concentrated in the female of the species. Males are its mere dregs and offscourings.'" He clasped his hands behind his back, his eyes widening as he spoke. "Each of you is capable, but you must cultivate within yourself a sense of honesty and shame." He reminded the girls to rinse their mouths out with tea when they said a dirty word. He discussed matters of personal hygiene and reprimanded them for spitting on the streets. Her father had a thick Jiangbei accent, and students often laughed when they heard him speak for the first time.

When Agnes was eleven, her mother was hospitalized after jumping off a two-story building and breaking her hand. The following Monday, her father opened his mouth in front of the student assembly, but no words came out, only a moaning sound. He covered his eyes with a fluttering hand. Immediately, a collection was started among students and faculty, a generous sum of money raised to pay for her mother's hospital bill. A story was posted outside on the newspaper wall in which a student praised Agnes's father for his selfless devotion to "a walking ghost" who had "very little expression on her face." Older girls came up to Agnes and pressed her hand. "Your poor mother!" they exclaimed in sad tones. They marveled at her father's goodness, assuring her that a kinder man could not be found.

Agnes intentionally flunked her entrance exams the next year so that she would not have to attend her father's school. She ended up going to a lesser school that was a half-hour commute by bus. Sometimes, she rode her old bicycle in order to save bus fare.

Her family lived in an outer courtyard in a three-room house without running water. Because her mother was sick, the school arranged for a maid to come tidy up their house and wash their clothes. The school's kitchen was only twenty yards away, and Agnes washed her face in the same cement basin where the vegetables were rinsed. Her father paid the cook a small sum to prepare their meals, which were always delivered to them covered with an overturned plate. At night they used candles during scheduled blackouts, and with the exception of her mother, who slept on a narrow bed surrounded by mosquito netting, her father, her brother, and Agnes slept on tatami floors.

Sometimes, when Agnes mentions her early life in Taiwan to her daughters, they look at her in astonishment, as if she had lived by herself on a deserted island. "That was the 1950s, right?" one of them asks. The other says, "You were so poor!"

"It wasn't so bad," Agnes replies. "Most everyone lived the same way, so you didn't notice."

What she remembers most from that time is following a boy in her choir whom she had a crush on. When she passed by him on her bicycle and the wind lifted her skirt, she was in no hurry to pull it down again. Some days, she picked up the cigarette butts that he tossed on the street and slipped the bittersweet ends between her lips. She kept a diary, and it was a relief to write down her feelings, but she burned the pages a few years later when not even the handwriting seemed to be her own. She did not want a record to exist. No one in the world would know she had suffered. Agnes thinks now of that girl bicycling around the city, obsessed and burdened by love. It isn't surprising that she never once suspected her father of having a secret life of his own.

Her parents moved to the United States after her father's retirement, and for nine years they lived in their own house in Bloomington, Indiana, a few miles from her brother's farm. After her mother's death, Agnes thought her father would be lonely by himself in the suburbs and suggested that he move to Washington, D.C., to be closer to her and her daughters. She was a part-time real estate agent (though she made most of her money selling life insurance), and she knew of an apartment building in Chinatown for senior citizens that was subsidized by the government. At Evergreen House, he could socialize with people his age, and when he stepped out of his apartment, he only had to walk a couple of blocks to buy his groceries and a Chinese newspaper.

Her father eagerly agreed to this plan. Six months after her mother died, he moved into Evergreen House and quickly made friends with the other residents, playing mah-jongg twice a week, and even going to church, though he had never been religious before. For lunch, he usually waited in line at the Washington Urban League senior center where he could get a full hot meal for only a dollar.

At seventy-eight, her father looked much the same as he did in Taiwan when Agnes was growing up. For as long as she could remember, her father had been completely bald except for a sparse patch of hair that clung to the back of his head. By the time he was sixty, this shadowy tuft disappeared, leaving nothing but shiny brown skin like fine, smooth leather. Her father had always been proud of his baldness. "We're more vigorous," he liked to say, "because of our hormones." He reassured Agnes that he would live to a hundred at least.

Every day, her father dressed impeccably in a suit and tie, the same attire that he wore as a principal, even though there was no longer any need for him to dress formally. "Such a gentleman!" Agnes's friends remarked when they saw him. He gazed at them with tranquility, though Agnes suspected he knew they were saying flattering things about him. His eyes were good-humored, clear, and benign, the irises circled with a pale ring of blue.

If anything, Agnes thought, her father's looks had improved with age. His hollow cheeks had filled out, and he had taken to wearing a fedora with a red feather stuck in the brim, which gave him a charming and dapper air. Maybe, too, it was because he now wore a set of false teeth that corrected his overbite.

Every other weekend, he took the Metro from his place in Chinatown to Dunn Loring, where Agnes waited for him in her car. He would smile at Agnes as if he hadn't seen her for a year, or as if their meeting was purely a matter of chance and not something they had arranged by telephone. If her teenage daughters were in the car, he would greet them in English. "Hello!" he smiled. "How are you?"

Her daughters laughed. "Fine! And how are you?" they replied.

"Fine!" he exclaimed.

"Good!" they responded.

"Good!" he repeated.

Agnes supposed the three of them found it amusing, their lack of words, their inability to express anything more subtle or pressing to each other. Her daughters were always delighted to see him. They took him out shopping and invited him to the movies. They were good-natured, happy girls, if spoiled and a little careless. Every summer, they visited their father in Florida, and when they came back, their suitcases were stuffed with gifts—new clothes and pretty things for their hair, stuffed animals and cheap bits of jewelry that they wore for a week and then grew tired of. Their short attention spans sometimes made Agnes feel sorry for her ex-husband, and she enjoyed this feeling of pity in herself very much.

In March, her father visited a former student of his in San Francisco. He came back two weeks later, overflowing with health and good spirits. He gave silk purses to the girls and a bottle of Guerlain perfume to Agnes. It was unlike her father to give her perfume, much less one from Paris. She asked him how he had chosen it. "A kind lady helped me," he replied soberly. By this, Agnes thought he meant a saleslady at the store. But later, as she was going through his suit pockets, emptying them of loose change and crumpled tissues and soft pads of lint—she planned on going to the dry cleaner's that afternoon—she found a sliver of light blue paper folded into eighths. It was a rough draft of a letter, without a date or signature, addressed to a woman named Qiulian. Her father wrote in a quaint, tipsy hand. His characters were neat though cramped, etched on the page as the ink from his pen was running out.

You cannot know how happy I was to receive your letter. I hope you are well in San Francisco, and that you have had restful days. I think of you often, perhaps more than I should. Like this morning, for instance, I wondered when exactly you had lived in Nanjing. Is it possible we lived in that city at the same time? I like to think that we passed each other on the street, I, a young man in his early thirties, and you, a schoolgirl in uniform with your hair cut just below the ear. We walked past each other, not knowing our paths would cross again—so many years later!

The cherry trees are in bloom here along the Potomac. I often find myself conversing with you in my head. Look at the falling blossoms, I say. Beautiful, yes? Some people, I know, don't have the courage for anything, but what is there to be afraid of? I thought I would spend the rest of my days alone. I can't help but think of the poet, Meng Chiao. "Who says that all things flower in spring?"

A few characters had been blotted out, a phrase added between the vertical lines of script. Agnes couldn't help but laugh, even though there was a slight pain in it, as with all surprises. How ridiculous that her father should be courting someone across the country. To be thinking of love when he should be thinking of the grave. She called up Hu Tingjun, her father's student in California. "So who is this Qiulian?" she demanded when he picked up the phone.

"Ah!" Tingjun said, his voice wavering. He had always been a little afraid of her since that time she had thrown a glass of water in his face. But he had a loose tongue, and Agnes knew he would not be able to resist the urge to gossip. "A real beauty from the mainland," he declared. "Your father has good taste."

Agnes allowed this to pass without comment. "And why is she so interested in my father? He doesn't have any money."

Tingjun laughed. "You underestimate your father's charms." He paused, and Agnes could hear him sucking his teeth. "I think she's had a sad life. You know what they say—every beauty has a tragic story."

Agnes frowned, switching the phone to her other ear.

"Her husband was an art history professor at Nanjing University," Tingjun said. "Struggled against, of course, and died in a reeducation camp. She married a second time, but this husband turned out to be a violent character—he beat her, I'm told, and she divorced him after a few years. She has two children from her first marriage, both of them in Guangzhou. She came here under a tourist's visa and is staying with an old friend from college."

"So she's been married twice already," Agnes said, "and wants to marry again. She doesn't have a very good track record."

"Have a heart, Shuling. What's so wrong with your father finding comfort in his last days? It's no good to be alone. No good at all."

"I never thought you were a sentimentalist," she said. "I wish I could hand you some tissues!"

Tingjun sighed. "You're always the same, Shuling."

When Agnes hung up the phone, she couldn't help but think of her mother, whom she had always loved more than her father, just as you love something more because it is broken. Her mother had lived to the age of seventy-one, longer than anyone had believed possible, defying the prognostications of doctors, the resignation of her children, and even her own will. Her father had never murmured a word of complaint in all the years he cared for her. In the mornings he prepared her a breakfast of pureed apples or boiled carrots. At night he brought her three pills—one sleeping pill, two that he had filled with sugar—and a tall glass of prune juice. Everything her mother ate had to go through a blender first. She chewed the same mouthful over and over again with slow awareness, sometimes falling asleep with the food still in her mouth. She once told Agnes that every bite she swallowed was like swallowing a small stone. The only thing she enjoyed putting in her mouth was her sleeping pills, and these she swallowed all at once without a sip of water. Perhaps Agnes respected this sickness in her mother more than her father's health, his natural exuberance, and his penchant for histrionics.

The day before her mother's funeral, Agnes remembered, she and her brother had gone to a store to look for watches. They had selected a gold watch with a round face, and her brother had asked the salesclerk if there was a warranty for how long it would run, which struck Agnes as funny since the watch was going on her mother's wrist. "Who cares whether it runs beneath the ground or not?" she said. Nevertheless, her mother had always liked to wear watches. They bought it for her because her old one was broken.

Then Agnes saw her mother lying in her coffin, the new gold watch ticking at her wrist. The sight of her mother lying in such a composed state, looking more content and peaceful than she did when she was alive, made Agnes desperate. She brushed her mother's cheeks and smoothed out her hair with increasing savagery, clutching her hand and kissing her cold lips, all the while smelling her powder and the undertaker's handiwork beneath the cloying scent of lilies.

At the funeral reception, her father positioned himself on a stool at the front door of his house so that anyone who passed by had to confront him. At one point, he sprung off his stool and ran across the yard to speak to his neighbor who had just come home from the store and was holding a bag of groceries. Agnes watched as her father waved his arms, his new suit a size too large for him, the cuffs dangling over his hands and flapping about his wrists. He squeezed his eyes and cried like a child, beating the side of his head with his palm. His neighbor set her bag down, took his hand between her own, and nodded in sympathy, even though she could not understand a word he was saying. Agnes's brother finally intervened, leading their father away so that the neighbor could go inside her house.

"Try to control yourself," Agnes told her father.

"You don't know what it's like to lose someone you saw every day of your life," he said, wiping his eyes.

When the funeral reception was over, after the visitors had departed and her father had shut himself up in his bedroom, Agnes and her brother stood in the backyard, looking at his garden.

"The two of them lived in their own world together," her brother said.

Agnes looked at the glossy tomatoes that hung like ornaments from the vines. The winter melons sprawled on the grass like pale, overfed whales. Above this, the sunflowers rose, their faces somehow human, drooping from their stalks. For the first time, she wondered about her parents, the quiet life they had lived in that home.

Agnes never asked her father about the letter she found. In October, he informed her that Qiulian would be flying down in a month and that they would be married in a civil ceremony at the courthouse. He wondered if Agnes would be their witness. Also if there was a restaurant in the area suitable for a small wedding banquet. No more than five tables, he said.

In the marriage bureau, there was a sign prohibiting photographs. Tiny pictures in pastel frames—a cheetah running, an eagle spreading its wings—decorated the walls. Agnes sighed as she looked at her watch. She got up from her seat and inspected a picture of a sailboat skimming along moonlit waters. The caption read: *You cannot discover new oceans unless you have the courage to lose sight of the shore.* This made Agnes laugh out loud, and the receptionist glanced up to look at her from her desk.

Her father arrived a moment later with his bride. He was beaming, handsomely dressed in a dark gray suit and platinum tie, two red carnations fastened to his lapel. He introduced them with mock solemnity, exaggerating the tones of their names, lifting himself in the air and falling back on his heels. Qiulian smiled at Agnes and told her that her American name was Lily. Everything Lily wore was white. There was her opaque white dress of crêpe de chine with its faintly puffed sleeves. Her pearl earrings and two strands of pearls wound closely around her neck. A corsage of white roses enmeshed in a swirl of white ribbon pinned to her chest. She had decided on white just as if she were an American bride, even though white was no color at all, what you wore to another person's funeral. Perhaps it was a sign of Lily's true feelings.

Agnes grasped her father's arm and pulled him aside. "How old is she, by the way?" It infuriated her that this woman was closer to her age than she had expected.

"That's top secret," her father said, adjusting his carnations. "She's very nice, isn't she? Do I look all right? What do you think of my tie?" He glanced over at Lily, who stood serenely looking at her shoes. She held a small beaded purse between both hands, and it seemed from her empty expression that she was pretending not to hear their conversation. "Incredible!" he muttered. "I'm supposed to feel less as I grow old. But it's the opposite . . . I feel more and more!" His eyes widened, and he knocked his fist against his chest. "Can you believe it? A seventy-eight-year-old heart like mine!" He walked back to Lily, smiling and patting her hand.

Agnes felt her skin begin to itch. She wanted to lift her sweater, scratch herself luxuriously until she bled, but the receptionist told them it was time, and they were ushered into a narrow green-carpeted room where the justice of the peace stood waiting behind a podium. Behind him was a trellis on which a few straggling vines of artificial clematis drooped. It was a halfhearted attempt at illusion, and, for this reason, it gave Agnes some relief. It startled her to think that she had once cared about the color of roses matching her bridesmaids' dresses. That day had been a fantasy with its exquisite bunches of flowers, so perfect they did not seem real. At one point, she had looked up at the sky and laughed. She had felt so light and happy . . . she had worn a white ballroom dress—and of all things—a rhinestone tiara! If photographs still existed of her in this Cinderella outfit, they resided in other people's albums, for she had torn her own into bits.

Her father was listening to the judge with an impassive, dignified expression, his hands folded neatly in front of him. Agnes thought Lily's smile belonged on the face of a porcelain doll. Her hair was cut in short, fashionable waves and seemed ridiculously lustrous for someone her age. Dyed no doubt. Neither of them understood what the judge was saying, and Agnes had to prompt them when it was time to exchange rings. When the justice pronounced them husband and wife, her father looked around the room, smiling good-naturedly. He thanked the judge with a bow of his head and took Lily gently by the elbow.

Her father visited less often after he was married. The few times he took the subway to Dunn Loring, he did not bring Lily with him. Agnes once asked him why, and he said Lily was quite popular at Evergreen House. "People are always inviting her out to restaurants," he said. "Or she goes over to other ladies' apartments and they watch the latest Hong Kong melodramas. What sentimental drivel! But she enjoys it, she can't get enough of it . . ." He told Agnes that one day, Lily wanted to eat *dan dan* noodles and nothing but dan dan noodles. "There was a restaurant we knew, but the owners were away on vacation. Qiulian suggested another restaurant, but when we got there, it wasn't on the menu and she refused to go inside. She dragged me from one place to another, but none of them served dan dan noodles. I was so hungry by this time, I insisted we go into the next restaurant we saw. But she said she wouldn't eat at all if she couldn't have her dan dan noodles. So we ended up going home, and I had to eat leftovers." Her father shook his head, though he was clearly delighted by Lily's caprice.

From her father, Agnes learned that Lily had studied Chinese history at the prestigious Zhejiang University. She liked to take baths over showers, used Pond's cream on her face at night, and sipped chrysanthemum tea in bed. She rarely bought herself anything, and when she did, the things she chose were charming and fairly priced. Her father gave Lily a monthly allowance of five hundred dollars, which was half the income he received from Agnes and her brother as well as from social security. Lily, in turn, sent money to her son, a book vendor, and to her daughter, a truck driver in Guangzhou.

More than a year passed, and Agnes never saw her.

In December, she walked by Lily almost without recognizing her. She had stopped in Chinatown to buy duck for a New Year's Eve party, and a small group of older women approached her on the street. She would not have paid them any attention if the woman in the gray raincoat had not paused in the middle of readjusting a silk scarf around her head to stare at Agnes. It took Agnes a moment to realize it was Lily. By that time, the women had passed, heading south in the direction of Evergreen House.

Agnes stood on the sidewalk, gazing absently at a faded brick building, its pink paint flaking off to reveal dark red patches. Even in the winter, the streets smelled of grease and the hot air blown out of ventilators. Behind a row of buildings, two looming cranes crisscrossed the sky. It was odd to think of someone like Lily living here. Agnes went inside the restaurant to get her duck, and by the time she stepped outside again, tiny flakes of snow were falling. She did not go back to her car but turned in the direction of her father's apartment.

Outside his door, she heard shrill voices and laughter, the noisy clacking of tiles being swirled along a table. The mah-jongg ladies, Agnes thought. Lily answered the door, her mild empty eyes widening slightly. Her mass of glossy black hair was perfectly manicured, and only her wrinkled neck betrayed her age.

"I saw you on the street," Agnes said. "Didn't you see me?"

"Yes," Lily said, pausing. "But I wasn't sure it was you until we had passed each other."

"The same with me." Agnes pulled off her coat and tossed it onto the sofa. "So, who are your friends here?"

"Oh yes, let me introduce you to my neighbors." The mah-jongg ladies half stood out of their seats, smiling at Agnes, but it was obvious they wanted to return to their game.

"Don't let me disturb you," Agnes told them. "Is my father here?"

"He's taking a nap," Lily said, taking her seat at the table.

The living room was brightly lit compared to the dimness of the hallway. It seemed like its own island of space as the afternoon waned and the windows darkened. The mah-jongg ladies chattered as they flung their tiles to the middle of the table. They were older than Lily, in their seventies at least, their hands plowed with wrinkles, with bright green circles of jade hanging from their wrists. Their fingers, too, were weighed down by gaudy rings, the stones shiny as candy, purple and turquoise and vermilion. "He ate oatmeal every day," a woman with badly drawn eyebrows was saying.

"I heard he took poison," another said, picking up a tile. She had thick, sour lips and wore red horn-rimmed glasses. "Didn't he lose everything?"

"No, it was a heart attack. His wife found him still sitting on the toilet! In the middle of reading a newspaper."

"He was too cheap to pay for his own funeral," the third one said. She had a sagging, magisterial face, her thick, white hair pulled back into a bun. "In his will, he donated his body to science."

The one with the false eyebrows knocked down all of her tiles. "Hula!" she declared.

There were startled cries. "I wasn't even close!"

"Did anyone have five sticks?"

Agnes smiled as she poured herself a cup of tea from the counter. These ladies were real witches, talking about people's ends with such morbid assurance—how could Lily stand their company? Perhaps she liked the attention, for she seemed to be the silent center of the group, the one the ladies exclaimed over and petted. Lily glanced over at Agnes from time to time, smiling at her. She seemed impatient for Agnes to leave.

"Well," Agnes said, after she had finished her tea, "he won't mind too much if I wake him." She walked across the room and opened the bedroom door, even though she sensed this was precisely what Lily did not want her to do.

Her father sat at his desk reading a newspaper, his bifocals drooping along his nose. A single lamp illumined his downturned head, and it seemed from his silence that he had been exiled here. His manner changed the moment he saw her. His face broke into an exuberant smile as he stood up from his chair.

"So what are you doing here? Come to pay me a visit?"

Agnes closed the door behind her. "I've brought you a duck," she said. "And to wish you a happy New Year."

"A duck? Did you go to the Golden Palace?"

"I did."

"That's the best place to go. They have better ducks than anywhere else. Number one ducks!" he said. "So plump! And with crispy skin."

Agnes looked at her father. "And how are you these days?"

"I'm fine!" he declared. "I'm good! Just look at me." He straightened his argyle sweater over his shirt and tie, then preened in front of the mirror, turning his head to one side and then the other.

"You don't play mah-jongg with the ladies," she said, glancing around the room. The furniture was mismatched—things that she had given him which she no longer had any use for. A chair from an old dining room table set. A desk with buttercup yellow legs. A massive dresser with gothic iron handles. It bothered Agnes to see her daughter's stickers still on one of the drawers.

"You know me. I'm not good at these sorts of games. I'm a scholar, I read things—like this newspaper," he said, waving it in the air. "Besides, they want to talk freely without me hanging about."

"What's that doing in here?" Agnes asked. "Is that where she makes you sleep?" In the corner, between the bed and the closet, was a makeshift cot covered with a comforter folded in half like a sleeping bag.

"The bed is too soft on my poor back," her father said. He pressed his hand against his spine and winced. "This way is more comfortable."

Agnes sat down on the thin cot, which bounced lightly. "So this is how she treats you," she said. "She won't even let you into her bed."

"Her sleep isn't good." Her father cleared his throat, setting the newspaper down on his desk. "She often wakes up in the middle of the night." He didn't look at her as he fiddled with the pages, then folded the paper back together. Agnes felt an involuntary stirring in her chest. She had avoided him all this time, not wanting to know about his marriage because she had not wanted to know of his happiness. But she should have known Lily was the kind of person who only took care of herself.

"How else is she treating you?" she asked. "Is she mistreating you in any way?"

"No, no," her father said hurriedly, shaking his head.

"Is she a wife to you?" There was a pause as he looked at her. "You know what I mean," she said.

"She complains of a pain," he offered hesitantly. "In her ovaries."

Agnes laughed. She got up and strode across the room, flinging the door open.

"Don't say anything," her father said. "Don't let her know what I've told you."

The mah-jongg ladies were laughing and knocking over their walls when Agnes burst into the room. She raised her voice above their chatter. "I'd like to talk to you!" she said to Lily.

For a moment, Lily pretended not to hear, continuing her conversation with the white-haired lady beside her. Then she glanced over at Agnes, her face a mask of porcelain elegance except for one delicately lifted eyebrow. "What is it?"

"Why aren't you sleeping with my father?"

The ladies' voices fell to a murmur, their hands slowing down as they massaged the tiles along the tablecloth. They looked at Lily, who said nothing, though her smile seemed to be sewn on her lips.

Her father clutched Agnes's arm, but she refused to be silent. "You married him, didn't you? He pays for your clothes and your hairdo and this roof over your head. He deserves something in return!"

Her father laughed out loud and immediately put his hand over his mouth.

Lily stood up, but the mah-jongg ladies remained in their seats as if drunk, their eyes glazed with the thrill of the unexpected. "Perhaps we can resume our games later," Lily said. The one with the horn-rimmed glasses stood up slowly from the table, prompting the other two to rise out of their seats. They looked as if they had been shaken out of a dream.

"Oh, my heavens!" the one with the eyebrows exclaimed as Agnes shut the door on them.

"Now," Agnes said, turning toward Lily and waiting for her to speak.

"I have an illness—" Lily began. "A gynecological disorder that prevents me—" Her gaze wandered to Agnes's father, who hovered near the bedroom door. "Well, in truth, he's an old man," she said, her expression hardening. "His breath stinks like an open sewer. I can't stand to smell his breath!" She snatched her scarf from the closet and wrapped it quickly around her head.

"If you don't sleep with him," Agnes said, "I'll send a letter to the immigration office. I'll tell them that you only married him to get a green card!"

Lily's hands trembled as she put on her coat. "Do as you like," she said, walking out the door.

Her father looked deeply pained.

"She won't refuse you now," Agnes told him.

"What has happened?" her father said, his voice shaking. "Who are you? You've become someone—someone completely without shame!"

"I should open up a brothel," Agnes declared. "That is exactly what I should do."

In February, her father called to tell her he wasn't sure whether or not his nose was broken. There had been a snowstorm two days before, whole cars sheathed in ice, the roads filled with irregular lumps, oddly smooth and plastic, where the snow had melted and then frozen again. In this weather, her father and Lily had gone out walking to buy groceries at Da Hua Market. Lily had walked ahead, and when she was almost half a block away, she turned around and asked Agnes's father to walk faster. He tried to keep up with her, but corns had formed along his toes and the soles of his feet. When he quickened his pace, he slipped on a smooth, deceptively bland patch of ice and hit his nose on the pavement.

When Agnes saw her father—a dark welt on the bridge of his nose, a purple stain beginning to form under his eyes—she couldn't help but feel a flood of anger and pity. You could have lived your last years in peace, she wanted to say to him. Instead she glanced at the closed bedroom door. "Is that where she's hiding?"

He looked at her morosely. "She left earlier because she knew you were coming."

In the hospital, Agnes noticed that her father walked gingerly down the hall, stepping on the balls of his feet without touching his toes or heels to the ground. An X-ray revealed that his nose was not broken after all. Agnes told the resident he was having problems walking.

"That's not an emergency," the resident replied. Nevertheless, she left the room to call in a podiatrist.

Her father grew excited when he saw the podiatrist. He began speaking to him in Chinese.

"I'm sorry," the podiatrist said, shaking his head. "I'm Korean. Let's take these off, shall we?" He lightly pulled off her father's socks. There were red sores all over her father's feet—along the sides and heels and in between the toes. But what shocked Agnes most was the big toe on his left foot. The nail of this one toe looked a thousand years old to her, thick and wavy, with encrusted yellow edges, black in the center and as impenetrable as a carapace.

"Older people's toenails are often like this," the podiatrist said, seeing Agnes's surprise.

Her father seemed oblivious to their comments. He was squeezing his eyes shut as the podiatrist worked on his foot, slicing the calluses off bit by bit with a small blade. Her father winced and jerked his feet up occasionally. "Oh, it hurts," he exclaimed to Agnes. "It's unbearable!"

"I know this isn't pleasant," the podiatrist said, looking at her father. He took a pumice stone out of his pocket and rubbed it gently against her father's foot.

When the podiatrist had finished paring away at his corns, her father covered his feet back up, slowly pulling on his socks and tying the laces of his shoes. He smiled at the podiatrist, yet because of his bruised nose, his face seemed pathetic and slightly grotesque. "It's better beyond words," he said.

In the parking lot, her father showed off by walking at a sprightly pace in front of her. "It's so much better now!" he kept exclaiming.

The doctor had told Agnes that the corns would eventually come back, but she didn't tell her father this. She was thinking how well he had hidden from her the signs of old age. That big toe underneath his sock. Since the time she was a child, she and her father had lived their lives independent of each other. She had never demanded anything of him, and he had been too busy with his work at school, so that by the time she was six, she had been as free as an adult. They left each other alone mostly because of her mother, whose sickness filled up the entire house and whose moods were inextricably bound with their own.

In the car, Agnes told her father that she thought he should divorce Lily.

"It's not as bad as that, Shuling."

"I hate how she humiliates you," she said.

Her father was silent, gazing out the window. "Love is humiliating," he finally replied.

When she dropped him off in front of his building, he did not immediately go inside but stood on the frozen sidewalk, waving at her. She knew he would stay there until her car was no longer in sight. It was his way of seeing her off, and he would do this no matter what the weather.

In June, her father called to see if Agnes had any photographs of his wedding banquet. He planned to present them as evidence during his interview with the immigration officer. Agnes could find only one photograph. She had dumped it in a shoe box to be lost in an ever-growing stack of useless pictures. Years ago, she had stopped putting her family's photographs in an album. Now whenever their pictures were developed, after her daughters' initial enthusiasm of looking at themselves, Agnes put the photos back into their original envelopes and tossed them into a shoe box.

In the photograph she found, Lily was caught looking away from the camera, her mouth oddly pursed, as if she were in the middle of chewing her food while smiling at the same time. A pair of chopsticks rested between her fingers. It was an odd moment. Lily appeared sociable yet removed at the same time. Her eyes were lively though they looked at nothing in particular. It was as if one had caught two versions of her in the same photograph.

Actually, there were two photographs of Lily that Agnes found. Two copies of the same picture. Agnes wanted to find a difference, something very small—a gesture of the hand, the curve of an eyebrow—but the two pictures were exactly alike. Another photograph of Lily would reveal another world. But there she was—Lily could never break out of the picture, an elegant woman caught in the act of chewing. Beside her, her father looked radiant, a little too well satisfied, two red carnations and a wisp of baby's breath pinned right over his heart. He was the only person in the photograph looking at the camera.

"Do you want to come over this weekend to pick it up?" she asked her father. "I'll drive you to your interview on Monday."

Her father hesitated. "You don't have to come in with me. You can just drop me off at the immigration office."

"Fine," Agnes said.

The morning of his interview, her father ironed his own dress shirt and put on a suit that still smelled of the dry cleaner's fumes. He shaved the tiny white hairs that had begun to sprout on his chin, and even sprayed himself with an old bottle of cologne that he found in a bathroom drawer. An hour before his appointment, he began to fidget, looking at his watch and pacing around the room. "Shouldn't we be leaving?" he asked.

"Sit down. We have plenty of time."

"I don't want to be late," he said, picking up his bag. "Lily will be waiting."

Agnes sat down, tapping a pack of cigarettes in her hand. This was one of her bad habits, which she blamed on him, even though he had quit smoking for twenty years now. "You realize, don't you," Agnes said, blowing smoke to the side away from him. "It's a certain fact. She'll leave you as soon as she gets her green card."

Her father cleared his throat and switched the bag to his other hand.

"You want her to stay, am I right?"

He sighed, heading toward the door. "Let's not talk about this anymore."

"I'm not taking you," she said. She flicked the ash off her cigarette onto a plate. "It's for your own good. I won't let her have it."

Her father shook his head. "Unbelievable," he said.

"I wrote a letter to the INS already. In the letter, I informed them that your marriage—your wife—is a fraud."

Her father closed his eyes, shaking his head. He began breathing heavily and grasped his collar.

"What would Mother say?" she said. "You were such an easy dupe!"

"You and her!" he said, looking at Agnes. "You make me want to die!" He hit his palm twice against his forehead. "I want to die!"

"You were so eager to jump into another woman's bed," Agnes said. "But you didn't know she wouldn't let you touch her. Not even if you married her!"

"A dirty old man," her father laughed. "Yes, I am a dirty old man! I sleep with whoever I want! I slept with our maids, you know that? It only cost fifty cents each time! Sometimes, I did it when you were in the house, and you never knew. It was like you were knocked out, and I wondered if you took your mother's sleeping pills. Because you never knew! You never knew!" He was talking so fast, spittle was forming on his lips.

Agnes felt her throat burning and tried to swallow.

"I slept with all of them!" her father repeated.

"I don't believe you."

"Yes!"

"Those women? They were old and fat . . ."

"Who cares? Their bodies were warm."

"Disgusting."

"Yes, everything is disgusting to you." Her father walked to the front door.

"Where do you think you're going?" she screamed.

He left the door open, and she watched him walk down the driveway with a jaunty step. She wondered if he even knew how to get out of the neighborhood. It was still morning, but the humidity was unbearable. She picked up the newspaper lying on the doorstep and went back inside. She would let him walk as much as he wanted. It would serve him right if he got heatstroke.

At eleven, the phone rang. It was Lily at the INS wondering where her father was. "He won't be able to make it," Agnes said, and she hung up the phone. But she felt herself shaking. Wasn't it obvious, wasn't it to be expected—a healthy, vital man married to an invalid for over forty years? And yet, she had never suspected. She remembered the speeches he gave, how everyone had called him a gentleman . . . and it was not what he had done that disturbed her so much as her own sickening ignorance. She felt as if a hole had opened up inside her chest, all the things she had known and believed slipping through.

Another hour passed, and still her father had not returned. What if he should simply lie down and die like a dog in the street? The thought made Agnes leave her house. She drove around her neighborhood, turning down streets that ended in cul-de-sacs. She felt something round and heavy inside her forehead, that it was splitting open from the heat . . . She turned out of her neighborhood onto a narrow two-lane road that dipped and curved without warning, and she couldn't help but feel dread growing inside her, a darkness that she wanted to make small again, half expecting to see her father lying on the side of the road.

She spotted him three miles farther down. He was walking at a much slower pace with his jacket along his arm. He had loosened his tie, and his white shirt was semitransparent with sweat. She slowed down and honked at him, but he kept trudging ahead, without turning to look at her. Agnes rolled down the passenger window. "Get in the car," she said, but he began to walk faster with small, clumsy steps. He was panting and bobbing his head with each step, intent on pressing forward, even though she knew his feet must be hurting him.

"It's useless to walk," she said, driving slowly beside him. "How far are you going to get, huh? Don't be foolish. Get in the car."

He shook his head, and she could see that he was crying.

"I'll take you back to your apartment. I promise, okay?"

He walked more slowly now, and she felt sorry for him, knowing there was nothing for him to do but give in. When she got out of the car, he was standing motionlessly by the side of the road, his arms hanging at his sides and his jacket on the ground. She touched his arm, and he blinked, looking around in bewilderment as she helped him into the car.

He began shivering as soon as he was inside the car, and Agnes turned down the air-conditioning. Neither of them spoke as Agnes drove to his apartment. At Evergreen House, he hurriedly got out of the car, searching his pockets for his keys. Agnes realized they had forgotten to get his bag at her house. Nevertheless, the security guard recognized him and let him inside the building.

When Agnes was twenty-two, she left Taiwan to study economics in Rochester, New York. She left her home and her parents with a feeling of relief. Her family life had become a source of embarrassment to her, and as her plane lifted into the air—it was the first time she had ever flown—she felt she was abandoning an idea of herself. She looked outside her window, the things she knew shrinking steadily away until all she could see were clouds, and she welcomed the prospect of being unknown in another part of the world.

In Rochester, she received a blue rectangle of a letter every other week from her father in Taiwan. On the front, he would write out her address in English with a painstaking, scrupulous hand. He told her about the vegetables he was growing in the courtyard, the Siamese cat that Agnes had left in their care, the state of her mother's health and the various foods she could keep down, news of her brother in the army, and updates of their relatives and friends, some of whom were leaving for the States. She would write back, sometimes enclosing a money order for twenty dollars. She could not afford to call them on the phone, but the few times she did, she heard her own voice echoing along the line, a high, unfamiliar sound, and this distracted her, made her think of all the distance her voice had to cross to reach their ears. Her parents always asked the same questions—*How are you? Are you eating well? Are you happy?*—until the static took over and their voices ended abruptly. Listening to the silence, she imagined their voices being dropped from a high space into the ocean.

She sent her parents a hateful letter once. They had set a date for her brother's wedding without consulting her, and it enraged Agnes to find out that she would not be able to attend. The next letter she received came from her mother, who rarely wrote at all after her fall. Her handwriting resembled the large, uncontrolled scrawl of a child or of someone who was right-handed trying to write with her left. She had copied Agnes's address so poorly, it was a miracle that the letter had arrived at all. *We received your letter in which you scolded us severely. Your father fainted after reading it, and it took him a long time before he could eat his dinner. He has heart trouble and cannot suffer any blows.* At the time, Agnes had been amused by her mother's lies. Her father had no history of heart trouble, and as for his fainting, she knew what a good actor he was. But it was her mother's last phrase that had come to haunt her. *He cannot suffer any blows.*

Agnes did not hear from her father for over a month, and in that time, she felt as removed from him as if he were living in another country. One day in August, she stopped by his apartment to give him a box of persimmons. Lily answered the door in gray slacks and a thin, watery blouse, a silk scarf wrapped around her head as if she were about to go out. "He's not here," she said coldly and began to shut the door.

"Wait—" Agnes said, putting her hand out.

Lily held the door open only wide enough for her face to be visible. The powder she wore could not quite hide the fine lines etched beneath her eyes, nor the age spots above her cheeks.

"Do you know when he'll be back?" Agnes asked.

"I have no idea."

"I'd like to wait for him if you don't mind."

"Wait for as long as you like," Lily said, turning away. She retreated to her bedroom and closed the door.

Agnes set the persimmons on the kitchen counter. Her father had hung red and gold New Year's greeting cards from the slats of the closet door. In the living room, he had decorated the walls with whimsical scrolled paintings of fruit and birds. She had always been somewhat relieved by his attempts to make the place more livable. Perhaps she was trying to console herself for the drab carpet and clumsy furniture, the sense of apology she always felt for things that were merely adequate. After two years, there was hardly any trace of Lily in the apartment, but this didn't surprise Agnes, as Lily had never intended to stay for long.

She paused outside the bedroom door before knocking. "I'd like to talk to you," she said.

"Come in then," a voice evenly replied.

Agnes saw Lily sitting on the side of her bed, a ghostly smile on her lips as she studied the scarf in her hands. She seemed like another person to Agnes, ten or fifteen years older at least, and it took a moment for Agnes to realize that her beautiful, shiny black hair was gone. Instead, wisps of ash-colored hair were matted together in places like dead grass. The sparseness of her hair revealed mottled patches of scalp.

"What happened?" Agnes blurted out. She couldn't help but stare at Lily's baldness.

"You didn't know?" Lily said. She touched her head lightly with a flat hand, her eyes vacant as she smiled to herself. "When I was struggled against, they pulled my hair out by the fistfuls, and it never grew back again. You would think it would grow back, but it doesn't always."

Agnes was silent for a moment. "Hu Tingjun told me about your first husband," she said.

"My first husband," Lily echoed, and it seemed to Agnes as if those words had lost their meaning to her. "Yes, my first husband was an avid collector of calligraphy. Did you know he had a work by Zhu Yunming that was more than four hundred years old? He said the characters flowed on the paper like a flight of birds. Like a wind was lifting them off the page."

Agnes shook her head. "I don't know much about calligraphy."

"This work was more than four hundred years old," Lily said, "can you imagine? My husband begged them not to destroy it. 'I'll give it to the state!' he said. But they said, 'Why would the state want such an old thing?' And they burned it before his eyes. Sometimes, I wish I could tell him, 'Is someone's handwriting worth more than your life?' I would have burned a hundred such pieces. You see, I'm not an idealistic person. There are things one must do out of necessity."

"My father is a foolish man," Agnes said.

Lily looked at her, twisting the scarf between her fingers. "Yet it's impossible to hate him. He doesn't have any cruelty in him."

"So you have your green card now."

"A few more months," Lily said.

"Where will you go after this?"

"California. My son is living there now."

"Does my father know?"

Lily nodded, dropping the scarf on the night table. "He's afraid, you see." She lay down on the bed, folding her hands over her stomach, her feet sheathed in brown pantyhose. "He knows his mind is fading, but he won't admit it. He shouldn't be allowed to live by himself much longer . . ." Lily closed her eyes. "I once told myself that I'd be happy, I'd never complain, if only I was safe. But I'm so tired of living here—I can't tell you how bored I am!" She curled up on her side, placed both hands underneath her cheek. "Do you mind turning off the light as you go out? I'm going to take a little nap now. It seems all I can do is sleep." She murmured her thanks as Agnes left the room, closing the door behind her.

Her father never mentioned Lily's departure, nor did Agnes say anything, both of them lapsing into a silence that seemed to make Lily more present in the room, just as her mother was often there in the room between them, in the air they breathed and the words they did not say.

One night, while her father was visiting, Agnes woke to find his light still on in his bedroom. When she knocked on his door, she saw that he was dressed in his suit and tie, his bags already packed, even though it was only two in the morning. She told him to go back to sleep, that it was still too early, and he smiled at her, waving at her from the back of his ear as he closed the door. She stood in the hallway, and after a moment, he turned off his light, but she knew he was sitting in the dark, waiting.

In January, the manager of Evergreen House called Agnes to inform her that her father had stopped paying the rent. "He gets confused," the manager said. "Sometimes, he doesn't recognize us."

Her father laughed when Agnes asked him about the rent. "Nobody pays rent here," he replied. Then he told her he suspected the manager of being a thief. "If anything happens to me, you should know that I have a hiding place for my cash. There's a brick in the wall which can be removed."

Agnes and her brother agreed it was time for their father to live with one of them. Their father didn't offer a word of protest as they thought he would. An airplane ticket to Indiana was purchased, and one weekend in February, Agnes went over to his apartment to help pack his things.

He answered the door in his slippers. The television was on, and he was watching a basketball game. His apartment smelled musty and sweet, like old newspapers. Perhaps it was the wood paneling or the brown carpet worn soft as moss. The sick sweetness emanated from deep within the wood. The carpet had inhaled odors that had been pressed in for years by slippered feet.

She took a suitcase from out of his closet and packed it hastily without too much folding. She did not like the intimacy of touching his clothes, as if he were already dead. He hung vaguely about her for a few minutes, then wandered out of the room. In a short while, he came back, looking around as if he were trying to find something. "What are you looking for?" she asked him.

He shook his head, closing his eyes, then left the room.

She finished packing two of his suitcases and dragged them to the front door. She found him standing on his balcony, watching a plane as it flew over the building. "That's the ninth one today," he said when she looked at him.

"You tell me what else you want to bring, and I'll send it to you."

"What's the use?" he said. "I don't need anything here. I probably won't live to see another year."

"Don't be so self-pitying," she told him.

In the elevator, there was an old man standing in the corner, both hands leaning against his walking stick. "Mr. Cao," her father said, smiling suddenly. "How are you? Let me introduce you to my wife."

"I'm not your wife," Agnes said, irritated. "I'm your daughter."

Her father screwed up his eyes, his fingers digging into his temple. Then he let out a loud, embarrassed laugh. Yet, he seemed delighted by his mistake. "My daughter," he said. "Please excuse me. Yes, of course, my daughter."

After she saw her father off at the airport, Agnes remembered the secret place he had told her about where he had hidden his money, and she decided to return to his apartment.

In the living room, she stared at the scrolled paintings on the wall. Melons with their curling vines, a powder-blue bird hanging on a branch too thin for its talons, a lopsided horse as fat as a cow scratching its neck against a tree. She took these scrolls off their hooks and rolled them up. Then she ran her hand along the wall, searching for a loose brick. She could not find one. She pressed her hands against the brick until the skin on her palms tingled with rawness. Anyone who saw her groping like this would think she was mad.

She looked in his desk drawers and underneath his mattress. She crawled around trying to find a loose spot in the carpet, but there was no part that would come undone. She could almost swear the carpet smelled faintly carcinogenic. Had he smoked a cigarette here? Maybe, after all, it was a habit he couldn't leave behind.

In his closet, she found a door to a crawl space that had been hidden by his clothes. She had to crouch through to get in. It was a place for storage and apparently had never been swept, the floor littered with sawdust. She couldn't see much of anything and went back for a lamp, which she left in the closet as far as the cord could reach. There was nothing in the space except an old crumpled shirt that she knew was not her father's. But then in the dim recess where the light barely reached, she saw a yellow shape, which turned out to be a suitcase, and just looking at it, she knew it was her father's, something her parents had used when they still lived in Taiwan. The suitcase lay on its side, and there were gashes in the fabric that he had covered up with duct tape.

Agnes sneezed twice when she unzipped the suitcase. She expected old clothes, maybe even the cash he had mentioned, but instead the suitcase was crammed full of letters. The envelopes were cold to the touch, permeated with the chill dankness of the room, as cold as a basement. Her father had thrown them in rather heedlessly, yet the letters had conformed to the shape of each other, she could see this in the indentations of the envelopes, pressed and stuck together like so many leaves. Little rectangles of blue paper, with red and blue stripes along the borders. *Aérogramme. Par avion.* There were long, slender envelopes with torn sides, the corners cut out with scissors where the stamps had been. She recognized some of the names on the envelopes—Jia Wen, Wang Peisan, Zhou Meiping, Wu Yenchiu—various friends and colleagues of her father, though she was unsure if any of them were still living.

In the pile, she recognized her own handwriting. Letters she had written to her father from Rochester. She had always been careless about her writing, and her characters now struck her as hasty and anonymous in their uniformity. She put the letter aside and searched through the pile for her mother's name. She felt a strange sensation similar to the hope she felt whenever she saw her mother again in her dreams. The envelope she reached for was brittle with tea-colored stains, fantastically bent, curling around the edges. Though her mother's name was on the front, the handwriting was unfamiliar to

Agnes. She pulled out a tissue-thin sheet of rice paper, folded vertically in thirds. The letter was dated February 19, 1946. Her mother wrote with a strong, fluid hand.

I have arrived safely in Yangquan. The doll you gave Shuling is quite beautiful and interesting. She is always playing with it, holding it in her hands, and I'm afraid she'll break it, so I put it in a glass jar so that she can look but not touch. Let her appreciate it more that way. Her appetite has improved lately. You would be amazed to see how quickly she moves about, how she turns left and right as she walks. She tries to talk, and I still don't understand her, but her hands point to different things, and I know what she wants.

Agnes couldn't finish the letter and slipped it back into its envelope. Better to forget, she told herself. Her fingers smelled of dust and old paper, and she stared vacantly at the suitcase full of letters. Had he left them behind for her? She wished she had never found them. On all the envelopes, his name. Hsu Weimin. Addresses she had forgotten and others she had never known. All the places he had ever lived. Yangquan and Hechuan and Nanjing and Taipei. Then the last places. Bloomington. Washington, D.C.

Agnes stood up, wiping the dust off her fingers. In the kitchen, she found an empty trash bag, and she returned to the crawl space, grabbing letters by the fistful and throwing them inside. How cold and brittle they were! She would never read them, she knew that, and just their presence was like a small stone in her heart. Nothing lasts, and she was not a sentimental person.

"You cannot blame me," Agnes said out loud, as if her father were in the room, watching.

Xmas in Las Vegas

DENIS JOHNSON

CARLO HAD ALWAYS WANTED to visit Las Vegas during Christmas. The place wouldn't be as crowded as in other seasons. Hotels would offer bargain rates. Lenore's kids were long gone—they didn't want to come home for Christmas. This seemed the time. Lenore didn't voice any enthusiasm for the idea, but she went along with it in the absence of a better plan. But she didn't feel altogether okay on the streets of Las Vegas at Christmastime. "I feel virtual," she said.

"What does that mean?"

"It's something the kids say. Whatever it means, it means the opposite of virtual. It means on the bogus or phony side of the spectrum."

"Well, if it means you don't feel down-to-earth, I don't feel down-to-earth, either. This isn't a place to feel down-to-earth. Vegas is another planet. The planet of glitz and giggles."

"Glitz and giggles," she said. She seemed delighted with this expression.

"I don't want to gamble," she said. "I hope we're not going to."

"I haven't gambled except for four times, and that was during my very first tour in the service," Carlo said. "Twenty-two years ago." Carlo had the numbers ready because this was a conversation they'd already had many times in consideration of this trip.

That first night, the twenty-third, they had a very good and very inexpensive dinner downstairs at the Sands Hotel and turned in early, and he and Lenore watched a movie on the big-screen TV. Lenore ate two small packs of M&M's while the film played. She'd brought them all the way from Cincinnati. Her innocent joy in the taste of M&M's was one of the things that made Carlo feel sentimental about his wife.

On the twenty-fourth, they woke to blue skies over Las Vegas. They'd had blue skies since the day before the trip began. The whole country was on a break from winter. They'd had an easy flight over, literally "clear sailing"—Carlo had taken the window seat and had not counted one cloud in the air between Ohio and Nevada.

They searched in the paper for a good show. They didn't find one. The big names were all on vacation. They'd expected that. It went with the discount prices and the sparse crowds of the Christmas season.

"Choose one for yourself," Lenore said. "Choose one with plenty of titties and rumps. They'll make me feel like dieting."

She and Carlo didn't have to go farther than right downstairs again, where they sat through a skateboarding extravaganza, a dozen helmeted and padded athletes jumping around impressively to the canned music of *Star Wars*, plus a small parade of extraneous undressed females. The drinks were cheap, and Lenore got halfway wrecked. She wasn't entirely serious, but she didn't let up: "What are we doing here? What are we doing here? We might as well gamble. I guess if we went broke, we could go home."

"Do you really want to go home?"

"Not really. I'm just looking for a reason why we're here. We came a long way, and it's not all free."

Later, Carlo woke briefly in the middle of the night. Beside him Lenore slept propped up on pillows, one hand resting on her stomach and holding the TV's remote control device. Beyond the foot of the bed the TV played without sound, and a readout in the screen's corner read 12:17 a.m., which meant Christmas had come. Lying there in the silent room, Carlo watched a scene from, he guessed, a movie, in which a young woman hung white laundry on a clothesline. Suddenly a look of utter shock transfixed the woman's features. She let go of a white shirt. A man walked into view, dressed in sooty rags. Meanwhile, the white shirt blew down a hill. The man and the woman embraced. A brief kiss—then lovingly they studied one another's faces. A long view now: the man laughed as he bounded down the hill, chasing the white shirt. Carlo took the remote control device from his wife's fingers. He had to pee. He wanted a bite of cold fruit. He wanted to smoke a cigarette. He didn't want to get sick, or have accidents, or be dead. He turned the television off. Holding the control device in his fingers, he fell asleep.

Christmas morning they woke up absolutely without any plans. Carlo felt apologetic about that, but he didn't apologize. He waited to see what Lenore had to say. What she had to say about it was nothing. Completely unconcerned. A day like any day: he woke up, and there was his wife beside him, watching the all-news channel with the sound off.

"Well," he said, "Merry Christmas."

"Same to you."

In a minute he asked her, "Do they ever say 'Xmas' anymore?"

"'Xmas?' I don't know."

"They used to abbreviate it down to 'Xmas.'"

"Hmm—you know what? I don't think I've seen a lot of that lately. I think they stopped. I think they decided it was offensive."

Carlo showered and stepped out and dried off with a white, fluffy towel. There were side-by-side sinks in the bathroom, with fixtures of gold plating, or fake gold plating—whichever, the gesture was appreciated. He turned on both faucets. Both gave out identical streams of water. He turned one off and brushed his teeth at the other. The toothpaste was something new Lenore had gotten. He'd never heard of this brand. Very pleasant, it was alive, it gave him a fantastic tingling sensation in his mouth. He rinsed and finished with some mouthwash, also new. It was horrible, like gargling gasoline. It jammed in his throat. He spat it out and rinsed his mouth, croaking, "Yuck! Ptooey! Ridiculous!"

Lenore must have heard him suffering, because she called from the bedroom, "Carlo? Hon?"

He found her sitting up, wearing a complimentary bathrobe, reading the hotel's bedside literature. "What is this crap?" he said, holding the jug in his hand. "This stuff is poisonous."

"I just grabbed it," she said.

"Well, do you mind if I throw it out?"

"Sure," she said. "It's just something I grabbed."

"Good. I don't want it around. I don't want to make the same mistake twice. There oughta be a law against this one. God!" he said. "I thought there were regulations." He replaced the cap tightly and threw it in the bathroom wastebasket. And he felt good thinking that in two or three hours, somebody paid to do it would come and take it away. He was crazy about this hotel. He got dressed and told her, "I need coffee."

He headed downstairs, still swallowing a bit of unpleasant taste. He sat at the lunch counter overlooking the main casino. He washed away the bad flavor with a cup of coffee poured for him by a redheaded waitress.

The main casino wasn't hosting much action currently—nobody at the craps or the roulette, only a couple of lone blackjack players at separate tables, and several diehards giving the slots a workout. One of the blackjack dealers, a young woman, sported a red elf's hat with the white ball on its peak. The casino seemed to be snubbing the holiday—maybe from spite, because it cut into their trade. Carlo saw no seasonal décor around the place. The elf's cap was perhaps the result of a personal decision.

Wow, he thought, forget about Christmas—they don't even have Xmas here.

Meanwhile, he wasn't sure the coffee tasted quite right. The horrible mouthwash must have maimed his taste buds.

He couldn't really blame Lenore for just grabbing things off the supermarket shelves and hurrying off on more important errands. Neither of them had time to do any serious shopping. They both worked eight-hour days, and in fact Lenore worked a bit more than that, also did a fair amount of traveling. When it came to the home front, they both contributed what they could.

They'd been married six years, and they got along fine with each other. He'd been single until he was forty years old, and now he liked being married. You hate the mouthwash, and there's somebody beside you to register the complaint. You don't go with it into the darkness of the grave.

Lenore had a good job, and she was an intelligent woman. She trained new employees for the Illinois-Indiana-Ohio region of Kinko's, the nationwide photo-duplication outfit, a quite sizable corporation. Carlo worked for Motor Vehicles.

What Carlo knew but hadn't told her, what he sensed about himself, was that on this trip at some point he was going to have sex with someone he wasn't supposed to.

He'd messed around in the service, he'd had a few experiences in foreign ports, enough to know that this was going to be dreary and it wouldn't turn out the way anybody expected it to, the way it advertised itself inside your mind. It wasn't going to be glitz and giggles.

The redhead poured and was already turning away when he asked her, "What's your name?"

She turned back. She wore a small name tag on her yellow uniform that said, CHARLENE.

"I'm sorry," she said, "what did you say?"

"Nothing."

"More coffee?"

"No, thanks. Not yet."

"Oh," she said, "I just gave you some, didn't I?"

"It's great stuff," he assured her.

The café's Muzak, at least, gave a nod to the nature of the season, faintly playing selections in the Christmas spirit. "I'll Be Home for Christmas" . . . the original "Rudolph," sung by Gene Autry . . . familiar carols done in every style—rockabilly, big band, the bland pop of the early 1960s. Right in the middle of this collection, they played "Papa Was a Rolling Stone."

"How about now?" the waitress said.

"Pour away," he told her. "And let me see that pack of Philip Morris—just to look at."

"You want to see it? Look at it?"

"Yeah."

"You just want to look at it?"

"Yeah. I'm just interested."

He hadn't handled a cigarette pack in years. He examined it. It was Christmasy, red and green, shiny, with an actual hologram on the front of it: the original Philip Morris bellboy, his hand cupped beside his mouth as he called out for Philip Morris. The friendly image floated right up toward your face. It turned this way and that, absolutely three-dimensional, not phony 3-D—not at all "virtual."

"I've never seen anything like it," he said.

"It's a promotional thing. It's a final farewell gesture. They're changing their name. No more Philip Morris. They're getting out of the business. No more coffin nails. Cancer. Death. It's all bad business."

"Do you remember the ads where this little man right here would say, 'Caaa-aall for Philip Mooooor-ris?'"

"No," she said, "I don't. I got no idea who that little head is supposed to belong to."

Carlo paid her for the pack, and she laid it out on the counter in front of him along with a book of the casino's matches. "Thank you," he said.

She poured him another cup of coffee while saying, "Hello and good morning," to a man who joined them at the counter now, sitting in the stool right next to Carlo's.

"So—is that a wedding ring?" the man said to Carlo first thing.

Carlo held his hand out before him and looked at the back of it, fingers spread, peering at the gold band on his left ring finger, and didn't exactly make an answer, not because he didn't know what to say about the ring, but because the man had only made one remark, and this was already an eerie conversation.

The man was gray headed, but thickly so, and had a young, smooth, dark face. The man said nothing further—got his coffee—but after a while held up his own left hand exactly as Carlo had done. He wore no ring on any of his fingers. Carlo sensed that something was coming.

"Spent five hours yesterday in a car with my ex-wife. We had to drive to Laughlin in this van I rented, get the stuff at her sister's house where it was stored—stuff from when we last lived together—had to get it over here to Vegas." He was quite earnest in his speech, almost urgent about it, but soft toned, and polite. "So we're tooling along in this rented van. Half our old stuff goes to my place, half goes to her place, et cetera. Spending a good bit of time together on this thing. And we got along fine. I wish I could've been that comfortable with her when we were married. Not that it would've made any difference, because from the first day we had no compatibility in the sack—but that's how it goes. Anyway, it was like two old friends. She asked me about some infidelities of mine that she had heard about. Repeatedly heard about. Rumors. I admitted I had an affair for eleven years with a woman in Boulder City, all during the time we were married. She asked me who, but I refused to tell her. I wouldn't involve another person. At that point—bam, flat tire. I lost it. Swearing, yelling, screaming. But I got over it in less than ten minutes, and I was calm again, and I dealt with the situation. After that we didn't talk at all for the last fifty miles. She was sort of crying. Well . . . she was hurt. People have their pride."

"Yeah . . ." Carlo lit up a cigarette for the first time in seven years.

"I got home, and my girlfriend is pissed because I just spent all that time in the car with my ex. I said fine, whatever you want, move out, whatever—but if you move out, you ain't coming back. . . . Who was it who originally said . . ." There was a long silence during which Carlo was only in love with his cigarette. "Said . . . Damn. Damn it, I can't remember the famous old saying I was going to say."

"Much less who originally said it," Carlo said.

The man laughed. He, like Carlo, seemed to have no reason for sitting at this counter.

The waitress came back with the glass pot and said, "Let me touch that up for you." As she poured, Carlo noticed she wore a diamond wedding and engagement set.

While the waitress busied herself busing tables, out of earshot, Carlo told the man, "I've got a curiosity about something. Don't be embarrassed."

"Hey. This is Las Vegas."

Carlo took that as some kind of reassurance. "When somebody goes to a massage parlor looking for more than just a massage—" Carlo stubbed out his cigarette in his coffee cup. "You know what I mean, right?"

"You're looking for a happy ending."

"I'm looking for a happy ending."

"You can get a massage anywhere. Right here at the hotel, probably. But not," the man said, "with the happy ending."

"But at a massage parlor—"

"Yes. At a massage parlor."

"I ask for a happy ending?"

"No," the man said. "To be completely sure, you gotta ask the girl for the erotic massage. With full release. Say to her, 'Do you perform erotic massage with full release?'"

"Wow," said Carlo. This phrasing felt very distant from anything he'd ever experienced. It seemed to come from so far away he could barely make sense of it. He said, "These girls—what time do they crank up?"

"Crank up?"

"You know."

"It's a twenty-four-hour town. There's no cranking up. It's always open."

"Aha, right," Carlo said, "I get it."

"But," the man said, "a massage parlor? I don't even know where you'd find one of those in this town. What you'll find around here is about a million call girls. Call one up. Call one up. They sell magazines full of their phone numbers—give them away free, actually, full of ads, and their pictures, and every other damn thing. Slip them under your door at your hotel!"

"Well, it was just a crazy impulse," Carlo said.

"That's what life consists of. Crazy impulses."

"Yeah."

"Go visit the old folks home. Pry open some old guy's eyelid and look in there to his brain. Guy's ninety-nine years old, he's in a coma. And you know what you're gonna see? He's thinking about the elusive female."

Carlo laughed. Their waitress had returned, and she told the man, "No more coffee for you! You need a cold shower!"

"Long as you're alive, brother," the man said, "and that's the simple truth. I used to say to myself, 'The car's not going to Boulder City tonight. No way. The car's not taking the Boulder exit. Not tonight. . . .'"

"Is that the same gal you ended up with?" Carlo asked.

"No. This one's a new one—if she comes back. I told her, no way, don't come back, but you know what *that's* worth. I'd love to say I'm done with her, but, come on—this is a moment of truth, I just dropped all but three dollars at the blackjack table. Sure, you say to hell with her, but you'll be back sniffin'. You'll be back for a sniff. Very few can stand the boredom of a certain kind of night, when you're just hanging around alone. Then—wham, you pick up the phone. You hop in the car. You head on over. And that goes on for years. Yeah . . . That pattern really stretches out on you.

"You meet a couple, they're like seventy-seven years old, you say, 'How'd you two work it all out—about life, and love, et cetera, now that you've hit your fiftieth anniversary?' Guy says, 'Work it out? No way! I'm gonna leave that bitch! She never has respected me!' And that's pretty much me. The nice lady doesn't respect me, but I'll go back and eat what she's dishing out just to keep from smelling my own stink. So: Now you've heard the truth. If I hadn't just lost fourteen hundred dollars at the tables, I'd probably have the strength to keep it up with my usual lies, but now you've heard the simple truth."

Carlo said, "Fourteen hundred dollars?"

"Yep, fourteen hundred. I'd call it a major reaming."

"Wow," Carlo said, "that's a lot of money."

"Welcome to Las Vegas," their waitress said, adding, "Viva Las Vegas!"

"I shouldn't mention it," the man said. "It's bad luck to mention bad luck."

"They comped you good, I hope," the waitress said.

"They comped me. I'm comped. I'm comped two nights and six meals. I'm comped half the way up my large intestine."

Carlo and the waitress fell silent. Carlo believed they were watching a man fall apart right before their eyes. But he also felt as if Las Vegas was, suddenly, holding out its arms in a wide welcome.

He paid and excused himself and went to the building's main entrance, where he'd seen a rack holding just the kind of ad sheet the man had talked about. Carlo stood before it for at least three minutes.

Lenore. She was dumpy, and she was pasty, and she was flouncy. Eight years back he'd been stationed at the naval recruiter's office in Cincinnati, working in a clerical capacity. He'd rented a duplex apartment Lenore owned, and for a couple of years she'd been his landlady and had lived next door. Now they were man and wife, and they lived together in her half of the duplex and rented the other half to a retired military man, a quiet, dependable widower and an excellent tenant.

He looked at the ad sheet clamped firmly in its receptacle. Where to go to study this thing? Where to hide, that was the question. They had restrooms down here in the casino. But he pictured himself locked in one of the stalls with this confidential material laid out on his thighs, turning its pages, and that was enough. He bent close, squinting at the sheet as a person might who had no idea what on earth it was, reading the banner ads on the front page. One advertised a Christmas special. A Christmas special! The image described itself: ACTUAL PHOTOGRAPH. Another showed a shapely woman in a negligee, with abundant brown curls and a face completely shadowed, thanks to a very poor printing job. She was saluting. Maybe she had a military background, like Carlo. Her phone number was printed large enough that he could read it easily, and it included a lot of 7s—a sign of good luck? "Actual Photograph." Was this blurry person the same one you met, if you arranged a meeting? Carlo couldn't guess her age. Blurred or not, he couldn't judge the ages of women under thirty. To him they all just looked amazingly young.

He memorized the phone number, stepped over to the check-in counter, and wrote the number down in his appointment book. He warned himself that somewhere not too far down the line he'd better blot this number from the page, because it was evidence. He didn't trust himself to get away with things.

Upstairs he was surprised to find Lenore exactly as he'd left her, sitting up in bed in her nightgown.

"What have you been doing?" he said.

"Calling everybody I know," she said.

"Calling? Really?"

Lenore was delighted. "Since you left, I've been on the phone nonstop. You wouldn't believe it! There's a special deal the phone company's offering through the hotel—ten-cent long-distance phone calls all day Christmas day. I mean *ten cents* per call! It's fantastic! I've talked to just about everybody I know."

"How are they doing?" Carlo asked. "How's everybody doing?"

"Good."

"Are they having a merry Christmas?"

"Everybody's having a good one," she said, punching another number.

He looked out at their view from the fourth floor, which he judged to be a drop of about forty-eight feet down to a wide avenue lined with huge multicolored signs doing the best they could, in the bright daytime, to pulse with garish light. Suddenly he started laughing.

"Where's the comedy?" Lenore said.

He shook his head. She went back to the phone. He'd only been laughing to remember something.

The morning they'd left, at breakfast, he'd found himself staring at the box Lenore had just poured her cereal from. The messages there on the back of it struck him as strange, or faintly silly. CHEERIOS—SHARING MEMORIES, one heading said. Another—SHARING 60 YEARS TOGETHER. And a third: SHARING 60 YEARS OF CHEERIOS MEMORIES. . . . Was he supposed to feel sentimental about a substance you dumped milk over and ate without thinking? He had told Lenore he thought it was ridiculous, and she'd said, "You know what's funny?—I like Cheerios now a lot better than I did when I was a kid."

He brought himself back to the situation at hand, and got his wife's partial attention as she talked to somebody. "I'm going out."

"No gambling!"

"Just a few well-placed bets."

He was kidding. She didn't hear him. "Great," she said, either to him or to the other party.

"Ten-four," he said as the door shut itself behind him.

At a payphone downstairs he got out his notebook and thirty-five cents.

The first thing he did when someone answered was to ascertain he'd rung the right number and had the right girl on the other end. He listened carefully to her voice. She sounded fairly nice, but she also sounded as if she'd just woken up. He said, "I hope it's not too early. And especially—you know—today."

"That's never a problem," the woman said. "Any day, all day."

"And you'd be available . . . around now?"

"Yes, I sure would be. Why don't we make it a date?"

"Uh, just to be sure—we're talking about a massage?"

"That's right. The works."

"I feel stupid saying this, but I guess I'm looking for—'a happy ending.'"

"That comes with the works. Satisfaction guaranteed."

"Okay—I just felt I had to ask, or I should ask."

"What hotel are you in?"

"The Sands," he said, "why? Where are you? Are you far away?"

"No. I can be there in twenty-five minutes."

"Oh, no—you can't come here," he said. "That wouldn't be good."

"Do you have some place in mind?"

"No. No, ma'am," he said. "No, miss."

"Bummer! All right, well, I'm at the Claymore. I'll meet you in the bar off the lobby of the Claymore. We'll sit down, and we'll have a drink. If you look okay, you can come up. If you don't look okay—you don't come up."

"How will I know you?"

"Just sit at the bar. My name's Jeannie. I'll find you."

"Should I tell you my name?"

"Whenever you want to. Don't worry, we're gonna get to know each other real well."

"Okay," he said, "well—my name's Carl."

"Have you done this before, Carl? Made a date on the phone like this?"

"Not recently," he said, "if ever."

"Then can I ask you a couple favors? Will you do me a favor and take a shower first?"

"Okay. Of course."

"And we're talking about cash."

"Cash, cash, yes. A cash transaction." But this idea of a shower—that was throwing him. "Does it count if I just showered about thirty minutes ago?"

"Thirty minutes?" She laughed. "I'll allow it."

"And, so—anything else? What else?"

"Most people are usually interested in the rate."

"Oh. Oh. Oh."

"If you're a rookie, I'd better let you know it's three hundred for an hour."

"Three hundred?"

"Three hundred, up-front. Cash only."

"You got it," he said.

"See? I'm as easy as pie," she said.

He took a cab to the Claymore. It looked not quite as fancy as the Sands. Inside the colors were different, but it was the same. He headed through the casino toward the bar without looking left or right. He understood that people labored day and night designing these places just to guide his feet toward a table or a machine and get him to make a bet. But they wouldn't have any luck with Carlo. He'd lost several paychecks in the service, playing blackjack, and just the thought of those old disasters still nauseated him.

He sat at the bar and said nothing. The bartender, an older man, seemed not to notice him at first. Carlo figured if it came to it, he'd ask for club soda. Or a Virgin Mary. He was nervous—even the tomato juice in a Virgin Mary might be hard on his stomach.

"You the guy looking for Jeannie?" the bartender asked.

"That's me."

"I'll call her room." The bartender got on the phone at the other end of the bar. He came back and said, "Two minutes."

And in just about two minutes a woman came in and said, "Who's looking for Jeannie?"

"I'm always looking for Jeannie," the bartender said, brightening at her entrance. She smiled at Carlo—he was the only other person here, after all—and he smiled back at the sight of her. She had short blond hair and a pretty, girlish face, with big eyes and a small nose and a small mouth. She was well made-up, and her hair was brushed, but she wore red sweatpants and a green parka and—as he glanced down—bright yellow house slippers.

"Here's Jeannie—reporting for duty," she said, and saluted.

He held out his hand. She accepted it, gave it a shake, leaned close, and kissed him very lightly on the cheek.

"Let's sit over here a sec," she said, and he joined her at a table. She folded her hands in front of her. "Welcome to my office, sir."

"Do you want a drink or something? While you size me up?"

"Not necessary. I can tell a mile away you're a sweetheart."

"Well," he said.

"If you've got the three hundred, you can fork it over now, and we'll head on up to my little crib. Not everybody gets to do that," she added, "only the sweethearts."

"So—pay you right now? Here?"

"That'd be the way," she agreed. "I owe this guy some money." She cocked her head toward the bartender, who didn't seem aware, any longer, of either of them.

Carlo gave her three hundreds. She went immediately to the bartender and spoke to him and handed him the money and kissed his cheek.

"On with the show!" she told Carlo, and he stood up, and she hooked her arm in his and guided him off toward the elevators. Carlo noticed a lot of people around—desk clerk, patrons, a janitor in a gray uniform standing right at the elevators beside a large, heavy floor-cleaning machine—but nobody seemed the least bit aware of Carlo and Jeannie as they waited for transportation upstairs.

"Excuse the getup. Soon as we get to the room I'll make some improvements."

"You look nice," he said.

"What a dude! Just for that, I'll be gentle."

The janitor didn't look at them, and when the elevator opened he made no attempt to join them onboard.

Carlo was used to feeling awkward in elevators. Jeannie was still talking as they stepped between the doors. "In town for long?"

"No, just a couple days. Just for Christmas."

"Terrific," Jeannie said. The doors parted. She stepped out saying, "This way," and, "When's that?"

They started trudging down a long hall, perhaps as long as a city block, although, because of the tunnel effect, it looked even longer. "What?" he said.

"I said, 'This way.'"

"But you said, 'When's that?' When's what?"

"When's Christmas?"

"This is Christmas," he said. "Today. Today is Christmas."

"Well, hey. Merry Christmas," she said.

"Merry Christmas." Carlo was aware of the numbers mounting as they passed, 315 . . . 317 . . . 319. . . . They were deep into the three-fifties before she called a halt.

He heard voices coming from inside her room, from the TV. It sounded like an old movie. Jeannie opened the door onto a room mostly pale olive green and orange, or salmon—also very pale and soothing. The movie on TV was in brilliant color with cheery yellow subtitles. She took the tag off the door and hung out the sign: PRIVACY PLEASE. The door shut behind them, and that was that. Here he was.

His young hostess smiled graciously—"One sec!"—and headed for the toilet.

Carlo read the bright yellow words of a man and a woman talking on TV. They weren't speaking French. He'd watched and enjoyed quite a few French movies, and to his American ears this was even more garbled than French. Maybe Russian. Polish.

"When I'm happy, I laugh! I dance! Nothing gets me down! And when I'm sad, I crash downward, my heart breaks, and I'm sure that God is a criminal."

He stood by the television with his head cocked, taking this in. He picked up the remote and found the mute button.

He was standing there foolishly when she came back in wearing a pink bra and pink bikini panties under a flimsy see-through negligee. Bare feet. No stockings.

She spread her arms and sang, "Ta-daa!"

He applauded softly with his hands.

"This way, please."

She guided him toward the bed and sat close beside him in a cloud of blossomy cologne. Carlo asked, "Do you come from a large family, Jeannie?"

"What?"

"I mean—is that why you like to keep the TV on, maybe? Are you used to a lot of voices?"

"I leave it on all the time. It fools the burglars."

"It fools them that you're French."

She laughed. "And now I have to be a boob and ask you your name again, because I'm sort of a boob with names."

"Carl," he said. "People call me Carlo, and don't ask me why. I've never figured it out."

"It's because people like you," she declared.

"Really?"

"When people give you a nickname, it's because they like you."

He stared at the tube. The yellow subtitle said, "*I want to weep. But I feel like I've wept already.*"

She picked up the remote. "Do you mind if I leave it on very softly?"

"No. Go ahead. How come?"

"I don't know. It's too quiet in here," she said.

She brought the voices up slightly.

"When it comes to subtitles," Carlo said, "I like white lettering better than yellow, even if it's harder to see. It seems to go better with the atmosphere."

"Well. I don't think there's a button for that, Carl."

This girl was funny! "What about some Christmas music?" He pointed to the radio on her nightstand.

But she shook her head. "That old Taiwanese clock radio? It sounds more like an insect."

The people on the tube went on softly and incomprehensibly. "So," Carlo said. "Was that actually you in the Actual Photograph?"

"That's me in the picture—before the recent fiasco at the hairdresser's. I've never been to the same one twice. They always murder me."

Now they stared at the movie. Nobody was saying anything at the moment. The man and the woman were exploring a sort of garden at night.

Housekeeping hadn't come yet. Maybe they wouldn't come today. After all, it was Christmas, although nobody in this town seemed to have been told. There were towels bunched on the floor, drooping from a chair. One of the sheets had gotten away and lay twisted like a rope. Jeannie had pulled the bedspread up over one pillow. The other was propped against the wall for sitting up in bed while watching television. Nothing in sight said, "Welcome to the whorehouse."

He noticed an ashtray or two, and smelled the stink of previous cigarettes. "Do you mind if I smoke?"

"No," she said, "do you mind if *I* smoke?"

"No."

"Well, gosh darn it," she said, "let's smoke!"

He laughed, and offered her one of his.

So far she'd shown high spirits, but dark circles around her eyes made her look soulful and mysterious.

"I think I got you up too early, didn't I?"

"No way, Carl. I'm up and down at all hours. Circumstances make the schedule."

They smoked. It was delicious. He could feel the nicotine gurgling in his fingertips.

"This is the scariest cigarette pack I've ever seen," she said. "Where'd you come from, Carl? The distant future?"

"Well, I don't know," he said.

She took a good puff, and exhaled, and appeared thoughtful before saying, "Why don't you strip down, and I'll relax you with a little back-rub? Then we'll take it from there."

"Let me think about this," he said.

"Would a little rubdown help you think better?"

"You're very attractive," he said.

"Thank you! One sec." She went to the closet and hung on to the door frame with one hand and stuck her feet, first one and then the other, into the darkness. She came back to the bed looking quite a bit more statuesque in bright blue pumps with tall spike heels. "I just got these beauties! Might as well put some mileage on."

"Great legs," he said.

"Thanks," she said. "They're all yours."

"All mine! Well," he admitted, "that's the most terrifying thing anybody ever said to me."

Great legs, definitely, and a pleasing shape, an ample, sweet-looking body. She was maybe a little flabby around the middle. Not that he minded in the least, but that's where she strayed from perfection.

He didn't feel particularly out of place, or confused, not even a tiny bit embarrassed. He just didn't know what he was doing here. He'd forgotten, more or less, where this moment had come from. He was trying to get back some sense of why he'd just given this nice woman slightly less than a week's salary after taxes, and then joined her here in her place of residence.

He was used to seeing luscious women in movies and magazines—standing there. He wasn't used to seeing them sit down, watching the flesh of their thighs widen as they sat on a bed beside him, or smelling the toothpaste on their breath.

"Carlo," she said.

"Yeah?"

"What's going on in that head of yours?"

"That's a mystery," he said. "Especially to me, sometimes."

"I hope you're not a nut!"

"I don't think so. Not the extreme kind, anyway. But can I just sit here a minute and sort of take it all under consideration?"

"You paid for an hour. It's your hour."

"It's just . . . I don't think I want to do this."

"Well, you paid for an hour," she said again. "Do you want a massage or something? Just a plain massage?"

"No," he said, "I—don't think I want a plain massage."

"Well, do you want to just go? I mean, listen. Whatever is your idea of a happy ending—I'm here for that."

"I appreciate it," he said.

"But no refunds!"

He didn't want to leave, at least not for a minute or two. It occurred to him maybe they could talk a little. What subject would come up between two people in a situation like this? It was like a private lesson of some kind. "I could ask you a couple things," he said.

"What?"

"Could I ask you," he said, "a couple things?"

"You mean you want to talk dirty?"

"I don't think I want to talk dirty," he said.

"Do you want to take a poll? Are you a pollster?"

"Nope."

"Well, then, what do you want to ask me?"

"Okay, let's see. Well, for one thing—what does 'Las Vegas' mean?"

"What do you mean?"

He shrugged.

"It means here."

"No, think about it—do you know what 'Las Vegas' means? Think about it."

"I never thought about it."

"Well, it's a foreign phrase, probably Spanish. A lot of our names mean something in a foreign language, and we hardly ever think about it. For all we know, 'Las Vegas' could mean 'The Idiots.'"

"Then they might as well come right out and say so in English," she said. "In the case of this town, that would be a good, appropriate name."

"How long have you been living here?"

"In Vegas? I'm back and forth. I'm off and on. Reno, San Francisco. I live in hotels. Sacramento . . . Up and down the line."

"But I just want to know how long—if you never thought about it—how *long* you haven't ever thought about it. How long have you been *around* Las Vegas, not thinking about what 'Las Vegas' means?"

"Four or five years, at least."

The idea of this young person living in a series of rooms like this one, embracing a wild style of life and getting along without disaster, astonished Carlo.

"Do I sound like a regular nut?"

"No. No. No. Not really."

"These are the kinds of things that pass through your mind at the Department of Motor Vehicles."

"Well, they should let you out to run around once in a while, Carlo. You need air!"

"So I *am* losing my mind."

"Hey, come on—so what? Whatever. It's nice to meet somebody who wonders what it's all about."

"Sorry."

"Or at least what 'Las Vegas' means."

"Do you think anybody ever thinks about these things?"

"Well, you do, obviously."

"I'd like to know if anybody else ever thought about them, or if I'm the only one. I'll give you another example." He dragged a pillow onto his lap. "Colors. I point to this pillow, and I say it's—what color would I say?"

"Blue. I don't know. Light blue?"

"Some form of blue. But 'blue' is only a *word* we've been taught to say when I point to that color. Maybe—inside my head—what I see would be red to you, and what you see would be—I don't know—purple, to me, or gray, to me, or any color at all. What we *say* is the same, but what we *see* could be completely different. Have you ever thought about that?"

"No."

"Am I way off in left field someplace? Or am I making sense?"

"You're making sense, but I think red is red and blue is blue. Otherwise we wouldn't call it 'red,' and we wouldn't call it 'blue.'"

"Jeannie, wait. Do you see what I mean? I could say 'blue, green, orange,' but what I see would be *your* idea of purple, black, yellow. We could be living in two completely different-colored worlds. And so could every other person on this planet. Same words, different colors."

He offered her a smoke. They lit up. Carlo said, "You know, I haven't smoked in seven years, until this morning. I should feel bad, but I don't."

"I know," she said. "I've tried everything, and this is the best stuff there is."

"I wish I'd never stopped."

"I know! I don't care how high they raise the taxes, I'll never quit."

"Okay," he said, "how about this one—taking the same idea a little farther. Maybe inside, when I say I'm sad, what I'm feeling is the same emotion you feel when you say you're happy. We *act* sad, we *say* sad, but who knows what we're actually feeling on the inside?"

"Same words, different feelings. Why not?"

"I realize it's a silly thing to bring up, more or less," he said, "but do you get it?"

"Same words, different colors." She was laughing at him. "Have you been to college?"

"A little bit," he said. "Just a couple courses in the service."

"I have," she said, "I've been to college. I went to college for almost two years."

"A college girl."

"Yeah."

"Do they talk about these things in college?"

"No," she said. "I really don't know what they talk about. That's why I left. What do you do?" she said.

"I work for the Ohio Department of Motor Vehicles," he said. "I administer the driving license exams, among other things like that."

"You mean the actual—" She lightly gripped an imaginary steering wheel.

"No, a cop does that. I do the other part, the written part. And various things. I'm an administrative assistant."

"How long have you been doing that?"

"I don't know," he said.

"You don't know?"

"I never counted it up," he was a little surprised to admit. He thought about it and said, "Seven years."

"Wow," she said.

"Before that I was in the navy," he said, "long-term."

"Did you count?"

"Uh. Yeah. Fifteen years," he said. "I quit re-upping after I got engaged. I don't think a married man should leave his wife and go to sea."

The direction of the conversation was making him sweat. He didn't like hanging around in this hotel room and thinking about Lenore, about the length of time they'd been together, about the decisions he'd made in his life.

The effect of being here was beyond that of a simple one-on-one conversation—he was perched on the peak of Mount Fuji with this stranger, and nobody within miles of them. He was stranded on a Japanese mountaintop with this attractive person who didn't know or care when Christmas came.

"Let me check out a couple of other things with you, see if you ever thought about them."

"I can pretty much guarantee you I didn't!"

"Do you ever feel like everybody knows something, and you don't?"

"More or less constantly!"

"Like there's one small, important fact, and you're the only person on earth who doesn't know it?"

"No. I feel that way at *parties*—around hip people, beautiful people, but not otherwise. . . ."

"*Is* there such a fact?"

"What fact?"

"Is there a fact," he said very carefully, "that you know, and everybody else knows, but I don't know it?"

She didn't answer right away. He was relieved to see her giving it some serious consideration. She thought a long time. He began to feel terrified.

"Well," she said, "if you don't know it, I don't know it, either."

"Think," he said. "Maybe it's so small, and to you so insignificant, that you don't even realize it. But to me it would be incredibly important."

"I know. But nothing comes to mind," Jeannie said.

"All right, good, fair enough, but, now, just bear with me, here. Just go along with the gag. Another question: Did you ever think that we're really living our whole lives backwards? That we start out as dust in the grave, that we form ourselves out of dust in our coffins, then we're unearthed, we're dug up, and then we start living as old people, and get younger and younger and younger, until we're children? And then babies? And then we crawl up inside our mothers, exactly in reverse of what we think? Wouldn't that explain why we see what happened to us as young people?—because it's actually the future, it's ahead of us, we can see it coming. And what we call the future is actually the past, it's behind us, and that's why we can't see it—because you can't see what's behind you."

Jeannie only cleared her throat—"Hm-mh. . . ."

"As far as the direction of time is concerned, what we call backwards is forwards, and what we call forwards is backwards. You can't see behind you—do you see what I mean?"

"I never thought about that."

"No? You never thought about any of this?"

"No. I'm still back at the part about the colors."

"But what do you think of it, as an idea? Am I wacky? Or do you think it could be possible?"

"That everything's backwards, but we think it's forwards? Sure. And upside-down, and all of that. I mean left, and right . . . sure. But—I'm sorry, what was your name again? I forgot!"

"Carlo."

"I forgot! Sorry, Carlo."

"What were you going to say, Jeannie?"

"We just go on acting like up is up and red is red, no matter *what* we *think*. None of it matters."

"It matters to me."

"You're not kidding. I can see that."

"It winds up like this," he said to her. "It gets pretty horrible. It comes down to this: Imagine a person whose heart is actually full of love, spending every day joyously, ecstatically married to somebody whose heart is absolutely filled with *hate*, and they both use the same word for completely opposite emotions."

Carlo had expected the unexpected, but he'd certainly failed to anticipate this. You head off into the morning, and you go here and there, and you find someone finally, and you talk, and you talk, and you talk.

And what does the other person say? She says nothing. She's completely silent, as Jeannie was right now. He wondered how long she'd be quiet if he stayed quiet.

Carlo wondered if she had ideas like this inside her. These might not be the circumstances, but in the right situation, what would surface? Given an opportunity to hold forth, what would she like to say?

"Cigarette?" he said.

"Thanks very much."

"Darn, I forgot I was going to stay quiet."

"Quiet? I'll definitely allow that!" she said.

He lit both their Philip Morris cigarettes with a match from the Sands Hotel and dropped the match into the ashtray beside her Taiwanese clock radio.

"Okay. Your turn," he said. "I've got twenty minutes here. You want to say anything?"

"Say what?"

"Anything. I was just taking all this in, this unusual get-together, reflecting on it, and thinking maybe when the usual thing happens, you don't get much of a chance to talk. You yourself. Jeannie. So . . ."

"This isn't that unusual," Jeannie said.

"It isn't unusual?"

"Every once in a while the usual doesn't happen. Every once in a while. You'd be surprised. And it turns out the guy just wants to talk. Really. It's true."

"About what?"

"Well, nothing. I don't remember. Personal stuff. Not the stuff you just talked about—not college stuff! . . . I mean, I get a real wide range of people in here. The entire gamut of modern civilization."

"Like who? What do they say?"

"The only one I remember right now was a guy who said he couldn't feel an ejaculation. He was numb."

"I see—numb," Carlo said.

"He was in a motorcycle wreck that did something to his spine. Everything was fine about him, except that he couldn't feel certain nerve endings, and he couldn't experience the pleasure of ejaculation."

Carlo said, "I see."

"And he ended up not wanting to do it, and we ended up—not doing it. Instead, he told me about how much he loved motorcycles, and how much he loved women, and how, by that time, he'd lost the power to be pleased by a woman, and he was scared to death of motorcycles. And, also, scared to death of women . . . I mean, I get 'em all. But, okay . . ."

She put her cigarette out and placed her hand gently on Carlo's knee as if to keep him still and continued. "Okay. Have you ever thought that there's a reason for everything?"

"I've never thought about it," he said.

"Have you ever felt that maybe you have a purpose, a reason for being just exactly you? That you were here to be listening, like the reverse of a newspaper, almost—you're here to receive the news that a person has found out. You're here to get the discoveries communicated to you. I mean, I just bounce around. I don't own much stuff . . . I don't live anywhere, I don't have anything, I don't *know* anybody, really—not very well—I hardly even *am* anybody, when you think about it. . . .

"Have you ever felt like you were almost just nobody? But it didn't matter, because you have this purpose, which is to be with other people? Have you ever kind of suspected that we almost don't exist, practically, except face-to-face with another person? Have you ever suspected that?"

"No, I've never exactly . . . suspected that," Carlo heard himself saying. Trying to follow all this just confused him. His thoughts were fuzzy, his head felt stuffed with cotton, with lint.

"Time's not quite over," she said.

"I just have one more thing to ask you about."

She laughed. "I think a shrink would be a lot cheaper. Or would it? Do they charge you a lot?"

"Just one more thing," he repeated, "and it's this: What if nothing exists? What if you're imagining all of this? I know you aren't, of course, because I know *I* exist. But *you* can't be sure. No one person can ever be sure about any of the others."

"Like, 'Life is but a dream.'"

"Exactly."

"Sometimes, it is."

"It is?"

"It sure was last night. While I was asleep. Everything that happened was a dream."

She struck him as quite a special kind of girl—steady, good-humored, generous of heart. He had an impulse to tell her this, to celebrate her qualities, but he knew he shouldn't start out saying something that could only lead to the question how such a nice person ended up working as a prostitute.

Jeannie cleared her throat just as she had before, "Hm-*mm* . . ."

"*Did* you grow up in a large family?" Carlo asked.

"Well, no, I grew up with my mom. A single mom. In pretty much the same places I hang around now—Sacramento, Reno, Vegas . . ."

"And what did your mom do? I mean, that sounds rude. What was she like? Or . . ."

"Oh," Jeannie said, "she was a gal pretty much along the same lines as me."

"Really? And what did she do?"

"For a living? She did pretty much the same thing I do."

"Wow. Really. No kidding," Carlo said.

Jeannie said, "*Now* I remember my dream . . . I was at a fast-food joint. I had a cup in my hand, but I couldn't find the right spigot to shoot the cream into my coffee. I was almost in tears. I was sort of whimpering. And there was somebody right beside me trying to do the same thing, and we both started laughing. We kept turning spigots and pushing buttons, and we were both laughing. And I said, 'God! This is so hard!'"

Carlo saw that his time was up. He didn't know if he was still allowed to talk. "They say we get messages from the unconscious mind," he said anyway, "via our dreams."

"I know."

"There are books about it."

"I know. But I'm not about to read a thousand-page book just to figure out the message."

"You're fun to be with," he said.

"I've always said so!"

"One more question? Last one?"

"Cross your heart," she said. "What's the question?"

"Well, suppose we went for another hour? Suppose, this time, we went for the works?"

"What fun!"

"Would that be another three hundred?"

"Let's talk about a discount," she said.

They worked it out. The two hours finished up at a total cost to Carlo of $400, and compared to what he'd always imagined of sex-for-pay in the tough town of Las Vegas, he felt he got the full value, and then some.

It started off awkward in a way that was funny, then it became all right for a while, and then it was awkward in a way that would have to be called, actually, awkward. And at one point it was getting so uncomfortable he had to stop. "What is it?" she said, and he didn't know what to say. And so he just continued again, feeling his elbows and knees on her sheets, his belly against hers, his chin pressing maybe too hard against the top of her head. He remembered his baldness. He felt like apologizing to someone who might be watching. He just continued, but this time, while he was making love to Jeannie, he thought about someone else, a fantasy woman who didn't exist.

But he got what he'd ached for, which was to touch her, or anyone like her. Her skin was smooth, very uniform, almost like rubber, but warm and living . . . not dark, but not pale, either—almost bright. He'd been so hungry to press against such skin, to kiss it and taste it, that even a few minutes of this—to say nothing of an entire hour spent naked with Jeannie—felt like lying down at last after an endless, pointless, exhausting day.

For a while afterward neither of them said a word. Carlo lay there bathed in sweat, lighting a Philip Morris cigarette and thinking, I'm so glad I started smoking again in time for this.

He couldn't help it now, his eyes were drawn to the tube, where a man hung upside-down by his ankles from the strut of a small plane.

A woman sat on a stump going thirstily at a slice of watermelon. She looked up. The strange dangling man flew past and grabbed her snack with one hand.

A longer view: the plane rammed a cliff face and exploded in a compact fireball.

Still longer view: a plume of smoke in an empty blue sky.

Carlo blew out smoke himself and thought once more: Just in time, I'm so glad, what a blessing.

These people on television looked familiar. Yes, he recognized them. He'd watched part of this same film last night, and here it was again the very next day. Perhaps they ran it repeatedly because it was a Christmas story—no way to tell, unless someone like Santa Claus or Jesus made an appearance. And now the next events were the very ones he'd already witnessed—the woman hanging laundry, the man approaching dressed in burnt rags, the two embracing, the white shirt tumbling on the wind down a hill.

When he left, Jeannie kissed him goodbye, and when the kiss was over, she yanked him back for one more, then shoved him away. "No more discounts. Call me."

"I probably won't," he said. "I leave town tomorrow."

"In that case, here's a freebie!" She pulled his hand to her breast and squeezed. Then she pushed him out the door, laughing at him.

"Ten-four," he said as the door closed.

He hiked down the long hallway and boarded an elevator. After he'd punched the button and it began to move, he had one of the crazier moments in his life, when he had no idea where this thing was taking him, whether up or down, right or left, maybe under and over like a Ferris wheel.

But how would he see it all later, looking back—assuming time ran forwards, and the past was really behind us. . . . Would he feel sorry for his deeds today? He couldn't guess. He guessed this much, however: This was no piddling little thing he'd done.

Twenty minutes later Carlo was back at the Sands. He looked around himself carefully as he made his way through the casino. He did not see one sprig of mistletoe. He didn't see any jingle bells, not one holly wreath, no tinsel, no candy canes, not the tiniest indication that Christmas had arrived. As a matter of fact he saw no way of figuring out whether it was day or night—no windows, no clocks. On the Muzak a rendition of "The Lonely Bull," originally made popular by Herb Alpert and the Tijuana Brass, was just finishing. Then came a vocal, Trini Lopez doing "If I Had a Hammer."

Back in the room, Lenore was dressed now, propped on the bed with the phone to her ear. As Carlo came through the door, she waved with her fingers and gave him a happy smile. He thought to himself: People are almost always cheerful around me.

"Back from outer space," he joked.

Lenore was watching the Weather Channel with the sound off. He stood beside the television and looked. The map was unblemished. At the moment, no snow fell anywhere in the continental United States. That didn't mean there wasn't plenty on the ground already, in places like Minnesota, North Dakota, Michigan . . . but right now the determination seemed to be that there just wasn't any weather.

Lenore was sitting up on the bed with her legs out straight in front of her, her shoes kicked off and her ankles crossed. She covered the phone's mouthpiece with the palm of her hand, and though the person on the other end therefore couldn't hear, still only mouthed the words *Hi, hon.*

The Third House

MARSHALL N. KLIMASEWISKI

ANGELA'S FAMILY OWNED three houses. Henry fell quickly in love with her. Her father was well funded, inheritably and otherwise, and engaged in writing a book. These were Angela's self-conscious phrases; she referred to her father as Mr. Jones. "What does he do?" Henry had asked, and she had said, "Mr. Jones is engaged in writing a book, Henry." Henry heard the irony, but chose to overlook it.

Mrs. Jones was a lawyer who couldn't work due to illness, and Angela's two elder brothers had died in a sailing accident. It was too much, really—too picturesque and romantically misfortunate—yet all apparently true. "Drowned, but not forgotten," Angela said of her brothers. Henry had no idea how to interpret her tone there.

She was twenty, six years younger than Henry, but it didn't show. She attended the college where Henry, sadly, cut the grass. He was sitting in on classes also, through the film department, and he worked for an ad agency in the city, but it didn't pay. She rowed for the crew team and wore her sleeveless jerseys on her way back from the river, or to class, or the library, and then to bed with him, too, when he asked. The muscles of her upper arms were long and glossy. Her habitual expression was a willing and absorbed smile, which seemed at first to soften the bite of her irony, but was, in fact, its most articulate feature. Henry had been in love before—you could say continuously, since adolescence—but never so decisively, or with so little encouragement. She accepted his romantic attentions without especially answering them; she seemed, he thought, hesitant to decline what she was due, although she might have been just as happy to leave these pennies in the till. One weekend she took him home to her family, apparently for the lark in it. "Mr. Jones will be fascinated," she said. "Be sure to wear this shirt."

The first house was in the woods in the best part of the state, with the trees bare much of the year and beautiful nonetheless. Even the trunks and crowns of Connecticut were not created equal: they were knobbed creatures, congested and dismal, to the north and east, hung with clothes or composed in clumps between highways, but as one traveled south and west toward the shore and the city, they gained balance, solemnity, and a winter sophistication, which might evoke (or, in Henry's case, install) childhood memories in black and gray, punched up by a touch of limbed menace. Angela's father had had this house built to his specifications. It was low and horizontal, discreet in front, with deep eaves; in back there were tall windows conveying panels of landscape. It was fitted to the slope, unless the hillside had been sloped to fit. The leaves from the trees were recently fallen and still bright. In the room where Angela's father sat—whichever it might be—there was a fire laid and moaning. The books had exploded from the shelves and settled on every surface like a pollen—they were damp on the edge of the tub and redolent beside the coffeemaker; hardbacks in drab cloth or older paperbacks with out-of-fashion covers, well handled but cared for, not shabby yet. Incredibly inviting. All weekend they slipped into Henry's hands. He flipped the pages, read a line or a paragraph, and everything he read seemed apt—appropriate to the Joneses, or their house, or both. *The large, low rooms, with brown ceilings and dusky corners*—this was James—*the deep embrasures and curious casements, the quiet light on dark, polished panels, the deep greenness outside, that seemed always peeping in, the sense of well-ordered privacy in the centre of a "property"*—. They smelled good, these books. Or not good in the right way.

Mr. Jones's book would be a study of James: a broad perusal through some narrow linguistic aperture, which he politely declined to explain. It was a dilettante's occupation, he said, a way to pass the time. He said so with a quick and clipped delivery that served modesty with beautiful rigor. He had taught once, at the same college that Angela attended, but he didn't any longer. He didn't work. He was engaged in writing a book. In the mornings he bustled forth from the mysterious back of the house—the region where Angela's mother lay (Henry had yet to be introduced)—to prepare the first stages of a breakfast that would linger until noon. Black coffee for his wife (and for Henry), tea for himself, pills and vitamins, oranges cut for the juicer. The table was laid with newsprint: the *Times* and the *New York Review of Books* and the *Guardian* a day late from London. Angela was studying in her room. Mr. Jones took coffee back to his wife. Then he sat with Henry and they read together. He wore halved lenses and his thinned hair was as the bed had left it. He was solicitous to Henry, but abstracted. He didn't seem to dislike him, or to be fascinated. He seemed not the slightest bit altered or disturbed by the company, which made Henry feel comfortable and welcomed, even if it was merely negligence. His small talk was professorial, to Henry's ear, gracious and well crafted, though his flat and dampened voice may have been most responsible for the effect—it leveled sentences into thick, sad slabs. He said, "I'm making toast here, Henry, and we have some apple butter—will you join me?" but it was as if he had said, "My sons died young, Henry, and my wife is an invalid—can you imagine?"

Around noon he always sat back and sighed and said, "Well." There was a breathy "h" sound coupled to the "w." He clapped his palms flat on his pants—a wonderfully decisive, preparatory gesture. Then he returned to the back of the house. Angela would emerge, sour and sharpened from concentration. She wanted to know how breakfast had gone. She wanted to know what they'd discussed. "Don't imagine he likes you," she said, and ate a crust of toast from her father's plate.

"He does, though," Henry told her. "He says he digs me."

She rubbed at one eye behind her glasses and scanned the articles her father had left exposed. "You think so?"

"'Henry,' he said, 'I'll speak plainly. I dig you. I'd like you to have my daughter.'"

She said, "We'll see," grinning only a little. She seemed truly disappointed, as if she'd left them alone together hoping for the worst. Despite her remorselessly lovely face, Angela's hair was kinky and unruly—she failed to wash it or comb it as often as most other girls her age, and she napped at the drop of a hat—so that it often trailed her like someone else's prank. She was even cynical about cynics, and could never be surprised, yet it was a comfort to feel that she should probably consult a mirror more often than she did. Henry wondered how long his novelty might last. He said, "Anyway, we don't need you, Mr. Jones and I. We don't need your approval, you know. We'll elope if we have to." When she ignored the joke, he unsuccessfully resolved never to tell her another again.

For the week surrounding Thanksgiving, she invited him to house number two. It was a cottage in Maine. There were as many books there, predominantly about sea voyages or polar expeditions—with maps inside the covers. There were fires burning in two rooms. A fire there was to dry the damp from your clothes and bake the salt into your skin. The pages of the books were often salty. The floors had warped so that they creaked or groaned in poignant, leathery phrases. Angela spent the better part of each day upstairs with her studies while Henry was downstairs with Mr. Jones. She had chosen chemical engineering—a discipline of great mystery without the slightest intrigue for Henry, as it was for her father—and though she could seldom get through three pages of a novel before falling asleep, she never dozed in front of her glossy, congested pages on thermodynamics and the principles of mass transport. Had Henry been invited to keep her father company? Maybe the invitation had been his idea. Henry listened to Angela's pacing from the room below, and sometimes he heard her mother as well, coughing or moving about, at the farther end of the house. He still hadn't been introduced to Mrs. Jones—hadn't set eyes on her, in fact—and neither Angela nor her father had bothered to apologize for this, or make an excuse. Mr. Jones would stop reading when they heard his wife stir, though he kept his head still and you could only tell by the way the focus drained from his eyes.

Mr. Jones didn't fish himself, but he would walk down the hill before dark—in no hurry, though it was always raining on this visit to Maine—to buy a good fish from the boats coming back. Angela would undress Henry while they watched Mr. Jones through the window and listened for her mother. They left their shirts on, but took the time to remove shoes. It was too disgraceful to stumble about with your pants bunched at your ankles. At least to Henry it was. Probably not to Angela. He stood behind her, and they watched her father's orange parka slip down through the break in the hedge, and then, in the reflection on the surface of the window, he saw her close her eyes and smile. She was a person who smiled when she was angry, Henry had learned. What he had taken for lust, initially, he recognized as anger now, though he didn't know exactly who or what she was angry at, and in certain ways he never would. When they were tired of standing, they lay on the warmed floor near the fire. The person on top watched for her father. She said he watched impatiently, but it wasn't quite true. It was enough, when he was alone with her, to know that her father would be there later as compensation, when Angela had retreated again.

Mr. Jones brought back a cod or a flounder. Lunches were haphazard (a crate of mangoes had been delivered through the mail, or there was soft cheese to spread; a ripe avocado without instructions) but Mr. Jones prepared elaborate dinners, Henry as his sous chef. Garlic and clarified butter and capers—ingredients unfamiliar to Henry, or translated into unfamiliar states, or simply handled with an unfamiliar reverence that rendered even the garlic exotic. Some evenings Angela joined them, but never Mrs. Jones. There wasn't a Thanksgiving turkey, or a mention of turkey, or anything that could possibly be mistaken for a trimming. Henry lied about this to his parents on the telephone that evening. It would have further damaged the poor impression they had somehow formed already, even though they hadn't met Angela or her parents. "Did they feed you?" his father asked first. "Your mother cooked enough for a small army," he said. And, "What did they feed you?" his mother wanted to know. *Who are these people?* was what they meant, of course. *Can we trust them?* There was the sound of machinery beside his mother, and the television turned up to overcome it. She was vacuuming while she talked—there had been an accident involving a cousin and cranberry sauce. "Put Mr. Jones on for a sec, Henry," she shouted. Henry told her, "No, he's out chopping wood," which was true—it was why he had chosen this moment to call. He stood in the far corner of the dining room, facing the windows, the spot in the house farthest from Mrs. Jones's room. But he had to shout, and the house was silent—he would certainly be heard. He wondered now just how quiet he and Angela had been, together in this same room earlier that afternoon. He watched Mr. Jones swing an axe sadly in the majestic drizzle. "I'll tell him you said thanks," he said, and had to repeat himself. "I got to go," his mother said. "But listen, get Angela to come here for Christmas, okay? I'll make a nice meal."

Angela had taken Cream of Wheat and a Rusty Nail upstairs to her mother after dinner. Her father carried wood in before Henry could help, and together they rebuilt the fire in the parlor. He said, "Play some music if you like," when he and Henry were alone together. The neighbor's cat had followed him in, and leapt up as soon as he formed a lap. The records were all of orchestras and their components—formal men not unlike Mr. Jones on the covers, involved in passionate or contemplative gestures, or bent over instruments that were strangely cluttered for the sounds they produced; also women caught open-mouthed in song. They were people who lived in houses like these, whose evenings sounded this way and lingered like so—Henry knew it. They belonged. Everything in this house belonged.

The characters in the books Henry took down from Mr. Jones's shelves belonged, too. It was a life from the right kind of book, the kind Henry had always loved, and by now he realized this was what had made it feel familiar despite the total lack of resemblance to his own life or to any household he'd ever visited. In the books he loved, it was usually raining, or it was snowing, and precipitation was a virtue. It was poorly lit, and there was a chill to burn off and a fire to do it at. There was an overlay of loneliness, or someone ill upstairs in a bed; there was a quiet history of disappointment or tragedy behind each scene. But attractive tragedy. There were affairs as well, of course. *Her father's life,* Henry read, in one of these novels, *her sisters's, her own, that of her two lost brothers—the whole history of their house had the effect of some fine florid voluminous phrase, say even a musical, that dropped first into words and notes without sense and then, hanging unfinished, into no words or any notes at all. Why should a set of people have been put in motion, on such a scale and with such an air of being equipped for a profitable journey, only to break down without an accident, to stretch themselves in the wayside dust without a reason?*

When the music began, Mr. Jones said slyly, "You're a Bach fan," as though Henry had been holding out on him.

"Who isn't?" Henry ventured.

His room upstairs was at one end of the hall. The damp cold bled readily through the old window casings. Angela never came to him at night, though he would listen for her and sometimes walk to the bathroom, hoping she was listening, too, and might be provoked. He wondered what she wore to bed here: what did the daughter in such a haunted family sleep in at the house in Maine? There were photos of the dead brothers downstairs. They looked both fragile and imposing: forthright tending toward hostile, though slim and small shouldered. Except that one was fair-haired and the other dark, they looked very much alike—matching expressions. Henry assumed their mother's illness was a product of their deaths—a very literary grief—but no one had said so. "Oh, don't ask," Angela had told him, offhandedly at first, but then her eyes had miraculously softened. She said, "See? If I start to *care* for you at all, then maybe I have to worry about what you'll think of my family. When we both know you're just not worth it."

"Try to resist me better," Henry said.

They had been on the beach—it was made of black and rounded rocks. The wind and salt made her skin feel tight when he touched her. Sometimes Henry remembered that there was a third house yet to come and could hardly believe his good fortune. It was in Baltimore, where Mrs. Jones had grown up. Angela said it was her favorite—almost the last thing she and her mother still agreed on.

The last night in Maine he dreamt himself asleep in this room, just as he was, then Angela's knock at his door. When he rolled over, she stood in the doorway in the short, filmy nightgown she wore at school, and with the light behind her he could see through both the gown and her flesh, her torso just a shade less translucent. She would relent, sooner than either of them expected. They would marry but without a ceremony, disappointing both families equally, if differently. She would be pregnant before she meant to be, too, and leave college, and he would get a paying job at a television station in Boston, setting them sufficiently apart from their families and the other accoutrements of what had seemed like an unfolding life and a desired, attainable future that even when they moved back to Connecticut, a few years further on, there weren't many binding expectations left to resist, or friends who had missed them, or familiar, promising roles available to be played still. They were happy enough for a long time, though they never resembled what they'd wished to become.

But when he woke, the knocking had turned into coughing, coming from the bathroom. It must be Angela's mother. Outside, the rain was blowing. Her breathing stuttered, and she seemed to be choking. Henry got up and went as far as the door to his room, but he couldn't bring himself to open it. Surely her daughter and husband were awake.

No one could sleep through that, could they? Her cough had a wet catch to it, a gluey stop. What would Henry say when he got to her? That morning he had finally met her—or had spoken to her, at least. He had taken her coffee up. Angela was in town; the phone had rung at just the wrong moment. "I can take it," Henry had said, and Mr. Jones had hesitated, considering, while the phone kept ringing. Mrs. Jones hadn't spoken when Henry had knocked at her half-open door. She had been standing by the window, smoking and examining her fingernails. When she saw him, she had turned away, obviously surprised, and said something quietly, to herself. Henry had prepared an elaborate, nervous introduction—*at last* and so forth, *a real pleasure, finally* . . . "Ah . . . shit," she had said, exhaling. She had a wide, soft face made pale by a frame of dark hair very much like her daughter's. She was younger than he'd expected—quite a bit younger than her husband, he guessed—and nice looking. Not ravaged at all. Henry set her coffee down on the bed table. "Pardon me."

"Yup. Thanks," she said, turning her face away further, fluttering a few dismissive fingers in his direction. She produced a cough to cover his exit.

Now he kept his hand on the door latch and listened. There was a last, decisive hack from the bathroom, then she spat. A single sob. Her breathing was heavy but regular again. She spat once more, then became very quiet. He intended to stay put until she had walked back down the hall to her room, because he was afraid she would hear him if he moved. But he was freezing, and she might have fallen asleep. He stepped carefully, and the floorboards creaked that much more. The bed creaked getting into it. He lay still and listened for her, with the rain falling against the window. It was hard to place the soft, intelligent face he had seen that afternoon (not as striking as her daughter's, but prettier) with such an obnoxious cough. Eventually, he fell asleep.

In the morning there was nothing amiss in the bathroom. In the kitchen Angela's father was pouring Henry's coffee already and brewing a second cup of tea for himself. He poked a finger at the folded paper. "Snow, they're telling me, Henry," he said. "If you can believe it. How did you sleep?" He stared—perhaps a challenge, as it seemed. Henry said, "Just fine."

Their shared breakfasts had become too comfortable and routine for the sour note to linger in the air long. Mr. Jones had been to the beach already to collect mussels. He gave the last lesson in what had been a weeklong course on the preparation of shellfish. The mussels that closed to the touch (never eat the others) would be debearded and scrubbed, and then sautéed with garlic and parsley stems and bay leaf and thyme. Served with the cooking liquid strained through a cheesecloth. Where did he learn all these recipes? Henry wanted to know, and Mr. Jones smiled and pointed approvingly—good question, yes, he had an answer for that. He said, "Now here's the thing. You're going to have to come back, you understand, and next visit I'm going to steal you away from Angela, and you and I will walk down to the docks together one afternoon. You'll see.

"Listen," he said, resting his hand on Henry's back, "if you don't come away from there with a better idea than crab cakes, it's your own fault."

A joke. Henry laughed with him. Evidently Mr. Jones didn't want to share Henry at all. Would Angela be impressed or disgusted? he wondered.

A bit later that morning there were footsteps in the hallway, and someone was coming down the stairs. Angela's father regarded the ceiling and folded his paper in anticipation. They were measured steps on the staircase, but then brisk enough rounding the corner. "Surprise," Mrs. Jones said, quietly, and carried it with a smile and shrug. "Don't get up."

Her husband had begun to, but he sat back down. "How are you?" he asked, with the floating indulgence that habit must have made of the question, and she said "good" in such a way as to close the topic. She poured herself coffee.

Mr. Jones watched her for a moment, then looked out the window, as if checking for snow. But the rain had stopped, and if anything, it looked like the day might clear. He seemed to remember his tea next, and turned all his attention to it.

Mrs. Jones sat down beside Henry, and swept the cat from the table with a backhand. She took a deep breath when she was seated—tired out from her journey, but satisfied with the destination. She wasn't quite as young as he had thought at first sight, but she *was* a pale and softened version of her daughter. The same dark hair, although hers was straighter and not as long as her daughter's, more orderly. There were soulful bags under her eyes—not unattractive, somehow. And her robe, which was a dark blue, draping satin, seemed inappropriately intimate.

She took up a portion of the newspaper, and across the table her husband made a momentary attempt to return to his own. A corner of her section had poked into the butter. It swung toward Henry's forehead when she turned the pages, and she didn't seem to notice, but Mr. Jones did. He fidgeted with his tea some more, then chose a mango from the crate. He didn't peel it, though—it sat on a magazine in front of him. There was a clock above the stove behind Henry that kept a loud, labored time. Henry wondered if he was expected to initiate a conversation. He wondered if Mrs. Jones knew his name. She turned her pages and sipped her coffee so comfortably that he might have assumed this was a customary morning, despite her absence the past week, except that Mr. Jones was so unmistakably disturbed. He was stealing sad glances at the pages laid on the table in front of Henry, but when Henry finally broke the silence, offering his section—"I'm done with it"—Mr. Jones was momentarily confused, then shook his head sternly.

The exchange seemed to provoke Mrs. Jones. She said, "I'm going to make French toast," and pushed back from the table. "Beat some eggs for me, Henry?"

"Right," he said, and followed her.

She asked him what they had all had for Thanksgiving dinner. Her husband let the cat out, then went into the parlor without a word, leaving Henry alone with her. Now, had he missed his turkey? she asked—perhaps to let him know that she had overheard the lie to his parents, although nothing in her manner seemed meaningful or sly. She kept sitting down as if to let him do the work, then remembering something else—she was never seated for more than an instant. "What did your mother cook?" she wanted to know. But she didn't pay attention to his reply. He kept his description as brief as possible, yet she still cut him off. "Here," she said, "dash of vanilla."

Then she said, "Oh, no." Henry had been pouring. "Too much milk," she told him.

"Mm. Sorry."

She took the bowl away, and dumped the eggs and milk down the drain.

"We'll start over," she said, but not unhappily.

Music began in the other room, and Angela's father came back. "May I help?" he asked.

She said, "Here." She was rinsing the bowl. "You do this, how 'bout?" To Henry she asked, "Can you set the table, do you think?"

There was a note of doubt to the question, or else he had imagined it. But sure enough, he managed to put the wrong forks out. She said, "Well I guess it's *like* dessert—French toast. Let's call it breakfast, though." She laid the correct forks herself while Henry stood aside. He had set four places, but she took one away.

Then she made "the boys" sit down at the table—out of her way, she said. Her whole mood seemed to brighten further, but her husband remained nervous. She said, "I have a bone to pick with you, Henry. You might as well know. It's not fair at all that you're leaving today, just when I'm feeling better. Angela and Mr. Jones got a whole week of you" (even she called him Mr. Jones) "while I laid in bed and had to hear all about your charms secondhand. Who wants juice?"

She wielded the pitcher, one hand on the back of his chair. The bread was frying and the syrup was warming and fragrant. The music was something sweet and delicate with a violin and piano. She said, "Talk to Angela," while she poured. Where *was* Angela, Henry wondered? "Tell her we can have you one more day, Henry. You could convince her if you wanted to, I'll bet." She just finished the sentence before a string of escalating coughs caught up with her.

Mr. Jones couldn't seem to contain himself any longer. The coughing set him free, and he took his napkin from his lap and stood. "Dear . . ." he said. "What are we doing, dear? This is . . . here." He reached across Henry's shoulder and tried, unsuccessfully, to take the juice pitcher from her hand. "Let me help you, please," he said, while she cleared the last of her cough. "This is, ah . . ." He laughed. "Come on now."

He had been tugging on the pitcher, but she wouldn't let go. She looked at him squarely and mildly—there was something impressive about it—while their four hands remained on the juice pitcher, suspending it above Henry's shoulder. Her smile had been expanding, slowly, and when she made a face—raising her eyebrows and crossing her eyes—Mr. Jones let go. She said, "No juice for Mr. Jones."

She turned back to the stove, and her husband sat down again. He picked his cloth napkin up from the table and refolded it in his lap. Henry thought they might share a look, but Mr. Jones returned to studying the window instead. He was a different man. Looking back on the morning later, that would be obvious as something available for Henry to take caution from, but he wasn't paying the proper attention as the events unfolded.

She served the French toast to the two of them, refilled her coffee, and sat down in front of her own empty plate. She moved now in the loose-jointed way that some people do when they've drunk too much; she fished a pack of cigarettes out of her robe and lit one. She smiled across the table at her husband—it was a perfect imitation of warmth—but he succeeded in never looking up at her. When she caught Henry watching the performance, her expression shifted and she leaned toward him, her chin turned away, and spoke out of the side of her mouth in a stage whisper. "Tell me *everything* you told Mr. Jones," she said. "The short version. I mean it, Henry. Catch me up on *you*."

There was a great deal of sly indulgence in her smile and in her lean. She ashed into her plate. And Henry smiled right back at her—in fact, he found he wanted to wink. This was the moment to pull away and recognize he was in the middle of a dynamic that had long preceded him; it was the right moment to be satisfied with having seduced Angela's father and consider her mother a negotiable obstacle. But something in the look she gave him suggested an acknowledgment of his success thus far—*I think you know me,* her eyes conceded; there was a touch of admiration, Henry imagined—as well as an invitation to one last challenge. She seemed to be saying, *My husband was easy, of course, but I want to be charmed, too, Henry.* And Henry might have resisted her if the resemblance to her daughter wasn't so present or the comparison, finally, he decided, so clearly in Mrs. Jones's favor. This was one thought he had, anyway, later on. This was one excuse. Another was that whatever he did next, it wouldn't have particularly made a difference, in the long run. We like to imagine the single step in some other direction would have been the first to a far different destination, but of course we make the same mistakes wherever we find ourselves, and our tendencies and weaknesses aren't subject to single decisions. It may be that any path we would have chosen—would have found ourselves drawn to, or inclined to trust—would have fed into a more or less identical landscape.

This morning would always be his introduction to his wife's mother—as he got older, the implied ceremony of the occasion seemed more meaningful to Henry—and he would have to remind himself, looking back, that there had been a few moments once, before he knew Mrs. Jones at all, when he'd imagined he could impress her. Sometimes he told himself if he had seen the third house before meeting her—the house in Baltimore that she'd bought on her own, where she'd lived alone before Mr. Jones, the house she'd return to when her husband was unexpectedly dead before her, selling the two she'd never cared for at contemptuously low prices—he might not have misjudged her so. It was an ordinary lump in an uncertain neighborhood, rendered dark by overhanging trees, with a sagging roof and clogged gutters and a tacked-on porch. It was the middle of three nearly identical houses at the end of a street roamed by busy, inconsiderate children. Mrs. Jones sat almost cheerfully by the windows or even on the porch of this house, disobeying her nurse, treating her daughter with the same polite indifference as ever—as if they were amiably agreed-upon enemies, or old friends who'd never cared for one another. But she was particularly talkative and vain with Henry at this house. *My charmer*, she called him. *Sit down here*, she said. "Ah, Henry," she sometimes said, when he told a story or carried a joke, "if only I had met you first. I'll bet all the girls tell you that." Flattery was the vehicle in which she preferred to convey her disapproval and mistrust.

On his initial visit there, not long after Mr. Jones had died, at a moment when Angela was out of the room, she had asked him what he thought of "the first house" now that he had finally seen it. She smiled kindly and mildly, sincerely interested in his opinion, and proud. She was almost ten years past the day he'd met her, but still pretty in a way that suggested vulnerability—it was still a persuasive disguise. By then he knew that her sons had been twenty-one and nineteen when they died; Angela had been thirteen. They weren't good people, these sons, according to Angela—they were self-involved and manipulative in the same way their mother was, quick with a slight, suspicious of women. But their mother had been a different person when they were alive, Angela said. She had loved them so forcefully that Angela herself, and her father too, had enjoyed a dose of surplus affection—as if the boys couldn't contain all she hoped to pour into them, and some had spilled over onto her daughter and husband. She wasn't an invalid before they died. She had liked her job and been good at it. She had kept an ambitious garden at each house. Since their deaths, she'd never stepped on a boat or stood on a dock, and beaches—in Maine or anywhere else—had entirely lost their appeal for her. She didn't like to see her grandson in a bathtub.

Henry didn't know what to tell her. The house was not quite ugly, but he couldn't see that it had any particular strengths, either—he could hardly imagine what to falsely praise—and what he found most discouraging about it was its mundane, upholstered resemblance to the ones he had grown up in. "It's homey," he said, finally, then had an inspiration and added, "I can see why Angela liked it, growing up."

Mrs. Jones had smiled—still kindly, it seemed, if indulgently, though how would he ever know? How to know what instincts she acted on, cruel or protective, and who could say what she had recognized and properly identified in Henry before anyone else had, or what affinities they might have shared under different circumstances? "You think it's ugly," she said, patting his hand—consolingly, perhaps. "You and Mr. Jones."

But in Maine, he was young. He had his heart's desire in sight and it included them all—the parents along with the daughter. "Tell me everything," she had said, and smiled memorably. And he didn't hesitate: he returned her smile, and Mrs. Jones leaned a little closer still, and Henry said, "Well," with Mr. Jones's "h" in it, and slapped his knees in imitation. He found himself doing these things without meaning to.

He said, "We've gone through Bach, and . . . Rachmaninoff." He was whispering. "We've given Henry James a good once-over, naturally." Her grin narrowed—as if to a point: *this is perfect*, she seemed to be saying to him, in that moment. *Oh, you're sharp.* "And, ah . . . we've covered flounder two different ways," he said. "A great deal on garlic. Mussels, of course. Then there was my trip to Martha's Vineyard when I was ten. Skinned the elbow," he said—he winked, and flashed his elbow. "And then the family sailing over from Poland, and Ellis Island. The house in Torrington. The plumbing fortune. All leading up to our shared affection for your daughter, I guess. That's . . ." But she was smiling differently now. "That's pretty much the short version of our week." And she was looking at Mr. Jones instead. When Henry looked, too, his own smile staled. He had half forgotten that Mr. Jones was in the room.

Mrs. Jones laughed a little—sweetly. She had made the game end before Henry realized it. She coughed once briefly and sipped her coffee, watching her husband through both. The record ended in the other room, and they heard the needle swing back into place. Mr. Jones put his silverware down on his plate and finished chewing. "Henry . . ." Mrs. Jones said, then turned back to him. "If you stay—Henry—you know . . . maybe you and Mr. Jones could dust off the skiff. He hasn't had anyone to sail with since he killed the boys, I'm afraid."

Mr. Jones sighed. He appeared tired and possibly disgusted, but not surprised. Henry began to feel sick to his stomach.

Mrs. Jones continued, ostensibly speaking to Henry, but watching her husband. "Wear a life vest is all I'm suggesting, darling." Mr. Jones pushed back from the table. "That's my advice. Going somewhere, dear?"

Her husband closed his eyes and sighed and said, "Pardon me."

"Oh, you lost him, Henry," his wife said, watching him turn away. "You *had* him," she said, her eyes still on her husband. "I could tell you had him."

Mr. Jones collected his parka from the peg by the door and pulled his boots on in no particular hurry. Henry needed to offer something, or take something back, but he couldn't imagine where to begin. "You were getting to be just like a son," Mrs. Jones was saying, "Henry. Except not dead. Will you be gone long, dear? I was hoping you'd do the dishes." As he crossed to the door, ignoring her, she said, loudly, "It's noble, Henry, to just walk away." She was actually looking at him now—at Henry—and he was so stupid that in that moment he still felt she was speaking to him, and that he might be expected to formulate a reply. "Silence is best, you know," she said. "Never give in." When Mr. Jones slammed the door behind himself, she began to cough.

Angela had overslept, she claimed. She said she woke to the sound of her mother shouting and then coughing. She slipped into the room and started the kettle going when Mrs. Jones was coughing still, Henry still sitting dumb at the table. She offered small spoon and china sounds into the silence when her mother was done coughing, and then she sat down with them and took up a section of the paper. In a little while she asked her mother, "Want your shawl from upstairs?" though she read while she spoke, disinterested. Mrs. Jones's gaze drifted just above the table, and she tapped at her lips, absently, with one finger. "Water's boiling," she replied at last.

Henry thought it was over—everything with Angela must be—and that he'd never had a chance. He should have known that. He'd gotten in over his head—anyone else in his position would have recognized it. In the car, driving home, Angela appeared to him in a different light: more or less mild and defeated, and not so mysterious or fierce as simply depressed, when compared to her mother. He'd often been surprised to find a trick door in the back wall of his love affairs, and when one day he stepped or stumbled through it, he would invariably be disappointed by the view from outside. He didn't dare tell her what had happened over breakfast, incorrectly assuming that she'd hear about it from her parents—or that she *hadn't* been asleep upstairs, of course, and had heard it all for herself. Wasn't that, in fact, the secret to life in that house? Hadn't it been the case all weekend? Half of him never stopped suspecting she had listened from her bedroom and left him to his fate, even when the next trip to her parents was proposed and, when he told her he couldn't go back there, could never face them again, she truly seemed not to understand. "They love you," she said, "for some reason. They wear me out, asking about you."

And a little later, when she wanted to elope (he'd known her indifference to his affection was a pose—why did its sudden disappearance surprise him?), she was convincingly mystified when he told her he didn't like the idea that half her attraction to him depended upon her parents' disapproval. She said, "No, that's *your* fantasy, dear. Not mine." And anyway, she wondered why he imagined she would ever have taken her parents' opinion into consideration?

In her last years, Mrs. Jones practiced the invalid's art of ill-timed imposition. She could be counted on to require an emergency visit (usually following the firing of a nurse) at any worst possible moment, and when she invited herself back up to Connecticut, she liked to buy the plane tickets before proposing the trip to her hosts. Angela would pretend to be determined to make her stay in a hotel, or to say that that sounded like a lovely trip, but unfortunately they wouldn't be available to see her those dates; but she also depended upon Henry to object to such measures and apologize for her mother. It was a banal marital dance they performed, like any other.

On what turned out to be both her last and her longest trip to Connecticut—all four endless weeks of December—Mrs. Jones's previously uncanny ability to sniff out the lies and arrangements devoted to Henry's affairs had blossomed into a broad and sloppy suspicion. "I'll just come for the ride," she kept saying, or "Why don't we all go?" She was wrong this time: a particularly lasting diversion had, in fact, just come to a premature end at the hands of a younger and unmarried rival, and Henry was desperately volunteering to shuttle his son between the busy appointments of a seven-year-old, not to free himself for other stops, but to be alone long enough to indulge his anger and continue the pressing and solitary debate he'd been having with his lover. "Who's he talking to?" Mrs. Jones asked Angela, whenever Henry was on the telephone. She devised petty reasons for Angela to call him at work, and when her daughter ran out of patience, she began calling herself, giving the secretary a false name, then hanging up as soon as she heard Henry's voice. None of this satisfied her, though, and when the unseasonably cold air turned arctic, up and down the coast, two weeks into her stay, she claimed she'd forgotten to leave the water running in her house and required Henry to drive down and check on it. There was nothing he wanted more than two days alone, and he almost agreed too readily, sending her suspicion off with him to Baltimore as well.

He spent the first third of his drive on thoughts of his lover (a production assistant on the last commercial he'd shot—a girl with excessively long legs and no patience and a brilliance for schedules and details; perhaps he'd never properly kept up with her), the second third on thoughts of his mother-in-law (what had sent her into this frenzy? in the past, her suspicions and little jokes had been coy and discreet, as if she'd never wanted to alert her daughter, only to let Henry know he could only fool one of them), and the last third on a scheme that came to him. A few years back, on a visit to Maine, while Henry and Mr. Jones sat in lovely, distressed Adirondack chairs and watched Angela keep Brian from stuffing pine needles in his mouth, Mr. Jones had suddenly turned and broken the habitual, uneasy silence between them to say, "I've finished my book."

He had whispered the news, and that fact combined with the gleam of pride in his eyes almost broke Henry's heart. "It that right?" Henry had said. "Congratulations! My goodness—I'd love to read it."

"Oh no," Mr. Jones had said, gaining control of his expression again. "No, it wouldn't interest you." But when Henry pressed, he was willing to supply the title: "The Tragic in James: Its Syntactic Delay." Henry received this with nothing more or less than incomprehension, but to Mr. Jones his expression must have looked like disdain, or something worse. "Well, that's only the working title," he'd added. "Anyway, it doesn't matter. No one will ever read it." And when Henry insisted they should all celebrate, at the very least, Mr. Jones had retreated entirely again to the high ground of failed eye contact and shadowy smiles from which he generally regarded his son-in-law. "In all honesty," he said, "it isn't really finished. I suppose I'd appreciate it if you'd keep this under your hat. I only meant to tell you, after all."

Then he never mentioned the book again—not to his wife, so far as Henry knew, and certainly not to his daughter. Either he never approached a publisher, or when he did, he was rejected, and when he died, Henry tried to urge Angela and her mother to search for a manuscript, but neither believed he'd ever really written anything.

So Henry would search. And in fact, who could say what he might find answers to in some drawer or closet of that stuffed house, cluttered as it was by too much of the furniture and too many of the books and paintings and debris of three houses? Henry was so diverted by the idea of finally ransacking the Joneses' past that he didn't quite process the sound he was hearing as he unlocked the front door, though it was clearly the sound of water. He found it streaming and foraging—it seemed sentient and even intent, a kind of infestation. It cascaded in thin falls down the wallpaper and dripped through the fixtures. It rippled in thick, dull syllables on the carpeted staircase. It took all day just to mop and drain the standing water and find workmen to join him for the heavy work the next day. He would have to telephone Mrs. Jones and get her permission to pull up the carpeting and throw away most of the furniture. Under the carpeting the floorboards might be warped. In the basement, a small lake settled darkly, smelling of mothballs and mold. He wondered if anything would be salvaged in the end.

That evening he halfheartedly poked into the crammed closets, where the sagging boxes peeled away in his hands, but the damp and the smells it brought forth made the familiarity of this house—of its fixtures and pull-shaded windows, its slipcovers and wallpaper patterns of repeating stagecoaches and stenciled flowers—more potent than ever. It felt as if he'd be unpacking his own past.

"The Tragic in James: Its Syntactic Delay"—how could such a topic possibly be interesting, anyway? Mrs. Jones and Angela were probably right—there probably wasn't a book at all, and of course Mr. Jones would have reserved the lie for Henry. No one else would have believed it. But even if such a book existed, how could it turn out to be revealing in the way Henry hoped? Would he give up even a glance at his lover, much less a few words from her ineloquent lips or the merest brush of her fingers, for the chance to read such a book? Henry had wished for the wrong things—he'd been granted his role in the wrong family and novel. He couldn't face the phone call to Mrs. Jones. He couldn't stay in the house, but a hotel room alone was out of the question, too. He laid the seat back in his car, in the driveway, with the heater running, on this street full of revving engines and strange calls in the night that might as well have been the one he grew up on, and he comforted himself with the thought that he was still young: there was still plenty of time for catastrophe and misfortune, for everything he'd chosen to fall out of his reach again.

Dancers

ELLEN LITMAN

THEY WERE TALL, GOOD-LOOKING, AND CARELESS. They arrived unexpectedly, descended upon Tanya's life, took up residence in her apartment. They seemed instantly comfortable there, as if it were the most natural thing for them to settle on the living room couch of somebody's apartment in Pittsburgh. They were dancers and nothing could be done about it.

Petya had told Tanya on Tuesday morning. He was eating the oatmeal she'd fixed for him, and she stood leaning against the microwave, coffee mug in her hands—she didn't eat breakfast. Petya said his high-school friend Senya was going to visit with them for a couple of days. "You remember," he said, "I've told you about him. The ballet guy."

She didn't remember, but that was all right; she liked when they had company. To others, she seemed like a private, solitary person, with her shyness, her eyeglasses, her quiet, concentrated look. People were afraid to disturb her, even Petya was afraid sometimes. She could tell he was a little worried now. She smiled to reassure him. It was good that this friend, this Senya, was arriving. They might all take a drive somewhere, go to a restaurant once or twice. Petya didn't like to eat out unless it was a special occasion. They did okay, money-wise—he was an engineer and she clerked at the medical center—but they were also saving for a house. Tanya's parents, too, always saved, ate out rarely and only at buffet types of places, and now they had a little house in Squirrel Hill. They called Petya a *sensible fellow*, and were glad because Tanya needed someone sensible. Tanya believed them and was also vaguely glad she had Petya.

Where was Petya's friend coming from? How long was he to stay? And what on earth were they going to feed him (their refrigerator in such a despicable empty state, you could roll a ball in there)?

"Don't you panic, *starushka*," said Petya. He called her that sometimes, *starushka*, a little old lady. She had recently turned twenty-six.

But Tanya panicked anyway. On her way to work and later at the office, she felt the sweet and tugging anticipation of something, an event. On her lunch break, she ran to the supermarket. She wanted bright holiday food: a frosty bottle of champagne, chocolates individually wrapped in crinkling foil, an enormous winter basket with ribbons. But the holidays were over, and she wound up instead with a splintery box of small, wilted tangerines.

The next night, Tanya and Petya drove to the Greyhound station. The New York bus had just pulled in, and there was Senya, sparkling with good-natured energy, rangy and blond, in a silvery winter jacket. He hugged them both, and Tanya felt swept up by the earnestness of Senya's hug. Then she saw the girl. The girl stood apart, watching the commotion with cool, guarded eyes. She wore a long leather coat and her red hair was gathered in a classic knot at the nape of her neck, the beautiful long neck with the fatigued tilt that Tanya had always associated with ballerinas.

"Why are you standing there, Ksyusha?" Senya said to the girl. "Look, this is Petya and this is Tanya."

She approached hesitantly, as if she knew they hadn't expected her.

"Nice to meet you," she said in a clipped, little voice. She offered Petya her hand and introduced herself—*Oksana*. They were to call her by her full and formal name.

On the way home, Tanya learned that Oksana was from someplace in Ukraine, that Senya had met her in Las Vegas, where both danced for six months in a Russian show called *Caviar*, that soon they would sign another contract—an agent from California had expressed interest, and also the artistic director of *Caviar* wanted them for his next show. They brought with them the tape of *Caviar*, and after dinner Oksana suddenly spoke up and insisted that they must, *simply must*, watch the tape. Tanya served tea in the living room, and they all sat in front of the big, humming TV and watched.

There were women in long *sarafans* and beaded *kokoshniks*. Cossacks with fake mustaches strutted in their dashing *sharovars*. Someone showed up dressed as a bear. There were modern numbers too, meant to represent the new, uplifted Russia: men and women in stark suits, marching pointedly and swinging their briefcases. At the end, girls in bright little skirts danced the cancan.

"Look at them," Tanya whispered to Petya. "Their legs grow from the same place as their teeth."

She meant it as a joke, the kind of joke Petya usually made himself. But Petya shrugged and even moved away from Tanya a little. Maybe he thought the legs were nice to look at, or maybe he was afraid that Senya and Oksana would overhear. But Senya and Oksana heard nothing. They were watching their *Caviar*—pointing, arguing—and blushing, agitated Oksana kept saying that *no, such-and-such was a good dancer . . . and once in the makeup room, Lida Gruzdeva told everybody . . . but it was a huge secret, like that time she got in trouble with Tikhonov, you remember that, right?* They were like two children just back from summer camp, still attached to the loud and communal way they had lived in Vegas.

Oksana's trunk stood in the hallway by the front door. The following night, coming home from work, Tanya bumped against it; it was the kind of dumb, clumsy thing she did a lot. The trunk was black and sturdy, with heavy metal patches around the corners; it had an old-fashioned bulk to it. Oksana said she never went anywhere without the trunk, not since her ballet-school days.

"Tell me about the ballet school," Tanya said, rubbing her bruised ankle.

"School like school," said Oksana. "Classes every day. Bad food. Cold bedrooms."

"You lived there?"

"The locals got to go home," said Oksana. Her home was three hours away by bus, and week after week she stayed at the school, returning home only during long breaks.

Oksana spoke with a teenage abruptness, like somebody forced to constantly explain boring and obvious things. She *was* a teenager, essentially. Barely eighteen. The way she spoke made Tanya feel old.

"I tried to get into ballet once," Tanya volunteered. "When I was seven. They didn't take me, said I had flat feet."

"The requirements are very specific," said Oksana. "Feet have to be well arched. Toes of equal length." She raised her foot and wiggled her toes to demonstrate. "Also the hips, wide so you can turn your feet to point outward."

She gave Tanya a quick once-over. "You've got the hips. But you're not tall."

"Well, nobody in our family is tall," apologized Tanya.

But Oksana wasn't listening anymore. Senya came into the room, and she half rose from her chair. Their love was in the annoying, devouring stage where the rest of the world was a mere nuisance. They needed each other all the time and urgently. They touched a lot; it was probably a dance thing.

Could Tanya love with such audacity, with sinking of the stomach and shaking in the knees? She had been seventeen when her family came to Pittsburgh. A plain, timid girl, she was virtually invisible. There was one excruciating year in high school, then college . . . Tanya had desperately wanted a boyfriend. She wanted a boyfriend to invade her life, to take control, to make her rare, unavailable, and thus desirable to others. She had seen it happen to her girlfriends.

Later that night Petya said that dancing was a bullshit profession. "No steady jobs," he said. "Look at them hanging, waiting for a contract. And Oksana? He'll dump her in a month."

He and Tanya were getting ready for bed. Tanya brought a basket of soft and toasty bed linens from the laundry downstairs. Sheets, pillowcases, a blanket cover. It smelled of safe, flowery confinement. No one was dumping anybody in their home.

But Petya said there was a couple in Montreal that had sort of adopted Senya. "You know," he said, "bored, wealthy people. Don't know what to do with their money. Get into silly matters, like symphony or pictures or ballet."

"Maecenas," said Tanya, "patrons of the arts."

"Whatever. *Senya's* people. He's one clever comrade, our Senya. They have a room for him up there, in their house in Montreal. Wallpaper, flowers on the table. Everything's proper. Money for college, too."

"And Oksana?"

"What Oksana? I'm asking you, *starushka*, is Senya insane to spoil a sweet situation like that? To bring along some girl, a silly Ukrainian broad, one meter seventy centimeters?"

Tanya took one corner of the fitted sheet and Petya took another. They pulled in opposite directions.

"Still," said Tanya, "I think they're in love."

"*In love*," he mocked her. "Don't you muddle honest people's heads, Tatyana."

That was Petya, practical, unsentimental. Nobody could muddle Petya's head. Relatives had introduced them when Tanya was a senior in college. He told her that he worked at Westinghouse. He made jokes about American incompetence. He seemed bored with his job, bored with America, perhaps even bored with Tanya. They went on four dates and she was growing bored with him too.

Then everything changed. One day Tanya met Petya's cousins, two huge slovenly guys, who were drinking beer from plastic cups at the bowling alley where Petya brought Tanya—*the American pastime, Tanyusha*. The cousins said it was a pleasure to meet her—Tanechka-Tanya—such a nice lady, too nice for a fool like Petya, and in college too! They said they didn't go to college. They were going to open a restaurant in Squirrel Hill. With a catering service.

Empty talk! said Petya. All of it! Dumb empty talk! He was taking Tanya home, and his voice kept breaking, he was so upset. He told Tanya that the cousins had been working in pizza joints, making minimum wage. They refused to understand that you were nothing, *nothing* without education. Two young, strapping guys, and not half-wits either . . . Tanya timidly pressed Petya's hand. And her heart, her poor heart, tired of waiting and being invisible, it faltered, it paused. But the next time she saw Petya, he was again his smug and catlike self—he made sleepy jokes and took Tanya to the movies at the Manor. She married him anyway, after a year of diligent dating, and the relatives said they were well matched.

The apartment began to carry traces of Oksana's presence. There was a plush toy dog she liked to cuddle with; there were her lace-up boots with shapely heels; there was a nylon ribbon she tied to the brass vanity in Tanya's bedroom. This was Oksana's peculiar, undeveloped idea of beauty, and Tanya was both frustrated and moved by it.

On Friday night Petya took Senya to the bowling alley, and Tanya and Oksana sat in the living room with a bottle of Baileys and a Victoria's Secret catalog. The *Caviar* tape was playing—those Cossacks again—and there was Oksana in her short, lime skirt and her dance shoes, tall and red-haired. One of the three prettiest girls in the show, she said.

A dancer in black elastic tights began a classical number. "Look," said Oksana. "That's Volodya."

By then Tanya knew the trajectory of Oksana's wayward past. The ballet school at first, then corps de ballet at a theater in Donetsk, and finally the American tour. It was during the tour that she had an affair with Volodya, the principal dancer. He was the one who persuaded her to stay.

They watched muscular Volodya do a robust pirouette. "Such a man!" said Oksana. "Such a wonderful, wicked man." And she groaned in a languorous, sexual way. After the tour ended, she and Volodya stayed in Philadelphia, in a ballet house with a dozen other unemployed dancers. The house belonged to Mickey the connoisseur, homosexual Mickey, who loved the dancers, kept them for free, and even helped them get jobs. Poor *gomic* Mickey, said Oksana. Come back anytime, he told her and Volodya, though he seemed to understand that they wouldn't. Not together anyway. After four months in Vegas, Volodya returned to Donetsk. He had a wife and a daughter there, and the wife was fed up with Volodya's touring.

"You didn't know?" said Tanya. In spite of herself, she was drawn into this little adolescent drama. "He didn't tell you about the wife?"

"I knew," said Oksana. "Everybody knew."

She spoke of men with the same assured precision she would use to explain some interesting pas de deux. Here was this girl, this creature, callow, yet experienced in ways that Tanya would never be.

A week went by, and the dancers showed no intention of leaving. But Tanya had already fallen under the spell of their artistic charms. With them around, life became brilliant and unpredictable. They did spontaneous, expensive things, like going to the Russian restaurant, Moscow Nights, or, at Senya's insistence, trying sushi for the first time. There was a weekend when they all went to the zoo, and there was a night when Oksana suddenly decided she needed a present for her godmother in Donetsk and they all got up and went to Monroeville Mall, even though it was after eight and Petya had an early meeting the next morning.

In the morning, Tanya, pale and lightheaded from lack of sleep, cooked quick, soundless breakfasts. At work, she talked about the dancers—that's what she called them, *those crazy dancers*—and what they'd done the night before. The girls at the office thought it was all very exciting. They wanted to know if the dancers were about to perform anywhere locally and if so would there be free tickets. Tanya tried to remain vague about that.

What the dancers did during the day was a mystery. Petya had taken them around Squirrel Hill, showed them a couple of cafés, some fancy boutiques on Forbes, a library. They could even take a bus to downtown. But the dancers never went anywhere. When Tanya returned from work, they were always in their home clothes, snuggled on the couch, napping or watching TV.

At night Tanya and Petya could hear them on that creaky living room couch. Tanya imagined their supple, capable bodies bending in all kinds of pleasurable positions. The sounds traveled from the living room: a trickle of laughter, Oksana's high-pitched and excited sobs. And next to Tanya was Petya, tossing, breathing heavily through his stuffed nose.

Petya couldn't sleep either.

"Have you seen her underwear hanging in the bathroom? What do you call those things anyway?"

"Thongs," said Tanya.

"Yes, thongs. Red. What's the deal with the red? What's the deal with the thongs? Don't they tear into your ass?"

"She likes them. It's sexy."

"One pair is sexy. Ten pairs is stupid."

"You're the one who's stupid," Tanya said, turning away from Petya. She suddenly had an urge to tell him that the gold chain he'd taken to wearing around his neck looked tasteless, that he'd gained weight, that the way he strutted around made him look like a small-town thug.

Something happened to Tanya whenever she watched Senya and Oksana together. They'd be standing by the window, pressed against each other—just the two outlines in the twilight—his body absorbing her small curves. Tanya's face grew hot. She noticed things about Senya: his hands, his bare feet, the way his jeans creased around his crotch when he sat. When he looked at her, she felt weightless and pretty.

After dinner, Senya would help Tanya in the kitchen. She washed the dishes and he stood in readiness with a dish towel. They worked side by side, silently, and their elbows sometimes touched. Tanya would say, Sorry. She could tell he was watching her—her neck, the side of her face. She would pull her hair back, tie it with an elastic—let him watch. He stood so close. Sometimes he stopped drying the dishes and just stood, looking at her.

"Were you really friends at school?" Tanya asked Petya one night. "You and Senya? Tell me how it was when you were kids."

Petya shifted in bed. "Settle down, Tanya. It's late and I don't remember."

"Come on, tell me," she said, reaching out and stroking his neck. "Te-e-ell me," she teased. She leaned on her elbow and let the strap of her nightgown slide down her arm.

Petya was not an inventive lover. He was straightforward with his needs and didn't know her body well. She believed it wasn't for a lack of generosity. He was too shy to explore or ask, and she was too shy to show him.

"You're obsessed with your Senya," said Petya.

She pulled back, right away feeling ridiculous. Remember who you are. Retreat into your poor, pudgy body—not fat, just poorly defined. She felt ashamed. Was that because Petya had unwittingly spoken the truth? Her playfulness, her fascination were misplaced.

"Go to sleep, Tatyana." He patted her shoulder reassuringly and fixed the strap of her nightgown. "I'm exhausted."

She pulled the blanket over her head.

She began to worry about the dancers leaving, going to California or Montreal. This was the end of their second week in Pittsburgh, and so far nothing had been mentioned, there were no signs, although they were now doing their exercises on the living room carpet, every evening. Tanya stayed out of their way. She liked to watch them from the adjoining dining room, the way they crouched next to each other, checking out angles and curves.

"Before thirty your body looks gorgeous," explained Senya. "But if you haven't been taking care, you turn thirty and it all begins: injuries, strains, onset of arthritis. Next thing you know, you have to go for a hip replacement. Right, Oksana?"

Oksana was on the floor with her legs up in the air, a perfect forty-five-degree angle.

"And one, and two, and three," counted Senya.

Petya was there too, right in the midst of it. He sat on the couch, his feet in ratty slippers almost touching Oksana's arm. Tanya had called him aside, whispered how he was probably distracting the dancers. He said it was his home, and if they were distracted they could go someplace else.

"Abdominal muscles are especially important," said Senya. He got on his knees next to Oksana, inspected the angle. "Nope. That's too high." He lowered Oksana's legs to thirty degrees.

"I can't anymore," said Oksana. She dropped her legs and covered her face.

"Come on. Let's go," said Senya. "One, two, three."

"I told you I can't." Oksana got up from the floor.

"That's because you've been doing nothing," said Senya. "And eating crap."

"Look at yourself first," said Oksana. She picked up her toy dog and went to hide in Tanya and Petya's room. They heard her click the latch.

"She refuses to understand." Senya turned to Tanya. "It's different for male dancers. We don't gain weight the same way."

That night, Tanya cooked them a healthy dinner. Chicken breasts, broccoli. She didn't want Senya to think she was feeding them bad food.

"Is this all we're having?" Petya poked at his broccoli. She gave him a look, which he received stubbornly, blankly. He wanted fried potatoes and herring and a special salad with mayonnaise. And beer.

She went and got him a beer from the fridge. "Happy now?"

"Happy."

"Tanya should take ballet lessons," said Senya.

Petya chuckled and choked on his beer. "Ballet," he said, clearing his throat. He and Oksana exchanged sniggering looks.

"I think she would enjoy it," insisted Senya. "She's got a graceful step."

"Graceful step," muttered Petya. "You hear that, *starushka*? We're sending you to do ballet!"

Tanya stared at her plate and tried to remember that this was Petya, that he didn't mean it, that he actually loved her in his own morose, idiotic way.

"Don't listen to him, Tanechka," said Senya. "What does he know? He's a boorish little fool."

She looked up slowly. Senya was waiting for her, his eyes were waiting, they were saying: It's *me*. Don't you *trust* me?

And she did. There was nobody else she could trust.

It was at the beginning of the third week that it dawned on Tanya that the dancers weren't going anywhere, that they had money problems, that there was, in fact, a whole money situation going on. She overheard little hushed arguments; she saw Senya frowning over his checkbook. The four of them had stopped going out. Now at night, they watched Russian films, the ones that Petya had rented from Three Bears and copied illegally using his cousin's second VCR.

They had got into the habit of arranging themselves in a certain configuration around the TV; each had a permanent spot and the configuration never changed. Petya and Oksana were both on the floor: Oksana on her stomach, Petya with his legs crossed, all of his remote controls gathered in a heap before him.

Tanya and Senya were on the couch; it felt awkward at first to be so close together, but he eventually got her to relax—stretch out and rest her head on his lap. Nobody seemed to care. Not even Petya. They were all dancers, all used to each other by then. Senya ran his fingers through Tanya's hair, massaged her neck. She told herself it didn't mean anything. It had nothing to do with her personally. It was just Senya, creative, uninhibited. Day after day it continued and then she didn't know what to think. Sometimes, during funny moments, she looked up at him and they laughed together. And there were other moments when his fingers tentatively and stealthily touched her face.

One evening after dinner, Senya sat at the table looking through the Sunday paper. Tanya was finishing up in the kitchen; she could see him from there, tracing inky listings of the help-wanted section.

"Tomorrow we're going to the Pittsburgh Ballet," said Senya.

"You are?" said Tanya. It wasn't really a question; she just felt like responding to his voice.

"To see if we can get a job for Oksana. Here, it says, Liberty something."

"Is that East Liberty?" Tanya said worriedly. East Liberty was a rough neighborhood.

"I know where it is," called out Petya. He was in the living room, reading about real estate.

"He knows," Senya said, entering the kitchen. His palms were stained with print, and he held them up to Tanya. He had a small smudge on his cheek too; she pointed it out. He turned his cheek to Tanya, as if she could, with her bare fingers, take care of the ink.

The next day Senya and Oksana went to the Pittsburgh Ballet. At dinner, Oksana said she'd had an interview and later watched a class. Nobody had offered her a contract.

"They said I can come to the classes."

"You should," said Senya.

"They are terrible," said Oksana. "Girls just stand there slack, and the teacher doesn't correct them."

"It's a different system," said Senya. "Anyway, I'm sure the troupe itself is very good, and that is what's important, Oksana, getting a contract with the troupe."

"A system?" said Oksana. "Don't talk to me about systems."

Tanya listened, embarrassed and strangely satisfied. They had been quarreling a lot lately. And Petya was quietly gloating too; he'd never liked Oksana.

Oksana went to three more classes that week, and each night it was like that.

"If that's how they teach ballet, then I don't know," she said on Thursday.

"That's not the right attitude," said Senya. "*Learn* from them. Take from them everything you can. If they see you're good, they'll give you a job."

"Nobody's giving me a job," snapped Oksana.

"Because you're not trying. They see the attitude."

"Shut up already with your attitude," said Oksana. "Nobody likes American ballet. Except for inept dancers, like yourself, who can't do good jumps."

"Inept?" said Senya.

"Yes! And everybody in Las Vegas knew."

They didn't speak for the rest of the night. Tanya wanted to be with

Senya, wanted to take Senya's hand, show him that she was on his side. But Petya led Senya away, probably to the bowling alley, where his cousins drank and said harsh things about women. Oksana started the *Caviar* tape. It couldn't be true what she had said about Senya. He was beautiful, he could jump. And even if he couldn't, it didn't matter, he was Senya.

On Sunday morning at breakfast, Senya said he was going to Montreal. He had to see his adoptive family; there was some business concerning his immigration status. He would leave first thing Monday morning, come back in a couple of days. Oksana was to wait for him in Pittsburgh.

From that little announcement Tanya concluded that the adoptive family didn't know about Oksana, and this made her happy. She had big plans for this Sunday, had talked Petya into driving to the house with a waterfall, a little road trip, with apple cider and a picnic basket. She thought of all the secret gestures she and Senya would be able to exchange.

But after breakfast Oksana and Senya started fighting. They went into Tanya and Petya's bedroom to argue, and Tanya waited and paced the living room. Their trip arrangements were falling apart, and Petya, who didn't want to go in the first place, was now annoyingly happy. In the afternoon it started to rain and there couldn't be any more talk of picnics and road trips. Oksana and Senya came out of the bedroom. Senya left to pick up a rental car. Oksana slept.

On Monday and on Tuesday Oksana went to her class. Her mood didn't improve. She hated the instructors and now, with no Senya around, she had to travel to the theater alone. At night she called Senya in Montreal and afterward cried. On Wednesday she stopped going to the theater. "It's a waste of time," she said. "There are no professionals there." She watched talk shows and slept on the unfolded living room couch. In the evening, she refused to eat dinner and instead sat in the bedroom at Tanya's vanity, putting on elaborate, predatory makeup.

Something changed in the way Tanya felt toward Oksana. Without Senya, Oksana became an encumbrance, an obstacle. Every time she went into the bedroom with the phone, Tanya found a reason to linger behind the closed door. She listened deliberately and didn't feel ashamed for listening. She hated Oksana's voice, small and stifled, full of little hysterics. "You asked me to come with you," said the voice. "You know I hate it here." Tanya imagined walking in and taking the phone away from Oksana. What would Senya think? He'd hear the pause, the different pattern of breathing. She'd say, "Hi, it's me." Or something else. Of course there would still be Oksana to deal with. Oksana with her prickly little love, her mincing affectations. Still, Tanya didn't want her out. As long as Oksana was there, Senya would come back.

A week had gone by. "How long is she going to stay with us?" said Petya. "I'm not a millionaire to feed an extra mouth. I'm not a charity."

"Don't ask me," said Tanya. "He's your friend."

"Friendship is friendship. But hey, Grandma, this crosses all the boundaries. This is simply insulting."

"He's *your* friend," Tanya repeated. It pained her to pretend that Senya was a stranger to her.

The days dragged on and Senya wasn't coming back. Tanya sank into apathy. "You've been kind of dull lately, Grandma," said Petya. But Petya didn't bother her. He wanted the usual things: meals, an orderly apartment, their weekly trips to the Giant Eagle. They drove to Monroeville, to furniture stores. He wanted to look for a new couch. Petya liked big, pompous stuff, chairs and couches that promised a long, settled life. Tanya in her coat, huddled on the edge of a leather love seat, yawned, looked around. Everywhere was monstrous furniture: sticky leather, loud print, something with flowers.

"This one? Or maybe that?" Petya rushed among couches. "Are you paying attention, Tanya?"

"Isn't this all terribly expensive?"

"I want to get the real thing," said Petya, "something that will look good in the house when we get one."

This is what she wanted to tell him: She didn't care about the couch or the house. Didn't want them. Didn't want Petya. The long, scheduled life, all its stages charted in advance by a committee of relatives. She didn't want *that*. I might not be around to share a house with you, Petya.

"You don't know what the real thing is," she said instead.

That night he got sick with a cold and she had to care for him, care for his sore throat. She stood in the kitchen boiling milk in a small pan and thinking about Senya.

They would have to move away, thought Tanya. Pittsburgh wouldn't do. Perhaps they would settle in Montreal. Somebody else would have to bring Petya his boiled milk with honey and a dash of mineral water. Tanya imagined herself in Montreal. She would dress smarter there, let her hair grow longer and wear it in a French braid. She'd get a job at some kind of office.

Senya had been gone for two weeks.

The milk began to boil. She turned it off and kept standing there, rocking slightly and aching.

"What's wrong with you?" Petya said, stepping in front of her. He wanted his milk. "What are you? Sleepwalking?"

The picture in her head got blurry: Montreal and Senya; her hair in a braid; she would have to learn French . . . "It's nothing," she said to Petya, and walked out of the kitchen.

He came back on Friday, early in the evening. Tanya had just returned from work and Petya wasn't home yet. She heard him from the kitchen: a knock on the door, the rustling of the coat, Oksana's little squeal. Oksana hadn't told anyone he was coming. Tanya stayed where she was; she didn't want to watch them together.

"Hello, Tanechka," Senya said, coming into the kitchen moments later.

"We didn't expect you," she said, and stopped, realizing it sounded wrong. "I mean it's great that you're here. We just didn't know. How are you?" She was stumbling.

"Good," he said brightly, and she heard something smooth and fake in it. He wasn't looking at her, was looking instead at the window, at the stove, at the pages of the week-old *Pittsburgh Post-Gazette* on the counter. "How are you guys?" he said. "How is Petya?"

"As usual," said Tanya. Her voice was sinking and she was suddenly dull, an old housewife in the kitchen. "Everything is as usual."

Back in the living room, Oksana emitted a polite little cough, as if to say, Your assistance is required here, Senya. He said, "Just a minute," and ducked out of the kitchen. He didn't return.

Forty-five minutes later Petya came home from the office, and they had dinner with the special Canadian beer that Senya had brought from Montreal. Very brown and bitter. He'd had a good time there in Montreal. The immigration business was settled; his surrogate family had missed him; he'd gone to see a hockey game.

Tanya took a sleeping pill and went to bed early. She said she had a headache, which was partially true. In the middle of the night she woke up and thought what a fool she was. Everything in her life was imaginary. She grasped at the tiniest signs of flirtation: a pause, a gesture, a tenuous smile. She pasted those together, convinced herself she had something whole. In the end, it was always a fluke, a delusion. She was invisible again. Next to Tanya, Petya was asleep and snoring, and she cried quietly until the tears exhausted her. All of her emotions were now spent.

But the next morning Senya took Oksana to the Greyhound station. It was a Saturday and he was sending her to Philadelphia. Oksana, her shoulders rigid with anger, had repacked her black trunk. She hugged Tanya and Petya like it was a formality. She thanked them, but there was something defiant in that too, as if she thought they were kicking her out.

"Should have done it a long time ago," Petya said when Senya and Oksana were gone.

"But why?" said Tanya.

Petya shrugged. "Got tired of her whiny ass?"

And just like that, Tanya had hope again. An idiot, she called herself, but the hope was already there, ringing in her ears, rippling before her eyes. She needed Petya to leave for a while, needed time to collect her thoughts. She tried to think of an errand for him, but Petya wouldn't move. Finally one of his cousins called, something about a car, a rusted muffler.

She was alone when Senya returned. He dropped in a chair, rubbed his eyes.

"Tired," he said. "All this driving."

She didn't know how to start, so she asked, stupidly, about Oksana. Senya said that Oksana would be all right in Philadelphia, that Mickey would take care of her.

"I'm sorry," said Tanya.

"Don't despair, Tanechka."

She suggested he have something to eat or take a nap, although she didn't really want him to sleep, she wanted to be with him like this, talking. Something important had to be said while it was just the two of them.

"That's okay, Tanechka. I need to head back."

"Back? Back to Canada?"

"To Montreal. I've got a job there."

"Dancing?"

"No, at a bank. Anyway, where is that bastard Petya? I want to say goodbye before I go."

"Don't," she said. "Please don't go yet." She looked down at her feet and waited for him to understand, her face turning excruciating crimson.

"Tanechka," said Senya. "You're one terrific girl."

He sat across from her, polite and regretful. Not a dancer. A clerk at a bank. Your balance has been exceeded. Nothing else would be said, she understood, no matter how long the two of them sat like this together, no matter how long she waited. She was still for a while, taking shallow, labored breaths, trying to deal with this final disappointment. Then she went to get the phone and the cousin's number.

That night, after Senya left, she found herself alone with Petya for the first time in many weeks. The apartment felt dead, as if some devastating energy had come and shaken it. Tanya sat in the dining room, her shoulders hunched. There was laundry to do and a meal to prepare.

"Oh, so good!" Petya said stretching. "So good when all the guests go home. What's for dinner, Tanya?"

She said, "I don't know," and started crying. I'm so tired, she kept repeating, so tired.

He was startled to see her cry like that; she almost never did. He came over and gently touched her shoulder. "That's okay," he said, "I know you're tired. They were here for a month. Longer even. Please, what do you want, Tanyusha? Do you want to order Chinese for dinner?"

She continued to cry, now because it was so unlike Petya to be gentle, and because it didn't make her love him any more. And yet she knew this would go on. This was what she had, what she would always have. The long succession of meals and couches and rooms, the sleepy murmur at the dinner table. And the slow, insipid feeling, swathing her, erasing her from the inside. She was wise and old enough to know that in the long run people didn't change.

"*Nu starushka*, stop this silliness," said Petya. "Come summer we'll drive to Montreal. Would you like that? We'll let Senya entertain us."

She nodded okay and tried to wipe her tears. She gave him her soft, reassuring smile. He was good and clueless. Come summer he would forget both Montreal and Senya. They both would forget.

The Photograph

HOWARD LUXENBERG

IT IS A STRANGE FEELING to see yourself paired in a photograph with the deceased. The dead man is my late uncle Jake. In the photo we are on the broad green lawn, by the arboretum, a trellis of wild roses serving as backdrop. I am in a tux with houndstooth tie and cummerbund; Uncle Jake is in a pale blue evening gown, a Dior, I believe. He has an arm draped over my shoulder in avuncular bonhomie. We are holding cigars and staring at the camera, mugging for it. One thin dark shadow creeps across the lawn at our feet. From the flagpole, I would guess. It's late afternoon in the photograph.

I can see the spot now, through the library windows. It's pretty much the same. The grass and the roses are paler in the sharp light of noon. The library is the only two-storied room in the house, so I'm sitting in the leather wing chair to compensate, I guess, for the vastness of this internal space. I like the library, but only if I'm in this chair. This is the room that most impresses guests. "I would kill for this room," a literary friend of Father's confessed once, and promptly fell into a thoughtful silence in which, I swear, she was working out exactly whom she would have to kill for this room to become hers. The wall facing the arboretum is mostly windows, twenty feet tall and paned. The three remaining walls are books, each tunneled by a door, and in one case a fireplace. (We once played Cask of Amontillado in that fireplace; I stood inside it while my brothers bricked me in with books until my screams brought Mother.)

You'll want to know about Jake's evening gown and his death. I'll get to that. Right now I want to tell you, selfishly, about how I feel seeing myself in this photograph. Strange is too vague. I feel out of place, as if I had worn the wrong clothes to a party. Dressed up when everyone else was casual. Or maybe the reverse: I imagine death is a more formal place than this. Still, that's not quite it. The picture looks to me like one of those marvels of modern special effects, where some of the characters are live actors and some are cartoons. I am the live actor, Jake is the cartoon. We're from two different worlds now. I can't quite explain it. Go find a picture of yourself with someone you love who's dead. You'll see what I mean.

Jake is the youngest of my father's three brothers. In the picture, he is in his forties. He is wealthy, like my parents, like all his brothers. Balzac said that behind every great fortune is a crime. The crime behind ours is the Civil War. The Blue and the Gray: we outfitted the Blue. Millions of shoddy, overpriced uniforms that lasted barely long enough for their owners to die in. Afterward we could afford to make better uniforms and price them fairly. We diversified into commercial uniforms: the grease monkey under your car is probably wearing one of our coveralls. That's all sold now, and invested. We live off the return.

Mother took Jake's death stoically, but hard. "He was like a sister to me," she admitted in an unguarded moment. Mother was a middle child, sandwiched between two boys. When she left home to marry Father she exchanged one barracks for another. Then she bore four boys, so that all her living relations were male. It must have been lonely for her, I realize now.

She so forgot herself with Jake that she had had a long confiding chat with him about her menopause. "I'm fine one moment, and the next I'm basting in my own juices."

"Yes. It's hell on silk. It's never quite right after you've sweated it. They're old-fashioned, but have you tried arm guards?"

"I want a girl." Mother expressed her desires in simple imperative sentences, the desire and its anticipated fulfillment joined. Had she wanted light, she would have said simply "I want light" in much the same tone as Jehovah's "Let there be light." In either case, there would be light. I don't mean she was spoiled or capricious, or that she expected to be waited on in her desires. "I want a girl" meant that she was about to embark on the process of adopting one; that she would overcome all obstacles with the firmness of her resolve and the resources at her disposal; and that her resolve and her resources were considerable.

"A servant?" Father misunderstood.

"No. Of course not. A girl of our own. A daughter."

"Oh."

"We'll have to adopt. You don't think I'm serious. I've thought about this."

"Okay." I have seen Father adopt this strategy before. The quick acquiescence to something of enormous moment, so that the burden of raising the obvious objections falls suddenly on the proposer.

Mother seemed not to have heard him. "Wouldn't it be nice to have a little girl?"

"Okay. Do it."

"Don't you want to think about it?"

"It's okay. Go ahead."

"We're talking about a person here. A change in our life."

"A daughter, to be specific. It's okay."

"You're bluffing. You don't think I'm serious. You think this is some postmenopausal burp or something. I'm serious. Don't pull that 'it's okay' shit with me."

"What shit? You want to adopt a girl. We need a coxswain for the family shell. Just make sure she's petite and not afraid of the water."

I didn't exactly witness this scene, of course. I'm imagining it, based on what I know of my parents' style of arguing. When we were growing up we used to Indian wrestle with Father. When we were very young, he would beat us by failing to counter our exertions, so that our own exuberance would throw us off balance. By the time we learned this stratagem we had moved on to other forms of competition.

Mother insisted we all come to dinner, and there she broke the news.

"You're going to have a sister." Unlike her desires, which were delivered in the imperative, her declarations always had a faint undertone of the interrogative.

I said, "You're pregnant? I thought . . ."

Mother saved me. "I am. Past menopause. We're adopting. Try to behave while we're in the process. You're the evidence that we're capable parents."

"Better go black market in that case." I don't remember who said this; it doesn't matter. We bantered about the unsuitableness of one or another of us as "evidence."

"Can't any of you be serious? I'm talking about your sister." Mother rose from the table at this point, as if she were going to propose a toast.

"To sister." I raised my glass.

"To sister." My brothers joined me. I think Father wanted to, but he knew better. Mother glared at each of us in turn. A look of such contempt, of such disgust, that it froze us in our spots. She left the table and did not return with dessert.

I'd seen this look before. It was Thanksgiving. The big dining room table groaning with food so perfect it looks lacquered. Pride of place goes to two huge turkeys, glazed to brown perfection. On their legs are these incredible lace doilies. I have no idea what they are called; you see them on rack of lamb. But these are more elaborate, they look like something you'd find in a poultry Victoria's Secret. This must be what Jake is thinking too, because when Mother hands him the carving knife and fork, and asks him to do the honors, he pauses. He stares at the turkey nearest him, draws our attention to it. He shakes his head. He puts the carving knife down. "I can't do it." Then he brightens. He grabs a leg in each hand and pulls them ever so gently apart. "But I'd love to take it upstairs and fuck the stuffing out of it."

Mother gave Jake a look of such withering contempt that it spawned its own name. After that Thanksgiving, whenever Mother got that look, we would caution each other: "Watch out for Mother: she's got that fuck-the-turkey look in her eyes."

On those occasions when he must dress up, Uncle Jake wears only women's clothes. No makeup, no wig. He doesn't shave his legs. I asked him why. "I like them. Besides, it puts everyone else at their ease; makes them less defensive. See, Ty, everyone's worst social fear is humiliation. They realize that any humiliation that befalls them will pale in comparison, and they are put at ease." It was true; I never went to a bad party with Jake.

I liked to hang around Jake at parties because he attracted women. The debs, burnished bronze by the sun, mouths full of perfect white teeth, faces flush with daiquiris and yearning. Or so I imagined. The bravest would leave her clutch and approach Jake, as if on a dare.

"Hi, I'm Sandy." A hand offered at the end of a straight arm.

Jake takes the hand, which is expecting to be shaken, and brings it to his lips. "I'm Jake. Pleased to meet you, Sandy." Then the inevitable compliment. (And why not? Sandy is beautiful, or at least pretty; charming and willing to be charmed, dressed so as to elicit an honest compliment.) "You look stunning. The earrings, the earrings are perfect."

This creates a certain confusion in Sandy, who must, she feels, return the compliment. The self-possessed ones bring it off without a hitch: "You look perfect yourself."

If she says this with a wry smile, and doesn't convulse into girlish laughter, I find myself smitten.

The other debs walk over and Sandy introduces them.

They are dying to ask. What? They don't know exactly. They want an explanation. If you are disfigured, or lacking a limb, people want to know why. You owe us an explanation.

"This is Tyler."

Most of us here are Tylers. But it's my given name as well.

"Ty." I correct him. "Just Ty. Ty Tyler."

Again the straight arm, dangling a hand, from Sandy. I shake it. I am not my uncle.

"You're wondering, where do I shop?" Jake always meets their expectations obliquely. "The S_____ shop." (I can never remember the name, and besides, it changes.) "The first visit is always the most difficult. They have to be brought up to speed. 'What size? Who's it for?' the clerk asks. 'Size twelve. For me.' There's usually a standoff at this point, although the better New York shops take it in stride. But in this case it's a first, because the clerk repeats herself. Brightens actually. 'Who's going to wear it?' I'm such a kidder, she thinks.

"'I am. I'm going to wear it.' Now she's flustered. She's looking for a catch, a way out. She sees one. 'Are you from one of those TV shows?' She's looking over my shoulder for an accomplice. 'What is this?'

"This is a man, attempting to buy a gown, to wear to his nephew's wedding. This doesn't happen very often, but it's happening now. It takes a little getting used to. The better shops offer their customers a little sherry. Perhaps you could join me in a glass."

"Would you like a drink? Can I get you a drink?"

Sandy wants a drink, or wants, rather, to accept his offer of hospitality, but doesn't want to stop the story.

I say: "I'll get drinks. Daiquiris okay?"

Jake continues: "I say to the clerk, 'I do this all the time, but you don't. I'm discerning, but I won't waste your time. I'd like to spend about two grand, but if we see something extraordinary, more is okay. Okay?' Sometimes the mention of money helps ground them."

Sandy's look says her gown cost considerably less than two grand. Jealousy or awe? I like Sandy. Let it be awe.

I said I'd get drinks but I don't. I stay to watch the rest of Sandy's reactions.

Look in vain for some defining instant that set Jake on his course of wearing dresses. Some childhood humiliation. Some adolescent misadventure. If you must have a reason, imagine this: Jake is thirteen, and is dressed as a girl for a costume party. The young lady of his current desire is disarmed by his sheep's clothing; a brief and poignant sexual encounter ensues—well, you get the picture: dresses are lucky for Jake. It never happened.

We are at the funeral home, making the arrangements. The pressing issue is this: what is the corpse to wear? A dark funerary suit, of course. I was sent to Uncle's pied-à-terre to retrieve the mortuary togs. I wanted to loiter among his private papers. I didn't. I went straight to his closet, mindful of my purpose. Forget black: there wasn't a suit of any color. Nothing but dresses, not even a pantsuit such as a smart young female broker might wear to a weekend lunch with a client. I reported back the news.

"Well, we'll close the coffin." Mother, ever the practical one, to the funeral director.

"As you wish. But he still has to wear something."

I was dying to ask why. I imagine the thought of being naked at his own funeral would have pleased Jake. Of course in that case he would have wanted an open casket.

"We'll have a suit made." It fell to Mother to enforce the proprieties. She swam the English Channel as a younger woman; getting a suit made in a day for a dead man didn't seem like much of an obstacle. She was reduced, after a dozen calls, to complaining that nowadays there were a few things money couldn't buy.

"Just put him in the Halston and close the damn casket." My Father.

The Halston cost four or five grand, and I knew mother intended to auction it for charity. She had always thought it needlessly extravagant and the auction was the chance to redeem it in her eyes. She wasn't about to stick it in the ground.

"Not the Halston."

"What then? Just panty hose and a bra?"

"The Halston's a red herring. Face the issue: is he going to be buried as a man or a woman?"

"He's a man. We can't do anything about that. The issue is his clothing."

"Had he left instructions, he would have insisted on a dress. Probably the Halston."

"We would have a judge vacate that request."

"Probably not." My brother, one of several family lawyers, corrected Mother.

The funeral parlor has recessed lighting, like an airplane's. How appropriate. The funeral director is an unctuous man smelling of too much aftershave. Polo, in our honor. Jake would have called him on it.

"May I make a suggestion?" The funeral director is addressing Mother.

"No." Then to me: "Get one of your suits."

"Won't fit." And not fitting.

Mother glares at each of us in turn: me, my brother James (the lawyer of the unfavorable legal opinion), Father, Polo the funeral director. Finally at Jake. The "fuck-the-turkey" look.

Mother swam the Channel from Calais to Dover, recapitulating a journey her ancestors had made shortly after 1066. They used boats. Six hundred years later a branch of her family crossed the Atlantic, starved, froze, endured, and planted their family on New World soil. The family flourished: it sprouted farmers and ministers; then judges, statesmen, physicians, bankers, and the occasional black sheep. It was a predominantly male line: some anomaly in the sperm or the conjugal habits yielded mostly men. I have three brothers. Father, as I've said, has three brothers. Father likes the idea of adopting a girl because the eight of us—he and his brothers, me and mine—could crew a family shell, but we lack a coxswain. A petite girl would be perfect.

"We are adopting a child, not a part of a boat." Mother.

But I see what my father sees: eight sturdy Tylers, two generations at the oars, average weight 205 pounds, ruddy with exertion, pulling together to the cadence called by a porcelain-complexioned girl, her ponytail gathered in a silver clasp. He sees it like a picture, gilt-framed, above the mantel, emblematic of everything he hopes we are.

You would think it a simple thing for a wealthy, connected family to adopt a child. Mother chooses an agency specializing in Asian children, because she's been advised the process is less complicated. But my parents learn at the adoption agency that they are old.

"How old are you?"

Mother sees the trap: "Old enough to raise a child." She is not used to being a supplicant; she doesn't know the forms.

The agency woman, young, heavy, frowns. "The ideal candidate is between thirty and forty. Studies show . . ."

Mother waves her off, but the agency woman continues her theme.

"Have you the energy to keep up with an active child? Most people think these children are docile, especially the girls, they've seen too many bad movies with that polite Oriental stereotype. But children are children. Little children are particularly active."

"Oh. I'm so glad you told me. I thought we'd just put her in the display case. It worked so well with my boys." Mother's anger is formidable. The mercy she generally shows the world ceases to flow; in its place a laser-guided vitriol searches for its mark. "How many children have you raised?"

"I have two kids."

"That's not what I asked. How many have you raised? How many have reached adulthood?"

"What?" The agency woman does not understand.

Mother presses: "How many? How many adults?"

"My children are four and six."

"Mine are twenty-two, twenty-four, twenty-seven, and thirty. Adult, alive, healthy, courteous, responsible. When you can say the same, in twenty years, if at all, you can pass judgment on my fitness as a parent."

Father is watching this with growing mortification. She's tipped the boat here. No coxswain will come of this exchange.

Later, in the privacy of the elevator, he says: "You certainly showed her."

"Do you think she hates us because we're white?"

"No, she hates us because we're rich."

Father had repaired a few breaches in his day, and was assessing the damage. Mother's harangue, while sharp, was essentially defensive. She had made no accusations or disparagements. That was good. It would play well when repeated and the tone declawed. He was already imagining the conversation with the adoption worker's supervisor. Mother's anger would become upset—not a calculated attack, but an overflowing from an internal wound. He was envisioning a hierarchy he would ascend, and with each step in that ascension his wife would become more the aggrieved party, until at the apex he would be face-to-face with someone as reasonable as he was. If not, at least then he would be free to lock horns with his adversary without feeling like a bully.

Not fit? Not fit? You could look on a globe, any globe, a small cheap one, and see the English Channel, a visible blue distance, and she had crossed it. Not fit? You could stand on the moon and see that separation from a quarter of a million miles away. Not fit indeed.

We are not a family of athletes. Rather we are perseverance incarnate, and sometimes that takes the form of athletics. So we tend to run and to row and to swim, activities too boring for real athletes. Our perseverance may be the virtue we make of a certain dullness, the reassurance we find in repetition. Mother with her oars of flesh, sculling across the Channel; father, uncles, brothers, plying our wooden oars. Sisyphean sports. Unwatchable sports.

Hardly Aphrodite. Mother standing in the foam at Dover. Her arms and thighs thick. A smile, but her eyes vague with fatigue. Her lips swollen and cracked. Splotches of Crisco, all that remains of her coating. As ugly a picture as she has ever taken. The record of the event.

I won't take you through all the stations of the cross, which is how Father began to refer to the adoption process. We'll just fast-forward to the meeting with the agency head. The crisis that morning was what to wear. Normally, this is not a problem; we are well versed in what is appropriate for all occasions. If you were visiting a self-important bureaucrat on official business you wore a conservative blue suit and a rep tie, something that would flatter his sense of solemn importance. Nothing too fancy, nothing Italian, nothing that would work against the phony seriousness of the occasion. But because we are wealthy, Father was afraid such a suit might take on an intimidating connotation. The sun was beginning to grill up a hot, unpleasant day. Father decided to wear the blue suit, but to carry the jacket and loosen the tie: proof that he could feel the heat just like the next man, suffer it in a democracy of men made equal by common sweat.

Mother eschewed her jewelry for this occasion; not even a watch, since time as well as money was the enemy. The thought of dyeing her hair had crossed her mind; she quickly obliterated the thought. She wore the most sensible-looking shoes she could find.

The meeting was in one of those ponderous modern buildings. Its architecture matched its purpose: monolithic blocky concrete with some whimsical touches that were intended to signal a humanity it didn't possess and could only guess at. It had guessed wrong.

The elevator hoisted them to their appointment. The director of adoption services was a thin black woman with a military carriage. She wore a single strand of pearls, identical to the ones Mother had left at home. (According to Father, it was all Mother could do not to call home and make sure hers were still in the jewelry case.)

Mrs. Starks did not offer to shake hands. She indicated they should sit in the two chairs facing her desk. There was nothing on her desk, not even a phone. An index card with the word *in* on it was taped to the corner. Father was recalibrating his opening remarks. He decided to let Mrs. Starks go first.

"Mr. and Mrs. Tyler. Repeat after me: 'I am fifty-six; Li is two.

When Li is twelve, I will be sixty-six. When Li is eighteen, I will be seventy-two.' You see the problem?"

Father says: "I see the prejudice."

The thing is, people don't wither under clever retorts, like they do in the movies. They just keep going. Father knows this; his remark escaped the usual vigilance he held over his speech.

"'When Li is eighteen, I will be seventy-two.' Just say it. I'm serious. Just say it."

Mother said: "When Li is eighteen, I will be seventy-two. When Li is one hundred and eighteen, I'll be one hundred and seventy-two. I'm sorry. I understand your point. I just don't agree with it."

"I'm sorry. I'm sorry you don't agree with it. Don't you want what's best for this child, even if what's best isn't you?"

The meeting seesawed back and forth, and grew less heated. Each side made small conciliatory gestures to the other's fundamental decency. They parted on decent terms, but without a child.

It was Jake who found May. "I got you a little girl. She needs a little work. She's four years old. May. May is her name." Mother was visiting him in the hospital, where he lay ravished by chemotherapy. Thin, without hair, he looked like a skull over which a nylon stocking had been stretched. Mother did not understand at first. "Her name is May. Your daughter."

How had he managed this, when all her resources, all her perseverance, had failed? She said simply, "How?"

"I cheated, of course. Still, the adoption, when you and John sign the papers, will be legal."

"How?"

"A million dollars and a future draft pick."

Later Mother would say he made some sort of deal with the devil. His arbitrageur of choice.

Mother summoned me and my brothers to a dinner, to meet May. Mother had prepared an elaborate Chinese meal, which I learned was actually Vietnamese. We ate in the formal dining room, which dwarfed the spring rolls and lemon chicken as it had never dwarfed the hams and turkeys.

"May escaped Vietnam on a boat not much bigger than this table. And less sturdy." Mother intended by this remark to enlist our sympathy for our new sister. It wasn't necessary: we were long past the age of tormenting the newest family members. May's problem would come from the opposite direction: we were all old enough to be her father, and she would be smothered in an avalanche of affection.

Jake died while I was away at college: my junior year abroad, in England. I meant to come home sooner. But we believe this of those we are fond of: they will last forever, or at least as long as we need them. I was old enough to know better and should have come sooner.

I flew first class. Jake would have approved. "You're rich; that's the simple fact. You didn't earn it, so you don't have to apologize for it. You're just a winner in life's lottery. It's a state of grace; live gracefully. Do good if you see the opportunity, but include yourself. I can't stand these rich folks who ride around in Fords and fly tourist to prove that money hasn't spoiled them. Money spoils you. Bear it like a man."

The stewardess was solicitous. People often ask the time of me, or directions. I have an approachable demeanor. It was Jake who pointed this out to me. We were in New York, walking down Fifth Avenue. A striking young lady stopped us. "Do you have the time?" Later I thought of a dozen clever responses; but I was surprised and answered honestly: "Yes." I looked at my wrist. "It's three twenty." She paused, thanked me, and was gone. Jake saw me puff up a bit—like I said, the woman was striking—and she had picked me to ask the time of. I was seventeen. Jake said, "Easy, Tiger. All she wanted was the time. And you look like the sort of decent guy who would give it to her without making her fish in your pants for a pocket watch." Seeing my wounded look, he added, "Sometimes the decent guys get the beautiful girls; it just takes them a little longer. This isn't the movies." The next day I received a package. A pocket watch and a note: "A more generous uncle, in a different century, would have sent you the girl."

The stewardess had that British knack of serving without being the least bit servile. "Going home for the holidays, Yank?" My drinking had made her familiar. It was curious.

"No. A funeral."

"So sorry."

"Yeah. Me too."

"Someone close?"

"My favorite uncle. Taught me all the manly arts. Cards, pool, playing the horses, drinking, smoking."

She patted my arm. The wine, and the drone of the flight, made me sleepy. I dozed.

This is how Jake died: slowly, with frequent bouts of hope, from pancreatic cancer. There was nothing particularly meaningful about Jake dying from this, rather than living, or dying in some other fashion. The nurses adored him; it was like the debs all over again. He was witty to the very end, for them. To Mother, he said, in a lucid moment of despair, "Do you believe this shit?" He was referring to the accoutrements of the final stage of his illness—the Levine tube, the catheter, the IV.

In the end, it was the Halston. You knew it would be. It fit poorly on his wasted body. We closed the casket. For Jake's sake, and for ours. He would not have wanted to be seen that way. He looked pathetic in it. But not everything that looks ridiculous is wrong.

Father commissioned a portrait of the Tylers crewing their eight. It is, when you get down to it, a portrait of Jake. He isn't in it; his spot is empty; his oar is shipped. The painter has softened May somewhat; you have to look very hard to see the disfigurement. Her face is shaded by a baseball cap, her black hair spraying out the back. Mother has given it pride of place: it hangs over the mantel in the library.

The Anthropology of Sex

MARTHA McPHEE

SHE WAS THE AGE I am now when I had an affair with her husband. I thought of her as all grown up—sagging flesh and a soft middle-aged body. Her cheeks drooped. There were smile lines about her mouth. Her age, thirty-seven, seemed impossibly far away and her life like a disease I didn't worry about catching since it only afflicted the old. I was nineteen and by the time I was her age I'd have my life figured out. I'd have children and a husband and a career, money in the bank, stocks, bonds, and my sister, Serena, living not too far away. I'd have everything we were promised by growing up American. And that future floated out there in my distance like an island. I didn't think about it much but I knew it would be there as surely as I knew that Bora Bora and Hawaii were out there, somewhere, with their palm trees and sapphire-blue skies and warm pacific oceans.

I had always wanted to have an affair. When Serena and I were little we invented a game, which we played with some kids down the street. The game was a variation on House and we called it Normal Day. In the make-believe we were all married to each other, leading normal lives—shopping, charging, drinking, fucking—and at the same time we were all having affairs. In the world of Normal Day, the trick was not to get caught. Like any affair there was an exciting period when no one knew and the secret was hidden tightly by the lovers.

Serena and I adored those words. We'd lie in bed and talk late into the night about Affairs and Lovers and Rendezvous and Trysts and Adultery and Betrayal. Any word that implied sexual deception. We tossed the words into the dark where they'd hang suspended long enough for us to muse over them, absorb them, make them ours. My sixth-grade English teacher had always said that if you use a word three times it's yours. Adultery, adultery, adultery.

The psychology was simple: Our mother left our father when I was four and Serena was six. She left him for Another Man (another term we loved—big and strong and tall and sexual). They had an affair and the affair broke our father's heart and the best explanation our mother had was that she had had to. She told us we would understand when we grew up and we wanted to grow up just so that we could understand. She said sex is too important, fundamental, the core. Sex, the word grew into enormous proportions. Every time I'd eat an apple to its core I'd think about the word, sex. SEX. Our mother left our father for the word. So Serena and I both aspired to affairs—noble aspiration that would lead us to a higher understanding and appreciation.

Her name was Gwen. Gwen, a solid middle-aged name. Her thighs were Jell-O-like. Her belly fleshy. (I look at my own body now and see hers, though of course I don't think of it so negatively anymore.) Thin strands of gray lined her hair. She was on her island, her Bora Bora. Half her life behind her, another half to go. (But the islands of the second half have less to do with perfection than with remedy.) God knows what she imagined her future to hold when she was a child. She was married to a very tall, dark-haired, blue-eyed philosophy professor seeking tenure at a small Maine college. They had a house on a cove filled with lobster boats. They had two cars and plenty of food. They spent their summers in Scandinavia. He provided for her, though she had a job at an art museum in a bigger town not too far away. Her husband's name was Jack and Jack was fucking one of his students. He fucked her in his office. He fucked her in the back of his small car—awkward and uncomfortable because they were both so tall. Outside, a world of blue skies and a beach strewn with driftwood. Lobster boats doing their lobster thing. A few egrets and a few seagulls. He fucked her in cheap hotels and he even took her to Grand Rapids, Cincinnati, and Sioux City to conferences of philosophy professors so he could fuck her there—upstairs in their hotel suite while downstairs a pack of professors discussed Kierkegaard, Nietzsche, Merleau-Ponty, Freud. They wandered the lobbies importantly in their rumpled tweed jackets. Kierkegaard was Jack's philosopher. He would claim that, "my philosopher," as if he owned the man. She lay on the big king-size bed and waited in silk underwear that he had bought her special for the occasion.

Her name was Isabelle, spelled the French way because her mother had a fascination with the country and spoke the language fluently and spoke it to Isabelle as an infant so she would have a head start. And Jack liked that, it made him think of Isabelle as French and exotic. Of course, Isabelle am I.

Was this Gwen's Bora Bora, her Hawaii? I met her once, before the affair started, outside a newspaper store on a Sunday. Snow everywhere, so bright you had to squint, and the magnificent bells of the church. My hand slipped into hers as we were introduced. I remember her hand was so small and warm and I could feel the bones. She was shorter than I and her smile so innocent seeming it was as if a little girl were lost in her face.

On the king-size beds of all the hotel rooms I'd call Serena to tell her about the shabby curtains that actually weren't shabby but described that way seemed more appropriate for an affair. "What's it like?" she'd ask. She had never had an affair. She had already met Nicholas, the man she would marry. I felt older, wiser, for once, holding an experience that she would have to feed on.

"I've met the wife," I responded, and described her lost face.

"I mean the sex," Serena said with a nonchalance that pretended she was not that interested, though I knew she was.

"He's old," I answered, polishing my nails a bright and alluring red. The smell of the lacquer made me heady. "He's old so it takes a long time."

"*Takes*," she repeated. "Is that a good thing?"

"I think of Gwen," I confessed. "Of her at home missing Jack while I lie beneath him. Of her watching us." Out the windows the cities all looked the same—short buildings with short water towers and smokestacks, dreary gray weather. A cold river flowing between banks of concrete.

"The potential for so much destruction," Serena said. I thought of myself as a mighty bomb, a Daisy Cutter. I could hear her typing. She always had to work while talking to me, as if to prove that I was secondary—or at least not central—that she had so much else in her life besides me. She was an aspiring poet in New York City, with a few poems in a few good reviews, all of which made her proud. I could hear sirens racing down Broadway. She always stayed on the phone. Sometimes we could stay on the phone so long we'd have nothing left to say but we'd stay there all the same just so that we could hear each other breathe. "The destruction you would cause if you went downstairs to the conference and introduced yourself," she continued. "Go," she dared. I could see her magnificent eyes pushing me. She was forever lining me up to risk everything, as if it would prove something. Perhaps my love for her or perhaps the simple sister truth: that if I were crushed I'd need her all the more. I was almost tempted to go downstairs because we were just playing with these people's lives.

Serena came to college to visit so that she could meet Jack. He had lunch with us in the student pub, in a dark corner booth. He came late, his big hands nervously working the lettuce in his sandwich because he knew he was being appraised—funny (and endearing) to see such a grown man intimidated by a girl. Serena's laserlike blue eyes held him for a long time in a silent conversation. Of the two of us she's the pretty one—long auburn hair, medium height, a dimple that catches the light each time she smiles, making her whole face sparkle. She cares enormously for her clothes and style—even presses her collars. Ever since I can remember I've been aspiring to her style, but I'm too lazy and never get it quite right so I give up and wear jeans.

I wanted her to approve of Jack, wanted her to want him, wanted her to be jealous, wanted him to fuck her—could imagine us lying in bed together talking about what it was like. I thought of Normal Day, of how she would always find new kids to play the game and when she ran out of new kids she married us off to stars: Steve McQueen, Paul Newman, O. J. Simpson (many years before he killed his wife). Finally Jack blushed and tucked his head in a bashful way and smiled.

"He's too tall," Serena would say later, dismissing him. But now to him she lifted her left eyebrow. She could do that. When we were children she would say that she had double-jointed eyebrows. "Kierkegaard is fabulous on love," she said.

"You would know," he said. The energy was kinetic between us, little jolts ricocheting from her to him to me. "As a poet, that is, of course, you would know about love."

I hadn't understood yet, of course, that Serena and I were playing with each other's lives.

I am Gwen's age now, thirty-seven. This past summer my husband, Lucian, our son, Serena and her husband, Nicholas, and their three girls rented a beach house for the month of July on Popham Beach, not far from where I went to college. I have a fondness for going back to scenes from my past. I don't avoid them. I don't turn them into mythic spots never to be visited again. Instead I return. Returning makes me feel like not too much is gone.

I had been to this beach many times before. It is one of the only beautiful sand beaches in the state of Maine, since a state park preserves most of it. The house we rented was an old Victorian on stilts with a wraparound porch and a turret overlooking dunes thick with dune grass and plovers and the gorgeous expanse of beach. Islands float just offshore, two of them connected to the beach at low tide by sand spits. The north end of the beach curves to meet the mouth of the Kennebeck. It is a pristine mouth, untainted by industry, and wide and deep enough to hold the Navy destroyers flowing down to the Atlantic from the Iron Works in Bath. The mouth is, I imagine, almost as it was in 1607 when its banks were colonized by the first pilgrims to this country—a history that makes this region noteworthy and thus proud. Here I first kissed Jack, a warm May day with big cottony Maine clouds and the whole world smelling of pine and salt. His lips tentative at first as they found mine, as if asking if this were all right, then finding in my response the authority to be bold, reckless even. Other students lurked about on afternoon strolls, adding to the daring pleasure of that first kiss. Jack had driven me to the beach for a walk and though I knew we would kiss I pretended to know nothing.

Lucian and I had a new Audi. He had a new BIG job as an editor in chief. We were both editors. Serena hoped someday he'd publish her poetry, which so far had not been published by a trade publisher. He did not like her work. He thought it overly emotional and embarrassingly revealing, but he did not tell her that. She also owned a restaurant in New York City, a small restaurant that served just one or two fabulous dishes per night—whatever Serena's fancy chose, since she was also the chef. It was more a hobby than a serious profession, though she was a fine chef—another thing she could do that I could not. Whenever she went on vacation she closed the restaurant down. Even so, when she was in town, it was packed; she was good at making people wait for her.

Our boy, Hunter, was a year old. We had plenty of food and had recently started to acquire stocks. It was a bull market so we thought only of stocks, never bonds, and it seemed our horizon was long. Serena and Nicholas convinced us to buy Intel and AOL and Cisco. We convinced them to buy Sun Microsystems and Qualcomm. We all had Lucent and Amazon. Not much translated rapidly into a whole lot more. The sky was a wonderful pale blue with depth and even when it rained the days were beautiful. We called those days mysteries because each one would be different. It would never simply rain. Rather there'd be a fog so dense you could not see your own feet or thunder and lightning would appear from a clear blue sky. We'd sit on the porch and watch the weather like some people watch a movie—the lightning dancing across the water, then the beach, then the dunes, approaching us. But we were not scared. Not even the girls were scared, though they ran through the house screaming, until Nicholas told them to quiet down.

Serena's daughters are three, five, and seven and they look exactly like each other and exactly like her. Even Lily, the firstborn. "She looks nothing like you," I used to tease Nicholas, because an old wives' tale has it that firstborns always look like the fathers so that the fathers stick around. It's supposed to be a biological trigger that dates back millions of years, an early paternity test. "Lily looks rather like Lucian," he'd say, teasing right back.

"If Lily were Lucian's child she'd be a boy," I responded. Another old wives' tale says that if a woman doesn't have an orgasm she is more likely to have a daughter. (As it turns out, our mother had three boys with her second husband. *Sex is too important, fundamental, the core.* If everyone were having great sex would there only be boys?) Our child looks just like Lucian. Nicholas smiled that half smile of his that sits on his lips full of knowledge and irony. Sometimes it could seem there was a whole world behind Nicholas that we did not know, that had nothing to do with Serena. Sometimes I found myself almost wishing he had another family, some deviant choice. Just a simple wicked thought, of how much she would need me if . . . But for Serena, Nicholas's mystery only added to his appeal.

When I first learned I was pregnant with a boy Serena asked repeatedly what we were going to do—as if the two of us were having the child. She bought books on the subject, poring over the details of how to raise a boy, making the prospect of a boy both frightening and irresistible. "A little penis inside you," she kept saying. "The way I like it," I'd respond. Sometimes it did feel like the children were ours, we spent so much time together. Her daughters wore our clothes, saved by our mother for thirty years in mothballs in the attic of our childhood home—a reckoning of hers with the promise of our future, that it would be brighter than the past she gave us. Serena clipped back her daughters' hair exactly alike with ribbons, the way our mother had done with us. Sometimes as the girls played it was as if Serena and I were seeing ourselves all over again.

We watched the rain, sipping wine on the wraparound porch of our rented summer home. "I suppose we've arrived," Serena said, lifting her glass for a toast. The rain stopped just as suddenly as it started and a full red moon rose over a lighthouse on one of the islands, the beauty making us feel lucky.

"Suppose?" Lucian noted.

"The ship," I said, pointing to it. The ferry from Nova Scotia passed on the horizon, lit up like a miniature Baccarat crystal ship. And though it appeared each evening, seeing it again always seemed like a surprise.

"The crystal ship," Lucian said. He is a small smart handsome man, shorter than I, with a strong jaw and bright brown eyes, thick blond wild hair, and a sense of humor that ripples out of him like heat.

"Suppose," Serena repeated definitively with that coy coolness of hers. "We're all waiting, as they say, for our ship to come in."

"It passes us by beautifully," Lucian said. It was now so quiet that, except for the waves, you could almost hear the ship chugging along, almost see the passengers dancing beneath the dazzling stars.

"Oh Lucian," Serena sighed, tilting her head back and offering him a sort of challenging stare, a stare that asked him now, What's not perfect about your life? She sat on the arm of his chair, her fingers resting lightly on the jeans above his thigh.

But I ignored the way Serena looked at Lucian. She'd been flirting with Lucian since I first met him. In fact, it was part of the initial seduction—a story we always loved to tell, that she even told as part of her toast at our wedding. I loved it because it showed our unity, how we were inextricably woven together like threads of a fine fabric. But I suppose she loved the story because it illustrated her triumph.

I met Lucian at a party on New Year's Eve. He was sitting in a room filled with men. I liked the way he sat in the chair, as if he owned it, feeling quite comfortable there. I liked the wild nature of his hair, how he seemed not to care about it, and even so it made him look dashing; I liked that the people surrounding him laughed because of something he had said. I found Serena and brought her to the room.

"There's one man here that I want. Find him," I said. She did not need to study the room. She walked directly over to Lucian, interrupted his conversation, and began to flirt furiously—all bubbly smiles and enthusiasm, exuding charm and desire. Nicholas was there but he wasn't paying attention. Serena's flirtations were their aphrodisiac. "You've got to have some trick when you've been with the same person twelve years," they'd say. Nicholas was also shorter than I, with short hair and magnificent light blue eyes and long feminine lashes so dark it always seemed he wore mascara, though of course he did not. Though he doesn't look it, he is a conventional type, an investment banker who spends long stretches of his time in Asia merging telephone companies, the reason Serena can afford to shut down the restaurant whenever she chooses.

Serena flirted with Lucian for the rest of the night, but slowly, slowly I inserted myself until I could see that Lucian was quite confused, then hopeful about a pair of sisters. With a kiss at midnight I claimed him unequivocally.

Serena for serene, of course. And she was. A placid face at thirty-nine. No wrinkles. No signs of undue worry. She was my closest friend. My love, my life. "You're the love of my life," I'd say to her. "You're the love of my life," she'd say to me.

Indeed we hated each other's friends, always telling each other why each other's friends were horrible. Nicholas never really loved me, nor I him. He was suspicious of me, always afraid somehow I'd manage to cheat him out of something. For a long time Lucian would insist that Serena was poison—afraid, I suppose, that she'd cheat him out of something. "She's dangerous," he'd say. "You're just jealous," I'd say. Her defense against attack was flirting, and she flirted with Lucian, knitting Lucian into her—her big eyes on him, so intensely interested in every word he uttered. It never occurred to me that she would flirt for another reason, that her flirting could be dangerous, that it could cheat Lucian of me. Friends for Serena and me were enemies, capable of annexing the best part of our country.

As children playing Normal Day we sometimes fooled the others by having an affair with each other. We sneaked off and touched tongues. Lightly and quickly at first. Serena's tongue was warm and had texture. A little bland, but soft and deep. At first we touched tongues because she promised me five cents. Then simply because we liked the sensation. I wanted to disappear in her tongue, become her tongue.

The tide came in and out like breathing, revealing the sand spits so quickly the crabs didn't have a chance to hide—those sand spits like arms reaching out from shore to the islands, clutching them. Hawaii? Bora Bora? The gulls swooped down and devoured the crabs. Their carcasses lay strewn about the isthmus.

On one of the two islands stands a mansion in a grove of pines. A wealthy man from Boston built it for his wife. The house is an exact replica of an old colonial house on an island in the mouth of the Kennebeck that faces the island of the wealthy Bostonian. His wife had liked that house so he had copied it for her so that she could look at the one she admired while being inside its replica. Not long after the house was completed, the wife was killed in a boating accident in the Caribbean. They had one young boy.

We sat in chairs close to the sand and read the paper. Nicholas was in Asia for a two-day deal. "Getting Serious About Adultery: Who Does It and Why They Risk It," I read aloud, holding the paper above my face to shield my eyes from the sun—and as I read the headline of the article somewhere and for some reason I regretted it. Like when you read an article on cancer and then realize you wish you didn't know the details, start to fear you have the symptoms.

"An appropriate article for us," Serena said with that dismissive nonchalance of hers, that what-you're-thinking-isn't-as-important-as-what-I'm-doing attitude of hers.

"Let's go for a swim," Lucian said, and jumped up. "Coming, darling?" he asked, and I thought he meant me, but it was Serena he was speaking to. And then, as if he realized his mistake, his eyes darted to me with a please-come look. Serena jumped up and followed him. They dived into the water as if it were warm. Something ugly was gnawing its way into my mind. I tried to push it out. I have a tendency to destroy happiness with fears of all the terrible things that can go wrong. "An apocalyptic imagination" is how Lucian describes mine—my ability to see the worst-case scenario as a fait accompli.

On his blanket the baby slept, making clucking sounds. Serena's girls were jumping about at the edge of the water, building sand castles and making noise—like a force, some intense weather system—all dressed alike in red bathing suits with white polka dots. Ribbons in their hair. If they were my children I'd yank those ribbons out. I wondered about them, about their being three. They fought all the time with Lily as the leader, and I wondered what their secret world was filled with. Did they think yet about Bora Bora? Sometimes I'd spy them studying the island of the Bostonian, hoping to see his son walking over the bald rocky slope from the ocean to the house—seduced already by wealth and pain.

The thing kept gnawing inside me like those holes the girls were digging in the sand; when they're deep enough the walls cave in, keep caving in until water swamps the hole. Lucian loves me, he loves, he loves, I thought, as if I were trying to convince myself. We had just made love while Serena watched the baby. We said we were going for a walk, but I knew she knew what we were doing. He loves me. My cheeks still flushed. The light lit his hair, turning it golden; their heads bobbed as they swam far out. I could hear the high pitch of their laughter. I was too afraid and cold to swim as far out as they could. I remember understanding just then, at that particular instant, as water brimmed over the surface of my hole, that Serena wanted to have an affair with Lucian—knew it like you just know some things, perhaps something I should have known for a long time now. It seemed my stomach fell a great distance, as on a roller coaster, and I wanted to disappear, become impossibly small. Every nerve alive.

"What's wrong?" Serena asked. She stood above me. The cold saltwater dripped off of her onto me. She was wearing a one-piece black bathing suit—a sort of 1940s style, square across the hips, a little like shorts hugging her butt, a halter at the chest loosely holding her big breasts. Her auburn hair fell in tresses down her chest. She would never show her tummy after the girls were born. It was scarred with ugly purple and black stretch marks ripping across her pale pink flesh—still full and flabby. She had made me rub belly balm, gooey and smelly, on my stomach so that the same would not happen to me. Then like a shot I wondered, Has she succeeded, has Lucian fucked her?

"Nothing," I said.

"I know something's wrong," she said.

If I lose her I'll have nothing, I thought.

"Should something be wrong?" I asked, looking up into her face, behind which was the big bright blasting sun—there to sting my eyes.

Lucian dripped cold water over the girls, making them shriek with delight and run away from him so that he'd chase them. They loved being chased by him. Already, like their mother, they were master flirts. "He's our other daddy," they'd say, because Nicholas was so often on the road.

There are some things you just don't suspect. I filled up with dread. I don't really know why then and not earlier or later or never. It was July 14, 1998. Bastille Day. Sometime in the afternoon. I had just turned thirty-seven. I was sitting on a beach in Maine reading an article on adultery. I put the paper down and watched my husband as he came back from the girls and his swim—tanned, slender body, wild hair, seductive full-lipped mouth. Was he screwing my sister? Because screwing it would be—all the more delightful for them because they were screwing me. I looked at Serena with her dark Italian glasses and stylish black bathing suit—left eyebrow rising over the frame of the glasses. Of the two of us I have the better body. I'm taller, thinner, tighter stomach from so many sit-ups. I stood up briefly, pretending to get something, just to remind myself, to show my body off in the bikini.

But then I felt ridiculous and old and sat down again. "What does the article say?" she asked.

"Why is adultery appropriate for us?" I said, quoting the article, trying to hide snappishness. She could always tell instantly when I went sour.

"My little sister's having fantasies?" she said, dismissing my paranoia before I had a chance to own it fully. She smiled, it seemed a little too triumphantly—as if she understood perfectly what was on my mind and was quite happy to have it there: she in there in my mind, belly dancing across it. She has a large ribbon mouth and when she smiles it breaks open like a dream to reveal her perfect white teeth and the promise of her good humor, that she'll settle it on you. The Maine water rolled bitterly over my toes. "We love that word, Adultery," Serena said to Lucian, and winked at me, trying to pull me back in.

"Normal Day," he said, and bent down to kiss me. Our mother had said that sex was the barometer of a relationship; if you weren't having any the relationship was in trouble. Lucian and I had plenty of sex. The idea of their affair was swallowed up momentarily with Lucian's kiss. "I prefer not to think about my wife having affairs," he said. Sometimes I'd tell Lucian that I wanted to be the other woman instead of the wife and mother. Sometimes we'd pretend that I was.

I laughed and everything seemed right again. Serena snatched the paper, skimmed the article and began to quote from it. "The human animal is built to love more than one person at a time. . . . We have the neurocircuitry that can lead us to adultery. . . . The big mystery in evolutionary terms is what do women get out of it?" Then she began to laugh, fits of it. She is even beautiful when she laughs, breaking into shards of light like a fountain.

"For men it's about spreading their seed, for women it's about protecting their offspring," I said. "That's the big mystery," I said—and though I was being ironic it occurred to me that ever since I met Lucian I hadn't wanted to have an affair.

"What can women possibly get out of it?" Lucian said, sitting down behind me and pulling me close to him, wrapping his arms around me tightly until I felt thoroughly loved and protected. *In Normal Day the trick was not to let the others know.* Serena watched us, though I tried not to look at her.

"If women didn't get anything out of it, Lucian, there'd be no one for you to have an affair with," Serena said.

"Serena," I said, unable to hide my distaste.

"Oh come on you two. Monogamy is not natural. Even Canadian geese, long believed to be the only monogamous animals in the animal kingdom, are not actually monogamous." For fifteen years, as far as I knew, Serena had been faithful. "This article is just another ruse to oppress women, using evolution as an excuse." Or had she? "What about pleasure? What about the sheer delight of the touch, the fingers, of someone new? Think of all the fabulously rich men out there whose pretty wives are screwing their riding instructors, Princess Di for example—those little intrigues are certainly not to protect their offspring."

"Nicholas, for example," I said, referring to a fabulously wealthy man with a pretty wife. She knew what I meant. We always knew what each other meant. We could never escape each other, no privacy in our thoughts. "The inherent high in betraying," I said, and then asked her if she ever thought about Normal Day, holding her with my sharp accusing eyes. I could no longer feel Lucian behind me. Lucian disappeared.

"You had the affair," she snapped, referring to Jack. "I didn't."

I had written a paper on Abel Jeanniere for Jack's class and it had won a national prize. It was about the French priest's radical position on sex, argued in his book *The Anthropology of Sex*. As a theological anthropologist he saw his task as one of "interpreting love beyond the schemas and stereotypes of (male-female) 'natures' in the truth and freedom of personal relations." In essence, he was investigating sexuality in marriage and raising it to heights it had not achieved before in the Catholic Church. He was making sexual intimacy a human requisite, scorning the doctrine that sex is for procreation alone and the belief that conjugal love is the death of the spiritual life. To lay the groundwork for harmony between human sex and spiritual freedom was a major advance. "To be fully oneself," Jeanniere repeats again and again, "is to know that one is for the other." This idea elevated woman to meet man as his equal—one for the other. To flee from woman-as-flesh is like using her as flesh, and subsequent freedom and creativity will not escape the shadow of this negation. Jack led me to Jeanniere and during long office hours we discussed, dissected, and contemplated the priest's intentions and then I wrote my paper and then it won its prize.

Because of the prize (which involved cash and a trip to Asheville, North Carolina, to read the paper) I was, for a short time, famous on campus. My whole life to this point has not been dominated by sex. SEX. I promise. I'm a book editor in New York City. I have one success followed by a run of disappointments and all that has nothing to do with sex. But it was Abel Jeanniere and sex that led me to meet Gwen a second time.

She had wanted to meet me. Jack told me so. She had heard him talk about me and she had heard me discussed among the faculty and she had seen my picture in the school newspaper and the local newspaper. It was odd that a young woman could write such a successful paper on a priest's ideas about sex. In my paper, I was interested above all in the inherent tension between the priest's preference for celibacy and his acute understanding, celebration even, of conjugal love. In the end of course, he prefers celibacy.

Jeanniere makes express reference to the need he feels to defend celibacy. He sees its justification as a search for "modes of intimacy beyond eroticism" and for "concrete but universal forms of love." The reduction of sexual desire and pleasure to "eroticism," and of eroticism to an animal instinct, serves his defense of celibacy by making room for the possibility of a higher relation than the sexual. Indeed, Jeanniere at times seems to place human sex ontologically apart from man as man. Sex posits itself to me for the sake of the species, and for me as an individual. "This is the exact point where I can affirm the strength of my own autonomous and personal position, or where I can renounce and lose myself in a nature that is mine but outside myself."

And so went my paper—celibacy leading Jeanniere out of the web of sexual complication to a higher state of clarity and perfection. (Note that I don't say *purity*. He would not have said *purity*.)

Jack talked to Gwen about me, told her that I was a gifted student—one of the few women in his class. I came to campus knowing exactly what I wanted to study, French and philosophy. I designed my own major combining the two and in three short years rearranged the entire department. In my sophomore year the man I worked with most closely, my adviser for this thesis that I had designed, died of AIDS. While he was sick and dying I continued to work with him. When he died Jack took over as my adviser and soon thereafter we began to fuck. For these reasons (all but the latter) I thought that Gwen wanted to meet me. I did not think that she wanted to meet me because Jack spoke of me incessantly.

I remember once we were making love on his living room floor. (He would not make love to me in their bed.) Our clothes were all over the place and someone walked through the front door and into the hall and started talking. A woman's voice that we both thought belonged to Gwen. I grabbed what I could of my clothes and raced away from the room, flying up the stairs and into the bathroom. Her bathroom, thick with her supplies. Rouge and tampons and pads and lipsticks and hair clips and her bras hanging from the shower rod and her underwear (big white overused underwear) and her socks and stockings. All the things that she wanted Jack to remove from her body, but there was no mystery left here and for an instant I felt sorry for her. Water dripped slowly in a leaky faucet. My heart raced. The window was too small to climb out of. The cabinet beneath the sink too small to squeeze into. The shower curtain one hundred percent transparent. Then I heard footsteps on the stairs. This was so terribly real. I wondered did I have time to dress. In my hands, I realized just then, of the clothes I was able to collect, I had only my bra and shoes—strappy high heels that I wore to be sexy. I put on my bra and crouched against the tub.

The door crept open slowly. My cheeks burned.

Caught, busted, snagged, as we used to say during Normal Day. Adrenaline rushing through every single one of us. The hunters and the hunted.

It was Jack. His face was serious. He told me to stand up. I stood up. He told me to put my shoes on. I put my shoes on. He told me to stand in front of the mirror and hold on to the sink. And I did. I could see him in the mirror. His chest pressed against my back and his mouth came to my ear. He whispered into it and his hands crept around my back and inside my bra, a lavender push-up bra that caused my breasts to spill from it. "You're going to feel me between your thighs now," he said. He pushed my back toward the sink so that I bent at the waist and then I felt him. He went in a little and then came out, in a little and then out until I pleaded. "That's right, that's right. Keep telling me what you want, kitten." His fingers were on my nipples. I felt like I was begging. I had no idea who was downstairs. I didn't care if it was Gwen. Let her see me like see this. My heart beat against my chest. "I want to hear you sing." I was begging, ready to scream. "Not too fast," he said, and moved away from me entirely. "Please," I said again, Gwen's big underwear staring at me. I wanted her to see me like this, wanted her to walk through that door. There was no stopping this. I was entirely his. He could do anything. "Tell me everything," he whispered, warm wet soft, coming into me again. "Just exactly what she would do to you?"

Were Serena and Lucian involved in this? So magnificent, like being cracked open and offered up to the universe. A life is being sacrificed for your pleasure. SEX. Exquisite, like glass breaking, shattering a thousand fractured parts of me to become completely whole and new again. My mother left my father for sex. I had no one to leave for Jack, but after that encounter, had I had a boyfriend I would certainly have left him for Jack. I almost wished I had someone to leave. "You have me to leave," Serena had said when I told her this story.

I met Gwen the second time at the main entrance to the philosophy department with Jack standing tall nearby. If I had asked Serena then about Gwen she would have said, "But of course Gwen knows. It's obvious. She might not admit it consciously. But she knows. If she didn't she wouldn't be interested in you." Serena loves to say that nothing gets by anyone. She says as well that we all know exactly what is going on. Did I already know about Serena and Lucian? For how long had I known? If we don't see something that is standing right in front of us it is only because we choose not to. We have that ability—to choose not to see.

Gwen and I shook hands. I was sweet. I smiled a big and young and toothy lying smile. I can imagine now what Gwen thought of me as she peered down on me from the wisdom of thirty-seven. A pretty and very young girl with her life in front of her and so much to figure out.

"I've heard so much about you," she said. Her smile was warm and tender, like her hand. She held on to mine for a long time. It felt as though she wanted to keep my hand. She studied me closely. I felt as if she were finding me in that bathroom. She was quite short. I looked her in the eyes. Hers were sympathetic. I was trying to figure out whether she knew. I loved that she kept my hand. I could feel Jack behind us, studying the moment as well. I loved the feeling of my hand clasped within hers as Jack watched on. It was as if our hands were communicating something, we were speaking back and forth to each other. A private conversation that Jack couldn't hear. I'd think about that conversation for years. I believe I was telling her that I did not love Jack. Never would. This was just a game. I'd break his heart—would I? Or was this just the hubris of youth? But at that moment all the destruction I had the potential to cause vanished. It was a long handshake. By the end of it Gwen understood something, that I was just a twerp, a punk. But she had held my hand protectively as well. "You're brave," she said. "Congratulations on your prize."

Later she'd tell Jack that I was lovely, that she felt sorry for me, that I seemed bright. She'd say many things about me. They'd discuss me over dinner. I'd be there at the dinner table, dissected. She couldn't get enough of me. She'd want to know what he thought would happen to me, what my grades were, did I ever talk about my family, did I have a boyfriend. I imagined, sometimes, that they talked about me while making love. She'd tell him that I was cute, pretty, so impossibly young. The fat, swollen cheeks of youth. And Jack would relay this all to me while we were fucking trying desperately to reignite the wilting sex. Gwen had accomplished her task; she had given her permission.

We fought that night, the night of the adultery article and the swim and the "Coming, darling?" First Lucian and I, then Serena and I, then Serena and Lucian. When Serena is mad at Lucian she simply stops speaking to him. When she is mad at me first she screams and then she gives me the silent treatment. The kids safely asleep, Serena making some elaborate meal for us to feast upon, I wondered ever so fleetingly what life would be like if she lived very far away from me, if our lives were not inextricably intertwined. And the thought blew in a soothing freshness, like that cold Maine water cleansing my toes. I imagined my family, husband, son, and I, in our own world, happily doing our own thing with no need for Serena. And thus I began a fight. It was easy to make Serena fight. She had many scabs to pick. I brought up her poetry, said, "Oh, Lucian should publish you," knowing well he wouldn't over his dead body, knowing well he thought her a wretched talent—not that extreme, but I was upset. I have a knack for making people feel bad, for picking their worst and most humiliating wound.

"Come on, Lucian. Why not?" I said. We were on our second bottle of wine, the remains of *risotto al funghi porcini* on our plates. The smell of Maine drifting through the windows making us cold. I would not give them my permission.

"Well, perhaps," Lucian said, trying to get out of it, giving me a please-stop look, not understanding fully the depth of my intentions.

"Let's schedule it. Set a date. Which poems would you choose? The one in which she talks about her bloody tampons?" I persisted. My face was red and ugly with the wine and the anger. And so on it went until my scheme worked and Serena declared that Lucian had no intention of publishing her and we were all drunk and fighting and crying.

"You don't like my poetry, do you?" Serena asked Lucian.

"Let's not fall into this, Serena," Lucian said calmly, saying her name with a familiarity as if he had said it to her privately many times. "Don't you see what she's doing?" as if it were the two of them were the pair.

"Is that true?" she asked.

He was silent.

"Lucian, is that true?" she asked again, saying his name as if she owned it. Everything rotten blossoming before me—one lover questioning the truth of the other. How long had I known? How often was I a part of her orgasm? What did he whisper into her ear? I knew of a man who cheated on his wife, called his wife while he was fucking his lover because hearing her voice in the midst of it all made the orgasm all the more complete.

"Just keep spreading your legs, darling," I said, "and he'll publish you." My gut pulled the rest of me inside out and into it.

Lucian shoved his chair back from the table and stood up and told me with eyes of hatred that I'd gone too far this time. "Why are you doing this?" he said with disgust. He stacked plates impatiently. If he were innocent he'd have laughed this off.

"Why are *you* doing this is what you should be asking," I said. I wanted to go back to the afternoon and do it all over, choose not to read that article, choose to stand up when he asked, "Are you coming, darling?" Yes, yes. I am.

Lily appeared at the foot of the stairs, her little sleepy face like a doll's. We became quiet. "I want my daddy," she said.

"He's in Asia," Serena said, barely noticing the girl.

"When's he coming back?" she demanded. "I want him back now."

"It's all right, dear," Lucian said, approaching her. For Lucian the children always came first. "He'll be back soon."

"I don't want you. I want my daddy," she snapped.

"Lily," Serena said. Lucian went outside and Serena followed him and then so did Lily. Those old wives, they say that children know the truth.

I lie on my bed in the turret. Outside the moon is so full and bright it seems like dusk. Low tide and those arms reaching greedily to the islands, mocking me. Bora Bora? Hawaii? I lie there for a long time before Serena comes. I cry a little, then make a bet with myself about what it means if she comes. If I hurt her she would not come. Then she appears and lies down next to me.

"You win," I say, and then get confused. "Or have you lost?"

"Why are you doing this?" she asks.

"You sound like Lucian," I say.

"I love you," she says. "You're it," she says—I'm all she has. My nose is pinching. I can hear my baby breathing. "You've done this all for nothing," she says.

"Have I?"

We lie there for a long time, listening to the light wind, the waves, the night. The moon continues its march across the sky. I remember an annoying man from college, a boy, really, who had close-set eyes and was unfortunately small; he made himself look even smaller by wearing outsized jackets. He walked around campus with a little notebook, taking notes, always needing to know everything about everyone and somehow finding out the information. He drew me a diagram once, when I thought my affair with Jack was my own big secret. The diagram had the names of dozens of our classmates, an intricate diagram with many crisscrossing lines leading from one name to another to another. With a pencil in his hand and his beady eyes lit with enthusiasm he showed me how I had slept unwittingly with a good portion of my class. He revealed this to me by informing me that Jack had slept with a girl named Cathy before he started fucking me, and Cathy, before fucking Jack, had fucked a good many others. His pencil started zigzagging all across the page and I began to laugh. I laughed hysterically, almost scaring the pathetic boy. I supposed he had wanted me to be upset by his revelation. Instead I saw Abel Jeanniere's celibacy lifting him beautifully above the intricate web of sex creeping through all our lives—mere mortals making messes of our lives. I laughed for the priest's endearing insight into our foolish fucking glee—generation after generation after generation. Not long after the births of the three boys my stepfather left my mother, running off with his young secretary. And I laugh again now, thinking of all this. I feel Gwen's long handshake giving me permission—understanding for the first time her wisdom. The laugh gives Serena permission to speak.

"Do you really think I could hurt you?" she asks, staring at the ceiling.

"Yes," I say, "because you already have. You've wanted me to believe in your affair."

"A bluff, you mean?"

"Did you want that power—if I wouldn't always love you most then I'd hate you most and thus still love you most?" A strong breeze comes through the walls and it seems the whole house moves.

"Where's Lucian?" I ask, getting a notion.

"He's walking," she says, understanding the notion. "He'll be gone awhile."

Those waves like a breath, like breathing, rolling in out in out tirelessly over the course of a day a year a life a millennium—whispering, brushing cool air over warm skin. Our bare arms barely touch. She smells like risotto, onions, and porcini, the sweet scent of wine, like you could eat her. Though it's light outside, it's dark in the room. I close my eyes. I can hear her breathing. I can feel her twisting toward me. I can feel her so close to my face, her lips on mine, her tongue on mine.

"Do you want to hear the truth?" she whispers.

"I already know the truth."

Dangerous Laughter

STEVEN MILLHAUSER

FEW OF US NOW RECALL that perilous summer. What began as a game, a harmless pastime, quickly took a turn toward the serious and obsessive, which none of us tried to resist. After all, we were young. We were fourteen and fifteen, scornful of childhood, remote from the world of stern and ludicrous adults. We were bored, we were restless, we longed to be seized by any whim or passion and follow it to the farthest reaches of our natures. We wanted to live, to die, to burst into flame, to be transformed into angels or explosions. Only the mundane offended us, as if we secretly feared it was our destiny. By late afternoon our muscles ached, our eyelids grew heavy with obscure desires. And so we dreamed and did nothing, for what was there to do, played Ping-Pong and went to the beach, loafed in backyards, slept late into the morning—and always we craved adventures so extreme we could not even imagine them.

In the long dusks of summer we walked the suburban streets through scents of maple and cut grass, waiting for something to happen.

The game began innocently and spread like a dark rumor. In cool playrooms with parallelograms of sunlight pouring through cellar windows, at Ping-Pong tables in hot, open garages, around orange and blue beach towels lying on bright sand above the tide line, you would hear the quiet words, the sharp bursts of laughter. The idea had the simplicity of all inspired things. A word, any word, uttered in a certain solemn tone, could be compelled to reveal its inner stupidity. "Cheese," someone would say, with an air of somber concentration, and again, slowly: "Cheese." Someone would laugh; it was inevitable; the laughter would spread; gusts of hilarity would sweep through the group; and just as things were about to die down, someone would cry out "Elbow!" or "Dirigible!" and bursts of laughter would be set off again. What drew us wasn't so much the hidden absurdity of words, which we had always suspected, as the sharp heaves and gasps of laughter itself. Deep in our inner dark, we had discovered a startling power. We became fanatics of laughter, devotees of eruption, as if these upheavals were something we hadn't known before, something that would take us where we needed to go.

Such simple performances couldn't satisfy us for long. The laugh parties, which sprang up here and there, represented a leap that we acknowledged as worthy of our hunger. The object was to laugh longer and harder than anyone else, to maintain in yourself an uninterrupted state of explosive release. Strict rules sprang up to eliminate unacceptable laughter: the feeble, the false, the unfairly exaggerated. Soon every party had its judges, who grew skillful in detecting the slightest deviation from the genuine. As long laughter became the rage, a custom arose in which one of us stepped into a circle of watchers and, partly through the stimulus of a crowd already rippling with amusement, and partly through some inner trick that differed from person to person, began to laugh, while the watchers and judges, who themselves were continually thrown into outbursts that drove the laugher to greater and greater heights, studied the roars and convulsions carefully and timed the performance with a stopwatch.

In this atmosphere of urgency, abandon, and rigorous striving, accidents were bound to happen. One girl, laughing hysterically on a couch in a basement playroom, threw back her head and injured her neck when it struck the wooden couch arm. A boy gasping with mad laughter crashed into a piano bench, fell to the floor, and broke his left arm. These incidents, which might have served as warnings, only heightened our sense of rightness, as if our wounds were signs that we took our laughter seriously.

Not long after the first laugh parties began to absorb our afternoons, there arose a new development, which threatened to overthrow the parties with effects of a more radical kind. The clubs, or laugh parlors as they were often called, represented a further effort to prolong and increase our laughter. At first they were organized by slightly older girls, who invited "members" to their houses and, in accordance with rules and practices that varied from club to club, produced sustained fits of violent laughter far more thrilling than anything we had yet discovered. No one was certain how the clubs had come into being—one day they simply seemed to be there, as if they had been present all along, waiting for us to discover them.

It was rumored that the first club was the invention of sixteen-year-old Bernice Alderson, whose parents were never home, who lived in a large house in the wooded north end of town, and who was said to have read in a history of Egypt that Queen Cleopatra liked to order a slave girl to bind her arms and tickle her bare feet with a feather. In her third-floor bedroom Bernice and her friend Mary Chapman invited the club members to remove their shoes and lie down one by one on the bed. While Mary, with her muscular arms, held the chest and knees firmly in place, Bernice began to tickle the outstretched body—on the stomach, the ribs, the neck, the thighs, the tops and sides of the feet. There was an art to it all: the art of invading and withdrawing, of coaxing from the depths a steady outpouring of helpless laughter. For the visitor held down on the bed, it was a matter of releasing oneself into the hands of the girls and enduring it for as long as possible. You had only to say "Stop." In theory the laughter never had to stop, though most of us could barely hold out for five minutes.

Although the laugh parlors existed in fact, for we all attended at least one of them and even began to form clubs of our own, they also continued to lead a separate and in a sense higher existence in the realm of rumor, which had the effect of lifting them into the inaccessible and mythical. It was said that in one of these clubs, members were required to remove their clothes, after which they were chained to a bed and tickled savagely to the point of delirium. It was said that one girl, sobbing with laughter, gasping, began to move her hips in strange and suggestive ways, until it became clear that the act of tickling had brought her to orgasm. The erotic was never absent from these rumors—a fact that hardly surprised us, since those of us who were purists of laughter and disdained any crude crossing over into the sexual recognized the kinship between the two worlds. For even then we understood that our laughter, as it erupted from us in unseemly spasms, was part of the kingdom of forbidden things.

As laugh parties gave way to laugh parlors, and rumors thickened, we sometimes had the sense that our secret games had begun to spread to other regions of the town. One day a nine-year-old boy was discovered by his mother holding down and violently tickling his seven-year-old sister, who was shrieking and screaming; the collar of her dress was soaked with tears. The girl's pale body was streaked with lines of deep pink, as if she had been struck repeatedly with a rope. We heard that Bernice Alderson's mother, at home for a change, had entered the kitchen with a heavy bag of groceries in her arms, slipped on a rubber dog toy, and fallen to the floor, and as she sat there beside a box of smashed and oozing eggs and watched the big, heavy, thumping oranges go rolling across the linoleum, the corners of her mouth began to twitch, her lungs, already burning with anger, began to tingle, and all at once she burst into laughter that lashed her body, threw her head back against the metal doors of the cabinet under the sink, rose to the third-floor bedroom of her daughter, who looked up frowning from a book, and in the end left her exhausted, shaken, bruised, panting, and exhilarated. At night, in my hot room, I lay restless and dissatisfied, longing for the release of feverish laughter that alone could soothe me; and through the screen I seemed to hear, along with the crickets, the rattling window fan next door, and the hum of far-off trucks on the thruway, the sound of laughter bursting faintly in the night, all over our town, like the buzz of a fluorescent lamp in a distant bedroom.

One night after my parents were asleep I left the house and walked across town to Bernice Alderson's neighborhood. The drawn shade of her third-floor window was aglow with dim yellow light. On the bed in her room Mary Chapman gripped me firmly while Bernice, bending over me with a serious but not unkind look, brought me to a pitch of wild laughter that seemed to scald my throat as sweat trickled down my neck and the bed creaked to the rhythm of my deep, painful, releasing cries. I held out for a long time, nearly eight minutes, until I begged her to stop. Instantly it was over. Even as I made my way home, under the maples and lindens of a warm July night, I regretted my cowardice and longed for deeper and more terrible laughter. Then I wondered how I could push my way through the hours that separated me from my next descent into the darkness of my body, where laughter lay like lava, waiting for a fissure to form that would release it like liquid fire.

Of course we compared notes. We had realized from the beginning that some were more skilled in laughter than others, that some were able to sustain long and robust fits of the bone-shaking kind, which seemed to bring them to the verge of hysteria or unconsciousness without stepping over the line. Many of us boasted of our powers, only to be outdone by others; rumors blossomed; and in this murky atmosphere of extravagant claims, dubious feats, and unverifiable stories, the figure of Clara Schuler began to stand out with a certain distinctness.

Clara Schuler was fifteen years old. She was a quiet girl, who sat very still in class with her book open before her, eyes lowered and both feet resting on the floor. She never drummed her fingers on the desk. She never pushed her hair back over her ear or crossed and uncrossed her legs—as if, for her, a single motion were a form of disruption. When she passed a handout to the person seated behind her, she turned her upper body abruptly, dropped the paper on the desk with lowered eyes, and turned abruptly back. She never raised her hand in class. When she was called on, she flushed slightly, answered in a voice so quiet that the teacher had to ask her to "speak up," and said as little as possible, though it was clear she'd done the work. She seemed to experience the act of being looked at as a form of violation; she gave you the impression that her idea of happiness would be to dissolve gradually, leaving behind a small puddle. She was neither pretty nor unpretty, a little pale, her hair dark in some elusive shade between brown and black, her eyes hidden under lowered lids that sometimes opened suddenly to reveal large, startled irises. She wore trim knee-length skirts and solid-colored cotton blouses that looked neatly ironed. Sometimes she wore in her collar a small silver pin shaped like a cat.

One small thing struck me about Clara Schuler: in the course of the day she would become a little unraveled. Strands of hair would fall across her face, the back of her blouse would bunch up and start to pull away from her leather belt, one of her white socks would begin to droop. The next day she would be back in her seat, her hair neatly combed, her blouse tucked in, her socks pulled up tight with the ribs perfectly straight, and her hands folded lightly on her maplewood desk.

Clara had one friend, a girl named Helen Jacoby, who sat with her in the cafeteria and met her at the lockers after class. Helen was a long-boned girl who played basketball, laughed at anything, and threw her head far back to drink bottles of soda, so that you could see the ridges of her trachea pressing through her neck. She seemed an unlikely companion for Clara Schuler, but we were used to seeing them together and we felt, without thinking much about it, that each enhanced the other—Helen made Clara seem less strange and solitary, in a sense protected her and prevented her from being perceived as ridiculous, while Clara made good old Helen seem more interesting, lent her a touch of mystery. We weren't surprised, that summer, to see Helen at the laugh parties, where she laughed with her head thrown back in a way that reminded me of the way she drank soda; and it was Helen who one afternoon brought Clara Schuler with her and introduced her to the new game.

I began to watch Clara at these parties; we all watched her. She would step into the circle and stand there with lowered eyes, her head leaning forward slightly, her shoulders slumped, her arms tense at her sides—looking, I couldn't help thinking, as if she were being punished in some humiliating way. You could see the veins rising up on the backs of her hands. She stood so motionless that she seemed to be holding her breath; perhaps she was; and you could feel something building in her, as in a child about to cry; her neck stiff; the tendons visible; two vertical lines between her eyebrows; then a kind of mild trembling in her neck and arms, a veiled shudder, an inner rippling, and through her body, still rigid but in the grip of a force, you could sense a presence, rising, expanding, until, with a painful gasp, with a jerk of her shoulders, she gave way to a cry or scream of laughter—laughter that continued to well up in her, to shake her as if she were possessed by a demon, until her cheeks were wet, her hair wild in her face, her chest heaving, her fingers clutching at her arms and head—and still the laughter came, hurling her about, making her gulp and gasp as if in terror, her mouth stretched back over her teeth, her eyes squeezed shut, her hands pressed against her ribs as if to keep herself from cracking apart.

And then it would stop. Abruptly, mysteriously, it was over. She stood there pale—exhausted—panting. Her eyes, wide open, saw nothing. Slowly she came back to herself; and quickly, a little unsteadily, she would walk away from us to collapse on a couch.

These feats of laughter were immediately recognized as bold and striking, far superior to the performances we had become accustomed to; and Clara Schuler was invited to all the laugh parties, applauded, and talked about admiringly, for she had a gift of reckless laughter we had not seen before.

Now whenever loose groups of us gathered to pursue our game, Clara Schuler was there. We grew used to her, waited impatiently for her when she was late, this quiet girl who'd never done anything but sit obediently in our classes with both feet on the floor before revealing dark depths of laughter that left us wondering and a little uneasy. For there was something about Clara Schuler's laughter. It wasn't simply that it was more intense than ours. Rather, she seemed to be transformed into a mere object seized by a force that raged through her before letting her go. Yes, in Clara Schuler the discrepancy between the body that was shaken and the force that shook it appeared so sharply that at the very moment she became most physical she seemed to lose the sense of her body altogether. For the rest of us, there was always a touch of the sensual in these performances: breasts shook, hips jerked, flesh moved in unexpected ways. But Clara Schuler seemed to pass beyond the easy suggestiveness of moving bodies and to enter new and more ambiguous realms, where the body was the summoner of some dark, eruptive power that was able to flourish only through the accident of a material thing, which it flung about as if cruelly before abandoning it to the rites of exhaustion.

One day she appeared among us alone. Helen Jacoby was at the beach, or out shopping with her mother. We understood that Clara Schuler no longer needed her friend in the old way—that she had come into her own. And we understood one other thing: she would allow nothing to stop her from joining our game, from yielding to the seductions of laughter, for she lived, more and more, only in order to let herself go.

It was inevitable that rumors should spring up about Clara Schuler. It was said that she had begun to go to the laugh parlors, those half-real, half-legendary places where laughter was wrung out of willing victims by special arts. It was said that one night she had paid a visit to Bernice Alderson's house, where in the lamp-lit bedroom on the third floor she had been constrained and skillfully tickled for nearly an hour, at which point she had fainted dead away and had to be revived by a scented oil rubbed into her temples. It was said that at another house she had been so shaken by extreme laughter that her body rose from the bed and hovered in the air for thirty seconds before dropping back down. We knew that this last was a lie, a frivolous and irritating tale fit for children, but it troubled us all the same, it seized our imaginations—for we felt that under the right circumstances, with the help of a physiologically freakish but not inconceivable pattern of spasms, it was the kind of thing Clara Schuler might somehow be able to do.

As our demands became more exacting, and our expectations more refined, Clara Schuler's performances attained heights of release that inflamed us and left no doubt of her power. We tried to copy her gestures, to jerk our shoulders with her precise rhythms, always without success. Sometimes we imagined we could hear, in Clara Schuler's laughter, our own milder laughter, changed into something we could only long for. It was as if our dreams had entered her.

I noticed that her strenuous new life was beginning to affect her appearance. Now when she came to us her hair fell across her cheeks in long strands, which she would impatiently flick away with the backs of her fingers. She looked thinner, though it was hard to tell; she looked tired; she looked as if she might be coming down with something. Her eyes, no longer hidden under lowered lids, gazed at us restlessly and a little vaguely. Sometimes she gave the impression that she was searching for something she could no longer remember. She looked expectant; a little sad; a little bored.

One night, unable to sleep, I escaped from the house and took a walk. Near the end of my street I passed under a street lamp that flickered and made a crackling sound, so that my shadow trembled. It seemed to me that I was that street lamp, flickering and crackling with restlessness. After a while I came to an older neighborhood of high maples and gabled houses with run-down front porches, where bicycles leaned wearily against wicker furniture and beach towels hung crookedly over porch rails. I stopped before a dark house near the end of the street. Through an open window on the second floor, over the dirt driveway, I heard the sound of a rattling fan. It was Clara Schuler's house. I wondered if it was her window. I walked a little closer, looking up at the screen, and it seemed to me that through the rattle and hum of the fan I heard some other sound. It was —I thought it was—the sound of quiet laughter, unless it was some trick of the fan. Was she lying there in the dark, laughing secretly, releasing herself from restlessness? Could she be laughing in her sleep? Was it only the motor of the fan? I stood listening to that small, uncertain sound, which mingled with the blades of the fan until it seemed the fan itself was laughing, perhaps at me. What did I long for, under that window? I longed to be swept up into Clara Schuler's laughter, I longed to join her there, in her dark room, I longed for release from whatever it was I was. But whatever I was lay hard and immovable in me, like bone; I would never be free of my own weight. After a while I turned around and walked home.

It wasn't long after this visit that I saw Clara Schuler at one of the laugh parlors we'd formed, in imitation of those we had heard about or perhaps had invented in order to lure ourselves into bolder experiments. Helen Jacoby sat on the bed and held Clara's wrists while a friend of Helen's held Clara's ankles. A blond-haired girl I'd never seen before bent over her with hooked fingers. Five of us watched the performance. It began with a sudden shiver, as the short, blunt fingers darted along her ribs and thighs. Clara Schuler's head began to turn from side to side, her feet in her white socks stiffened; and as laughter rushed through her in sharp shuddering bursts, one of her shoulders lifted as if to fold itself across her neck. Within ten minutes her eyes had grown glassy and calm. She lay almost still, even as she continued to laugh. What struck us was that eerie stillness, as if she had passed beyond struggle to some other place, where laughter poured forth in pure, vigorous streams.

Someone asked nervously if we should stop. The blond-haired girl, glancing at her watch, bent over Clara Schuler more intently: After half an hour, Clara began breathing in great wracking gulps, accompanied by groans torn up from her throat. Helen asked her if she'd had enough; Clara shook her head harshly. Her face was so wet that she glowed in the lamplight. Stains of wetness darkened the bedspread.

When the session had lasted just over an hour, the blond-haired girl gave up in exhaustion. She stood shaking her wrists, rubbing the fingers of first one hand and then the other. On the bed Clara Schuler continued stirring and laughing, as if she still felt the fingers moving over her. Gradually her laughter grew fainter; and as she lay there pale and drained, with her head turned to one side, her eyes dull, her lips slack, strands of long hair sticking to her wet cheek, she looked, for a moment, as if she had grown suddenly old.

It was at this period, when Clara Schuler became queen of the laugh parlors, that I first began to worry about her. One day, emerging from an unusually violent and prolonged series of gasps, she lay motionless, her eyes open and staring, while the fingers played over her skin. It took some moments for us to realize she had lost consciousness, though she soon revived. Another time, walking across a room, she thrust out an arm and seized the back of a chair as her body leaned slowly to one side, before she straightened and continued her walk as if nothing had happened. I understood that these feverish games, these lavish abandonments, were no longer innocent. Sometimes I saw in her eyes the restless unhappiness of someone for whom nothing, not even such ravishments, would ever be enough.

One afternoon when I walked to Main Street to return a book to the library, I saw Clara Schuler stepping out of Cerino's grocery store. I felt an intense desire to speak to her; to warn her against us; to praise her extravagantly; to beg her to teach me the difficult art of laughter. Shyness constrained me, though I wasn't shy—but it was as if I had no right to intrude on her, to break the spell of her remoteness. I kept out of sight and followed her home. When she climbed the wooden steps of her porch, one of which creaked like the floor of an attic, I stepped boldly into view, daring her to turn and see me. She opened the front door and disappeared into the house. For a while I stood there, trying to remember what it was I had wanted to say to Clara Schuler, the modest girl with a fierce, immodest gift. A clattering startled me. Along the shady sidewalk, trembling with spots of sunlight, a girl with yellow pigtails was pulling a lollipop-red wagon, in which stood a soft, jouncing rhinoceros. I turned and headed home.

That night I dreamed about Clara Schuler. She was standing in a sunny backyard, looking into the distance. I came over to her and spoke a few words, but she did not look at me. I began to walk around her, speaking urgently and trying to catch her gaze, but her face was always turned partly away, and when I seized her arm it felt soft and crumbly, like pie dough.

About this time I began to sense among us a slight shift of attention, an inner wandering. A change was in the air. The laugh parlors seemed to lack their old aura of daring—they had grown a little familiar, a little humdrum. While one of us lay writhing in laughter, the rest of us glanced toward the windows. One day someone withdrew from a pocket a deck of cards, and as we waited our turn on the bed we sat down on the floor to a few hands of gin rummy.

We tried to conjure new possibilities, but our minds were mired in the old forms. Even the weather conspired to hold us back. The heat of midsummer pressed against us like fur. Leaves, thick as tongues, hung heavily from the maples. Dust lay on polished furniture like pollen.

One night it rained. The rain continued all the next day and night; wind knocked down tree branches and telephone wires; in the purple-black sky, prickly lines of lightning burst forth with troubling brightness. Through the dark rectangles of our windows, the lightning flashes looked like textbook diagrams of the circulation of the blood.

The turn came with the new sun. Mist like steam rose from soaked grass. We took up our old games, but it was as if something had been carried off by the storm. At a birthday party in a basement playroom with an out-of-tune piano, a girl named Janet Bianco, listening to a sentimental song, began to behave strangely. Her shoulders trembled, her lips quivered; mirthless tears rolled along her cheeks. Gradually we understood that she was crying. It caught our attention; it was a new note. Across the room, another girl suddenly burst into tears.

A passion for weeping seized us. It proved fairly easy for one girl to set off another, who set off a third; boys, tense and embarrassed, gave way slowly. We held weep fests that left us shaken and thrilled. Here and there a few laugh parties and laugh clubs continued to meet, but we knew it was the end of an era.

Clara Schuler attended that birthday party. As the rage for weeping swept over us, she appeared at a few gatherings, where she stood off to one side with a little frown. We saw her there, looking in our direction, before she began to shimmer and dissolve through our abundant tears. The pleasures of weeping proved more satisfying than the old pleasures of laughter, perhaps because, when all was said and done, we were not happy, we who were restless and always in search of diversion. And whereas laughter had always been difficult to sustain, weeping, once begun, welled up in us with gratifying ease. Several girls, among them Helen Jacoby, discovered in themselves rich and unsuspected depths of unhappiness, which released in the rest of us lengthy, heartfelt bouts of sorrow.

It wasn't long after the new craze had swept away the old that we received an invitation from Clara Schuler. None of us except Helen Jacoby had ever set foot in her house before. We arrived in the middle of a sunny afternoon; in the living room it was already dusk. A tall woman in a long drab dress pointed vaguely toward a carpeted stairway. Clara, she said, was waiting for us in the guest room in the attic. At the top of the stairs we came to a hallway covered with faded wallpaper, showing repeated water wheels beside repeated streams shaded by willows. An unpainted door led up to the attic. Passing under shadowy rafters that slanted down over wooden barrels and a folded card table leaning against a tricycle, we reached a half-open door and entered the guest room. Clara Schuler stood with her hands hanging down in front of her, one hand lightly grasping the wrist of the other.

It looked like the room of someone's grandmother that had been invaded by a child. On a frilly bedspread under old lace curtains sat a big rag doll wearing a pink dress with an apron. Her yellow yarn hair looked as heavy as candy. On top of a mahogany chest of drawers, a black-and-white photograph of a bearded man wearing a fedora sat next to a music box decorated with elephants and balloons. It was warm and dusty in that room; we didn't know whether we were allowed to sit on the bed, which seemed to belong to the doll, so we sat on the floor. Clara herself looked tired and tense. We hadn't seen her for a while. We had hardly thought about her; it occurred to me that we'd begun to forget her.

Seven or eight of us were there that day, sitting on a frayed maroon rug and looking awkwardly around. After a while Clara tried to close the door—the hinges creaked, and the wood, swollen in the humid heat, refused to fit into the frame—and then walked to the center of the room. I had the impression that she was going to say something to us, but she stood looking vaguely before her. I could sense what she was going to do even before she began to laugh. It was a good laugh, one that reminded me of the old laugh parties, and a few of us joined her uneasily, for old-time's sake. But we were done with that game, we could scarcely recall those days of early summer. And, in truth, even our weeping had begun to tire us, already we longed for new enticements. Perhaps Clara had sensed a change and was trying to draw us back; perhaps she simply wanted to perform one more time. If she was trying to assert her old power over us, she failed entirely. But neither our halfhearted laughter nor our hidden resistance seemed to trouble her, as she abandoned herself to her desire.

There was a concentration in Clara Schuler's laughter, a completeness, an immensity that we hadn't seen before. It was as if she wanted to outdo herself, to give the performance of her life. Her face, flushed on the cheek ridges, was so pale that laughter seemed to be draining away her blood. She stumbled to one side and nearly fell over; someone swung up a supporting hand. She seemed to be laughing harder and harder, with a ferocity that flung her body about, snapped her head back, wrenched her out of shape. The room, filled with wails of laughter, began to feel unbearable. No one knew what to do. At one point she threw herself onto the bed, gasping in what appeared to be an agony of laughter. Slowly, gracefully, the big doll slumped forward, until her head touched her stuck-out legs and the yellow yarn hair lay flung out over her feet. After thirty-five minutes someone rose and quietly left. I could hear the footsteps fading through the attic.

Others began to leave; they did not say goodbye. Those of us who remained found an old Monopoly game and sat in a corner to play. Clara's eyes had taken on their glassy look, as cries of laughter continued to erupt from her. After the first hour I understood that no one was going to forgive her for this.

When the Monopoly game ended, everyone left except Helen Jacoby and me. Clara was laughing fiercely, her face twisted as if in pain. Her skin was so wet that she looked hard and shiny, like metal. The laughter, raw and harsh, poured up out of her as if some mechanism had broken. One of her forearms was bruised. The afternoon was drawing on toward five when Helen Jacoby, turning up her hands and giving a bitter little shrug, stood up and walked out of the room.

I stayed. And as I watched Clara Schuler, I had the desire to reach out and seize her wrist, to shake her out of her laughter and draw her back before it was too late. No one is allowed to laugh like that, I wanted to say. Stop it right now. She had passed so far beyond herself that there was almost nothing left—nothing but that creature emptying herself of laughter. It was ugly—indecent—it made you want to look away. At the same time she bound me there, for it was as if she were inviting me to follow her to the farthest and most questionable regions of laughter, where laughter no longer bore any relation to earthly things and, sufficient to itself, soared above the world to flourish in the void. There, you were no longer yourself—you were no longer anything. More than once I started to reach for her arm. My hand hung in front of me like a fragile sculpture I was holding up for inspection. I saw that I was no more capable of stopping Clara Schuler in her flight than I was of joining her. I could only be a witness.

It was nearly half-past five when I finally stood up. "Clara!" I said sharply, but I might as well have been talking to the doll. I wondered whether I had ever spoken her name before. She was still laughing when I disappeared into the attic. Downstairs I told her mother that something was wrong, her daughter had been laughing for hours. She thanked me, turned slowly to gaze at the carpeted stairs, and said she hoped I would come again.

The local paper reported that Mrs. Schuler discovered her daughter around seven o'clock; she had already stopped breathing. The official cause of death was a ruptured blood vessel in the brain, but we knew the truth: Clara Schuler had died of laughter. "She was always a good girl," her mother was quoted as saying, as if death was a form of disobedience. We cooperated fully with the police, who found no trace of foul play.

For a while Clara Schuler's death was taken up eagerly by the weeping parties, which had begun to languish and which now gained a feverish new energy before collapsing decisively. It was late August; school was looming; as if desperately we hurled ourselves into a sudden passion for old board games, staging fierce contests of Monopoly and Risk, altering the rules in order to make the games last for days. But already our ardor was tainted by the end of summer, already we could see, in eyes glittering with the fever of obsession, a secret distraction.

On a warm afternoon in October I took a walk into Clara Schuler's neighborhood. Her house had been sold; on the long front steps sat a little girl in a green-and-orange-checked jacket, leaning forward and tightening a roller skate with a big silver key. I stood looking up at the bedroom window, half expecting to hear a ghostly laughter. In the quiet afternoon I heard only the whine of a backyard chainsaw and the slap of a jump rope against a sidewalk. I felt awkward standing there, like someone trying to peek through a window. The summer seemed far away, as distant as childhood. Had we really played those games? I thought of Clara Schuler, the girl who had died of a ruptured blood vessel, but it was difficult to summon her face. What I could see clearly was that rag doll, slowly falling forward. Something stirred in my chest, and to my astonishment, with a kind of sorrow, I felt myself burst into a sharp laugh.

I looked around uneasily and began walking away. I wanted to be back in my own neighborhood, where people didn't die of laughter. There we threw ourselves into things for a while, lost interest, and went on to something else. Clara Schuler played games differently. Had we disappointed her? As I turned the corner of her street, I glanced back at the window over her dirt driveway. I had never learned whether it was her room. For all I knew, she slept on the other side of the house, or in the guest room in the attic. Again I saw that pink and yellow doll, falling forward in a slow, graceful, grotesque bow. No, my laughter was all right. It was a salute to Clara Schuler, an acknowledgment of her great gift. In her own way, she was complete. I wondered whether she had been laughing at us a little, up there in her attic.

As I entered the streets of my neighborhood, I felt a familiar restlessness. Everything stood out clearly. In an open, sunny garage, a man was reaching up to an aluminum ladder hanging horizontally on hooks, while in the front yard a tenth-grade girl wearing tight jeans rolled up to midcalf and a billowy red and black lumberjack shirt was standing with a rake beside a pile of yellow leaves shot through with green, shading her eyes and staring up at a man hammering on a roof. The mother of a friend of mine waved at me from behind the shady, sun-striped screen of a porch. Against a backboard above a brilliant white garage door, a basketball went round and round the orange rim of a basket. It was Sunday afternoon, time of the great boredom. Deep in my chest I felt a yawn begin; it went shuddering through my jaw. On the crosspiece of a sunny telephone pole, a grackle shrieked once and was still. The basketball hung in the white net. Suddenly it came unstuck and dropped with a smack to the driveway, the grackle rose into the air, somewhere I heard a burst of laughter. I nodded in the direction of Clara Schuler's neighborhood and continued down the street. Tomorrow something was bound to happen.

End of Messages

LUCIA NEVAI

MAYBE IT'S ME, but a funeral seems like the worst occasion to sell anyone a grand piano, let alone the bereaved. I held father's service in Ludlum's best funeral home, though Ludlum being a down-at-the-heels industrial wasteland, some might say that's redundant. I'm working my way through the receiving line, dodging insults, personal and professional. I'm taking angry confrontations, passed off as condolences, on the chin. The hostility I've lived with all my life is clear. The family physician recommended tranquilizers, but I wanted to get through this on the truth. The truth is a drug, too.

I hustle my guests through the line. I offer no surface resistance. "Yes, he deserved to suffer." If only it had been you. "Yes, he was a tough old bird to the end." He could have eaten you for lunch. "Yes, I look old." And you haven't changed in twenty years? I am willing to see through everything, until my piano teacher is standing before me.

Don Widden still wears a beret, but the act of donning it daily with a dare-to-be-different attitude for the past twenty years has resulted in such an exaggeration of the angle that it excites worry: will it fall off? Exaggeration has also occurred in Don Widden's face. False expressions of aesthetic delight and fake paternal approval have frozen his features in a semblance of ready-made understanding: one eye offers warmth, the other sincerity; the raised eyebrows convey the notion of an intellect that has been interestingly, if only partially, aroused; the smile is a wide, held-still, quivering "Cheese"; a solicitous dimple threatens to turn flirtatious should further intellectual arousal occur.

Don Widden's hair is short and gray. When I had my crush on him, it fell to his shoulders in wavy, auburn curls like Lord Byron, whom he often quoted: *O chestnut tree, great-rooted blossomer, are you the leaf, the blossom or the branch? How can we know the dancer from the dance?*

As always around him, I regret my looks. I have father's chunky, pugnacious face. My nose, like his, is rough with bumps. My hair is now rat-gray, but I still part it down the middle and pull it off the forehead, right and left, with blue plastic Flintstone barrettes. I have a cold sore on my lower lip, which I've slathered with Vaseline Petroleum Jelly. I'm wearing a neck brace to reduce the stabbing twinges that occur when turning my head. In lieu of black, I'm wearing Father's kilt from his bagpipe days, the family tartan, Cameron Erracht Old. Yes, we're Scots. We're tight-fisted, melancholy, bellicose lovers of life. My crutches are behind me, propped up against the funeral home credenza. I broke my ankle on the hospital steps chasing down the nurse who let father die.

To prove he's not just any old Tom, Dick, and Harry at this funeral, Don Widden offers me a hug, and not just any hug, a long hug. Some would call it inappropriate. With my face actually pressed up against his embroidered Nepalese wool vest, it becomes obvious that he could use a bath. Finally, he swings his torso away, grabs my elbows in his hands, and cocks his head. I worry about the beret falling off. He looks into my irises for roughly a count of five, then says, "*Doth sorrow lean her drooping head?*"

Drooping head, drooping head. If Don Widden ever interjected this quote into a piano lesson, it wasn't mine. I remember everything this man said, and he said a lot. He talked through half of every lesson and still charged Dad as if he hadn't. As a result, I only practiced half of what he told me to. Crush or no crush, I wasn't a fool. The trick was figuring which half. If I guessed wrong, I went for the bluff. This only failed once, the week he asked to hear no. 31 from the *Czerny Exercise Book for the Left Hand.* I had practiced only the Sarabande from the Partita no. 3 in A Minor. I positioned myself at the edge of the piano bench, straightened my spine, took a deep, calming breath, raised my hands to the keys of the prized ebony Steinway concert grand, and sight-read through both pages of no. 31 for the first time, producing with a straight face an excruciatingly error-filled, comically plodding noise beyond description.

Now, I feign recognition of the drooping-head quote, raising my eyebrows and smiling a slow, bittersweet smile. Out of the depths of my memory (damn you, Dad, for dying and taking the lid off this) comes the image of something I would prefer to forget. At dusk in Mr. Widden's living room, after we talked heart to heart straight through my hour, he spurred me to confide my secret fears. As I did, he leaned ever closer, listening intently. An electric charge filled the room. When our chins were only a few inches apart, he said, "May I?" He brought his lips to mine. He did this the week before I went off to college.

The obvious wounds me now. He kissed everyone. Still, I forgive the man. His life has not panned out.

At nineteen, Don Widden was poised for success, filled with promise, winner of the Ludlam Youth Talent Award sponsored by the Rotary Club, sent to Manhattan to study with Joshua Lifshin, celebrated student of Horowitz. That was the summer the ragweed count rose to the highest level in history. Don Widden had hay fever. His eyes teared, his cheeks erupted in hives, and he sneezed uncontrollably. He cut back on the frequency from twice weekly to once. Then one warm, bright evening in July, he sneezed straight through his lesson. Lifshin asked him to quit.

Sadly, young Don put away his sheet music and zipped his backpack. Meanwhile, Lifshin sat down to play the Stravinsky Suite Italienne for piano and violin. Itzhak Perlman was visiting friends across the courtyard. Perlman, hearing those interesting, intelligent, Russian chords, that brazen, brilliant melody, whisked his Stradivarius out of its case, stepped out onto the balcony across the way, and played the violin part. Residents on all twelve floors stopped chopping chives or watching *The MacNeil/Lehrer Report* or reading a *New York Times* best seller, and assembled on their balconies to enjoy the duet. Lifshin and Perlman went on to perform the "Chanson Russe," the Divertimento, and the Siberian Dance Suite.

"Bravo, bravo," the New Yorkers roared, coming to a full standing ovation on their balconies, under the thickish, starless, orange layer of diffracted urban light known in Manhattan as a summer night—I've seen it and it's not natural. It's tiring to feign recognition. My bittersweet smile is shrinking to bitter. The woman behind Don Widden is shifting her weight rapidly to demonstrate impatience. "Excuse me," she says three times. You're excused.

"We *will* catch up later," I say to Don. I want him to visit me in the weeks to come, to discuss the eternal mysteries of music.

"I loved your father," the woman before me says. In her clingy coral knit, she's pushing eighty, ignoring the unofficial rule that wrinkles and cleavage should be mutually exclusive. Her waist has been yanked there by Olga of Sweden with an effort so extraordinary, all you notice is the effort. She glows with a vital, deeply ingrained self-love, evenly distributed over her surface.

"Thank you," I say.

"Literally," she says. She's proud of herself—there might be a smirk on her lips. It's hard to tell—the orange lipstick goes outside of the lines. I have the right to remain silent. "I just wanted you to know," she says. "In case you ever need to talk about it." She's through with me. She moves through the arch to the buffet without looking back.

Reception at the funeral home to follow interment, were the words I chose to conclude the obituary. If I hadn't, only a handful of people would have showed, judging from Dad's ninetieth birthday. I wanted a massive send-off, a front-page photo of a dozen troopers saluting a great gold tomb on its way to the cemetery, snarling traffic for hours. Through the arch in the great hall, among other delicacies, are a hundred pounds of jumbo shrimp flown in fresh from the Gulf Coast of Alabama, piled at the base of an enormous ice sculpture that spells D-A-D. The top curves of both Ds are melting a bit. A crack, a hairline emotional fracture, forms in me. I miss him. My hero, my general, my mainstay, my champion, my friend.

The receiving line is still fifty strong. The foyer door opens with urgency and gusto. In runs Lisa, my ex-best friend and a judge in our county court. She's hearing testimony today from a surprise witness in a controversial case involving a child slave-labor ring up on the mountain. Lisa has adjourned court specifically to console me. Lisa is 100 percent class. She's smart, she's just. Her blond two-tone highlighted hair brings out the beauty in her olive skin. In her black suit and pearls, she is attractive, elegant, poised. She is also pressed for time and cuts the line. *Let bygones be bygones*, her eyes clearly say, as she elbows her way toward me. I want to, but before I forget, I need to remember. Something was said five years ago that ended the friendship.

The woman before me now has a musty odor as if she's slept in her clothes for three days. She claims she worked for me at the quarry as a bookkeeper and never got a bonus. "Thank you," I say when she tells me I've gained weight.

We are in the bluestone, fieldstone, and granite business. Our only competitor is the Mafia. Unlike the rest of Ludlum, father was not intimidated by the threat of unlimited surprise violence from the Italians. "When they threatened to kidnap you," he told me often, "I said, '*Help yourself*—you'll be doing me a favor.'" He laughed his cruel laugh. Father said things he didn't mean. He was blunt, strong, and, except for those bumps along his nose, good-looking. He had a fragility or two beneath all that overt strength and bravado. I was confused about what made father tick until I realized the key to father was rage. A hot molten core of rage motivated him to act, even if he were acting the part of a gentleman. He didn't care what bridges he burned. Something of that came through when he talked to the Mafia.

What backed him up? He was a Scot. Scotsmen have hard heads, literally and figuratively. The so-called Glasgow handshake is an enthusiastic, head-on banging of skulls that would give 99 percent of the men on the planet a concussion. Scotsmen stand firm. That is their defense *and* their offense rolled into one. Although they possess deep imaginative power, it does not show up in their choice of combat. Combat is primitive. A Scot today still loves a club. This, too, came through in father's talks with the Mafia.

Our quarry is northeast of Ludlum. Some would call it a blight. Father and I thought it was beautiful. We never got tired of the sight of that little row of men and the trucks traversing the great cross section we had dynamited into our planet, dislodging beautiful chunks of quality stone, hoisting them by crane into our ten-ton trucks, easing them in low gear up the roads that crisscrossed the raw inside of the earth to the sales yard above. When Father was dying, we discovered we both liked the scratchy feeling of breathing in stone dust—it had the taste of money.

Unlike 99 percent of fathers and daughters, we had closure. After a lifetime of snide put-downs from him with never a compliment, never a word of praise, my father lay in his hospital bed, humbled and sedated, poked from head to toe with plastic tubes, clear fluids dripping in, cloudy fluids dripping out, and told me the greatest moment of his life was all my doing.

It occurred during the Father Daughter Fall Classic at the North East Golf & Country Club on the seventeenth hole in the third and final game. Dick Riggs and his daughter, Kelly, were in first place with two under par. We were in second place with four over. People were already congratulating Dick and Kelly. Swarms of club members and a pack of reporters from the local papers were following them. Maybe all that attention and reassurance made them relax too soon. Maybe it was just our year.

The seventeenth hole has a long, uphill fairway with a pond on the left. The green is also uphill with a stand of woods on the right. Dick's drive got him in the pond. Unbelievably, once he got on the green, he took two putts to sink the ball. Kelly's drive was a slice that overshot the green and landed in the woods. To get out, she chose a nine iron. Kelly Riggs is one of the few people in the club who knows what to do with a nine iron. She lined up the shot to land high on the green, so the ball would roll neatly down into the cup, a strategy that worked on the fourth hole and again on the thirteenth. Then she whiffed it.

I got my ball in the hole in two—and Dad came up with a hole in one. Everyone saw it—there was none of that questioning of Dad's scores that went on during the regular golf season. Going into the eighteenth hole, we were four under par to their four over. We won. Did anyone shake our hands? Did they feature us on the front page of the paper? No, they showed the Riggses jumping for joy when they both birdied the thirteenth hole.

The way a community deals with its rich is 100 percent hypocritical. They come fawning at you for donations in the tens of thousands for something they promise to name after you. You give it. Bridges, stadiums, libraries—pretty soon, everything's in your name. The more things in a community in your name, the less credit you get. The person who gets the credit is the one who asked you for the check. Your money is theirs to distribute as they see fit. They believe you don't really deserve your fortune. It wasn't vision, hard work, skill, intelligence, or perseverance. It was luck. You took advantage. You cheated. You stole. Rich people, I am trying to tell you, are an emotionally deprived, persecuted minority.

"Fa-Lo-For-Ho," Lisa says when we are finally face-to-face, our secret password invented the night we sat in her parents' attic and cut our palms with manicure scissors to become blood sisters. Wild, lonely gales of hysterics—made by me—echo through the funeral home.

"Is it . . . devastating?" she asks, when we have both dried our eyes. Lisa's manner always lures me toward love. I want to let bygones be bygones. The effort she's made to appear here and now in my hour of need should be proof enough of her good intentions, but something makes me hold back.

"It's a blessing," I say, the way people do to eliminate real feeling.

Lisa's disappointed. She looks at my crutches, my neck brace, my cold sore. She hesitates to leave my side. "Let me know," she says, "if there's anything I can do." Unlike 99 percent of people who say that, Lisa means it. After my auto "accident" (a hit-and-run involving a stolen UPS truck at night—the Mafia stop at nothing), she brought me homemade chicken soup, *Glamour* magazine, and a new video game.

"We'll talk," I say, in a tone that means we won't.

Here's Belle, Dad's cleaning lady for forty years, with a new man friend, a shrunken thing with soft shoulders and a hard kyphosis, one of the statistically few men afflicted with severe osteoporosis. Halfway down his spine, his Harris Tweed sports jacket flies out on a tangent. Belle takes his arm to underline what a catch he is. Belle is pushing seventy, and she looks good. Her blue eyes sit in her face like they should—no hyperthyroidal bugging out, no yellow film, no disappearing into a cubist nightmare behind trifocals with distracting frames. She glows with health, probably the result of a lifetime of happy, light physical labor.

"We just came back from Peru," she says. She's competing with me—I say nothing. "We were both bowled over by Lake Titicaca," she says. I'm sure you were, between your titi and his caca. "We came back a day early for this," she says. She makes it clear she's here out of the goodness of her heart and not because Dad was good to her, in fact, perhaps Dad was the opposite. "Well, good luck to you," she says with a lingering emphasis as if to imply, *You're going to need it.*

Last in line is my father's sister. She's obese and doesn't quite know where her body ends. She rolls into me, bumping up against my chest like a large, white, fluffy tumbleweed. I lose my balance—easily done with a broken ankle. I land on the floor with a soft thud. She towers over me, asking if she is in father's will. "We haven't read it yet," I say, though we have. My father didn't like his sister. The gift he left her was an insult, the inheritance version of getting a lump of coal in your Christmas stocking. He left her $650. When the lawyer read me that, I roared. She tells me now she needs an eye operation—she needs a deposit to schedule the surgery. "Medicaid should cover that," I tell her.

"I don't like their surgeon," she says. He probably doesn't like you either. I look for the funeral director—someone's got to help me get up. He's in the foyer, reading the guest book with an expression somewhere between boredom and prurience, while he chews on a fingernail. "Help, Mr. Ornstrom, help," I yell. Because I am paying him, he does. I go looking for my piano teacher.

I see him at the buffet, talking to an earnest young girl with long brown hair. I have no idea who she is or why she is attending my father's funeral. I pull rank. "How *have* you been?" I say to my piano teacher in a commanding voice as I place my right crutch on this girl's shoe. Because I am the bereaved, she says nothing, not oven *ow*, just eases her toe out from under the crutch with a series of small, determined yanks and backs away. My piano teacher is reaching across an old woman to dip a shrimp in cocktail sauce. In the process of bringing it to his lips, he drops a blob of sauce on her bare arm. Both her hands are full. She looks at it, then at him, and licks it off.

What follows next as we try to establish our former dishonest intimacy is as awkward, dissonant, and excruciating an exercise as my sight-reading of Czerny so long ago. He pushes the shrimp into one cheek. He's chewing to beat the band and wiping the dripping cocktail sauce from his lips as he says, "*Look you with mad disquietude on the dull sky?*"

"I do, I do," I say. I make up a poignant tale. I say I went looking for this very kilt in Father's trunk up in the attic, only to find it dry-cleaned, pressed, and hanging in my closet, safety-pinned with a note from Father, *Wear for me.*

"How atavistic!" he says. I make a mental note to add that word to my vocabulary. His eyes dart to the buffet. He wants another shrimp.

To hold his attention, I think of another lie. "I'm thinking of going back to the piano," I say. "As a grief thing." "Really!" His brain goes into calculation mode, sending his irises all herky-jerky. "I cannot believe what a coincidence this is!" he says. "I'm selling my grands! You could buy both!"

"I could, couldn't I." My tone is a sarcastic monotone, rich in disappointment and despair. "Excuse me while I sit down," I say. "It's been a long year."

I fasten my armpits over the rubber pads of my crutches and swing myself away. In the director's study, I find a club chair. I seat myself to undergo this unwelcome, rapid, radical revision of my personal history. Here comes the subject, Don Widden, kneeling before me to describe *again* the tone of the concert grand—warm, delicate, clear, no overtones in high or low registers. It's a Steinway Model AIII with a square tail built in 1914, he says. As if I hadn't taken my lesson on it every week for six years. As if he hadn't played me my first Satie on those very keys one spring evening when the sky was the color of molten lava. He says the concert grand is worth sixty—I can have it for forty. The baby grand, he'll throw in for another twenty.

There it is, the number. In any given conversation, as a rich person, you're always waiting for the number. My face clearly shows that I have taken offense, but he only sees cash when he looks at me. And because of this man, I gave up my engagement.

It happened at a dinner party in my honor at the home of my fiancé's parents. I decided to charm the erudite guests with the only erudite story I knew, the story of my piano teacher witnessing a spontaneous duet between Itzhak Perlman and Joshua Lifshin that July night in Manhattan.

As I spoke, the accountant sitting on my left kept glaring at me. He gasped, rolled his eyes, and uttered numerous dismissive harrumphs. He was a small, bent, densely packed man, so utterly rounded and planed and abraded and neutered by numbers in boxes on pale green paper with light blue lines that no one except a client could possibly be proud to be seen with him—not a mother, not a child, not a wife. He happened to be a classical music buff. "Don Widden never won the Ludlam Rotary Youth Talent Award," he said, interrupting me when he could stand it no longer. "And if he had, he would never have studied with Lifshin. Lifshin never taught in Manhattan. Lifshin came from Austria directly to Chicago. He lived there for two years, then moved to Los Angeles."

I was furious. He might as well have said Lord Byron was short, fat, and lame. "You are a liar and a cad," I said. My fiancé's mother remained calm. She was a very statuesque and cultured woman, not beautiful per se, but brave enough to wear her white hair extremely short to better display her museum-quality turquoise-and-silver Navaho earrings. "Ted," she said to my beau in a quiet, queenly aside.

My fiancé leaped to her side. He was statuesque and cultured, too. They were nose to nose. They had the same nose. Some would call it a beak. I did not like the complicity between them. They were of one mind. What kind of husband would be of one mind with his mother? "Do something," she said.

My fiancé walked around the dining room to my chair and pulled it away from the table with me still in it, still talking. I was rattling off the very compositions by Stravinsky that Don Widden had heard the great duo play.

"Siberian Dance Suite?" the accountant screamed. "There's no Siberian Dance Suite by Stravinsky. There's no Siberian Dance Suite by anybody."

"Agatha has not been feeling well," my fiancé said.

"I feel fine," I said. He kept pulling me backwards, away from the table. I grabbed the linen tablecloth and held on. A chaos of china, crystal, and silver hit the floor. As I hoped, the accountant got the worst of it. The engagement was officially broken the following day.

That was only the first time. Every year since then, out of loyalty to Don Widden, I have made myself a laughingstock. Just last month, I spoke at the dedication of the new science wing we donated to the college. I gave the usual science-is-the-future spiel, then closed with my favorite quote from Lord Byron, the lines on the chestnut tree. Several people in the audience laughed contemptuously. A heckler yelled, "Get it right, you philistine! It's Yeats!"

Don Widden still rents the one-bedroom house he rented when I took lessons from him, but it is no longer in a marginal neighborhood. It's in a poor neighborhood. Subsidized housing has sprung up around him. His neighbors are all on welfare. If there is a stabbing in Ludlum, it happens within a stone's throw of Don Widden's house. None of the wealthy people in town feel comfortable sending their children to his house for lessons. He has to go to them. Half the time his car doesn't work. Last winter, father and I drove past him as he was pedaling an old bicycle up a snowy street to a Tudor mansion with ice in his eyebrows and a line of snot swinging like a pendulum from his nose. I cringed and ducked.

"Sixty thousand dollars for two pianos worth ninety," Don Widden says again, "no delivery charge." Those three last words have a dramatic effect. Everything larger than life about Don Widden deflates in a vulgar, comical, final, reverse trajectory, like a balloon released at the neck, farting its way through the air in drunken loop-de-loops, only to land—flaccid, spent, and no more fun—on the floor.

What happened with Lisa happened soon after she asked her husband for a divorce. She invited me to her home—there was something she wanted to discuss with me over a glass of wine. I didn't like the sound of that and I put it off for a while.

The night I finally went, something bizarre had just occurred. Lisa's husband had removed "half the furniture" as agreed, but he had come in with a chain saw while she was in court and removed the bottom half. Their furniture was terrible to begin with—all new, all colonial, all from Sears. All had that identical lathe work, stained brown and coated with high-gloss polyurethane, which, even when both halves were there, did not create the effect of a noble past but of a troubled future. And now, with only the top half sitting on the floor, the insistent decorativeness was twice as psychotic.

We drank our wine. I kept waiting for Lisa to broach the difficult subject she had alluded to on the phone. I thought she was going to ask me for money.

"Aggie," Lisa said finally. "Are you aware that your father has a telephone problem?"

"He does not!" I said. I was affronted. "I just called him an hour ago," I said. I'm afraid my voice was strident.

"Not with his telephone equipment," Lisa said, "with how he uses it." Lisa looked at me with disarming directness. "He says nasty things presumably while getting his rocks off," she said.

"Lisa," I said. My tone was dismissive. "I'm sorry for all you are going through right now."

She punched the play button on the answering machine on the kitchen counter. Some crank had left a message inviting Lisa to accept him amorously in ways that no self-respecting woman would allow even her mate to suggest, let alone a stranger. A few of the descriptions of Lisa's anatomy were startlingly accurate, which told me the caller was her ex-husband disguising his voice. She had extremely thin hips. The caller suggested invasive activities that might have caused those bones to break.

When the beep sounded and the answering machine cut the caller off, I could breathe again. The message was graphic, and I was glad it was over. The next message was him again. Picking up his hairy log where he'd left off. He called five times. Her blank was like blank. He wanted to blank with her blank until she blanked. Never in my life was I more exhausted, ashamed, defiled, and relieved than when the eerie prerecorded electronic man inside Lisa's answering machine finally said, *End. Of. Messages.*

"There were more at court," Lisa said. "My secretary intercepted them and saved them so that I could decide how to proceed."

I wasn't happy with Lisa making me listen to filth that she had brought on herself by choosing a husband with so many different problems, but she needed a friend, and *Fa-Lo-For-Ho* stood for "Faith, Love, Forgiveness, Hope."

"Lisa," I said. "That was disgusting. But *that* was not my father."

Her eyes bugged out. "Aggie!" she said. "Have you lost your mind? I mean, defend him. Apologize for him. Minimize his behavior. Protect him. But deny that that is his voice? An obscene phone call is a felony."

"You have never been more mistaken," I said. I stood up, poured the undrunk bottom half of my wine out of the glass into the sink and down the drain. We didn't speak again.

Of course that was father's voice on Lisa's answering machine. And Lisa wasn't the only one. It was the only good thing about dad being dead. End of messages. Don Widden remains on bended knee before me, reporting the outrageous prices comparable pianos have gone for on eBay. I listen with the springy, weightless wisdom of a recently unburdened heart: none of what he says is true.

When I was growing up, I asked father what my mother was like; he said only that she was a gold digger. It was our cleaning lady who told me how beautiful she was. She was thirty-two to his fifty-four. She had me, then left us both. Any father is a god when your mother leaves you. People don't understand that, especially when a lot of money is involved.

In the foyer, I see Olga of Sweden on her way out the door. Father made a last-minute alteration to his assets—a savings account with a balance of $50,764.00 was closed out. It could have been for her. If so, she deserted him, too, at the end. There was a number father kept calling. His voice was so weak it was nearly inaudible. He kept leaving the same message—he was failing, would she please come. Never had father looked so out of his element as when he understood he would soon be dead. In his eyes, I could see *a heart chilled into a selfish prayer for light.* Whether Byron said it like that or at all doesn't really matter anymore.

There's Lisa, putting on her coat. I thought she was long gone, but she believed me when I said, "We'll talk." There's something burdened about her shoulders, something forlorn about her chin. She looks bereft. *Let me know if there's anything I can do.* Something of the giddy, ego-shedding rush of the convert toward baptism inhabits me. I seize my crutches and swing past Don. Lisa's out the door before I'm halfway to it. There's a crowd. Everyone's leaving at once. I'm going to have to hurt some people to catch up with Lisa. "Move it, dirtbag," I say to my aunt. I hobble out the front door. Lisa is backing out of her illegal spot on the grass. I'll never make it down the steps in time. I yell her name from the top step in a bellow so animal and urgent, I myself am moved. She hits the brake and looks my way.

I, Maggot

MARK JUDE POIRIER

MY MOTHER RARELY SPOKE of my father's family history, but when she did, she spoke in threats: "Ask one more question about that cousin-fucker, and I'll kick the queer right out of you!" or "I'll kill Mr. Maggot if he ever shows his inbred face around here again!" Because I had never heard the terms *cousin-fucker* or *inbred*, I was intrigued. I was ten. I knew what *fucker* meant; a teenage neighbor boy had shown me confusing, shaky videotapes of himself fucking a fat girl from the street over. I couldn't imagine fucking any of my three cousins, not even Bill, whose round shiny biceps stirred me in ways I knew, even at ten, I shouldn't be stirred.

My thirst for knowledge led me first to the dictionary, which didn't fully answer my questions, and then to my mother's closet, where I knew she had hidden a shoe box of old photos, clippings, and letters—important things.

I was more familiar with my mother's closet than my mother was. Her wardrobe was not that extensive, and I had memorized her dresses, blouses, tube tops, shoes, even undergarments. Don't think that I'm a cross-dresser, because I'm not. I never got into that. I was more into organization, so stepping into my mother's closet was both frustrating and exhilarating. I had no siblings, no friends except for the teenager who fucked the fat girl on tape, so I'd often spend hours reorganizing this closet while my mother was at work, Xeroxing or doing whatever it was she did in the strip mall office full of agents who rented out other strip malls. I carefully arranged the dresses—only twelve—by season, then subarranged them by color, light to dark. They were equally spaced, hanging three inches apart from one another. I measured with a yardstick, marked the rod with chalk. The shoes: also by season, then by heel height. But, before I organized anything, I took mental pictures of where everything was so I could perfectly restore the messiness after I had my fun. I had to. If my mother knew I had been in her closet, she would have clobbered me.

I found the box right where I had seen it last: behind a pair of scuffed red pumps. (Oh, how I wanted to buff and polish those hideous shoes!) I knew which man in the photos was my father. I had the same nose as he did, a dimpled three-balled proboscis, a nose I would later learn branded me as a cousin-fucking, maggot-loving, meat-wreath-building piece of inbred trash. My favorite photo of him, a photo I was smart enough to later swipe the night before my mother sent me down to UCLA, at age fourteen, to take part in the Feminine Boy Project, shows him washing his car, a bright cerulean sports car—a TR7, I recently determined after extensive Internet research. He's wearing Levi's and a T-shirt with rolled-up sleeves. Butch. Me, except butch. Not forced butch—real butch. Today, the photo is framed in a tastefully basic frame of dark oak, on a crisp, light blue matting. It sits on my desk next to the computer on which I type this.

The other photos, even the other photos of my father, held no interest for me. My mother, graduating from junior business college in a hideous lavender cap and gown; a small home my parents had once rented in Nova Scotia; me, minutes after my birth, my foreskin intact. The letters were boring. A few from former boyfriends, one of whom wrote that he missed my mother's "hot titts [sic]." There was, however, a ten-page document, handwritten in a loopy script, rolled tightly, and tied with a red ribbon. It was composed in an obscure French dialect—of course, I didn't know that then, when I was ten; I just knew it was a foreign language. I eventually swiped the document, as well, and brought it with me to UCLA when I was fourteen.

The Feminine Boy Project: forty boys, ages six to eighteen, prancing, diddling, tickling, wanking, mincing—all under the careful and close supervision of two psychiatrists, whom I shall call Dr. X and Dr. Y. We feminine boys lived in a small dormitory that had formerly been used to house visiting football and basketball squads from the PAC-10. The very thought that some big dumb jock from Arizona State or Stanford had once slept in the very bed I was sleeping in, had once sat at the desk where I sat, had once lathered his muscles in the shower where I showered, sent me into a high state of arousal. There were big, clunky early-eighties video cameras mounted on the walls in each room. I'm quite sure now that Dr. X and Dr. Y had once been feminine boys themselves and that their research was nothing more than fodder for their prurience.

The Feminine Boy Project was San Francisco's Castro District in miniature, so it prepared us well for the life that awaited us. The boys who were most masculine, or who had developed the skills necessary to come across as masculine, were the ones we all wanted. None of us wanted a prancing Nellie like ourself. The more masculine boys—MMBs—only wanted boys like themselves. That left a bunch of frustrated young fags, each of us getting bitchier as the days passed.

Dr. X and Dr. Y fawned all over the MMBs, especially the post-pubescent ones, granting them special privileges, buying them gifts of body oil and wrestling singlets. We received nothing except three drab meals per day, all of which tasted of musk because, as I later learned, they were laced with testosterone. Yogurt: testosterone; jelly toast: testosterone; cheese pizza: testosterone. The hormones caused several of the boys to develop beer guts, hairy necks, and shrunken testicles but did nothing to help eliminate lisps, expressive hands, or fits of girlish giggling.

After weeks of shoving seminars, basic math and science courses, two hours per day of physical education where we were smacked into learning to throw perfect spirals, I discovered that I could sneak out after dinner for a few hours and stroll about the UCLA campus.

The fourth-floor restroom in the university's main library was where I learned that there are some butch men—mostly closet cases—who prefer the company of girly boys. After a few months of ritualized abuse from strangers in stall three, I explored more of the campus, and eventually found my way to the French department, where I met Emille Gaudette, PhD, the crackpot Canadian dyke who would eventually translate the papers I had stolen from my mother's closet.

Emille was a visiting professor from a small island close to the island from which my father's family hailed. I was a smart kid, if I do say so myself; I knew that I needed someone from the Nova Scotia area to translate the papers, and I asked the secretary, a man I recognized from the fourth-floor restroom scene, if UCLA was home to anyone like that. He directed me to Emille's office.

Emille's door was ajar, and there she sat: a grotesquely obese blob, her blubbery wrist cinched by a man's thick digital watch. She ate pungent sardines from a can. Colette paperbacks were stacked on her desk in precarious towers. She wore a green pantsuit, with a large set of keys affixed to her belt. I had never seen a dyke before, so I was a little taken aback, but the social skills I'd learned at the Feminine Boy Project came in handy, and I introduced myself.

"I have heard about that Project of Feminine Boys," she said in a husky French accent. "I think it is vile, and I have written several letters to the chancellor in complaining."

"It's not that bad," I told her. "Some of the older guys are cute."

We chatted a few more moments, and then I asked her about the papers. She was intrigued, ran her finger along her hairy upper lip. "My childhood was very near to the Island of Prince Robert," she said. "Bring me the papers tomorrow."

I did, and the translation follows:

I, MAGGOT
BY JEAN POIRIER XII
TRANSLATED FROM THE FRENCH BY DR. EMILLE GAUDETTE

On the northwest corner of our island, the Island of Prince Robert, where in winter the wind lashes us so hard that our teeth freeze and crack and dislodge from our purpled gums, where the Gulf of Saint Pierre is gray with millions of dead octopuses, where each of us bears the surname Poirier or Gaudette and, responding to some atavistic itch, curls up with his cousin to stay warm and perpetuate the bloodline, the Spring Meat Wreath custom continues—and will continue despite the protestation of my younger brother Barthelmew.

Throughout winter, each of us in this seaside hamlet of Parmonte dreams of the tinkle of maggot chimes. When the days begin to elongate, we happily prepare by breaking shovels and choosing meats.

Three meats must be used in the braiding: beef, pork, and horse. If no horse is available, as has often been the case, dog can be used, but only if the pork is substituted with lion of the sea. Beef is always available. Pork is not. Moose may be substituted for pork, but not if horse is unobtainable. In this case, snake is used in lieu of horse—which pleases many, as the snakes are easily braided, especially the thin Nova Scotia ice snake, sometimes called the Saint Pierre ice eel, although it is a reptile, not a fish. Thus there are myriad possibilities for the meat wreaths, each producing its own odor and sound.

Barthelmew drinks soybean milk from boxes emblazoned with Chinese characters. He will not sit at the table with the rest of the family—my father, my sister, and me—if any product of animal is being consumed. He does not eat ice cream, of course. Most cookies are made with eggs, so he avoids them. The colored marshmallows in some American breakfast cereals hold their shapes with the help of gelatin that is made from the hooves of various ungulates. He eats no soup prepared with beef or chicken stock—and what palatable soup is not? Barthelmew rides a ferry every few weeks, even in the darkest and coldest months, across the bay to Newfoundland—a six-hour voyage, sometimes through bergs of ice the size of skyscrapers—to buy his animal-free food products from hippies who escaped to our hemisphere for political reasons. Barthelmew eats in his bedroom with the door shut, which my father and I find disrespectful to my sister, who painstakingly prepares our meals. My sister often cries.

The antics of Barthelmew are especially tiresome now because the Meat Swap is in full swing. I search for the best strips, adhering closely to the rules of combination. There is a surfeit of horse this year! Tough bands of the most sinewy cut hang from hooks above many of the booths. I prefer the traditional beef, pork, and horse wreath, as the dog and lion of the sea tend to fall rather quickly, and the hypersalinity of snake blood causes the snake flesh to cling to the meat frame long into summer. I have seen well-preserved and maggot-free snake meat hanging on family doors in July. Imagine waiting until late summer to hear a round of maggot chimes! The availability of horse this year is a good omen: the summer will be long and wet, and the winter short and dry.

Today Barthelmew marches through the Meat Swap holding a placard: IF YOU ARE GOING TO KILL ANIMALS, AT LEAST EAT THEM. He does not utter a word, just paces by the booths, abiding the jeers from angry meatmongers, hiding his face behind his stringy hair. Someone flings a liver at the back of his head—a wet slap.

I promenade along the cobblestones of Parmonte, my white canvas trousers blotted with the blood of the three animals. I step over hundreds of traditionally broken shovels, playfully kicking a few to the curb. My meat satchel is full and heavy. Cousins wave to me from windows and stoops. Their fingertips are bloodstained, their springtime grins wide and honest. Meat is in the air. It is palpable.

The man—considered a man if he is at least fourteen years of age by the first of January—and his winter cousin braid meat together. They make one wreath. The wreath is officially the property of the male and will hang on the door of his house, on the door of the house of his father, or on the door of the house of his oldest brother. The winter cousin is permitted to stay with the man until they both hear the first tiny peals of the maggot chimes. The man builds the frame of the wreath with branches and nails. The winter cousin is permitted to nail the braided meat to the frame, but traditionally it is the task of the man.

We speak French. Our pallor is like the milk of cows, and our hair color ranges from mahogany to tar black. Our hair is thick. No man balds. There are six nose types among us: coned, hooked, hooked cone, conical upward hook, downward hook, and the dimpled three-balled proboscis. My father, my sister, and I were each blessed with the conical upward hook, that of my sister being the daintiest. Barthelmew has the dimpled three-balled proboscis. He is nineteen and has never taken a winter cousin. I believe he is a homosexual.

My winter cousin Doreen waits for me on the front porch, holding her meat satchel like a newborn, rocking it. She has daubed her full bosom with blood, the conventional gesture to indicate she is willing to be my winter cousin again next year. This makes me happy, as she told me in March of last year that my knob-loving needed improvement. I found the appropriate pamphlets in the office of the town physician, studied the diagrams and photos, and went to work that night, her soft thighs pressing my ears flat against my head. Now, the maroon smudge across her cleavage and her coquettish smile tell me that my knob-loving has improved. Barthelmew has never loved the knob of a winter cousin.

According to lore, the original meat wreath was hung in 1874 by Jean Poirier to win the heart of Geraldine Gaudette, the town beauty. The Gaudettes were poor. The children, including thirteen-year-old Geraldine, were gaunt and often ravaged by impetigo, lice, and Canadian sallet worms. But the beauty of Geraldine shone through her afflictions. When young Jean noticed her, he was smitten. Each night, he sneaked meat morsels over to her window. He exchanged the napkin-wrapped meat for transfenestratory kisses. The father of Geraldine was a proud man, and when he learned of the amatory transactions of his daughter, he forbade her from accepting the meat. He forbade Jean from setting foot on his property and threatened to kill him with a garden shovel.

Jean began to hoard meat scraps under his bed until he had enough to make a silent statement—the original meat wreath. But the meat was not braided; it was nailed to a circular board in clumps. Jean felt the rotting meat was a perfect badge for the hateful restriction—if Mr. Gaudette chose to deprive his daughter of the meat, it should openly rot. Each morning, as the Gaudette children passed the Poirier house on their way to school, they stared at the carrion. They smelled it, too, and when they gagged, they would be reminded of their scornful and hapless father, the man who could not provide them with meat of their own. Geraldine never gagged. She breathed in the sweet rotten stink like ambrosia, and her grubby collar was wet with tears by the time she reached her desk at school.

One afternoon, upon returning from school, Jean noticed a maggot plop from the carrion. A moment later, another fell. They squirmed at his feet as their parents buzzed around his head. The falling maggots gave him an idea: the rotting meat was not enough by itself; he needed something beautiful to represent the love he felt for Geraldine. Beautiful sounds! Chimes!

He first tried a cowbell, built a little wooden frame for it and placed it under the falling maggots. Maggots did hit the bell, but the sound was barely audible. Next he hung many small bells of the type usually reserved for reins on holiday sleighs. When the maggots hit these bells: sweet little pings. But the sounds were unsatisfactory to Jean, not quite loud enough. He went to the toolshed and pounded the cowbell into a flat sheet, the clapper and all. When he put down the hammer, the cowbell was the size of a large dinner plate, and as thin as paper. He sawed small notches around the edge of this flat sheet. To these notches he tied the jingle bells with the laces from his old church boots. Using eight sticks, he rigged his new work under the wreath. The final product looked like a miniature wood and metal trampoline.

He waited for the maggots to fall, and when they did, the sound was beautiful: melodious and rich, a politely tuned gong sound followed by the happy jingle of the holiday bells. When bits of carrion fell, the sound was equally sonorous, but deeper, more pronounced.

That night, Jean tiptoed across the lawn of the Gaudettes, ducking behind trees and bushes. He knocked lightly on the window of Geraldine and told her to meet him on his front porch. There, next to the maggot chime, outside the door, Jean had prepared pillows and blankets. They spent the remainder of the night in the arms of each other, listening to the maggot chimes, every note sending a charge through their intertwined bodies.

As he had done every morning since he learned Jean was interested in his daughter, Mr. Gaudette woke in the darkness with nervous energy coursing through his veins. He stretched, put on his boots, and walked down the hall to check on Geraldine. Her sleeping pad was vacant.

He draped a coat over his wool underclothes, grabbed a shovel, and ran to the house of the Poiriers, where he found his daughter and her paramour.

As the first rays of sun stretched across the dewy spring grass, Mr. Gaudette stomped his boot on the shovel, easily bisecting the esophagus and larynx of Jean. The vertebrae separated with ease. The moist cracking sound woke Geraldine, and she screamed.

Nine months later, she gave birth to the first Poirier-Gaudette, a boy she called Little Jean.

Doreen and I braid the meat in my bedroom after spreading newspaper over the floor. The braiding symbolizes the perpetual union of Jean, Geraldine, and Little Jean. Doreen is a tight braider; her three meats become one. Watching her hands as she tugs the wet tendons fills me with joy. Another winter with her! Our wreath is handsome, and I pull the velvet tarp off the maggot chime. Only one group of Poirier-Gaudettes makes the chimes. They live behind the tallest hill in Parmonte, in a large barn. The men in the group have bulging forearms on which they tattoo images of their winter cousins. The women in the group are said to have the largest knobs on the island. I have never taken a winter cousin from the chime group, so I cannot verify the knob information. For his fourteenth birthday, a boy is given a maggot chime by his father, who walks over the hill the night before. The boy becomes a man in a brief, secret ceremony. I am not at liberty to divulge the details of the sacrament, but I can say that it is painless and quite pleasing. Barthelmew refused to participate in the ceremony. My father is still disappointed.

I carry the wreaths, and Doreen carries the chime. I hang the wreaths, and Doreen places the chime. We smile. She licks my neck. Her tongue is warm.

Tonight, my sister, who has never been taken as a winter cousin because of her lazy eye and clubbed foot, prepares the Spring Meal: pheasant stuffed with sweetly marinated beef cubes, glazed in molasses, served on a bed of raisins, chestnuts, and woven bacon strips. And à la carte, she serves us zesty venison muffins, steamed broccoli, and russet potatoes. While the main course my sister prepares is quite traditional, she strays from the norm for dessert and carries in a large prune and maple pie, still steaming from the oven.

My father watches wistfully as Doreen places her fork on her lap, wipes her face with a napkin, and licks my neck. My sister mimes the procedure, licking the air. We leave a portion from each course of the meal on the windowsill to attract men to my sister. Someday she will be braiding meat with a man, I am sure. Someday a man will love her knob. I tell her this. I remind her that her fine cooking will win over any man. My winter cousin and my father agree. My sister smiles and begins to clear the table when we hear a shriek from out front.

I first see tall flames, then Barthelmew amid them, flailing madly like a caged monkey. Some of the broken shovels are not burning, but the fire is big enough to engulf him. Flames dance from his back and legs. His charred head smokes. His shrieks become louder, more pained, higher in pitch and more infantile. Then they stop. I hear the crackle of the fire. He crumbles. His seared head lies flat against the lawn.

My sister screams. My father screams and stomps his feet. My winter cousin does not scream; she gasps, then begins to breathe quickly.

I smell Barthelmew. The stink of Barthelmew is thick. It gathers in my throat and I taste it. I taste him.

A note is nailed to the door just below the meat wreath. Three words in the jagged scrawl of Barthelmew: A FINAL PROTEST.

Where is my maggot chime?

END

Postscript:
I read the translation in Emille's office a few days later, and was horrified when Jean was murdered and Barthelmew burst into flames. Emille did not try to comfort me directly, only said, "The story of Jean is an excuse for inbreeding in a small gene pool. And it is unclear if Barthelmew actually died. I have read other documents that indicate he constructed a large puppet of meat and burned that in his stead. He made his family think he burned, but he lives happily with his man-lover on a small farm of organic vegetables in Oregon, United States." Not true, I'm sure, but a nice unexpected gesture from a macho woman like Emille.

That night, in the dorm, I gathered several boys from the project, and I read them the translation. Silence followed. Several boys' cheeks were streaked with tears—for Barthelmew, the tragic lovers, or all of them, I don't know, but there was a beautiful solidarity among us until stupid Dennis dramatically flipped the blond bangs from his eyes and asked, "What's 'knob-loving' mean?" I wanted to punch him. Honestly. But I realized that was probably what Dr. X and Dr. Y had been conditioning me to do, so I sat on my hands.

Shades of Mango

NATASHA RADOJCIC

THE PARCHED EASTERN EUROPEAN summer of '81 dries up the riverbanks that hum with the buzz of newborn mosquitoes, and the shriveling crops warn of a barren harvest, but Mother and I are saved from scarcity. Her most distinguished brother, the firstborn Malik, has been appointed Ambassador to Cuba and he has bought our plane tickets.

Malik is a real success, the pride of our family. Tito, the president of our righteous and brave country, appointed him to this position himself, and honored him with a gold pin. Fidel Castro complimented the proficiency of his Spanish, and his picture appeared in an important Cuban newspaper.

Take the bad girl with you, the aunts advise. Being under the same roof with a serious, respectable man will be constructive. I have one suitcase, filled with homely and humble outfits designed to steer me in the right direction.

I miss the European drought. Breathing in Cuba feels like inhaling water. We arrive and the shirts stick to our bodies, which seem too tall and too white among the short brown people who greet us on the tarmac. Uncle fits among them like Gulliver. He seems happy to see Mother, even happier to see the pretty, pale all-girl choir here to represent Yugoslavia at the International Youth Festival. Uncle loves pretty women and marvels at the way their elongated limbs fuss about in the heavy sun.

Let me help you with your suitcase, he tells one of them, the one Mother pointed out as vulgar during the flight. The driver takes our baggage.

There are no seasons here. No such change around the girth of the planet; just the exhausting morning heat, then rainy afternoons, followed by the evening heat. The perpetual water flow has transformed my skin and my hair. Both grow thicker, heavier. I cut my T-shirts, shorten a pair of pants way above my knees. The frumpy skirts are still inside the suitcase.

I spend the first few boring mornings playing soccer against the cook's assistant. A grown man of maybe forty lets me dribble the deflated ball between his legs and beat him. A swift career move, as he has his eye on the soon-to-retire driver's position. Getting on the ambassador's good side is a wise choice. Those who drive have access to gas coupons. Just like at home, gas is everything in Cuba.

After a month I am slowly settled. The kitchen is my haven. I love the clank of the dishes, the hissing of the pans, the piercing chatter of the house parrots. The way they fret each time the sizzling oven door opens and the scorching steam surges through their cages.

Lupe, the main cook, serves me cheese sandwiches. Makes the gardener laugh. I don't know his name. He is chocolate-dark, and he never sits down while I am around and never looks at me directly.

Mother stays away from the kitchen, says the jungle heat makes her want to eat more, which is bad for the waist. Aunt Ludmila thinks it's bad to spend time with the help. It's common, she says. She has blossomed since we arrived here. Our Muslim names mark no shame at all; the color of the skin is the chief distinction in this land. We are the whites, better than everybody. Here Aunt Ludmila's paleness is priceless.

At home, the feeble pasty color of her skin was often blamed for Cousin Juma's mental condition. Juma was born with a gaping hole in her stomach, a belly open to the world. Aunt Ludmila claimed her to be a miracle, a precious miracle destined to be cherished. She was kept concealed from the world. In the darkness of her room, Juma read the *Encyclopedia Britannica* and memorized every detail about the beautiful actresses. When she was allowed at the family dinner table, she spun intricate stories. Her favorite was Harlean Carpentier, born March 3, 1911, in Kansas City, which was not in Kansas at all. Juma told us that young Harlean, believing she was soon to be a huge star, adopted her mother's maiden name and rebaptized herself as Jean Harlow. Then in 1932 her husband Paul Bern's unfortunate death shook Hollywood.

There were rumors of suicide. Of secret liaisons. Of a young lover. Jean Harlow was five feet three inches, 36-26-36, 108 pounds, Juma said. None of us had a clue what a foot, an inch, or a pound meant. I imagined they were something wonderful, if they introduced the lovely Ms. Harlow into the company of Ava, the raven-haired, green-eyed vixen who married Frank Sinatra; Rita, who, Juma taught us, was actually Mexican; and of course the French sex kitten, petite Brigitte, who loved animals as much as she loved cutting her wrists with razors.

I hardly ever see Uncle. He is always at the port. The ships under the Yugoslavian flag carry special cargo from Russia, things that keep the Communism in the Caribbean afloat, he says. It's an honor.

During the afternoon downpours I swim in the oval-shaped pool. When it starts to thunder Mother orders me inside. She is afraid of lightning. Afraid of my getting electrocuted. It had happened to me once already. A toaster rattled my teeth. Mother says the lightning is like millions of toasters. I try to ignore her, but when the sky thuds are too loud for her, the pool gate turns up locked. Then I kill my time wandering about the enormous hallways of our splendid two-story mansion, with an octagonal ballroom and endless staircases. The original residents must have been prosperous. Pious, too, since they built the house so close to the church. I can see the sharp steeple from my window. The sugar fields are on the other side. They are monitored by the army.

I seek clues, traces. Who was the husband, I wonder? Was the wife gentle and sweet? What color were the children? Did they learn to walk early? Or were they brawny like me, and walked late, when the poor legs were strong enough to carry all that body, as Mother anguished? What were the secrets the musty tropical concrete witnessed? Lovers? Treasures? I find nothing.

There is a door in the ceiling in the middle of the kitchen. I ask Lupe what's up there. She points her pretty brown eyes sharply at me and says harshly, *nada*. Then she returns to ripping the feathers off the dead chicken that had been soaking in the boiling water. She tugs on the bird severely. Its broken neck dangles off the kitchen table. I am surprised. Several days before, I watched Lupe tenderly hand-feed

Kotorita, one of the parrots, struck down by a bird disease. She used a cotton towel to clean her beak, eyes, and feet. Lupe is even nice to Juma. She smears the yellow ham fat over toast when Aunt Ludmila isn't watching. It's Juma's favorite food, and she calls Lupe "Lupita," which means little and sweet.

I sneak the ladder from the broom closet during the afternoon siesta. Uncle is snoring in the shade of the cabana. The Cuban rum inebriates him much faster than Bosnian plum brandy. The thumping showers outside the window muffle the screeching of the attic cover as I lift it up. At first I see nothing. A bleached plywood storage room with bags of flour, beans, and rice and bottles of oil. The dried meats Mother and I smuggled across the border hang against the wall. We brought five sheep legs. One has already been served. There are only three hanging. Cubans are not permitted to buy meat and I understand why they would steal.

There are two tiny windows. The raindrops bounce off the beefy leaves, barely moving them. Some sort of jungle bird squawks and flutters away through the downpour. From the window in my bedroom at home in Yugoslavia I could see a single poplar, stripped of its greenness by the freezing eastern wind. And far beyond the poplar, the sooty Danube coiling behind the dirty cargo trains lugging coal from Hungary.

There is a big stain on the windowpane. Without getting closer I recognize blood. I once saw a freshly beheaded rabbit stain a windowpane. My screaming grandmother, the executioner, blamed the dull knife for not slicing the artery right. The drops of color on this windowpane are the same. Somehow I know they didn't sprinkle from a rabbit's throat.

I climb down quietly, and run into Lupe's concerned face. She knows to whom the drops belonged. "*No se preocupe*," I say, and offer her my hand. "*Sílencio*."

Before dinner I carefully examine the walls in the den. The Communists destroyed all the portraits. Several new coats of paint haven't covered the dents where they hung for generations. After we sit down to eat, under the chandelier bigger than my childhood bed, I ask Uncle who lived in the house before the Revolution. The damn capitalist bourgeois, he grunts. The exploiters. Those who took more than they needed from the poor, much more than they needed. How are we different, I wonder, but have the good sense not to ask.

My going to school is postponed. I am relieved. I can't understand a word, and even the tallest boys are shorter than I. I'll be starting the English school next month, Mother warns, which means harder math, law, and physics. She's made grand plans for my future. Cuba is a great opportunity, she says, it will open many, many doors for me.

The embassy is giving a huge banquet and even Fidel is expected to attend. Our house is in uproar for three days with preparations. Special soldiers armed with heavy machine guns snoop all over the house. One of them tries to get a better look while I am swimming. Our cocker spaniel barks him away. The dog hates uniforms.

Aunt Ludmila's been hard after Lupe and the extra help employed to assist with the banquet. She clutches at her reddening throat, a thing she does when she is nervous, and she screams after she tastes a sauce Lupe made.

"Disaster, disaster," she cries. "You can't expect a girl, a Cuban girl, to understand complex European dishes."

"Sorry, *señora*." Lupe looks at the floor embarrassed. I am angry. I want to grab Aunt Ludmila by her badly dyed hair. I want to yank hard and scream back, European? You grew up barefoot chasing runaway cows and sucking bee sting venom out of your calloused feet. Leave Lupe alone. But I am too much of a coward and resign to offering Lupe a consoling look.

A young boy signed up to bring in the baskets of vegetables and wine gapes before the colossal Viennese cake. Cubans get coupons for flour in the *líberta*, ration book. The cake had devoured fifty eggs, three pounds of sugar, and three pounds of butter. There is very little flour left in the bag, the same size bag apportioned to an average Cuban family for a month's supply.

"Get out of here, little idiot," Aunt Ludmila bellows.

I catch Lupe's glance. Ludmila may be dim and slow at times, but she is usually not cruel. At least never in front of strangers. She must be worried that Cousin Juma might find a way to escape the woman hired to keep her in her bedroom, a nurse of some sort, and start on the famous actresses and embarrass our country. Or that Fidel Castro, a reputed admirer of redheads, might fall for my mother, who by far outshines the legendary Hollywood beauties, and create an international scandal. From Juma I learned that the mighty Rita Hayworth was really short and drank too much. Mother is tall and I have never seen her drunk.

For days, dressmakers discreetly visited her room, measured her delicate waist, her regal shoulders, her perfect legs. With sharp needles, their fine hands shaped the fabric to fit Mother's beauty. The help is so wonderfully cheap and accurate around here, Mother says. She is a daughter of an illiterate woman, born in a house without indoor plumbing, and yet she bears her newfound distinction with the ease one might attribute to generations of careful breeding.

The outcome is exceptional. My mother is ravishing. I want to kiss her like the men have kissed her before and forget how ugly I am. She shimmers in a green gown, her light burgundy tresses held up with the diamond pin that we, the compassionate and just visitors from a Communist sister country, recently purchased with illegal Western European currency from the impoverished Cubans on the street.

Benya, the driver, is assigned the task of driving me to the ice-cream parlor and a movie during the first hours of the banquet, until my bedtime. Mother wants Juma to go with us. She says it would do her good to be independent, get out of the house, even if the nurse comes along. Then there is some commotion upstairs. Juma, who's been agitated since the morning, is in the hallway naked. The soldiers are peeking from under their humbly bowed heads, suppressing laughs. The nurse is complaining in a fast-paced Spanish. "*Maldita sea, arruinar!*" Ruined. Her only sweater has been bitten through and she's had enough.

Together, Mother and Aunt Ludmila regain control over the unfortunate family heritage. The crazy girl is briskly wrapped in a tablecloth. Mother brings her best brush and offers to untangle Juma's hair. As does everybody else, Juma melts before Mother and concedes. The ebony handle glides slowly up and down as Aunt Ludmila offers her daughter some sweet lemonade. Juma refuses, but changes her mind after Mother tells her fresh lemon is good for acne. I wonder what kind of lemonade makes an agitated person so sleepy, so quickly. As Juma's eyes close, Mother puts the brush down and looks at Ludmila the same way Lupe and I sometimes do.

I follow Benya, who is telling something very strict to the soldiers, down the stairs to our Ford LTD, the only American car I have ever been inside. I love the car and I have washed it twice. I am glad Juma is not coming. I'd rather eat my ice cream and watch my movie in peace.

The streets are brimming. Benya drives slowly toward old Havana, cursing—"*Maricon . . . cono*" at the traffic. The International Youth Festival is at its peak. Everyone is outside. On the corner of Obrapia and Aguiar I see some of the Yugoslavian choir members.

"Let's stop. *Por favor,*" I ask Benya.

He looks at me, then at the girls and I whisper, "I won't tell, won't tell. I didn't about the blood on the attic window either." He looks at me again and I see he knows what happened to the people, and that maybe he too thinks it wasn't right.

"Okay."

The girls are gathered around a Cuban band. The drummer has only one arm and is beating the other conga with his foot. There are three guitar players. The girls are wearing their stage clothes—long, plain black velvet skirts, starched white shirts. They are singing, "*Guantanamera, guarira guantanamera.*" The sweating air juices up the fabric, and the clothes don't look so plain anymore.

The girl Mother pointed out as cheap, the one whose suitcase Uncle offered to carry, the pretty Gordana, is spinning around while the men are clapping. She has taken her bra off. I can see her nipples through her shirt, darker and bigger than Mother's exquisite pink dots. The men around her get louder each time she lifts her arms up and they can get a better look. "*Oshun Kole-Kole, Oshun Kole-Kole,*" they chant to the wicked sorceress, the lady of the river, the goddess. I think maybe it's not so bad to have big, dark nipples like Father's Gypsy grandmother, or these coffee-colored people, and I promise to try not to curse the two brown spots I see growing in the mirror.

A young man snakes slowly out of the crowd toward Gordana. He is darker than the rest, black like charcoal, and shirtless. He grabs her by her hand and starts swirling her around like I have never seen before. The Cubans are clapping even harder, and the drummer is beating faster and shaking the stump of his arm and sweat clamps Gordana's shirt to her nipples, and the crowd is now screaming, "*Kole-Kole, Kole-Kole!*" moving their hips, until Benya touches my shoulder and says, "*Vamanos.*"

"*No, no, por favor*, let me look, let me look please." He smiles and whispers, "I'll go get the ice cream, so we have something to take home."

"*Gracias.*"

I am alone in the crowd. No one is watching me. I shake too. Scared at first; scared that Mother will come looking, making sure I eat the right kind of ice cream and that there are no dangerous toasters or lightning in Old Havana. Then I am no longer afraid, and I start to shake, to bend, to quiver, and an older bronze-colored man comes near me, leans over: "*un poquita blanquita.*" He rubs his dirty hand up toward my shoulder.

"What are you?" he asks.

"*Gitana,*" I say.

He throws his head back, shining his blackened gums; his fedora falls on the ground. "I knew it," he says, "I knew it. One of us."

The night is longer, even hotter than the afternoon. The endless Cuban summer night, tossing, sweating, rolling, thinking about Gordana's dancing partner's chest. The music accompanying the banquet downstairs is stifling. I am ashamed of myself, ashamed of my shaking. I want ice cream. I want my bad mouth full of cold ice cream. I would bite into it and press my teeth into it until it throbs and erases the afternoon, the blackened gums, *Gitana*, *Kole-Kole*, and the sweat.

Benya left a paper box filled with vanilla in the freezer. I refused it when he offered on the drive back. Didn't want to be a child. I do now. I want to feel like a little girl again, want my ice cream. There is a strange change in me, and while I tiptoe downstairs toward the kitchen, past the armed soldier falling asleep with his head propped up against his machine gun, past the servants wearing tuxedos, I no longer want to bend my head down and look away like I used to.

I peek inside the ballroom. The dresses and suits whiz by me, methodically, deliberately. The rhythms claim conquest. People of this room have won. The crystal glasses glitter over the coy smiles of the expensive ladies, and assured gentlemen mix their important stories into the sweltering mustiness.

Mother is the star. She is dancing with Fidel, whose green uniform is flat and not at all luscious compared to her dress. I am proud she outshines him. Hand grenades and a pistol hang around his waist. I change my mind about him falling for Mother. It's not that I'm afraid. No—I grew up around weapons. No, this is not fear. The armed bearded man whose hands are on Mother's body had something to do with the stain in the attic. I am sure. I don't want him touching her.

The kitchen is empty. I sit behind the door and feel tears, a terrible bubbling of tears. Something is irrevocably lost. Lupe passes me without noticing. I can see how uncomfortable she is in the stiff gray dress Aunt Ludmila made her wear for Fidel. Then she sees me and gently whispers, "What is the matter, child, don't cry here." Her hands, tired from chopping, pulling, cleaning all day long, offer a hug. I obey like a little girl. I can still be nice and kind to Lupe. But her hug is no longer enough.

I ride my bike and listen to the youth choir practice every day. I wear makeup. Mother is happy I wear makeup, says she was worried I'd stay a boy forever. Aunt Ludmila disapproves, says it's too early. "If she is allowed to paint herself now, what will ensue at seventeen, eighteen?" Ensue? This big word angers me. I steal her lipstick in retaliation. She wears red and it's the color I want. I put it on once I'm outside, using the bike mirror. My lips are red, and the older Cuban ladies say "*Puta*" when I go by them. Their husbands, I think, don't mind as much.

The beggar ladies smile at me. "*Que bonita,*" one of them calls me. I come back the next day and sit with her. "*Que bonita,*" she calls me again, and strokes my hair with her fingers, her nails cracked from sleeping on the street concrete. The following day I find her passed out. I take my lipstick and put the red on her mouth. She wakes up startled and grabs my arm like a drunk man would, but then she recognizes me, "*Bonita*," and smiles and falls back to sleep with red *puta* lips smiling.

I sit in the back of the concert hall and watch the choir girls. They are tired. The conductor has heard that Brezhnev, the Russian president, might show up for the final performance. The posters of him shaking hands with Fidel hang over the entire length of Havana's skyscrapers. If Brezhnev liked the girls, it could mean a good chance for the conductor at the musical academy in Moscow. The conductor is also a championship swimmer, a sharpshooting winner, and a legend in long-distance running. He will not stop. The rehearsing is ceaseless. The girls are complaining they'll have no throats left to make a peep with if the bushy-eyebrowed Russian does show up. Finally they are dismissed. Gordana's dark-skinned dance partner helps her off the stage.

Like me, he is always around. Sometimes he fixes a stoop or returns a beer to the ice bucket. But mostly he waits for her. His name is Roderigo. They talk with their heads close together like lovers in the movies.

A little more than a week later Uncle starts coming. He arrives alone without Benya. Never offers to drive me home. The crowd of dark Cuban builders with tools parts as he passes. Everybody calls him *Señor*, even if we are all Communist and equal now. Gordana is impressed. I notice he too relishes her big nipples.

Soon she no longer talks sweetly to Roderigo. She is nice to me when Uncle is around. When he leaves she acts like I don't exist. She tells others she always knew she was worth noticing, even if she is poor, her father a dirt-covered miner and her mother a nothing. A girl like her is destined to marry somebody important with his own American car and an important job, somebody everybody calls *Señor*. He promised he'd leave his wife and his idiot daughter.

He says that to every girl, I want to tell her, upset she called Juma an idiot. The party would never allow him to leave Aunt Ludmila, daughter of a war hero who was a close confidant of Tito's. I decide not to speak. She'll find out soon enough, like all the ballerinas and actresses who caught Uncle's eye before her.

In the beginning Gordana and Uncle are careful. She sneaks first into the janitor's room nobody uses. He enters behind her. Later they both come out a minute or two apart. He looks the same. Her hair is a little messier. Then they become sloppier, careless. The zipper on her skirt stays open and the color of his cheeks matches her blush. *Puta*, I want to call him.

There are yellow and white flowers, Uncle's favorite, on the stage the day before the weekend break. Gordana throws her choir cloak off. Her pretty arms gesture *I'll be back in a few days* to Roderigo. He saddens with disappointment. She slips into the front seat of our Ford. The car drives away, the space between her and Uncle's heads narrowing. I sit down and wait. One of the stage builders, the one with the hump in the middle of his back, walks over and whispers to Roderigo. He kicks the ice bucket, yelling, "*Puta, puta!*" Then he sits down in the middle of the slush and seems lost.

Only diplomats can buy Coke. It comes all the way from Germany. I bring a can to him and offer a sip. He looks up at me, at the can, at my pretty dress, and then at his friends who are laughing, "*Vendetta, vendetta.*" I know they are coaxing him to revenge his honor but I don't care. Being close to him makes me forget all of them, everything.

Every day I steal money and food, cans of ham, expensive French cheese, half-empty jugs of wine left over from our dinners. Lupe knows what I am doing. She tells me, "I will cover for you." I give her a big hug and run outside into the shade under a mango tree where he waits.

At first we just ride our bikes. He leads. I follow far behind. He brings along a bruise-colored blanket.

"*Playa?*"

"*Sí.*"

The ocean is loud and we are alone. We sit for a while and listen. Then he lays me down on my back, and spreads my legs, like Cousin, except gently.

"Are you hurting, *me amor?*"

I know what he is asking me and I am not about to admit I am not. So I cry as if I were, and he relaxes and is happier than he would be if he knew someone else has hurt me before him. Gordana is prettier, and has big nipples, and if I didn't have something better than her, all the coupons and ham in the world wouldn't help.

We hide. We look for a different place, somewhere we haven't been yet. Always carrying the same blanket. The canal, the cane fields, the back of his friend's house where every gutter leaks. We return to the beach. The hot wind blows over the dunes when it's not raining, and rolls the dry seaweed in front of us. If we are alone, he washes me in the water after. If the salt burns between my legs, he blows on it like Mother did when I was very small and I had a cut that needed to be washed out with alcohol. Sometimes he brings an empty beer bottle filled with fresh water and then it doesn't burn.

"Blow on it, anyway," I say.

"Do you like it?"

"I like it a lot when it doesn't hurt."

"How long will you be in Cuba?" he asks me after a month as he kisses my forehead.

I pull away from being treated like a child.

"A year, maybe."

"And then?"

"Home, I guess."

"You will leave me?"

"I don't know."

"If you do, I will curse you."

"I thought it's against the Party to curse," I say.

He doesn't answer for a while and I forget the question.

"The Party," he finally says.

I see he is afraid to say more.

"I don't know anything about your family," I say.

The story follows. His father was a famous drummer, left his mother when they were little. She worked in the factory, fending alone for her hungry children. He is proud of her. And loves her. He makes a strange face when I tell him Mother left Father. A woman to leave a man? He's never heard of such a thing. What kind of men do we breed in the Cold Country? Not real men, for sure? He turns his brown back away from me. Only weaklings are left behind by their wives. Your father must have been a softy man, a woman.

I am mad at him for saying such things about my dad, and I tell him he would never be able to come to the house, and how Uncle says the darkies are obstacles for Cuba, lazy, useless, promiscuous.

Now he is angry, and tells me he only came because I am rich and have coupons and how I would never forget him because he was my first, and he would forget me as soon as he turned his back. I laugh. Oh, I'd forget. It was not my first. Men have wasted my time before. I see I have injured him, but I continue. Gordana rides in our Ford every day, sits in the front seat while Uncle has his fingers under her black skirt. She lets him, she lets an old wrinkled man touch her like that for chocolate and a drive in a fancy new car. Uncle even asked about the young darky rumored to have been her lover. "How could you even ask?" she said, frowning, "How can anyone like a man darker than this chocolate?" and she waved the bar in front of him. Uncle apologized for insulting her and took her to the Tropicana show, the most famous show in Havana, where poor people like Roderigo cannot afford to go.

He is on top of me again, stronger, like Cousin now, forcing my arms back, legs apart, and he is crying "*Puta, puta!*" and I am crying "*Te amo,*" and he bites my skin, but then he kisses me, "I am sorry, I am sorry," and then there is more pleasure than ever.

I am bleeding. There are stains on my underwear brown and pasty, like espresso pudding. I don't know what it is. I bled once before, the first time Cousin hurt me. This could be the monthly thing I heard about. The thing that washes out a woman. But it could be something else, something to do with Roderigo. I can't ask. I sneak into Uncle's room and steal several socks. I use one at a time to keep the pudding from spreading. I throw the socks in the public garbage can at night when I go on my bike ride.

I don't tell anyone. Not a soul. Those are my secrets. The socks, Roderigo, all of it. But the rumors have their own way of accumulating and spreading. Slowly at first. The gardener trimming the bushes in the middle of the night to avoid vicious sun sees a black shadow sliding under the mango tree. Keeps it to himself at first. Then he sees it again. Tells the cleaning lady, the young mistress is into voodoo. "Voodoo," she mocks. "She is into what every hot little rich *puta* in this part of the world wants. A *negrino*. I turn up her unmade bed every morning. No voodoo keeps a girl from sleeping."

I hear a rumble of voices in the kitchen one night. Concerned voices.

"It's a disease. It's wrong." I recognize the gardener's nasal singsong. "A rich white girl and a poor black boy."

"Certainly not a new story," Lupe objects. "But I worry. She's not fifteen yet, won't be until the fall. Her mother should get her out of here."

"One of the men should warn the boy," the gardener says. "So he doesn't end up in more trouble than he can handle. What he's doing is crazy. The Party would never allow the marriage."

"Marriage?" Lupe's angry voice shakes the kitchen walls. "What are you talking about? She's not fifteen!"

I ignore the rumors. Mother asks nothing. She spends less time at home. She seems tired and pale. I wonder if being around Fidel wears her out. Roderigo wants me to come and meet his family, wants to meet Mother. When I tell him no his eyes are full of tears. Then I tell him, next time, and he holds me, his body tense and distant as if he knows I am lying.

Three days before school starts, Uncle bursts into my bedroom and grabs me—"You little slut"— by the hair and throws me on the floor. My head hits the upholstered edge of the chair. I almost laugh at him, it didn't hurt.

Ludmila holds Mother back at the door. Uncle kicks me, and I crunch up in a ball. Then Cousin Juma jumps at Aunt Ludmila, and Mother twists away and tackles Uncle. "Stop it," she screams. He turns around and clutches her hands, "Dear, dear, you shouldn't be here, you should be in bed, you are terribly sick, my dear." He turns to me, "Look what you did to your mother, she is sick, sick because of you, her womb is killing her, the womb she carried you in, you no-good whore, see how pale she is."

"Stop it," she whispers.

"Don't tell me not to tell her," he hollers. "She should know what she's done. Your Mother is dying, you terrible, terrible little slut!"

I can smell the rum on his breath, and I know he is drunk, and I am hurting everywhere, and Cousin Juma is screaming, screaming, hitting herself on the face, scratching herself, and her arms are bleeding. "Daddy stop, stop, please," she cries. He only stops because he is tired. He looks at me, tells me, "You make me sick, you make everyone sick," and he leaves the room.

Minutes pass before anyone speaks. Mother sits on the floor with her face down. Aunt Ludmila is leaning against the door holding on to the frame. Cousin Juma is on the floor licking her bleeding forearms and humming. Mother crawls over to her and touches her head.

"That's a pretty song sweetheart," she says.

"Aha."

"Don't do that." She moves Juma's mouth from her arm. "It'll get infected."

I sit in the corner and nobody looks at me.

It's official by the next afternoon—we are leaving. Somebody has packed our bags and piled them neatly by the door; we are flying in the morning. They thought I would fight and scream, but I am just sitting down in my room. Someone carries our bags to the car and loads it. The trunk screeches as they force it closed. I write silly things on a piece of paper, trying to phrase a goodbye to Lupe, to Benya, to Roderigo, but I don't know what to say.

I go over to Juma's room. She is bobbing on the bed, repeating, "Sorry-Sorry, Sorry-Sorry." I take my brush out of my purse. It's old and scratched and not at all as elegant as Mother's. I offer my best pins. She accepts.

"Pretty," I whisper. She likes it when I call her pretty. "Listen to me," I say.

She draws near and tunes in to me.

"You are not as stupid as they think. Just don't drink any of their tea and lemonade. That's what makes you stupid."

She drops her chin lower.

"I mean it," I say, and turn toward the door.

"Lovely," she calls.

I stop. Our eyes lock.

"Thank you."

Aunt Ludmila leads me to make sure there is no scene and mutters, "Please be quiet in front of the help. We have been embarrassed enough by your shenanigans with the poor darkie boyfriend. The shame could get all the way to the Central Committee, all the way to Tito's ears. It could ruin us all." I nod obediently. Lupe touches my arm as I walk by, and it takes everything I have in my legs to continue. Benya is not driving, Uncle is. Mother hides her eyes from me, and I stumble humbly into the car.

The flight back is long and the stewardesses are nice. They know we are related to somebody important, they saw the car was allowed all the way to the plane steps. Mother sits all the way in the front, away from me.

We break in Prague in the transit hotel near the airport. Mother goes to bed and doesn't come down to lunch. At least in here we can mingle with people, she says. Here our passports are good enough for mixing in. We don't have to sleep hunched over in the airport seat with our heads in our hands like we had to in Canada, where people from Communist countries are not like other respectable citizens.

She says she doesn't want to leave the room until dinner, and will I go to that nice lady at the gift desk to buy a watch for Mother's youngest sister.

"I promised her a Bulova," she says.

I have never been entrusted with such a task, and I buy the watch that costs exactly as much as I have in my hands. A watch is a watch, what do I know. I think nervously of Mother in the bed upstairs. A young Czech woman with skin even paler than Mother's wraps the round Bulova with Roman numbers inside a square box.

Mother wakes up for dinner and, sick or not, she is still lovely in her claret dress. The hotel manager walks up to us instantly.

"Please, follow me," he says.

He serves us beluga with bread and butter himself. I ask for mango, and both he and Mother give me the what is wrong with you look—you strange girl, asking for mango in landlocked Czechoslovakia, don't you know this is Europe?

I push the food around my plate.

"Why aren't you eating?" It is the first question Mother has asked me in months.

"Not hungry."

"Don't worry." She touches me gently the way Lupe touched Kotorita. "It will pass. Everything passes quickly when you're young."

I look down at the table.

Back in the room she tumbles onto the bed exhausted again.

"You can lie down next to me if you want," she says.

I cuddle next to her and hold her tight.

"Are you hurting from Uncle Malik?" she asks.

"No. I'm just afraid."

"Of what?"

"I don't know."

She kisses me.

We lie in silence as the planes roar over our transit room. The runway lights are blue and red and orange. They flicker over the thin blanket that covers her body.

"What is my Father like?" I ask after a while.

She turns on her back. The orange light falls on her face. She looks healthy that way.

"I didn't know him very well," she says.

"Aunt Dika says he's a liar."

"Everybody has an opinion."

"Dika doesn't lie."

"Everybody lies."

She closes her eyes slowly and it seems like she is asleep. I wait. Her chest moves slowly up and down for a while as the fourth plane whistles outside. I return to my bed.

"Make sure you are covered well," she says with her eyes closed. "This is not Cuba."

I sneak under the blanket and the sheets are cold and I wonder how many people have slept on them, and were they as unhappy as my Mother is, and were they as scared as I am, and were they pretending to sleep although the clocks are upside down and it's only lunchtime in Havana.

Mother turns on her hip. The blanket falls into the crescent of her waist. Her breathing changes, gets faster. I think she's crying. I go back to her bed and hug her again. She seems thinner than a minute ago. I kiss her the way she used to kiss me when I was little and she thought I was sleeping, on the back of my head right where the hair disappears into the neck.

"Sleep, *Mamita*," I address her the same way the little Cubans address their mommas. She is relaxing. I whisper, "I too left my heart in Cuba," but she says nothing and she just shakes a little as the muted sobs rattle her body. "Don't worry," I tell her, "I am here. *Guantanamera*," I sing, "*guarira guantanamera, ne se preocupe niña, te amo, te amo, te amo.*"

Christ, Their Lord

STACEY RICHTER

WHAT WERE WE THINKING? Well, it was June. June! One hundred and eight degrees every day. We had been looking for over six months. The house had a pool. A pool! The sign beside the curb said *reduced.* Then there was the adorable 1950s-ness of it—the pink and white tile bathroom, the spangled Formica in the kitchen, the flying-saucer light fixtures. And this business about the tyrannical neighborhood association, about the streets being closed to cars and filled up with hay carts and carolers and schoolchildren and tourists, hay carts loaded with mentally handicapped adults bellowing with marvel at the shiny, shiny lights, here in the subdivision of Yuletide Village, which so kindly puts on a display of holiday lights for the community for three weeks every winter—spreading the cheer, spreading it like manure—we thought, what did we think? We thought I could handle it. But Jesus fucking Christ.

Outside in the street, I can hear people caroling—*caroling*, the most odious of verbs. And yet:

The Cuervo Gold
The fine Colombian
Make tonight a wonderful thing.

Trevor loves Christmas! He associates it with huge boxes filled with presents, glazed hams, furry mittens, hypnotic lights, pecan pies made just for him. I associate it with empty passageways in deserted malls where "Jingle Bells" plays over and over, followed by a glockenspiel version in Walgreen's and "Deck the Halls" piped into the parking lot, rendered by chipmunks. Meanwhile, edging in from the side, is a memory of my mother sitting me down and instructing me how, as a Jewish child, to properly sing Christmas carols:

O come all ye faithful, joyful and triumphant
O come ye, oh come ye to Bethlehem
Come and behold him, born the king of angels
O come let us adore him,
O come let us adore him,
O come let us adore him! Christ THEIR *lord.*

Something happens to people's brains in the Sun Belt. I believe the constant overload of vitamin D has softened my skull and turned me nice, so that I've started to act like a nice person—though maybe with a little more of it I will overdose and just come into my own nastiness. For it is innate, at my core. The true flowering of my being is bored and acidic and annoyed with the incredible idiots who surround me, always talking about themselves.

As an antidote I decide to read more great books so that I can keep company with the likes of Shakespeare, Virginia Woolf, Plato, but this time around Socrates strikes me as repulsive, the kind of man who does not shower, does not cut his toenails, and cannot stop disabusing his neighbors of various innocently held notions. He picks food out of his teeth while explaining exactly how and why they are stupid asses—until finally they get so sick of his shit that they *execute* him.

Obviously, this is somewhat extreme. But killing one's neighbors. Now there's an idea.

Next door to the west are Jim and Cindy Nickle. She's a kittenish, fifty-year-old schoolteacher with long legs, dyed hair, and eyes loaded with mascara. I find Cindy's girlishness loathsome—her fakey hostess patter, fluttering lashes, house pride, her complete and utter dedication to the veneer—it's all freakishly like a Cheever story, but without the antique furniture. She talks and talks—the subject is Christmas decorations! Because the bad thing is starting, the very, very bad thing. Her husband, Jim, is handsome yet inert, a chair-sitter. "Jim thinks I'm terrible!" she says. Jim leafs through a magazine. Every now and then, perhaps preemptively, Cindy cries, "Jim, Jim, stop!"

In the first week of December we enter the casual, laid-back ambit of Christmas hell. The neighborhoodwide decorations go up.

The cherry pickers give me hope. They are sort of intriguing, with the men wobbling up there in plastic tubs stringing lights along the branches of the Aleppo pines, big shaggy yeti that do not evoke the tannenbaum. Then, one by one, our neighbors begin to erect elaborate dioramas in their yards. Apparently, there is a contest. Cindy Nickle rings the doorbell and makes me come out and pretend to admire her Wise Men, which are wooden cutouts, decaying and faded like my mental companion Socrates. For some reason, when I look at them I go into a trance; this reminds me of the experience I had with the dead paloverde beetle under the stairs, three inches long and disgusting, eerily reminiscent of half a baked potato. I couldn't tear my eyes away from it. I just stood there for five minutes, zombied-out, staring, thinking: *Ick! Ick! Ick!*

Possibly the pot smoking is not helping things.

A few words about Trevor: he is not my husband. We do not plan to marry. We do not plan to reproduce. We keep separate bank accounts and when we go out to dinner we ask the server to split the check on two cards. In any other neighborhood, in any other part of our mildly liberal desert town, our relationship would be unremarkable. However, we've masochistically chosen to live in the most conservative subdivision we could find, a little slice of *I Love Lucy* and *Leave It to Beaver*, a relic inhabited by school principals and policemen and old, old ladies; plumbing contractors documenting the evils of fluoridated water; a gnarled minister; people with flagpoles in their lawns and RVs entitled *Windpasser* or *The Invader* parked in their side yards. We ourselves seem so strange by contrast that the neighbors occasionally walk out of their houses and look at us if we are, for example, doing some yard work out front wearing black T-shirts and black shoes with Walkmans attached to our heads. What are we? Satanic fornicating animal mutilators? And then there is the parade of homosexuals and curators and musicians and freelancers and enviro-activists and hunchbacks and dwarves and other unmarried people who occasionally visit us, our friends and acquaintances, degenerates all.

Anyway, Trevor. He is so cute. He has a dent in his chin and curly hair that sits flat against his head, like the marble hair on Michelangelo's

David. Anyone who can do funny voices as he can deserves a medal. Sometimes I think he would drink fourteen martinis every night if he didn't think it would displease me, but he works hard all day in his little home office, designing Web sites that help people buy important things, like patio-misting systems, and is funny and sweet and only occasionally teases me about the dark hair growing out of the mole on my neck. I'm absolutely certain that he loves me, but sometimes, to make sure, I follow him from room to room like a hungry little dog.

You'd think that the Nickles would have a nicer Christmas display, as everything else in and around their property is polished and controlled in a manner that makes a person wonder when Jim and Cindy stopped sleeping together. The poodle clip of their hedge, the Tombstone roses twined carefully over the trellis around the door—chuppa style, the style of my people, greedy eaters of borscht and chopped liver, and three slices of rye bread with that—for the Nickles everything must be outwardly nice. Must be nice! Of course, there's their thirty-five-year-old son who still lives in the back house, a sort of converted shed with an air conditioner completely conjoined to the double-brick exterior via rust. I've looked inside: cot, dorm fridge, bong, cable box, a stack of comic books hiding a larger stack of porn. The son himself is as pale as a cave creature though his palms have a faint orange glow from a diet of processed cheese snacks.

That he is roughly my contemporary disturbs me.

And that together we have been doing some bong hits.

I need a special sticker on my car now to get in and out of the neighborhood in the evening. The sticker designates me as an accursed resident of Yuletide Village as I honk and scowl and inch my way at five miles per hour through the smiling and entranced crowds touring the holiday lights, until I manage to startle a lady in a three-wheeled Handy Cart out of the way and turn into my own driveway—a pool of darkness in a sea of light. For we have no decorations. No crèche, no baby Jesus, no rebellious Star of David. No animatronic carolers jerking to-and-fro like drunken frat dudes, no Charlie Brown in a snowsuit, nothing to delight children or adults or disabled adults or grandparents or sullen adolescents with creamy sentimental centers who are not really so tough. What we offer the holiday crowd is this: a little of nothing for no one.

I fiddle with the tape player in the dash. I've been experimenting to see what kind of music cancels out Christmas music. I had hopes for hip-hop and thrash metal, but I've discovered that it's the mellow, pot-smoking music of the seventies that neutralizes merriness best. I sit for a minute in the driveway, cranking it. Steve Miller sings: "Some people call me the Space Cowboy / Some call me the Gangster of Love . . ."

As I make my way from the carport to the kitchen door, a random man yells at me. "What kind of a jerk doesn't celebrate Christmas?"

"My kind of jerk," I mutter back.

In the evening, Trevor sits me down. He says he has a suggestion regarding the decorations. He wants us to have some.

"Nothing elaborate or stupid. Maybe just a string of lights."

What Trevor doesn't understand is that My Hate is heartfelt and true and not something to be disregarded. My Hate must be respected. It is stately and grave and very sad, like an elephant in leg irons.

"I don't think so."

"Okay." Trevor sighs. "How about a log?"

We're sitting beside the flagstone fireplace, beneath the amoebae-shaped overhead lamp, in the bliss of our pure, never-renovated fifties living room. I'm wearing a puffy dress and an apron. He's drinking a martini from an angular martini glass. Previously, I had been in the back house doing bong hits with the Nickles' revolting bat child, who's happy for the company I guess. I guess no one has ever talked to him voluntarily. I knock at the window and stand outside as we pass the bong back and forth. I think it's clear to both of us that the interior of the shack is totally encrusted with semen and could be described as such, like some kind of nouvelle cuisine entrée, monkfish, and that it would be wholly unacceptable for me to set foot inside. So I stay out in the yard, leaning against the parts of the shack that have been rinsed by rainwater. The Bat Boy and I agree that the marijuana makes the lights look more interesting.

"A log?"

"Yes."

"A log and only a log?"

"Yeah. Here's the thing. It's pagan."

Trevor shows me an article from a Christian newspaper called *Good News*. It explains that Jesus was not actually born in December, but in midsummer. The article goes on to urge Christians to stop celebrating Christmas because it is a pagan holiday bequeathed to us by hairy Druids who worshipped trees, wine, beasts, mind-bending herbs, and the holy fertility of vaginas.

"Those pagans sound just like Hell's Angels."

"Kinda," Trevor says, with some doubt in his voice.

I dust off my apron and pick out a log from the bin of firewood beside the fireplace and carry it out the door. There are maybe a hundred pedestrians on the sidewalk in front of our house at that hour, gawking at the decorations on either side, bundled up, singing, holding cups of spiced cider, faces awash in golden light—and they all turn to look at me when I open the door. Who am I? I might be Santa! Trevor leans against the doorway pinching a martini glass like Cary Grant. I walk to the center of the lawn. I heave the log from my chest and it thuds into the center of a square of winter grass and lodges there. A log and only a log.

It looks rather festive.

Sometimes I wonder what the Bat Boy thinks about all this. It's hard to tell. As I open the gate between our yards and approach the shack he bounces up and down like I'm his favorite babysitter and says, "Dude, guess what? Guess what? I watched *The Twilight Zone* marathon today!" He's pudgy, with close-set eyes sunk deeply into his head. His face is greasy and sometimes a hair protrudes from his nose. Weirdly, the Bat Boy has great enunciation, giving him an air of maturity undercut by his tendency to mouth breathe, to chuckle vacantly, to rehash eighties slang. He often shields his eyes with his hands while we're talking, as though I am a blinding light. I don't mind, as he's so nauseating that I can barely bring myself to look at him full in the face anyway.

"Any good?"

"Bitching," he enunciates.

I lean against the windowsill of the back house and accept the bong while in the background, wafting on the breeze, floats the statement: "It's a holly, jolly Christmas." The bong is made of blue plastic and the little bowl is packed with pungent sinsemillian. The Bat Boy gets it from Fat Man, who comes by once a week, a lifetime supply of adipose rolling around beneath his T-shirt—one of his few other visitors.

The Bat Boy gestures toward the bong and says: "It's like it sucks your brain out, puts it in a Cuisinart, then pours it back in your skull all smooth."

Indeed, he is correct. I look out over the Nickles' backyard and feel the smooth-brain beauty of night in the desert, crisp but not cold, the moon above like a spotlit Chihuahua, the Christmas lights blinking in the neighborhood beyond, so unreal. So totally fake, the cheer and goodwill and such. The Bat Boy starts his strange, guttural chuckle. In some moments he seems just slightly off in his manner, as though he'd spent a few seminal years in another country—maybe France. Then he talks about going to the salad bar with his mother and filling his plate with raisins and I realize that there's something deeply wrong with him. I'm worried for the Bat Boy. He's thirty-five and has never done his own laundry. My God, who wouldn't be worried for the Bat Boy? He's clearly in the throes of something universal and corrupt. He smells sour. He doesn't floss. He looks at me with his sunken eyes. I'm probably the only woman who has ever spoken to him more than once, aside from his mother. He knocks the bowl against the side of the shack and the ashes sprinkle out. I have a question for him.

"You know that song 'Jingle Bells'?"

The Bat Boy nods.

"What kind of weird grammatical thing is going on with that 'jingle'? What is it? Is it an imperative verb? An adjective? The horse's *name*?"

The Bat Boy stares at me blankly, then says, "It's the bells." He chuckles and adds, "They jingle."

That is what the Bat Boy thinks of all this.

Later his mother tells me that he can play "Flight of the Bumble Bee" on the piano flawlessly. But nothing else. Not even "Chopsticks."

Elsa comes over and talks and talks but doesn't listen, as is the way with Elsa. She's an artist with willowy arms, neck, and legs and a big fat ass that I would never dream of mentioning if I liked her better. She paints transgressive portraits of dead animals (as, curiously, have nearly all the artists I've ever known). Trevor finds her sort of relaxing. "Because you never need to worry about making conversation when Elsa is around."

"I know people who would kill for this audience," she says.

"Audience?"

"These crowds outside. These hordes of people. Where can you find a gathering like that? An audience that possesses the gaze, that sees, yet without anticipating art or even beauty."

"They're just here to look at our log." Trevor is sipping a cocktail called a Gibson, which is a martini containing something that isn't an olive—possibly a cotton ball.

Elsa continues on as though no one else had spoken. "Yet they come to behold, to witness a visual experience. Something transcendent, beyond the seasonal. Beyond the Santa or the Rudolph or the tripartite Snow Man."

"I don't really think of it as transcendent. More like torture."

Elsa fixes me with her chilly stare. "Right. Well, you can whine about it, or you can use it as inspiration to make something better." Elsa bites a nail. "You should do something with this. You should make a statement."

"A statement?"

"Exactly. Like art. Like some really motherfucking intense art." Elsa walks to the window and flings open the curtains. She gestures toward the bedazzled neighborhood overrun with children and carolers and grandparents and horseys. They all look back in at us through the window. "What is this, if not a vernacular form of installation art?"

"Christmas decorations?" I venture.

Elsa looks at me with disdain, as is the way with Elsa. "Get out of your head," she advises. "Get out of your head and into the world."

I'm mellowing out with Steely Dan's "Gaucho," trying to block out the caroling, when my mother calls. My mother—always helpful, always striving. She's the last of that generation of women who were not expected to have jobs or even hobbies. Therefore she's been forced to hurl herself into the business of others, endlessly, day and night, just to keep herself busy, the poor thing. She's become fascinated by the holiday occupation of our neighborhood.

"Wouldn't it be terrific if you had kids of your own," she says. "They'd be so excited!"

"I'm sure they'd be apoplectic. But wouldn't you want them to be more Jewish?"

"Of course, but I'm thinking about the lights. Lights don't have religion. They're universal."

"They twinkle." I start to laugh, because I'm stoned. Which is basically the only time that I get along with my mother.

She starts to laugh too. "They do! We had beautiful lights on the house on Lawndale Avenue when I was a girl."

"What?" I stop laughing. "What?"

"And angels. Fabulous, golden angels."

"What did you say?"

"I said 'angels.' Don't worry, they were nondenominational. There are plenty of angels in the Old Testament."

"You never told me this."

To honor our Jewish heritage, and according to my parents' wishes, my own girlhood was spent without lights, trees, stockings, Santa, eggnog, or goodwill of any kind. My parents generally spent Christmas day doing yard work while my brother and I watched undesirable Christmas specials on TV. An effort was made to substitute Hanukkah, but it drifted around on the calendar from year to year in a way that made it hard to take seriously.

"I didn't tell you? That's funny. I must have mentioned the tree?"

"What are you saying? That you had a Christmas tree?"

"Oh, well. Not every year."

"You had a tree?"

"It's not important. It just occurred to me that Grandma might still have the angels in her garage. Maybe we could send them to you. You could put them on the lawn."

"I don't want them."

"I'll just poke around."

"Did you hear me just say I don't want them?"

"Well that's fine. That's not a problem. The last thing I want to do is go digging through bins of my mother's garbage."

The nondenominational angels arrive in a giant box two days later, overnighted. For some reason, perhaps because Trevor is busy working, I decide to take one over to show to the Bat Child. It's evening. The lights are just twinkling on and the police barricades that keep out nonlocal traffic (with the exception of horse-drawn hay carts) are just being set up. Christmas hangs in the air like a fetid odor. I have a terrible feeling in my stomach, true dread, as though I will always be exiled. I will be stuck in the most horrible place imaginable, a seventies fern bar, while everyone else is happy and full of cheer. Everyone else is gathered in front of the fire, decorating a tree, singing about love, while I sit alone on a dirty wooden bench with my feet scraping the orange shag carpet, droning *Christ their lord.*

The Bat Boy slides open the window and hands me the bong. He has the waxy look of the unwashed and a fold of belly hangs out from under his shirt. I accept the bong and press my mouth to the plastic tube. It only takes a moment to realize that what we are smoking this evening is some truly choice marijuana, deeply spectacular. I look in the bowl. Within is a half-burned bud, sparkling with resin. The Fat Man has outdone himself. Almost immediately upon exhaling I possess a clarity that allows me to see the nature of things in their truest, deepest aspect.

"Good weed."

The Bat Boy nods sagely. "Most definitely. Excellent. Fat Man called it 'Truth Teller.'"

I nod. Yes, truth. It's everywhere.

"I've been smoking it all day." He looks into the middle distance and says, "Now I understand."

I giggle.

"Beam me up," the Bat Boy says, and I giggle harder. I feel something under my arm and look down to see the angel. I hold it up to show the Bat Boy. The angel has a sweet, porcelain face, like a genderless doll. It's as big as a three-year-old. He/she is dressed in golden robes that end just above a pair of little black slippers. The Bat

Boy and I stare at the angel for a while. I can see the deepest, truest aspect of things, and what I see is this: the angel is adorable.

The Bat Boy shrinks back into his shack and, in his clipped voice so full of wisdom and stupidity, says, "Holy shit. That thing is evil. Get it away from me."

Then he withdraws into the shack and snaps the window shut.

One advantage—the only advantage—to The Occupation is that it provides an excess of light, people, and police protection that allows me to walk around my own neighborhood alone at night. Therefore I am feeling very independent and stoned as I amble around later that evening, looking at the Santas dragging their bellies on the rooftops, the reindeer pawing the air, the lampposts striped like candy canes. I go all the way to Gavin Road, and it's getting so cold on the way back that I have to put my hood up. The streets are half-empty but the lights are still going full force, twinkling like demons. Some people have really gone all out. One family has filled their front yard with polyester batting, to give us desert-dwellers the feeling of snow. Little soft-sculpture children throw "snowballs" at a floppy soft-sculpture man. Other homeowners have barely tried or tried strangely and failed, like the inhabitants of the house decorated entirely in blue lights, glowing like a gigantic bottle of Windex.

When I'm nearly home I notice that someone is following me, darting behind me from tree to tree like a secret agent. Who is it? Why, it's the Bat Boy! Why is he following me? Because no other girl has talked to him in twenty years, so of course he's madly in love with me.

I guess I forgot to mention that.

Because nature abhors a vacuum, we put the angels on the front lawn, halfheartedly, propped beside the log. They are not properly lit. They are not staked to the earth and could be stolen. We are not trying very hard, due to My Hate, and I feel stupid and hypocritical to be trying at all, but Trevor has been bitten by the spirit of the season and thinks the angels are cute, and who am I to extinguish his joy and cheer and tell him not to drink so much? Why shouldn't he drink gallons and gallons of martinis? God knows I'm getting stoned often enough with the Bat Boy who's probably imagining me posed in revolting sexual tableaux involving elves even as I stumble back into our swank, fifties living room with a slack jaw and bloodshot eyes, smelling like bong water. At this, Trevor fails to blink an eye. He has never asked where I go every night when I slip out the sliding glass door and disappear for thirty or forty minutes. I don't think he's even noticed.

But he does notice this: several days after we put the angels in the yard, we come home from an outing to find that someone has been tampering with our angels. Someone has been *fucking* with them, more accurately. There are four angels. We find that two of them have been buried head-down in the yard so that their little legs are waving immodestly in the air. The other two are splayed, cruciform, across a couple of prickly pear cacti, their garments rent by thorns. Oh my. It looks quite uncomfortable. But that's not all! Someone has been very busy. Written largely across the lawn, in tiny white lights held down by wires, is the word "Evil." An extension cord snakes over to an outdoor outlet on the side of the Nickles' house.

"Wow," says Trevor. "Wow. When did you do this?"

"I didn't."

Trevor follows me into the house saying, "I don't get you," and, "Did you do that to piss me off?" and, "That's actually psychotic," while I keep repeating that I didn't do it. But Trevor will not believe me until I finally break down and explain about the Bat Boy and the bong and the semen-encrusted shed and the evenings we've spent together, passing crackers smeared with orange paste back and forth through the sliding window, passing the blue bong back and forth, talking, giggling, until Trevor starts to get a wounded look around the eyes. Then finally he does understand, and goes into his office and says he doesn't want to talk to me right now.

"Hey," I say through the door. "Hey, why don't you come out for a minute. Do the Chinese restaurant waiter! Do the angry Belgian pastry chef!"

I wait. Nothing.

I guess Trevor is not going to do any funny voices for me today.

Later I sit in the splendor of our perfect fifties living room, in the dark, listening to the crowd shuffle by outside our picture window. Sometimes I hear nothing and sometimes I hear a kind of angry murmuring, the kind that might be made by a group of men in Klan outfits. For the moment I have switched to martinis. I imagine the gaze of the public falling upon our angels with buried heads. Our angels impaled on prickly pear. Maybe this is educational: when bad things happen to good angels. Everyone now and then I peek out the window. The log is still there! Valiant little guy. People are throwing trash at our display to express their displeasure. A couple of people ring our doorbell, hoping to express their displeasure in person.

I'm enjoying my martini. I can understand what Trevor sees in them. It's like smoking pot, but with more hostility and extra trips to the bathroom.

The next morning I get up and start picking trash out of our front yard, feeling a trifle ill. The neighborhood looks truly desperate in the light of day, with everyone's decorations turned off and washed-out in the flat desert light, the road littered with piles of horseshit bisected by tire tracks. There is nothing like Christmas in Arizona, azure skies and 72 degrees, to make the world look fraudulent. Someone has put a Big Gulp cup over the foot of one of the angels. It smells somewhat uriney, and I'm wondering if someone actually *peed* on one of the angels when a feeling comes upon me, a little engine of prissiness. I decide what I'm going to do. I'm going to tell. So I march next door and ring the Nickles' bell.

Cindy answers wearing a ruffled green and red bathrobe. She already has her eye makeup on, and she's talking on the phone. She makes me wait for a while and then rolls her eyes and tells me she's on hold—can I be quick?

I tell her that I think she should know her son has made an unholy diorama depicting the graphic torture of angels on our lawn.

She gives me a level gaze. "Floyd didn't do that. Floyd likes to stay in the back house."

"Yeah, but the thing is, he did."

She presses her lips together. "Floyd likes to stay in the back house. Jim! Jim?"

Jim's voice floats through the door. "What?"

"Honey, where does Floyd like to stay?"

He echoes her singsong tone: "Floyd likes to stay in the back house."

She looks at me through wide, mascara-framed eyes. "See?" And then she closes the door.

That night a police cruiser stops in front of our house and sits there with its lights flashing against our window for a while and then drives off. More trash is thrown. The doorbell rings twice. I ignore all this and spend the hours of The Occupation watching a movie called *Endless Summer 2*, about a pair of suntanned boys who roam the planet surfing beautiful, blue waves. Every now and then I get up and go listen at the door to Trevor's office. He's in there, tap-tapping on his computer.

Of course, the obvious thing to do is to remove the angels. Why not? Really. I've already tried twice. But each time I end up just standing on the lawn, staring at them, just staring like a zombie. I cannot do it. I just can't. We had good times together, the Bat Boy and I, smoking out, gazing off at his old tetherball pole with the withered globe at the end, his mother's voice whining across the yard from the big house. There is no sanctuary like the sanctuary of outsiders; there is no fellowship like the fellowship of the scorned. Deep inside we all have a Bat Boy, echolocating inside an empty cave, forever shunned, hated, misunderstood, smelly, flinging our ardor unsuitably, desperately, making strange things in the hope of attracting love. Who am I to say this is wrong?

Furthermore, we're in agreement. Christmas is evil.

Days pass. Somewhere, elsewhere, someone is opening the little doors of an Advent calendar. Trevor will not move the display and I will not move the display and it's obviously bothering him. I infer this when Trevor stops talking to me altogether.

"Hey!" I say as he passes me in the hallway, "Who's the slowest mouse in the whole world?" But he doesn't even look tempted to break down and do the voice of Slowpoke Rodriguez, the stereotypical

Warner Brothers mouse whom I generally nix as too offensive, though Trevor does his accent so well.

I have forsaken the Bat Boy and his sticky weed for several days because I am a person of conscience and morals and his behavior has weirded me out. But Trevor won't talk to me, and our friends are off doing Christmas things that don't involve us, and no one likes me anyway, I've decided. I'm ill-tempered and bitter. Like Socrates, I cannot stop disabusing people of various joyously held notions and beliefs. Who wants to indulge my scowling? Nobody. Of course, people are warm and full of spirit at this time of year, but I am lonely, lonely—if only I had a wonderful little dog to look at me with adoring eyes, while I work alone in my drafty room and Trevor works next door, alone in his drafty room—I think about this until, finally, I feel so forlorn and sad that I decide to go back.

The light is on in the Bat Boy's shed but he's nowhere in sight. Usually he's waiting for me, leaning against the sliding window like he's ready to take my order. I pad across the grass and look inside. Bat Boy is lying on his back on his cot beside a reading lamp. One hand is at his side, touching the bong. His face is relaxed. What is he doing? He's staring at the ceiling. I tap the glass.

In one movement, the Bat Boy swings his feet to the floor and starts loading up the bong. He leans over, chuckling softly, and slides the window open.

"I thought you weren't coming back."

"No, I'm here."

"Dude," he says, with sadness, "I thought you weren't coming back."

"Floyd."

"You're going to love this herb."

"Floyd."

He chuckles. "That's my name, don't wear it out."

"Okay, I just have to ask you. Did you do that to our angels? Did you, uh, *reconfigure* them?"

"Yeah, yeah. Wicked, isn't it?"

"Sort of. Some people don't like it though."

"They're just bugging."

"Yeah. They are. They're bugging on our doorstep."

"My mom and dad are totally bugging. They don't like it AT ALL." He chuckles and hands me the bong.

I take a hit of the sweet, sticky smoke. "Really? It's better than their lame-assed Wise Men."

"You think?"

"My God. A thousand times better."

The Bat Boy's hand creeps across the windowsill until it rests on top of my own. He squeezes. I'm pretty certain he's been picking his nose with those fingers. But for some reason, I squeeze back.

Elsa starts hanging around, taking photographs. At first she's half-angry, half-excited that we've taken her advice and created some really motherfucking intense artwork in the yard.

"I can't believe it," she keeps saying, and also: "I hope you're telling people this was my idea. I want full credit." Elsa on this particular afternoon is wearing a parka splattered with paint and a pair of shorts she found in the garbage—she makes sure to tell us this, because she wants us to know that she thinks buying clothing is repulsively bourgeois. "This is great," she keeps repeating, snapping away with her camera, "this is anti-everything. Anti-religion, anti-neighborhood, anti-beauty. I can't believe your neighbors haven't lynched you."

If I could wedge in a word, I would wedge in the word *yet*.

Eventually Elsa stops talking long enough for me to explain that in truth, we didn't make the motherfucking intense angel thing. Trevor nods. He's not talking to me, but he'll talk to Elsa.

"We didn't make it. We just leave it there," he says. "We want full credit for that."

"It was our neighbor," I chime in. "Our autistic, pot-smoking, dysfunctional neighbor whose parents keep him in a little shack and pretend he doesn't exist."

"Oh my God," says Elsa, and stands there for a second, momentarily struck dumb. "That is so unbelievably cool."

Another day passes, another little door opens, and presto, it's Christmas Eve. What makes stupid things happen? Every schoolchild knows the answer to this: drugs mixed with alcohol. Even as I resume smoking pot, I keep up with my martinis, until finally all the lines get a little blurrier. All the elves get a little sillier. Okay, fine: I'll say it. On Christmas Eve, the Bat Boy and I get stoned and make out. He grabs my hand and looks at me with adoring eyes, then, while chuckling, he leans toward me until his lips are pressed against mine. I stand on the outside of the shack. He stays on the inside. We pull apart. He looks at me with his sunken eyes and says, "Dude." After a while I decide I'm cold and join him on the inside. I don't know what I'm thinking. I guess I want something new on a crisp, winter night: two people united in hate for the holidays. I think it could make the world shine and/or twinkle. I can't say I recommend it. Kissing the Bat Boy is like mouthing something that has been stored in a trunk for a very long time. Still, I feel assured that no one has been there before me, and no one would be there after; that for him at least, this is something very special. A sackful of joy.

Before I go, he says, "Don't leave."

"I have to."

"Let me come with you."

"Absolutely not." I climb back out the window and into the blurriness of his yard.

What can I say? There is no sanctuary like the sanctuary of oddballs taking refuge in one another. There is no loyalty like the loyalty of the scorned.

Two days later, the shack is empty. The bong is nowhere in sight. It's empty the day after, and the day after that. I corner Cindy in the driveway, who cheerfully tells me that Floyd the Bat Child has finally moved out. Out! He's moved in with his girlfriend, Elsa Hammer, a lovely girl and a fantastic artist. Did I know her?

"I thought Floyd liked to stay in the back house."

"Let me tell you a little secret." Cindy leans closer until I'm swimming in her perfume. "Floyd hated the shack. He always hated the shack. But we couldn't have him in the house. Not all day long."

"I thought he liked it. I thought he wanted his privacy."

"Are you crazy? He detested it out there."

"No."

"Yes. He wanted to be in the big house with us," Cindy touches a smug finger to the corner of her mouth, "but he was getting too old. We thought he should be independent."

"I don't believe you. It was his shack. He loved it."

"Floyd," says Cindy, "always hated that shack." And then, singing out: "Jim, what did Floyd hate?"

Jim's voice floats out of the big house: "The shack."

Eventually, Trevor starts talking to me again. Even after Christmas is over, I keep listening to my CD of the Steve Miller Band and Trevor makes up new words to the chorus: "I'm a joker / I'm a smoker / I'm a real estate broker." He mixes up a few martinis and we drink them together and then I do interpretive dances on the flagstone patio while he watches for a while, then goes inside to finish up some work. I dig the angels out of the yard and put them in the trash. Christmas is finally over, New Year's is past, Valentine's Day, Easter. The days get longer and hotter. In the afternoons I put on my suit and float around in the pool, looking up at the clouds, feeling pissed off and betrayed while telling myself I shouldn't. What's the big deal? All Floyd did was use art to get chicks, as millions of painters and poets and guitar-playing boys before him have. Isn't that why people make things in the first place? To say all the things that have such power but sound so tame when we say them flat out: that we want love, that we're lonely, that we hate the shack, that we've always hated the shack, that we're afraid we're in the process of wasting our lives.

As for me, I've decided that I do not hate the shack, that I shall not conduct a life spent hating the shack. Yuletide Village is where we live. We picked this god-awful place, and a series of events will be happening here every December. Why can't our part of it be pagan? What did Elsa say—if you don't like something, you can complain about it, or you can make something better yourself? Fine. We can venerate our own gods. In our yard there will be no cheer, no light, no hope, no merriness. But I've decided there will be drunkenness, wild beasts, potent herbs, vaginas, and log after log after log.

We are designing the display now.

Such Fun

JAMES SALTER

WHEN THEY LEFT THE RESTAURANT, Leslie wanted to go and have a drink at her place, it was only a few blocks away, an old apartment building with leaded windows on the ground floor and a view over Washington Square. Kathrin said fine, but Jane claimed she was tired.

—Just one drink, Leslie said. Come on.

—It's too early to go home, Kathrin added.

In the restaurant they had talked about movies, ones they'd seen and ones they hadn't. They talked about movies and Rudy, the headwaiter.

—I always get one of the good tables, said Leslie.

—Is that right?

—Always.

—And what does he get?

—It's what he hopes he'll get, Leslie said.

—He's really looking at Jane.

—No, he's not, Jane protested.

—He's got half your clothes off already.

—Don't, please, Jane said.

Leslie and Kathrin had been roommates in college and friends ever since. They had hitchhiked through Europe together, getting as far as Turkey, sleeping in the same bed a lot of the nights and, except once, not fooling around with men or, as it happened that time, boys. Kathrin had long hair combed back dark from a handsome brow and a brilliant smile. She could easily have been a model. There was not much more to her than met the eye, but that had always been enough. Leslie had majored in music but hadn't done anything with it. She had a wonderful way on the telephone, as if she'd known you for years.

In the elevator, Kathrin said,

—God, he's cute.

—Who?

—Your doorman. What's his name?

—Santos. He's from Colombia someplace.

—What time does he get off is what I want to know.

—For God's sake.

—That's what they always asked. When I was tending.

—Here we are.

—No, really. Do you ever ask him to change a lightbulb or something?

Leslie was searching for the key to her door.

—That's the super, she said. He's another story.

As they went in, she said,

—I don't think there's anything here but scotch. That's OK, isn't it? Bunning drank up everything else.

She went to the kitchen to get glasses and ice. Kathrin sat on the couch with Jane.

—Are you still seeing Andrew? she said.

—Off and on, Jane said.

—Off and on, that's what I'm looking for. On and off is closer.

Leslie came back with the glasses and ice. She began to make drinks.

—Well, here's to you, she said. Here's to me. It's going to be hard moving out of here.

—You're not going to get to keep the apartment? Kathrin said.

—Twenty-six hundred a month? I couldn't afford it.

—Aren't you going to get something from Bunning?

—I'm not going to ask for anything. Some of the furniture—I can probably use that—and maybe a little something to get me by the first three or four months. I can stay with my mother if I have to. I hope I don't have to. Or I could stay with you, couldn't I? she asked Kathrin.

Kathrin had a walk-up on Lexington, one room painted black with mirrors on one wall.

—Of course. Until one of us killed the other, Kathrin said.

—If I had a boyfriend, it would be no problem, Leslie said, but I was too busy taking care of Bunning to have a boyfriend.

—You're lucky, she said to Jane, you've got Andy.

—Not really.

—What happened?

—Nothing, really. He wasn't serious.

—About you.

—That was part of it.

—So, what happened? Leslie asked.

—I don't know. I just wasn't interested in the same things he was interested in.

—Such as? Kathrin said.

—Everything.

—Give us an idea.

—The usual stuff.

—What?

—Anal sex, Jane said. She'd made it up, on an impulse. She wanted to break through somehow.

—Oh, God, Kathrin said. Makes me think of my ex.

—Malcolm, said Leslie, so where is Malcolm? Are you still in touch?

—He's over in Europe. No, I never hear from him.

Malcolm wrote for a business magazine. He was short, but a very careful dresser—beautiful, striped suits and shined shoes.

—I wonder how I ever married him, Kathrin said. I wasn't very foresighted.

—Oh, I can see how it happened, Leslie said. In fact I *saw* how it happened. He's very sexy.

—For one thing, it was because of his sister. She was great. We were friends from the first minute. God, this is strong, Kathrin said.

—You want a little more water?

—Yes. She gave me my first oyster. Am I supposed to *eat* that? I said. I'll show you how, she said, just throw them back and swallow. It was at the bar at Grand Central. Once I had them I couldn't stop. She was so completely up-front. Are you sleeping with Malcolm? she asked me. We'd hardly met. She wanted to know what it was like, if he was as good as he looked.

Kathrin had drunk a lot of wine in the restaurant and a cocktail before that. Her lips glistened.

—What was her name? Jane asked.

—Enid.

—Oh, beautiful name.

—So, anyway, he and I went off—this was before we were married. We had this room with nothing in it but a window and a bed. That's when I was introduced to it.

—To what? Leslie said.

—In the ass.

—And?

—I liked it.

Jane was suddenly filled with admiration for her, admiration and embarrassment. This was not like the thing she had made up, it was actual. Why couldn't I ever admit something like that? she thought.

—But you got divorced, she said.

—Well, there's a lot besides that in life. We got divorced because I got tired of him chasing around. He was always covering stories in one place or another, but one time in London the phone rang at two in the morning and he went into the next room to talk. That's when I found out. Of course, she was just one of them.

—You're not drinking, Leslie said to Jane.

—Yes, I am.

—Anyway, we got divorced, Kathrin went on. So, now it'll be both of us, she said to Leslie. Join the club.

—Are you really getting divorced? Jane asked.

—It'll be a relief.

—How long has it been? Six years?

—Seven.

—That's a long time.

—A very long time.

—How did you meet? Jane said.

—How did we meet? Through bad luck, Leslie said—she was pouring more scotch into her glass. Actually, we met when he fell off a boat. I was going out with his cousin at the time, we were sailing, and Bunning claimed he had to do it to get my attention.

—That's so funny.

—Later, he changed his story and said he fell and it had to be *somewhere*.

Bunning's first name was actually Arthur, Arthur Bunning Hasset, but he hated the Arthur. Everyone liked him. His family owned a button factory and a big house in Bedford called Ha Ha where he was brought up. In theory he wrote plays, at least one of which was close to being a success and had an off-Broadway run, but after that things became difficult. He had a secretary named Robin—she was called his assistant—who found him incredible and unpredictable, not to mention hilarious, and Leslie had always been amused by him, at least for several years, but then the drinking started.

The end had come a week or so before. They were invited to an opening night by a theatrical lawyer and his wife. First there was dinner, and at the restaurant, Bunning, who had started drinking at the apartment, ordered a martini.

—Don't, Leslie said.

He ignored her and was entertaining for a while but then sat silent and drinking while Leslie and the couple went on with the conversation. Suddenly Bunning said in a clear voice,

—Who are these people?

There was a silence.

—Really, who are they? Bunning asked again.

The lawyer coughed a little.

—We're their guests, Leslie said.

Bunning's thoughts seemed to pass to something else and a few minutes later he got up to go to the men's room. Half an hour passed. Finally Leslie saw him at the bar. He was drinking another martini. His expression was unfocused and childlike.

—Where've you been? he asked her. I've been looking all over for you.

She was infuriated.

—This is the end, she said.

—No, really, where have you been? he insisted.

She began to cry.

—I'm going home, he decided.

Still, she remembered the summer mornings in New England when they were first married. Outside the window the squirrels were running down the trunk of a great tree, headfirst, curling to the unseen side of it, their wonderful bushy tails. She remembered driving to little summer theaters, the old iron bridges, cows lying in the wide doorway of a barn, cut cornfields, the smooth slow look of nameless rivers, the beautiful, calm countryside—how happy one is.

—You know, she said, Marge is crazy about him. Marge was her mother. That should have been a tip-off.

She went to get more ice and in the hallway caught sight of herself in the mirror.

—Have you ever decided this is as far as you can go? she said, coming back in.

—What do you mean? said Kathrin.

Leslie sat down beside her. They were really two of a kind, she decided. They'd been bridesmaids at one another's wedding. They were truly close.

—I mean, have you ever looked at yourself in the mirror and said, I can't . . . this is it.

—What do you mean?

—With men.

—You're just sore at Bunning.

—Who really needs them?

—Are you kidding?

—You want me to tell you something I've found out?

—What?

—I don't know . . . Leslie said helplessly.

—What were you going to say?

—Oh. My theory . . . My theory is, they remember you longer if you don't do it.

—Maybe, Kathrin said, but then, what's the point?

—It's just my theory. They want to divide and conquer.

—Divide?

—Something like that.

Jane had had less to drink. She wasn't feeling well. She had spent the afternoon waiting to talk to the doctor and emerging onto the unreal street.

She was wandering around the room and picked up a photograph of Leslie and Bunning taken around the time they got married.

—So, what's going to happen to Bunning? she asked.

—Who knows? Leslie said. He's going to go on like he's going. Some woman will decide she can straighten him out. Let's dance. I feel like dancing.

She made for the CD player and began looking through the CDs until she found one she liked and put it on. There was a moment's pause and then an uneven, shrieking wail began, much too loud. It was bagpipes.

—Oh, God, she cried, stopping it. It was in the wrong . . . it's one of his.

She found another and a low, insistent drumbeat started slowly, filling the room. She began dancing to it. Kathrin began, too. Then a singer or several of them became part of it, repeating the same words over and over. Kathrin paused to take a drink.

—Don't, Leslie said. Don't drink too much.

—Why?

—You won't be able to perform.

—Perform what?

Leslie turned to Jane and motioned,

—Come on.

—No, I don't really . . .

—Come on.

The three of them were dancing to the hypnotic, rhythmic singing. It went on and on. Finally Jane sat down, her face moist, and watched. Women often danced together, or even alone, at parties. Did Bunning dance? she wondered. No, he wasn't the sort, nor was he embarrassed by it. He drank too much to dance, but really why did he drink? He didn't seem to care about things, but he probably cared very much, beneath.

Leslie sat down beside her.

—I hate to think about moving, she said, her head lolled back in weariness. I'm going to have to find some other place. That's the worst part.

She raised her head.

—In two years, Bunning's not even going to remember me. Maybe he'll say "my ex-wife" sometimes. I wanted to have a baby. He didn't like the idea. I said to him, I'm ovulating, and he said, that's wonderful. Well, that's how it is. I'll have one next time. If there is a next time. You have beautiful breasts, she said to Jane.

Jane was struck silent. She would never have had the courage to say something like that.

—Mine are saggy already, Leslie said.

—That's all right, Jane replied foolishly.

—I suppose I could have something done if I had the money. You can fix anything if you have the money.

It was not true, but Jane said,

—I guess you're right.

She had more than sixty thousand dollars she had saved or made from an oil company one of her colleagues had told her about. If she wanted to, she could buy a car, a Porsche Boxster came to mind. She wouldn't even have to sell the oil stock, she could get a loan and pay it off over three or four years and on weekends drive out to the country, to Connecticut, the little coastal towns, Madison, Old Lyme, Niantic, stopping somewhere to have lunch in a place that, in her imagination, was painted white outside. Perhaps there would be a man there, by himself, or even with some other men. He wouldn't have to fall off a boat. It wouldn't be Bunning, of course, but someone like him, wry, a little shy, the man she had somehow failed to meet until then. They'd have dinner, talk. They'd go to Venice, a thing she'd always wanted to do, in the winter, when no one else was there. They'd have a room above the canal and his shirts and shoes, a half-full bottle of she didn't bother to think of exactly what, some Italian wine, and perhaps some books. The sea air from the Adriatic would come in the window at night and she would wake early, before it was really light, to see him sleeping beside her, sleeping and breathing softly.

Beautiful breasts. That was like saying, I love you. She was warmed by it. She wanted to tell Leslie something but it wasn't the time, or maybe it was. She hadn't quite told herself yet.

Another number began and they were dancing again, coming together occasionally, arms flowing, exchanging smiles. Kathrin was like someone at one of the clubs, glamorous, uncaring. She had passion, daring. If you said something, she wouldn't even hear you. She was a kind of cheap goddess and would go on like that for a long time, spending too much for something that caught her fancy, a silk dress or pants, black and clinging, that widened at the bottom, the kind Jane would have with her in Venice. She hadn't had a love affair in college—she was the only person she knew who hadn't. Now she was sorry, she wished she had. And gone to the room with only a window and a bed.

—I have to go, she said.

—What? Leslie said over the music.

—I have to go.

—This has been fun, Leslie said, coming over to her.

They embraced in the doorway, awkwardly, Leslie almost falling down.

—Talk to you in the morning, she said.

Outside, Jane caught a cab, a clean one as it happened, and gave the driver her address near Cornelia Street. They started off, moving fast through the traffic. In the rearview mirror the driver, who was young, saw that Jane, a nice-looking girl about his age, was crying. At a red light next to the drugstore where it was well lit, he could see the tears streaming down her face.

—Excuse me, is something wrong? he asked.

She shook her head. It seemed she nearly answered.

—What is it? he said.

—Nothing, she said, shaking her head. I'm dying.

—You're sick?

—No, not sick. I'm dying of cancer, she said.

She had said it for the first time, listening to herself. There were four levels and she had the fourth, stage Four.

—Ah, he said, are you sure?

The city was filled with so many strange people he could not tell if she was telling the truth or just imagining something.

—You want to go to the hospital? he asked.

—No, she said, unable to stop crying. I'm all right, she told him.

Her face was appealing though streaked with tears. He raised his head a little to see the rest of her. Appealing, too. But what if she was speaking the truth, he wondered? What if God, for whatever reason, has decided to end the life of someone like this? You cannot know. That much he understood.

John Ashcroft : More Important Things Than Me

JIM SHEPARD

CREATIVE SELF-DOUBT

When people have honest questions about where I stand or what I'm doing—in politics, it happens all the time—I've learned not to take it as an insult. In fact, I often find that their concerns mirror reservations I might have had on my own. Their honesty helps me clarify the situation. Nobody wins when anyone holds grudges.

ELECTABILITY

Folks say, "Here's a fellow who doesn't spook moderates, who's actually electable." That word pops up a lot: electable. Paul Weyrich had some people over one night and we were lounging around out on his porch and he suggested that I was more than just presentable; I was a guy who could go on Jay Leno and play a couple of tunes with the Oak Ridge Boys.

Pessimists claim my only base is the pro-family, religious vote. They say, "Where else can he go? The country club? The boardroom?" My answer is that those aren't the only places to look. My answer is that I'll take my chances with the American people. I served two terms as governor in a Democratic-leaning state, I had a national profile as a Senator, and, yes, I have support among what the media calls the Religious Right. In my gubernatorial reelection I carried 64 percent of the vote, the best showing of any Missouri governor since the Civil War.

MY PRINCIPLES

My principles are out there for everyone to peruse, and always have been. Whenever I get more than four people in a room, I tell them:

You examine the record, and let me know if you find anything that's contradictory or troublesome. And if you think you do, you come back to me, and we'll clear it up on the spot.

In the Senate, I fought against national testing standards, activist judges, and the nomination of a pro-abortionist Surgeon General.

I forced the first floor vote ever on term limits and had to fight my Majority Leader to do so. I wrote part of the welfare-reform law allowing states to deliver services through churches and private agencies.

I promoted the defunding of the NEA. The average guy who wants to go down and see Garth Brooks, he doesn't get a federal subsidy, but the silk-stocking crowd that wants to see a geometric ballet in Urdu, they get a break on their tickets.

When it came to bills, I didn't trim and I didn't pork things up, whether the doors were closed on the session or not.

And I keep reiterating, wherever I go: it's against my religion to impose my religion on others.

ETHICS

I tell people that I know about scandal. During my second term as governor, I had an overeager staffer who, when he heard about my boy's need for some books on Queen Elizabeth for a homework assignment, called the state librarian at home and got her to open the library after hours. The press got ahold of the story, like they get ahold of everything, and I quickly took responsibility. Around the house we call it Homeworkgate and joke that we learned from our mistake. A columnist for the *St. Louis Post-Dispatch* wrote about the whole thing, "If a state ever had a less exciting governor than John Ashcroft, I never heard about it."

TURNING HEADS

I hear that I first started turning heads after the charges became public that Monica Lewinsky had turned the President's. Most everyone in my party maintained a code of silence in the early going. I did not. I said publicly in an address to the Conservative Political Action Conference that January, "Mr. President, if these allegations are true, you have disgraced yourself and the Office of the Presidency, and you should resign now."

That's what I said. It bears repeating: "Mr. President, if these allegations are true, you have disgraced yourself and the Office of the Presidency, and you should resign now."

ATLANTA

If I had one problem when I was running for President, in perception terms, it was Atlanta. Atlanta was a nightmare. I dropped the ball there and I'm the first to admit it.

I was nervous. I started right in, once introduced, on principles, and what I stand for, and there was a point a paragraph or two into my notes when I realized that the silverware wasn't going to get any quieter, and flop sweat set in. I was fighting a losing battle with overdone filet mignon for everyone's attention.

It didn't help that Forbes was going on next and that he got about ten standing ovations for saying mostly the same things. *Steve Forbes.*

A nightmare. I get the shivers going back over it, I don't mind admitting.

"Shiver shiver shiver," Janet says, sometimes, late at night, lying next to me.

ETHICS

It's fashionable, I guess, for people to talk down Jimmy Carter, but let me say this: Jimmy Carter was an unimpeachable straight shooter who restored people's trust in the Presidency. And don't think the American people couldn't use a little of that particular medicine right now.

THE TRANSPORTS OF LOVE

Hollywood likes to showcase the tyranny of romantic infatuation—how two people might abandon their friends, family, and beliefs all in the name of an overpowering emotion—but my father didn't raise me that way. He wasn't a stoic and didn't despise emotion. He believed that delayed gratification was an essential practice for success in life. He always said, "Don't jeopardize the future because of the past."

A woman from a national magazine wrote that I had a Boy Scout's haircut and a choirboy's magnetic machismo. I wrote her a note explaining that I appreciated the joke, and that I didn't think magnetic machismo was what we needed in a President at that particular point.

HELPMATE

Janet says that after God she puts family first, everything else second, and nothing third. During the campaign for the Senate she was asked if she minded being a helpmate. "No," she said. "The same way I don't mind being a math professor or writing textbooks."

SEX

Once in a diner a fry cook said to me—I guess in an attempt to destroy his customer base—"I'll tell you one thing: I'm not getting any tonight." What I should have answered was something I thought as I drove away: that our country was affluent in sex but bankrupt in love. Prostitutes have a sex life. Animals have a sex life. Human beings should have a *love* life.

The right results come first from working hard to make the right decision, and then working even harder to make the decision right.

THRIFT

Missouri remains one of the cheapest places to buy gas in America. My staffers tease me because I've been known on drives home to run the tank down to near empty so I can save a few dollars by filling up on the other side of the Mississippi.

WHY I SUPPORTED THE DEATH PENALTY AS GOVERNOR

I was the ultimate appeal to correct error, not reward regret, emotion, or even religious conversion. Becoming a Christian removes us from *eternal* penalties.

PUBLIC CIVILITY

The original rules of debate for the Constitutional Convention in 1787 did not allow conversation when another member spoke. No reading of any kind was permitted during debate, and no one was allowed to speak twice unless everyone else had spoken once.

THINGS TO WORK ON

We're all works in progress. I know that I sometimes don't make a sufficiently forceful impression. I know that I can seem to people, as Janet likes to put it, too settled on my own road. There's a little motto painted onto the serape of a toy donkey on my desk: "*We're all here to learn from one another.*" I look at that motto every day.

RECURRING DREAMS

Janet notes that I'm thrifty even with my dreams. I tend to have the same one for weeks running. They stay in my head. My most recent one features Barney Thomas, one of my father's oldest friends, who's sick now. My father called him The Judge when I was growing up.

R&R

I give visitors to my office copies of my ten-song tape, *The Gospel (Music) According to John*, which I composed and produced myself.

FRIENDSHIP

Harry Truman said, "If you want a friend in Washington, buy a dog."

FRIENDSHIP

When I was State Auditor of Missouri, I had seats on the fifty-yard line for Tigers games. When I lost reelection, I couldn't get into the end zone.

AS THE SEASONS CHANGE

Growing up I never imagined that I would one day need a man to work five days a week just to organize my schedule, let alone that I'd have an after-hours recording that goes like this: "Hello, I'm Andy Blake, scheduler for Attorney General of the United States John Ashcroft. If you'd like to request an appointment, please fax your request to the following number . . ."

AMBITION

The Presidency is like running the mile. You have to run the first few laps, and run them hard, before you know if you're really even in the race.

In 1998 Paul Gigot asked, in the *Wall Street Journal*, "Richard Nixon and Watergate helped make a president out of an obscure Democrat named Jimmy Carter. Can Bill Clinton and Monica Lewinsky do the same for an equally unknown Republican?"

THE JUDGE

Two months ago he sent a letter I still haven't answered. Usually I'm a bear on correspondence. I haven't even finished reading it.

In the dream he's as nice as can be. He quotes the first line of his letter: "So, John, the sawbones has come through with the bad news that apparently I've got the lung thing everyone's been worried about."

MODERATION

Do we think a four-time murderer is only "moderately" dangerous?

Are drugs in a schoolyard only "moderately" a problem?

In combat, do we want our fellow soldiers to be "moderately" brave?

Are we so sure that "moderation" is always a good thing?

THE LONG VIEW

Includes the understanding that the verdict of eternity stands above the verdict of history.

FALSE PRIDE

I'm constantly on the lookout for it.

LOSING TO A DEAD MAN

My theory about elections is mirrored in what I hold about all of life. For every crucifixion, a resurrection is sure to follow—maybe not immediately, but the possibility is always there.

MELANCHOLIA

I became Governor ten years ago. Twelve, I guess. Time flies.

THE HARD ROAD

Like anyone else, there are weaknesses I've had to overcome to get to where I am today. A reporter once said that I speak like I'd rather be gigging fish on the Osage, and I dropped him a note telling him that that was because it was true: I would.

SECRET DISCOURAGEMENTS

Distractions don't seem to want to leave me in peace when my faith in myself is shaky or my defenses low. Janet calls them The Secret Discouragements. I think:

—In a February 1998 poll of registered Republicans in New Hampshire, 0 percent named me as their first choice for the nomination.
—Even John Kasich got 2 percent.
—I'm not a natural self-promoter.
—I don't like the way I look when I eat.

UNFINISHED PROJECTS

The letter on my computer is entitled *Untitled.* So far it has the address and no date and two lines: *Dear Barney: It was terrible to hear about your terrible news.*

ALWAYS ON OFFENSE

During my first term as governor, Missouri landed both the Royals and the Cardinals in the World Series. There was speculation as to who I'd be rooting for. I rooted for both. My wife and I made a special hat the night before, half and half, red and blue, with bills on both sides. I flipped it around between innings to the team that was batting. An editorial the day after accused me of indecisiveness or double-dealing or both. But a letter writer from Hannibal hit the nail on the head: There was another way of looking at it, he said. Governor Ashcroft is just always on offense. And he was right.

JOHN ASHCROFT IN THE POCKET OF BIG TOBACCO

Who pays for years and years and years of government litigation? Who is it that foots the bill so the trial lawyers can pocket billions?

ON BEING PART OF A PERSECUTED MINORITY

Most of those who criticize me for my religion haven't even taken the time to discover just what my religion is. The Assemblies of God is a Pentecostal denomination, so I know what it's like to be a part of a minority and mocked for one's beliefs. When the mockers come after me, I refer them to two bumper stickers distributed by AG pastor Fulton Buntain: IT'S NEVER TOO LATE TO START OVER AGAIN and IT'S ALWAYS TOO SOON TO QUIT.

ON PUSHING THAT LIBERAL ROCK UP THE HILL

I used to tell my son when he got frustrated about his math scores: "You know, there are times that maybe God will call us to do something that doesn't have an apparent success about it at the moment."

LEARNING ABOUT VALUES

My father was a pastor and a college president. I remember as a very young boy hearing his early morning prayers and tiptoeing downstairs to sit beside his knees. So that I was shielded by his body as he pleaded for my soul.

LEARNING ABOUT VALUES

The day before he died, in the presence of a small group of family and friends, he reminded me that the spirit of Washington is arrogance, and that the spirit of Christ, on the other hand, is humility.

LEARNING ABOUT VALUES

He was on the sofa, and struggled to get up to help family and friends pray over me. I said, "Dad, you don't have to struggle to stand and pray over me with all these friends." He said, "John, I'm not struggling to stand; I'm struggling to kneel." And he left that couch and came and knelt with me.

WHY SHOULD WE BELIEVE IN THE RESURRECTION?

After losing my first race for Congress, I was appointed State Auditor. After losing the election to maintain that post, I was elected State Attorney General. After losing the election as chairman of the Republican National Committee, I was offered the candidacy as U.S. Senator. After losing the reelection campaign for U.S. Senator, I was appointed Attorney General of the United States.

LEARNING ABOUT VALUES

My role models are: Jesus Christ, Abraham Lincoln, J. Robert Ashcroft, Barney Thomas, and Janet Ashcroft. With no apologies, and in that order.

STANDARDS

No schoolteacher could have gotten away with the behavior that Bill Clinton did. No principal, no college president, no corporate president. That he wasn't forced to resign tells me that our standards for the Presidency are lower than they are for virtually any other job in America. And that, to me, is a disaster.

DECEPTION

How can we expect individuals to be faithful to us if they're not faithful to the people in their own families?

GOVERNMENT

Revival isn't something that comes from government. Government is not an agent of spirituality. But it can be a moral force. It's said you can't legislate morality. Well, I've got news for those who say that: *all* we should legislate is morality. And we certainly shouldn't legislate *im*morality.

WHAT'S IN MY HEART

Have I been the man I could be? No. What's in my heart? What do I spend my time thinking about? Could I at any moment make a clean breast of it to people; let them see, *so here's what I've been thinking*?

I get teased for starting every staff meeting with that phrase: "So here's what I've been thinking."

HAVING GOOD MEMORIES

Is like having gold in your spiritual bank. Nothing can take the place of them. Nothing can diminish them. Nights I can't sleep I remember floating on my back with Dad down the little stream behind our farm, the sun on our faces, the leaves spiraling overhead. When one of my colleagues from across the aisle is going on about this or that victimized minority, I remember my father and The Judge taking three straight Saturdays to help me with my soapbox racer. Their faces come back to me when I don't expect them, and when I do. Their faces are a gift I have to be strong enough to carry.

MR. PERFECT

Janet gets a kick out of it whenever a publication decides I'm Mr. Clean or Mr. Perfect or whatever they've decided to call me. She's happy for me but she always makes a wry little list of recent shortcomings to keep my head from swelling. "All well and good, Mr. Perfect," she said after the most recent article, in the *Southern Partisan*, "but you still haven't called Barney back."

UNFINISHED PROJECTS

Dear Barney:

- terrible to hear about your terrible news
- don't want to lecture an old lawyer on the law
- know full well that spirit of Christ is humility
- imagine how it felt to read you never thought you'd "find Bob Ashcroft's son in the pocket of Big Tobacco"
- full slate
- sleeplessness

· wanting to write forever, feels like. Took stock, made notes, as way of preparing self
· really took stock
· City on the Hill

DAD'S TWENTY-ONE LIFE LESSONS

4
Silence sometimes shouts.
#5
Creative self-doubt fertilizes the field of creativity.
#7
Never eat your seed corn.
#8
When you've considered all your options, work to expand your options.
#11
The lives of father and son are intertwined; when one dies, the other is diminished.
#12
A father should not only pass on his strengths, wisdom, and insight, but also how to handle weaknesses, failures, and insecurities.
#13
When you have something important to say, write it down.
#15
Little things mean a lot.
#21
Saying goodbye is a way of beginning to say hello.

#22

When I was eight, my father took me to the sleepy Springfield airport, once a World War II training field. He was an amateur pilot. We walked up to a 1941 Piper Cub, climbed in, and took off. A few minutes later, he shouted over the engine noise: "John, fly the plane for a while."

"What do I do?" I shouted back.

"Grab the stick and push it," he said. I did. We went into a sickening dive. He pulled us out. He had a good chuckle, and I had a good lesson: actions have consequences. And when I put my hand to something, I can make a difference.

THE MELANCHOLY TRUTH

Each of us is required to exercise leadership, even if it's limited to our personal relationships.

GROUNDSWELLS OF SUPPORT

The Judge said when a politician claims there is a public outcry for him to run for office that it means that his mother and father think it is a good idea. A groundswell of support means that an aunt and uncle agree.

My houses are filled with plaques and honorary pictures, keys to various cities: temporary acknowledgments of the offices I held, not indications of the man I am, or hope to be.

FLATTERY

Think about it: virtually any positive remark you could make about Jesus would be true.

THE LONG VIEW

I try to adopt a forward-looking approach, focusing on what I might become, not on what others are saying about me today.

ATTITUDE OF GRATITUDE

My father didn't allow us to use the phrase "I'm proud of . . ." "Say you're grateful for it," he always said. "Not proud."

God doesn't ask us to sacrifice our children to Him. He sacrificed His Son for us. Pride doesn't enter into it here. Gratitude is the appropriate response.

INNER RESERVES

Six weeks after my brother's funeral, my father had a massive heart attack.

WHAT FAMILY IS ALL ABOUT

My brother had lived in the same town, and used to drop in on him every other day. My father told him he didn't need to feel as if he had to come by all the time. My brother answered that a phone wouldn't work for what he wanted, because sometimes he just wanted to lay eyes on him.

GOOD FORTUNE

The story of the Asian man who commissioned a work of art to represent good fortune, the artist free to choose any form or method of representing it. He chose three lines of calligraphy:

Grandfather Dies
Father Dies
Son Dies

The wealthy Asian said, "How can this represent good fortune? Everyone dies!" The artist said, "The good fortune is in the sequence."

GULLIBILITY

When someone promised my father something, he assumed that that person was telling the truth. Every so often someone would say to me, "Your father sure was gullible." But who'd want to be raised by a cynic? Believing in the best and giving others the benefit of the doubt may not be the most astute financial advice, but it's the only spiritual advice.

DESPITE EVERYTHING

Despite everything, I could hear sometimes in my father's voice the way a certain insecurity invaded his thoughts. A few times he said to me, "If I weren't a college president, I wonder if anyone would still care about my opinions."

CARRYING THE BALL

When people say pictures don't lie, they fail to realize that our favorite pictures try to suggest that our best moments are persistent moments.

They're not. We might have looked like that for a second, but then our hair moved, our clothes wrinkled, our expressions got tired, our faces sagged back to normal.

WRITING

There's something about being able to put writing down and pick it back up that makes it special. Maybe we have a struggle getting what we need to get out face-to-face, or on the telephone. Maybe the deliberate pace of writing allows us to express ourselves more clearly.

THE REASON FOR DISCIPLINE

The very nature of Judeo-Christian culture is choice driven.

SUNDAY SCHOOL

When I was in Sunday school one of our songs went like this:

Be careful, little eyes, what you see;
Oh, be careful, little eyes, what you see.
For the Father up above is looking down in love;
So be careful, little eyes, what you see.

PUNCTUALITY

My father was never on time: he was always *early*. On time was not an option. If you weren't early you were late. We were always the first to church, the first to school, the first to work.

MORE IMPORTANT THINGS THAN ME

Because of his ministries, he was never home in the summer. At Little League I'd look up and see all the other dads. As I got older I realized that the most important thing my father ever taught me was that there were more important things than me.

ROAD TRIPS

Once I was an appropriate age, I was regularly invited to go along on his ministry trips. Everyone talks today about getting involved in their children's worlds. My father invited me into *his*.

HINDSIGHT

For a while, I thought he was ignoring me. It turned out that he was *building* me.

RESPECT

Once when I was twelve I had just heard him address a group of college students, and he turned to me and said, "What do *you* think, John?" He asked my opinion. You know what that said to an adolescent boy?

When I traveled with him, he quizzed me about tensions or contradictions in any of the concepts he'd been dealing with. I wanted to be able to respond correctly, so I listened as if nothing else mattered.

OUR OWN LITTLE PRISONS

Do yourself a favor: the next time you're driving with someone and you see that faraway look in their eyes, and you wonder what's going on in their heads—*ask*.

COURTESY

Even in his latter, potentially lonelier years, my father was passionate about taking the pressure off people. He was always adamant about one part of his dinner invitations: "Come when you can and leave when you want to."

DISCOVERY

I'm a fan of the discovery school of education. When education focuses exclusively on comprehension, a crucial spiritual element is lost. An educated person is someone who's become addicted to the thrill of discovery. If someone tells me they're feeling prematurely old, I tell them: buy a telescope, go visit a new culture, work through a college textbook.

OPEN YOUR EYES

There's a spot on a twisting farm road near our place in Greene County where, at the right time of year, in the right weather, tarantulas make their crossing. Most drivers don't even notice, but I like to stop and watch, and I've been known to pick up one or two and take them home to Janet. I'll set one on the kitchen counter when I know she's coming. She'll scream loud enough to make me think it's all been worthwhile, but she doesn't appreciate it. She tells people that it's a family joke that I enjoy and she endures.

"Why would you do that?" someone might ask. That's the wrong question. We saw something new. We enlarged our lives.

COOKIES

My father never let people leave without putting something in their hands. He developed a signature gift, a plaque he had produced for the sole purpose of giving away. The calligraphy read *As long as he sought the Lord, God made him to prosper.* I've never been sorry for anything I've given away (whereas the same is not true for anything I've kept or purchased).

Once I was back in Missouri, I visited The Judge four days running. I said to him, "Is there anything I can do for you?" He said he could go for some chocolate chip cookies. I went back to the house and started assembling the ingredients.

"What are you doing?" Janet wanted to know.

I told her I was making cookies. It was something I wanted to do for myself. She watched for a while and then went about her business.

The stirring, the mixing, the baking started paying me back. I started to process my prayers and work through my anger at the cigarettes that had shortened his life. I underbaked the cookies so they'd be good and moist. I made them small to stack in a Pringles can. I delivered them when he was asleep.

GENEROSITY

Political liberals take the admonition to be generous in giving as an admonition directed toward the government. In actuality, it's the reverse. Real givers are people who enjoy giving away their *own* money.

Beware the generosity of those who make a living giving away *other people's* money.

STAYING ON MESSAGE

All the good groups in the world, and a few bad ones, bring their causes, purposes, and bills to my office virtually every day, and if I don't happen to speak out on their particular concern at least once a week, I get asked, "What happened to you? Why are you silent? Don't you care?"

What some of these groups don't understand is the necessity of staying on message. Try to do everything and you end up doing nothing. It's like physics: if you don't concentrate your force, you don't penetrate the wall. Some issues have other senators as their champion, and I may stand behind them as a strong supporter. What each of us has to do is determine the primary emphasis of our calling. A good colleague of mine understands this: he says he has 365 titles but only two speeches. My father repeated the same things his entire life. Because he stayed so focused, it was impossible to be around him for any length of time and not know what he believed in.

WRITE IT ON YOUR HAND

Character is what you're made of when everything else that might hold you up evaporates on the spot.

MEMORIES WITH STAYING POWER

Everyone was standing when I noticed my father lunging, swinging his arms, trying to lift himself out of the couch, one of those all-enveloping pieces of furniture that tends to bury you once you sit in it.

GOODBYES

Back in Washington in our little one-and-a-half room apartment, in an alley just off Second Street, Janet and I had just fallen asleep when we heard a rattling of the iron bars on the door. She thought it was someone trying to break in. I said, "No. It's my dad." The next morning we heard the news.

GOODBYES

I was told that in the emergency room, he finally said to the doctors, "Boys, you better just quit. You're hurting more than helping."

Everyone who knew him joked about his goodbyes. He waved like a person stranded on an island. Fifty, a hundred yards down the road, you'd look back, and he'd still be waving, his arms going like he was helping to park a jet.

GOODBYES

As a boy, on days when there were no Little League games, I'd get a bat and a dinged-up softball and go into a field by myself and play All-Time Home Run Derby. It was always the same six guys in a round-robin: Mel Ott, Ernie Banks, Eddie Matthews, Ted Williams, Jimmy Foxx, and Mickey Mantle. I'd bat for each and after each swat I'd have to troop after the ball and find it. "What're you doing?" Janet finally said, after having watched me from the kitchen window for about twenty minutes.

HELLOS

I stood there in the field, holding my softball like an apple. Somewhere I'd lost my bat. Janet was wiping her hands on a dishtowel as she walked across the alfalfa stubble. There were apple trees and behind them a beautiful twilight, with our farm spreading out around us. A contrail made a quiet little line across the sky. I was Attorney General of the United States. My father was sitting on my bed. He was telling me that things don't *happen*; they're *made* to happen. He had his palm to my face. He had only my welfare in mind. This was the only world we knew. This was the world that was swept away.

SOURCES INCLUDE:
Atlanta Journal and Constitution (6/25/01, editorial)
New Republic (6/29/01, "Washington Diarist: My Boss the Fanatic," by Tevi Troy; 12/22/97, "The Gospel According to John," by Jason Zengerle)
National Review (3/23/98, "Mr. Clean," by John J. Miller)
Speech to CPAC Annual Meeting (3/6/97, "Courting Disaster: Judicial Despotism in the Age of Russell Clark," by John D. Ashcroft)
Congressional Record (5/8/96, "The Team Act," by John D. Ashcroft)
CNN *Crossfire* (5/19/98, "The Tobacco Wars Head to the Senate Floor"; 2/25/98, "Clinton and Lewinsky: Will We Ever Know the Truth?")
Charisma and Christian Life ("A Capitol Christian," by Gary L. Thomas and Jennifer Ferranti)
Lessons from a Father to His Son, by John D. Ashcroft and Gary L. Thomas (Thomas Nelson)

Squatters

JULIA SLAVIN

MARCH IS A BIG MONTH FOR SQUATTERS. It's getting on to tax time. They look at what they've got and want something better, to feel taken care of for all they pay. Pottery Barn says they have one. "It's a feeling, Kay," the manager tells me. "There's a presence." That's all you need to hire me. Those premonitions are usually right. I look around the store. Nothing's out of place but you always find something. Even the most fastidious leave a thread of them behind. In the employee washroom: the blue plastic cover of a Bic shaver. A man. I tell the manager to lock up as usual. In the morning the problem will be gone. At dusk, I head over to Montgomery Plaza. George, my People Mover driver, got here before me.

"Not expecting more than one tonight," I tell George.

"One or a hundred and one makes no difference to me, Kay." I lean against the Mover a few moments to watch the sun dip behind Old Navy.

"Good one tonight, wouldn't you say?" I ask George. "Nicely jaundiced?"

"Not like Ikea."

"Apples and oranges, George. There's no topping an Ikea sunset."

"Home Interiors?"

"Palladium red. Best & Company?"

"Peach schnapps. Need my help in there?" George asks.

"Nah. Bachelors are easy." I go to work. The mall is always cold and so is everyone. We can't get warm. There's no difference between March and September or January or July anymore. Only one season now: air-conditioning. We disconnect it in our apartments, block the vents in the office, it bleeds through. It blasts from the buildings onto the parking lots. We can't stop it in our cars. All day long we shake.

I open Pottery Barn with my master key and step into dining. I love seeing how the squatters rearrange the displays. The nerve. Not only do they make the stores their own, they make them *more* their own. I see the Gilbern table is set for two with the Calypso pottery and the Bugatti stemware and the Saratoga flatware. A single rose in a bud vase. Is it possible there's a second squatter that I missed? A woman? Couldn't be. Women always leave something behind to reveal themselves.

I come upon my squatter in bed. He's in periwinkle pajamas from the Men's Store, reading a Classic Edition of Dickens's *Oliver Twist* that he took down from the shelf of the display. He looks up from the book as though I'm his wife just home from the office.

"Comfy?" I ask. "Where's the other one?"

He shakes his head. "It's just me."

"Why is the table set for two?"

He shrugs, embarrassed. "Seemed homier that way."

I look around the room. He's even hung his clothes on the dumb butler. "Nice bachelor pad."

"I'm not hurting anybody," he says. "I always leave everything just the way I found it."

"Yeah, squatters always say that. But you're trespassing. You're breaking the law. Get up. You're going to The Corner." He gets up, but he walks past me. "Where do you think you're going?"

"To get something to eat." Trouble. I should have brought George. I follow him back to dining. He opens a bag from Ben & Jerry's, puts *Roy Orbison's Greatest Hits* on the Yamaha. "My name is Roy, too." He serves us mint chip ice cream in the Hattiesburg bowls. Normally, I don't eat anything cold, but it's my favorite flavor and why not, it's a slow night. "And your name is Kay Martin."

"You know me?"

"I read the profile in *Security Week*."

"Did you now?"

"They had it in the display, upstate. On the Savoy console. Remember that collection?"

"The weathered look. Compartments for practical storage. Discontinued last May."

"I'm impressed."

Like most squatters, a repeat offender. Once you squat, you never stop. You move store to store. Like a roach. The trip to The Corner does nothing but slow them down, no matter what the district lords think. "I liked the article," he says. "They were right about your calves." He looks at my legs under the table. I've never been attracted to a squatter before. There was Max who set up as a bartender in Bath & Beyond. I used to go in for a nightcap and tell him my worries before I got pressure from the firm and had to send him out. And there was the goon from Sports Authority, but I didn't know he was a squatter. He told me he *worked* there. That was during a period of personal weakness. I gave up ownership of my *self*, overidentified with *him*. I fancied myself a shadow athlete, carrying his Power Bars around in my purse, reminiscing about the good old days when Olberman and Patrick anchored Sports Center, incorporating excruciating idiom into my vocabulary like "Put the biscuit in the basket" and "Nothin' but net." And worse, I *believed* I liked sports. But this squatter . . . Just look at him with his crew cut that's grown out into a wedge, chocolate chips fixed between his teeth.

"Why do you do this?" I ask over a second helping of ice cream.

"They just make everything so nice here," he says. It's true. They put the Wilmington armoire with the Tribeca collection, mix contemporary with antique, practical and fanciful. A sisal rug beneath a beaded mirror, a collector's quilt discreetly hung over the arm of the Josephine chair-and-a-half, linen swags on iron rods and sconces and throws, and look at this! Velvet floor pillows. Combinations I try and just can't get right. So I try again with Dorset slipcovers and pasha rugs, Palo Alto lamps and Audie chairs. Oh, and the Breckinridge collection. What a clunker. In the store it was classic and opulent, matched with the Longfellow rug. At home, a jumble of failure. Storage lockers on the highway, packed with my mistakes.

"Can I ask you for a favor?" he says. "In return for the ice cream?" I knew this was coming. Nothing's free. "I'll leave after dessert. After I straighten up, of course. But can I take my own car? Will you let me skip The Corner?"

"If you like." What the hell. I still get paid. He thanks me, gazing into my eyes while I finish my ice cream. I want a boyfriend. I want to be irresistible instead of the Hydra who scares them away. I want someone to paw at me and bug me to take off my clothes. I want someone to complain that we never have sex anymore when I think we have sex all the time, someone who will get pouty and miserable when I point out all the times we had sex during the past week. I pull my napkin out of the ring and wipe my mouth. "I suppose you're going to try to get me into bed now, too," I say.

He glances at the clock on the Kipfer sideboard. "It's eleven thirty. I usually watch Leno."

George gives me a ride to my car. "I thought the premonitions were always right," he says.

"Usually, but not tonight," I say. "Everybody's so jittery these days with the new tax code." George drops me off, wishes me better luck.

I drive home, molecules splitting, every electron in my body vibrating with the heat of possibility. I park in the underground garage, change into Asics and charge up the twenty-seven floors. I turn on the lights just in time to catch my little black dependents running for cover. "One of these days I'm gonna get you leeches!" I put on my parka and snow boots, turn on the kettle for tea and look around for a place to sit. But there's nowhere I want to sit. So, like every night, I stand until I can't stay awake any longer. I want an apartment without bugs. I want an apartment that's decorated. I try, I do. I like green but it's the wrong green and it makes the beige look yellow and I don't like yellow unless it's the sun. I tried a leaf motif on the couch and chair-and-a-half. It clashed. I tried draping upholsteries over the arms of chairs, a sponge pattern on one wall, creative tiles and borders, throw rugs and runners and candles and screens. I made a mess. But I have a good view. You can see clear out to Ikea, with all of its promise of something better, of getting it right. A thousand extra for the western exposure. Worth every nickel for the sunsets and for Neiman's and Nordstrom and Krispy Kreme and Saks. And at night, when the lights come on through the far reaches of the district, it's like standing over the stars.

"Where are you?" Roy asks on his little Nokia phone. I can see him in the Pottery Barn window looking all around the mall.

"Over here. No, here. Victoria's Secret." I'm dressed in a peach blossom merry widow, seamed stockings, a silk shorty robe. He gasps over the crackling cells.

"Good God. I thought you were one of the mannequins. You look like what's-her-name from the catalog." He presses his hand against the glass.

"Come over," I say.

"You mean, leave here?"

"I've got the master key." I lift it out from between my Miracle Cups.

"Oh, baby. Baby, I think I love you."

"I love you."

"I want you to live with me."

"Where?"

"Here."

"Ha! You know what they do to crooked plaza cops? Come here," I say. "There's a satin-covered chaise in dressing room three. A floor-to-ceiling antiqued mirror. Flattering light."

"I just want to look at you. From here." He slips his hand down the front of his pajamas. "Take off your robe."

Back at the firm, my desk is out in the hall. I storm into my boss Ewan's office. "You're really going to fire me?"

"I didn't fire you. I just moved your desk out in the hall." Some Computer Fraud chicks flit by Ewan's office in their Jil Sander suits. Computer Fraud gets everything. They get cappuccino makers and recumbent bikes, plush rugs and maritime desks, Mont Blanc pens all around. They get Prada and Zegna, Armani, Chanel. They get western exposures. I get harsh morning light and Nine West.

"How am I supposed to work?" I ask.

"Could be worse. Could be in the parking lot." He points out the window. I look down at McCoy from Infidelity, shuffling and stacking papers on his desk in space 6, spraying his head with a bottle of SPF 50. "You haven't clinched in a month," Ewan whispers. "March is almost over. The Home Store wants to switch to the Brown Firm." Then he starts one of his coughing fits, which means now get the hell out of my office. Cough, cough, cough, cough, cough. He throws back a swig of Dimetapp.

I call Roy on his cell phone.

"Tough day?"

"Yeah."

"Come home."

I slouch into Pottery Barn and see he's set the table with the Palmetto mixed 'n' matched with the Seville. *Percy Sledge's Greatest Hits* plays on the stereo. He's tossing a bowl of spaghetti from Sbarro and there's salad from Everything Yogurt. A fruit tart from The French Baker on a domed cake plate. Wine from The Spirit of Wine. He rubs my shoulders, then serves the spaghetti. We eat pie. We watch Leno. We have sex. I wake at three.

"Where are you going?" he asks.

"Home," I say, getting dressed.

"Home is with me."

"You could come too."

He switches on the Tuscan floor lamp, leans back against the Kalorama bolster pillows.

"You have bugs and sad greens and bad air."

I get quiet, buttoning the cuffs on my sleeves, remembering the fate of my dear old mentor, Sammy Verghese, the toughest heat in the district. Clinched more in a year than I did in a decade. Taught me everything I know. Then the July 4 Macy's bust. He went in and didn't come out. Ewan made me do the bust myself. Found Sammy shacked up in a Hawthorne bed among the Avalon highboys and Clementine rugs. Ewan sent him out to The Corner. Mixed him in with the general population, the very people he'd busted time and again. I kiss Roy good night, lock up, and leave.

It's a clear night after a fine day but the parking lot is freezing. The sun can't get through the air-conditioning anymore. To break the monotony, I drive home through the parking lots, to see if I can make it the whole way without leaving the plazas. George bets me ten bucks that I can't. In fact, I can, except where I cross a wide pike to drive underground and park.

The bugs are in full swing. Having a gay old time on my Delancey couch, I see, dropping down from the shades, crawling up the walls.

They don't bother to hide anymore when I turn on the lights. I must have fallen asleep standing up again because I wake with daylight in my eyes, folded in on myself, a crumpled dollar somebody dropped in the center of the living room floor.

I do a few busts. There are the newlyweds at Fabulous Flannels that I've been putting off just because they seem so happy, the career girls at Comfort In Down, and oh, hell, I hate this, Milt at Home Depot.

"Why, Kay? Why? I never hurt anybody."

"I'm sorry, Milt."

"I'm too old to begin again."

"You'll land on your feet."

"And I gave you all those breaks on winches and bolts."

"You've been a good friend." I slap the side of the People Mover and George drives out to The Corner.

Roy and I eat mint chip ice cream on the Kaiser divan and watch *20/20*. A piece that blows the hatch on kitchen handymen. I move uncomfortably in my seat.

"What's wrong?" Roy asks.

"The couches at Domain are cushier," I say.

"What were you doing over there?"

"They think they have a squatter but I couldn't find anything. They have a lot of big soft pillows with tapestry coverings. Boy, they've got a great set dresser on their payroll. She does upholstery draping. It's warm and inviting."

I feel him go rigid.

"I'm sure it's . . . *lovely*."

"What's the matter?" I ask.

"I happen to like *this* couch, that's the matter."

"I wasn't suggesting . . . well, to be perfectly honest, it is a little cold here and I was thinking . . ."

"I like it here."

"I was putting an idea on the table, you don't have to get snippish."

"What makes you think you can just come in here and start regulating things?"

"I was telling you about my day."

"I'm not a Domain person. I'm a Pottery Barn kind of guy."

"All right, all right. Sorry I brought it up."

We haven't been getting along lately. Small things set him off. He's constantly cleaning up after me, making me feel unwelcome. We haven't had sex in days.

I wash the dishes in the employee lounge and tell him I'm going out. I head east toward Bloomingdale's. The mall is deserted. My Via Spagas thump a tom-tom on the brickwork to a Muzak "Going Up the Country" by Canned Heat. A new store, Denim Interiors, is set to open its doors in the morning, a venture with Levi Strauss. The display shows a sectional couch with zippers and pockets for a newspaper, a stonewashed love seat with a button fly, faded armrests with rips and patches, belt loops round the hassock. It's just a matter of time before they'll be calling me to remove a cowboy who's moved in, hung his boots up on the calf skull, a Lone Star in a chair pocket, playing *Hank Williams's Greatest Hits* on the Bang & Olufson. I walk by Lewis of London. A squatter with her newborn in a sliding rocker. I know her. Natalie. A chronic squatter. I busted her at Perfect Patios ten years ago. Within one week she got clinched at Maurice Villency, upstate. Soon she was back here, a stint at The Door Store, Scan, Macy's, even a couple of nights back at Patios. A pathetic case. And now she's dragging around a family. A toddler sleeps in a Pretty Penny youth bed and her baby nurses in the slider. I stop and watch. Having a baby was never something I wanted to do. I didn't want to put my body through all that rewiring. I thought if I ever did have a kid I'd adopt, and not a baby, a two- or three-year-old, something already formed. But I look at the way the baby is gazing up at her mother, the way Natalie is smiling down at her, and I'm hit with the deep ache of want.

"We could make it work," I say.

"How? Where would we put the thing? In a drawer?"

"Sure. My mother kept us in drawers. She lined them with towels and soft blankets. Lewis of London has . . ."

He slams his paper down on the Prairie bench. "I do not want to hear about Lewis of London. I did not sign on for any of this."

"Where are you going?" I cry.

"The Cheesecake Factory."

"Can I come too?"

"It's a free goddamn country." I chase him through the mall, by Bon Voyage and Hold Everything, through the revolving door at The Cheesecake Factory. He gives his name to the hostess and we settle in at the bar for the forty-five-minute wait. He turns his back toward me. Everything about his body language says stay away. The girl to his right has fake tits. I look at myself in the mirror over the bar. I'm puffy and blotched. I shouldn't wear sea foam, it's wrong for my pallor. He orders Irish coffee with an extra shot of Lusivit. I've never seen him drink before. I don't like men who drink. The nice ones get mean. The mean ones get nice. Which kind is he? I don't know. I order hot chocolate. We drink in silence. He looks at the fake tits.

"I don't feel much like cheesecake, after all," he says finally. We pay for the drinks and walk out into the mall.

"We were doing fine," he says, looking in the window at Guess? "We were happy. Why do people have to push relationships up to failure? Why does the Peter Principle always have to be employed?"

"I want a family," I say.

"We were a family. You and me."

I would feel less lonely if I were alone.

"I want a domestic situation," I say. "I look around. Everybody is wrestling with their domestic situations but me. I'm forty-one. All I have is my job. I want something more."

"You had me. What was that?"

I can't answer.

He leans against his car, a gold Delta 98 in mint condition. Such a good parking space, a shame to give it up.

"Where will you go?" I ask.

"Upstate." I look inside the car. There's not a fleck of dirt. Not a book or a map or an empty Styrofoam cup or a used-up air freshener. The passenger seat and backseat look never sat in, the seat belts laid out on the leather for no one. The car reveals nothing about him. I think of my Honda Civic with its missing front light, the rear bumper held on by duct tape, the 7-Eleven cups and Applebee's flyers, the feng shui beads hanging from the rearview mirror, the ripped pair of L'eggs on the dash. Roy could be anyone, so I know I won't miss him when he's gone. As he drives off I still don't miss him. I go back in the mall, pulling every trick I can think of to circumvent Pottery Barn.

Back at the firm, I don't even have a desk anymore. Just a little tray and a folding chair. At the other end of our suites, a party in Computer Fraud. Robison cracked another mail-order scam. They've got a band and strippers and a cake and champagne. I look over at McCoy trying to clear a jam in the Infidelity copier. Coman picking his teeth in Embezzlement. I should just say, "The hell with this," and walk out. But no one would hire me now. I make a decision. I'm going to do my job.

"To think I took you in and you do this to me now."

"This is not your home, so you didn't take me in."

"Hmph!" The old woman shuffles out of Domain with her sack of clothes.

"Okay, people, let's go." Scores of humans groan and climb up from the couches and chair-and-a-halves, from between the stacks of Persian rugs and wall-to-wall carpets in the home furnishing section of Macy's.

"Ah, back to nature." I rip open the Velcro on the Himalayan tents at Hudson Trail Outfitters. I hate the tent jobs. The hippie squatters never clean up after themselves.

"Oh, man."

"Yeah, yeah, there's more wilderness out at The Corner, now move it. Load 'em up, George, I'm heading over to Furni*cheer*!"

Ewan moves my desk back into an office. In fact, I get a window with a western view of the district. Ocher sunsets, saffron light, flashes of zinc. I sit with my feet crossed on the sill, drink decaffeinated chai and watch the passing world. I realize how being with Roy weakened me. Being with Roy made me forget how good I was at my job, made me lose my *self*. How I subjugated myself to be with him. Living at Pottery Barn, indeed. What kind of a life was that. Where was my dignity. Pathetic.

Nighttime. I sit in the plaza lot for a few minutes and breathe the evening air. Tonight is the Lewis of London job. I hate busting families. It's my job, I tell myself. What they are doing is wrong, I tell myself. And if they can't take care of themselves the state will take care of them. I lock my doors, walking against traffic toward the mall.

"Did you see it tonight?" I'm startled by George calling out from the Mover.

"Nicely methyl," I say. "Good bariums, subtle yolks."

"I meant the way the ball seemed to split open in the end," George says. "The Schweinfurt in the flares, the Impressionism of the blast."

"Yep, it was darn aesthetic tonight. Tall, dark, and handsome. Easy on the eyes."

"You weren't watching, Kay."

"I was too, George."

"Need my help?" I don't like the way he's looking at me.

"Nah. It's just families."

"Want the gloves?"

"When have I ever worked with the gloves, George?" He shrugs. I go to work.

It's early, ten o'clock, but they are all in bed. I shine the flashlight in their eyes. They look out from the beds dully, but I know they must be frightened to death. I turn on the lights. "Pack up, people. We're going to The Corner." They struggle up, already dressed in their clothes. They expected me. Natalie packs some onesies in a diaper bag. A man lifts up his daughter from a dream. A set of twins climbs down and out of the Seafarer bunk. A dog stretches his back and yawns. Natalie's older kid steps up.

"Can I bring my bear?" he asks. He's a cute little guy and I fall for him right away, who wouldn't, with that wide gap-toothed smile and those mournful brown eyes, the kind of kid you're likely to see on a billboard in an ad for snack cakes, an amber hue to his skin that seems to cast light all around him. I crouch down so I'm close.

"You can bring anything that belongs to you," I say. The kid takes a long look at the bear, lays it down on the Lil' Pilots bed, covers him up, whispers goodbye . . .

Well, now, a scene like that would crack a fault in any heart. Even the most hard-boiled.

"I'm driving out to The Corner alone?" George asks. "Ten days before tax deadline?"

"Some nights you come up empty," I say.

"How long we been doing this together, Kay?"

"Twenty-three years, George."

"You got something you need to tell me?"

"No, nothing, George." I can't look him in the eye.

"Jesus and George love you, Kay."

"I appreciate that." I send him on his way.

The motion of the sliding rocker makes Natalie's baby, Angelica, drop off quickly. I hand her up to Natalie, who lays her in the Flora bassinet. In the back of Lewis's, Olivia yells at her twins to stop jumping off the top of the Seafarer bunk, it's not safe. The boys' dad comes in from work and they rush to him. Did you bring us something? Just me, he says. Oh, hell, they say. Don't say hell, he says. Natalie asks if I want soup. It's fresh. There's plenty. Alexa, a fifteen-year-old, lies on the Aurora canopy bed. She hates school, she hates her friends, she thinks she's ugly. "Kids can be mean," I call over to her. "Especially teenagers." It seems to help. The kids sleep. The adults sit in the rockers, drinking Canada Dry and white wine, discussing the kids, the district elections, whether or not it will rain.

The good times go by too quickly.

My boss, Ewan, does the job himself. He looks down at me in the sliding rocker and shakes his head. "The best plaza cop I ever had," he says.

"Don't act so surprised, Ewan. Even you can look around this store and see how nice they make everything."

I step up into the People Mover, find a spot among the bodies and sit on the floor next to Natalie. People sit or lie on their luggage. I have nothing. We jerk back, then settle as the truck moves out. "They're taking us to The Corner," Alexa cries. "They split up families. They make you work. You live in places with terrible bugs."

"No, no," I assure her. "It's nothing like that." It's just a low open shelter, I tell her, on the edge of the district, at the beginning of the desert, though I've never actually made the trip myself. I was always satisfied to turn the problem over to George as soon as I got the folks in the People Mover. And then for George to turn the problem over to the next guy. We drive for a long time. My mind fills with inopportune, anxious thoughts. I need clothes. I need a bath. I need food. I need Advil. I need dental floss and Robitussin and Coppertone and Tums. I need Tampax and Bactine and Pantene and Crest. I need a hat. I climb up on an upside-down egg crate so I can look out a crack in the side of the People Mover. The landscape fills with some of the bigger chains, then the car dealerships, then the strips, then the miles and miles of self-storage facilities, bunkers protecting our mistakes. And far out in the district, the outlets. Thank God I never had to work the outlets. The dregs of Squatterville, George calls them. Some real roughnecks, count your blessings, he always said. The trip goes on and on. We start to warm in the natural air. People remove their sweaters, take babies out of blankets, kick off their shoes, startle at the sweat generating on their skin. What is that smell? Where is it coming from? Why, it's the smell of each other. What a heavenly scent. I realize I've spent years trying to find such a smell, delicious and earthy, a strange subterranean plant.

Two men climb up on the egg crate, their heads pressed together looking out the crack.

"What do you see?" a woman asks.

"I see a sign for Oxenbury," one of the men says.

Oxenbury! My hometown! In my mind's eye I can see the streets, the parks, the houses of my childhood home. The drugstore owned by Doc Shapiro, the soda fountain next door. My mother pulling turnips in the front of our house, my father just coming home. Would it all still be there? The field where I kissed Jerry Ackerman? The swings where Kate Rendall and I played? My school? Our church? No air-conditioning except at the movie theater. In those days we sweated, our mouths parched, we burned in the sun, knocked senseless by the bullying heat. If I could just see my old street. I stand and beg the men to let me climb up and look out the crack just for one moment. But they won't move and one of them glares down at me. Lord help me, it's Nestor. The biggest, meanest, most recidivist squatter in the district, up from the outlets. You name it: Bedside Manor, Cotton Connection, Ikea,

The Christmas Store, Workbench, the Bastille Day Crate 'n' Barrel bust. I shrink from the weight of his stare. Controlled, eyes locked on mine, he says, "You. You are from Oxenbury?"

"Yes," I say.

"Then you have already *seen* Oxenbury." I lower myself down to the floor and look around the Mover. Everyone looks worried. But we will be fine, I know, we'll start again, we'll get it right. This is just a mild hassle, that's all, like no parking, or a flat tire or a shade of yellow that looked attractive on the paint wheel but putrid on the wall. A setback, nothing more.

Will They Kill You in Iraq?

ANTHONY SWOFFORD

IT IS NOVEMBER OF 1990 and Corporal Arthur Schitzler is a member of the Sixth Combat Service Support Battalion, First Marine Division, currently deployed to Saudi Arabia. He's a mechanic who works on five-ton trucks. Bolts and bloody knuckles. Fifteen gallons of oil per engine. It amazes Arthur how much oil those monsters gobble.

He is a pogue, in the rear with the gear. During peace, the pogue is the lowest life-form in the Marine Corps, according to the grunt. The grunt hates the pogue because the pogue maintains the vehicles that transport the grunt to the field, and if there is anywhere in the world the grunt does not want to be, it is in the field. The grunt wants to be on base, drinking from five-dollar cases of Michelob. Or on liberty, screwing local whores or the wives of pogues who are on deployment. On Okinawa, the grunt does not want to be in the Northern Training Area humping through triple-canopy jungle. The grunt wants liberty in Naha, drinking at exotic bars called Café Paris or Club Manhattan or the Omaha Underground. In those bars, the grunt will meet Japanese girls who attend Naha University, and he'll beat the shit out of pogues who may or may not get in his way. But at war, especially a desert war, if the five-tons are not working the grunt will have to hump hundreds of miles in order to find the enemy. During a desert war, the grunt loves the pogue.

Arthur has a recurring dream: He rides shotgun in a five-ton full of grunts on their way to a battle. The engine starts to choke and cough and burn out. This is because he has forgotten to put oil in the engine. The truck stops. Arthur pulls his entrenching tool off of his pack and digs a hole. Eighteen inches down he finds a stream of oil. He dips his

Kevlar helmet into the stream and pours the oil from his Kevlar into the engine, fifteen gallons' worth. He gets the grunts to their battle and they slaughter the Iraqis. He is the hero. He likes this dream.

A reporter from a San Francisco news station arrives at Sixth CSSB headquarters to conduct taped interviews with Bay Area military personnel deployed in Saudi Arabia. The reporter, John Logan, has permission to interview Arthur, who is from Walnut Creek. Arthur grew up watching Logan deliver the nightly news into his home.

Logan and his camerawoman are set up in a GP tent near the XO's hootch. The XO, a major, is sad that he is not from the Bay Area. He wants to say hello to his wife and children and ailing mother. He considers lying to Logan but decides against it for fear of losing rank and respectability. Eventually, the major will resign from the Marine Corps when it is discovered that he regularly wears medals and ribbons he did not earn and that while year after year he scored the lowest marksmanship grades with both the rifle and pistol, he wore expert badges for both weapons. After his separation from the Marine Corps, he will hang himself in the bathroom of the VFW in Big Timber, Montana.

The major stands outside the GP tent to make sure Corporal Schitzler does not smear him.

Arthur knows the major is there because every few minutes someone will yell, Good day, sir, and the major will reply softly, And you. Arthur considers the major a supreme asshole, melted down from human form and poured into a casting in the sphincter foundry at Quantico.

Arthur sits on a cot and Logan sits a few feet opposite him on another cot. The cots are made of canvas, with aluminum frames. While Logan's camerawoman adjusts the generator-run lights and pats Logan's forehead with makeup, Arthur reads some of the various phrases of graffiti that have been written on the cot with U.S. Government black ballpoint pens: *1st Mar Div Kix Ass; Suzi Rottencrotch is a friend of mine; KEEP YOUR FILTHY HANDS OFF MY WIFE.* Arthur remembers watching Logan deliver various breaking news stories: Reagan's shooting, they stopped *Scooby Doo* for that one; the bombing of the marine barracks in Lebanon, *Gilligan's Island* lost to the terrorists;

a young dead navy ensign dumped onto a tarmac from a hijacked plane somewhere in Africa, and the short-lived soap opera *Santa Barbara* cut short. Two weeks later, when the officer's body arrived in Virginia or wherever the dead bodies arrive, the soap opera was interrupted again. Arthur had stood at attention in front of his TV and saluted the ensign's flag-covered coffin. That day, Arthur decided he would join the navy when he turned eighteen. When he went to the navy recruiter's office, the recruiter was at the nearby sports bar watching a monster truck competition. The marine recruiter pulled Arthur into his office and impressed on him the importance of manliness and honor, two things the recruiter assured Arthur he would always be short on if he joined the Squids. The recruiter added, "The navy is the taxi for the Marine Corps. We find out where the wars are and the navy takes us to them. And they cook for us while we float on their ugly fucking ships. Good chow though. Better than ours."

Logan wears khakis and a green argyle golf shirt with the word TITLEIST over the left breast pocket. Arthur thinks, Titillate, I wish Connie Chung were here. Or even Joan Lunden. Arthur heard once that newscasters often wear shorts or dirty jeans or underwear below the camera view. He'd never watched Koppel or Rather or Pauley the same way again.

Logan is sweating, just as Arthur and the camerawoman are, and he is angry. He says, "Goddamn, June, isn't there some makeup that won't drip down my fucking face in this heat?"

June says, "Sorry, John. It's over a hundred degrees. You're just gonna glow, okay?"

Logan says to Arthur, "So, how the hell are you, hard charger? You're the guy from the East Bay, right?"

"Walnut Creek. My family used to sit around and watch you give the news."

Logan says, "Great, another family brought together by John Logan. Your parents, they were the ones who chose me over Stephen Pickens and Sherry Martinez, right?"

"My mom is crazy about you. My dad thinks you're a puffer, but he watches you anyway."

"A puffer, as in a fairy? Tell your dad I've sucked more than my share of dicks for a straight guy, but that's what it takes in this business. But you see her, you see Juney, that goddamn sexy camerawoman? Right now I'm fucking her. And you're gonna go to sleep tonight on a dirty cot just like we're sitting on and you're gonna jerk off, right?"

"Something like that."

June says, "Don't believe a word he says. He's been trying to screw me for six years. He's taken me everywhere, Afghanistan, Lebanon, Moscow, the crumbling East Berlin, all for nada. Tonight, he'll toss off just like you. Or maybe he'll find some happy sailor."

"All right," Logan says, "let's do this interview. Now, I want you to talk to me just like you do your buddies. I'm gonna ask you questions and you answer as if that camera isn't even there. Pretend we're old pals putting back a few at the Enlisted Club. Juney, let's roll."

Logan asks Arthur, "Do you consider the assassination of Saddam Hussein to be a justifiable, attainable goal for the Joint Forces?"

"I think you're asking the wrong guy. I fix trucks. Assassination can always be justified by someone. Or even large groups of someones. Entire nations. Sure, it's justifiable and attainable. All I've got to worry about is changing tires and oil. I'll tune up the truck they drive to Baghdad. No problem."

"Do you consider Southwest Asia to be an appropriate Area of Operations for the American military?"

"I consider the entire world an acceptable AO for the American military." Arthur knows the major will love his answers. Arthur has been trying for a month to get on the manifest of marines being sent to the nearby Texaco encampment for Thanksgiving. The American workers are hosting marines for three days over the holiday. The lucky chosen will eat home-cooked turkey dinners and drink liquor and beer, and who can know, maybe even fuck some aging geologist's wife or daughter.

Logan says, "Tell me a little about Walnut Creek, what you miss. What you'll do when the ball game is over."

"I have trouble with the term 'ball game.' I find it insulting to both baseball and war. You people and your goddamn sports analogies. I miss my parents. I miss the sunset over the Pacific. I miss Gloria Sayler."

"Is that your girlfriend, Gloria?"

"Kind of a girlfriend. A neighborhood girl. We hang out and eat hamburgers, you know, wholesome stuff. Nationwide Freezer Meats in Moraga is our favorite place. We go there after baseball games."

"You play any sports, besides whacking your willy? Grinding the beef?" Logan laughs at himself. "Sorry, buddy," he says. "Just kidding."

June says, "Okay, enough dick humor. Back on track, little man."

Logan asks, "What kind of reading material do you have over here?"

"Well, my mom just sent me Orwell's *Homage to Catalonia*, but I haven't started it. Gloria sent me a book of plays by Sartre recently, but I traded it for a box of Nutter-Butters."

"You don't like the French?"

"I think the best things the French have given us are baguettes, berets, and vanilla-scented whores. I had one once on liberty in Paris. She took an American fifty and a bottle of Pinot Gris. And she smoked all of my cigarettes. But I was only smoking because I was in Paris."

"Have you had any contact with French forces, the famous Foreign Legion?"

"No."

"Would you ever consider joining the Foreign Legion? Those boys get a lot of action."

"Sure, I'd look into it if I had a reason to leave the U.S. As of now, I'm planning on joining the American Legion and the VFW. Word is they sell draft beer for seventy-five cents and top-shelf whiskey for two bucks."

"Have you been overseas? Okinawa? The Philippines? Thailand?"

"I've been on a West Pac. We stopped in the PI and Korea, and we spent about a month on Okinawa. Pretty countries, all three."

"What is the cost of a woman in Olongapo versus Paris? I'm thinking of taking a trip. This is off the record."

June says, "Nothing is off the record."

Arthur says, "The deals in Olongapo were astounding, I must tell you. Fed, fucked, and drunk, in any order, overnight, for ten American. I felt like a thief. I often paid double or triple, because I could. The women are nice. They really are. I'd warn them against you. I'd have them fix you up with a boy and roll you."

Two weeks later, when the news station runs their special report *The Bay Area and the Persian Gulf Conflict*, Arthur's portion of airtime consists of him saying, "I'll tune up the truck they drive to Baghdad. No problem. I think the best things the French have given us are baguettes, berets, and top-shelf whiskey for two bucks. Of course, I was only smoking because I was in Paris. Fed for ten American. I felt like a thief. I'd have them fix you."

After graduating from the California College of Arts and Crafts in Oakland, Mary Slater continues working her job at SF MOMA. She sells admission tickets and pushes memberships that include exclusive invites to Friday Night Art Films and the Saturday Night Jazz Improv Project. She regularly has sex with Martin Font, who also graduated from CCAC. He works the espresso cart in the mezzanine of the museum. Mary is a photographer and Martin is a painter. They rarely talk about art. They talk about rising rents in the city and trying to land a job with BART, as the BART system has the strongest, most corrupt union in the state after the prison guards. Mary's father was a prison guard who died during a riot at Folsom in 1979. She was eleven years old. She misses her father.

The Thursday night *The Bay Area and the Persian Gulf Conflict* airs, Mary is home rather than out for dinner and drinks with Martin Font, where she is most Thursday nights. Martin is a prick, she decided that afternoon. She always pays for drinks and dinner while he leers at the waitresses. Despite her wage of $7.37 an hour, Mary's money problems aren't especially stifling because of the prison guard union and the manner in which they take care of the children of their fallen comrades.

Mary has had her television since she was twelve years old. It is a thirteen-inch color Sony that has lost its sound. Mary watches the news with disinterest. Tanks rolling across a horizon. Helicopters landing in the middle of the desert, blowing sand hundreds of feet in the air. Marines marching across lonely dunes. Between the images of the machinery and the groups of men, there are quick shots of individuals. The men move their mouths nervously, shrug their shoulders, look down at the ground. She has never cared all that much about what the military does. She'd rather not see war and violence perpetrated by her country. She votes but feels that she has little say after that. She's not going to protest, not going to write letters. She might someday look into photojournalism as a way to make a living, maybe report from a war zone or two. She tries to think of the names of a few famous war photographers but she cannot.

Corporal Arthur Schitzler's face appears on the screen. She sits on the couch and stares at the television. Corporal Arthur Schitzler, Walnut Creek, appears at the bottom of the screen. She does not know why, but she thinks, I need to know this man, I may love this man. This confuses and frightens her.

Corporal Arthur Schitzler's face is gone from the screen and John Logan reappears, clean as ever, white shirt, red tie, blue suit jacket.

On the cover of *Photo* magazine Mary writes, *Corporal Arthur Schitzler, Walnut Creek.*

She showers and calls her friend Melissa, whom she meets at Drago for drinks.

Mary tells Melissa about Corporal Arthur Schitzler.

Mary says, "It's something about his face. He looked honest. I know it sounds corny, but he really did, honest and sad. It's got to be better than loving a happy fabulist."

Melissa advises her to look through the Walnut Creek listings for Schitzler, and to call however few there might be, until she finds his parents. Mary decides she will not go to work until she tracks down Corporal Arthur Schitzler's overseas address. That's what she calls him, Corporal Arthur Schitzler. Someday she will call him Arthur, and Arty, and Shitso.

Mary and Melissa drink five whiskies each. As they pull cash from their purses, a German tourist and his friend snatch the tab from the bar and insist on paying.

Mary and Melissa leave Drago with the two Germans. They walk along Market Street toward the Germans' hotel room. The women are drunk and so are the Germans.

The hotel is near the UN. The Germans tell elaborate lies about the work they do for their government. The hotel room is done in brushed sheet metal—the walls, the ceiling, all of the furniture. "This hotel is very industrial," one of the Germans says, as he pushes *play* on the bedside CD player, and German industrial music pours from the speakers. Mary pulls from her purse a stale poppy-seed bagel that Martin Font gave her the day before. One of the Germans removes a six-pack of German abbey ale from the refrigerator. Melissa and the Germans drink ale on the bed while Mary nibbles at her bagel, sitting at the metal desk.

One of the Germans says, "It's good to party in America. American party girls are fun. No questions."

Mary says, "There are always questions. Who is your mother? Is your father a good man?"

Melissa begins to kiss one of the Germans. Mary turns away and pulls hotel stationery and a pen from the desk drawer. She begins to compose the letter she will write to introduce herself to Corporal Arthur Schitzler. Dear Sir. Dear Corporal. Dear Arthur.

Melissa is on her back with both of the Germans. One has a hand down her pants and the other is fondling her breasts. Mary realizes that Melissa is passed out. The Germans are very involved in their molesting. They are smiling at one another in their stupid tourist way, as though Melissa's body is an amusement park. They don't notice Mary grab a bottle of ale in each hand. She walks to the bed and hits them both over the head with a bottle at the same time. The bottles break and glass and ale spill all over Melissa and the bed and the Germans.

One of the Germans is bleeding. Both are knocked out. Neither will die. Neither will remember any of the evening after leaving Drago. They will travel by train to Portland and Seattle and Vancouver and have similar experiences in each city. Drunkenness, women, molestation, assault. The German who is currently bleeding will be arrested in Vancouver for rape. He'll be tried and convicted, and he'll spend a few years in jail. After the trial, his fiancée will marry his travel companion.

The breaking of the bottles and the ale-sopping of her clothes awakes Melissa. She refastens her bra, adjusts her shirt, and buttons her pants. She hugs Mary.

Melissa says, "Fuck. I drank way too much. Let's get a cab to your apartment. I don't want to go home to Tom tonight."

Arthur is on the manifest for what the command is calling Turkey Liberty. The night before Turkey Liberty begins, he has to finish a fifty-point inspection on a five-ton. At item thirty-three, Check Tire Pressure, he calls it quits. He climbs into the cab and pulls the afternoon's mail from his cargo pocket.

Gloria Sayler writes him once a week. She never writes more than a page. Gloria's mother is an administrator for an HMO, and she mails Gloria's letters from her office. The metered postage stamps have company messages printed next to them: HIGHEST NURSE-TO-PATIENT RATIO IN CALIFORNIA! FORTY CENTS OF EVERY DOLLAR GOES TO PATIENT CARE! ASK YOUR DOCTOR FOR AN ALLERGYSMART GUIDE!

Gloria Sayler is not promising anything, but she is not completely discounting the possibility of a pleasant, sex-filled reunion for the two of them. She was excited to see him on television; her entire family watched. They weren't sure if what he said made any sense, but it was nice to see his face on the screen. It's nice to have a hero from the neighborhood. WC High played the tape the next morning for homeroom. She is sure that when he comes back there will be a parade, and he'll probably get a key to the school, or something like that.

Mrs. Schitzler writes Arthur seven or eight letters a week, sometimes ten. He only reads one or two a week. The envelopes are always stuffed thick, sometimes so thick that she has to throw on extra postage for the next ounce. Mrs. Schitzler writes that she too has seen him on television. His father had been late at work that night, getting ready for a big sale, but she saw the report. She was so excited, she couldn't figure out the taping function on the VCR. They are hoping to get a tape from the television station so his father can watch it. She writes that Arthur looked handsome, that his desert camouflage utilities reminded her of the suits he used to wear, the uniformity and crispness of the lines. She thinks that the marines should consider accessorizing the uniform with an ascot. It would be a very civilized look. Arthur wonders if maybe his mother isn't thinking of one of the generals or colonels when she writes about the uniformity of the lines. He knows that the day before the interview he washed his utilities by hand and that they were still dirty and wrinkled when he spoke with Logan.

Arthur's adoptive parents, Mr. and Mrs. Schitzler, work at the Nordstrom in Walnut Creek. His father is the head of Men's Suits, and his mother is the head of Women's Shoes. They are well-dressed people. Arthur grew up wearing fashionable clothes. He wore suits to the public school. His shoes were shined by Oscar and Pedro, the Filipino shoeshiners at Nordstrom. Because of his appearance, Arthur's peers ridiculed him.

Arthur carries one black-and-white photo of his biological parents. He pulls the photo out of his wallet and sets it on the dash of the truck. His biofather is sitting sidesaddle on a motorcycle, and his biomother is standing on the gas tank, which is decorated with flames. She is wearing a jean jacket with nothing underneath, and cutoffs. She wears no shoes on her dirty feet. She is pregnant with Arthur. She is an angry young Navajo woman. Her name is Screaming Eagle. Arthur shows no genealogical attributes of the Navajo other than jet-black hair and skimpy beard growth. His father wears a straw cowboy hat. He is Anglo, of mixed ancestry. Arthur doesn't know his biofather's name. On the back of the photo, written with black ballpoint pen in confused penmanship of sixth-grader quality, the inscription: *me an screaminn eagle on my hog*. The printing on his father's black muscle shirt, either an advertisement for a whiskey or a Latin American anarchist's call to arms, is unintelligible through the grainy haze of the 110 film. He wears cutoff jeans and dusty black combat boots. Occasionally, Arthur longs to meet his biological parents. He wonders if they saw him on television, if somehow they might know who he is. Maybe they've secretly followed him from the orphanage. Maybe the middle-aged, dark-skinned waitress at Nationwide Freezer Meats is Screaming Eagle. Stories surface all the time about a waitress at a diner having served her long-lost father Special Number Five for fifteen years without him knowing the relation, and one day she sets down his plate of meat loaf and asks, Did you ever live in Walla Walla? Did you ever know a Miss Lodice Jones?

After the war, Arthur will go to Nationwide Freezer Meats for a burger with Mary Slater. This will be their first date. The dark-skinned, middle-aged waitress will not be there. When Arthur inquires about her, the owner will say, while scrubbing his grill, "Fuck, man. I don't remember all the broads who work for me. She's working at some other shithole burger place, whaddaya think?"

In the morning, Arthur lines up in formation with the other ninety-nine marines on the Turkey Liberty manifest. More than a few deals have gone down in order to secure a slot. Little Snooty, a corporal from Supply Company, traded ten new smut mags, eighty dollars in cash, three bottles of whiskey, and a forty-five-day light-duty chit with a sergeant in Admin in order to get his name on the manifest.

The captain reports to the major, "All present and accounted for."

The major says, "Gentlemen. You are the ambassadors of the Marine Corps. Conduct yourselves accordingly. These American families want to see in your eyes the death stare of the protector. Give them this. Use your utensils correctly. Say yes sir and ma'am. Alcohol is illegal in the Kingdom of Saudi Arabia. The consumption of it is punishable by death or something worse. If your hosts offer, you must refuse. There have been rumors that these homes will be filled with prostitutes or just plain easy women. This is incorrect. If you make lewd advances, I will find out and you will go up on Office Hours. If you debase the Marine Corps, you will suffer the wrath of the Uniform Code of Military Justice. Do you understand me, gentlemen?"

"Yes, sir."

A Humvee leads a caravan of Land Rovers and Volvos into the battalion headquarters. Fifty families will take two marines each for the holiday weekend. The families hope to host marines from their home state or even their home city. The major commands the marines to get on line in alphabetical order of state of origin. There is one marine for Alaska, five for Arkansas, ten for California, seventeen for Texas. There are no representatives from Hawaii, Maryland, Nevada, South Dakota, or Vermont but a fairly even distribution throughout the remaining states.

The marines are on line and twenty feet across from them the families are standing. Most of the family men are in their late thirties or early forties. Their wives are good and plump blond midwesterners, svelte tan ladies from West Coast beach towns, severe women from the eastern seaboard, big-haired Okies and Texans, dark Southeast Asians from the various poor island nations. The children are small, confused versions of their parents.

Arthur has been on line like this twice before, once in the whorehouse in Paris, France, and many years earlier when he was seven weeks old and Mr. and Mrs. Andrew Schitzler adopted him from an orphanage in Paris, New Mexico.

The orphanage is brightly lit. The waxed floors reflect the overhead fluorescent lighting, and through the halls children run, singing. Mr. and Mrs. Schitzler are led to the newborn room by the stout head nurse, named Freeser. Freeser has worked here for fifteen years. The state of New Mexico might approve a couple for adoption, but that does not mean Head Nurse Freeser will. Her checklist is less conventional. She's not concerned with family history and current or cross-generational mental illness. She cares about what you will name the child, that you will not allow a girl to wear lipstick and short skirts until she leaves your home with a husband, that the boy will wear suits and answer yes sir and yes ma'am.

There are six newborns, from the age of three weeks to seventeen weeks. The children are in cradles. They are wrapped with white swaddling clothes. The Schitzlers think they want a boy. There are two boys. One will not stop crying and the other is quietly edging his way into a sleep. The Schitzlers and Freeser stand over this boy. He has a scratch of black hair on his head and his hands are balled up in fists. Mr. Schitzler nudges a finger into the boy's tiny right fist and the boy tugs at his finger. Mrs. Schitzler does the same with the boy's left hand and the boy tugs. They smile at one another and Nurse Freeser smiles as well and says, "What will you name the boy?"

Mrs. Schitzler says, "Arthur. He will be Arthur."

Mr. Schitzler says, "Yes. Arthur. He'll be a tough knuckle-duster, and the women will love him."

Freeser says, "Arthur is a fine name. Let's finish the paperwork."

After the paperwork, Freeser hands the Schitzlers a black-and-white photo of Arthur's parents. It is the photo of pregnant Screaming Eagle standing on the motorcycle, and straddling the motorcycle, Arthur's father. But the photo is a lie. Freeser bought the photo for five cents in a dime shop in Las Cruces. She spent days looking through junk shops and dime shops and antique shops for suitable photographic progenitors for the young male newborn now named Arthur Schitzler.

Arthur is in the home of Mr. Charles Highsmith, a geologist for Texaco, his wife, Lawlie, and their two sons, Sammy and Shawn. The other marine is Little Snooty. Arthur doesn't know Little Snooty's first or last name, he only knows him by what everyone calls him, Little Snooty. Little Snooty is four feet ten inches tall. He received a height waiver in order to join the marines. His nose is always running. Little Snooty is from Fresno, hell of all Central California hells. People who leave Fresno do so only briefly before returning to die long, lonely deaths. Or they return dead.

The Highsmiths have lived in Saudi Arabia for ten years. They both grew up in San Diego, received their geology degrees from the state university, and moved quickly into the business of making a family.

Lawlie says, "The two munchkins are great, but I'm tied up now. We'll ship 'em off to college in six and seven years and then we're gonna sail around the world. Right, Charlie-boy?"

Charles says, "Yes, babykins."

Charles is at the bar mixing four gin and tonics. A gin and tonic doesn't seem like a real drink to Arthur, more like a spritzer or a shot of mouthwash. How could someone be drawn and quartered over gin?

The Highsmith home is a split-level stucco structure with a two-car garage. The builder, Pierce & Pierce & Pierce of Winnemuca, Nevada, has built variations on the same floor plan in Master Design Communities in twenty American states and three oil-rich countries.

The Highsmiths have a black leather couch, love seat, and recliner. Their barrister bookcases are filled with fascinating pieces of native art from Indonesia and similar islands where geologists work for Texaco. The art is made from gourds and bull horns and hair and dried shit, both animal and human. Once a year the Highsmiths vacation in Manhattan, and framed prints from various exhibitions at the major museums hang from the walls. Schiele. Picasso. Magritte. Seurat. Kandinsky. Hopper.

The drink is strong, the first that Arthur has had in four months. Little Snooty, with his supply connections, has been drinking whiskey regularly since arriving in-country. The Highsmith boys are upstairs playing Atari, and occasionally their arguments spill downstairs, where one of the parents pulls them apart and mediates the dispute, threatening various forms of punishment both monetary and physical.

Little Snooty is sunk into the couch, looking through a *National Geographic*, and Charles assists Lawlie in the kitchen. Arthur pours himself another drink and returns to the recliner.

Little Snooty says, "Check out the titties on this Amazonian monster. Goddamn."

Arthur says, "Come on, man. I stopped looking at that shit in sixth grade. I thought you were the battalion connection for porn mags."

"I am. I'm the connection for everything. It's just, well, there aren't any porn mags in this house. But how about that sweet-assed Mrs. Highsmith? Hey, Mother, want another? I mean, shit, I never seen nothing like that around San Diego. I must be going to the wrong clubs."

"You probably go to the whale club, right? Searching out those hefty wives whose jarhead husbands are on a West Pac?"

"Hell, no. I never screw marine wives. I go down to Coronado and screw squid wives. Man, those poor fuckers out at sea for a year and their wives running around, giving that shit away. Dumbfucks. Marry their goddamn high school sweetheart from bumfuck nowhere and think she's in San Diego with the checkbook and she ain't gonna be spending all the money and running around getting fucked. Shit."

"They're not all screwing around. I know some guys whose wives are faithful."

"You seen their pictures? Faithful West Pac wives are horse-ass ugly. Ugly women don't get the dick outside of marriage. Maybe once or twice before the wedding they get lucky, some dude makes a huge mistake, but that shit don't happen often. It messes up the balance. Ugly women can hang that pussy on the mailbox and the goddamn mailman will pass it up!"

"You're all talk, man. It's boring. Talking about fucking and bitches and drinking and fighting. When's the last time you got fucked? About four months ago, just like the rest of us."

"I got some sooner than that. You forget, I'm Little Snooty. And what else you gonna talk about? We're jarheads, man, about to go to war, how else are we supposed to talk? It's just like the war movies. Except, in every other lousy war the U.S. has ever fought they've had bars and whores, and so did the movies. They'll make some boring-ass art films about this war. Moving pictures of sand dunes and shit. Anyway, I did my time as an altar boy. That's the wrong damn altar. I'm trying to lighten things up. Put all the shit into perspective."

Little Snooty flips through another *National Geographic*.

Arthur smells the turkey and what he thinks is baked squash. He tops off his drink. Arthur thinks, Little Snooty is right, it is how we are supposed to talk. Killers. Fighters. Fuckers. How we are ordered to think. The major and his orders, ambassadors of the corps? Goddamn animals, every one of us. And then we go into a home, and what then? Eating like pigs at the table. Fuck this and fuck that and goddamn bitches and look at these titties. No wonder the mothers of America hate the corps. The corps kills their baby boys. Mothers of America meek and mild, say goodbye to your sweet child. Little Snooty was probably a sweet child back there in Fresno. His mommy loved him, and his sisters, and the older girls from the neighborhood who protected him from the bullies. And then there is no one protecting him, all he's got is the killer mentality that's been sewn on his shoulder, and he must hide his heart.

Arthur wanders into the kitchen. Lawlie looks like a good cook, whatever that means. She is bent over the stove, telling Charles to go to page 575 of the cookbook and tell her again the baking time for the squash. There are three wooden spoons on the surface of the stove, each with something in their bowl—bisque, potatoes, squash. The spoons are arthritic looking and burnt along the handles. Two pies are on top of a butcher block, covered with wax paper. Lawlie's menu is attached to the refrigerator door with a peach-shaped and -scented magnet. Arthur recalls his mother's magnet, a lady beetle with the antennae missing. Garlic mashed potatoes. Cranberry relish. Corn-bread stuffing. Shrimp bisque. Apple-sausage-stuffed butternut squash. Maple-glazed parsnips. Pears in red wine. Pumpkin cheesecake. Pecan pie. They never write turkey.

Lawlie says, "The Texaco commissary brings in all the items to make a Thanksgiving dinner right out of *The Joy of Cooking*. I grew up with a different menu, but I've adapted over the years."

Charles says, "Texaco takes care of its own. Here we are in Saudi Arabia, having a holy American holiday dinner. It's amazing."

Arthur says, "Yeah, it looks great."

Charles says, "Hey, buddy, how 'bout you fill us up at the bar and call the boys and Snooty in. Mom'll be ready for us in a shake."

The Highsmiths are a praying family. At the dinner table, they all join hands. Arthur holds Lawlie's hand on his right. It is a fine small hand, even pretty, a little damp because she just washed, and he is happy to be holding it despite the prayer. He runs his thumb over her wedding diamonds. On his left he holds Sammy's hand, which is sweaty and sticky, covered with jam. Charles asks God for a quick and decisive victory over the menace to the north. He hopes the fine marines he's honored to feed will be watched over, and so too the precious natural resources that allow him to support his family.

The Highsmith boys behave themselves during the meal. Two bottles of red wine are gotten through. Charles and Lawlie ask Arthur and Little Snooty the types of questions parents ask a boy before he takes their daughter out on a first date. When Arthur clears his second plate of food, three gin and tonics and three glasses of wine into the day, he is smashed. He excuses himself upstairs to the room that has been prepared for him, and he takes a nap.

While Charles and the boys are washing the dishes, Little Snooty and Lawlie are upstairs screwing. Arthur thinks he hears a woman coming in the next room but decides it's just a dream, and he tries to navigate his way back into the dream. Little Snooty will have sex with Lawlie three or four times a day over the next few days. Usually, they'll have sex in the garage, in the cargo area of the Land Rover. When Little Snooty is not screwing Lawlie, he looks through a *National Geographic* or calls international phone sex lines—011-EZE-SLTZ, 011-FRE-GRLS, 011-ASS-LOVR. At the end of December, after the Highsmiths' phone bill arrives and Lawlie admits to Charles her infidelity with Little Snooty, Little Snooty will go up on Office Hours charges for Conduct Unbecoming a Marine. He'll be busted to private and through monthly payroll deductions he'll pay the Highsmiths' phone bill. Little Snooty will say again and again, "They can take my money and my rank but they can't take back those sweet fucks. I might die a private, but least I won't die unfucked for six months like all you all other motherfuckers."

Mr. Highsmith will attempt to drive into the Sixth CSSB compound for a few words with Little Snooty. The MPs will turn him away. He'll return the next day, and every day for three weeks after. He'll drive around the compound blaring, from speakers mounted on his hood, a Psy Wars tape he has prepared for Little Snooty: "You short little

Fresno fuck. I'm gonna find you back in the States and kill you. I'm gonna chop off your dick and feed it to a rat. I'm gonna shove a starving weasel up your midget ass." The MPs will allow Mr. Highsmith three or four trips around the compound each day before they run him off. When he stops his Psy War assault on Little Snooty, most of the marines from the Sixth CSSB, including Little Snooty, will miss it.

Arthur wakes from his nap and heads downstairs. Little Snooty and the Highsmiths are playing Monopoly. They invite Arthur to join in: they'll give him a few minor properties, a utility, and double the normal starting cash, but he says no thanks. He'd like to make a collect phone call to the States if that's possible. It's morning in California, and his parents will be watching parades on television. He serves himself a slice of pumpkin cheesecake and pours a double whiskey and water at the bar. He takes the cordless phone, along with the drink and cake, upstairs to the room he's staying in.

Mr. Schitzler accepts the call. He is happy to hear from his son. He and his wife are drinking mimosas and watching the parades.

Mr. Schitzler says, "Your mother and I miss you, son. I watched the tape from the news yesterday. You look healthy. They must be feeding you well."

Arthur tells his father he is being hosted by an American Texaco family. Mr. Schitzler thinks this is a fine idea. His father recites the items on his mother's menu. Her menu is not all that different from Lawlie's. No bisque though, but a sweet potato soup. Arthur's mother gets on the phone. She is overjoyed. She sounds like a teenage girl hearing from her first crush.

Arthur's mother tells him that they had been receiving phone messages from a girl named Mary Slater, and that two days ago, after none of her calls were returned, this Mary Slater showed up at the front door.

Mrs. Schitzler says, "She is very pretty. She saw you on the news and she needs to tell you something. I gave her your address and, because I had extras, one of your boot camp photos and also two of your senior portraits. One of you in the tux, the other of you wearing the red sweater."

Arthur is running through his head the name Mary Slater. He doesn't know her. He can count on one hand the number of women he knows in the States. The number of women he has slept with, he can count on the same hand.

Arthur says, "Mom. She says she saw me on TV and she tracked you down. Isn't that kind of crazy? Did she look strange?"

"Oh no, honey. She was very nicely dressed and made-up. I could very well have sold her her shoes. They were Mary Janes. Prada or Vuitton. Classic."

"Where does she live?"

"The city. I think the Mission. She moved there from Oakland recently. She went to CCAC. She's a photographer. She works at SF MOMA."

"Jesus, Mom. Did you invite her in for a drink?"

"It was midmorning. We had mimosas on the porch. We're having lunch next week."

It is the middle of February. Arthur and Mary Slater have exchanged a dozen letters. She has sent snapshots of herself and photos from her portfolio. Arthur is very impressed with her mind and her art and her beauty.

Arthur is busy performing fifty-point maintenance checks on five-tons. The UN deadlines for complete Iraqi withdrawal from Kuwait have passed. American planes are dropping thousands of tons of bombs a day on Iraqi positions throughout Kuwait and Iraq. Grunts have been involved in firefights near the Kuwait/Saudi Arabia border.

The Sixth CSSB has moved its concertina-wire encampment fifty klicks north since Thanksgiving. Arthur had his last shower six weeks ago. His desert camouflage utilities are bleached nearly white from sweat and sun. There are greasy hand marks on his uniform where after packing bearings or replacing an oil pan gasket he has wiped his hands on himself rather than on a rag.

He sits in the passenger seat of a five-ton. Mary's photos are leaning against the windshield, three snapshots of her and her triptych of a Moroccan beggar family. When he finishes with each truck he climbs into the cab and writes a few paragraphs to Mary. This letter is seventeen pages long. He has three more trucks to work on before the convoy is ready to roll northward with troops and supplies. After he finishes the last truck he will send the letter to Mary and tell her it might be the last she hears from him for some time.

Three days ago, Saddam Hussein's soldiers lit fire to the underground oil pipelines in Kuwait, and fires blaze nonstop from the pipes. The black smoke billows a mile high, and the sky alternates between black and gray and an empty white color. Occasionally, a slight rain of oil droplets falls.

Arthur completes a page to Mary. The oil is falling and he rolls down the window of the five-ton and holds the page out, where it collects pinpricks of oil. The oil doesn't obscure his words, but his penmanship does look odd—three or four dots on the *i*'s, *t*'s that look like citrus trees, droplets gathered around the intersection. He leans his head out the window and stares straight up. The sky looks like the inside of a chimney or the detonation of a bomb.

Arthur has finished the inspections and sent the letter to Mary. The war is under way. He is riding shotgun in one of the five-tons that is part of a fifty-truck supply and troop convoy. The truck in front of Arthur is full of grunts, pink-faced and weary. Their weapons are loaded with full magazines. When the oil rain falls, the grunts pull their helmets down over their faces. With their helmets and bulky flak jackets, they look like hard-shelled insects.

The convoy is supporting Task Force Grizzly, a two-regiment force that has had great success with the enemy thus far. Thirty hours into the ground war, Grizzly is kicking ass and taking hundreds of prisoners who have been surrendering in conjunction with Geneva Convention rules: barefoot, with their boots slung over their necks, waving a white cloth or T-shirt, with no weapons on their person.

The convoy heads north through the desert and moves as most convoys do, in fits and starts. The drivers are supposed to maintain two hundred yards between each truck but the excitement over what seems like an easy victory has helped close that tactical gap. The feeling that they are going somewhere, that things have finally been decided, is overwhelming. The drivers casually talk back and forth on their radios, clogging the frequencies.

Arthur hears the whistle of incoming rounds. He thinks he is imagining this distinct sound, but when truck three in front of him, the one

Little Snooty is riding shotgun in, explodes, he knows the whistle is real. Two more explosions. Arthur's truck is loaded with small-arms ammunition. He and the driver debark and run south. The supply captain lies flat on the deck outside of his truck and yells at them to get down. They do.

The supply captain is on the radio to the Fire Direction Center, screaming, "Drop some shit on them! Drop some fucking shit on them!"

The truck in front of Arthur's takes a hit. The grunts were standing, trying to get a good look at the exploded vehicles. The truck lies burning on its side and the grunts' bodies are spread out in a twenty-meter half-moon of flesh and flak jackets and weapons. All are dead, along with the driver and the mechanic. Three other vehicles are on their sides as well, burning.

An A10 Warthog comes in low, its guns blaring, and it fires a volley of missiles at the Iraqi tanks that were blowing the convoy to nothing. The enemy assault ends.

Arthur double-times to Little Snooty's vehicle. Burning wooden crates of medical supplies are still secured to the bed of the toppled truck. A few other marines arrive and stare at the wreckage. They can hear the bodies burning in the cab; flesh sizzles and small pops cause embers to rise from the flames, which climb out of the cab through the passenger window frame. A marine next to Arthur is holding an e-tool at his side. Arthur grabs the e-tool and shovels sand into the cab while the other marines begin to toss sand on the burning medical supplies using e-tools and helmets.

The fire is extinguished. Inside the cab, Little Snooty's body lies on top of the driver's body and they are both badly burnt and covered with sand. Arthur cannot recall the driver's name. A sergeant peers into the cab and says, while crying, "Goddamn. This is Little Snooty's truck, ain't it? Goddamn. Little Snooty." He pulls out his 9mm pistol and fires a fifteen-round clip into the cab.

Little Snooty is given a full military funeral at Sunset of the Pines Mortuary in Fresno. His parents, after the few months it takes to process such paperwork, receive a two-hundred-thousand-dollar check from Servicemen's Group Life Insurance. They build a new home with this money. They also receive a check from the Marine Corps for Little Snooty's final pay, minus the seven hundred dollars still owed toward the Highsmiths' phone bill.

Arthur and Mary are in bed in their house in Walnut Creek, a few blocks away from the house Arthur grew up in. They are having loud, satisfying sex.

Mary teaches photography at CCAC. Arthur owns a garage where he makes most of his money from smog inspections and the costly repairs required to pass the state emissions tests. Sometimes he feels as though his entire life has been about oil and fuel and dangerous emissions.

There is a fireplace in their room, and on the mantel sits Mary's triptych of the Moroccan beggars and the snapshot of the two people Arthur believes are his biological parents. Also, there is a photo of Arthur taken a few days after the war ended. He'd just jumped out of a field shower, and he is naked but holding his helmet over his crotch. Behind him, the oil fires burn.

After the convoy is hit, they proceed slowly north to Al Jaber Airfield in southern Kuwait, secured by the infantry that afternoon. There is not much work to do. Mostly the marines talk about the bad luck of being the first in and the last out.

Every few days Arthur rides shotgun in a five-ton transporting war prisoners to the airfield at Riyadh, where the prisoners will spend a week before being flown to Iraq. On the drive to and from Riyadh they pass the burnt hulks of the five-tons from the convoy. One morning on the way to Riyadh Arthur has the driver stop when they come upon the debris. He orders two prisoners off the truck and marches them to the cab of Little Snooty's vehicle. With his pistol he motions the men to sit down. He sits down with them. The men are tired and sad. They were treated badly by their government and are about to return to their country, having failed that government.

Arthur says, while pointing at the cab with his pistol, "My buddy died in this truck. Well, not really my buddy. But I knew him. He was a good guy. Little Snooty. I don't even know his real name. He was crazy. Some geologist had us over for Thanksgiving. He fucked the poor guy's wife for three straight days."

The men look at one another. One of the men has a thick, handsome beard, dark black with flecks of gray.

Arthur asks, "Do you have children?"

He knows it is useless. He wishes he'd gone to the Arabic classes S-2 conducted. He removes the magazine from the pistol and clears the chamber. He puts the pistol to his temple and dry-fires five times.

"Will they kill you in Iraq?"

The men look at him confusedly.

He inserts the magazine, chambers a round, and places the muzzle against the bearded Iraqi's temple. He points toward Iraq and makes firing noises, "Bang. Bang. Bang." The man is weeping.

Arthur says, "I'm sorry. But will they kill you in Iraq?"

He shoves the pistol into the sand until it is buried but one corner of the grip. He fires, and the earth around the weapon erupts. The Iraqis run toward the transport truck. Arthur tries firing again, but the pistol has malfunctioned. He works his finger uselessly against the trigger.

Eros 101

ELIZABETH TALLENT

Question one: *Examine the proposition that for each of us, however despairing over past erotic experience, there exists a soul mate.*

Answer: Soul? In some fluorescent lab an egg's embryonic smear cradles a lozenge of eponymous silicon, the vampiric chip electromagnetically quickened by a heartbeat, faux alive, while in a Bauhaus bunker on the far side of campus, a researcher wheedles Chopin from a virtual violin, concluding with a bow to her audience of venture capitalists, but for real despair, please turn to Prof. Clio Mitsak, at a dinner party in her honor, lasting late this rainy winter night, nine women at the table, women only, for the evening's covert (and mistaken: you'll see) premise is that the newly hired Woolf scholar will, from her angelic professional height and as homage to VW, scheme to advance all female futures, and the prevailing mood has been one of preemptive gratitude, gratitude as yet unencumbered by actual debt and therefore flirtatious, unirksome even to Clio, its object. Clio who, hours ago, hit the button for auto-charm, safely absenting her soul (*there*) from the ordeal of civility. Gone, virtually, until dessert. Set down before her, the wedge of cake, lushly black as creekbed mud, parting under the tines of the fork, brings her to her senses, but then she's sorry, because the whipped cream is an airy petrochemical quotation of real cream, and the aftertaste of licked-tire-tread provokes an abrupt tumble into depression. It is an attribute of the profoundest despair not to realize it *is* despair. Kierkegaard. Mitsak. She's vanished down that rabbit hole known as California and her cell never cries *text me*. Her past, rare for a lesbian, has gone dead quiet; her exes have adopted Chinese infants abandoned in train stations. Desire's deserted the professor (she is the deserted train station), and this candelit table strewn with cigarettes ashed in saucers and wineglasses kissed in retro red makes her want to cry out a warning. Nine innocents commencing the long romance with academia's rejections: Well, she has everything they long for, and look at her. Old! Old! Old! Old! Old! Alone! Alone! Alone! Alone! It's not really there, is it, such stupidity, on the tip of her tongue? Yes it is—(she's drunk)—but look, she's saved, struck dumb by a voice.

The voice can't be described as *honeyed.* It doesn't intend to flatter. Neither gratitude nor the least career-driven taint of ingratiation figures in its tone. The voice belongs to the woman at Clio's left, whom Clio has succeeded, since seating was reshuffled for dessert, in not noticing at all. Such gaps or rifts in social obligation are the prerogative of charisma, with its sexy, butterfly-alighting attentiveness, its abrupt, invigorating rudeness, the masochistically satisfying cold shoulder turned toward any less than stellar presence. Regretfully, Clio concedes (as perhaps the voice, fractionally wounded, implies) that she has managed to ignore beauty.

Q: *Briefly explicate Rilke's lines "All of you undisturbed cities / haven't you ever yearned for the Enemy?"*

A: When that beautiful voice says, "Selfish us, we've kept you up too late. You're tired," Clio, not yet ready to confront the source, steadies the bowl of her wineglass between two fingers and a thumb, observing the quake of her pulse in the concentric wine rings. The voice qualifies, thoughtfully: "No, *sad*," italicizing with the pleasure of nailing emotion to its right name, and at this ventured naming, Clio feels the startled relief of the very lonely, whose emotions, unless they trouble to name them to themselves, run around nameless. Immediately following relief comes panic, not at all an unusual progression, for there's no panic quite like the panic of having found something you'd hate to lose. Now we come to that asocial moment when the inkblot of private gesture, proof of exigent emotion, stains the unfolding social contract: Clio can't look at this woman. Not yet. Realizing it can only seem strange, she closes her eyes. A person whose composure is not only a professional asset but an actual cast of mind may become a connoisseur of her own panic, just as, for a Japanese gardener, the random scatteration of cherry petals on raked gravel possesses an inimitable beauty:

so behind her closed eyes Clio experiences, as counterpart to dismay, a sneaky delight at her own downfall. The Enemy!

Q: *The absurd and the erotic are mutually exclusive modes of perception. That is, no love object can be both ridiculous and beautiful. True or false?*

A: The voice's owner, perceiving an invitation in Clio's empty glass, leans in with the bottle, startling Clio, whose closed eyes have prevented awareness of her proximity. Clio jumps, diverting the airborne artery of wine, which leaps about, bathing her wrist, spattering her dessert plate, splashing from the table's edge onto her black silk lap. The voice's owner fails to right the bottle until wine rains from the table's edge, pattering into flexing amoeba shapes on the polished floor, the voice's owner apologizing manically—yet as if she anticipated some need for apology?—and setting the bottle down with a thump. *I'm so so sorrrrry.* It is Clio's lap that the voice's owner bends toward, still uttering wild *sorries,* so that Clio's first image of her happens to be of the parting of her hair, a line of skin as naked as if a fresh-peeled twig had just been unearthed. As for her hair, it is red and in torment, copious, strenuous, anarchic hair, writhing, heavy, ardent, gorgeous hair tricked into confinement, knotted at the nape of a neck so smooth and white its single mole seems to cast a tiny shadow. The tip of Clio's tongue so covets the mole, which stands out like one of the beads of Beaujolais on Clio's own wrist, that Clio scarcely experiences the swabbing of the napkin at her lap—thus, for the sake of the imagined, missing out on the erotic thrill of the actual, and immediately repenting this, the first loss within the kingdom of true love.

"This is *so* not working," says the woman, trying to blot at Clio's wrist while Clio memorizes every detail of the profile of her future. Too much forehead, baldish and exposed-looking, as is often true of redheads, a long nose with a bump at its tip, the smart arch of the lifted eyebrow, thick eyelashes dark at their roots, fair to invisibility at their tips. A fine chin. A neat and somehow boyish ear, exposed by the ferocious tension of the trammeled hair. Why boyish? Unearringed, Clio notes, not even pierced, just a sexy virgin petal of lobe. Under the fine chin, the hint of a double, a softening in a line that should ideally run tensely along the jaw to the downcurve of the throat. This is true of redheads as well, Clio thinks, this appearance of fattiness or laxness in certain secret places, as if the body, where it can, resists the severity of the contrast between pale skin and vivid hair, and asserts a passivity, a private entropy, counter to the flamy energy of red. Clio is forty-two to the other's twentysomething: fact. Fearful fact.

"Don't worry, we can get you cleaned up," says the younger woman, "so come on," standing to seize Clio's wrist, leading Clio down a long and shadowed hall, the din of apologies—everyone's, chorused yet random, like Apache war cries—fading behind the two of them, then gone entirely, Clio surrendering to the sexiness of being *led*, for the other hasn't released her wrist and hasn't turned around, Clio Eurydice, prisoner, or child, intently reading the text of this most unexpected of persons, the Beloved. Under Clio's hot gaze the knot of passionate hair at the Beloved's nape, screwed so tight in its coil, releases red-gold strands flaring with electricity.

Q: *The following quotation is taken from Wittgenstein's* Philosophical Investigations:

> [A] face which inspires fear or delight (the object of fear or delight) is not on that account its cause, but—one might say—its target.

Discuss.

A: Prof. Mitsak's new condominium comes with its own scrap of California, backyard enough for two spindly fruit trees, a lumpy futon of gopher-harrowed turf, and an inherited compost heap. It's still winter, the trees' tracery of bare branches unguessable as to kind, but Prof. Mitsak thinks of them as plum trees because sex, for her, was born with a theft: of her grandmother's plum jam, the old woman watching, from the corner of an eye, the child's fingers crooking over the jar's rim, sliding into the lumpish, yielding sweetness, the old woman giving the harsh little laugh peculiar to that kind of vicarious delight, witnessing a pleasure one essentially disapproves of, which costs one something—in her grandmother's case, a steely domestic rigor and a wicked Methodist conviction about the virtue of self-deprivation were both held in check for the duration of Clio's self-pleasuring. The child must have trusted the old woman would tolerate this display of sensuousness, but how could she have known? It will be spring by the time the trees, if their blossoming proves they're not plum, can disappoint Clio, and by spring she hopes to be eating and sleeping again, done with writing and rewriting letters, real, insane, ink-and-paper letters, she never sends, through twisting herself into yoga asanas meant to impress the younger, suppler Beloved, who will never observe these contortions. In Clio's previous experience of heartbreak, she's been its cause. All this is new to Clio, and, as she says to herself, she's not good at it. She's a bad sufferer, graceless, tactless, wincing, vindictive, a forgetter of goddaughters' birthdays, a serial umbrella loser. Winter rains down on her head, pelting her with the icy spite of finality: she will never tilt a bottle toward the mouth of a Mei or Ming, or click wedding ring against steering wheel in time to Mozart. Her most parodied gesture becomes the quick, convulsive shake of the head with which she assumes the lectern, flicking raindrops across her notes, rousing the microphone to a squalling tantrum as water pings against electronics. In each lecture Clio seems to be trailing after some earlier, smarter, more competent Clio, even as she had followed the Beloved, she of the Sturm und Drang hair, down the fatal hallway. How can love do this, divorce one from oneself? One's old, reliable, necessary self? All winter, this is the single relief built into every pitiless week: white-knuckling it at the podium, Clio suffers the loss of something other than the Beloved.

Fridays can be very bad. Those Fridays when faculty meetings are held, Clio must, as often as not, encounter the Beloved—as junior faculty, her attendance isn't always required, but there is this pain, certain Fridays, of having to sit on the far side of a slab of exotic wood from some plundered rain forest, studying the span of the Beloved's cheekbone, a revelation of human perfection. Like human perfection, shadowed. The corner of the Beloved's mouth has an unwarranted tendency to break Clio's heart. That is, the corner of this mouth now and then deepens into a near-smile. Suppose everyone were capable of disarming everyone else thus, by the merest turn of a head, by the flicker of an eyelid or the premonition of a smile, then all relations would be grounded in wonder, then everyone would be taken hostage by the immensity of what it is possible to feel.

Q: *True or false: In narrative, desire is scarcely born before it encounters an obstacle; neither can exist without the other.*

A: Following the Beloved down that dim hallway, *you*, in your Questioner's detachment, would have kept your wits about you, and would have observed, on the fourth finger of the Beloved's left hand, the diamond whose mean-spirited glint was hidden by the wonder veiling Clio's mind. Well: she is only a character, much of her own story is lost on her.

In that Ladies' designed for blissful immersion in one's own reflection, the professor stripped bare, the Beloved rinses her trousers under a golden faucet. She twists and wrings out the trousers, then carries them to a dryer on the wall, tapping its round silver button, dangling Clio's black legs in the sirocco, so they weave happily, gusting into the Beloved's own body, then fainting away.

"Really, you don't have to do this. You should be out with the others."

"*I* spilled the wine all over you."

This washerwomanly penance is cute, they both think.

"Why did you say, before, 'sad'?" Clio asks.

"Maybe everyone is, when a dinner party lags on and on. If we had a reason to leave, we'd leave. If we don't have a reason, that's sad. You don't seem to have a reason. Or"—she catches herself—"is it rude to say that?"

When she turns the professor makes a fig leaf of her hands. "It's honest."

"And I was surprised, you know? One always thinks of famous people as having everything figured out. Here. You can try these now."

Q: *Susan Stewart writes: "The face becomes a text, a space which must be 'read' and interpreted in order to exist. The body of a woman, particularly constituted by a mirror and thus particularly subject to an existence constrained by the nexus of external images, is spoken by her face, by the articulation of another's reading. Apprehending the face's image becomes a mode of possession. . . . The face is what belongs to the other. It is unavailable to the woman herself."*

A: What was the question?

Q: *What do you make of that?*

A: Clio, done hiking her trousers up, finds the Beloved in a lazy stretch, the real and mirrored Beloved's arms lifted, fingers interlaced, palms ceilingward, fox-red tufts of underarm hair bristling, little black dress hiked midthigh high: flirtatiousness or ravishing unselfconsciousness, and for Clio, no knowing which. So deep is her confusion that she cracks her knuckles and then remembers how she had hated it when her *mother* did that. Several small wildfires of desire are adroitly stamped out, Mother's is so derisive a shade, and Clio was never out to her. It is the perfect antidote to desire, skinny Mother materializing, upright backbone and the witty incision of her neat, ungiving Methodist smile. Just *try* thinking back through this woman.

It's then that two blazing wings of sensation touch down on Clio's nape, and the Beloved's palms begin to move in soft circles, massaging, worrying at the tension they find, digging in, the Beloved's thumbs closing in on the axial vertebra, so that Clio feels the three-dimensional puzzle-piece of bone click as if newly wedged in place, her entire skull balanced most vulnerably upon the knife's point of sexual alertness, Clio afraid to move or make a sound for fear of dislodging the hands, startling them into flight, so appalling would their loss be. She is aware that savage loss is the counterpart and shadow of this raw arousal and yearning, which she can scarcely trust even as she leans into it, wondering what this means, this sensual charity, and unable to ask, such is the din of sensation, so wholly grateful is she for the cleverness of the Beloved's hands.

"Shiatsu."

"Shiatsu," echoes Clio.

"Mmm. Good for what ails you."

The Beloved's reflection squints at the real-world Clio over her shoulder, to which she administers a comradely slap. Dismissed.

What ails me? Clio wonders. *Loss. Aging. Remorse.* You *are good for that.*

So this is the dark side of Eros. Always before it was Clio who inflicted the first reality check. The pangs foreshadowing abandonment, the subtly poisonous forewarning: Clio dealt those out.

Now we come, though it doesn't look like it, to our epiphany, for

Clio, academe's androgynous roué, contriver of seductions, far-flung affairs, and prolonged breakdowns—here and now, Clio encounters a possibility never before entertained: she's been unkind. Careless with others' hearts. A waster of time and a despoiler of affection. As of this moment, that Prof. Mitsak is dead. Just ask Clio, absorbed in this mirror's vision, herself and her one true love, the radiant-haired object of all future dreams, now rubbing a finger across a front tooth. Clio puts her hands on those shoulders and turns the slender black-sheathed body around. She thinks *heart-stopping* of the weird seizure, like an appalling inward death, of her own breath in her throat, and then all self-narration, even the faint stabs at description that accompany the worst emergencies, stops. Though the red mouth tilts toward her, lips parting, the eyes remain open. Dazzling, desirous, repelled, unreadable.

Q: *Compare/contrast the roles of "body" and "soul" in the act of kissing.*

A: This eyes-open kiss is clumsy: neither body nor soul can readily forgive that. Seduction, it turns out, requires an almost Questioner-like detachment to insure grace. To become a character in the story is to fall from grace. It's as if Clio, in her previous affairs, was always narrator, never simply down in the story, at the mucky, hapless level where she knew only as much as anyone else. Or less. It could be the Beloved needs a narrator, not simply a floundering fellow character. Her teeth grate against the Beloved's, a terrible, nails-on-blackboard sound from which they both recoil.

Q: *Comment briefly on the following quotation.*

> Perhaps it was to that hour of anguish that there must be attributed the importance which Odette had since assumed in his life. Other people are, as a rule, so immaterial to us that, when we have entrusted to any one of them the power to cause so much suffering or happiness to ourselves, that person seems at once to belong to a different universe, is surrounded with poetry, makes of our lives a vast expanse, quick with sensation, on which that person and ourselves are ever more or less in contact.

A: Nadia is her name, Nadia Nadia Nadia Nadia Nnnnnnn—*ahhhhh*—deeeeee—uh.

All that drear winter of La Niña, it feels to Clio as if she's trying to keep a wine cork submerged in a bathtub using only one thumb, so dodgy and haywire is this love. Tamped-down love offers not sublimated energy but an exhausting impatience: before long, she's sick of obsession's two-lane Nebraska highway. She welcomes any distraction, even this folder, plunked down on her desk by a junior colleague, untenured, younger even than the Beloved. Fading back toward the doorway, this colleague announces in an injured tone: "We really need to know what you think." *We*, the women. Not that the junior women will be voting on this appointment, but they will have the chance to voice their opinions. Renee, though standing—on the far side of Clio's desk—crosses her legs, a habit of hers. When sitting down she hangs one leg over the other, hooks a toe behind a calf, and strains for ease, a gauche, brain-driven woman whose particular mix of ethnicity baffles Clio. African American? Vietnamese? And Czech? Irish? Dutch? Some unprecedented cat's cradle of deoxyribonucleic acid granted her that shapely mouth, pugilist's menacing nose with flaring nostrils, oily fawn skin marred across the cheekbones by an orange-peel stippling of adolescent acne. That acne, severe and untreated, suggests a raisin-in-the-sun, down-home poverty, valiantly tackled and, at this point in her young career, deeply repudiated. If Renee ever had an accent, it's gone. Not quite gone: some suggestion of backwater lulls and day-dreamy delta vowels remains, despite the reign of that impressive will. To suggest a chic she's far from possessing, Renee's left ear is multiply pierced and, adorned with wires and rings, seems more alert than the other, more attuned to signals and nuances. It is to this ear that Clio says, "Calm down. I'll read it. Just calm yourself, Renee."

"You don't seem to get it. You were our only chance."

In this chilly pause, Clio, love's insomniac, fails to suppress a yawn. Renee, fervent with insult, closes in, hurling herself into Clio's office's only unoccupied seat, a meanly proportioned straight-backed chair designed to discommode students who would otherwise linger in Clio's aura of disdainful indifference. Throwing one leg over the other, leaning in, slapping the folder, Renee begins, "We expected so—"

Clio says, "'So'?"

What the hell is the expression stamped on the fine, ethnically inscrutable features. "So much of you, when you came. That you would, not *mother* exactly, at least *care* about our careers. *Open doors* for us. Use your influence with the men, whose basic wish, it can't be lost on you, is that we'd all just go away. What kind of life is this? Helena's bulimia's *a lot worse*, Trish chain-smokes unfiltered Camels, Ellie must be running ten miles a day, Nadia—Nadia's a weird shadow of her former self."

"A shadow?"

"Me, I fantasize obsessively about burning down this building."

"But Nadia? You were about to say why she's a shadow?"

"Even to confess this fantasy probably gets me on about five different lists right now."

"I haven't noticed anything wrong with Nadia."

"Well: you seem to be avoiding her."

"No. No no. Not avoiding her. Why would I avoid Nadia? No."

"Avoiding all of us then."

"You seem to have found me."

"Right at home in this building I burn down, in my dreams, ten or eleven times a day."

"If you burn it down what will you do?"

"Ha! Even in daydreams I blow out the match. Even in my head, where you'd think I'd have no fear, I can't touch the flame to the shitty carpet. This place! Can't you get a little more involved? Without some input soon, things around here are gonna go in a truly ugly direction. Word here in River City has it that sentiment's running against Nadia's tenure. Why, you wonder? Why? Would you like the figures on just how many junior female faculty this place has ever tenured? Because I'd like to give you that figure. I like that figure for its impressiveness. It's a very round number. Big fat succinct zero. And against that zero is pitted the one person who can conceivably intervene without risking her entire future, except that person, you, refuses to be pitted."

"I will," Clio says.

"You will?"

Down the hallway, a door opens, closes, and is locked, the homeward-bound deconstructionist whistling merrily, the melody trailing down the floor before vanishing into the elevator, not without lodging itself in Clio's mind. *Miss my clean white linen, and my fancy French perfume.*

"I will start paying attention," Clio says distractedly. "I will pit myself."

"Because I fear the consequences for Nadia if that zero's allowed to rule. Look, did I—?"

"Did you?"

"Offend you."

"There's truth in what you said." Gently, but sick of gentleness, disliking the baiting way this woman hangs her sentences in the air.

"Sorry." A pause while this antagonist wonders how far she can push her luck. "But we *really need you*, is the thing."

"Don't be."

"I would open a florist shop," Renee says. "After I burned this building down. If you must know."

"You know what I think of?" Clio says—not, in the moment, even faintly surprised, though in lucid retrospection she will marvel at this question, at having done, next, something so unlike herself, telling a truth, and why, when no good comes of such slips? "A bookstore on a downtown corner in some small town. Rare books, first editions."

"But you're famous. You're fine. You're not at their mercy." *You have everything I want.*

"There are days, lately, when I don't love books."

"You're losing your soul."

Clio reflects on the justness of this observation, and is struck to find herself agreeing. "People open bookstores because they want their souls back."

"Yes they do. I know bookstores where people have *gotten* them back."

They laugh, and then don't know what to do.

"Why did you come in now? About my pitting myself? Why never before?"

"Nadia. She just seems a little *off*. Girl's spending all her time scheming ways to persuade men who don't even know she exists that they owe her a *yes*. The vote's next week."

"Right. Of course." Clio had known, but forgotten, that this was looming, perhaps because, in the cool scholarly part of her soul, and inadmissable though it is, she doesn't much like Nadia's work. Trusting this secret assessment, with the rest of her soul so compromised, would be unwise, she knows, and she's intended, all along, to vote yes, venturing arguments that will make it hard for her male colleagues to vote no. Clio's meant, in short, to do the right thing, or at least the least *wrong* thing. Whichever way it goes, this meeting can cause pain: the pain of Nadia's being granted tenure and remaining near but unpossessable, the pain of Nadia's being refused tenure, thus vanishing forever from Clio's life. If not even a starry glimpse of the object of fear and desire is possible, what will become of that life?

And yet, freed on this, the first afternoon in our story that can safely be called *spring*, lugging her laden briefcase, Clio surrenders to bliss hidden within each Friday, taking the stairs in long-legged, traipsing descent, her voice pitching *up!* and *up!* precariously, caroming off cinder block as if the stairwell were a gigantic cement shower stall, quick with resonance, echoing and amplifying:

"Oh I

"Could drink

"A case

"Of you!"

You! flung into the rainy outer world as Joni Mitchell, trailing rags of her ethereal voice, charges across the asphalt only to find, wading in a slow circle around a rusted-out, tail-finned wreck of a car in the flooding parking lot, Nadia, head bent under the assault of the rain, carrying a sodden shoe box, now and then pausing to hammer with her fist at the car's Bondo-dappled hood. Clio suffers a curious twist of emotion she can't at first recognize, which then comes dismayingly clear. Before, encountering Nadia unexpectedly, she's experienced a number of emotions—shame of a particularly rich, basking intensity, or a pitiless, wired kind of happiness—but never before has any response to Nadia been as mild and lucid as this: disappointment. Dismaying, because while shame and happiness can be explained, in regard to Nadia, what can disappointment mean? An emotion so small and—ordinary.

"This is all I can *fuck. Ing.* Take." *Fuck* and *ing* are blows.

It's been two months since they have exchanged more than cautious *hi*'s, passing in the hall. "Keep hitting like that, you'll hurt your hand."

"I locked myself out. Do you *fuck ing* believe it?"

"Come get in my car. You can use my cell."

"This had to happen in front of you." Nadia begins to cry. "When all I want—"

"When all you want?" More baiting sentences? Did the junior women catch this from each other?

"Is to be like you, you know. So to*gether*. So far above the shit and disarray."

Nadia wanted not to *have* but to *be* Clio, it seems. *Not at their mercy.* Not at anyone's: a girl's dream. "I lose keys," she says, and tries to catch Nadia's wrist before she can bang on the old car again, but too late: a ruckus of reverberating metal, and the rain drumming steadily on the Chevy's roof and hood, Clio sheltering Nadia's head, now, under an impromptu roof of briefcase.

"Get in my car and we'll figure out what you should do."

"I can't get in your car, I'm soaking."

"You're shivering. Come on."

In Clio's BMW, with its kid-glove leather and customized quiet, German meticulousness exerts its power to heal the psyche, and Nadia grows calmer. Ducking into the passenger side after Clio unlocked its door, she'd absently relinquished the old shoe box with bulging sides, wound around with duct tape and curiously heavy. Covertly, Clio tries shaking the box.

"Hey!" Nadia cries, and snatches the box away, giving Clio a wild look—accusation and darkening sorrow are in the look, leading her to confess, "This box has my heart in it."

"Your *heart*?"

Nadia leans forward in her seat and rests her forehead against the lid of the box, communing with whatever's inside. After a moment she says clearly, "My little cat." Droplets chase down the spiraling madrone twigs of wet red hair to patter onto the box's cardboard, where they appear as fuzzy, swiftly dilating dots. Her face hidden, she says, "Who loved me for *me*."

There is nothing to say to this, and nothing to dry either of them with, Clio the bad, the negligent mother in the quasidomesticity of the car's interior. Wanting to help but unable to think of anything, Clio sets the wipers going. Fans of visibility flash open and swipe shut, melodically. Around them, the drenched and shining asphalt reveals streaks of rare brilliance, as if light is drilling down into a medium infinitely soft and black, and the other cars stranded here and there across the lot possess the sharp-edged perfection of abandoned houses—of houses where you can see in one window and all the way through, out another window. Clio turns on heat, not just because Nadia's still shivering; suddenly it seems important that they not be fogged in by breath, and she's worried about the strangeness of Nadia's behavior. "The cat is," Clio says delicately, "*in* the box?"

"Dead," Nadia says to the box.

"Nadia, I'm sorry."

"Fuck, what a word," Nadia says. "*Dead.* Onomatopoetic."

"I'm so sorry."

At last, to Clio's relief, Nadia sits up. "I knew something was wrong all night and I took her in first thing this morning. To the vet, I mean. It was an okay experience, really. They give her this shot and she goes all soft in my hands. This little velvet sack from which all fear just, *sssst*, leaks away. I'm holding her, I'm stroking her, they give her the other shot then. The death shot."

Q: *In the light of your answers to the previous questions, formulate a definition of "beauty."*

A: "I'm sorry," Clio says again, meaning to convey an anxious, electric empathy, though she can't help it: such grief seems faintly ridiculous to her, and even diminishes the younger woman. Is there a fugitive whiff—carnal, catlike?—of decay in the car? She hadn't known Nadia had a cat, but in her experience cats, belonging to lovers or exes or lovers' exes' exes, come with relationships—never before sealed in a box, though. Clio wants to apply the balm of her cool hand to Nadia's forehead, to the temple, where the growth of new hair forms a minute clockwise whorl, like the illustration of the birth of a star, the tiny hairs strung with impossibly fine condensation. For no reason a phrase of Woolf's comes to Clio: "'Reality' . . . beside which nothing matters." Reality for Clio seems born of that fine, nearly invisible star on the Beloved's temple, and if she wants more than anything to touch it, for the sake of what the other must be feeling, she resists.

Q: *"At the center of each person," D. W. Winnicott writes, "is an incommunicado element and this is sacred and most worthy of preservation." Can this belief be reconciled with erotic love, and if so, how?*

A: She resists. "Where can I take you?" she asks, hating to interrupt this silence, the easiest intimacy they are ever likely to achieve.

Provoked by sympathy, her instinct to redeem herself warring with the haywire wretchedness of grief, Nadia begins to cry again. "Hey, hey come on, it's all right, it really is," Clio says. "I can take you wherever you need to go."

Still Nadia weeps into her hands, not with her hands clasped to her face but rubbing and swiping at it compulsively, as if her hands wanted to *work* on grief, to knead and knuckle it out. This at least—the loss or death of cats being a staple of lesbian discourse—*is* familiar.

"The trouble is I don't know where to go. Or what to do with her." Nadia's voice has a rasp in it, deprivation meeting and marrying remorse, the tone of the truly, bitterly disconsolate. The dead cat smell is stronger now. Nadia says, "I live in this *box*, this apartment, seventh floor, I don't own any of the ground. There's no place to put her." She clears her throat. "I thought of stealthily burying her on campus, maybe in one of those old eucalyptus groves. That's why I brought her. I was actually walking around with her under my arm, looking. But I thought, what if the campus police find me burying this little box of cat? Won't it be ludicrous, won't it get me in trouble, won't they just anyway stop me? Plus what can I dig with? It's not like I own a shovel. What a fucked-up *life*. I hate my *life*. I can't even call someone and say, 'My cat died,' because everyone I know would feel some kind of irony about the situation, like they would never be caught driving around with their cat in a box, like it could never happen to them. Even Billy. He wouldn't mean to, but he'd convey his—I'm sorry, I'm ruining your beautiful leather."

Billy, Clio remembers, is the boyfriend, who teaches at Columbia, and seems to be mostly a phone presence in Nadia's existence, but as such, sufficient to prevent other entanglements. For example, with Clio.

"He would convey his what?" She can't help this little viper of voyeurism, uncoiling.

"He never liked the cat. So—his re*lief*."

"Oh, no."

"He's going to try not to show it but he's going to be *glad*."

"Surely not, Nadia."

"He's going to think, ah, now we can live together, no impediments."

"The cat can't have been much of an impediment."

"He can be *fussy*. The cat, for some reason, liked peeing in his shoes."

"Listen, I think we should go to my place. I have a backyard. Maybe you'd like to bury your cat there. It's a nice backyard. Shady in summer, when the trees leaf out." Clio promises "plum trees" even as she wonders whether the silken gentleness she's always managed to spin from the straw of her soul for Nadia would vanish at the first scent of cat piss arising from a Manolo Blahnik. Well: not a problem for this lifetime.

"You'd want my cat in your backyard? Why?"

"You need to get her into the ground, right? I don't mind if you use a little of my backyard. I think it's a good use for it."

"How can we bury her in rain like this?"

"Under umbrellas?"

Umbrellas are what they use, taking turns digging and sheltering, Clio glad to break in her Smith & Hawken spade, the soil yielding pebbles of asphalt and shards of glass but mostly giving way easily enough, not difficult to dig a fair-sized hole in, though the bottom has begun to seep before Nadia lowers the sodden box, and because Nadia begins to cry again, it's Clio who shucks the first spadeful onto the darkening coffin, petals falling in a sudden gust and sticking to the cardboard, Nadia crying harder, Clio's lower back beginning to ache and her own eyes to brim. Why is she crying? Suddenly the sadness is a volatile force, impersonal but owning Clio completely, a howl lodged, just barely contained, in her throat. In the virgin spade, the muck glistens like cake.

When Clio is done tamping the earth over the grave, she asks Nadia if she'd like to come in, and Nadia assents. Barefoot, she prowls past the floor-to-ceiling bookshelves with scarcely a sideways glance. Clio can't help registering her failure to read titles or pull out a single one of the Woolf firsts with their fragile, charming Vanessa Bell jackets.

In the kitchen Nadia pauses at the refrigerator door. "Wow. All these Chinese babies."

"My godchildren." Each morning, with her first cup of coffee, she stands before the collage of fat-cheeked faces, snowsuits and tutus, trying to make sure she's not forgetting another birthday.

"All girls?"

"In China girls get abandoned, so the parents can try for a boy."

"Do you like kids?"

"Only those."

"I can't imagine what it would feel like, abandoning your baby." She imagines: "Like ripping your heart out with your bare hands." She taps several pictures. "These are cute, these tiny violins."

"Suzuki method."

"I want kids."

"Why don't you get out the wine? But let me pour."

"Ha."

Bringing two wineglasses filled to the brim, she sets one by Clio and sits in the nearer of two cubes of chrome and black leather.

Clio says, "I'll make a fire. Get you warmed up." She busies herself with crumpling newspaper and arranging kindling into a tipsy pyramid—for some reason thinking, as the lit match wavers, of Renee—she's in luck, the fire catches nicely, and Nadia comes to sit cross-legged beside her, the bath towel now slung over her shoulders boxer style. She rubs the back of a freckled hand across her cheekbone, leaving a streak of wet grittiness. Clio looks away so she won't be tempted to take the towel's corner and erase that streak. She doesn't want to ask if she can, but simply for things to unfold, or not, as Nadia wishes. Nadia hugs her shins, fire gazing, and says, "I was crazy. You saved me."

"I want something for you."

"Something *for* me? What?"

"You might not understand this, or think it has anything to do with me—and probably it doesn't—but what I want is your happiness. However you want to go about obtaining it. Whatever shape it takes in your imagination. The funny thing is I can want this without knowing anything about it. How you'd even define happiness. Whether you even think it exists."

"What about your happiness?" Nadia says. "Say something happened. Would you be all right if it happened only once?" So, when it comes down to it, she's someone who likes to know what she's getting into. Clio had believed, wrongly, she would prefer not-knowing, risk, improvisation. Perhaps her hair improvises so ardently she feels she must insist on control, elsewhere.

"I don't know." She rues her honesty. "Yes."

"You would? Even if we can't see each other after this?"

"Yes."

"Because this can't turn into a *thing*." Nadia sticks to interrogation: unwillingly, Clio realizes she might be good at it. "I don't want you to get hurt, do you see that?"

"I'm fine."

"Because I'm straight."

"You know I love you," Clio says, "that I loved you the moment I saw you," and then she says, "and you know that's true," and hugs her own shins, the two of them fire-gazing in parallel universes, waiting for what will come next.

Q: *Tell me.*

A: The Beloved's nipples are terra-cotta, her vagina is coral, her hair, floating as it dries, a torrent freed from gravity, roams the air around her face with an unruly will of its own, her high forehead serene in spite of this changeling hair, her little breasts swinging and bumping her whippet rib cage, the mole on her neck vivid, her kneecaps flushed bright pink by the fire's heat as she crouches above the professor, and if Clio wants to think this night the most beautiful she will ever live through, who can disagree? All conspires to insure the Beloved's tenure: Why would Clio dissent? Let us say that the *yes* she scrawls on a slip of paper, one of several dozen slips collected by the chair, was inevitable. Let's agree that no love should be judged by its duration, and that what Clio learns this isolated night is of rare worth in what Keats calls the school for souls. In Eros 101. But there is another vantage point, the future, which finds Clio dreaming she's lost something and can't find it no matter how she searches. She wakes to find she's bitten her lip until it bleeds. Amoebas of blood stain the pillow slip, and when, later that day, Clio discovers the wedding invitation lurking in her departmental mailbox, she bangs her forehead against the wall of her office in sorrow urgent as autism. Nadia's bridegroom is handsome in his tux—maybe there is, in fact, a slight fussiness in the meticulous shine of his shoes and the primly satisfied set of his mouth; of the two of them, bride and groom, his is the more conventional prettiness. After a boomingly musical interval all heads turn to follow the (newly tenured) bride's progress down the aisle, getting farther and farther away, and the only thing Clio wants to do, there in her pew, is scratch at her own arms, smear ashes across her face, maul and mark her body forever, but a hand clasps hers. This clasp conveys restraint, tolerance, calm. It's Renee's hand, for not long after Clio sat down, Renee slid into the pew beside her, craning her neck to take in the fanciness of the flowers at the altar, concluding, "Swanky." Then, in a whisper: "Mimosa. Interesting choice."

The two trees in Clio's yard prove to be not plum but cherry, merely ravishing. Even the inexhaustible Woolf, in the following days and weeks, holds no interest for the professor. Much, much later it will occur to Clio that though the box seemed to her to possess sufficient weight, and in handling the box she'd seemed to sense inside it something both lolling and stiff, she'd never actually seen the cat. In fact, the lid had been taped down, the box had been defensively wound around and around again with duct tape. Does it matter that she might have been cheated into *yes*? If it wasn't the cat in the box, what can it have been? Something with the density of the once-alive, with a certain compactness, the weight of dark muscle—say, Clio's heart. It might as well have been her heart, she parted with it so completely that night, and it's so long—so bitterly long before she will see *that* again.

Q: *Does she ever see it again?*

A: Sweet Questioner, you care. Clio doesn't really see it again until two years later when, rolling over in bed, lifting herself on an elbow to gaze down her pugilist's nose at Clio, Renee reels off the ingredients of her fawn skin, handsome mouth, and eerie green eyes. Black, Lakota Sioux, Welsh, a little Norwegian. One mystery solved, at least. And look, beyond the ken of this exam they never run out of things to say to each other, though one spends her days leafing through old books, the other up to her elbows in sweet peas and tuberose, cattleya and quince.

Q: *Read the following quotation from Simone Weil's* On Human Personality.

> If a child is doing a sum and does it wrong, this mistake bears the stamp of his personality. If he does the sum exactly right, his personality does not enter into it at all.

Argue that this does, or does not, have implications for love.

The Way the Sky Changed

AMANDA EYRE WARD

I HAD HEARD ABOUT THE RIB, of course, but I did not expect it to be at the Smiths' Christmas party. Yet there it was, on the mantel, sandwiched between a bowl of cinnamon-scented potpourri and a holly sprig. Merry Christmas! Here's our daughter's rib.

There were pictures of her all over the house. Maybe they had always been there, I don't know. But the one of Kat with me, before our senior prom—it was too much. I stood in the kitchen and drank Scotch fast. My husband would have told me to take it easy, pardner, but he was gone too, and not even a rib to show for himself. My mother came into the kitchen and took in the scene: me, a ham sandwich, an empty glass.

"How are you?" she said. She raised her eyebrows.

"The ham is delicious," I noted.

"From Harrington's in Greenwich," she said.

"Really?" I said.

"Same as last year," said my mother. I nodded. "Same as the year before that," she said.

"Is that right?" I said.

"Yes," said my mother.

In the dining room, I found Callie. She was pregnant and miserable. She wore a Burberry headband and her roots were showing. "I've never been sober at one of these before," she said. "It's hell."

I laughed. "You might have a husband, but at least I can drink," I said. Callie turned those brown eyes on me.

"Why do you go and say things like that?" she said. I shrugged. "Did you call the therapist?" she said.

"Yes," I said, "I made an appointment for next Thursday."

"Really?" said Callie.

"Yes, really," I said. "What am I, a four-year-old?"

"I'm glad," said Callie, touching my arm. "Laureen has really helped me. Laureen and the Zoloft."

"I wonder why a rib," I mused.

Callie sighed. "What?"

"It's just so . . . random. Why a rib? Why not a collarbone?"

Callie looked at her shoes. Her feet were puffed out of them like pastry.

"How are you feeling?" I asked.

"What?"

"I mean with the baby and all. Do you feel tired, still?"

"Yes," said Callie.

"Me too," I said. "But I'm not pregnant," I said.

"No," said Callie. "You're not."

We had thought about it, Paul and I. There had always been a reason to wait. Money, the right timing, Paul's bonus, my big new writer. Fucking Hal Underson, whose novel finally went to a crappy little press in St. Louis. I had had high hopes for Hal, a movie deal. My 15 percent of Hal was about three hundred dollars. So we'd waited.

"No," I said to Callie, "I'm not."

Callie's husband, George, came up behind her, holding out a mini quiche. "Yummy," he said, pushing the morsel toward Callie's mouth.

"Get it away from me," said Callie.

"Suit yourself," said George.

"Suit yourself?" I said. "Are we really old enough to say 'suit yourself'?" I laughed, but then realized that both George and Callie were sober.

"Lucy," said George, licking his fingertips, "there's a guy I'd like you to meet. He's in arbitrage, nice guy."

"George!" said Callie. "She's not ready to date yet." She looked at me, shaking her head in apology.

"Sure I am," I said. "What's this guy's name?"

"Lewis."

"Oh," I said. "Lewis? Are you sure?"

"He is nice," admitted Callie.

"Nice dull?" I said.

"No, nice like he's not an asshole."

"Is he my type?" I said.

Callie and George looked uncomfortable. "I have a type," I said. "And it's tall and blond. Ponytailed, actually."

George cleared his throat. "But Paul is . . . I mean, Paul was . . ."

"Just because I married a short Jew doesn't mean I can't have a type," I said. I laughed, but it came out strangled. "I'm not crying," I explained, "I'm just tired."

"I'll give him your number," said George. "Lewis."

"Well, I'm off to the bar," I said. I left Callie and George feeling sorry for me and worried about me. They had enough to worry about, and I wished they'd just ignore me, just treat me like a rib in the corner of the room.

My mother drove me home from the party. She asked me if I'd like to stay over at home. "I have a home," I said.

"I meant my home," she said.

"Spend the night in my old room, like I'm fifteen?" I said. "No spank you."

"You should really watch it with the booze," said my mother.

"Like father like daughter," I said.

"You know something," said my mother as she dropped me off.

"No," I said, "I don't know anything."

"Well, I'll tell you," said my mother. "You were difficult until the day Paul found you, and then you sweetened for a while. I thought you had changed. But it was just Paul, all along."

I closed my eyes, and things seemed spinny. I forced them open and my mother was watching me. "It's been over a year," she said, "and now it's up to you to save yourself."

I nodded. "I hear you," I said, and then I threw up.

I had nightmares about Paul's bones coming to find me. I didn't want them, though I had brought his green plastic hairbrush to the police station in a fit of sentimentality. The word around town was that once they matched the DNA, the police would knock on your door with the news. In my town, that fall, we waited.

I guess I hadn't really believed that Kat was gone until the rib arrived. Kat, who had walked hand-in-hand with me to kindergarten, her brown hair swinging, who had taught me to kiss, pressing her own dry lips to mine. Kat!

Lewis the nerd called the next week. My assistant, Cindy, came into my office. "Lewis Freed on Line Two," said Cindy.

"Take a message," I said.

She shrugged pertly. Cindy. This gal was all about pert. She came back not a minute later. "He says he's made reservations at Caroline's Comedy Club for Thursday," said Cindy.

"Yuck," I said.

"It's fun," said Cindy.

"You've been to Caroline's Comedy Club?"

"This guy I dated? Frank Drury? He was big into comedy. It's fun, really."

"Give me that number," I said. I called Lewis in arbitrage. I'll be honest: I don't know what arbitrage is. I've lived in New York my whole life, but my father was a lawyer and so was Paul. Arbitrage just never factored in. Lewis answered the phone. I explained that I would not be able to go to Caroline's Comedy Club. "George told me you'd be difficult," said Lewis.

"Excuse me?"

"Lucy, I've already bought the tickets. It's just a comedy club. I'll pick you up after work?"

"Oh, okay," I said.

But first there was Laureen, the therapist. She told me to let go of regrets. I told her my mother said I had never been a very nice person. She told me to let go of fear. I told her about the comedy club, and she thought that was a good idea.

Caroline's Comedy Club was crowded and smoky. Lewis held my arm as we wound our way to our seats. One table leg must have been shorter than the rest; the table kept tipping all around. I was tired before our drinks arrived. "So what did your husband do?" asked Lewis. I thought this was a funny way to begin a date.

"Lawyer," I said.

"My wife sold software," said Lewis.

"Your wife?" I said.

"Kendall," said Lewis. "She was on Flight 11."

"I didn't know," I said. What did I want with some widower, I thought. "Jesus, I'm sorry," I said. The waitress returned with our order. She was a bit sour, but I guess you don't have to be funny to serve the drinks.

"Where was he?" asked Lewis. "Your husband?"

"The North Tower," I said.

His eyes were dull. "Kendall was in business class," he said. I nodded. "Did he . . . did you talk to him?" asked Lewis.

"No," I said. He nodded, and drank his martini quickly. We ordered another round.

The first comedian had bad skin. He told a bunch of jokes about his mother, and then a bunch of jokes about how dumb Cajuns are. I had never met a Cajun, so these jokes were wasted on me. It seemed that Cajuns fished a lot. We sipped our drinks sadly, and after the first comedian had finished, I told Lewis I was simply exhausted, and I went outside and hailed a cab.

Paul and I used to watch the news after work and drink wine. There was a plane crash in Kansas one night. "If you were in a plane going down," I said, "I would not want you to call me. I'd rather remember all the good times. Not one last crappy phone call, you know?"

"I don't know," said Paul. "I might want you to call me."

"Well, don't call me," I said. "I'm not interested."

I think about Paul, trapped in the searing building. I tried to call his cell phone in the end, but there was no answer. I know that he wanted to call me, to say goodbye. I know he didn't jump. Well, I don't officially know, but that's what I think. Maybe he fainted. Maybe it wasn't as bad as I am pretty sure it was. I wish he had called me. I wish I could say to him, I'm sorry. I wish he had taken a sick day, or crashed his car. But his car was parked at the station when I finally got home from the city. There was his coffee mug. There was the napkin from his English muffin, marked with a butter stain.

Lewis called me at work in the morning. "I thought the comedy club would be a good idea," he said, "but I guess maybe it wasn't."

"It was fine," I said.

"I'd like to see you again," said Lewis. This surprised me.

"How about cheeseburgers?" I said.

"How *about* cheeseburgers," said Lewis.

He took the train out, and we went to the Rye Grille and Bar. "I've never been to Rye," said Lewis. "Scarsdale, yes, but never Rye."

"It's a nice place," I said. When Jan came to take our order, she looked surprised to see me with a date, then angry, then sad.

"What do you recommend?" Lewis asked Jan.

"Oh, get a cheeseburger," I said. Paul and I always ordered cheeseburgers.

"The tuna steak sandwich is good," said Jan. She looked Lewis up and down. He was cute in a preppy way: the tousled hair, ruddy skin. If you watched him, you could see how he'd looked at five, chasing after frogs or whatever.

"The cheeseburgers are really the best," I insisted.

"I think I'll try that tuna steak sandwich," said Lewis. He looked up at me with a smile, but must have seen something in my face. He blinked, and I looked down at my menu. "Wait," said Lewis, reaching out and touching his fingers to Jan's arm, "I've changed my mind."

She wheeled around and raised an eyebrow.

"I'll have a cheeseburger, after all," said Lewis.

"You might even want to try the fried onions on top," I said.

"Oh," said Lewis, "okay."

The following Saturday, Lewis asked me to go antiquing with him in Connecticut. "There's a great diner in Roxbury," he said, "and then we can go for a hike along this river." I preferred to spend my Saturdays gardening, but I went along. Lewis brought a pair of ladies' hiking boots. They fit me perfectly, and this seemed to make Lewis very happy. I wore my own socks, however. We drove up to Connecticut in Lewis's Volvo wagon. He played tapes of Nina Simone and held my hand when he was not shifting the gears. "I packed a picnic lunch," he confided. "Pâté and grapes and even that pinot noir."

"What pinot noir?" I said.

He looked flustered. "Oh, you'll like it," he said. He squeezed my hand.

The scenery grew beautiful. Barns and cows and men selling peaches. Lewis pulled into the parking lot of an antique store called Mason's. He opened my door and took my hand. "Come on," he said, "I have a surprise for you."

I followed Lewis into Mason's. It was a drafty old store filled with dusty crap. Lots of nautical-themed stuff, and a bunch of that Fiesta-ware. Lewis hustled toward the back, and I pretended to be interested in some old cough medicine bottles. There was music in the store: Billie Holiday. I liked that.

It wasn't long before Lewis came back. "It's all arranged," he said, his eyes shining. He took my hand, and led me to a back room. Once there, he gestured to a huge mirror. It was surrounded by an ornate frame. It was unwieldy and ugly.

"Sweetheart," said Lewis, "it's yours."

"The mirror?" I said.

He nodded, tears in his green eyes.

"Oh Lewis," I said, "it's just what I've always wanted."

"I know," said Lewis. He took me in his arms, and whispered, "Sweetheart, I know." After this exchange, we went to a grassy spot and ate the pâté and drank the pinot noir. Lewis did not kiss me.

My mother came over the next day. "What on earth is that?" she said, pointing to the mirror, which was propped up in my front hallway.

"A mirror," I said. "Lewis gave it to me."

"My God," she said. "It's hideous."

"Well, okay," I said.

"What are you making?"

"Beef Stroganoff."

"Oh sweetie," said my mother. I stirred the pot, and added salt.

"Would you like some pinot noir?" I asked my mother.

"Pinot noir?" said my mother. "I only drink pinot grigio and you know it."

"People can change," I said.

"Did you hear about the femur?" said my mother.

"Oh God," I said. I closed my eyes. "You know what," I said, "I don't want to hear about any femur."

"This isn't any femur, Lucy," said my mother. "It's Doug Greenman's femur."

"Jesus Christ," I said. I had once given Doug a blow job in the back of his father's Porsche.

My mother shook her head. "Tragic," she said, "just tragic. But they're burying theirs, not putting it on the mantel."

I kept stirring. "That smell," said my mother. "That smell makes me think of your father."

"Really?"

"He used to love beef Stroganoff. Don't you remember when I'd make it for him? Just as he came home from work I'd have it ready. He'd call from the station and say, 'Is dinner ready?' and I'd say, 'Yes, dear,' and I'd pack you and your brother in the Oldsmobile and we'd go get your daddy. I'd put you to bed while he had his cocktails and watched the news, and then we'd eat together." The light coming in my kitchen window made my mother's face glow. "That was a good time," she said.

"I used to make it for Paul," I said. "I never knew why."

She smiled at me sadly. "This is just a bad time, honey," she said. "But then it will be a good time again."

"What if it's just going to get worse?" I said.

She looked down at her tiny Gucci pumps. She opened her hands and then pulled them into fists.

That night, after eating three helpings of my beef Stroganoff, Lewis asked if he could sleep over, and I said yes. I gave him a pair of Paul's pajamas, and of course Paul's toiletries were all still lined up in the cabinet. Lewis was bigger than Paul, so he just wore the pajama shirt and his boxers. He smelled all wrong with the right toothpaste.

Laureen was not pleased with the news of my love interest. "What is Lewis like?" she asked me.

"He bought me a mirror," I said. She pursed her lips.

"This does not sound like a healthy step forward," said Laureen. I told her that I felt better.

"Feeling better does not always mean feeling healthier," said Laureen. I told her I would keep that in mind.

Lewis's apartment was cluttered, filled with books and papers. Kendall, it turned out, had been a software salesperson who had wanted to be a poet. I was never much for poetry, but Lewis told me which ones to read to him, and how to pronounce the words I didn't know. Lewis made elaborate ethnic meals: Indian, Greek, Ethiopian. Kendall had always made the *injera* bread, and I couldn't get the hang of it, so I found a restaurant on Amsterdam and I just picked it up on my way over. Her shoes fit me, which was a bonus: Kendall had had very good taste in shoes. I began jazzing up my outfits with her Fendi heels and Sigerson Morrison slingbacks.

I was there, at Lewis's apartment, that Saturday morning. The plan was to go out to Kendall's favorite breakfast spot, Café Con Leche, and then to go to the Hayden Planetarium, one of Lewis's childhood haunts. Lewis had once sat through three star shows in a row. He loved the way the sky changed. I was surprised he could still look up.

Kendall had not liked coffee, so I usually brought instant in my purse. I was boiling water when the buzzer rang. I pressed the intercom button. It was the NYPD, said a nice-sounding man. Oh, fuck, I thought. What I do not need is Kendall's femur hanging around.

"Lewis?" I said. "It's the NYPD."

Lewis came out of the bedroom, pulling on a pair of Paul's sweatpants. "Let them in," said Lewis.

I am not a stupid woman. I know that Paul was at work on September 11. He had kissed me, had caught the train on time. He was at his desk, because he was the sort of man who woke each morning and went where he was supposed to go. Paul was dead. Unless he drove his car to the station, took the train to the plane, and flew to Vegas.

Lewis appeared to be having trouble breathing. He bent over and put his hands on his knees, then straightened. He rolled his head to one side and then the other. "Oh, God," said Lewis, "oh fuck, fuck, fuck." His face was pale: we both knew what was coming. We had two minutes, maybe three, before the cops came to the apartment door.

"Lewis," I said, "Lewis, I have something very important to tell you."

"What?" said Lewis. "What is it?" Paul's sweatpants were too short for Lewis. Half of his shins showed, and his ankles were not elegant, as Paul's had been.

I felt sick. I took Lewis's hand. "If anything ever happens to you," I said, "I want you to call me. Please, please call me."

"I will," said Lewis, "of course I will, I promise."

"I mean it," I said, "I was wrong about Kansas."

I was crying, it seemed. Lewis pulled me to him. His heart was hammering against his ribs. I heard footsteps in the hallway, coming toward us. "I'll call you," said Lewis. His breathing was ragged. "I will. But there's something you should know."

There was a knock at the door, a sharp, professional rap. There was shuffling, a clearing of a throat.

"I'll call you, but it won't make any difference," said Lewis. "It's all the fucking same, in the end."

He let me go, abruptly, and then he unlocked the door and opened it. "Mr. Lewis Freed?" said the cop. He was an older man, with lines in his face. His eyes were sad and tired.

"Yes," said Lewis.

"May we come in?" said the cop.

Lewis looked at me. I closed my eyes. Paul, a Vegas showgirl on his lap. Kendall, writing poetry, snacking on *injera* bread. I opened my eyes, and Lewis was looking into them. We both knew it was time to find out what remained.

Han Gahp

JUNG H. YUN

THERE WAS A MUDSLIDE, two villages away. A meat calf was lost, and four horses found.

"In a field," the boy said. "All of them, see? Four wild horses, buried up to here." He pressed his finger to his nose and held it there until she looked.

"And then what?" Mee asked.

"Then twelve men came. Twelve big men, and they tried to pull the stallion free, but he just kept sinking, so one of the men shot him. Shot the rest of them too." He stared into his empty cup as if he'd forgotten something. "My parents would like you to come visit. They said we can celebrate the birthday you missed."

Mee smiled, and the boy made an effort to smile back.

"It's been a long time. Are they well?"

He shrugged. "The same, but that was some storm, wasn't it? Did you notice how the rain, how it fell sideways? Like everything was turned around?"

Mee eased herself up from the table and carried her breakfast plate to the sink. "Eighteen days of rain," she said. "I've never been inside for so long." She lifted the lid of the trash bin, then stopped, righting herself before the boy could see. "Tell your parents," she said, scraping her leftovers into a pot, "I'll come by soon."

"Today?"

"No, today I'm going to town. But tomorrow, maybe."

The boy stood up and pushed his chair neatly against the table. "I'll tell them tomorrow, then. You'll definitely come tomorrow."

He smiled again, wider this time, and she thought to call him "nephew" as he said goodbye, but he wasn't a nephew. Only a cousin of the multiplied sort, the kind with names too married and married over to remember well. She watched from the doorway as he ran down the hill, slipping twice in the swampy grass. A poor farmhand, she thought, but still a good, pleasant boy. Not like his brothers. Least like his parents, their manners so pinched and proud. She waited until he disappeared from view, leaving the village spread below with its yellow, wasted fields. Fields cut to hectares and half hectares and halves and quarters of those. All of them now drowned.

Mee picked up her walking stick and hung the worn leather loop around her wrist. She taped a note to her postbox:

WENT TO TOWN.

So no one would worry.

Firs and black pines hung limp in the heat. Sunlight pierced through their branches. Mee walked beneath the forest's ragged canopy, resting often in its shade. By noon, she reached the locked gates of the mine. Its hum had gone quiet, and she wondered when the road would be cleared so the men could return to work. Not soon, she thought. The storm had left its waste at every step. Split trees and branches, birds scorched by lightning, and suddenly butterflies, their wings pressed open by the rain. She had never seen so many. Large and small, opal and pearl, some eaten by insects and others left whole to dry. She walked over them and around them, studying their frail bodies in cracks of light.

"It's no use," a man called.

Mee looked up and saw an old man sitting against a tree. At his feet were dead rabbits.

"Just step on them," he said. "It's faster that way."

"Do you know why they're here?"

The man held out a canteen and shook it at her. "Come and rest," he said. "You'll never make it past the next hill without some water."

Mee folded her hands behind her back. The boy's visit had distracted her; she carried only a walking stick and money pinned inside her pocket. "I don't want to bother you," she said.

The man waved her forward. "You're not a bother. Come rest awhile." He cleared a place for her to sit and handed her the canteen.

The water tasted warm and metallic, but she was grateful for a drink.

"I found these," he said. He pulled three wild plums from a sack and gave her one. "The skins are too hard to eat, so you have to peel them." He dug his nails under the skin, pulling away curled slivers of pink and throwing them to the grass. "They're a little tough, but the juice is sweet." He pushed the plum whole into his mouth.

Mee took a small bite and felt the scrape of pit against her teeth. "So many butterflies. Do you know where they came from?"

"Moths," he said. "Silkworm moths." He set one of the rabbits on his knee and tied a piece of twine to its neck. "My son was trying to breed them here. Almost had enough before the storm came and ripped the roof off his hatchery." He tied the loose ends of the twine to a branch and lifted it, dangling the rabbit by its neck. "Makes them easier to carry," he said. "I found three of them on the road, still fresh."

Mee looked at the scrawny rabbit, its stomach bloated from rain. "Why is it we've never met before?" she asked.

"We only came two months ago. My son bought a piece of land, just up the road. You?"

"I live across that valley over there."

"No, I meant do you have children?"

"Oh, yes. Yes. I have a daughter. And three grandsons too."

"Three! How lucky. Do they all live at home?"

Mee took another bite of her plum. She chewed it slowly. "They all live in America."

The man's eyes widened. "Are you the one? The one with the doctor in America?"

She nodded.

He set the branch down and the rabbit's wet ear grazed her leg. "I've heard about you," he said. "A doctor! Your daughter must be very rich. She must send you lots of money."

Mee put the lid on the canteen and handed it back to the man. "You've been so kind," she said, "but I have to see the postman before he closes. He's very strict about closing on time."

"Are you expecting something? Something from your daughter, maybe?"

She stood up, her legs heavy and stiff. "It was my birthday last week. My sixtieth."

The man slapped his hand against his knee. "Your sixtieth! Your *han gahp* must have been big, the biggest ever. Could all of your relatives make it through the storm?"

"My daughter's very busy. Besides, she always sends nice gifts, and this one I'm sure will be very big." She brushed a leaf off her skirt. "I should go now. Thank you for the water."

Mee stood up and walked back to the road, stepping gently over a bright white moth. She turned and caught the man watching her, his expression curious. He waved and she continued on, less careful of where she stepped, but careful still.

Manners confused her. She no longer understood them, the way hers differed from theirs. The poorest saw no harm in prying. They considered it polite to comment on her wealth, to take interest in the details. It was the kind of talk that embarrassed her, though she couldn't deny her good fortune. She needed nothing that she could think of. Her house was grand compared to her neighbors'. The roof was shingled with clay, not tin. She had hot water that ran through copper pipes, and a stove and refrigerator brought by truck from Seoul. There was too much food in her pantry, once-worn clothes in her closet, and the storekeeper always offered her credit though he knew she didn't need it, though he refused it to everyone else. Her daughter sent one million *won* at the end of each month, always without reminder, and always more than she could spend in her village, a dot of a place with nothing to do and few good things to buy. Only a small movie theater two kilometers away and a store that sold western-style dresses and hats that she had no place to wear. The balance of each month's check she put into a tin, then two tins and three tins and now eight tins stuffed with thousand and ten-thousand notes. Thirty-two million *won* in all, nineteen years worth of time.

Mee stopped at the edge of the road and bent to her knees beside a stream. Rotting crab apples and plums floated along its slow current. She untied the scarf from her neck and stared at the red silk square, the strange curled design that her daughter said was so popular in America. The fabric was smooth against her fingers, prettier than anything she could buy for herself, prettier still because her daughter bought it.

But the trouble these gifts caused. The dyed and woven clothes with labels that none of the village women could read, but always wanted to inspect. The heavy feather-filled coats that kept out the cold. The bolts of fabric sent by fancy postman for tablecloths too fine to use. Colors so bright that she was always seen against the tans and browns of her neighbors. She pushed the scarf into the water and wrung it tight, then wrapped the cool fabric around her neck.

"Hello again!"

She turned and saw the old man coming fast behind her, his branch strung with rabbits bouncing on his shoulder.

"I was hoping to find you, and so close to home." He pointed to a thicket of mulberry bushes. The faint outline of a house stood behind its ragged green leaves.

"Let me help you," he said. "If this gift is as big as you think, you won't be able to carry it back alone. Let me get my son to help. He can bring his wheelbarrow."

"That's very kind, but—"

"I insist. There's nothing he can do today. All of his moths are gone. Besides, no taxi will bring you home till this road is cleared. Please," he said, pushing her toward a muddy footpath. "I'll tell my son to join us. He'll be happy to help."

"I'll pay him," she said.

The man shook his head. "You don't need to do that. We're neighbors now."

He led her down the path toward the house, a small gray shed slapped together with concrete brick. Weeds and wild mushrooms grew in thick patches near the front steps.

"Come inside," he said, setting his rabbits on the grass. "My son must be looking at his hatchery again. You can rest up in here while I get him."

She followed him through the open door into a windowless room. On one side was a table, two chairs, an icebox and stove. On the other, bamboo sleeping mats with blankets stacked on top. Cookery lay about the floor collecting rainwater. And in the open closet, clothes folded on a shelf and a single wire hanger from which hung a suit.

"See that?" he asked. He pointed to the dark brown jacket, a cream-white tie draped over the shoulder. "My son gave me that for my *han gahp*, just like he should. We lived farther west then, but all my family came. Dozens of them, from everywhere. And my nieces cooked the best food. Roast pork and dumplings and three kinds of sweets. We had so much, we had to give it away the next day, even the beer and wine." He ran his hand down the tie, brushing a dried spider from the fabric. "It made me wish I could have done more for my father when he turned sixty. My mother too. Their *han gahps* were nothing compared to mine."

"I'm sure you did your best."

He shrugged. "I tried, but still—" He dropped the tie and turned to her. "I'm sorry. I shouldn't talk like this."

"Why?"

"Because you didn't have a *han gahp* of your own."

She took the sleeve of the jacket and rubbed the prickly wool between her fingers. "We should go now, I think."

Water dripped from the edge of the roof, splattering the steps with rust-colored spots. Mee stood in the doorway, waiting for the man to return with his son. It occurred to her that only the dumbest of men would raise silkworms in a place that rained six months of the year and snowed three more. Still, she would offer the son money. He would need it now to live. Her neighbors too, their soybeans and hay and barley all drowned. Even the smallest of their vegetable gardens carried off by the storm. Soon they would come to her door by the dozens. Or they would send their children to invite her for meals or tea or wine. They would talk to her and feed her and refill her glass and compliment her good fortune, and they would make her ask if she could help them, which she always did. Interest-free, for as long as they needed it.

Mee shook her head. It was coming again, another season of debts, the life spans of which she dreaded because she knew that no one liked to owe. And no one liked the person to whom they owed. So her neighbors would avoid her for months at a time, saying nothing more than "good morning" and "goodbye" until they repaid the five or ten thousand that allowed them to eat. Always with a minimum of conversation, always with money so worn, it could hardly be tendered again.

She imagined what the women would say after seeing the son with his wheelbarrow, following her home with some fancy new thing they could never afford. Their husbands would see too, walking back from their fields with shovels and picks slung over their shoulders, their eyes narrowed until she turned to face them. Mee wondered if it was unkind, parading herself in front of them like that, but her birthday had been spent alone. Not a single visitor came up her hill. Not even the postman, whose car was too old to make the trip well on the driest of roads. She spent the day thinking of her father's *han gahp*, how she and her siblings prepared for weeks in advance. She was pregnant then, and could only make wreaths while her sisters cooked and her brothers carted supplies. But they were long, thick wreaths, each flower sewn from six pieces of fabric, and when they hung above the banquet table, her mother said it looked like a real celebration, and all of the guests complimented her father for raising children who gave their thanks so well.

Mee looked at the suit hanging in the closet. She knew the man would be buried in it, as it was meant to be, just as her father was buried in the suit that she and her siblings gave to him. But this man would live longer than her father, who passed the year after his *han gahp*. People lived longer now.

She slipped out the door as the man returned with his son.

"Here he is," the man said. "Strong as a horse. He can help you."

The son introduced himself with a quick bow from his waist. "We should leave now," he said, "if you expect to finish this before dark."

Mee thanked him, but the son was gone, pushing his wheelbarrow over the footpath, cutting tracks through the mud.

"Was he unhappy to do this?" she whispered to the old man.

"Oh, no. He was glad to come. But he's not much for talk. All he does is think of his moths."

"They're all gone? Not a single one left?"

"That's the good news. He found some cocoons in the hatchery, a dozen of them at least." He pointed to the sun. "If she stays out long enough, they might open, give him a few moths to breed for next season."

Mee reached into her pocket. "You should let me pay him for his trouble. He should be home now."

The man swung his arm under hers, lifting her sagging back as she walked. "I told you that wasn't necessary. My son farmed for fifteen years before he decided to raise silk. And I farmed for fifty before him. It's always something with farmers. Rain is the least of it."

She looked at his fingers resting near her elbow, the way the tips pressed into her skin. She thought it was better than fine. "Then I'll make you and your son dinner," she said quietly. "Afterward. You can come to my house and I'll make you both dinner, if you like. I have this stove. Four rings to cook on. I can never use them all for myself."

"See?" he nodded. "How good this turned out? We meet a new friend, we get to see that village we never have time to visit. And we'll be hungry by the time this is done. So we have the storm to thank for this, don't we?" He patted her arm and let go. "Why don't you tell my son? We've never been asked to take a meal with anyone here. Tell him, please. He'll be so excited."

Mee quickened her step and caught up to the son several meters ahead. "Excuse me."

The son looked at her, then back again at the road. "My father says you're the one with the doctor in America."

"Yes," she said, winded. "I—"

"How did that happen?"

"She went to school there. University too."

"But how?"

"I used what my husband left me, so she could study." The wheelbarrow shot a stone at her knee. "Would you and your father like to have dinner at my home when we finish?"

"So why live here then? Why not move?"

"Because I grew up here. And my daughter, she says I might not like it in America, the way people do things."

The son shook his head. "If I could leave, I would. Take my father with me. This place is for the pigs."

"But he said you had good news. He said you found some cocoons to hatch for next season."

The son leaned toward her. "My father," he whispered, "likes to pretend. Likes to make good out of everything, even wet cocoons. My mother said it was his worst habit."

"But the sun," she said. "When you put them in the sun, maybe they'll dry."

"Dry? If only it was so easy. A drop of water on a cocoon, it's like dipping them in oil. Kills them all just the same." He stopped and picked a stone from his shoe. "I suppose I could eat afterward."

Houses began to crowd each other along the road. Then shops appeared with colorful metal signs. Pharmacies and laundries and lunch counters serving noodle soups and cold barley tea. Men with bright red faces sat outside wine parlors playing cards while women swept dust and broken window glass from their homes.

Mee knocked on the postman's door and he cracked it open slowly. The dog chained in the side alley tipped back its head and howled.

"Shut up, you!" the postman shouted. "I haven't slept well in weeks," he said. "That damn dog hasn't stopped barking since the rain started. I have half a mind to—" He shook his head, opening the door wide. "I'm sorry. You didn't come to hear me complain. You've come for your package."

Mee left the man and his son on the street and walked into the small office. Boxes and bags of undelivered mail sat on every surface. She squeezed between waist-high stacks that teetered as she passed and stood idly in a corner.

"I'll never catch up," the postman said, searching through the shelves behind his desk. "I have no one to help me, and that dog won't let me sleep, and my car is filled with water—" He smiled tightly. "I can't stop myself today, can I? Nothing but complaints."

Mee looked down at her mud-caked shoes. Usually, she let the postman tell her his troubles until he had none left to tell, but she could hardly think of him now. She wondered if she should make a soup for dinner, if she had enough salted shrimp for seasoning, if she should buy an extra head of cabbage to shred in the broth, if she should use her plain dishes or her fancy ones.

"Here it is," the postman said. "I kept it in a special place so I could find it easy for you."

He handed her a box wrapped in brown paper, stamped with bright seals from the places it came. It was smaller than she expected, but heavier than it looked. She removed the envelope taped to the box and found a card inside, white with a yellow cake on the cover. Her daughter signed it, adding that the gift was something useful, and her grandsons signed too with fat, cloudlike letters that slanted across the page. Stapled to one side of the card was a familiar yellow check, drawn from the national bank, but written out in the amount of three million *won* instead of one. She picked up the box and tore the paper from one end. Beneath it was a picture of a telephone.

Mee's breath caught in her chest, and the postman looked up from his mail.

"Something wrong?" he asked.

She ignored him, lifting the flap of the box to find a moss-colored telephone inside. The same as the picture.

"No. Nothing's wrong. My daughter, she—outdid herself this time."

"We should all be as lucky as you," the postman said.

She thanked him as she made her way back to the entrance. The door clicked into place behind her and the lock turned quickly from within. The man and his son stared at the package under her arm as she joined them in the street.

"Is that the gift?" the man asked.

She nodded. "A telephone."

The man tilted his head to one side.

"I live on a hill," she said. "It costs a lot of money for them to run lines to a hill." She took the check from her pocket and held it out to them. "She sent this too."

The son's eyes followed the string of numbers from left to right. His mouth opened slightly, then snapped shut.

"A telephone is a very good gift," the man said quietly.

"It is. There's not even one in our village yet, but when the lines are run, I can talk to my daughter all the time, and my neighbors—they can come to me if they want to use the phone."

The son lowered his wheelbarrow. "So I came all this way for nothing?"

"Never mind, never mind," the man said. "Be quiet now."

Mee's cheeks burned. "I'll pay you," she said, pulling out her money. "How much do you want?"

The man placed his hands over hers, squeezing them tightly. "Put that back now. We don't need it, I told you—"

"Whatever you think is fair," the son said.

"No, don't do that. We don't need your—"

Mee pressed the money into the son's hand. "Here. Take it."

He looked at the thick stack of bills, then at her. "What's all this? I didn't ask you for a loan."

"It's not a loan," she said. "It's for your time. Yours and your father's."

She turned to the old man, trying her best to smile. His expression stopped her cold. Mee knew the look on his face. Knew it better than anything, so she chose not to see. Instead, she lifted her eyes to the last of the day's light, to the violet slowly overtaking the blue, and when the man said "goodbye" and the wheelbarrow creaked across the road, Mee hardly noticed. She saw only the absence of clouds in the sky, promising a night still and clear. Clear as if the storm had never come.

CONTRIBUTORS

DOROTHY ALLISON is the author of the novels *Bastard Out of Carolina* and *Cavedweller*.

STEVE ALMOND is the author of two story collections, *The Evil B. B. Chow* (Algonquin, 2005) and *My Life in Heavy Metal* (Grove, 2002) and the nonfiction book *Candyfreak: A Journey through the Chocolate Underbelly of America* (Algonquin, 2004). His new novel, cowritten with Julianna Baggott, is called *Which Brings Me to You.* It will be published in spring 2006. His favorite music can be found at www.bbchow.com.

AIMEE BENDER is the author of three books: *The Girl in the Flammable Skirt*, a *New York Times* Notable Book of 1998; *An Invisible Sign of My Own*, a *Los Angeles Times* pick of 2000; and a new collection, *Willful Creatures*. Her short fiction has been published in *Harper's, McSweeney's, Granta, Story*, GQ, the *Paris Review*, and other journals, as well as heard on PRI's *This American Life*. She lives in Los Angeles and teaches creative writing at USC.

DAVID BENIOFF worked at a variety of jobs, including nightclub bouncer, high school English teacher, and radio deejay, before selling his first novel, *The 25th Hour*, in 2000. Viking published his collection of stories, *When the Nines Roll Over*, in October 2004. He is currently writing his next novel, scheduled for publication in the summer of 2007.

His screenplays include *The 25th Hour*, directed by Spike Lee; *Troy*, directed by Wolfgang Petersen; and *Stay*, directed by Marc Forster. His future projects include adaptations of *The Kite Runner* and *For Whom the Bell Tolls*, as well as *Wolverine*, based on the popular Marvel Comics superhero.

PINCKNEY BENEDICT grew up on his family's farm in Greenbrier County, West Virginia. He has published two collections of short fiction and a novel. His stories have appeared in, among other magazines and anthologies, *Esquire*, *Zoetrope All-Story*, the *O. Henry Award* series, the *New Stories from the South* series, *Ontario Review*, the *Pushcart Prize* series, and *The Oxford Book of American Short Stories*. He wrote the screenplay for the feature film *Four Days*. He is a professor in the English department at Hollins University in Roanoke, Virginia.

AMY BLOOM is the author of the novel *Love Invents Us* and two collections of stories: *Come to Me*, nominated for a National Book Award, and *A Blind Man Can See How Much I Love You*, nominated for the National Book Critics Circle Award. Her first book of nonfiction is a collection of essays on gender and culture: *Normal: Transsexual CEOs, Crossdressing Cops, and Hermaphrodites with Attitude*. Her books have been translated into many foreign languages. Her stories have appeared in *Best American Short Stories*, *Prize Stories: The O. Henry Awards*, and numerous anthologies here and abroad, and she has won a *National Magazine* Award for Fiction. She has written for the *New Yorker*; the *New York Times Magazine*; *O, The Oprah Magazine*; the *Atlantic Monthly*; *Vogue*; *Slate*; and *Salon*, among others. She lives in Connecticut and teaches at Yale University. Her upcoming novel will be published by Random House in 2007, followed by a story collection in 2008.

ROBERT OLEN BUTLER is the author of ten novels and three collections of stories. In addition to a Pulitzer Prize in 1993 and two National Magazine Awards in 2001 and 2005 (all for fiction), he has received a Guggenheim Fellowship, as well as the Richard and Hinda Rosenthal Award from the American Academy of Arts and Letters. He teaches creative writing at Florida State University. The severed-head pieces herein are six of sixty-two such very short stories that will be published in a volume called *Severance* by Chronicle Books in the fall of 2006.

DEBORAH EISENBERG's most recent collection of stories is *Twilight of the Superheroes*. She lives in New York City, but part of the year she teaches at the University of Virginia.

RYAN HARTY's stories have appeared widely in literary magazines and have been anthologized in *The Pushcart Prize* and *The Best American Short Stories*. His story collection, *Bring Me Your Saddest Arizona*, won the John Simmons Short Fiction Award and was published in 2003. He is at work on a novel.

HOWARD HUNT is the author of *Young Men on Fire* (Scribner, 2003), hailed by Booklist as "*The Great Gatsby* meets *Sex in the City*—a wonderful, fun, strangely real look at the wealthy young in New York today." He currently lives in Prague, where he is working on a collection of short stories.

FRANCES HWANG has held fellowships at the Fine Arts Work Center in Provincetown and the Wisconsin Institute for Creative Writing, as well as a residency at the MacDowell Colony. Her stories have appeared in *Glimmer Train*, the *Madison Review*, and *Best New American Voices 2003* and *2005*.

DENIS JOHNSON has published fiction, verse, articles, and plays. He lives in Idaho and Arizona.

MARSHALL N. KLIMASEWISKI's stories have appeared in the *New Yorker*, the *Atlantic Monthly*, the *Yale Review*, *Ploughshares*, and elsewhere. His first novel, *The Cottagers*, will be published by Norton in May of 2006, and a collection of stories titled *Tyrants* will follow. He teaches at Washington University in Saint Louis.

ELLEN LITMAN was born in Moscow, Russia, where she lived until 1992. She holds an MFA from Syracuse University, and she was a fiction fellow at the Wisconsin Institute for Creative Writing. Her fiction has appeared in *Other Voices*, *Ontario Review*, *Gulf Coast*, and *TriQuarterly*. She currently lives in Boston and teaches at Babson College.

HOWARD LUXENBERG's stories have been published in *Other Voices*, *Gettysburg Review*, the *Iowa Review*, and *Alaska Quarterly Review*.

MARTHA McPHEE received her MFA from Columbia University. She is the author of the novels *Bright Angel Time*, a *New York Times* Notable Book in 1997, and *Gorgeous Lies*, nominated in 2002 for a National Book Award. She teaches at Hofstra University and lives in New York City with her husband, the poet and writer Mark Svenvold, and their two children. Her third novel, *L'America*, will be published in the spring of 2006.

STEVEN MILLHAUSER is the author of ten works of fiction, including *Edwin Mullhouse*, *Martin Dressler*, and *The Knife Thrower and Other Stories*. His most recent book is *The King in the Tree*, a collection of three novellas.

LUCIA NEVAI's short fiction has been published in the *New Yorker*, *Zoetrope All-Story*, the *Iowa Review*, *New England Review*, and other periodicals. She is the author of two collections of stories, *Star Game*, which won the Iowa Short Fiction Award, and *Normal*. Born in Iowa, Nevai now lives in upstate New York.

MARK JUDE POIRIER grew up in Tucson, Arizona. He is the author of two short story collections, *Naked Pueblo* and *Unsung Heroes of American Industry*, along with the novels *Goats* and, most recently, *Modern Ranch Living*.

NATASHA RADOJCIC was born in Belgrade, came to New York City on her own in her twenties, and stayed. She is the author of two novels, *Homecoming* and *You Don't Have to Live Here*, both published by Random House. Her nonfiction writing has appeared in the *New York Times*, the *Boston Review*, and *Ms.* magazine.

STACEY RICHTER is the author of *My Date with Satan*, a collection of stories.

JAMES SALTER is the author of the novels *Solo Faces*, *Light Years*, *A Sport and a Pastime*, *The Arm of Flesh* (revised as *Cassada*), and *The Hunters*; the memoirs *God of Tin* and *Burning the Days*; and the collections *Last Night* and *Dusk and Other Stories*, which won the 1989 PEN/Faulkner Award. He lives in Colorado and on Long Island.

JIM SHEPARD is the author of six novels, most recently *Project X*, and two story collections, most recently *Love and Hydrogen*. He teaches at Williams College and in the Warren Wilson MFA program.

JULIA SLAVIN is the author of *The Woman Who Cut Off Her Leg at the Maidstone Club and Other Stories* and the novel *Carnivore Diet*.

ANTHONY SWOFFORD is the author of *Jarhead*. His writing has appeared in the *New York Times*, *Harper's*, the *Guardian*, and elsewhere. He is currently working on a novel to be published by Scribner. He lives in New York City.

ELIZABETH TALLENT, author of a novel and three story collections, has recently completed a new novel. She teaches in Stanford University's Creative Writing Program.

AMANDA EYRE WARD is the author of the novels *Sleep Toward Heaven* and *How to Be Lost*. She lives on Cape Cod with her husband and son, and is currently writing a novel set in Cape Town, South Africa.

JUNG H. YUN was born in Seoul, South Korea, and grew up in Fargo, North Dakota. She graduated from Vassar College and the University of Pennsylvania, and is currently an MFA candidate in creative writing at the University of Massachusetts-Amherst. In 2003, she won second place in the *Zoetrope All-Story* Short Fiction Contest and was a finalist for the *Glimmer Train* Short Story Award for New Writers. Currently, she lives in Montague, Massachusetts, where she is working on a collection of short stories.

COPYRIGHT NOTES

"The Breakup Vows," copyright © 2003 by Steve Almond. First published in *Tin House* no. 15.

"End of the Line" from *Willful Creatures* by Aimee Bender. Copyright © 2005 by Aimee Bender. First published in *Tin House* no. 21. Reprinted by permission of Doubleday, a division of Random House, Inc.

"Mudman," copyright © 2005 by Pinckney Benedict. First published in *Tin House* no. 23.

"Zoanthropy," copyright © 2003 by David Benioff. First published in *Tin House* no. 14. Reprinted by permission of the William Morris Agency, LLC.

"I Love to See You Coming, I Hate to See You Go," copyright © 2004 by Amy Bloom. First published in *Tin House* no. 19. This story will appear in Amy Bloom's third story collection, to be published by Random House.

"Severance," copyright © 2004 by Robert Olen Butler. First published in *Tin House* no. 20.

"Revenge of the Dinosaurs" from *Twilight of the Superheroes* by Deborah Eisenberg. Copyright © 2006 by Deborah Eisenberg. First published in *Tin House* no. 17. Reprinted by permission of Farrar, Straus and Giroux, LLC.

"Why the Sky Turns Red When the Sun Goes Down," copyright © 2002 by Ryan Harty. First published in *Tin House* no. 13.

"Sovietski!" copyright © 2003 by Howard Hunt. First published in *Tin House* no. 16. Reprinted by permission of International Creative Management, Inc.

"The Old Gentleman," copyright © 2005 by Frances Hwang. First published in *Tin House* no. 22.

"Xmas in Las Vegas," copyright © 2003 by Denis Johnson. First published in *Tin House* no. 15.

"The Third House," copyright © 2004 by Marshall N. Klimasewiski. First published in *Tin House* no. 21.

"Dancers," copyright © 2004 by Ellen Litman. First published in *Tin House* no. 20.

"The Photograph," copyright © 2003 by Howard Luxenberg. First published in *Tin House* no. 17.

"The Anthropology of Sex," copyright © 2003 by Martha McPhee. First published in *Tin House* no. 15. Reprinted by permission of the Wylie Agency, Inc.

"Dangerous Laughter," copyright © 2003 by Steven Millhauser. First published in *Tin House* no. 17. Reprinted by permission of International Creative Management, Inc.

"End of Messages," copyright © 2005 by Lucia Nevai. First published in *Tin House* no. 23.

"I, Maggot," copyright © 2003 by Mark Jude Poirier. First published in *Tin House* no. 15. Reprinted by permission of the Wylie Agency, Inc.

"Shades of Mango," copyright © 2004 by Natasha Radojcic. First published in *Tin House* no. 18.

"Christ, Their Lord," copyright © 2004 by Stacey Richter. First published in *Tin House* no. 21. Reprinted by permission of International Creative Management, Inc.

"Such Fun" from *Last Night* by James Salter. Copyright © 2005 by James Salter. First published in *Tin House* no. 22. Reprinted by permission of Alfred A. Knopf, a division of Random House, Inc.

"John Ashcroft: More Important Things Than Me," copyright © 2003 by Jim Shepard. First published in *Tin House* no. 14.

"Squatters," copyright © 2004 by Julia Slavin. First published in *Tin House* no. 18. Reprinted by permission of International Creative Management, Inc.

"Will They Kill You in Iraq?" copyright © 2004 by Anthony Swofford. First published in *Tin House* no. 18. Reprinted by permission of International Creative Management, Inc.

"Eros 101," copyright © 2004 by Elizabeth Tallent. First published in *Tin House* no. 20.

"The Way the Sky Changed," copyright © 2004 by Amanda Eyre Ward. First published in *Tin House* no. 21.

"Han Gahp," copyright © 2005 by Jung H. Yun. First published in *Tin House* no. 22.